OURSELVES
AMONG OTHERS

Cross-Cultural Readings
for Writers

OURSELVES AMONG OTHERS

*Cross-Cultural Readings
for Writers*

EDITED BY

Carol J. Verburg

FOREWORD BY

Sol Gittleman

Provost, Tufts University

A Bedford Book

ST. MARTIN'S PRESS · NEW YORK

*For my mother and
my late father, with thanks.*

Library of Congress Catalog Card Number: 87-060595
Copyright © 1988 by St. Martin's Press, Inc.
All rights reserved.
Manufactured in the United States of America
1 0 9 8 7
f e d c b a
For information, write St. Martin's Press, Inc.
175 Fifth Avenue, New York, NY 10010
Editorial Offices: Bedford Books of St. Martin's Press,
29 Commonwealth Avenue, Boston, MA 02116
ISBN: 0-312-00354-4

Bedford Books of St. Martin's Press

Publisher: Charles H. Christensen
Associate Publisher: Joan E. Feinberg
Managing Editor: Elizabeth M. Schaaf
Developmental Editor: Stephen A. Scipione
Production Editor: Chris Rutigliano
Copyeditor: Susan M. S. Brown
Book Designer: Anna Post
Cover Designer: Volney Croswell

Cover Art: M. F. Husain. *Cage* V. Oil on canvas. 68 × 78 inches.
From the Chester and Davida Herwitz Family Collection.
Map Designer: Richard D. Pusey

ACKNOWLEDGMENTS

Chinua Achebe, "Civil Peace," from the book *African Short Stories* edited by Chinua Achebe
and C. L. Innes. Copyright © 1973 by Chinua Achebe. Reprinted by permission of Doubleday, a division of Bantam, Doubleday, Dell Publishing Group, Inc.

(Continued on page 666)

FOREWORD

Americans have never really given much thought to other countries. After all, this nation stretches for more than 3,000 miles from one ocean to another, and almost all our ancestors left other places to come here. Does it really matter a great deal that many American high school students believe that the language of Latin America is Latin, or that few of us understand the cultural differences between the Iranians and the Iraqis, or that there is a reason why the Poles fear the East Germans as much as they do the Russians? We just do not take much time to examine the past, or to deal with a world getting more and more dangerous and increasingly in need of communication. The fact is, though, we live in a global village, and we have to understand our international neighbors as if they were the people next door.

Whether we live on the coasts of the United States or in the middle of its continental landmass, none of us can escape the meaning of Bhopal and Chernobyl. Technology has forced each of us to come to grips with people halfway around the world. Once we threw spears at each other, then we learned to shoot, and now we can destroy the earth. To assure that our grandchildren survive to have their own grandchildren, we must begin thinking about how the peoples of the world deal with their problems, think about themselves, and share a mutual concern for survival. To give us all a chance, we must learn to deal with each other as fellow inhabitants of the same town. We can't afford to dehumanize, to stereotype, or to accept the traditional prejudices of times past. We don't have to like each other, but we do have to understand why we act the way we do — what Islamic fundamentalism is, how Vietnamese culture differs from other Southeast Asian cultures, what it is like growing up in Israel or the Soviet Union. More than ever before it has become essential for every educated person in this country not only to be able to locate Kabul, the Strait of Hormuz, or the nations bordering on South Africa but to know the concerns and values of the people who live there as well. We need to understand the mind of the Afrikaner as well as the world of the Namibian.

For American college students this quest for understanding can begin as early as first-year orientation exercises and should continue throughout the college years. Ideally it will include not only classes in cultural anthropology, foreign languages and literatures, world history, and international relations but also the opportunity to travel abroad under the auspices of university programs. This quest should involve all students, from liberal arts majors to those in the health sciences and professional disciplines. It has been my experience as an educator involved in the development of such curricula that students from all walks of college life are eager to see through the often dehumanizing glut of information they face every day to the real human issues at stake. They welcome the chance to recognize the human strands that link them with other people from other cultures in other parts of the world. Not surprisingly, the working world students face after college is also paying increased attention to the international scene, and has a corresponding interest in students who are familiar with it.

Ourselves Among Others expands the borders of the first-year composition classroom to provide American students with views of other people around the world as well as their views of us. The readings focus on themes that compel us to examine ourselves as part of the human family, as parents and children, as men and women, as friends and enemies. The rich variety of material ranges from stories and essays to reportage, interviews, and autobiography. Yet every reading is included for a common purpose: to help us better understand the concerns and values of our coinhabitants of the global village.

By looking at others, we will also better understand ourselves. Americans are by nature people in a hurry, who do not spend much time looking backward. Although we are an immigrant nation, we have always told the next wave of immigrants: Be like us, learn American values quickly — whatever "American values" may mean. Increasingly, however, we have come to accept that we are a multicultural nation with a past and that we can examine that past to learn about our connectedness to the larger world, which will be with us for the rest of our lives.

Even reading the newspaper today is an exercise in global education, in confronting a complex world where demands will be made on the responsible citizen as never before. That education must never end, because into the twenty-first century and beyond, knowledge of each other's values will be the main guarantee of the world's survival. Nuclear proliferation has made it a certain fact that many nations will have the capacity to do away with traditional enemies. But because nations are no longer islands independent of each other, every nation shares the responsibility to prevent such destruction from happening. Only through reason and understanding can we save each other. Only through the experience of sharing cultures, values, and the sense of common family can we succeed.

Sol Gittleman
Provost
Tufts University

INTRODUCTION

Provost Sol Gittleman of Tufts University has suggested in his foreword the urgent reasons for encouraging students to become better informed about the "global village" we live in. By learning to see themselves as citizens of the world they will inherit, by responding to the concerns of its other inhabitants, they become capable of making informed, humane choices when they enter that world. In college there is no earlier or more apt opportunity to encourage this widening of vision than in first-year composition classrooms, where students are expected to read carefully, think deeply, and then to write clearly about what they have read and thought. Traditionally they have been asked to read, think and write about themselves — as citizens of a particular country, the United States, and as heirs to Western knowledge, attitudes, and assumptions.

Ourselves Among Others extends these traditional geographic and cultural boundaries to encompass the rest of the world. Without losing sight of themselves, students will witness lives in thirty-seven other countries, discovering what it means to grow up in post-colonial Africa, to fall in love in China, to balance career and family in Japan, to participate in a revolutionary struggle in El Salvador, to live in a woman's compound among Afghan refugees. By thinking and writing about these selections, students will connect with lives that often differ crucially from their own, but just as often startlingly resemble theirs. They also will have the chance to sample some excellent contemporary prose by writers as diverse as Gabriel García Márquez, Nadine Gordimer, Amos Oz, Nathalie Sarraute, and Wole Soyinka.

The sixty-five readings in *Ourselves Among Others* have been chosen and arranged to illuminate what it means to live in today's global village. The selections focus on universal human experiences and concerns; the parts proceed in an order that corresponds to an outward movement into larger and increasingly complex social spheres. From the closeness of family life in Part One, the readings move through adolescence to the verge of adulthood in Part Two to the sometimes conflicting pressures of love and gender roles in Part Three. How people respond to the demands of their livelihoods (Part Four) opens into how they cope with the demands of the political systems that regulate their lives (Part Five). Part Six details the dramatic consequences when those systems fail and the results are political violence or outright war — an immediate and chilling reality that much of the world wakes up to every day. Finally, Part Seven explores what it means to be abroad in a world where easy generalities about East and West, communism and capitalism, and the Third World have become clearly inadequate.

Given the overwhelming amount of compelling writing from, and about other cultures, it seemed essential to limit the scope of *Ourselves Among Others* to those genres of most practical use to composition students. About three-quarters of the selections are nonfiction — essays, interviews, reportage, autobiography — presenting stimulating information on, and current or historic insights into, the contemporary world. The remaining selections are short stories, also chosen for both content and craft. Perceptive and skillfully written, the stories depict cultures through the passionate and prejudiced eyes of "insiders" — writers who, by holding up a mirror to their compatriots, reveal much about the internal qualities of their cultures to "outsiders."

On a more strictly pedagogical level, the selections in *Ourselves Among Others* were chosen because they provide fresh resources for classroom discussion and writing assignments. Students can assess the distinctive thinking, experience, and voices of non-American writers, whose assumptions about what is significant, what is praiseworthy, what is amusing or sad or frightening may contrast with — or may echo — corresponding American assumptions. In some instances students will discern hidden biases that color one person's views of someone else's customs; in others, they will recognize the common fears, delights, and frustrations of being human in any culture. Using the selections as a starting point, students also can see how personal experience may serve as raw material for an expository essay, as well as identify rhetorical patterns and strategies to analyze or use as models for their writing.

Although the book primarily aims to introduce students to writing from and about a range of foreign cultures, *Ourselves Among Others* does not overlook the breadth of American experiences within the United States. It seemed desirable to provide familiar ground from which students could commence their explorations of other cultures as well as a closer-to-home demonstration of the variety of human situations, attitudes, and opinions. Accordingly, each of the first six parts opens with a series of excerpts called *Observations: Looking at Ourselves.* These "short takes" by writers such as Annie Dillard, Ellen Goodman, William Least Heat Moon, Mario Puzo, Richard Rodriguez, and Alice Walker explore each part's theme *within the United States.* Voices less well known, but often equally eloquent, comment on experiences from living on welfare to nursing in Vietnam. (Part Seven, because it intersperses American and non-American accounts of "feeling foreign" inside and outside the United States, does not begin with *Observations.*)

All the selections in this book, whether they enlighten, intrigue, challenge, or even offend students, will reward their attention. To encourage the reader to make the effort that good writing demands, selections are preceded and followed by material that places them in context:

Prereading: Each piece opens with a headnote on the author and his or her culture: its location, history, and current status. When one country is represented by several selections (examples include the Soviet Union, China, and Japan), different appropriate background information precedes each piece. Multiple headnotes on a single culture are cross-referenced so that students can look up additional data as they wish.

Postreading: Detailed questions following each piece are designed to help students pick out and examine the aspects — factual, rhetorical, and thematic — that most deserve scrutiny. Questions are of two types: Explorations, intended to stimulate thought and discussion, and Connections, focusing on relations between pieces, including main selections and *Observations.* These are followed by writing suggestions (Elaborations). Like the selections, the questions and assignments are likely to prompt readers to evaluate, and reevaluate, their assumptions about how the world works.

If the abundance of new material in *Ourselves Among Others* seems daunting at first glance, be assured that a comprehensive instructor's manual is available. Prepared by Kathleen Shine Cain of Merrimack College, the manual includes a general introduction that discusses teaching possibilities and provides suggestions for launching the course; sample syllabi; brief introductions to each part, suggesting various subthematic combinations and listing familiar American readings that instructors may wish to consult; discussions of all Explorations and Connections questions, paying particular attention to possible student reaction on more controversial pieces; additional questions and assignments following each part, including journal suggestions and essay and research assignments; a rhetorical index; and additional resources, including an index to headnote information and a concise list of reference materials.

Like every book, *Ourselves Among Others* has been a collaborative effort. I wish to thank the many reviewers who commented on various drafts: Nancy K. Barry, University of Iowa; Robert J. Connors, University of New Hampshire; T. Obinkaram Echewa, West Chester University; Jeanne Gunner, University of California, Los Angeles; Edward A. Kline, University of Notre Dame; James Moore, Minneapolis College of Art and Design; Michael G. Moran, University of Rhode Island; Sr. Sheila Rausch, College of St. Benedict; Robert A. Schwegler, University of Rhode Island; Bruce Southard, Oklahoma State University; Josephine Koster Tarvers, Rutgers University; Amy Tucker, Queens College; Sauling C. Wong, University of California, Berkeley; and Winifred Wood, Wellesley College. All their suggestions were appreciated, and many helped to shape this final version. I'm especially grateful to Kathy Cain of Merrimack College, who has been not only an excellent reviewer but a valued partner as the author of the instructor's manual. Charles H. Christensen of Bedford Books deserves thanks from all teachers of English for his commitment to publishing outstanding, innovative books, and from me for his inspiration and support on this one. Steve Scipione has been a tireless filler of cracks, sounding board, and right-hand man; his help was invaluable. Chris Rutigliano cheerfully and conscientiously steered the book through production. Nearly everyone at Bedford pitched in at some point — thanks to all of you, particularly to Joan Feinberg, Matthew Carnicelli, Ellen Darion, Nancy DeCubellis, Elizabeth Schaaf, and Mary Lou Wilshaw. I was also lucky to work again with designer Anna Post and copyeditor Susan Brown; and I appreciate Mary Hoffman's help clearing permissions.

Most of all I'm grateful to the people whose writing appears in this book, many of whom have persisted in their craft against obstacles unknown in the United States. For me, and I hope for you as a teacher or student of writing, *Ourselves Among Others* represents an unexpectedly rich opportunity to share new experiences and insights, as well as to find out firsthand what's going on elsewhere in the global village.

C. J. V.

CONTENTS

FOREWORD   *v*

INTRODUCTION   *ix*

A NOTE ON TRANSLATIONS   *xxiii*

1. THE FAMILY: *Cornerstone of Culture*   *1*

OBSERVATIONS: LOOKING AT OURSELVES
*Bill Cosby, Michael Novak, Carol Kleiman, Jane Howard, Claudia
Wallis, Ellen Goodman   3*

SRI DELIMA, *Black-and-White Amah*   *9*

A Malaysian journalist reminisces about Ah Yoong, the Southeast Asian Mary
Poppins who drilled her in proper behavior and loved her unreservedly.

BRUNO BETTELHEIM, *Why Kibbutzim?*   *14*

For pioneering Israeli kibbutzniks, a crucial step in creating a new society was
designing a radically new way to bring up future citizens.

RUTH SIDEL, *The Liu Family*   *21*

"All students study for the revolution, not just for grades," declares a teenage Red
Guard. In Mao's China, the family was one more means to serve the
motherland.

GYANRANJAN, *Our Side of the Fence and Theirs*
[SHORT STORY]   *28*

An Indian family's curiosity about their aloof new neighbors is tinged with
suspicion: "What sorts of things do they talk about, and why are they always
laughing?"

JOHN DAVID MORLEY, *Acquiring a Japanese Family*   36

Through his Japanese roommate, a British student in Tokyo accumulates an
invisible grandfather, an anxious mother, and an aunt and uncle fleeing rumored
earthquakes with their parrot.

CAROLA HANSSON and KARIN LIDÉN, *Liza and Family*   48

A Soviet working mother speaks frankly about such universal issues as day care,
divorce, birth control, and the difficulties of trying to be an ideal parent.

VINCENT CRAPANZANO, *Growing Up White
in South Africa*   58

"Children don't notice the color of their friends' skin," says Hennie, an Afrikaner.
"You only become aware of it when you're told that you're big now and must not
play with Coloured girls anymore."

WOLE SOYINKA, *Nigerian Childhood*   66

A Nobel Prize-winning novelist and playwright recalls his family's special blend
of Nigerian tribal magic and Church of England Christianity.

GHOLAM-HOSSEIN SA'EDI, *The Game Is Over*
[SHORT STORY]   76

In a poor Iranian village, two boys play a comic but dangerous game of
disappearance and deception when they plot to avenge a father's nightly beatings.

2. COMING OF AGE:
Landmarks and Turning Points   101

OBSERVATIONS: LOOKING AT OURSELVES
*Jack Agueros, Gail Sheehy, Tom Wolfe, Richard Cohen, Olga
Silverstein*   103

NATHALIE SARRAUTE, *My First Sorrow*   109

For a French schoolgirl, an essay assignment opens the door into an entrancing
new world where language and imagination have more power than reality.

MISHIMA YUKIO, *The Boy Who Wrote Poetry*
[SHORT STORY]   115

Confronted by a friend's anguish, a youthful Japanese writer begins to suspect
that his gift for metaphor is an empty talent without experience to back it up.

SOPHRONIA LIU, *So Tsi-fai*   127

"What happened to all of us that year in sixth grade, when we were green and young and ready to fling our arms out for the world?" A boy's suicide in Hong Kong twenty-three years ago still haunts a fellow student.

LILIANA HEKER, *The Stolen Party* [SHORT STORY] *132*
An Argentine girl, proudly enjoying a birthday party at the house where her mother is a maid, recoils from a thoughtless gesture of gratitude.

VLADIMIR NABOKOV, *From* Speak, Memory *139*
In this reminiscence of his Russian boyhood, the author relives the horrible afternoon when he learned that his father would soon face death in a duel.

MARIO VARGAS LLOSA, *Sunday, Sunday* [SHORT STORY] *145*
Bitter over a romantic rivalry, a Peruvian teenager challenges his best friend to a drunken dare that nearly drowns them both in the fog-shrouded Miraflores sea.

VED MEHTA, *Pom's Engagement* *162*
When she reaches the approved age for marriage, an Indian girl is plucked from her sheltered childhood and betrothed by her parents to a stranger.

MARJORIE SHOSTAK, *Nisa's Marriage* *172*
A !Kung tribeswoman recalls her reluctance to leave her mother's hut for her husband's, and her gradual discovery that being a wife is less painful than she thought.

AMOS OZ, *If There Is Justice* [SHORT STORY] *180*
Home on his first leave, an Israeli soldier struggles to recapture his old closeness with his mother, his friends, his kibbutz, and the boyhood he left behind.

3. **WOMEN AND MEN:** *Images of the Opposite Sex* *193*
OBSERVATIONS: LOOKING AT OURSELVES
Adam Smith, Dena Justin, Joe Kane, Gloria Steinem, Susan Brownmiller, Gayle Early, David Owen, Amy Gross, Anne Roiphe *195*

ISAK DINESEN, *From "Daguerreotypes"* *204*
A Danish writer's description of the four types of woman recognized by nineteenth-century gentlemen suggests the persistent usefulness of these types for understanding how men wish to perceive women.

SANTHA RAMA RAU, *Boris's Romance*   *213*

While living in Moscow, an Indian writer and her American husband learn
about Russian courtship customs from a young friend whose description is based
on painful experience.

BEVERLEY HOOPER, *Falling in Love with Love*   *220*

"I have this feeling, here in my heart. . . . Is it love?" As China's doors open to
the West, an Australian writer finds that its young people's hearts are opening to
old-fashioned Hollywood romance.

OCTAVIO PAZ, *My Life with the Wave*   [SHORT STORY]   *234*

A Mexican poet narrates the tragicomic tale of a man who falls in love with
an ocean wave and is both elated and tormented by her tempestuous
charms.

SIMONE DE BEAUVOIR, *Woman as Other*   *241*

To this French writer, woman's historically subordinate status derives from man's
primordial tendency to divide all existence into the Self and the Other.

ALBERTO MORAVIA, *The Chase*   [SHORT STORY]   *249*

Recognizing that his wife's most potent attraction is her wildness, an Italian
husband realizes that to tame her would be to lose what he loves best.

NAILA MINAI, *Women in Early Islam*   *256*

Muhammad, the founder of Islam, emerges as a thoughtful man strongly
influenced by his independent first wife and their shared commitment to
women's rights.

CHERRY LINDHOLM and CHARLES LINDHOLM,
Life Behind the Veil   *267*

Two anthropologists studying Muslim women on the Pakistan frontier look into
the reasons behind their strict seclusion and note their ingenuity in bending the
rules.

YASHAR KEMAL, *A Dirty Story*   [SHORT STORY]   *279*

In a rural Turkish village, a mountain girl bought to be a farmhand's wife
becomes a victim of the local youths' lust and the local women's condemnation.

4. WORKING: *We Are What We Do*   *303*

OBSERVATIONS: LOOKING AT OURSELVES
*Alice Walker, Mario Puzo, Richard Rodriguez, Elliot Liebow, Bruce
Weber, Marge Piercy, Russell Baker, Betty Friedan, Studs
Terkel*   *305*

ANDREW H. MALCOLM, *Snowbird* 313

In a dogsled trek across the Yukon, an Indian guide who can read trail signs and talk to animals teaches a journalist how to live in the Canadian wilderness.

ZHANG XINXIN and SANG YE, *The Hunter* 321

A delegate to a Communist party conference looks back over half a century of trapping leopards and tigers — and dodging politics — in the mountains of China.

R. K. NARAYAN, *Trail of the Green Blazer* [SHORT STORY] 331

An Indian pickpocket's pride in his professional skill is damaged by his discovery that lifting a wallet is easier than putting one back.

SHIVA NAIPAUL, *The Palmers* 337

To a Kenyan tea planter and his wife, "home" is England, where servants understand their duties and laborers can be trusted to stay on the farm, where they belong.

EZEKIEL MPHAHLELE, *Tradition and the African Writer* 344

A South African writer explains the dilemma of trying to reconcile one's ancient tribal heritage with a modern education designed by European colonizers.

DAVID PLATH, *Tomoko on Her Television Career* 351

Straddling two traditions, a Japanese television producer recalls her narrow escape from an arranged marriage and her struggle to carve out a media career.

SATOSHI KAMATA, *Six Months at Toyota* 360

Western admirers of Japan's business practices may be shocked by this journalist's account of working on an auto factory assembly line.

HEDRICK SMITH, Skoro Budet — It'll Be Here Soon 374

"Storming" is Russian factory workers' term for the monthly cycle of waiting for parts, frantically assembling their quota of products, and celebrating payday with vodka.

JILL GAY, *Patriotic Prostitutes* 383

Where U.S. troops fought and vacationed fifteen years ago, prostitution mushroomed into a growth industry, which today is actively nurtured by Southeast Asian governments.

THELMA FORSHAW, *The Demo* [SHORT STORY] 391

An Australian immigrant trembles with fearful memories of his native Europe when a political demonstration threatens his shop, the core of his identity.

5. **CITIZENS:** *Government For and Against the People* 403

OBSERVATIONS: LOOKING AT OURSELVES
*Frank Trippett, Vicki Williams, William Least Heat Moon,
John Kenneth Galbraith, Robert Nisbet,
Annie Dillard* 405

DAVID LAMB, *The New African Chiefs* 414
Zaire's Mobutu Sese Seko is one of the new generation of African leaders who combine native and European techniques to rule as "half-god, half-chieftain."

JAMES FENTON, *The Philippine Election* 422
A British poet recalls how he came to the Philippines to investigate the islands' exotic reputation and wound up covering the overthrow of dictator Ferdinand Marcos.

JULIO CORTÁZAR, *Regarding the Eradication of Crocodiles from Auvergne* [SHORT STORY] 436
"No one has ever admitted seeing a crocodile in Auvergne," reports an Argentine exiled to France, "so that from the start any attempt to exterminate them is surrounded with difficulties."

GERMAINE GREER, *In Cuba* 441
A tour of the Western Hemisphere's first Communist country convinces an Australian feminist that Cuba represents a genuine people's revolution, a beacon to other developing nations.

LIANG HENG and JUDITH SHAPIRO, *Chairman Mao's Good Little Boy* 450
During the ideological tempests of China's Cultural Revolution, a family learns the hard way that Chairman Mao's eyes are on every breath you take, every move you make.

NADINE GORDIMER, *Africa Emergent* [SHORT STORY] 465
Friends from a multiracial South African theater troupe must weigh loyalty against safety when a net of apartheid, suspicion, and danger closes around one of their members.

GUZEL AMALRIK, *A Visit with Andrei at the Labor Camp* 479
The wife of an imprisoned Soviet dissident, allowed a brief reunion with her husband, fights bitter cold, harassment, and the anguish of seeing him malnourished and maltreated.

JANINE WEDEL, *Polish Line Committees*   *488*

Faced with a shortage of consumer goods under their Soviet-dominated
Communist government, Poles respond with ingenuity and cooperation.

GABRIEL GARCÍA MÁRQUEZ, *Death Constant Beyond Love*
[SHORT STORY]   *493*

As Senator Onésimo Sánchez plods through Colombian villages toward the end
of his last campaign, his bleak cynicism is pierced by a bolt of love.

6. WITNESSES TO WAR: *Soldiers and Survivors*   *503*

OBSERVATIONS: LOOKING AT OURSELVES
David Byrne, William H. Sullivan, Mark Baker, William Broyles, Jr.,
George Gilder, Barbara Ehrenreich   *505*

CZESLAW MILOSZ, *American Ignorance of War*   *513*

"Are Americans *really* stupid?" Eastern Europeans ask a Polish poet, shocked at
the naïveté of a people whose assumptions have never been shattered by a foreign
invasion.

DORIS LESSING, *The Afghan Resistance*   *519*

A British novelist talks with Mujahideen warriors, their leaders, and their families
about Afghanistan's fight to oust its Soviet-sponsored government.

ROGER ROSENBLATT, *Children of Cambodia*   *530*

In a refugee camp for Cambodians in Thailand, an American journalist hears
some of Southeast Asia's most appalling war stories from its youngest victims.

SHELLEY SAYWELL, *Women Warriors of El Salvador*   *540*

Maria and Ileana are both twenty-five, both mothers, both newly widowed,
and both guerrilla fighters recuperating in Canada from torture in
Salvadoran prisons.

ALBALUCÍA ÁNGEL, *The Guerrillero*   [SHORT STORY]   *556*

"Now you'll see, Felicidad Mosquera, when they all arrive with their machetes,
threatening, asking you where in hell has he hidden himself, then you'll
confess." A Colombian short story gives an inside look at interrogation.

MILOVAN DJILAS, *Ideas Against Torture*   *560*

A former official in the Yugoslav government turns his experience into steps by
which other torture victims can cling to sanity and life.

FRANK O'CONNOR, *Guests of the Nation*   [SHORT STORY]   *564*

Two young Irish soldiers play cards and argue about religion with their English
hostages until a twist of events forces their friendship up against the wall.

RYSZARD KAPUŚCIŃSKI, *Carlotta*   *576*

In an MPLA outpost in Angola, the boys were joyriding on a captured tractor
and the girls were doing their hair when the enemy appeared out of nowhere.

CHINUA ACHEBE, *Civil Peace*   [SHORT STORY]   *584*

After Nigerian troops have quelled Biafra's attempt to secede, an odd camaraderie
arises between a roving band of thieves and the man whose "egg-rasher" check
they steal.

GÜNTER GRASS, *Resistance*   *591*

A West German writer argues for steps to ensure that the world war in which he
came of age is truly the world's last war.

7.   WE ARE ALL FOREIGNERS   597

PAUL HARRISON, *The Westernization of the World*   *599*

Given our world's spectacular cultural diversity, why are men around the globe
wearing identical suits and ties to work in identical offices?

V. S. NAIPAUL, *Entering the New World*   *606*

The author relates his encounter with an Ivory Coast poet whose father had sent
him to the French colonial school not to become a "white man" but "to enter
the new world, that's all."

EDWARD T. HALL, *Proxemics in the Arab World*   *611*

To understand why both Arabs and Westerners accuse each other of pushiness,
we must recognize the contrast in their concepts of personal space.

KATE MILLETT, *Arriving in Tehran*   *621*

Iran after the shah's downfall is no liberated democracy, finds an American
feminist, but a remilitarized zone of armed militia, sandbagged hotels, and
shrouded women.

GUAN KEGUANG, *A Chinese Reporter on Cape Cod*   *630*

From its vending machines to its employment ads, the United States strikes a
visiting journalist as an overwhelming barrage of options.

ORVILLE SCHELL, *Shanghai* 635

To a pair of Chinese teenagers, the United States is a faraway magic land of Fords and Dodges, Camels and Lucky Strikes, and that most prized of all status symbols, Levis.

ANDREA LEE, *The Beriozka* 644

For foreigners, the Soviet diplomatic store is a source of scarce luxury items; for Russians, it is a tantalizing glimpse into consumer paradise.

DAVID K. SHIPLER, *Western Things* 649

Although we like to think the Russians envy our democratic government and personal freedom, an American journalist asserts, what they really covet is our stereo systems and designer jeans.

STANISŁAW LEM, *Being Inc.* [SHORT STORY] 656

In this review of an imaginary American novel, a Polish science fiction writer envisions a future in which the only kind of life that cannot be arranged is an unarranged life.

GEOGRAPHICAL INDEX 671

INDEX OF AUTHORS AND TITLES 673

A NOTE
ON TRANSLATIONS

The three excerpts that follow come from different English translations of the same Iranian short story, originally written in Farsi. As you compare them, keep an eye out for differences and also for unexpected similarities. What do you learn from these passages about the choices a translator must make?

1

Hasani himself told me. He said, "Let's go over to my place tonight." I'd never been to their place, nor had he to mine; that is, I'd always been too afraid of what my father would do to ask him over, and he, he too, feared his father. But that night being unlike other nights, I couldn't get out of it; Hasani was mad at me, he imagined I no longer liked him, I wasn't his friend — so I went; it was the first time I had set foot in his place. We always ran into each other outdoors; mornings I would go by his little shanty and would whistle loud like a bulbul,[1] with a pretty bulbul's whistle that he himself had taught me. And so, it was as if I had whistled, "Come on, Hasani, it's time to get going." Hasani would pick up a can and come out. Instead of saying Hi, we would box with each other a bit, with firm, respectable punches that hurt. So had we arranged — whenever we would see each other, whenever we would part, we would box. Unless we were angry with one another, or we had cheated each other. Next we would set out and pass among all the little hovels and plunge into Body Washer's Hollow, where city garbage trucks dumped refuse, and we would delve into the trash; one day I would gather some tin and Hasani a little glass, and another day Hasani would gather some tin and I a little glass. Now and then we would come up with something better, an empty vegetable oil can, a baby's bottle, a

---

[1] A Persian songbird, probably a nightingale, frequently mentioned in poetry. — ED.

broken doll, an odd useless shoe, a perfectly good sugar bowl with a handle missing, or a plastic pitcher. Once I found a golden talisman bearing a Koranic verse such as would be hung around a baby's neck, and Hasani had once found an unopened package of imported cigarettes. Whenever we became tired, we would go to the side of the hollow where the big terrace was which ended at Hajj Timur's Kiln, that no longer operated and was in ruins, that was abandoned to God's care.

> – "The Game Is Over"
> Gholamhosein Saedi
> Translated by Robert A. Campbell (1978)

◇◇◇◇◇

2

Hasani himself asked me. He asked me to go to their hut that evening. I had never gone to their hut. He had never come to ours. I'd never asked him to, because I was scared of my pa. He was scared of his pa, too — a lot more than I was of mine. But that evening was different. I had to go. Hasani would feel hurt and get angry at me if I didn't. He would think I didn't like him anymore and wasn't his friend. That's why I went. That was the first time I set foot in their hut. We always met outside. Our huts were in a cluster of squatters' huts. I'd stop by their hut in the morning and whistle — a pretty whistle he had taught me. This was our signal. It was like saying, "Come Hasani! Time to go to work." Hasani would pick up his bucket and come out of the hut. Instead of saying hello, we would fistfight for a spell — nice, hard blows that hurt really good. We fistfought when we met, and we fistfought when we parted — except when we were mad at each other for some reason.

Hasani and I would walk past the huts until we reached the pit near the home where they washed the dead. The garbage trucks emptied the garbage in that pit. Hasani and I went to the pile every morning. Some days I would collect tin cans, Hasani would look for broken glass; some days he would look for tin cans, I for glass. Once in a while we would find something better, an empty margarine can, a pacifier, a broken doll, a shoe, a plastic pitcher, or even a sugar bowl with just a tiny crack. Once I found an amulet and Hasani an unopened pack of imported cigarettes. When we got tired we would go to the other side of the pit, past Hadj Teimur's kilns — which were not working anymore and had been abandoned.

> – "The Game Is Up"
> Ghulamhusayn Sa'idi
> Translated by Minoo S. Southgate (1980)

⟨◇⟨◇⟨◇⟨◇⟨◇⟩

3

Hasani said it to me himself: "Let's go over to my place tonight." I'd never been to their place. He'd never been to mine. What I'm getting at is, we were always too afraid of our fathers. He was a lot more afraid than I was. But that night it was different: Hasani was mad at me. He imagined that I didn't like him anymore, that I wasn't his friend. So we went. Usually we just met each other outside. In the morning I would go to their little shack and give a long-drawn-out whistle that Hasani had taught me. When I whistled, Hasani would grab a can and come out. Instead of saying "Hi," we would fight a little. We would hit each other hard so it hurt. That's how we'd decided to behave, and whenever we met, or whenever we left each other, we would fight like that — unless we were either angry or had tricked each other.

After that we'd go running between all the little shacks and drop into Body Washer's Hollow. The city garbage trucks dumped their trash there. We'd root around in the trash. One day I might pick up some tin, and Hasani might find some glass. Now and then we'd get our hands on something better, like an empty salad oil can, a baby's bottle, a broken doll, a useful shoe, a perfectly good sugar bowl with a handle broken off or maybe a plastic pitcher. Once I found a gold charm with a verse from the Koran on it. Like from a baby's necklace. Hasani had found a full pack of foreign cigarettes. When we got tired, we'd go to the side of the hollow where there's a big flat place: Hājji Timur's Kiln's at the far side of the terrace. They didn't use it anymore. It was ruined.

– "The Game Is Over"
Gholam-Hossein Sa'edi
Translated by Robert Campbell (1981)

What structural differences, such as paragraph and sentence breaks, do you notice in these three translations?

What contrasts in emphasis can you identify? That is, where is a detail included by one translator and not another? What ideas are condensed by one translator and spelled out by another?

Which passages in each translation do you think are more successful than in the other two? Which translation do you like best overall, and why?

OURSELVES
AMONG OTHERS

*Cross-Cultural Readings
for Writers*

PART ONE

THE FAMILY

Cornerstone of Culture

OBSERVATIONS:
LOOKING AT OURSELVES

Bill Cosby, Michael Novak, Carol Kleiman,
Jane Howard, Claudia Wallis, Ellen Goodman

❖❖❖❖❖

Sri Delima, *Black-and-White Amah* (MALAYSIA)

Bruno Bettelheim, *Why Kibbutzim?* (ISRAEL)

Ruth Sidel, *The Liu Family* (CHINA)

Gyanranjan, *Our Side of the Fence and Theirs* (INDIA)

John David Morley, *Acquiring a Japanese Family* (JAPAN)

Carola Hansson and Karin Lidén, *Liza and Family*
(SOVIET UNION)

Vincent Crapanzano, *Growing Up White in South Africa*
(SOUTH AFRICA)

Wole Soyinka, *Nigerian Childhood* (NIGERIA)

Gholam-Hossein Sa'edi, *The Game Is Over* (IRAN)

ALL OVER THE WORLD, FAMILIES ARE THE MEANS BY WHICH NEW members of a society start learning its rules. From this introduction come the child's earliest ideas about what is "normal" and what is "strange." Human beings are astonishingly adaptable. Thus, as we scan different societies, we see children — and their parents — playing a wide variety of roles.

Just as the family's structure and dynamics change from one society to another, so does the writer's focus. What is significant about families? unusual? amusing? inspiring? tragic? We open with a range of *Observations:* Bill Cosby on why people have children; Michael Novak on capitalism's impact on the American family; Carol Kleiman's frustrations as a divorced mother; Jane Howard with creative ideas for pseudofamilies; Claudia Wallis on our national preoccupation with day care; and Ellen Goodman assessing the family as "social glue."

As we see how writers of different nationalities approach this universal institution, we look into the heart of culture. Sri Delima presents an alternative to day care in "Black-and-White Amah," a reminiscence about the devoted, domineering nurse who shaped her early years in Malaysia. The question of how and by whom children should be reared receives another answer in Bruno Bettelheim's "Why Kibbutzim?" the collective strategy of the Israeli kibbutz. Ruth Sidel reports in "The Liu Family" that China under Mao Zedong also cast the family as a political keystone, but there the concept was applied quite differently.

The dogmatism of the Chinese Cultural Revolution has echoes in Gyanranjan's short story "Our Side of the Fence and Theirs," where an Indian family watches their new neighbors for breaches of the social code. The identification between self, home, and family also infuses John David Morley's "Acquiring a Japanese Family." In Japan the word for "home" can also mean "myself."

The urban Soviet family, like the Japanese, is close not only by tradition but by necessity, because housing is scarce. In "Liza and Family" Carola Hansson and Karin Lidén interview a Moscow working mother whose safety net is her relatives. The extended family is equally significant to Hennie, a descendant of Voortrekkers profiled by Vincent Crapanzano in "Growing Up White in South Africa." Hennie's family taught him *manlikheid* — manhood — and racism. Wole Soyinka's "Nigerian Childhood" depicts a black Anglican household where British propriety is cheerfully mixed with African magic. Finally, in Gholam-Hossein Sa'edi's chilling short story "The Game Is Over," poverty and parental abuse spur two Iranian boys to an act that staggers their whole village.   ❧

OBSERVATIONS:
LOOKING AT OURSELVES

1

It seems to me that two people have a baby just to see what they can make, like a kind of erotic arts and crafts. And some people have several children because they know there are going to be failures. They figure that if they have a dozen, maybe one or two will work out, for having children is certainly defying the odds.

– Bill Cosby
Fatherhood

◇◇◇◇◇

2

We live in lucky times. So many, so varied, and so aggressive are the antifamily sentiments in our society that brave souls may now have (for the first time in centuries) the pleasure of discovering for themselves the importance of the family. Choosing to have a family used to be uninteresting. It is, today, an act of intelligence and courage. To love family life, to see in family life the most potent moral, intellectual, and political cell in the body politic is to be marked today as a heretic.

Orthodoxy is usually enforced by an economic system. Our own system, postindustrial capitalism, plays an ambivalent role with respect to the family. On the one hand, capitalism demands hard work, competition, sacrifice, saving, and rational decision-making. On the other, it stresses liberty and encourages hedonism.

Now the great corporations (as well as the universities, the political professions, the foundations, the great newspapers and publishing empires, and the film industry) diminish the moral and economic importance of the family. They demand travel and frequent change of residence. Teasing the heart with glittering entertainment and gratifying the demands of ambition, they dissolve attachments and loyalties. Husbands and wives live in isolation from each other. Children of the upwardly mobile are almost as abandoned, emotionally, as the children of the ghetto. The lives of husbands, wives, and children do not mesh, are not engaged, seem merely thrown together. There is enough money. There is too much emotional space. It is easier to leave town than to pretend that one's lives truly matter to each other. (I remember the tenth anniversary party of a foreign office of a major newsmagazine; none of its members was married to his spouse of ten years before.) At an advanced stage capitalism imparts enormous centrifugal forces to the souls of those who have most internalized its values; and these forces shear marriages and families apart. . . .

An economic order that would make the family the basic unit of social policy would touch every citizen at the nerve center of daily life. The family is the primary teacher of moral development. In the struggles and conflicts of marital life, husbands and wives learn the realism and adult practicalities of love. Through the love, stability, discipline, and laughter of parents and siblings, children learn that reality accepts them, welcomes them, invites their willingness to take risks. The family nourishes "basic trust." From this spring creativity, psychic energy, social dynamism. If infants are injured here, not all the institutions of society can put them back together.

> – Michael Novak
> "The Family Out of Favor"
> *Harper's*

◇–◇–◇–◇–◇

3

One summer day, my son Robert, then five years old, took me by the hand and asked me to go outside with him.

Holding on tightly, he carefully walked around the house with me, looking at doors and windows and shaking his head. There was something he didn't understand.

"Mommy," he finally asked, pressing my hand with his warm, chubby fingers, "is our home broken?"

His words shot through my body, alerting every protective instinct, activating my private defense system, the one I hold in reserve to ward off attacks against women and children.

"Oh, Robbie," I answered, hugging him, "did someone tell you that we have a broken home?"

"Yes," he said sweetly. "But it doesn't *look* broken!"

"It's not," I assured him. "Our house is not broken and neither are we."

I explained that "broken" is some people's way of describing a home with only one parent, usually the mother. Sometimes there was only one parent because of divorce, like us. "There are still lots of homes like ours. And they're still homes."

Robbie looked relieved and went to play with his friends. I stood there, shaking with anger.

What a way to put down a little kid and me, too, I thought. I supported my three children, fed and clothed them. I was there for them emotionally and physically. I managed to keep up payments on the house. Although we struggled financially, we were happy and loving. What was "broken" about us?

> – Carol Kleiman
> "My Home Is Not Broken, It Works"
> *Ms.*

◇◇◇◇◇

4

Whatever "support systems" may be, the need for them is clearly urgent, and not just in this country. Are there not thriving "megafamilies" of as many as three hundred people in Scandinavia? Have not the Japanese for years had an honored, enduring — if perhaps by our standards rather rigid — custom of adopting nonrelatives to fill gaps in their families? Should we not applaud and maybe imitate such ingenuity?

And consider our own Unitarians. From Santa Barbara to Boston they have been earnestly dividing their congregations into arbitrary "extended families" whose members are bound to act like each other's relatives. Kurt Vonnegut, Jr., plays with a similar train of thought in his fictional *Slapstick*. In that book every newborn baby is assigned a randomly chosen middle name, like Uranium or Daffodil or Raspberry. These middle names are connected with hyphens to numbers between one and twenty, and any two people who have the same middle name are automatically related. This is all to the good, the author thinks, because "human beings need all the relatives they can get — as possible donors or receivers not of love but of common decency." He envisions these extended families as "one of the four greatest inventions by Americans," the others being *Robert's Rules of Order*, the Bill of Rights, and the principles of Alcoholics Anonymous.

This charming notion might even work, if it weren't so arbitrary. Already each of us is born into one family not of our choosing. If we're going to devise new ones, we might as well have the luxury of picking the members ourselves. Clever picking might result in new families whose benefits would surpass or at least equal those of the old.

> – Jane Howard
> "All Happy Clans Alike"
> *Atlantic Monthly*

◇◇◇◇◇

5

With both Mom and Dad away at the office or store or factory, the child-care crunch has become the most wrenching personal problem facing millions of American families. In 1986, 9 million preschoolers spent their days in the hands of someone other than their mother. Millions of older children participate in programs providing after-school supervision. As American women continue to pour into the work force, the trend will accelerate. "We are in the midst of an explosion," says Elinor Guggenheimer, president of the Manhattan-based Child Care Action Campaign. In ten years, she predicts, the number of children under six who will need daytime supervision will grow more than 50 percent. Says Jay Belsky, a professor of human development at Pennsylvania State University: "We are as much a society dependent on female labor, and thus in need of a child-care system, as we are a society dependent on the automobile, and thus in need of roads."

At the moment, though, the American child-care system — to the extent that there is one — is riddled with potholes. Throughout the country, working parents are faced with a triple quandary: day care is hard to find, difficult to afford, and often of distressingly poor quality. Waiting lists at good facilities are so long that parents apply for a spot months before their children are born. Or even earlier. The Empire State center in Farmingdale, N.Y., received an application from a woman attorney a week after she became engaged to marry. Apparently she hoped to time her pregnancy for an anticipated opening. The Jeanne Simon center in Burlington, Vt., has a folder of applications labeled "preconception." . . .

Fretting about the effects of day care on children has become a national preoccupation. What troubles lie ahead for a generation reared by strangers? What kind of adults will they become? "It is scaring everybody that a whole generation of children is being raised in a way that has never happened before," says Edward Zigler, professor of psychology at Yale and an authority on child care. At least one major survey of current research, by Penn State's Belsky, suggests that extensive day care in the first year of life raises the risk of emotional problems, a conclusion that has mortified already guilty working parents. With high-quality supervision costing upwards of $100 a week, many families are placing their children in the hands of untrained, overworked personnel. "In some places, that means one woman taking care of nine babies," says Zigler. "Nobody doing that can give them the stimulation they need. We encounter some real horror stories out there, with babies being tied into cribs."

The U.S. is the only Western industrialized nation that does not guarantee a working mother the right to a leave of absence after she has a child. Although the Supreme Court ruled last January that states may require businesses to provide maternity leaves with job security, only 40 percent of working women receive such protection through their companies. Even for these, the leaves are generally brief and unpaid. This forces many women to return to work sooner than they would like and creates a huge demand for infant care, the most expensive and difficult child-care service to supply. The premature separation takes a personal toll as well, observes Harvard Pediatrician T. Berry Brazelton, heir apparent to Benjamin Spock as the country's preeminent guru on child rearing. "Many parents return to the workplace grieving."

– Claudia Wallis
"The Child-Care Dilemma"
Time

◇—◇—◇—◇—◇

6

They are going home for Thanksgiving, traveling through the clogged arteries of airports and highways, bearing bridge chairs and serving plates, Port-a-Cribs and pies. They are going home to rooms that resound with old arguments and interruptions, to piano benches filled with small cousins, to dining-room tables stretched out to the last leaf.

They no longer migrate over the river and through the woods straight into that Norman Rockwell poster: Freedom from Want. No, Thanksgiving isn't just a feast, but a reunion. It's no longer a celebration of food (which is plentiful in America) but of family (which is scarce).

Now families are so dispersed that it's easier to bring in the crops than the cousins. Now it's not so remarkable that we have a turkey to feed the family. It's more remarkable that there's enough family around to warrant a turkey.

For most of the year, we are a nation of individuals, all wrapped in separate cellophane packages like lamb chops in the meat department of a city supermarket. Increasingly we live with decreasing numbers. We create a new category like Single Householder, and fill it to the top of the Census Bureau reports.

For most of the year, we are segregated along generation lines into retirement villages and singles complexes, young married subdivisions and college dormitories, all exclusive clubs whose membership is defined by age.

Even when we don't live in age ghettos, we often think that way.

Those who worried about a generation gap in the sixties worry about a generation war in the seventies. They see a community torn by warring rights: the Elderly Rights vs. the Middle-Aged Rights vs. the Children Rights. All competing for a piece of the pie.

This year, the Elderly Rights fought against mandatory retirement while the Younger Rights fought for job openings. The Children Rights worried about the money to keep their schools open, while the Elderly Rights worried about the rising cost of real estate taxes.

The retired generation lobbied for an increase in Social Security payments, while the working generation lobbied for a decrease in Social Security taxes. The elderly wanted health care and the children wanted day care and the middle-aged were tired of taking care. They wanted the right to lead their own lives.

At times it seemed as if the nation had splintered into peer pressure groups, panthers of all ages. People who cried, not "Me First" but, rather, "My Generation First."

But now they have come home for Thanksgiving. Even the Rights are a family who come together, not to fight for their piece of the pie this day, but to share it.

The family — as extended as that dining-room table — may be the one social glue strong enough to withstand the centrifuge of special interests which sends us spinning away from each other. There, in the family, the Elderly Rights are also grandparents and the Children Rights are also nieces and nephews. There, the old are our parents and the young are our children. There, we care about each others' lives. There, self-interest includes concern for the future of the next generation. Because they are ours.

Our families are not just the people (if I may massacre Robert Frost) who, "when you have to go there, they have to let you in." They are the people who maintain an unreasonable interest in each other. They are the natural peacemakers in the generation war.

"Home" is the only place in society where we now connect along the ages, like discs along the spine of society. The only place where we remember that we're all related. And that's not a bad idea to go home to.

> – Ellen Goodman
> "Family: The One Social Glue"
> *Close to Home*

SRI DELIMA

Black-and-White Amah

"Black-and-White Amah" originally appeared in Sri Delima's news-paper column "As I Was Passing" for *The New Straits Times* in Kuala Lumpur, Malaysia. Born in 1936, Sri Delima was educated at the University of Malaya in Singapore. Her diverse writing includes critiques of the local arts and cultural scene; she also acts in her own radio plays.

Sri Delima laments in another of her columns: "There was a time when, if you went abroad, you had to explain painfully that Malaya was somewhere southeast of India and southwest of China. (Later it helped to say 'south of Vietnam.')" Foreigners' confusion is perhaps understandable. The Malay Peninsula extends southward from Thailand, east of the Philippine Islands and north of Indonesia. In 1824 the British and Dutch split their holdings in the islands around the peninsula, known as the East Indies. The southern Dutch East Indies became independent in 1945 as Indonesia. The northern British East Indies — plus the Malay Peninsula — evolved into the Federation of Malaya. In 1963 the federation became an independent constitutional monarchy within the British Commonwealth under the name of Malaysia. It comprised the Malay Peninsula (including Singapore at its tip), Sabah (North Borneo), and Sarawak, until Singapore dropped out in 1965. Malaysia's present total area is a little larger than New Mexico; its climate is tropical; its people are approximately 47 percent ethnic Malays, 34 percent Chinese, and 10 percent Indians.

British rule, though it lasted less than a century (1874–1963), had a profound influence on Malaysia. Some of its effects are visible in Sri Delima's essay: the English language; unity among scattered regions and races; and colonial class consciousness and dependence on servants. The "black-and-white amah" is the Malaysian counterpart of the British nanny, a woman hired to care for small children. *Tuan* and *mem* are titles given to high-ranking officials and their wives.

The elders in my clan speak nostalgically of the old "family retainer" type of servant, the kind that after a while became more "family" than "retainer."

She — when it was a she — regarded you as her very own, for did

9

she not watch over you when you were a baby, protecting you from mosquitoes and evil spirits and the newfangled notions of your young parents?

It was from her you learnt your first words and heard your first tales of magic. From her too you got the first spank on your naughty little bottom to set you on the path of virtue and grace and pretty manners.

Yet let anyone else in the house so much as flick that precious bottom,   4
and she leapt to your defense like a mother-tigress and consoled you with sticky sweets and stickier kisses.

Or if it was a he, what did you not learn from him in the way of skills and knowledge of the world? From kite flying to rambutan raiding you owed him all the basics.

When it was his turn to take you to school and hang around the premises till the time came to take you home again, he did it with as much loving patience as his female counterpart, and a lot more style. He was always dressed to kill for the occasion and greeted people on the way with elaborate courtesy, regaling you immediately afterwards with stories of their idiosyncrasies.

She's and he's alike, these retainers retained their protective affection for you all their lives and yours. Often their children grew up with you and the ties remained strong down the generations.

My mother was fiercely modern and would not have her children   8
brought up by "old traditionalists who wrap babies up like Egyptian mummies and feed them on mashed bananas."

When at thirty-three she had me, her first living child, it was a "black-and-white amah" for me or nothing. Ah Yoong's salary must have swallowed up half my parents' combined income, but they cheerfully scrimped to give their beloved offspring as good a start in life as the *tuans'* and *mems'* children.

The clan's oral literature contains stirring accounts of battles between Ah Yoong and my mother on the one side and grandmas and great-aunts and miscellaneous elders on the other side.

Wrap in *bedung* or leave free, feed on demand or to schedule, mashed bananas or mashed potatoes, sleep with an elder or alone in a cot, play barefoot in the garden or with socks and shoes on, etc., etc., etc.

Ah Yoong and my mother won most of the battles. But the inevitable   12
day came when they fought each other and Ah Yoong stalked off with bag and baggage and black umbrella and all.

I yowled day and night and broke out in a rash, but by the time my

mother had swallowed her pride enough to send emissaries to coax Ah
Yoong back, a *mem* and *tuan* had already snapped her up and taken her
on transfer with them, destination unknown. So there went my chance
of being blindly loved for a lifetime.

My rash turned out to be chicken pox rather than separation shock
and my fickle child's heart soon semiforgot Ah Yoong. The war and the
Japanese Occupation came and went, then one day in 1946 who should
appear but Ah Yoong, looking not a day older but a lot more prosperous,
all aglitter with gold and jade.

I had been a plump three-year-old when she left and now I was a
skinny ten, but she recognized me at once and smothered me with hugs
and kisses and even tried to carry me in her still-strong arms.

She had come, she said later, just to see whether we had come through   16
the war all right. She had been singularly fortunate, she said, smiling
her sweet gold-tooth smile at our teasing about her finery. After half-
suffocating me again, she vanished from our lives.

How I envy a friend's friend whose old servant is with him to this day.
He, ungrateful fellow, deems it a mixed blessing.

I see his point, though. He is a senior executive accustomed to command respect and deference. He gives a grand reception in his gracious
split-level home, and in the midst of it all out pops his old servant with
a glass of milk and says, waving her finger chidingly: "Now be a good
boy, Young Master, drink your milkie-milk."

Still I consider him lucky and so does our common friend, who has
been changing servants about once a fortnight these past few years.

"You would think I was some sort of ogress, the way they have been   20
walking out on me," she sighs.

Far from being an ogress, she is the gentlest and most thoughtful
creature you could hope to know. It is just the changing times, I tell her.
Domestic service as a career has gone out of vogue — and I am not sure
it is not a good thing.

Except for the "black-and-white amahs" — for whom you pay the
earth and still worry lest they leave you for someone who offers the sun
— today's servants are mostly young girls out to make a bit of money to
help their families or to splash on clothes before they get married and
settle down.

They are young people in a hurry — restless, ready to fly off at the
slightest dissatisfaction. So what do you do? The need is more yours than
theirs, so you have to do acrobatics to catch and hold them.

My friend has listed some of the "musts"s and "must not"s of the   24
game. The "must"s include: free access to transistor radio, television set,
and telephone; neighbors with servants; easy transport to and from town;
weekends off and long stretches off around festivals; and a salary a girl
can mention without blushing to her status group in the servant hierarchy.

The "must-not"s comprise: grumbling when two days off stretch into
six or a girl keeps having to go home because relatives will keep falling
ill and dying; noticing that a particular relative seems to have died more
than once; commenting on cuisine disasters or cobwebs in corners; and,
taboo of taboos, absentmindedly switching to another channel when a
Malay, Hindi, Chinese, Tamil, or Egyptian film comes on.

I am passing this list to another friend. She is swotting up[1] on the
subject, as someone is bringing along a prospective servant to her house
soon. She wants to be ready with the right answers when the prospective
servant interviews her for suitability as an employer.

EXPLORATIONS

1. What is Sri Delima's attitude toward Ah Yoong, her "black-and-white amah"?
   According to her essay, what are the main benefits to a child of having such
   an amah? What are the benefits to the parents?

2. From what sources did Sri Delima gather the information in "Black-and-
   White Amah"? At what points in the essay does she move from personal
   experience to outside data and vice versa? Look closely at each of these
   transitions. How does Sri Delima use them to establish the universal relevance
   of her own experience?

3. Another technique Sri Delima uses to reach a wide audience is varied persons:
   Parts of her essay are written in the first person (*I*), parts in the second person
   (*you*), and parts in the third person (*she* or *he, they*). What advantages does
   she gain as a writer from using each of these persons?

4. As a newspaper columnist, Sri Delima must catch her readers' attention. One
   way she does this is by including vivid details in her essay. For example,
   instead of writing simply "Ah Yoong stalked off," she writes, "Ah Yoong
   stalked off with bag and baggage and black umbrella and all." Find at least
   three more places in "Black-and-White Amah" where specific details help Sri
   Delima to make her point. What is the impact of each of these descriptions?

---

[1] A British expression for studying. — ED.

CONNECTIONS

1. Claudia Wallis's *Observation* describes some American parents' child-care dilemma. What aspects of this dilemma are solved for some Malaysian parents by the "black-and-white amah"? What aspects remain unresolved?

2. Which concept of the American family presented in the *Observations* appears closest to the Malaysian family depicted by Sri Delima? On what evidence do you base your answer?

ELABORATIONS

1. "Domestic service as a career has gone out of vogue — and I am not sure it is not a good thing," writes Sri Delima. This statement could be made in a number of countries besides Malaysia, including the United States. What biases and assumptions does it reflect on the author's part? Why do you think caring for other people's homes and children has "gone out of vogue" as a full-time occupation? Write an essay on domestic service as a career option: its past, present, and potential pros and cons.

2. Recall a caretaker, such as a baby-sitter or a grandparent, who played a memorable role in your childhood. Using as many specific details as possible, write an essay comparing and contrasting your caretaker's role with that of the black-and-white amah in Sri Delima's essay.

BRUNO BETTELHEIM

Why Kibbutzim?

Newsweek has called Bruno Bettelheim "one of the world's outstanding authorities on childhood emotional development and disorder." The author of numerous books, articles, and essays, as well as a monthly column for the *Ladies' Home Journal,* Bettelheim was born in Vienna in 1903. In 1938 he received his Ph.D. from the University of Vienna; and the Nazis took over Austria. Bettelheim was sent to the concentration camps at Dachau and Buchenwald. Released the next year, he emigrated to the United States and became a naturalized citizen. In addition to serving as a professor of education, psychology, and psychiatry at the University of Chicago, he headed the university's Sonia Shankman Orthogenic School from 1944 until 1973. He also coproduced a motion picture, *The Kibbutz.* He now lives in California.

"Why Kibbutzim?" comes from Bettelheim's 1969 book *The Children of the Dream,* which he wrote after spending seven weeks studying communal child rearing in the Israeli kibbutz. These collective farms (singular *kibbutz,* plural *kibbutzim*) were first established by Palestinian Jews even before the United Nations officially created the state of Israel in 1948. Jews fleeing discrimination and persecution all over the world had been migrating to this strip of land on the eastern Mediterranean coast, seeking to reestablish the ancient Jewish homeland. After World War II more than a million refugees flocked here. Creating kibbutzim was one concrete way of helping to build a new and better future. In a country of 7992 square miles which includes the Dead Sea and the Negev Desert, and only a fifth of which is arable, kibbutzim have been practically as well as politically crucial. Today they remain a way of life for a significant minority of Israelis, and a cornerstone of Israeli culture.

(For more background on Israel, see p. 180.)

From its very very inception the purpose of the kibbutz movement, for both sexes, was first and foremost to create a new way of life in a very old and hostile land. True, the raising of a new generation to this new way of life was soon of crucial importance, but of necessity it took second place. Because unless the first generation created the society, how could it shelter any new generations? It was this older generation that subjected itself to great hardships and dangers, that first reclaimed the land, wresting harvests from a barren soil, and later fought the war that gained them statehood.

Today, apart from the still pervasive problem of making fast their new statehood, there is still the war for social ideals to be waged. But those ideals are harder to maintain when the problem is no longer one of creating a homeland, but of maintaining themselves as a splinter group in a land swept up in a booming economy. Such ideals are specially hard to preserve when the surrounding population is by now so largely concerned with acquiring the more convenient life that goes with a higher standard of living. The kibbutz parent, in his devotion to ideals, may be likened to our own early Puritans; except that these latter-day Puritans are not surrounded by a wilderness but by modern city life, which makes things a lot harder.

Kibbutzniks have never been more than a tiny minority in Israel. Nevertheless they have played a critical role there, both as idea and reality, out of all proportion to their numbers. For example, in 1944 Henrik Infield, in his book *Co-operative Living in Palestine*, places the total membership of all kibbutzim at about sixteen thousand. Twenty years later their numbers had grown to about eighty thousand, living in about 250 kibbutzim, but they were still only about 4 percent of the population of Israel. Yet this 4 percent accounted for some 15 percent of all members of the Knesset (Israeli parliament).

Even if the kibbutz stood for no more than a small sect, living by its esoteric convictions and trying to raise its children by these lights, their devotion to lofty ideals would command respect. But for Israel they do much more than that, since they still provide much of the national ethos, and the best part of it. As many thoughtful Israelis told me: Were it not for the kibbutz dream of a better society, there would be nothing unique left about Israel. Having created a refuge where Jews can live free of persecution, Israel would be nothing more now than just a tiny new nation.

(Though written before the 1967 war, I see no reason to change this statement. The Arab-Israeli conflict is no longer a matter of the majority group persecuting a minority of its own citizens, but of two or more nation-states at odds over territorial rights. That one is smaller than the others does not make war and persecution the same thing, which they are not.)

It is also a nation with only one tenuous claim to the land: namely, that some two thousand years ago it was occupied by the spiritual ancestors of those who again hold possession now. This is not much of a claim compared to the uniqueness Jews felt, and which kept the Jews going during the two thousand years they were homeless.

All this has, in fact, led to many contradictions from which Kibbutz life still suffers: In reclaiming the land, as in creating the state of Israel, kibbutzniks displaced Arab neighbors and fought them though violence was contrary to their socialist convictions. Kibbutz founders wanted Israel to be an ideal state, free of all exploitation, where life would proceed in peace close to the biblical land. But the realities of the Middle East force Israel to be a garrison nation geared to defense, if not a war; a capitalist nation with many of the unpleasant features of a new nation trying to industrialize in a hurry.

I know that they also suffer from another contradiction, because they are keenly aware of it: Since they are atheists, they cannot base their claim to the land on the biblical promise that gave it to the Jews. The Jews needed a homestead. How desperately they needed it was made clear first by Hitler, and then by the plight of the Jews in Arab countries. But no other land was acceptable to the religious group, and no other land offered asylum to areligious Jews. So it had to be Israel, whether for political or emotional reasons. 8

In the face of all this contradiction and conflict, then, is where the kibbutz ethos makes a difference. It stands for utter devotion to the idea that once again Jews in Israel must not only create a new model of the good and just life, but actually live it — when need be at the cost of great personal hardship — or die for it if they must. Certainly the six-day war vindicated kibbutz child-rearing methods and made it once again a symbol of all that is best in Israel. Not only did the kibbutz provide an inordinate percentage of the officer corps, it also suffered stagggering losses. Some 4 percent of the Israeli population lives in the kibbutz, and kibbutzniks thus accounted for some 4 percent of the fighting force. But while about eight hundred soldiers fell in the war, two hundred of them came from the kibbutz (most of them born and raised there). Thus the 4 percent kibbutz segment of the Israeli army suffered 25 percent of all casualties. This was the true measure of their heroism, courage, and devotion to duty. Once more, as in the settling of the land and the war of liberation, the kibbutz ethos gives special meaning to the lives of Israelis today.

It is in this context of self-elected mission that the entire phenomenon of the kibbutz must be understood, and flowing from it, what the parents do or do not do in raising their children. . . .

How did the kibbutz way of raising children come about? First, it seems that kibbutz founders did not trust themselves to raise their own children in such a way as to become the carriers of a new society. To quote [Stanley] Diamond:

> The collective method of child rearing represents a rejection of the family, with particular reference to the parental roles. . . . It was felt that the family itself has to be banished, in order to rear the "new Jew." . . . [Kibbutz founders] were moved by the desire to create a new generation that would be "normal," "free," and "manly," unsullied by the exile. . . . They did not think themselves worthy of rearing such children within the confines of their own nuclear families, and they dared not trust themselves to the task.[1]

Thus the realization of their larger dream depended on this new and uniquely brought up generation. But the new generation, and the unique way of bringing them up, were an afterthought, an accident. The kibbutz — a society that devotes its all to the future, and hence to its children, that has turned upside down all traditional modes of child rearing to realize its goals — started out as a society that had no interest in children whatsoever and no room for children in its life.

While this in no way invalidates the educational method, it accounts for many contradictions that cannot be understood except from its unplanned inception. We are faced with the anomaly that what started as a nuisance, because it stood in the way of the founders' main purposes — to execute an idea — has become a central feature on which the idea's survival now depends.

As Joseph Baratz (1954) tells the story of Degania, the first kibbutz, the original kibbutzniks (of whom he was one) wanted no children in their community. Most of the settlers did not even want to marry, because "they were afraid that children would detach the family from the group, that . . . comradeship would be less steadfast." Therefore it was seriously proposed that all members should oblige themselves not to marry for at least five years after joining the kibbutz, because "living as we do . . . how can we have children?"

When the first child was born in the kibbutz "nobody knew what to do with him. Our women didn't know how to look after babies." But eventually "we saw it couldn't go on like this. . . . By the time there were four children in the settlement we decided something must be done. It was a difficult problem. How were the women both to work and look

---

[1] In *Social Problems*, Vol. 5, No. 2, 1957 and *Dissent*, Vol. 4, 1957. — Ed.

after their children? Should each mother look after her own family and do nothing else?" The men did not seem to feel strongly either way.

> But the women wouldn't hear of giving up their share of the communal work and life. . . . Somebody proposed that the kibbutz should hire a nurse . . . we didn't hire a nurse, but we chose one girl to look after the lot of them and we put aside a house where they could spend the day while the mothers were at work. And so this system developed and was afterwards adopted in all the kibbutzim, with the difference that in most of them the children sleep in the children's house, but with us [at Degania] they stay at night in their parents' quarters. . . . Only recently have we built a hostel for children over twelve where our own children live.[2]

This is how the famous communal education of children began.   16

I myself questioned the founding generation: I wondered why the original group, so intent on creating a new way of life, had given no thought to their own continuity by planning for the next generation. The answer was always the same as the one given in published accounts by the earliest settlers: "Founding the settlements, cultivating the land was so arduous, so much a grown-ups' task, that we could not think about children." I cannot help feeling that part of the original attraction of a thus-defined task might have been that it left no place for children. Because if one does not think of having children, it is because one has no wish for them at the time, and not because the task at hand is so arduous.

If my speculation is valid, one might carry it a step further and say that the founding generation knew they had no wish to replicate the family as they knew it, and of this they were entirely conscious. But despite their rejection they could not think of how else to raise children. Hence to them, the decision not to form families meant not to have children. If so, then kibbutz life was attractive to those who for this or other reasons did not wish to have children. My assumption seems supported by the incredibly low birthrate in the early days of kibbutz history, which contrasts sharply with other settings in which a people live in hardship and danger and nevertheless produce many children.

It would seem, then, that chance and a desire for quite other things dictated the child-caring arrangements made hastily, piecemeal, and with little plan or thought; arrangements that were later formalized into dogma, as is probably the origin of most dogmas.

---

[2] In A *Village by the Jordan* (London: Harville Press). — ED.

EXPLORATIONS

1. Bettelheim writes, "The kibbutz parent, in his devotion to ideals, may be likened to our own early Puritans." What similarities is he referring to? In what ways do you think "modern city life . . . makes things a lot harder" for the kibbutz parent than for the Puritans?

2. Most of Bettelheim's paragraphs open with a topic sentence which is followed by supporting evidence. Look at four or five paragraphs in "Why Kibbutzim?" What different types of evidence does Bettelheim use? Which type(s) do you find most persuasive?

3. Bettelheim speaks of "the kibbutz dream of a better society." Based on his description of how kibbutzim came to exist and how they operate, what kind of "better society" does "the kibbutz dream" seem to represent? What are its ideals and goals as a culture and for individual members of the culture?

CONNECTIONS

1. The kibbutzim described by Bettelheim and the "black-and-white amah" described by Sri Delima represent contrasting parental attitudes toward child rearing. What cultural and personal values and goals underlie the differences in these two approaches? (Refer to both the selections and their headnotes.)

2. What statements in Michael Novak's *Observation* suggest that some contemporary Americans share the qualms about having families which Bettelheim attributes to the Israeli kibbutzniks? According to Novak and Bettelheim, how are Americans' and Israelis' reasons for avoiding this commitment similar and different?

ELABORATIONS

1. Bettelheim quotes Stanley Diamond: "The collective method of child rearing represents a rejection of the family." What specific aspects of the traditional nuclear family do you think the early kibbutzniks rejected, and why? Based on "Why Kibbutzim?" and the *Observations* on pages 3–8, as well as your own knowledge of life in nuclear families, write an essay about the practical and psychological conflicts between work (or political activism, or any other time-consuming commitment) and traditional parenthood.

2. According to Bettelheim, the kibbutz's communal approach to child rearing derived from the potential parents' wish for their children to be better, stronger, and happier than they were. Do you think American parents share this wish?

If so, what strategies do they pursue to fulfill it, and how well do they succeed? If not, what are their goals for their children? Drawing on Bettelheim's analysis and the *Observations* that open Part One, write an essay on the aims and dreams of American parents (or some specific segment thereof) and their impact on American children.

RUTH SIDEL

The Liu Family

Ruth Sidel graduated from Wellesley College and the Boston University School of Social Work. She now lives in Riverdale, New York, where she has worked extensively with emotionally disturbed children. Sidel and her husband, Victor, have twice visited China as guests of the Chinese Medical Association. Their first trip, in 1971, produced Sidel's much-praised book *Women and Child Care in China: A Firsthand Report*. The second trip, in 1972, yielded *Families of Fengsheng: Urban Life in China*, from which "The Liu Family" is taken. Her most recent book is a study of poverty in the United States, *Women and Children Last* (1986).

Since "The Liu Family" was written, daily life in China has changed dramatically. The ancient Chinese Empire underwent a massive upheaval in 1949, when Communist forces took over the government. Under Chairman Mao Zedong, the Revolution entered a new phase — or, more accurately, a series of new phases, each with its own set of ideological and practical goals. "The Liu Family" is a vivid portrait of family life during the Cultural Revolution, the last and most repressive decade of Mao's regime. Mao's death in 1976 ended his twenty-seven years in power and ushered in yet another political, economic, and social transformation, which is continuing today.

Sidel follows the Chinese custom of giving a person's family name first and given name second. *Peking* and *Mao Tse-tung* are old spellings of *Beijing* and *Mao Zedong*.

(For more background on China, see pp. 220, 321, and 635.)

"All students study for the revolution, not just for grades," declared Liu Shu-min in a quiet yet firm voice. "They usually do not think about how high their grades are but just about what their real knowledge is — for without real knowledge one cannot join the construction of the motherland!" Liu Shu-min, a lively girl of seventeen, with eyes at once smiling and serious and long dark pigtails which swing just below her shoulders, is the third oldest of the five Liu children.

Having completed six years of primary school and three years of lower middle school, she is currently in the first year of higher middle school. In her gray jacket, blue pants, green socks, and black canvas shoes she walks a few short blocks to school every morning, arriving just before

7:30. Shu-min has a long, busy day at school beginning with early-morning exercises and including classes in mathematics, chemistry, physics, English, physical culture, politics, and health. She returns home for lunch and a short rest at 12 noon, returns to school at 2:30, and then stays after classes are over at 4:00 for physical exercise until 6:00.

The wide red band Shu-min wears on her left arm indicates that she is a member of the Red Guards. When she was younger, she was picked as a "Little Red Guard," and then in 1968 at the age of thirteen Shu-min was again chosen by her classmates and approved by the leaders of the Red Guards. She and her fellow Red Guards are a far cry from the Red Guards of 1966, 1967, and 1968 who traveled long distances from home to *ch'uan-lien*, "exchange revolutionary experiences," who carried on long, intense political disputations with their teachers and with their fellow students, and who, as the vanguard of the Cultural Revolution, gathered en masse in Tien An Men Square in Peking waving and shouting, *"Mao Chuhsi wansui!"* ("Long live Chairman Mao!") as they were greeted by him. These days Shu-min and her fellow Red Guards help their classmates who may be having difficulty with their schoolwork or with their political studies; they visit historical places, museums, and parks so that they may better understand the revolution; and they help to keep order in school by preventing the five "don't wants": throwing stones, fighting, breaking school windows, playing with sticks in school, and going out of the school gate between classes.

Like the original Red Guards, Shu-min studies the writings of Mao   4
Tse-tung and tries to use his teaching to mediate the quarrels of her fellow students. When asked to describe how she resolves quarrels between her classmates, Shu-min replied seriously, "I help them to understand the situation through their studying and applying Chairman Mao's work. We encourage them to make a 'self-criticism' and then ask them to unite." Who is chosen to be a Red Guard? According to Shu-min, "If you study Chairman Mao and your other subjects well and if you unite with your classmates well, you can be a Red Guard." According to another teenager who is not a Red Guard, "Red Guards have to be better than the other kids. They have to do good things and stop bad things. They have to do everything first and set an example. They have to be brave."

But it's not all studying and mediating disputes for Shu-min. Although she spends part of her free day, Sunday, washing clothes, hers and those of others in her family, she also likes to be with her friends, to go to the movies (*The Red Detachment of Women* is her favorite), and to go high jumping. She high jumps both in school and on the Peking Municipality high-jumping team. Shu-min had a ready answer and a broad smile when asked what she would like to do when she finishes higher middle school. She wants to "join the People's Liberation Army and then become a doctor." She quickly added that if this was not possible, she would do anything that was needed by her society, but after graduation her first plan is to apply to the P.L.A.

Shu-min lives with her thirteen-year-old brother, her eleven-year-old sister, and her parents in a small three-room house at the far end of a courtyard in Peking's Fengsheng Neighborhood. An older sister of twenty-four, unmarried, is a factory worker who sometimes lives with the family but usually stays in the factory dormitory. An older brother, age twenty-one, is a member of the People's Liberation Army and is stationed in South China.

To visit the Lius' one-story home, one walks down a dusty lane with high gray walls on both sides. Opposite a sign written in colored chalk that reads, "Actively carry on the sanitation movement; always keep this neighborhood clean," is the entrance to a large courtyard in which six other families also live. The smooth paths of the courtyard are surrounded by lush green bushes and trees — pomegranate plants laden with fruit, seven-foot-tall sunflowers, and small plants in wooden tubs. The bottom third of the Lius' house is gray brick, and the rest is constructed of wood painted red and green. Three small steps lead to a porch from which red pillars rise to support the slanting gray-tile roof. Just inside the front door is the main room with a stone floor and white stucco walls. A map of China and some framed pictures of the family hang on one wall over a high table on which rest a thermos bottle and glasses for tea. An electric pendulum clock set in wood hangs on another wall next to some straw baskets; a fluorescent light hands from the ceiling, and above that a single unadorned light bulb burns. The Lius sleep in this room as well as in the other two rooms, and carefully folded quilts with red-flowered designs are stacked on the beds. By the window goldfish swim lazily in a tank set on a desk.

Shu-min's father, Liu Yen-tung, is a forty-six-year-old skilled worker   8 in a factory in the east suburb of Peking. Dressed in a blue shirt, blue pants, and black sandals in the Indian summer of September in Peking, he is a handsome man with a broad smile and an open manner who looks younger than his forty-six years. Shu-min's mother, Chang Hung-chuang, on the other hand, looks nearly ten years older than her forty-nine years; she has a worn thin face and a worried look and is dressed in a white blouse worn over baggy blue pants. She does not work outside of the home but remains there taking care of the family. She is quiet and lets her husband do most of the talking.

Every morning Comrade Liu takes his breakfast in a small restaurant in the neighborhood and then bikes off to work at 6:30. It takes him one hour to get to work. The factory used to be located near his home, but when it was enlarged in 1959, it was moved from the West District of Peking, where the Fengsheng Neighborhood is located, to an eastern suburb. When asked if he would prefer to live closer to his place of work, Comrade Liu replied that his oldest daughter works near where they live and their children are in school here, so he would prefer to remain here and commute to work. His wife and children eat their breakfast of gruel and noodles at home, and the children then go to school — Shu-min to higher middle school, her brother to middle school, and the youngest child to primary school. They all have lunch at home with their mother, and then, after returning to school for the afternoon, the entire family eats dinner together in the evening. Just outside of the house Comrade Chang does the cooking in a tiny area which includes a coal-fed one-burner stove and a small storage space for simple cooking utensils. For dinner the Liu family enjoys many kinds of vegetables, particularly eggplant and cucumbers; they also eat some meat, chicken less often because they do not enjoy it, but fish very often because they like it.

In the evenings the children do their homework, and they all enjoy listening to the radio, playing Chinese chess, and reading the newspaper. They also very much like to go to the movies and try to go once or twice a week.

Comrade Liu works a six-day week; Friday is his day off. He spoke easily about his financial affairs. He earns 112 yuan per month (a beginning worker commonly earns approximately 35 yuan per month, and the average worker earns about 60 yuan per month), and his oldest daughter earns 33 yuan per month (1 yuan equals approximately 40¢). The implication was clear that they combine these two salaries in order to provide for the family. They pay 8 yuan per month for rent and 1 yuan per month for electricity and water. If Comrade Liu should become ill, he would go to one of the three clinics his factory maintains; for minor illness he goes to the health station in his shop. If his wife is ill, she goes to the Fengsheng Neighborhood Hospital nearby, pays the entire amount, and then is reimbursed for one half of the amount from her husband's factory. The children do the same except for minor illnesses, which are cared for in school free of charge.

As the Lius and their visitors are sitting in their home talking of their 12 medical care, a little girl about three years old with a doll-like face, wearing a brown corduroy jacket, light-colored pants, and a pink ribbon in her hair, wanders in and climbs up on the bed. Li Hsiao-hung lives in the same courtyard and is so comfortable in the Liu home that she seems like one of their children. She sits swinging her legs from the high bed, soberly looking around, and when a visitor brazenly picks her up to give her a hug and to practice meager Chinese, her eyes only widen farther. She wanders into other bedrooms with the Lius, their guests, and representatives of the neighborhood committee, all of whom seem to know one another intimately. Each bedroom has two beds piled with folded quilts, a large chest, and a small chest of drawers with a mirror hanging on the wall nearby and, next to it, a picture of Mao Tse-tung. Outside of the Liu home are large tubs of goldfish; the Lius say that they belong to a neighbor next door who does not have any children.

The lanes and courtyards of the Fengsheng Neighborhood are quiet on a weekday morning. Children are in school, most of their parents at work, leaving only a few older women, retired workers, and small children around the courtyards. Just before noon children stream out of the nearby schools and start home for lunch, some walking two-by-two, some running and shouting, others talking in small groups, the red scarves of the Little Red Guards and the red armbands of the older Red Guards standing out vividly in the crowds. Midafternoon is once again quiet, sleepy, but starting at four o'clock, children and adults begin streaming home, bicycle riders stirring up the dust of the narrow lanes, ringing their bells insistently to warn pedestrians out of the way. The streets become jammed with shoppers buying food. But by midevening dinner is over, and by nine or ten the courtyards are quiet once again.

The Liu family and six other families live together in their courtyard; these seven families are part of the fourteen thousand families who make up the Fengsheng Neighborhood in Peking.

EXPLORATIONS

1. In the opening paragraph of "The Liu Family," what does Liu Shu-min mean by "real knowledge"? From what sources has she apparently gotten her information about what "all students" in China think and do? Would you, as an American student, classify Liu Shu-min's statements in this paragraph as "real knowledge"? Why or why not?

2. What facts in "The Liu Family" has Sidel evidently gleaned from her own observations? What information appears to have come from interviews? from other sources? Which types of information do you find most interesting? most convincing?

3. In her third paragraph Sidel includes two Chinese phrases, along with their translations. In the rest of the essay she simply translates Chinese into English. Find the two Chinese phrases in paragraph 3. What effect(s) do they have on Sidel's essay? Why do you think she chose these particular expressions out of all the possibilities to include? How would the essay's impact be different if Sidel had not quoted any Chinese terms?

CONNECTIONS

1. "The Liu Family," like Bruno Bettelheim's "Why Kibbutzim?" is a report on a controversial foreign culture by an American observer. What is the main purpose of Sidel's essay? of Bettelheim's? To what extent, and in what ways, does each essay reveal the author's view of the political system in the country under study?

2. China and Malaysia are both Asian nations but with very different histories, political systems, and social structures. What similarities (if any) can you find in the attitudes toward the family described in "The Liu Family" and Sri Delima's "Black-and-White Amah"? What aspects of the Lius' family relationships do you think Sri Delima would criticize? What aspects of the Malaysian family depicted by Sri Delima do you think the Lius would criticize?

3. In her *Observation*, Ellen Goodman calls family "the one social glue" in the contemporary United States. According to Sidel's description, what is the main social glue in Mao's China? What roles are played by the family? In what ways is Chinese society evidently more cohesive — better glued — than ours? In what ways does China's high social cohesion strike you as more desirable and less desirable than our looser structure?

ELABORATIONS

1. Both the Chinese family described by Sidel and the kibbutzniks described by Bettelheim are participants in the creation of a new society. What goals and values do they have in common? How and why do they differ? Write an essay comparing and contrasting the Israeli vision with the Chinese, focusing on the family structure and practices each culture has chosen to carry out its revolutionary principles.

2. What aspects of your life would seem most odd and fascinating to Chinese readers? Suppose a Chinese sociologist were to study your family. Write an essay following Sidel's format, but replacing her description of Liu Shu-min, her schedule, family, home, and ideals with a description of your own life. Most important, how do your activities and priorities reflect the principles of the American Revolution, as Liu Shu-min's reflect the principles of China's Revolution?

GYANRANJAN

Our Side of the Fence and Theirs

The son of a renowned writer, Gyanranjan was born in 1936 in Allahabad, India, where he received his M.A. from Allahabad University.
Although he began his literary career as a poet, he published his first
short story in 1960 and was soon hailed as representing the new writing
of the sixties. "Our Side of the Fence and Theirs" is the title story from
his first collection, published in 1968 and translated from the Hindi by
Gordon C. Roadarmel. A second collection followed in 1971. Today
Gyanranjan continues to work mainly in the story form.

With a third of the area of the United States, India has three times
its population. The Indian civilization is one of the world's oldest, dating
back more than five thousand years. European traders discovered this
South Asian peninsula in the sixteenth century; by the mid-1800s the
British had wrested control from the native rajas. After World War I,
Mohandas "Mahatma" Gandhi led his people in nonviolent resistance
and civil disobedience. Since independence in 1947, India's central family has been that of its first prime minister, Jawaharlal Nehru, whose
daughter Indira Gandhi (no relation to Mohandas) succeeded him and
was in turn succeeded by her son Rajiv.

(For more background on India, see pp. 162 and 331.)

Mukherji has been transferred and no longer lives in our neighborhood. The new people who moved in have no contact with us. They
appear to be Punjabis, but maybe not. It's hard to know anything about
them.

Ever since they arrived, I've been strangely anxious to find out about
them. For some reason I can't stand staying detached. Even on journeys
I have to get acquainted with the other travelers. Perhaps it's just my
nature. But no one at our house is indifferent to those people. We're
respectable, honorable people. Having young women in the home, we're
forced to understand everything and to be constantly aware. We're full
of curiosity, and keep forming impressions based on the activities of our
new neighbors.

I'd like to invite the whole family over to our house and be able to
come and go at their place. But probably they're completely unaware of
my feelings. Their life is an unusual one. They spend a good part of the

day sitting around on chairs set on the firm ground near the veranda of their house. Those chairs remain outside all the time, even at night. They're very careless, but the chairs have never been stolen.

On one side of our house, there's a government office and a high brick wall. Behind us is the back of a two-story apartment building and, in front, the main street. As a result, we have no real proximity with any other family. The new neighbors seem like certain people found in big cities who establish no connection with others and keep strictly to themselves. Both this city and the neighborhood are quiet and peaceful. People come and go at a leisurely pace and stroll around casually, since life has no great urgency. That's why we find our neighbors strange.

I went outside. Those people were having morning tea, at the late hour of nine. Besides the husband and wife, there's one girl who must be their daughter. One always sees these same three people, never a fourth. The daughter may not be pretty, but she's a well-mannered young woman. If she used the right makeup, she might even look pretty. I've noticed that she laughs a lot — and frequently. Her mother and father laugh also. They always look happy. What sorts of things do they talk about, and why are they always laughing? Are their lives so full of delightful circumstances which keep them laughing? Or are they insensitive to the harsh, realistic circumstances of life? Amazed, I compare my family with the neighbors.

They startle me by suddenly bursting into laughter. I'd been concentrating on the rose beds, but now my trowel stopped. Their laughter seemed unable to stop. The girl rose from the chair and stood up, handing her teacup to her mother for fear of spilling it. Instead of standing straight, she was doubled over. Something funny in the conversation, perhaps a joke, must have set off the explosion of laughter. The girl, helpless with laughter, was unaware that her dupatta[1] had slipped off one shoulder. The movement of her bosom was visible — free and unrestrained. This was too much! Her mother should have scolded her for that carelessness. What kind of person was she not to mind? But maybe, unlike me, none of them had even looked in that direction.

Daily a kind of mild compulsion grips me, and my helpless fascination about the new neighbors grows. I'm not the only one. Puppi is very curious too, and keeps praising the material of that girl's kurtas.[2] My brother's wife also glances periodically from the kitchen toward their

---

[1]A long, thin scarf worn over the shoulders. — ED.
[2]Long, loose shirts. — ED.

house, and Granny even knows when the neighbors have bought water chestnuts or squash and when the stove has been lit. Nevertheless, those people don't show a scrap of interest in us.

The girl never looks in our direction, nor do her parents. It doesn't   8 even seem intentional. So the thought of them conversing with us is remote and unimaginable. Perhaps they don't need us in their world. Maybe they consider us inferior. Or maybe they fear trouble because of our proximity. I don't know to what extent that could be true, however, since the sight of a young man in the vicinity doesn't seem to fill her parents with the fear which my father feels for Puppi at the sight of my friends.

We never hear a radio at their place, while ours blares constantly. There's bare ground in front of their house, with not even a blade of grass. Our house has a lawn, along with a vegetable garden and beds of strong-smelling flowers. Why doesn't that girl make friends with my sister and my sister-in-law? Why don't her parents mix with mine? Why don't they notice us drinking tea out of cups prettier than theirs? What they ought to do is add us to their list of acquaintances. They should be interested in everything of ours. Next to the fence, on our side, there's a big tall tamarind tree with fruit six inches long hanging from it. Girls are crazy about tamarind fruit, and yet this neighbor girl never even looks over longingly. She's never given me the satisfaction of breaking a piece of fruit off the tree.

I keep waiting. . . .

Our neighbors evidently have no problem that might make them want to seek our help. Perhaps the little internal problems that exist in our home and others don't exist in theirs, which is astonishing. None of the three ever appears worried. The girl's father must frown occasionally, and at times her mother must get upset, but nothing can be seen or heard from our place. Possibly the girl has some secret and private corner in her heart — some complication or emotional conflict. Maybe so, maybe not. Nothing definite can be known.

A light usually burns at night in their middle room, where Mukherji 12 and his whole family used to sleep. Apparently even indoors they sit together and talk. They must have an endless supply of stories and material for conversation. A sigh slips from my lips. In our house the talk deals only with the weather, mosquitoes, the birth of children, the new wives of relatives, kitchen matters, and ancient divine heroes who obliterate the present.

The fence between our houses is a barrier only in name. It's only a foot-high ridge of dirt with some berry bushes, a long stretch of dry twisted wild cactus, and some unknown shrubs with white ants clustered around the roots. In between, the ridge is broken in several places. Paths have formed, used by the fruit and vegetable sellers as well as the sweeper woman and the newspaper vendor. The postman and milkman have been using these paths for years. Despite the damage from dogs and cats coming and going and from animals grazing on the plants, the fence remains much the same as ever. Until a short time ago, Mukherji's daughter Shaila used to take this route bringing books over to me. It's such a convenient and simple fence that we can easily ride bicycles through the gaps from one side to the other without dismounting. And previously we used to pass through that way, but no longer, because our neighbors interpret a fence as something uncrossable.

They've been living here for three months. . . .

I often move my desk outdoors for study. At this time of year the outside air is lovely, like ice water in an intense summer thirst. But studying there is difficult. My eyes leap the fence and my mind hovers around the neighbors' house. A young and unattached girl. Cheerful and fearless parents. If only I'd been born in that home! That's the way my mind wanders.

At times the neighbor girl sits outside all alone, doing some work or doing nothing. Occasionally she strolls over to the wall on the other side of her house. Elbows propped on the wall, she watches the street. Then she returns. Loafers from other neighborhoods come into our area a lot. Not that there's any lack of them in our neighborhood too. But she always seems innocent and free, walking with small swaying steps.

At our place, in contrast, my sister-in-law takes Puppi along even when she goes outside to get flowers for worship. She's scared outside the house and in it too. She's kept scared. A sharp eye is kept on Puppi also. One time the neighbor girl's father put his hand on his wife's shoulder in the course of conversation, and Puppi was immediately called into the house on some pretext. That scene produced an uproar at our place. Such shamelessness! Gradually people in our house have begun considering the neighbors quite dangerous.

With the passing of time, the attraction toward the neighbors has changed into dislike, though they might as well be nonexistent as far as we're concerned. In time, however, our family has made the neighbors a focal point for all the evils in the world. Our eyes cross the fence thousands of times in what has become a part of our daily routine. A new distress has crept into our minds, added to our other worries. I, too, waste a lot of time, but not a glance from there ever falls this way.

Somewhere nearby a diesel engine, finding no signal to proceed, stands shrieking. The novelty of the sound is startling. For a while all of us will talk about nothing but the diesel engine.

Yesterday those neighbors had not been home since noon. A few   20
guests were staying at their place, but there was no hustle and bustle — just the usual carefree atmosphere. I rose and went inside. Sister-in-law was drying her hair. Then, I don't know why, she teased me slyly, connecting me with the neighbor girl. Smiling to myself, I went outdoors. Just then the girl and her mother returned, probably from the bazaar, carrying some packages. The father must have remained behind.

Both that evening and this morning people kept coming and going there. But it couldn't be considered a large number of people. Their house has the atmosphere of some ordinary festival celebration — just faintly. We were all astonished when the milkman reported that the daughter's marriage took place last night. It was some man from the other side of town. She'd had an Arya Samaj[3] wedding. My sister-in-law threw me a teasing look of sympathy, and I started laughing. I laughed openly and freely, thinking what dreamers we all are.

Now and then three or four people would arrive at their house. They'd go inside, then come out a little later and go away. They were mostly serious and restrained people. At times children gathered, shouting and running around, but otherwise there was no commotion — as though everything were taking place easily and smoothly. There was no way to know just what was happening, nor how.

At our house this has been a day of great uneasiness. After several hours, the girl emerged. She was wearing a sari, maybe for the first time. She stepped out on the veranda straightening her sari and carrying a coconut. Her swaying walk was restricted considerably by the sari and she moved forward with an eye on each step. She hadn't veiled herself in any way, nor, even with her husband walking so close to her, did she show any of the embarrassment and coquettishness of a traditional bride. Her husband looked like some friend of mine. No one was weeping and wailing. Several times the girl's mother kissed her warmly on both cheeks.

---

[3]A reform sect of Hinduism that stresses a return to the principles and practices found in the Vedic scriptures. — ED.

The father patted her head. The girl's eyes could no longer conceal a shimmer of tears reflecting her excitement over the new life ahead.

Squirrels were darting across the fence from one corner to the other. Mother expressed amazement to me over the girl's failure to cry. According to her, the girl had become hardened by her education and had no real love or attachment for her mother and father. "They're all like that these days . . . with not one tear for those who struggled and sacrificed to raise them."

I was not interested in listening to such things. I observed that Mother was enjoying the sun, shifting her position to stay in the patches of sunshine. Then Father made a pronouncement — "In the old days, girls would cry all the way to the edge of the village. Anyone who didn't was beaten and forced to cry. Otherwise her life at her husband's home could never be happy." Father feels very distressed that things are no longer like that. "The old days are passing and men's hearts have become machines, just machines!" At such times his voice grows sharp, and the wreckage of Kali Yug, this Age of Darkness, dances before his eyes.

A few small isolated fragments of cloud have appeared in the sky over our home and then passed on. The parents and relatives reached the gate and were waiting to give the girl a last farewell. The boy's party had brought a Herald car for the groom which looked like a colorful room. That colorful room glided slowly away and was gone.

Granny was the most astounded of all and kept muttering to herself. This marriage made no sense at all to her. "No fanfare, no uproar, no feasting. What's the point of such stinginess! And besides, not even asking the neighbors on such an occasion. What's happening to mankind? Good god!"

Having said good-bye to the girl, the people walked back to the house. Each carried out a chair and sat down outdoors. Ever since the girl's departure, her mother had been a little sad and subdued. A few people kept her company, probably trying to cheer her up. My friend Radhu swore that he could prove the girl was a woman of the world. I felt only the sadness of an intense loss. A sort of strange emptiness — an emptiness at being left behind and an emptiness produced by Radhu's loose talk about the girl. Absolutely unfounded! Maybe talking about a girl's misconduct provides a kind of depraved satisfaction. But perhaps in one corner of my mind, I, too, like my family, can't tolerate the behavior of the neighbors.

Night is sloughing off the cover of evening. The people who were seated around a table across the fence have risen and dispersed. As usual, a light is burning in the middle room of the neighbors' house. Their night has become peaceful and quiet as usual, and there's no way to know how they're feeling about the absence of one member of the family. At our house, though, the bazaar of neighbor-criticism is doing a heated business.

EXPLORATIONS

1. What are the social functions of the Indian family as Gyanranjan depicts it? Based on "Our Side of the Fence and Theirs," how would you describe Indian parents' responsibilities to their children, and children's obligations to their parents?

2. Gyanranjan's narrator gives only fragmentary information about himself and his family members in terms of such standard characteristics as name, gender, age, relationship, and appearance. What can you deduce about the narrator and the other members of his household from clues in the story? What aspects of people does the narrator seem to think are more interesting and important than these "standard" characteristics?

3. How would you describe the narrator's attitude toward the family next door? Looking back through "Our Side of the Fence and Theirs," note each place where the narrator judges the other family's behavior. What sense do these judgments give you of what kind of people the next-door neighbors are? What sense do they give you of the narrator and his family in comparison?

4. The only dialogue in "Our Side of the Fence and Theirs" comes near the end of the story. Technically, *dialogue* means speech between two or more characters, such as a conversation or argument. How do the quoted speeches in this story diverge from that definition? What role do these speeches play in the story? How would the story's impact change if Gyanranjan used true dialogue throughout the story?

CONNECTIONS

1. Which of the two families in "Our Side of the Fence and Theirs" seems more like the Liu family of Peking? Why? Which judgments by Gyanranjan's narrator about the family next door do you think Liu Shu-min would agree with? Which judgments would she disagree with?

2. Neither "Our Side of the Fence and Theirs" nor Sri Delima's "Black-and-White Amah" was written for an American audience. What customs does

each author refer to which are apparently familiar to his or her readers but unfamiliar to you as a foreigner? What assumptions does each author make about his or her readers' values which do not hold true for you? How do these "insider" references and assumptions affect your response to these two pieces of writing?

3. What views expressed in the *Observations* about the family's functions and values are echoed by the narrator's family in "Our Side of the Fence and Theirs"? What views expressed in the *Observations* are embodied by the family on the other side of the fence?

ELABORATIONS

1. "We're respectable, honorable people," declares Gyanranjan's narrator. On the basis of "Our Side of the Fence and Theirs," write an essay describing the values, habits, attitudes, and relationships that the narrator's family apparently believes define a "respectable, honorable" Indian family.

2. With his first sentence, Gyanranjan lets us know that this is the story of someone who believes his life is shaped by events outside his control. We learn by paragraph 2 that the narrator wishes he could get to know the family next door but feels powerless to do so. Most of us have had similar experiences. Write a narrative essay about a situation in which you wanted to become better acquainted with someone but felt prevented from doing so by family or social pressure.

JOHN DAVID MORLEY

Acquiring a Japanese Family

"John David Morley was born in Singapore in 1948 and was educated at Merton College, Oxford. His first job was in Mexico, as tutor to the children of Elizabeth Taylor and Richard Burton. Then he went to Germany to work in the theater, and by the age of twenty-four had begun to develop an interest in the drama — and later the general culture — of Japan, and to teach himself the language. He went to Japan on a Japanese government scholarship, to study at the Language Research Institute of Waseda University, Tokyo. Since then he has made his home in Munich, where he works for Japanese television as a liaison officer and interpreter, researching TV documentaries. He has translated some thirty Japanese scripts into English and German."

"Acquiring a Japanese Family" comes from Morley's semiautobiographical novel *Pictures from the Water Trade: Adventures of a Westerner in Japan* (1985), as does the preceding paragraph about the author.

Japan has intrigued Westerners since its self-imposed isolation was ended in 1854 by U.S. Commodore Matthew C. Perry, who forced the opening of trade. At that point this 2360-mile archipelago off Asia's east coast was ruled by the shoguns, a succession of military governors who had dominated Japan since 1192. Before the shogunate came the empire, which supposedly began in 660 B.C., and which reestablished itself in 1868. Today Emperor Hirohito is Japan's head of state, in a parliamentary democracy led by Prime Minister Yasuhiro Nakasone. Japan consists of 4 main islands and over 3000 smaller ones; almost three-fourths of the country is hills and mountains, many of them dormant or active volcanoes. While Japan remains ethnically homogeneous, contact with the West has spurred enough cultural and economic change to give this nation the highest growth rate in the industrialized world.

(For more background on Japan, see p. 115.)

Boon did not like the Foreign Students Hall where it had been arranged for him to live, and on the same evening he moved in he decided he would move out. . . . But the decision that he did not want to live there was one thing, finding somewhere else to stay was quite another, and this in turn would have been impossible or at least very difficult if he had not happened to meet Sugama a few days after arriving in the country.

The introduction was arranged through a mutual acquaintance, Yo-shida, at the private university where Boon was taking language courses and where Sugama was employed on the administrative staff. They met one afternoon in the office of their acquaintance and inspected each other warily for ten minutes.

"Nice weather," said Boon facetiously as he shook hands with Sugama. Outside it was pouring with rain.

"Nice weather?" repeated Sugama doubtfully, glancing out of the   4
window. "But it's raining."

It was not a good start.

Sugama has just moved into a new apartment. It was large enough for two, he said, and he was looking for someone to share the expenses. This straightforward information arrived laboriously, in bits and pieces, sand-wiched between snippets of Sugama's personal history and vague profes-sions of friendship, irritating to Boon, because at the time he felt they sounded merely sententious. All this passed back and forth between Sugama and Boon through the mouth of their mutual friend, as Boon understood almost no Japanese and Sugama's English, though well-intentioned, was for the most part impenetrable.

It made no odds to Boon where he lived or with whom. All he wanted was a Japanese-speaking environment in order to absorb the language as quickly as possible. He had asked for a family, but none was available.

One windy afternoon in mid-October the three of them met outside   8
the gates of the university and set off to have a look at Sugama's new apartment. It was explained to Boon that cheap apartments in Tokyo were very hard to come by, the only reasonable accommodation available being confined to housing estates subsidized by the government. Boon wondered how a relatively prosperous bachelor like Sugama managed to qualify for government-subsidized housing. Sugama admitted that this was in fact only possible because his grandfather would also be living there. It was the first Boon had heard of the matter and he was rather taken aback.

It turned out, however, that the grandfather would "very seldom" be there — in fact, that he wouldn't live there at all. He would only be there on paper, he and his grandson constituting a "family." That was the point. "You must *say* he is there," said Sugama emphatically.

The grandfather lived a couple of hundred miles away, and although he never once during the next two years set foot in the apartment he still managed to be the bane of Boon's life. A constant stream of representa-tives from charities, government agencies, and old people's clubs, on

average one or two a month, came knocking on the door, asking to speak
to grandfather. At first grandfather was simply "not in" or had "gone for
a walk," but as time passed and the flow of visitors never faltered, Boon
found himself having to resort to more drastic measures. Grandfather
began to make long visits to his home in the country; he had not yet
returned because he didn't feel up to making the journey; his health
gradually deteriorated. Finally Boon decided to have him invalided, and
for a long time his condition remained "grave." On grandfather's behalf
Boon received the condolences of all these visitors, and occasionally even
presents.

Two years later grandfather did in fact die. Boon was thus exonerated,
but in the meantime he had got to know grandfather well and had become
rather fond of him. He attended his funeral with mixed feelings.

Sugama had acquired tenure of his government-subsidized apartment   12
by a stroke of luck. He had won a ticket in a lottery. These apartments
were much sought after, and in true Japanese style their distribution
among hundreds of thousands of applicants was discreetly left to fate.
The typical tenant was a young couple with one or two children, who
would occupy the apartment for ten or fifteen years, often under conditions of bleak frugality, in order to save money to buy a house. Although
the rent was not immoderate, prices generally in Tokyo were high, and
it was a mystery to Boon how such people managed to live at all. Among
the lottery winners there were inevitably also those people for whom the
acquisition of an apartment was just a prize, an unexpected bonus, to be
exploited as a financial investment. It was no problem for these nominal
tenants to sublet their apartments at prices well above the going rate.

Boon had never lived on a housing estate and his first view of the tall
concrete compound where over fifty thousand people lived did little to
reassure him. Thousands of winner families were accommodated in about
a dozen rectangular blocks, each between ten and fifteen stories high,
apparently in no way different (which disappointed Boon most of all)
from similar housing compounds in Birmingham or Berlin. He had
naively expected Japanese concrete to be different, to have a different
color, perhaps, or a more exotic shape.

But when Sugama let them into the apartment and Boon saw the
interior he immediately took heart: this was unmistakably Japanese. Taking off their shoes in the tiny boxlike hall, the three of them padded
reverently through the kitchen into the *tatami* rooms.

"Smell of fresh *tatami*," pronounced Sugama, wrinkling his nose.

Boon was ecstatic. Over the close-woven pale gold straw matting lay   16
a very faint greenish shimmer, sometimes perceptible and sometimes not,
apparently in response to infinitesimal shifts in the texture of the falling
light. The *tatami* was quite unlike a carpet or any other form of floor
covering he had ever seen. It seemed to be alive, humming with colors
he could sense rather than see, like a greening tree in the brief interval
between winter and spring. He stepped on to it and felt the fibers recoil,
sinking under the weight of his feet, slowly and softly.

"You can see green?" asked Sugama, squatting down.

"Yes indeed."

"Fresh *tatami*. Smell of grass, green color. But not for long, few weeks
only."

"What exactly is it?"   20

"Yes."

Boon turned to Yoshida and repeated the question, who in turn asked
Sugama and conferred with him at great length.

"*Tatami* comes from *oritatamu*, which means to fold up. So it's a
kind of matting you can fold up."

"Made of straw."   24

"Yes."

"How long does it last?"

Long consultation.

"He says this is not so good quality. Last maybe four, five years."   28

"And then what?"

"New *tatami*. Quite expensive, you see. But very practical."

The three *tatami* rooms were divided by a series of *fusuma*, sliding
screens made of paper and light wood. These screens were decorated at
the base with simple grass and flower motifs; a natural extension, it
occurred to Boon, of the grasslike *tatami* laid out in between. Sugama
explained that the *fusuma* were usually kept closed in winter, and in
summer, in order to have "nice breeze," they could be removed altogether. He also showed Boon the *shoji*, a type of sliding screen similar
to the *fusuma* but more simple: an open wooden grid covered on one
side with semitransparent paper, primitive but rather beautiful. There
was only one small section of *shoji* in the whole apartment; almost as a
token, thought Boon, and he wondered why.

With the exception of a few one- and two-room apartments every   32
house that Boon ever visited in Japan was designed to incorporate these
three common elements: *tatami*, *fusuma*, and *shoji*. In the houses of

rich people the *tatami* might last longer, the *fusuma* decorations might be more costly, but the basic concept was the same. The interior design of all houses being much the same, it was not surprising to find certain similarities in the behavior and attitudes of the people who lived in them.

The most striking feature of the Japanese house was lack of privacy; the lack of individual, inviolable space. In winter, when the *fusuma* were kept closed, any sound above a whisper was clearly audible on the other side, and of course in summer they were usually removed altogether. It is impossible to live under such conditions for very long without a common household identity emerging which naturally takes precedence over individual wishes. This enforced family unity was still held up to Boon as an ideal, but in practice it was ambivalent, as much a yoke as a bond.

There was no such thing as the individual's private room, no bedroom, dining- or sitting-room as such, since in the traditional Japanese house there was no furniture determining that a room should be reserved for any particular function. A person slept in a room, for example, without thinking of it as a bedroom or as his room. In the morning his bedding would be rolled up and stored away in a cupboard; a small table known as the *kotatsu*, which could also be plugged into the mains to provide heating, was moved back into the center of the room and here the family ate, drank, worked, and relaxed for the rest of the day. Although it was becoming standard practice in modern Japan for children to have their own rooms, many middle-aged and nearly all older Japanese still lived in this way. They regarded themselves as "one flesh," their property as common to all; the *uchi* (household, home) was constituted according to a principle of indivisibility. The system of movable screens meant that the rooms could be used by all the family and for all purposes: walls were built round the *uchi*, not inside it.

Boon later discovered analogies between this concept of house and the Japanese concept of self. The Japanese carried his house around in his mouth and produced it in everyday conversation, using the word *uchi* to mean "I," the representative of my house in the world outside. His self-awareness was naturally expressed as corporate individuality, hazy about quite what that included, very clear about what it did not. . . .

The almost wearying sameness about all the homes which Boon vis- 36 ited, despite differences in the wealth and status of their owners, prompted a rather unexpected conclusion: the classlessness of the Japanese house. The widespread use of traditional materials, the preservation of traditional structures, even if in such contracted forms as to have become merely symbolic, suggested a consensus about the basic requirements of daily life which was very remarkable, and which presumably held implications for Japanese society as a whole. Boon's insight into that society was acquired very slowly, after he had spent a great deal of time sitting on the *tatami* mats and looking through the sliding *fusuma* doors which had struck him as no more than pleasing curiosities on his first visit to a Japanese-style home.

Sugama, Yoshida and Boon celebrated the new partnership at a restaurant in Shinjuku, and a week later Boon moved in.

The moment he entered the apartment a woman who was unexpectedly standing in the kitchen dropped down on her knees and prostrated herself in a deep bow, her forehead almost touching the floorboards, introducing herself with the words "*Irrashaimase. Sugama de gozaimasu . . .*"

Boon was extremely startled. He wondered whether he should do the same thing and decided not, compromising with a halfhearted bow which unfortunately the woman couldn't even see, because she had her face to the ground. She explained that she was *o-kaasan*, Sugama's mother.

Sugama had a way of springing surprises — or rather, he indicated his intentions so obtusely that Boon usually failed to realize what would happen until it was already in progress — and so for quite a while Boon assumed that there must have been a change in plan, that the mother had perhaps joined the household as a stand-in for the grandfather. He greeted her in fluent Japanese (he had been studying introductions for the past week) and promptly fell into unbroken silence, mitigated by the occasional appreciative nod. Boon for his part hardly understood a word of what Sugama's mother was saying but she, encouraged by the intelligible sounds he had intially produced, talked constantly for the best part of an hour, and by the time Sugama eventually arrived Boon had become resigned to the idea that his talkative mother was going to be a permanent resident.

The misunderstanding was swiftly ironed out. No, *o-kaasan* had only come up to Tokyo for a few days (from whatever angle of the compass one approached Tokyo the journey to the capital was described as an elevation) in order to help with the move.

Sugama's mother was a small, wiry woman in her late fifties. Her teeth protruded slightly; like most Japanese women, even those who had very good teeth, she covered her mouth with her hand whenever she laughed. She was a vivacious woman and laughed frequently, so one way and another, with all the cooking, cleaning, and sewing she also did during the next four days, her hands were kept continually busy. She was of slight build but very sound in lung, with the effect that when she laughed it resounded throughout her whole body, as if the laugh were more than the body could accommodate. Perhaps this laughter drew Boon's attention to a girlish quality she had about her, despite her age and a rather plain appearance. He often watched her working, and in the spare, effortless movements of a woman who has performed the same tasks so many times that not even the tiniest gesture is superfluous there was also something unexpectedly graceful.

On the far side of the *fusuma* Boon often heard them talking late into the night. Night after night she sawed away at him with her flinty, abrasive voice. In the mornings Sugama was moody, the atmosphere in the house increasingly tense. Boon was left guessing. Gradually, in the course of weeks and months, Sugama began to take him into his confidence, and in retrospect he learned what must have been the subject of those nightly conversations.

O-kaasan's most pressing concern was that her son, at the advanced age of twenty-eight, was still unmarried. Boon couldn't see what the fuss was about, but Sugama was slowly coming round to his mother's view, who was quite sure it was a disaster. "The wind blows hard," he announced mysteriously, apparently by way of explanation — Boon himself had to blow pretty hard to keep up with conversations on this level. He said it was up to Sugama to decide when and whether he wanted to get married. It wasn't anybody else's business. Sugama would clearly have like to be able to agree with this facile advice and just as clearly he could not, entangled in a web of sentiment and duty of which Boon was wholly ignorant.

The promptings of filial duty which caused Sugama such heartache and which to Boon were so alien demanded of Sugama a second, even more painful decision. He was the *chonan*, the eldest son, thereby inheriting the obligation not merely to provide for his aging parents but to live with them in the same house. There were two alternatives open to him. He could either bring his parents to live with him in Tokyo or he could return home to his province in the north. A house in Tokyo large enough to provide room for grandfather, parents, Sugama, and — sooner or later — a fourth generation family was out of the question; on his present salary he would have to work for several lifetimes in order to pay for it. A one-way ticket home came a great deal cheaper, which was just as well, since the only job awaiting him at the other end would be poorly

paid and with even poorer prospects. Such was the path of righteous-
ness. . . .

O-kaasan had only just packed her bags and gone home when — as
usual without any forewarning — Sugama turned up late one evening
accompanied by an old man, his wife, and an enormous cardboard box.
Boon was sitting in his pajamas eating noodles out of a saucepan when
these unexpected visitors arrived. Consternation. The old lady caught
sight of him and dropped her bag (very probably she had not been
forewarned either), immediately prostrating herself on the floor in the
deepest of deep bows, old-style obeisance with the added advantage of
concealing momentary shock and embarrassment. The old man was no
slouch either. Palms on the floor and fingers turned inwards he bobbed
his head up and down several times in Boon's direction, apologizing
profusely every time he came up for air. All this happened so quickly
that the astonished Boon didn't even have the presence of mind to put
down the saucepan he was holding, and he sat there in his pajamas
uneasily aware that he was the most unworthy object of the visitors'
attentions.

Sugama came forward rather sheepishly, stepping in cavalier fashion
between the prone bodies on the kitchen floor, and explained who they
were.

"My grandfather's brother — younger brother — and wife."   48

"Not your grandfather?" asked Boon doubtfully, always alert to the
possibility of misunderstandings when Suguma ventured into English.

"No, no *not* my grandfather."

"Your *great*-uncle, then."

"Ah! *Great*-uncle? *Great* uncle?"   52

Sugama paused to digest this new word, mustering his ancient relative
with pursed lips. It was clear what was passing through his mind.

Boon was still not reassured. He kept an eye on the ominous cardboard
box, quite large enough to accommodate a third, perhaps enfeebled
relative, and wondered what else was in store for him.

"What are they doing here?"

"Earthquake," said Sugama simply. Boon fetched his dictionary and   56
Sugama, reverting to Japanese, sat down to explain the situation.

At about nine o'clock that evening his great-uncle had called him in
his office (Sugama worked a late shift) with the startling news that a
major earthquake was imminent. How did he know? His wife had told
him so. How did she know? A fortune-teller she regularly visited and in
whom she placed absolute confidence had seen it in his cards and crystal

ball. She was terrified, and having personally experienced the Great Kanto
Earthquake of 1923 in which over a hundred thousand people had died
she was not taking any chances. Her fortune-teller couldn't predict exactly
when the earthquake would occur, but it might be at any time within
the next three days; the greatest likelihood of its occurrence was forecast
for midnight on the following day. The two old people ran a little shop
in the downtown area of Tokyo where many of the houses were flimsy
wooden structures which tended to slump and collapse very easily, even
without the encouragement of an earthquake. But their great-nephew,
they heard, had just moved into a marvelous modern building that was
supposed to be *earthquake-proof*. Could they come and stay for a few
days? Of course, said Sugama. So without more ado they bundled their
worldly goods into the largest available box and Sugama brought them
over in a neighbor's truck.

As a matter of fact there had been a slight tremor the previous evening.
It was Boon's first. He had been standing in the kitchen helping himself
to another glass of whiskey when the floor unaccountably began to sway
and a set of irreproachable stainless steel ladles, which until then had
given him no cause for complaint, started rattling menacingly on the
kitchen wall. Boon had replaced the whiskey and made himself a cup of
tea instead.

Great-uncle and his wife knelt on the *tatami* listening to Sugama's
recital, wagging their heads and smiling from time to time, as if allowing
that there was something rather droll about the situation, but also wanting
to be taken absolutely seriously. However, with every moment they spent
in the apartment this became increasingly hard to do, for the eccentric
old couple seemed to be guided by a mischievous genius — they belonged
to nature's blunderers, everything they touched turned to farce. Their
great-nephew had just finished his dramatic account when there was a
shrill call of *ohayo!* (Good morning) from the kitchen, and all eyes turned
to the neglected cardboard box.

"Oh dear! The poor thing!" crowed the old lady, getting up at once   60
and pattering over to the box. She pulled open the flap and gently lifted
out a bright yellow parrot. The indignant bird rapped her knuckles a
couple of times with the side of his beak and settled frostily on the tip of
her finger.

Sugama, Boon, the elderly couple, and the yellow parrot housed
together for the next three days. Once he had provided his relatives with
a roof over their heads Sugama took no further interest in them and was
unaccountably busy for as long as they stayed there, leaving the house

earlier and returning later than usual. His prodigiously long working hours impressed great-uncle and worried his wife, who took to preparing nutritious cold snacks for the laboring hero before retiring for the night. Sugama did justice to these snacks with the same appetite he applied himself to his work, warding off their anxieties with careless equanimity.

"You've got to hand it to him — he certainly works hard," said great-uncle at breakfast one morning, just after Sugama had left the house.

"Ah," replied Boon noncommittally. He knew perfectly well that Sugama's overtime was not spent at the office but at mah-jongg parlors in Nakano and Takadanobaba.

In the meantime Boon was left to study the evacuees and the evacuees Boon with mutual curiosity. On the whole he had the impression that they were rather disappointed in him. At first they looked at him as if he had descended from another planet, but when it became obvious that he was not going to live up to these expectations their interest declined into an attitude of gently reproachful familiarity. For Boon did not sleep on a bed, he dispensed with bacon and egg, he knew nothing about baseball, ate rice and drank green tea with relish, and was unpardonably fond of dried cuttlefish and raw squid, foods which foreigners were commonly supposed to regard with horror and loathing. Altogether Boon was not as Boon should be, and they were rather disconcerted.

This attitude — a national prejudice, really — that foreigners and the Japanese way of life must almost as a matter of principle be wholly incompatible was something Boon encountered time and again. Under the cover of courtesy, of polite considerations for differences in tastes and customs, many Japanese would gleefully reveal their own select cabinet of horrors, confronting their guest with fermented bean curd or prawns drowned in sake not as something he might care to sample but as a kind of ethnological litmus test: if he found it indigestible and swiftly turned green this would be taken by them as confirmation of their own cultural and racial singularity. With barely concealed triumph the host would commiserate with his victim, invariably remarking *Yappari, nihonjin ja nai to* . . . (Ah well, unless one is Japanese . . .). . . .

On the fateful morning great-uncle took cover under the *kotatsu* earlier than usual and sat tight for the rest of the day. His wife went about her household tasks as briskly as ever, but when there was nothing left for her to do and at last she knelt down beside great-uncle at the little table it became evident how restless she really was. From time to time she laid down her sewing, listened intently, sighed, and picked it up again. As the evening wore on and the tension began to mount, Boon couldn't resist cracking a few jokes, which great-uncle good-humoredly deflected at his wife. It was only to set her mind at rest that they had come to stay, he assured Boon. Women couldn't resist fortune-tellers, but it was just a lot of nonsense after all; and for good measure he made a few jokes himself at her expense. Boon was not deceived. Throughout the evening great-uncle helped himself to the bottle of fine old malt whiskey, originally intended as Sugama's present, much more liberally than he otherwise did and by midnight he was in true fighting spirit, his face shining with such particular splendor that his wife's attention was diverted from the impending destruction of Tokyo to the threat of great-uncle's imminent collapse.

There was no earthquake that night, but the old lady couldn't quite believe this and for two more days she sat it out in her nephew's apartment waiting for the dust to clear. Sugama was dispatched, like a kind of dove from Noah's Ark, to report on the state of the world, and it was only after he had personally confirmed that the house in downtown Tokyo was still in perfect order that she consented to their departure. Boon particularly regretted the loss of the parrot, which spoke few words of Japanese but those very frequently, thus improving his pronunciation of the language.

EXPLORATIONS

1. According to Morley's account, what is the attitude of Japanese adults to the older members of their family? to the younger members? How are Sugama's obligations as a family member different from those of a typical twenty-eight-year-old American?

2. Morley tells his story from the point of view of Boon, a fictional English visitor to Japan. At what points in the narrative does Boon act and react like a stranger in a strange land? At what points does he behave (or try to behave) like a Japanese native? In what respects was it probably easier for Morley to write this narrative in the third person than the first person? — that is, to depict Japan through Boon's eyes instead of his own?

3. Morley has interwoven information about Japanese customs with the story of Boon, Sugama, and his family. How would the impact of "Acquiring a Japanese Family" change if the factual sidelights (for example, or interior decoration) were omitted? What information in this narrative do you as a reader find most striking and memorable?

CONNECTIONS

1. Like Gyanranjan in "Our Side of the Fence and Theirs," Morley tells his story from the viewpoint of someone whose attitude contrasts with that of his housemates. What similarities in personality do you notice between Gyanranjan's narrator and Morley's Boon? How are their roles in their respective households alike and different? How are their functions as point-of-view characters alike and different?

2. Scarcity of space is a major influence on life in Tokyo, as it is in Peking. In what ways do the Communist Chinese described in Ruth Sidel's "The Liu Family" approach this issue differently from the capitalist Japanese? What attitudes and tactics do the two cultures share? How does the family's function as "social glue" appear to differ in Japan and China?

3. What concepts of how the family functions (or should function) appear in both "Acquiring a Japanese Family" and Michael Novak's *Observation?* Which of these concepts are depicted by Novak as endangered in America and by Morley as thriving in Japan? What factors can you identify as having influenced the family's divergence in these two cultures?

ELABORATIONS

1. Much of the information Morley gives his readers about the Japanese family is indirect: for example, his discussion of the interior of Japanese homes and the concept of *uchi*. After carefully rereading "Acquiring a Japanese Family," write an essay describing Japanese attitudes toward the family: its social role, its influence on the individual, and the responsibilities and privileges of family members.

2. Morley writes: "The most striking feature of the Japanese house was lack of privacy; the lack of individual, inviolable space. . . . It is impossible to live under such conditions for very long without a common household identity emerging which naturally takes precedence over individual wishes. This enforced family unity was still held up to Boon as an ideal, but in practice it was ambivalent, as much a yoke as a bond." Write an essay applying Morley's statements to the Israeli kibbutz-versus-family dilemma described by Bruno Bettelheim in "Why Kibbutzim?"

CAROLA HANSSON
and KARIN LIDÉN

Liza and Family

Carola Hansson and Karin Lidén are natives of Sweden. Living on the northeastern edge of the Soviet Union, they have been moved by their interest in women's position there to visit the USSR many times. In addition to *Moscow Women* (1983), in which the following interview appears, they have translated material by exiled Leningrad feminists for a book published in Sweden in 1981. At present Hansson works for Swedish television and lives with her husband and children in Uppsala. Lidén works as a writer and consultant for Swedish radio and lives with her husband and child in Paris. "Liza and Family" was translated from the Swedish by Gerry Bothmer, George Blecher, and Lone Blecher.

The Union of Soviet Socialist Republics is the largest country in the world, covering a sixth of the earth's land area and featuring every climate but tropical. Nominally this sprawling nation is a federation of fifteen republics under a central Communist government which took power in 1917, after the czar's overthrow. Political, economic, and social reforms have been ambitious, but change is not always fast or smooth. Although nearly all legal economic enterprises are state owned, for example, a huge illegal black market flourishes, and imported goods are prized. Traditional values persist, but in new forms. "Liza and Family" illustrates the daily contradictions faced by one young Soviet worker-mother.

Hansson and Lidén interviewed Liza in her Moscow apartment. She is twenty-eight, an editor for a publishing house. "She doesn't walk into the room; she makes an entrance," write the authors. "She seems delighted to see us and to play the role of hostess. . . . She is wearing a long, tight, ruffled dress with a turn-of-the-century look and platform sandals. She invites us to sit down in her kitchen, one of the most impractically arranged we have ever seen. The stove is in one corner, the small sink in the other, and in the middle, with hardly any space to move around, is a small table. A few watercolors depicting beautiful Russian summer landscapes are tacked up on the walls, a reminder of what exists outside this bleak high-rise kitchen."

(For more background on the Soviet Union, see pp. 139, 213, and 649.)

Tell us something about yourself.

I'm twenty-eight. I have a degree in literature and work for a publishing house. I have a son, Emil. I had a husband, who was an artist, but now he's gone. We got married in 1970 and divorced in 1975, I think.

I own my apartment, which my father bought for me, since it's so difficult to get an apartment here; for someone my age it's totally impossible. I lived here with my husband, and now I live here alone.

What is your daily routine like? Can you tell us what you did yesterday, for instance?

4

I got up at seven o'clock and went to work. Mostly I have to travel during rush hours; the streetcar was so crowded that I was almost knocked down . . . horrible.

Oh no! Yesterday was Monday! I woke at six, pulled my child out of bed, packed a bag full of stuff for the whole week, and then he and I took off for the subway. The *two* of us were practically knocked down. A woman was sitting and reading and wouldn't give up her seat, even though my son was squashed against the doors. He almost fell on her, and I tightened my grip to keep him from falling and getting hurt. I told him, "Emil, a child could die in front of that woman while she sat there reading. Don't you ever be like that." It took us fifty minutes to get to the day-care center.

I took him inside and undressed him and then I had to rush off to work. He cried, "Mama, I don't want to stay here. I want to go home." I said, "Emil, sweetheart, please stay in the day-care center now. I'll come and get you soon. I'll pick you up on Friday." And yesterday was Monday. It was terrible, but I had to hurry off to work.

I left him crying. The teachers took him by the arm and brought him over to the group because I couldn't stay to comfort him. I picked up my things and put my shawl over my head. Outside it was still rush hour. And I was going to the opposite end of Moscow. It was another hour's trip, and I was already late for work. When I dashed out of the subway I was planning to transfer to a bus, and I felt as if I were about to have a minor heart attack. But the bus was just pulling away, so I had to run instead, knowing I'd be in trouble because I was late. I was trying to work out a scheme. If only there were an open window at my office so that I could throw my stuff in and crawl in after it! That way no one would know I was late.

However, the windows were closed, and I quickly ran in. There was

8

a lot of work on my desk. First on the agenda was a weekly report. There was also a lot of mail, proofreading, and editing. Then I had to race around to various departments, pick up files, etc. After lunch I became terribly drowsy because I had hardly slept all night long. I was absent-minded and couldn't seem to pull myself together. Later when I felt I couldn't stand it any longer we sent someone for a bottle of wine. Sometimes we do that where I work. Yesterday, toward the end of the day, we drank a big glass of port to clear our heads.

Then, exhausted, I dropped by my parents' since I hadn't prepared any food at home. I knew they would have something for me. Afterwards I watched television — one of those series. I was too tired to think or read, although I had a book that had been hard to get my hands on. It had been such a difficult day. So that's what my day was like yesterday, a typical Monday.

So Emil's at the day-care center all week. Is he there at night as well?

Yes, it's called weekly boarding school. I could pick him up on   12
Wednesdays, but it doesn't seem to work out. If I fetch him after work we don't get home until eight. He goes to bed at nine, and then I have to get up at six to get him back to the day-care center. The rush again, the mobs. That isn't good for him. He might catch influenza since he wears his little fur coat in the subway, although it's terribly hot and he's soaked with perspiration when we get into the street to walk to the center. As a result he has a cold almost the whole winter.

Does he like the boarding school?

It's O.K. By Friday when I pick him up he's happy. He's been playing with his friends and it's hard to tear him away. He's gotten used to it. But on Monday it's the same story all over again.

Doesn't his father spend time with him?

No, he rarely sees his father. The situation is complicated. When the   16
baby was born I gave him my surname. I decided that since I had had to carry the whole burden and I suffered the most, I wanted to give him my name. His father was very upset that the boy didn't have his name. They almost never see each other, although Emil is the image of his father. He never gets anything from him, but I do get alimony, 35 rubles a month.[1]

---

[1]One ruble (divided into 100 kopeks) is currently equivalent to around $1.36.

How do you spend your free time?

Saturdays and Sundays are mostly devoted to my child. When he sleeps I have some time to read, but a lot of my energy goes into him. Free time? Yes, on weekdays after work. Of course I'm tired, but at least I can do as I please. Sometimes when I have a few moments I try to write; I couldn't imagine not writing. I'll probably write all my life — how regularly I don't know, since I don't have the time. But when I have a free evening I write poetry.

How much time do you spend on your household? Shopping, for instance.

I have an easier time than most because of my parents. When I can't   20
bear to do the shopping — because as sure as anything I'll start arguing with someone, complain to the manager, or hit somebody; that's just the way I am — and when I can't stand the mass of people, the crowd, the confusion, and I need to be alone, I go to my parents' and my mother feeds me.

My relationship with my parents is very good. Of course we argue, but we argue with an understanding of each other, because I'm like them in my way of thinking. We always enjoy each other's company. I share my most intimate thoughts with them — especially with my father. When we talk I don't feel that he's older than I am — we're the same age in our souls.

When I was a child that feeling was even stronger — one of us could tell what the other was thinking, even if we were apart. It's said that Blok[2] had a similar relationship with his mother; for me it's with my father.

I remember that when I was about five, he was going through a difficult time. I was in a country day-care center; I was restless and couldn't sleep — I sensed that Papa was having a hard time. Then we went to Moscow and I asked him why. Something had happened. I remember the incident so clearly. A poet — he's dead now — had written an article criticizing him. I didn't understand any of this, since I couldn't read, but I sensed that Papa was in trouble. We had always been able to communicate — even better before I was married. Then we used to travel together. He is a poet and often makes public appearances. I appeared on the stage with him and read his poems.

---

[2]Alexander Blok (1880–1921) was a Russian Symbolist poet.

In this country when children leave their family they seldom think   24
about their parents; children and parents usually don't understand each
other. The children take off when they're about seventeen and get married. When children and parents have to live together they live as neighbors in a joint or communal apartment.[3] But the children have to obey
their parents. There's a saying in our country: If you spit on old people
you spit on your country; if you spit on your ancestors you spit in your
own face.

Were you born in Moscow?

Yes. Six of us lived in a room twenty square meters in size, which
was part of a communal apartment. It was Mama's room. Papa wasn't
born in Moscow; he came from . . . the frontier you could say, from the
country. He married my mother and settled down in that room. There
was also Mama's sister, Grandmother, and I, and then my brother,
Alyosha, was born. As a young girl Mama had lived in a whole apartment.
Then in 1937 her father was put in prison. If my grandmother had
divorced him she could have avoided going with him and could have
stayed with her three children. But she didn't think it was right to divorce
him after he was jailed, so she went to prison for eight years as a family
member of an enemy of the people. When the children were left alone
they were forced to leave their apartment, which consisted only of two
rooms — small ones at that — even though her husband had had an
important position in the government. They were kicked out, and my
mother, who was sixteen at the time, was left with two small children.
Her youngest sister was three, and the authorities wanted to put her in
an orphanage, but the family pleaded with them, and finally she was
allowed to stay. She had a very interesting life, my aunt, but you came
to talk about me. . . .

Can you envisage a life without children?

Definitely not. If a couple already in their forties haven't heard the   28
sound of children's voices in their home, life is meaningless, period. Of
course it's obvious that the woman suffers the most. Formerly, among
the peasants, divorce was granted on these grounds, and I think that was
right. One should have children, no matter how difficult the situation.

---

[3]Because of the continued shortage of housing in Moscow and other large cities, it is still
common for several families to share an apartment with a communal kitchen and bathroom
but separate living/sleeping quarters.

Also, because of the low birthrate, Russia is wasting away . . . although I myself don't intend to give birth to a second, third, fourth.

Would you like to have more children?

Yes, but I don't have a husband. If I did, I'd have a second and a third. I would want a girl because they're so much closer to their mother.

How would you find the time?

I would leave the children in one of the weekly boarding schools. 32 What else can you do? Tsvetayeva[4] had three children, but she kept on writing.

You just said that the birthrate was low in the Soviet Union. What could be done to raise it?

To raise the birthrate one has to raise wages. They're so low now that women can't afford the luxury of two or three children.

What is a good mother?

Naturally, a good mother has to take care of her baby, take it out for 36 walks and make sure it develops physically. But she should also give the child moral guidance — a feeling that life has a spiritual dimension. A mother who is concerned only with the child's health and safety is not a good mother. Of course she has to be a social being as well — she has to suffer the sorrows of her people. Then her child will turn out well. I'm quite convinced of that.

And how would you define a good father?

A good father? I know only one example of a good father, and that's mine. In the Soviet Union the father usually loves the wife above the children, but a good father ought to put his children first. When I was a baby my father always used to carry me in his arms at night. He didn't worry about his time, although he wrote a lot — carrying me on his arm. A father should spend as much time with his child as possible, and not only treat it as a child, but as an adult. Perhaps my husband would have made a good father, but after six months he was conscripted. He was twenty-seven, and it was his last call of duty. He was gone for a year, and I was allotted 15 rubles per month. When he returned, the child

---

[4]Marina Tsvetayeva (1892–1941) was a Russian poet. — ED.

was a year and a half old already, and he was like a stranger to the child. Things just kept on getting worse and worse between us until we divorced.

I was much closer to my father than my mother, but I feel that for a son a father is absolutely necessary. I can't imagine my own childhood without my father, and I don't know what I would have done without him. I have a feeling that he gave me everything.

Do you consider yourself a good mother?   40

No, I'm a disgusting mother! I bring up my son on the run. I get tired of trying to keep him amused and give him a pencil so that he can keep himself busy drawing.

However, I do try to teach him the love of work. That's the most important thing one can teach a child — aside from spiritual and ethical values, of course. But I don't see these qualities in my son, and therefore I consider myself a bad mother. I should have taught him better.

Do you think one ought to give boys and girls a different upbringing?

No. I believe that girls ought to be taught to cook, clean, and do   44 housework, but so should boys. People ought to be free and independent, but not arrogant. There's not really much difference between a boy and girl, except that boys have to develop more physically, and that of course is the father's job.

Do you have contraceptives in the Soviet Union?

We have the I.U.D., although it isn't used very much. Women who want one have to stand in line a long time. We try not to use the pill because of the possible danger to a future fetus. Some also use aspirin, but that's also considered to be dangerous.

But above all we have many abortions. They're horrible, absolutely horrible. But what's the answer? Our contraceptives aren't any good. There are condoms, but they're so repulsive and bad that we would rather go through an abortion. . . . The first Christians copulated only in order to procreate. In my opinion abortions are punishments for our sins.

Have you ever had an abortion?   48

Yes, many — seven. It's hard both physically and psychologically. Now that it's done with drugs there's no pain, but it's hard on the psyche.

How are women affected?

There are painful repercussions. There's no way of thinking about anything else when you're pregnant and you have to wait two months for an abortion. Then the aftermath is difficult. It affects not only your sex life, but also life in general. Sometimes I fear that I may be pregnant again; then I can't think about anything else, can't write, can't read, can't do anything.

People say that when a woman gives birth to a child she gets younger, 52 and when she has an abortion she gets twice as old. So I have become seven times as old! . . . The only concern doctors seem to have is to make abortions relatively painless. Previously no drugs were given. But the dread of pregnancy still remains stronger than anything else.

How did you react when you discovered that you were pregnant the first time?

I was hysterical. It was totally unexpected, since I didn't believe . . . I couldn't imagine that children were conceived that quickly. No one had told me anything. I got together with my husband, and I got pregnant immediately. It was so strange and unexpected that I had an abortion, though naturally I should have had that first baby. I went through with the second pregnancy and mostly felt fine, but I developed toxemia. The delivery was very difficult. They don't use any drugs, gas, anything. None of the women around me wanted them either. I begged for a cesarean, howled like an animal, couldn't stand the pain any longer. I screamed so much that they finally had to give me something to induce labor, and I had terrible contractions and kept on screaming until there was blood in my mouth.

A friend had a baby two months later and told me that an old lady who had taken a three months' course told her how to prepare for each contraction. She gave no drugs, but only explained in what position my friend should lie. They also give massage, but that doesn't help. One feels like an animal.

My baby was born in a special clinic, but still. . . . During the delivery 56 I was badly torn, but they didn't even sew me up. Recently I went to a gynecologist who asked me whether I had given birth in the country — but in fact I gave birth at a special clinic in the capital.

Did you feel that the pains you suffered affected your relationship to the child?

No, I felt it was quite normal. I knew that it would hurt. I was so happy to see him that I forgot it all.

EXPLORATIONS

1. Commenting on the Soviet women they met, Hansson and Lidén note that all of them "had very definite opinions . . . [but] these opinions were riddled with contradictions." What contradictions do you notice in Liza's opinions about motherhood and fatherhood? parent-child relationships? the functions of the family?

2. Liza mentions some Soviet views and customs that seem conservative by American standards and others that seem radical. Choose three practices or attitudes in "Liza and Family" that clash with your values. What practical aspects of life in Moscow appear to have caused or encouraged each one?

3. An interviewer's skill lies in her or his ability to ask questions that elicit interesting information. Look at the questions asked by Hansson and Lidén. Which ones seem designed to bring out general facts about Soviet life? Which ones seem to come from the authors' on-the-spot curiosity? What other factors can you discern behind the questions in this interview?

CONNECTIONS

1. After reading "Liza and Family" and John David Morley's "Acquiring a Japanese Family," what similarities do you notice between parent-child relationships and responsibilities in the Soviet Union and in Japan? To what extent, and in what ways, do you think these similarities are related to the housing shortages in Tokyo and Moscow?

2. Ruth Sidel's "The Liu Family" paints a very different picture of Communist society from "Liza and Family." Which differences in the family's social role seem to derive from contrasting Soviet and Chinese attitudes? In what ways do you think differences in the interviewers' techniques affected these two portraits of family life?

3. How do Liza's problems as a working mother compare with those of the Americans in Claudia Wallis's *Observation*? How do the available solutions appear to be different in these two cultures? How are parents' priorities different?

ELABORATIONS

1. What advantages do Hansson and Lidén gain from presenting "Liza and Family" in interview format? Look back at "The Liu Family" or "Acquiring a Japanese Family" to see how Sidel and Morley make different use of interview-based information. Then write an expository essay about Soviet family life based on Hansson and Lidén's interview with Liza.

2. The "black-and-white amah" described by Sri Delima, the kibbutz described by Bruno Bettelheim, and the weekly boarding school described by Liza all represent different approaches to child care. Write an essay comparing and contrasting these three strategies, with emphasis on their relative benefits (as cited by the authors) to parents and to children.

VINCENT CRAPANZANO

Growing Up White in South Africa

Vincent Crapanzano, born in 1939, is a professor of anthropology and comparative literature at Queens College and the Graduate Center of the City College of New York. The author of two books on the Moroccan people, he served as consulting editor for *Culture, Medicine and Psychiatry* and for *The Psychoanalytic Study of Society*. Crapanzano has also published recent articles and reviews in the *New York Times Book Review, Philadelphia Inquirer, Times Literary Supplement,* and *Chicago Tribune*. Between trips to Paris with his wife, writer Jane Kramer, Crapanzano makes his home in New York City. "Growing Up White in South Africa" comes from his 1985 book *Waiting: The Whites of South Africa*.

Covering the continent's southern tip, the Republic of South Africa is about twice the size of Texas. Bantus (blacks) are a majority of the population, which also includes Afrikaners (whites of Dutch descent), Asians (mostly Indians), and Coloureds (mixed Khoisan and white descent). The region's native Khoisan tribes — formerly known as Bushmen and Hottentots — had been joined by Bantus from the north by the time Dutch settlers arrived in the seventeenth century. When the British seized the Cape of Good Hope in 1806, many Dutch trekked north and founded two new republics, the Transvaal and the Orange Free State. Hennie, the man interviewed by Crapanzano in "Growing Up White in South Africa," is descended from these Voortrekkers. They and their white countrymen have kept political control by means of *apartheid*, a policy of racial separation that severely limits blacks' access to jobs, housing, income, and influence.

(For more background on South Africa, see p. 344.)

Hennie, the third of three brothers and a sister, was born in 1924 in a small town in the northwestern Cape near the Namibian border. His great-grandfather on his father's side had trekked into the Orange Free State. He was a restless sort of man who, like so many of the Voortrekkers, never seemed satisfied with the land he was farming. "He kept moving on," Hennie explained. "Those Voortrekkers were nomads. They could never settle down. The grass was always greener on the other side. And it often was. Trekking ran in their blood, and I suppose it runs in mine too. I've never lived in any one place for very long. We're not like the people in Wyndal. They've been on the same farm for generations. They have a sense of family history. It's in their homes and on their land. I am the seventh generation born here but I don't know where my ancestors came from. I don't even know where my mother's father was born."

Hennie's grandfather left his father in the Free State and settled down with his two brothers in the northwestern Cape. They staked out a vast farm in an area that was so dry — it was a desert really — that they moved around it according to where the rains fell. "They would settle down with their sheep where it had rained until the springs ran dry and there was no more pasturage. Then they would move on. Some of those farms were over forty thousand morgen.[1] Ours wasn't that big. I don't know how big it was. I'm not sure anyone did. It wasn't big enough though. There was a long drought. It lasted seven years. It rained on the neighbors' farms but not on ours.

"My grandfather was a stubborn old bloke. He wouldn't sell, but his sons didn't much fancy sheep farming. They sold off the few sheep they had left. My grandfather had given them a few sheep when they were kids — that was the custom — and it was those sheep that they sold. I don't think that between them they got more than two hundred rand, but land was cheap in those days and they were able to buy fifteen morgen of completely undeveloped land right along the Orange River. My dad had a lot of faith in irrigation farming. They started clearing the land, stumping the great trees out. They had to level it, too. For the first two years they planted just enough to keep themselves going. It was difficult, and eventually my uncle got out of the venture and started a cartage business with an old ox wagon and some donkeys. They hadn't built the railway to the southwest yet, and there was a lot of work for him, but the business petered out. Then he moved to the South West to look for diamonds, but I don't think he ever saw one. He was starving to death when my dad finally bought him a little plot of land.

"We used to have two and a half, sometimes three, crops a year. We would underplant one crop with the next so that as we reaped one, the other was already growing. We wanted to make maximum use of the land. The soil was so rich we had to fertilize only once a year. We always had something to eat, even during the Depression. We weren't rich, but

---

[1]A morgen is a Dutch unit of land area equal to 2.116 acres. It comes from the Middle Dutch *morghen*, "morning" — a morning's plowing.

we were never really poor. My dad used to say he would never again farm more than a stone's throw from a river.

"After my dad married and had children, he sold the farm and bought another one, a smaller one, nearer town. It was about six morgen, but his kids could go to school by donkey cart. By the time I went to school, he had sold the second farm and bought an even smaller one, right in town. I used to walk to school. The farm was only about three morgen, but it could be even more intensively cultivated. The railway was in by then, and we used to ship fruit and vegetables up to the South West. It's very dry up there, and vegetables were so expensive that people began to write to my dad and ask him to send them ten bobs' worth a week. It wasn't long before the shops got hold of his name and started ordering through him. When I took over the farm, I stopped the small orders. It was easier that way. And then later a friend of mine and I started our own shop up there. We captured the market in no time."

Hennie remembers little of his childhood, and what memories he has seem flat to me, fragmented, and devoid of those resonances that make memories come alive. I was not surprised. Many of the Afrikaner men with whom I talked seemed unable to re-create the first years of their life in a vibrant fashion. I attributed this, without sufficient evidence, I suppose, to the presence of an authoritarian father who was never to be questioned.

"In the Afrikaans tradition you do what dad tells you," Hennie explained. "You don't question him. You want to be like him. There is a tremendous identification between father and son. The son puts on a show of masculinity. We have a special word for it in Afrikaans: *kragdadigheid*, 'power,' 'strength.' 'Potency,' I think, is the best translation. The son must show his potency, his *kragdadigheid*, before his father. He must show it, but he can't question his father's *kragdadigheid*. There's the rub."

Hennie laughed. "This all began in the early days, when people were living in a frontier situation. Once you started shaving, once you started growing a beard, you were considered a man. Now you could go with your dad on some of his hunting expeditions. You were allowed to ride with a rifle. The rifle was more or less a sign of manhood. And we have in our history, I believe, an example that has inspired more youth than anything else. That is the story of Dirkie Uys. He was only about twelve years old when his dad was mortally wounded by the Zulus. He stood over his dad until help finally arrived. Now, you see, that is *the* example for youth. The great thing was to prove your manhood, your *manlikheid*.

And really it's a stupid sort of thing and carried to stupid extremes. 'If you can hold your liquor, then you're a man' sort of thing. If you're really a man, you don't need to prove it.

"Now, in many ways, my brothers and I were brought up differently. My dad never forced us into anything. If my brother wanted to go to university, that was all right. He never told him he had to become a minister. In the old Afrikaner tradition, the first clever son always became a minister. The next one became a lawyer or a teacher, and the third took over the farm. My dad never insisted that we go on with our schooling. I'll never forget, one day my eldest brother complained to my father that his teachers didn't know what they were talking about. My dad told him he didn't have to go back to school if he felt that way. Of course, he was back at school early the next morning. That was the way my dad was. He wasn't very strict, I suppose, given all the mischief my brothers got into. I was only given a hiding once. I can remember it, but I can't remember why. I think that my mother was more of the disciplinarian in our home.

"Of course, I was sort of catapulted into manhood when my dad died. I was only thirteen. My eldest brother was already up in the Transvaal in the mines, and my second brother was at varsity. I had to go to school and manage the farm by myself. My mother — she had always been rather ill — took to her bed after my father died. I hardly remember her during those years anywhere but in bed or, on summer evenings, on the stoep, staring out over the fields onto the river. That lasted two or three years.

"She was, in her way, a gutsy lady. She was over ninety when she died. She could talk to you on nearly any subject. The week before she died she took part in the talent contest they had in her old-age home. She had five books of poetry on her deathbed — she was already looking for a new poem to recite at the next do they were going to have at the home.

"During those years I was the man around the house. I just suddenly 12 realized that I had extra responsibilities. I had to accept this. What else can you do? Your dad has died, and you just have to carry on. I don't think I thought about it very much. So, you see, in some ways, my dad's death protected me from having to prove my manhood. I didn't have to play rugby to prove that I was a man. That's what rugby's all about, you know."

Hennie had no time for rugby. He insists that after his father's death he managed the farm by himself. His brothers were away; his mother

was ill; his uncle was not much of a farmer. He rarely mentions any
relatives when he talks about his life immediately after his father's death,
though there were some: cousins on his father's side and his mother's
two brothers, who lived nearby. Nor does he mention the Coloured farm
workers. Hennie prefers to remember himself alone.

I asked him who took care of him when he was a child.

"My sister Katrin did. We never had a nanny as such. There was a
Coloured girl who stayed with us. My parents adopted her, and she grew
up with the rest of us.

"There were Coloured people who lived on the plot next to us, and I   16
played with their kids. Naturally, my first friends were Coloured. Children
don't notice the color of their friends' skin. You only become aware of
it when you're told that you're big now and must not play with Coloured
girls anymore. I was about ten, I suppose, when I became aware of the
fact that people had different-color skin. It didn't much matter. My
parents were friendly with the *volk* who lived around us. My mom used
to visit them, and they would visit us too. There was nothing odd about
that! And yet somehow . . . Well, I remember there was a European
who had married a Coloured woman. They didn't live too far from us.
They had a lot of goats, and the goats kept getting into our yard. I chased
them back one day and I told the European that my dad said he should
be more careful with his goats. I called him *outa*. You only call Coloureds
outa. He corrected me, and I said, 'But you're married to a Coloured
woman.' I had to depart in a hurry. That was my first awareness of color,
and I suppose that is why I always remember it. It is from moments like
this that you become aware of differences. You begin to think about it.
You begin to notice that there are certain people who are different and
live differently.

"It started with the first settlers. South Africa was never colonized to
the extent that Jamaica was for instance. For many years there was a very
small minority battling against tremendous odds to keep their identity
and their way of life — in a world around them that was terribly different.
There are a lot of laws that we have today that got started then in that
struggle. If an African or a Coloured man raped a white woman, he
would be hanged. If a white man raped a Coloured woman or an African,
he probably wouldn't even have had to go to court.

"In my younger days I was like a little rhino. I just went charging
through life, and what didn't suit me, I kind of brushed out of the way.
And if I didn't like you, I'd tell you in no uncertain terms. And if you
didn't grasp it, I'd hammer it into you. When my father and his brother

moved to town, they were only the sixth European family up there. All the land belonged to the Coloureds, and they had to buy it from them. My dad and his brother always used to say that they had tamed that part of the world. They hammered those others into submission. I suppose I shouldn't laugh, but that was the way it was in those days.

"I've been wondering whether I should tell you this or not, but as we're on the subject, I might as well. Everything about my family wasn't always respectable and good. When my uncle came back to farming, he grew a lot of watermelons. You get to know your watermelons. You've got to keep an eye on them to see which are ready for picking. My uncle suddenly found that some of his melons were disappearing. So one night he sat up in the bushes to see who was helping himself to them. There was a tremendous storm that night, and in the lightning my uncle could see this bloke coming toward him and eventually he recognized him. He was one of those very cheeky Coloureds who used to boast that no white man had ever hammered him. My uncle watched and waited and caught him red-handed. The bloke tried to make a run for it, but before he could get over the fence, my uncle had him down and was punching away at him. Then he started pulling out his hair — his eyebrows even, every bit of hair on his body. And when he ran out of hair, he pulled out his pocketknife and began stabbing him, just little stabs, on his inside thighs. The bloke couldn't walk for weeks.

"Now, I'm not telling you this with pride. But as a child, it made a 20 tremendous impression on me. You see, here's a guy who boasted that no white man had ever hammered him, and then one of your own relatives — one you respect — puts him in his place. You want to imitate him. You don't even think about it. You do it automatically until something happens to make you really think about what you're doing. It just can't come from within. It's got to come from outside — from God. You need the courage to change.

"We've got to teach our children to question why they're doing the things they do. But when I was in school we just sat there like a lot of little birds with our mouths open, and the worms were stuck down. That was that. We never asked questions."

EXPLORATIONS

1. How would you describe Hennie's attitude toward his father? On what specific statements do you base your conclusions? What appears to have been the role of Hennie's mother in the family? The role of his brothers? his sister?

2. Crapanzano's rendering of Hennie's story combines exposition and dialogue. Presumably everything the author knows about Hennie comes from interviews; thus, Crapanzano had to decide where to quote and where to paraphrase what Hennie told him. Look closely at a long paragraph or a pair of paragraphs in which Hennie and Crapanzano both talk about the same topic — Hennie's ancestral history, for example, or the Afrikaans concept of masculinity. In what ways does Crapanzano's voice differ from Hennie's? What information does Crapanzano tell us that is better suited to his voice than to Hennie's? How would Hennie's quoted statements lose or gain impact if rephrased in the author's words?

3. Hennie narrates most of his and his family's experiences in the first or third person (*I* or *we*; *he, she,* or *they*). In a few places he shifts to the second person (*you*). Whom does Hennie mean by *you*? How do the tone and purpose of his narrative change when he switches into the second person?

CONNECTIONS

1. Hennie, like Liza in Carola Hansson and Karin Lidén's "Liza and Family," sometimes talks about himself as a person in charge of his life; at other times he seems to feel overwhelmed by forces beyond his control. What outside forces do Hennie and Liza cite as obstacles in their paths? What impact of these forces on himself or herself does each speaker regret most?

2. Crapanzano's first two paragraphs describe a South African attitude toward home and family that contrasts sharply with the Japanese attitude depicted by John David Morley. What specific differences can you identify between Hennie's family situation and Sugama's? In what ways has geography probably helped to create these differences? Which differences are likely to derive partly from Hennie's being a generation older than Sugama?

3. What resemblances do you notice between the attitude of Hennie's family toward their neighbors and that of the narrator's family in Gyanranjan's "Our Side of the Fence and Theirs"? How are these families' internal dynamics similar? How would you characterize each narrator's feelings about his father? about the female members of his family? What connections (if any) do you perceive in each family between members' attitudes toward each other and toward people outside the family?

ELABORATIONS

1. Imagine you are a journalist assigned to write an article about "the family as social glue" based on the information in "Growing Up White in South Africa." Your article should be a short essay describing how the Afrikaans family functions. Assume that the data provided by Crapanzano are accurate, but do not quote more than a few brief phrases from either him or Hennie. Use your own best judgment to paraphrase and interpret Hennie's statements.

2. "The child is father of the man," wrote the poet William Wordsworth. We are shaped by our parents, and our childhoods shape our future as adults. Choose a problem imposed on Hennie by his upbringing, and on children in general by adults, that concerns you: too much or too little parental control, ineffective forms of discipline, inadequate role models, narrow-minded teaching. Write an essay identifying the ways in which this problem is likely to shape a future generation of American adults, and suggesting some potential solutions.

WOLE SOYINKA

Nigerian Childhood

Playwright, poet, novelist, and critic Wole Soyinka won the 1986
Nobel Prize for literature. He was born Akinwande Oluwole Soyinka near
Abeokuta, Nigeria, in 1934. Educated in Ibadan, Nigeria, and at Leeds
University in England, he studied theater in London and had a play
produced there. Returning to Ibadan, Soyinka became co-editor of the
literary journal *Black Orpheus* and was instrumental in the development
of a Nigerian theater. He has taught drama and comparative literature at
the universities of Ibadan, Lagos, and Ife in Nigeria; he holds an honorary
Doctorate of Letters from Yale University and has been accorded major
literary prizes in England, including the prestigious John Whiting Award.
Soyinka's career was interrupted by two years in prison for allegedly
supporting Biafra's secession from Nigeria (see p. 584). "Nigerian Childhood" comes from his 1981 autobiography *Aké: The Years of Childhood.*
A pluralistic nation of many tribes (Soyinka is a Yoruba), Nigeria lies
in the large curve of Africa's western coast. Its early cultures date back
to at least 700 B.C. Portuguese and British slavers began arriving in the
fifteenth century. In 1861 Britain seized the capital city of Lagos during
an antislavery campaign and gradually extended control. Nigeria regained
its independence a century later and is now a republic within the British
Commonwealth. British influence remains strong; the nation's official
language is English. For all but four years since independence, Nigeria's
governments have been military.
"Nigerian Childhood" takes place about twenty years before the end
of British rule. At that time Soyinka lived with his father, the headmaster
of the Anglican Girls' School in the town of Aké; his mother, whom he
nicknamed Wild Christian; and his sister Tinu. "Bishop Ajayi Crowther"
is Samuel Adjai Crowther; Enslaved in 1821, freed and educated by the
British, he became the first black African bishop of the Anglican Church.

If I lay across the lawn before our house, face upwards to the sky, my
head towards BishopsCourt, each spread-out leg would point to the inner
compounds of Lower Parsonage. Half of the Anglican Girls' School
occupied one of these lower spaces, the other half had taken over
BishopsCourt. The lower area contained the school's junior classrooms,
a dormitory, a small fruit garden of pawpaws, guava, some bamboo, and
wild undergrowth. There were always snails to be found in the rainy

season. In the other lower compound was the mission bookseller, a shriveled man with a serene wife on whose ample back we all, at one time or the other slept, or reviewed the world. His compound became a short cut to the road that led to Ibarà, Lafenwá, or Igbèin and its Grammar School over which Ransome-Kuti presided and lived with his family. The bookseller's compound contained the only well in the parsonage; in the dry season, his place was never empty. And his soil appeared to produce the only coconut trees.

BishopsCourt, of Upper Parsonage, is no more. Bishop Ajayi Crowther would sometimes emerge from the cluster of hydrangea and bougainvillea, a gnomic face with popping eyes whose formal photograph had first stared at us from the frontispiece of his life history. He had lived, the teacher said, in BishopsCourt and from that moment, he peered out from among the creeping plants whenever I passed by the house on an errand to our Great Aunt, Mrs. Lijadu. BishopsCourt had become a boarding house for the girls' school and an extra playground for us during the holidays. The Bishop sat, silently, on the bench beneath the wooden porch over the entrace, his robes twined through and through with the lengthening tendrils of the bougainvillea. I moved closer when his eyes turned to sockets. My mind wandered then to another photograph in which he wore a clerical suit with waistcoat and I wondered what he really kept at the end of the silver chain that vanished into the pocket. He grinned and said, Come nearer, I'll show you. As I moved towards the porch he drew on the chain until he had lifted out a wholly round pocket watch that gleamed of solid silver. He pressed a button and the lid opened, revealing, not the glass and the face dial but a deep cloud-filled space. Then, he winked one eye, and it fell from his face into the bowl of the watch. He snapped back the lid, nodded again and his head went bald, his teeth disappeared, and the skin pulled backward till the whitened cheekbones were exposed. Then he stood up and, tucking the watch back into the waistcoat pocket, moved a step towards me. I fled homewards.

BishopsCourt appeared sometimes to want to rival the Canon's house. It looked a houseboat despite its guard of whitewashed stones and luxuriant flowers, its wooden fretwork frontage almost wholly immersed in bougainvillea. And it was shadowed also by those omnipresent rocks from whose clefts tall, stout-boled trees miraculously grew. Clouds gathered and the rocks merged into their accustomed gray turbulence, then the trees were carried to and fro until they stayed suspended over Bishops-Court. This happened only in heavy storms. BishopsCourt, unlike the

Canon's house, did not actually border the rocks or the woods. The girls' playing fields separated them and we knew that this buffer had always been there. Obviously bishops were not inclined to challenge the spirits. Only the vicars could. That Bishop Ajayi Crowther frightened me out of that compound by his strange transformations only confirmed that the Bishops, once they were dead, joined the world of spirits and ghosts. I could not see the Canon decaying like that in front of my eyes, nor the Rev. J. J. who had once occupied that house, many years before, when my mother was still like us. J. J. Ransome-Kuti had actually ordered back several ghommids[1] in his lifetime; my mother confirmed it. She was his grandniece and, before she came to live at our house, she had lived in the Rev. J. J.'s household. Her brother Sanya also lived there and he was acknowledged by all to be an òrò,[2] which made him at home in the woods, even at night. On one occasion, however, he must have gone too far.

"They had visited us before," she said, "to complain. Mind you, they   4
wouldn't actually come into the compound, they stood far off at the edge, where the woods ended. Their leader, the one who spoke, emitted wild sparks from a head that seemed to be an entire ball of embers — no, I'm mixing up two occasions — that was the second time when he chased us home. The first time, they had merely sent an emissary. He was quite dark, short and swarthy. He came right to the backyard and stood there while he ordered us to call the Reverend.

"It was as if Uncle had been expecting the visit. He came out of the house and asked him what he wanted. We all huddled in the kitchen, peeping out."

"What was his voice like? Did he speak like an *egúngún*?"[3]

"I'm coming to it. This man, well, I suppose one should call him a man. He wasn't quite human, we could see that. Much too large a head, and he kept his eyes on the ground. So, he said he had come to report us. They didn't mind our coming to the woods, even at night, but we were to stay off any area beyond the rocks and that clump of bamboo by the stream."

"Well, what did Uncle say? And you haven't said what his voice was   8
like."

Tinu turned her elder sister's eye on me. "Let Mama finish the story."

---

[1]Wood spirits. — ED.
[2]A kind of tree demon.
[3]Spirit of a dead ancestor. — ED.

"You want to know everything. All right, he spoke just like your father. Are you satisfied?"

I did not believe that but I let it pass. "Go on. What did Grand Uncle do?"

"He called everyone together and wanted us to keep away from the place."   12

"And yet you went back!"

"Well, you know your Uncle Sanya. He was angry. For one thing the best snails are on the other side of that stream. So he continued to complain that those òrò were just being selfish, and he was going to show them who he was. Well, he did. About a week later he led us back. And he was right you know. We gathered a full basket and a half of the biggest snails you ever saw. Well, by this time we had all forgotten about the warning, there was plenty of moonlight and anyway, I've told you Sanya is an òrò himself. . . ."

"But why? He looks normal like you and us."

"You won't understand yet. Anyway, he is òrò. So with him we felt   16 quite safe. Until suddenly this sort of light, like a ball of fire began to glow in the distance. Even while it was still far we kept hearing voices, as if a lot of people around us were grumbling the same words together. They were saying something like, 'You stubborn, stiff-necked children, we've warned you and warned you but you just won't listen. . . .'"

Wild Christian looked above our heads, frowning to recollect the better. "One can't even say, 'they.' It was only this figure of fire that I saw and he was still very distant. Yet I heard him distinctly, as if he had many mouths which were pressed against my ears. Every moment, the fireball loomed larger and larger."

"What did Uncle Sanya do? Did he fight him?"

"*Sanya wo ni yen?* He was the first to break and run. *Bo o ló o yǎ mi, o di kítìpà kítìpà!*[4] No one remembered all those fat snails. That *iwin*[5] followed us all the way to the house. Our screams had arrived long before us and the whole household was — well, you can imagine the turmoil. Uncle had already dashed down the stairs and was in the backyard. We ran past him while he went out to meet the creature. This time that *iwin* actually passed the line of the woods, he continued as if he meant to chase us right into the house, you know, he wasn't running, just pursuing us steadily." We waited. This was it! Wild Christian mused while we

---

[4]If you aren't moving, get out of my way!
[5]A ghommid; a wood sprite which is also believed to live in the ground.

remained in suspense. Then she breathed deeply and shook her head with a strange sadness.

"The period of faith is gone. There was faith among our early chris- 20 tians, real faith, not just church-going and hymn-singing. Faith. *Igbàgbó*. And it is out of that faith that real power comes. Uncle stood there like a rock, he held out his Bible and ordered, 'Go back! Go back to that forest which is your home. Back I said, in the name of God.' Hm. And that was it. The creature simply turned and fled, those sparks falling off faster and faster until there was just a faint glow receding into the woods." She sighed. "Of course, after prayers that evening, there was the price to be paid. Six of the best on every one's back. Sanya got twelve. And we all cut grass every day for the next week."

I could not help feeling that the fright should have sufficed as punishment. Her eyes gazing in the direction of the square house, Wild Christian nonetheless appeared to sense what was going on in my mind. She added, "Faith and — Discipline. That is what made those early believers. Psheeaw! God doesn't make them like that any more. When I think of that one who now occupies that house . . ."

Then she appeared to recall herself to our presence. "What are you both still sitting here for? Isn't it time for your evening bath? Lawanle!" "Auntie" Lawanle replied "Ma" from a distant part of the house. Before she appeared I reminded Wild Christian, "But you haven't told us why Uncle Sanya is *òrò*."

She shrugged, "He is. I saw it with my own eyes."

We both clamored, "When? When?"   24

She smiled, "You won't understand. But I'll tell you about it some other time. Or let him tell you himself next time he is here."

"You mean you saw him turn into an *òrò*?"

Lawanle came in just then and she prepared to hand us over, "Isn't it time for these children's bath?"

I pleaded, "No, wait Auntie Lawanle," knowing it was a waste of time. 28 She had already gripped us both, one arm each. I shouted back, "Was Bishop Crowther an *òrò*?"

Wild Christian laughed. "What next are you going to ask? Oh I see. They have taught you about him in Sunday school have they?"

"I saw him." I pulled back at the door, forcing Lawanle to stop. "I see him all the time. He comes and sits under the porch of the Girls' School. I've seen him when crossing the compound to Auntie Mrs. Lijadu."

"All right," sighed Wild Christian. "Go and have your bath."

"He hides among the bougainvillea. . . ." Lawanle dragged me out of 32 hearing.

Later that evening, she told us the rest of the story. On that occasion, Rev. J. J. was away on one of his many mission tours. He traveled a lot, on foot and on bicycle, keeping in touch with all the branches of his diocese and spreading the Word of God. There was frequent opposition but nothing deterred him. One frightening experience occurred in one of the villages in Ijebu. He had been warned not to preach on a particular day, which was the day for an *egúngún* outing, but he persisted and held a service. The *egúngún* procession passed while the service was in progress and, using his ancestral voice, called on the preacher to stop at once, disperse his people, and come out to pay obeisance. Rev. J. J. ignored him. The *egúngún* then left, taking his followers with him but, on passing the main door, he tapped on it with his wand, three times. Hardly had the last member of his procession left the church premises than the building collapsed. The walls simply fell down and the roof disintegrated. Miraculously however, the walls fell outwards while the roof supports fell among the aisles or flew outwards — anywhere but on the congregation itself. Rev. J. J. calmed the worshippers, paused in his preaching to render a thanksgiving prayer, then continued his sermon.

Perhaps this was what Wild Christian meant by Faith. And this tended to confuse things because, after all, the *egúngún* did make the church building collapse. Wild Christian made no attempt to explain how that happened, so the feat tended to be of the same order of Faith which moved mountains or enabled Wild Christian to pour ground-nut oil from a broad-rimmed bowl into an empty bottle without spilling a drop. She had the strange habit of sighing with a kind of rapture, crediting her steadiness of hand to Faith and thanking God. If however the basin slipped and she lost a drop or two, she murmured that her sins had become heavy and that she needed to pray more.

If Rev. J. J. had Faith, however, he also appeared to have Stubbornness in common with our Uncle Sanya. Stubbornness was one of the earliest sins we easily recognized, and no matter how much Wild Christian tried to explain the Rev. J. J. preaching on the *egúngún*'s outing day, despite warnings, it sounded much like stubbornness. As for Uncle Sanya there was no doubt about his own case; hardly did the Rev. J. J. pedal out of sight on his pastoral duties than he was off into the woods on one pretext or the other, and making for the very areas which the *òrò* had declared out of bounds. Mushrooms and snails were the real goals, with the gathering of firewood used as the dutiful excuse.

Even Sanya had however stopped venturing into the woods at night, accepting the fact that it was far too risky; daytime and early dusk carried little danger as most wood spirits only came out at night. Mother told us that on this occasion she and Sanya had been picking mushrooms, separated by only a few clumps of bushes. She could hear his movements quite clearly, indeed, they took the precaution of staying very close together.

Suddenly, she said, she heard Sanya's voice talking animatedly with someone. After listening for some time she called out his name but he did not respond. There was no voice apart from his, yet he appeared to be chatting in friendly, excited tones with some other person. So she peeped through the bushes and there was Uncle Sanya seated on the ground chattering away to no one that she could see. She tried to penetrate the surrounding bushes with her gaze but the woods remained empty except for the two of them. And then her eyes came to rest on his basket.

It was something she had observed before, she said. It was the same, no matter how many of the children in the household went to gather snails, berries, or whatever, Sanya would spend most of the time playing and climbing rocks and trees. He would wander off by himself, leaving his basket anywhere. And yet, whenever they prepared to return home, his basket was always fuller than the others'. This time was no different. She came closer, startling our Uncle who snapped off his chatter and pretended to be hunting snails in the undergrowth.

Mother said that she was frightened. The basket was filled to the brim, impossibly bursting. She was also discouraged, so she picked up her near empty basket and insisted that they return home at once. She led the way but after some distance, when she looked back, Sanya appeared to be trying to follow her but was being prevented, as if he was being pulled back by invisible hands. From time to time he would snatch forward his arm and snap,

"Leave me alone. Can't you see I have to go home? I said I have to   40 go."

She broke into a run and Sanya did the same. They ran all the way home.

That evening, Sanya took ill. He broke into a sweat, tossed on his mat all night and muttered to himself. By the following day the household was thoroughly frightened. His forehead was burning to the touch and no one could get a coherent word out of him. Finally, an elderly woman, one of J. J.'s converts, turned up at the house on a routine visit. When she learnt of Sanya's condition, she nodded wisely and acted like one who knew exactly what to do. Having first found out what things he last did before his illness, she summoned my mother and questioned her.

She told her everything while the old woman kept on nodding with understanding. Then she gave instructions:

"I want a basket of *àgìdi*, containing fifty wraps. Then prepare some *èkuru* in a large bowl. Make sure the *èkuru* stew is prepared with plenty of locust bean and crayfish. It must smell as appetizing as possible."

The children were dispersed in various directions, some to the market   44
to obtain the *àgìdi*, others to begin grinding the beans for the amount of *èkuru* which was needed to accompany fifty wraps of *àgìdi*. The children's mouths watered, assuming at once that this was to be an appeasement feast, a *sàarà*[6] for some offended spirits.

When all was prepared, however, the old woman took everything to Sanya's sickroom, plus a pot of cold water and cups, locked the door on him, and ordered everybody away.

"Just go about your normal business and don't go anywhere near the room. If you want your brother to recover, do as I say. Don't attempt to speak to him and don't peep through the keyhole."

She locked the windows too and went herself to a distant end of the courtyard where she could monitor the movements of the children. She dozed off soon after, however, so that mother and the other children were able to glue their ears to the door and windows, even if they could not see the invalid himself. Uncle Sanya sounded as if he was no longer alone. They heard him saying things like:

"Behave yourself, there is enough for everybody. All right you take   48
this, have an extra wrap . . . Open your mouth . . . here . . . you don't have to fight over that bit, here's another piece of crayfish . . . behave, I said . . ."

And they would hear what sounded like the slapping of wrists, a scrape of dishes on the ground, or water slopping into a cup.

When the woman judged it was time, which was well after dusk, nearly six hours after Sanya was first locked up, she went and opened the door. There was Sanya fast asleep but, this time, very peacefully. She touched his forehead and appeared to be satisfied by the change. The household who had crowded in with her had no interest in Sanya however. All they could see, with astonished faces, were the scattered leaves of fifty wraps of *àgìdi*, with the contents gone, a large empty dish which was earlier filled with *èkuru*, and a water pot nearly empty.

No, there was no question about it, our Uncle Sanya was an *òrò*; Wild

---

[6]An offering, food shared out as offering.

Christian had seen and heard proofs of it many times over. His companions were obviously the more benevolent type or he would have come to serious harm on more than one occasion, J. J.'s protecting Faith notwithstanding.

EXPLORATIONS

1. What is the relationship in Soyinka's family between Anglican religious beliefs and traditional African magic? At what points in "Nigerian Childhood" do parents use each of these belief systems to control or teach children? At what points do the childrens' beliefs guide them toward "good" behavior?

2. "Stubbornness was one of the earliest sins we easily recognized," writes Soyinka. What other virtues, failings, and rules of behavior have these children evidently been taught? Cite specific evidence for your conclusions.

3. What aspects of Soyinka's narrative make it clear that he was an adult when he wrote "Nigerian Childhood"? What passages indicate that he is telling his story from a child's rather than an adult's point of view?

CONNECTIONS

1. Both "Nigerian Childhood" and Vincent Crapanzano's "Growing Up White in South Africa" are set in cultures where native African and colonial European influences are mixed. Judging from these two accounts, which culture has accommodated its dual heritage more successfully? On what evidence do you base your opinion?

2. When Carola Hansson and Karin Lidén asked "What is a good mother?" Liza answered that, in addition to providing physical care, "she should also give the child moral guidance — a feeling that life has a spiritual dimension. . . . She has to be a social being as well — she has to suffer the sorrows of her people." What actions and statements by Wild Christian fit this definition? What actions and statements by Soyinka suggest whether he believes Wild Christian is a good mother?

3. What child-care role is evidently played by "Auntie" Lawanle in the Soyinka household? How does her role compare with that of Sri Delima's "black-and-white amah"? What functions in both cultures seem to be reserved for the mother?

ELABORATIONS

1. Soyinka's matter-of-fact narration of magical events helps us as readers to understand the plausibility of these events for the people involved. By showing rather than explaining his and his family's belief in "the world of spirits and ghosts," Soyinka encourages us to sympathize with, if not share, that belief. Could an outside reporter tell these stories as convincingly? Write an imaginary interview with Soyinka (you might use "Liza and Family" as a model), or a brief essay about his family's blend of magic and Christianity (you might use "The Liu Family" or "Growing Up White in South Africa" as a model). Try to portray the young Soyinka's acceptance of magical events as a reasonable attitude.

2. When you were a child, were you afraid of imaginary monsters? Have you or a friend ever had an encounter with a ghost? Write a narrative essay about an experience that most American adults would respond to with skepticism, depicting it (as Soyinka does) as a real event.

GHOLAM-HOSSEIN SA'EDI

The Game Is Over

Widely considered Iran's leading writer, Gholam-Hossein Sa'edi was born in Tabriz in 1935. He became involved in political activities while studying medicine (he is a psychiatrist) and was later imprisoned and tortured by the shah's regime. Many of his writings were banned. He was eventually released and allowed to come to the United States; he has since returned home. Sa'edi is one of the founders of Iran's modern drama and theater, and has written numerous plays as well as short stories, film scripts, and anthropological monographs. "The Game Is Over" (*Bazi tamam shud*) first appeared in the Tehran publication *Alifba* in 1973. The following translation from the Farsi, by Robert Campbell, was done for Sa'edi's American story collection *Dandil* (1981).

Sa'edi's homeland, the Islamic Republic of Iran, lies south of the Soviet Union and northeast of Saudi Arabia. Iran is an expanse of large salt deserts and mountains dotted with oases and forest areas. Long known as Persia, it was conquered repeatedly over its 4000-year history. The British and Russian empires vied for influence there in the nineteenth century; Afghanistan was severed from Iran by the British in 1857. The shahs (father and son) ruled from 1925 to 1979, when conservative Muslims took power under the aged religious leader Ayatollah Ruhollah Khomeini.

(For more background on Iran, see p. 621).

I

Hasani said it to me himself: "Let's go over to my place tonight." I'd never been to their place. He'd never been to mine. What I'm getting at is, we were always too afraid of our fathers. He was a lot more afraid than I was. But that night it was different: Hasani was mad at me. He imagined that I didn't like him any more, that I wasn't his friend. So we went. Usually we just met each other outside. In the morning I would go to their little shack and give a long-drawn-out whistle that Hasani had taught me. When I whistled, Hasani would grab a can and come out. Instead of saying "Hi," we would fight a little. We would hit each other hard so it hurt. That's how we'd decided to behave, and whenever we met, or whenever we left each other, we would fight like that — unless we were either angry or had tricked each other.

After that we'd go running between all the little shacks and drop into Body Washer's Hollow. The city garbage trucks dumped their trash there. We'd root around in the trash. One day I might pick up some tin, and Hasani might find some glass. Now and then we'd get our hands on something better, like an empty salad oil can, a baby's bottle, a broken doll, a useful shoe, a perfectly good sugar bowl with a handle broken off, or maybe a plastic pitcher. Once I found a gold charm with a verse from the Koran on it. Like from a baby's necklace. Hasani had found a full pack of foreign cigarettes. When we got tired, we'd go to the side of the hollow where there's a big flat place: Hājji Timur's Kiln's at the far side of the terrace. They didn't use it any more. It was ruined.

There were all these big wells on the terrace — not just two or three, but well after well after well. Once I got the idea of counting them two by two. After we counted fifty, we got tired of it and quit. Every time we went to the wells we played these games that were fun. We would lie down and crawl up to where our chests were over the wells, and then we'd make funny noises. The noises would echo in the wells and come out again. Every well was different and would answer us with a special sound. Mostly we'd just laugh into the well, and instead of laughs, we'd hear cries coming back out. We'd get scared, and we'd laugh some more, louder, but the crying just got louder too. Hasani and I would be alone, mostly. Other kids hardly ever came to the hollow. Their mamas wouldn't let them. They were scared they'd fall in a well or get hurt some other way. But Hasani and me, it wasn't just that we'd gotten bigger, or that we always came home with sackfuls of stuff. Our mamas didn't mess with us any more. They never said anything.

That afternoon, the one before the night I went to Hasani's place, Hasani came out, and he was really low. He was wrinkling his forehead. You could see he'd been crying a lot. He didn't feel like doing anything. His heart wasn't in it. When we went to the hollow, he just wandered around, poking at the trash with his stick. He swore at his dad some. I knew what had happened. His dad had come home from work at noon and been really mad. He had argued with his boss and been fired, and when he got home he had jumped Hasani and beat him like there was no tomorrow.

We'd heard Hasani yelling. My ma had sworn at Hasani's dad. She said, "Why are you beating an innocent child?" I saw the marks the belt had left on his shoulders, and a place under one eye that had gotten swollen and turned black and blue. Every night when Hasani's dad came home, before he changed clothes or washed, he would beat Hasani. He would beat him with his fists. He'd kick him. He'd use a club, or a rope,

4

or a belt. He swore at Hasani and beat him till he cried bloody murder; you could hear him scream all over the place.

The neighbors would go running up. They'd swear, "May I die and you die," and make him let him go. Hasani's dad would beat him every night, but my dad would only beat Ahmad and me once or twice a week. Like when he was feeling bad, or things at the shop hadn't gone well, he would take it out on us. He'd beat us till suppertime. My ma would take to crying and carrying on and saying, "You bastard! Why are you killing my children! Why are you crippling them!" My dad would turn around and start taking it out on her. She'd yell, "Children, get out, get out!" By the time we'd got out, my dad would have calmed down. He'd just sit real quiet in a corner and chew on his mustache, and he'd say, "Call the children and let's guzzle down something."

But Hasani's dad didn't bother the other kids. He just beat on Hasani, and his ma would never say, "Get out!" Because Hasani's dad would always block the door and lay into him just like that. He would hit and kick him all over. He'd grab his head and pound it on the wall.

That was the first day he'd taken it out on Hasani around noon. Hasani   8 was really down, so I tried to cheer him up. I said to him, "Let's go up there." We got out of the hollow and went to the flat place where the wells are. We sat down beside one. No matter what I tried, he didn't say anything. He just stayed gloomy. I even lay down by the well and stuck my head in, and I made noises like a cow and a puppy, and I laughed and cried and did everything I knew how to do. But would you believe it? Hasani just sat there frowning. He kept hitting his toes with his stick. At last I whistled to him in our private code, "Hasani, what's with you?" Hasani didn't answer. I called again, "Hasani, Hasani." He turned around and said, "What?" I said, "What are you being so cross for?"

"Why should it be for anything?"

"By God, stop your frowning. What are you frowning for?"

"I didn't make myself start frowning. How can I quit?"

I got up and said, "Come on, get up and let's do something so you'll   12 cheer up."

Hasani, who was still hitting his toes with his stick, said, "Like what?"

I thought a bit, but couldn't come up with anything to bring him around. I said, "Let's go to the road and watch the cars."

"What for?"

"Let's go and count the hearses like we did the other day. Let's see   16 how many go by in an hour."

"As many as go by, go by. So what?"

"You want to go on top of Hājji Timur's Kiln and throw rocks?"

He said listlessly, "I don't feel like it. If you want, go by yourself and throw rocks."

I sat down on a heap of garbage. No way was he going to listen to what I was saying. I said, "Better yet, get up, let's go to the square. There's lots to see."

"What's there to see?"

"We'll look at movie posters, then we'll go back of Stone Cutter's Square, and watch Sagdast the Dervish do magic tricks."

"By the time we get to the square it'll be dark."

"So we'll take a bus."

"With what money?"

"I've got twelve *riāls*."

"Keep it for yourself."

"Let's go get something to eat, OK?"

"There's no point in eating anything."

I was at my wits' end. I went on looking around, and my eyes fell on Shokrāi's garden. I said, "Hey, Hasani, do you want to go steal walnuts?"

"Yeah, since I haven't been beaten enough today, let's go get caught by the gardener."

A while went by. Neither of us said anything. Two men showed up from behind the kilns. They stood around and watched us for a while, and then they headed for the garden and jumped over the wall. First there were yells. Then we could hear some men in there laughing. I said to Hasani, "Why are you mad at me?"

He said, "I'm not mad at you."

We shut up again. Hasani went on hitting his toes. I said, "Cut that out. Are you going crazy?"

He said, "All right. But it doesn't hurt."

"Now you say something."

"I don't know anything to say."

Angrily, I shouted, "You're getting pretty sickening. Get up, let's go."

We both got up and got going. While we were walking along between the wells, I said, "Hasani!"

"What?"

"Out with it. Whatever you want, whatever's on your mind, spit it out."

"I want to beat the crap out of that father of mine."

"Great. Well, go beat the crap out of him."

"I can't do it all by myself."   44

"Of course you can't."

He stopped all of a sudden and asked me, "Will you come with me so we can give him what's coming to him?"

I thought a bit. Hasani's dad hated children. You couldn't so much as look at him. He'd never say hello back to you. He'd just go by glaring. My dad would say that this bastard's crazy, a bit cracked, unsound of mind, you might say. Now how was I going to jump him? And if I didn't do it, Hasani would be mad at me. I didn't want Hasani mad at me. I was turning this over in my mind when Hasani said, "Don't you want to help me?"

"Why not? I want to. I want to a lot."   48

"Then why don't you answer me?"

"So how are we going to jump him?"

"You come over to our place tonight. We each hide in a corner. When he comes after me, all of a sudden we attack and grab his legs and knock him down and wipe him out!"

"And then what?"   52

"And then nothing. Just he'll know what it feels like to be beaten. I'll be happy."

"OK."

So that's how we wound up at his place. It was just about sunset, the time when the sky is turning gray. Hasani's dad hadn't shown up yet. Hasani's ma told us to go bring water for them. We went and got the water, and then we just waited, shifting from foot to foot. Finally we saw Hasani's dad way off. He was bent over, with a bag across his shoulder. Hasani said, "Here comes the son of a bitch." We went running off. We took a short cut and got to his shack. Hasani's ma was sitting outside cooking tomatoes over the primus. Hasani's little brother was sitting with his ma's arm around him. He was bawling. We went in the yard and set the pitcher of water by the window, then walked into the house. Hasani's ma yelled from outside, "Hey, Hasani, light the lamp."

Hasani lit the lamp. His little sister had gone to sleep in a corner of   56
the room. I said, "What do we do now?"

"Nothing. Just sit there by the door and don't do nothing."

I sat and waited. Hasani sat on the other side of the room. There was no sign of his dad yet.

Hasani said, "Don't forget, just grab his leg."

"What are you going to do?"   60

"First I'll punch him in the jaw, then I'll jump him and beat him into the ground."

Fear grabbed hold of me. I didn't know how things were going to end up. I was waiting like that when we heard his dad yelling outside. He started shouting, "You filthy slut, I hadn't come yet. What are you cooking dinner for?"

Hasani's ma said, "What the hell am I supposed to do? You always want to wolf something down when it gets dark."

Hasani's dad shouted, "Are you and your whelps eating too, you slut?"   64

Hasani's ma cried out, "Help, people! Help! Would to God you get crippled and your legs broken at the roots."

Hasani said, "You hear?"

"Hear what?"

"He's kicking my ma. The crazy pig!"   68

We heard Hasani's dad start yelling, "What's this little bastard doing hanging around here?"

"So where's he supposed to hang around?"

"How should I know, somewhere else, some other corner."

He came into the yard and set his bag and junk beside the door. He   72
started coughing and spitting up phlegm. He cursed under his breath, then picked up the water jug, sloshed some water around his mouth, gulped some down and came toward the room. He took off his shoes. My heart had stopped beating. As his dad came in, Hasani looked just like a cat that's scared, half-crouching and inching back. His dad gnashed his teeth and snarled. Hasani, who was pinned up against the wall, said, "What are you going to do?" His dad said, "Nothing. What can one do with you, you snot-nosed little brat?" All of a sudden he noticed me. He looked me over from head to foot and twirled his mustache. I was terrified. I began edging back without getting up. "Glory be, what's this fat baboon doing here?" he sneered.

"He's my friend, Abdul Āghā's son."

"I don't care what piece of shit's son he is. What's he doing in my house?"

"I told him he could come."

"You mean the wretches don't have a hole of their own to crawl in?"   76

"Sure they have a house, a much nicer one, too."

"So how did he wind up here?"

He turned on me and yelled, "Get up, beat it, go crawl in your own shack."

Full of fear, I was getting up, when he said, "Move it!"

Hasani said from the back of the room, "He's not going. He stays here."

Hasani's dad turned around and clenched his fists. He headed for Hasani. "You fruit of adultery, you've become so brazen you're standing up to your father?"

Hasani's little sister woke up with a start and ran in panic out of the room. Hasani's dad was moving in and raising his fists, when suddenly Hasani shouted, "Come on!" I charged in. As Hasani's dad brought his fists down, Hasani jumped to one side. His fists hit the wall. I lunged and grabbed his leg. Hasani got loose from his dad and grabbed the other leg. We both yanked, and Hasani's dad fell on us shouting. First a fist connected with my head, and then another fist got Hasani's. Then he hit both our heads at the same time. The two of us wriggled out from under him. Hassani, swearing under his breath, kicked his dad in the side, and we both lit out the door. The guy kept yelling, "Now I'm really going to get you bastards. You couldn't take it, so you're going after your hit man to finish me off?"

He took after us. Hasani's ma stood by the lantern wailing. She didn't   84
know what to do. We went right past her and flew like the wind up a back path to the hollow. We heard Hasani's dad shouting, "Catch them! Catch them!"

He ran a few steps behind us, and then he stood still, swearing and wailing. It had gotten dark. Nobody came after us, and nobody seemed to feel like catching us. We jumped into the hollow, panting. We took each other's hands and waited to see if Hasani's dad or anyone else would show up and grab us. I said to Hasani, "We better get out of the hollow."

"Yeah. Or you'll see the bastard coming along with a club in his hand. Then we've had it."

We climbed up out of the hollow and sat down on a little rise. While we were catching our breath, I said to Hasani, "We did a good job of getting away from him."

"It's a shame we couldn't really work him over."   88

"When do you want to go home?"

"Go home? The hell I want to go back home! God, he's just waiting for me to go back so he can get his hands on me and really tear me to pieces."

"So what do you want to do?"

"Nothing."   92

"Where will you stay the night?"

"Nowhere. I've got nowhere to go."

"Come on over to our place."

"Right, fall into *your* dad's clutches. Those bastards are all alike. 96
There's not a shred of mercy in them."

"If you don't go back tonight, what will you do tomorrow? What will
you do day after tomorrow? Finally you'll have to go back."

"I'm not so sure. One of these days you'll look and see I've up and
gone somewhere else."

"Like where?"

"Wherever."   100

"To do what?"

"How should I know what I'll end up doing? I'll become an apprentice.
I'll run errands. I'll be a porter."

"You're just a kid. Nobody will hire you."

"Why not!"   104

"Because you don't know how to do anything."

"So I don't know a trade. I can wash and sweep in front of stores."

"Anyway you'd have to be bigger for them to hire you."

"I could still collect trash and sell it."   108

"Where'd you sleep nights?"

"In the ruins."

"It's no good. A day, two days, OK. Finally you'll die of hunger or
something will happen to you."

"Never! I won't die. I'll go and beg and survive."   112

"Right. So keep on dreaming. They'll take you and put you in the poor-
house. Have you forgotten about the kids at Asadul and Ābji-ye Rezā?"

"So what should I do?"

"I don't know. It seems to me you should go back home."

We both shut up. The moon had come out, and most everywhere was 116
brightly lit, except for the dark holes of the wells that nothing could light
up. You could see lanterns here and there among the shacks. Hasani
looked at them and said, "There's no going back home now. He'd peel
the skin off my head."

We were quiet again and listened to the crickets. Hasani all of a
sudden jumped up and said, "Listen, I've got a plan. You get up now
and run like hell to the houses and start crying and carrying on and
yelling and start a commotion and say Hasani's fallen in a well."

I jumped up with my heart in my throat. I cried, "You mean you
want to throw yourself in a well?"

"You think I'm such a jackass that I'd go throwing myself in a well? You just say I've fallen, and then you'll see my dad pass out cold. Then you'll see him get his."

"And then?"   120

"And then nothing. I'll go and settle down somewhere."

"Then they'll go search the wells."

"They can't search all the wells. So what if they look in one or two? Finally they'll get tired and guess that I've died. Then they'll get together and cry for me, and read out of the Koran. My ma and dad will beat their heads and say nice things about me."

"Hasani, this isn't a good thing to do."   124

"Why isn't it?"

"If your dad just wastes away, or your ma dies of grief, then what will you do?"

"You're imagining things. It's not like that at all. I know them better than that. They won't waste away and they won't die of grief. When they've finally made mincemeat of themselves and beaten their heads and chests, you come quietly and let me know. I'll go running home. When they see I'm alive and I haven't fallen in the well, you don't know how happy they'll be. I think my dad will make peace and not beat me any more."

"Well . . ."   128

"Well what?"

"Well, I'm afraid of your dad. I'm afraid that after I say this stuff, he'll get me and kill me."

"What do you have to do with my dad? When you get to the houses, start yelling and beating your head and say, 'Hasani's fallen in the well! Hasani's fallen in the well!'"

"Then I'll have to cry. What if I can't?"   132

Hasani looked me up and down and said, "You're such a jackass! In the dark who'll know if you're crying or not?"

"OK. Then what will you do?"

"I'll go sit in some cranny of the kiln."

"And when you die of hunger?"   136

He asked me, with his voice full of surprise, "You mean you won't bring me water and bread? Huh? You really won't come?"

"Sure I'll come."

"Fine, so get going."

I was starting off when Hasani said something else. "What is it?" I 140 asked.

"Don't forget I'm hungry. Bring me some bread and water in the morning."

"OK. I'll come for sure."

"Good. So go!"

I still hadn't made my mind up to go or not. Hasani grabbed my hand 144 and said, "First come here. I'll show you where I'll be."

We were on our way to Hājji Timur's Kiln when some dogs came at us. We took care of them with rocks. Then we went around the wells and went into the last oven. Its roof had fallen in, and nobody would have believed anyone could possibly be staying in there. Hasani said to me, "I'll stay right here. OK?"

"OK."

He said, "Don't wait around. Get going. Don't forget to really really yell."

"Right. OK." 148

I walked around the kiln and went between the wells. Then I dropped into the hollow. A bunch of dogs were running around. They ran away when they saw me. My throat was clogged with dust. I drank a little water from the tap. I remembered that I had to run harder and to yell bloody murder.

I jumped up and rushed screaming toward the shacks. There was a crowd around our place. I didn't know what was going on. You would have thought from hearing me that Hasani had really and truly fallen in a well, I raised such hell and wailed so loud. The crowd milled in my direction. I saw my dad and Hasani's dad. They seemed to lunge at me at the same time. I wailed in a tear-choked voice, "Hasani! Hasani!" Hasani's dad, standing there with a club in his hand, asked, "What happened to Hasani? Huh? What happened?"

"He fell," I wailed, "He fell! He fell!"

I started crying in earnest, tears pouring down my face. 152

Hasani's dad shouted, "Where did he fall? Tell me, where did Hasani fall?" I yelled, "In the well, he fell in the well!" For a minute everyone was silent, and then a strange murmuring rose up. A jumble of voices near and far shouted, "Hasani's fallen in the well! Hasani's fallen in the well!"

People lost their heads and didn't know what to do. Those who were in their houses came pouring out. Some brought lanterns. Everyone set out running toward the upper part of the hollow. I was stretched out on the ground wailing when my dad bent over me and took my hand to pull me to my feet. He said, "Get up. Come on, let's see, which well did he fall in?" We had just started running when several men surrounded me. They ran right along with my dad and me, asking over and over, "Which well? Which one did he fall in?"

We passed the hollow and got to the wells. The moon had risen higher, and the holes of the wells had gotten darker and deeper. Everyone was standing around. Hasani's father swayed like a willow. He grabbed my arms and shook me, saying, "Which one? Which one?"

Before I could answer, he threw himself onto the trash heap and began   156 wailing loudly. Two or three men went up to him. Abbās Charkhi kept trying to comfort him, saying, "Don't worry a bit. We'll have him out of there in no time. Nothing's the matter. Don't cry. Take it easy, we'll find him soon."

By the time Hasani's father had calmed down, another commotion had begun. The women came weeping. Hasani's mother was in front of them all, beating her head and clawing at her face, moaning from the bottom of her heart, "My Hasani! My Hasani! My Hasani!"

She said other things you couldn't make out. Abbās Charkhi came closer and said to me, "Listen, child. Tell us which one he fell into."

"I don't know."

Hasani's father rushed me, shouting, "Bastard! Say what really hap-   160 pened to my child!" Āghā Ghāder held him back and told him, "Get a hold of yourself. Let him say what happened." I swallowed my sobs and said, "Hasani's dad caught us and he was going to beat us up."

Hasani's father broke in: "Just tell us where he fell!"

"Hurry up and tell us!" yelled my dad.

Abbās Charkhi said, "Let him have his say, man. How did it happen?"

"We got away and came here. Hasani was way in front of me. We   164 were both running. Hasani was afraid his dad would catch up and grab us, so he ran faster than me. I turned around and looked in back of me and saw he wasn't coming. Nobody was coming. I yelled, 'Wait, Hasani!' But he didn't wait. Just then all of a sudden he screamed and fell."

Hasani's dad said, "Where did he fall!"

I said, "I thought the earth had swallowed him up. I called and called, but he didn't answer. However much I looked, I couldn't find him."

Hasani's dad just shouted again, "Which one did he fall in!"

Abbās Charkhi said in a mean voice, "How should he know which   168 one he fell in? Let's go find him ourselves."

Then he turned to the men and said, "Get moving. Come ahead. Be careful!"

As they set out, they stopped talking. No one cried. No one shouted.

Only Hasani's mother moaned softly, while the other women kept telling her, "Be calm, sister, don't fuss, they'll find him now and get him out."

Some people kept going, "Shhh." You'd think Hasani was sleeping and might wake up. They went up to several wells, and then Hasani's dad lowed like a cow, "Hasani, Hasani." He was so mean and nasty that if maybe Hasani had really fallen in a well and could get out, he would grab him and start hitting and kicking him again. Abbās Charkhi said, "Calm down a bit. Cool down and let us get on with our work."

Someone said out of the dark, "We must have rope and lanterns. We   172 can't go into wells empty-handed."

Several people went running to the houses. A couple of lanterns were brought up. Abbās Charkhi took one of them. He stretched out by one of the wells, and held it over the hole. Everyone had made a circle around the well. Abbās, with his head in the well, said in a muffled voice, "I don't think he's fallen into this one."

So they went to the next well. This time it was Mosayyeb who stretched out flat and held the lantern over the well. He said, with his drawn-out voice like a peddler's, "Where are you, child? Where are you?"

There was no answer. They went on to the third well. Then to the fourth well. Then to the fifth well. Then to the sixth. Then they split up into two groups, then into four. They brought extra lanterns, seven or eight of them, and a lot of rope. Several people started tying knots in the ropes. The more they went on with no sign of Hasani, the madder they got, and the more they would argue. After a while they called everyone to one well, I mean Abbās Charkhi called everyone, and everyone ran up to it. Abbās had gone out of his wits. He said, "I think he's here. I heard something. It's as if someone is crying in there." Everyone fell silent. Several people stretched out and stuck their heads into the well, listened, and said, "Yeah. That is it."

Hasani's dad started raising hell. He said, "Hurry up, hurry up. Get   176 my boy out of there! Get my boy out!"

Mosayyeb said, "Who will go down?"

Ghāder said, "The well is old. It might cave in."

Hasani's father said, "By God, it won't cave in. Go on in, go in and get him out."

Everyone looked at one another. Abbās Charkhi said, "No one's man   180 enough? I'll go myself. Pass the rope and let's see."

Abbās wife cried out from where the women were, "Not you, not you! You can't! You don't know how!"

Abbās shouted angrily, "What business is it of yours, you bitch? Shut up, I can't let the boy die in there!"

His wife shoved everyone aside, ran up and clung to Abbās, saying, "I won't let you. I won't let you. By God, I won't let you!"

Abbās slapped his wife hard and said, "Get lost, you're being impos-   184 sible."

Then he shouted firmly, "Rope!" They brought rope and tied it around Abbās's waist. Then they tested the knots one by one. Abbās said, "Be careful. Don't let go of me on the way down."

Several men said, "Don't worry. We'll be careful."

Abbās got ready. He grabbed one of the lanterns, bent over, and looked down the well. Then he handed the lantern to someone and said "*Bismillāh*" loudly. Everyone prayed then. Hasani's dad raised his hands to the sky and said, "O most Merciful of the merciful, O Grandfather of Hosein the Oppressed, O Grandfather of Fātemeh the Pure, O Grandfather of Khadijeh the Magnificent, bring up my child alive, bring Hasani back alive!"

Abbās was hanging there in the well with his elbows resting on the   188 rim. He said, "Watch that rope closely. When I jerk on it, pull me up." His wife started crying behind us. My ma comforted her. Then Abbās went down. Five or six of the men held the rope. They clutched it tightly and let it go handspan by handspan. They muttered things to each other. Hasani's dad was walking around in circles, saying things like, "O God! O God!" I had completely forgotten that Hasani was at the kiln. In the bottom of my heart I was saying, "Oh, if only Hasani were in there, and Abbās wouldn't come out empty-handed, and everything would be OK!" After a while, my dad, who was holding the rope with the others, said, "Haul it up. Haul it up. Haul it up."

Rahmat said, "What for?"

"The rope is shaking. Are you blind or something?"

Everyone stopped talking. They started drawing up the rope. Hasani's dad was peering over the heads of the others and waiting for Abbās to appear. Then Abbās's two hands gripped the rim of the well. He drew his elbows up the rim, hauled himself over it, and flung himself across the ground. Ghāder asked, "Wasn't he in there? Wasn't he in there?" Hasani's dad wailed and started to cry and groan. Abbās rolled over and sat up. He said, "I was suffocating."

Ghāder said, "That's all?"   192

"All there was in there was the carcass of a fat dog."

Mosayyeb said, "You're sure?"

"Imbecile, can't I tell Hasani from a dead dog?"

He got up and took the rope off his waist. Everyone got together again 196
and went to another well, then to a third, then to a fourth. They divided
again, and then again. They would kneel over each well, calling Hasani.
At that point I sneaked off and headed for the houses, slipping through
the shadows and byways so that nobody would see me. I drank some
water from the tap and then went behind the tin wall. I crept into our
own place. No one was there. I scooped up a loaf of flatbread and a
pitcher without a handle. I scurried out, and, when I got to the tap
again, I drew some water. I passed the hollow, turned at the road, and
reached Hājji Timur's Kiln just where Hasani was staying. I peeped in
and called him softly. He didn't answer. I called him again. He didn't
answer. I called him loudly. There was nothing. I was afraid. Then I
said to myself, "God forbid he should mistake me for someone else." I
started whistling and right away I heard Hasani's whistle over my head.
He was stretched out on the platform and was watching me. I said, "Hey
Hasani!"

He said, "Come up carefully."

I handed him the pitcher, got hold of the bricks of the wall, and
climbed. We both crawled slowly forward and sat by the bottom of the
kiln's chimney. I said, "Hadn't we decided that you would wait down
there?"

He said, "I climbed up to see what was going on."

"You know what would happen if they saw you?"   200

"No way. No one will see me."

He began to laugh. I asked, "What are you laughing for?"

He said, "I'm laughing at my old man, at all of them. Look at them,
the way they're running around."

He pointed to the terrace of the wells. Some people with lanterns in 204
their hands were going this way and that around the wells. Others seemed
to be glued to one well. They weren't moving.

I said, "We've done something very bad, Hasani."

"Why?"

"Your dad's killing himself. You don't know the state he's in."

"Don't worry, he won't kill himself. What's my mother doing?"   208

"She's beating her head and chest. She keeps crying."

"Let her."

"You don't know how it is. Abbās went down a well, and instead of
finding you, he found a fat dog's body down there."

"He's found his father's body."   212

We both laughed. I took out the bread, and we split it up and ate it. I wasn't thirsty, but Hasani gulped down some water. I said, "Now shouldn't we go down to them?"

He said, "For what?"

"To get the thing over with. They can't go through all those wells one by one."

"It's much too soon. Let them try."   216

"Someone might fall in a well and die."

"Don't worry. They all have dogs' lives and nothing'll happen to them."

"This is an awful thing we've done."

He turned and looked me up and down, and said, "Isn't it an awful 220 thing they do, always going around and beating us before supper?"

"For God's sake, cut it out, Hasani. Come on, let's go back."

"I can't go."

"Why not, then?"

"Supposing I go back. What will I say?"   224

"Say you'd gone to Shokrāi's garden to eat walnuts."

"Then they'd find out you were lying."

"I'll say, how would I know where you'd gone. I thought you'd fallen in the well."

"No. They'll know for sure and it'll be all over for us."   228

"By God, let it be. Come on."

"I'm not coming. I can't come."

"Then I'll go and say Hasani hasn't fallen in a well, that he's staying at Hājji Timur's Kiln."

He turned, looked at me angrily, and said, "Fine. Go and tell. From 232 then on we'll have nothing to do with each other. You'll see me when you see the back of your ear."

"Then when do you want to go back to your house?"

"The day of mourning, when they read the Koran for me. All of a sudden I'll come in. That will feel so great!"

"Don't talk garbage. What'll be so great about it?"

"It's so obvious. When everyone is beating their heads and chests, I'll 236 just quietly saunter up, walk in real nonchalant-like, and say *'Hello!'* First everyone will be scared. They'll cringe. The women'll scream. The children will run away thinking I've come back from the next world. Then when they see, no, it's just me, I'm alive, I see, I laugh, I move my hands and feet, they'll all be happy. They'll leap in the air. They'll fall on the ground. They'll keep hugging me and kissing my face. You don't think that's any fun? Really?"

We went on staring at the people going around the wells with their

lanterns. Now and then I would hear men or women shouting. I said,
"So I guess I'll be going back."

"Go on, but don't let them know where I am."

I crawled down from the recess on all fours. I looked around and
jumped to the ground. I passed by the roadside, dropped into the hollow,
and climbed out again. Everyone had formed a circle around one well.
I went running up to it too. I saw my mother pounding on her head and
wailing. The men had a rope hanging down the well. I squeezed through
and got to the brim. I saw Abbās saying to the other men, "Haul up!
Haul up!"

Ghāder asked, "What for?"   240

"Are you blind or something? Can't you see it's shaking?"

Everyone fell silent and started hauling on the rope. Behind me
Hasani's father was beating on his chest rhythmically. He was saying, "O
Great Khadijeh! O Prophet Mostafā! O Stranger of Strangers! O Lord of
the Martyrs!"

Then I saw my dad with his elbows on the rim of the well drawing
himself up. He had turned black from head to foot and was gasping.
Abbās said, "Lie down. Stretch out and catch your breath." Several men
got hold of my dad under the arms and stretched him out beside the
well.

II

The next morning, no one went to work. Everyone was worn out and 244
went back to their shacks. They hadn't found Hasani. Abbās Charkhi
said, "It's no use. No one can search all the wells."

They had just been through the deeper wells that opened into one
another and had sewage running through them. In their black depths
weird things had been seen. Ustā Habib had run across some creature,
about as big as a cow, with four tails and a dead man's head between its
teeth, going here and there. The Sayyed had run into a bunch of naked
people covered with wool clinging to the sides of the well. When they
saw him, they dived into the sewage and disappeared. Mir Jalāl had seen
with his own eyes huge, black wings that flew around by themselves.
They said weird noises had come from the very depths, like the sounds
of cats wailing, and the laughter of women you couldn't see. Several of
them had even heard cymbals and trumpets, like they play on the Day
of Āshurā. They'd heard wailing and crying behind them.

Abbās said it was no use, it was all over, there was no way to find

Hasani. So then they went back home, tired and sleepy, and dazed. Everyone but Hasani's dad, who kept on wandering around the shacks, jerking his head right and left, forward and back, pounding his hands together and saying, "Did you see what happened? Did you see how my child has gone away? How he's died young?"

Hasani's dad wasn't wailing and crying any more. Instead he began worrying about pointless things, like the roofs of the houses, the dark openings of tombs, covered barrels lined up against the walls, stains on the gunny sacks hanging in front of the houses. Now and then he would stop and bend over to pick some stupid thing off the ground — a scrap of tin, or a broken glass, or a worn-out shoe. He would fiddle with it, and then throw it away and go after something else, muttering, "Now they're eating him. It's all over. My Hasani is finished."

I walked around him several times. It was always the same. He 248 wouldn't see me, or he would see me and not care. After a few minutes of this, I remembered that Hasani would be hungry and waiting for me. I went to our place. Everyone was asleep. My dad had flopped over so that his muddy feet stuck out. I snitched a loaf of bread and a fistful of lump sugar that were in easy reach, and went out again. Everything was sullen and gloomy. I saw Hasani's dad standing behind a house scraping his fingernail across something on the wall. The sun was up and lighting everything. I got to the tap and drank some water. No one was around. I dropped into the hollow, and, past the upper end, I made it to Hājji Timur's Kiln. I headed for the recess, knowing Hasani was there. Hasani was sleeping. When I called him, he woke up with a start. He got scared and shouted, "Who is it? Who is it?"

"Don't worry," I said, "it's just me."

He sat up. He looked different. His eyes were sunken, and his hands shook. I said, "What's up with you? Anything happened?"

"I dreamed that I fell in a well, and whatever I tried, I couldn't get out."

"It's your own fault. You were the one who wanted to keep up this 252 game. You dad has cracked up."

He didn't say anything. He just dragged himself outside. We both sat in the sun. I handed him the bread and the handful of sugar. He hadn't finished his water. He picked up the pitcher, gulped down some water, and splashed some over his face. As he woke up more, he asked, "How have things gone?"

"They're sure now you've died," I said.

"What did you do?"

"I didn't do anything. I didn't say anything."   256
"Now what do they want to do?"
"They haven't decided on anything."
"Aren't they going to read the Koran for me?"
"I don't know. I haven't heard anything."   260
"I think they'll do it this afternoon."
"Where do you get that?"
"Do you remember when Bibi's grandson died? They read the Koran
the day after."
"If that's how it goes, this is your big day all right."   264
"Yeah. God, let it be today. I can't handle any more of this."
"God willing, this will be the day."
"You won't forget to come tell me?"
"No, why should I forget? But get yourself ready for a real beating."   268
"No way. I'll just make them happy."
"Go right on thinking that. You'll see."
"Want to bet?"
"What's the bet?"   272
"If they get sore about like why am I alive and didn't die, and they
jump me and beat me up, you win, and if they're glad, I win, and you'll
get a real thrashing from me."
"That's just great. I've gone through all this for you, and in return
you want to beat me up?"
He laughed and said, "I'm kidding. I'll buy you an ice cream."
"OK. You're on."   276
He tore off a piece of bread and stuffed it in his mouth. He asked,
"Now what do we do?"
"Nothing," I said. "You stay in this cranny, and I go to the house to
see what happens."
"If the reading is tonight, you'll let me know?"
"Sure."   280
Hasani's reading was that afternoon, in front of the houses. Abbās had
nailed a piece of black cloth on the end of a stick and had stuck it into
the ground at the head of the square. Everyone was sitting outside, the
women on one side, and the men on the other. People from other places
had been told, and were coming in batches. From Yusof Shāh Hollow,
from the tenements of Sarpich, the kilns of Shamsābād, the hovels of
Shotor Khun and Mollā Ahmad Hollow. They were all strangers, and
they were dressed in every color you can think of. As they would come
into the square, the women would run up to Hasani's mother. She was

sitting with her scratched and bloody face in front of their house. She wasn't crying any more. She was beating her head and sometimes pounding her chest. As the women came up to her, they would begin to cry, tearing at their own faces and saying, "Dear sister, dear sister, what has befallen you, what has befallen you?"

Hasani's dad was sitting in front of our place, not sitting exactly, but sprawled across the ground, staring ahead senseless. Whoever came and understood who the dead boy's father was, went up to him and said, "*Salām.*" Not hearing an answer, he would turn away and go sit down. Abbās, who was standing, bellowed, "Fātiheh!"

The men recited the Fātiheh, the Opening of the Koran. Ustā Habib went around the crowd with a pitcher, giving water to the thirsty. Two old men had come from Ghoribā Hollow with a pouch of tobacco. They were rapidly rolling cigarettes in newspaper and setting them on a tray. Bibi's oldest son Ramazān was passing the tray among the people. Everyone smoked, and everyone drank water, except Hasani's dad. He didn't do either. He just kept running his tongue over his lips, and sometimes he would spit on the ground.

An hour had gone by when a lot of people showed up running from 284 the road. Everybody turned and looked. Abbās shouted, "The Gypsies of the Black Tents from Elders' Hollow are coming. Let's go meet them."

Several people took off. The Gypsies, panting hard, came running. A lot of them were holding banners. There were several old men in worn-out clothing running in front of everyone. They beat their breasts and looked nervous. Among them was a thin *ākhond*[1] with a long neck and a small turban. The women came behind, all of them barefoot and dusty. As they got to the little square, the sounds of prayers rose up. The men and women separated. The women ran shrieking toward Hasani's ma, and the old men greeted his dad. He didn't answer. Then the *ākhond* went off to sit on the steps of our place. Esmāil Āghā shouted, "Make prayers! Make them loud!"

Everyone offered prayers. The *ākhond* said in a hoarse, nasal voice, "Be seated, all be seated, all be seated. Be seated so that we may weep and recite the doleful story of Ghāsem son of Hasan, how he found martyrdom at Karbalā, in remembrance of this other unfortunate youth." First he read a strange prayer, and then he started reciting the story. All at once, people started crying and wailing. Everyone cried. The men

---

[1]One learned in religious matters; a mullah.

cried. The women cried. Their children cried. Even I cried. Only Hasani's dad did not cry, but kept wandering here and there, running his tongue over his parched lips. The crying got louder and louder. The Gypsies rose and bared their chests. The *ākhond* rose and bared his chest. He said in a loud voice, "Now to rejoice the Lord of the Martyrs and the dear unfortunate one, we will beat our breasts."

He began reciting songs of mourning. The Gypsies began beating their breasts. The other men stood up and bared their breasts and began beating them. The women shrieked even louder, as they stood arm in arm, wailing. Suddenly I remembered: Now is the time. Now I must go tell Hasani.

No one was paying any attention to me. No one was paying any 288 attention to anyone at all but himself or herself. I slipped away quietly. First I backed away, then I turned and ran. I wiped away my tears. When I got to the tap, I drank some water. Then I dropped into Body Washer's Hollow and climbed out. No one was around. I started running again. Running like the wind, I went around the wells and kept on. My heart was full of dread. Sweat was pouring down my face when I reached Hājji Timur's Kiln, circled around, and made my way to Hasani's niche. Hasani was stretched out on the platform. When he saw me he stood up, stepped out, and said, "What's going on?"

"They're mourning for you," I said.

"What are they doing?"

"People have come from everywhere and they're beating their chests for you."

He stared at me for a moment and said, "What are you crying for?" 292

"For you."

"You're such a jackass! You knowing I was alive and hadn't died!"

"It's all the fault of the *ākhond* the Gypsies brought along. He made everybody cry."

He clapped his hands together in delight and said, "So it's time, right?" 296

"All right, I think it's time."

"Now we'll see who wins the bet."

"Would to God that you win."

He laughed and said, "Run, we're off!" 300

He broke into a run. And then so did I. We both charged ahead, but Hasani was flying like the wind. He ran so fast no one could have caught up with him. I kept shouting, "Hasani! Hasani!"

He called back, "Hoo! Hoo!"

Then, suddenly, I don't know what happened — how can I say what happened? Hasani hit his foot against a pile of rubbish, and — just like that — he fell. He fell right into a well. I thought — I mean I didn't think Hasani had fallen in a well — I thought the earth had swallowed him up. I ran up. There was no Hasani. Hasani had fallen in a well. In a huge well, bigger than all the rest of them. My tongue became tied in knots. I wanted to shout "Hasani!" but I couldn't. I had no voice. My mouth wouldn't open. No matter how hard I tried, I couldn't say "Hasani!" I sat on the heap of garbage and held my shoulders. I couldn't catch my breath. Three times I pounded my head on the garbage, and then I got up, not by myself, but it seemed like something picked me up and set me on my two feet. I started to run again. Faster than ever, faster than Hasani had run. I wished I had jumped and fallen in a well. All of a sudden, I found myself running down the road. When I reached the tap, I caught my breath, my tongue came untied and I said softly, "Hasani! Hasani! Hasani!"

As I came up to the square, the breast-beating had come to an end. 304 Everyone was sitting quietly facing each other. Ramazān was passing out cigarettes among the men, and Ustā Habib was going here and there carrying the pitcher of water. I shrieked, "Hasani! Hasani! Hasani!" I pounded my head hard with my fists and rolled on the ground. Everyone got up and mobbed me. Abbās, who was the first to get to me, took my hands so I wouldn't beat myself and asked me, "What happened? What happened?"

I shouted, "Hasani. Hasani fell in the well."

I rolled over and bit the ground. First there was a murmuring, and then a clamor. Everyone tried to calm me down. They kept saying, "OK. OK. May God have mercy on him. Don't hit yourself any more. Be calm." I shouted, "Just now he fell, just now, this very minute he fell, Hasani fell in the well!" My dad pushed the others away and came up to me, saying, "Shut up, child. Don't make things more painful for his father and mother."

"He fell, he fell in the well before my eyes."

"I said shut your mouth. Be silent, you little jackass."   308

He picked me up and gave me a hard slap on the ear. Esmāil Āghā pulled my dad back and roared, "Don't hit him, you son of a bitch. Can't you see he's out of his head?" He took me in his arms and said, "Calm down, calm down."

Ustā Habib handed Esmāil Āghā a glass of water, and he poured it over my face. However hard I fought to get free from the arms of Esmāil Āghā, it was no use. Several people helped him keep me from getting away. I was wailing loudly, "Hasani fell! He fell in the well! Hasani! Hasani!" when Esmāil Āghā clapped a big hand over my mouth, and they all dragged me into our own house. As I was dragged past Hasani's dad, I looked at him and pointed at the wells with my hand. He didn't look at me. He wasn't aware of me. He just went on staring ahead. As we went into my house, Esmāil Āghā said, "Be still, child. Everyone knows Hasani was your friend. You liked each other a lot. Now what can one do? This was the will of fate."

I yelled, "He fell just now! He fell just now!"

I tried to break away and get out, but they didn't let me. My dad said, 312 "What do we do with him? Huh? What do we do with him?" Esmāil Āghā said, "He's gone mad. It's best we bind his hands and feet." So then they bound my hands and feet. I started to wail. My dad said, "What do we do about his wailing?" Esmāil Āghā said, "We'll gag him." They gagged me and tossed me into a corner. My dad rubbed his hands together and said over and over, "What will I do? My God, my God, if he stays this way, what the hell am I to do!"

Esmāil Āghā said, "Don't worry. Right now we'll go ask the *ākhond* of the Gypsies to write out a talisman for him. Then he'll improve."

Ustā Habib said, "If he doesn't get better, we'll take him to the shrine at Shāh 'Abdol 'Azim."

My dad moaned a long-drawn-out moan, and began walking in circles, saying, "O Imam of the Age, O Imam of the Age, O Imam of the Age!"

Esmāil Āghā said, "Better we leave him alone. Perhaps he'll come 316 around."

They left the house and fastened the door. The sounds of the gathering's prayers rose up again, and the *ākhond* of the Gypsies read the eulogy in his hoarse, nasal voice.

EXPLORATIONS

1. Sa'edi starts his story with a suggestion from Hasani, the significance of which becomes evident only later. What sentence in his first paragraph does the author use as a transition out of the present? Where and how does he make the transition back into the moment of Hasani's suggestion? What does Sa'edi accomplish by jumping around in time rather than telling his story in chronological order?

2. Sa'edi lets us know immediately that Hasani and the narrator have already been influenced by the violence in their families. What signs of this influence

do you find in paragraph 1? Over the next few pages, what other speeches and actions by the story's characters reveal their attitudes toward physical and emotional abuse within the family?

3. What is your response to the ending of "The Game Is Over"? How would the story's impact be different if Hasani did manage to show up at his own funeral? What tactics does Sa'edi use to make his readers curious about how Hasani's parents and others will react to his miraculous return? Did these tactics succeed in diverting you from guessing the story's ending?

CONNECTIONS

1. What similarities do you notice between Wole Soyinka's Nigerian childhood and the Iranian childhood depicted by Sa'edi in "The Game Is Over"? At what point in Sa'edi's story does the idea arise of escaping from poverty and frustration into a world with other possibilities? What particular parallels between these two narratives make it possible to imagine Sa'edi growing up in a family such as he describes here, and then escaping, like Soyinka, to become a successful writer? What important handicaps do Sa'edi's characters face which Soyinka did not?

2. Hennie in Victor Crapanzano's "Growing Up White in South Africa" talks about the concept of manhood passed down from father to son, and the ways a son learns to show he is a man. How would you describe the concept of manhood Sa'edi's characters are learning from their fathers? In what ways is it similar to Hennie's? In what ways is it different?

3. In his *Observation*, Michael Novak writes: "The lives of husbands, wives, and children do not mesh, are not engaged, seem merely thrown together." What causes does Novak identify for this problem in upwardly mobile America? What causes does Sa'edi identify for this problem in the Iranian village of "The Game Is Over"?

ELABORATIONS

1. Imagine you are a journalist covering Hasani's tragic story for a magazine or newspaper. Based on "The Game Is Over," write an account of the boy's fate, its apparent causes, and its implications for other children like Hasani. (Your "article" may take either an expository or an argumentative form.)

2. Friction, as we all know, is part of family dynamics. Nearly every young

person living with his or her parents or guardians feels tempted at some point to leave home because of a conflict. Write an essay about an experience which caused you to leave home either permanently or temporarily, or to seriously consider leaving. What do you think of your decision in retrospect? How did the experience affect you as an individual? as a family member?

PART TWO

COMING OF AGE

Landmarks and Turning Points

**OBSERVATIONS:
LOOKING AT OURSELVES**

Jack Agueros, Gail Sheehy, Tom Wolfe,
Richard Cohen, Olga Silverstein

◇—◇—◇—◇

Nathalie Sarraute, *My First Sorrow* (FRANCE)

Mishima Yukio, *The Boy Who Wrote Poetry* (JAPAN)

Sophronia Liu, *So Tsi-fai* (HONG KONG)

Liliana Heker, *The Stolen Party* (ARGENTINA)

Vladimir Nabokov, *From Speak, Memory* (CZARIST RUSSIA)

Mario Vargas Llosa, *Sunday, Sunday* (PERU)

Ved Mehta, *Pom's Engagement* (INDIA)

Marjorie Shostak, *Nisa's Marriage* (BOTSWANA)

Amos Oz, *If There Is Justice* (ISRAEL)

As each of us progresses from infancy toward old age, we continually encounter change — in our circumstances, and in ourselves. Sought or unsought, good or bad, all change creates stress. Particularly disruptive are shifts from one phase to another: from childhood dependence into adult self-reliance, from solitude into companionship, from intimacy into loss.

The playwright George Bernard Shaw wrote that when you learn something, it feels at first as if you've lost something. The passage from youth to maturity for most of us is a matter less of age than of moving from ignorance into awareness, from innocence into experience. Sometimes the change is marked by a ritual (formal or informal); sometimes we only notice it afterward. *Observations: Looking at Ourselves* offer a sampling of rituals and turning points in the United States: Jack Agueros on a Puerto Rican boy's alienation from the American dream, Gail Sheehy on pulling up roots, Tom Wolfe on young people leaving home, Richard Cohen on a father-son awakening, and Olga Silverstein on today's generation of women and their mothers.

The accounts of coming of age in other cultures are arranged in roughly chronological order. We begin with an inner dialogue by French novelist Nathalie Sarraute, who recalls how she discovered the potent pleasure of writing as a schoolgirl in "My First Sorrow." A Japanese writer's moment of self-discovery carries ominous overtones in Mishima Yukio's short story "The Boy Who Wrote Poetry," an account of the author's realization that brilliant metaphors do not make a poet. Still more disquieting is Sophronia Liu's bitter recollection in "So Tsi-fai" of a classmate's suicide during sixth grade in Hong Kong.

In Liliana Heker's short story "The Stolen Party" an Argentine maid's bright, spunky daughter is introduced to class prejudice. Social distinctions are viewed from the other end of the scale by Vladimir Nabokov in "From *Speak, Memory*," his vivid reminiscence of confronting his father's mortality shortly before the Russian Revolution.

Mario Vargas Llosa's short story "Sunday, Sunday" takes us from the brink into the heart of adolescence with a Peruvian teenager's ambitious — and dangerous — plunge into romantic rivalry with his best friend. A contrasting view of courtship is presented by Ved Mehta, who describes the Hindu rituals and the emotional shock that marked his sister's involuntary coming of age in "Pom's Engagement." Marjorie Shostak's "Nisa's Marriage" is a !Kung woman's account of being forced into social adulthood before physical puberty. Finally, Amos Oz's short story "If There Is Justice" shows a young Israeli soldier returning home to his kibbutz for the first time since his baptism by fire. ◇

OBSERVATIONS:
LOOKING AT OURSELVES

1

My mother kept an immaculate household. Bedspreads (chenille seemed to be very in) and lace curtains, washed at home like everything else, were hung up on huge racks with rows of tight nails. The racks were assembled in the living room, and the moisture from the wet bedspreads would fill the apartment. In a sense, that seems to be the lasting image of that period of my life. The house was clean. The neighbors were clean. The streets, with few cars, were clean. The buildings were clean and uncluttered with people on the stoops. The park was clean. The visitors to my house were clean, and the relationships that my family had with other Puerto Rican families, and the Italian families that my father had met through baseball and my mother through the garment center, were clean. Second Avenue was clean and most of the apartment windows had awnings. There was always music, there seemed to be no rain, and snow did not become slush. School was fun, we wrote essays about how grand America was, we put up hunchbacked cats at Halloween, we believed Santa Claus visited everyone. I believed everyone was Catholic. I grew up with dogs, nightingales, my godmother's guitar, rocking chair, cat, guppies, my father's occasional roosters, kept in a cage on the fire escape. Laundry delivered and collected by horse and wagon, fruits and vegetables sold the same way, windowsill refrigeration in winter, iceman and box in summer. The police my friends, likewise the teachers.

In short, the first seven or so years of my life were not too great a variation on Dick and Jane, the schoolbook figures who, if my memory serves me correctly, were blond Anglo-Saxons, not immigrants, not migrants like the Puerto Ricans, and not the children of either immigrants or migrants.

My family moved in 1941 to Lexington Avenue into a larger apartment where I could have my own room. It was a light, sunny, railroad flat on the top floor of a well-kept building. I transferred to a new school, and whereas before my classmates had been mostly black, the new school had few blacks. The classes were made up of Italians, Irish, Jews, and a sprinkling of Puerto Ricans. My block was populated by Jews, Italians, and Puerto Ricans.

And then a whole series of different events began. I went to junior high school. We played in the backyards, where we tore down fences to build fires to cook stolen potatoes. We tore up whole hedges, because the green tender limbs would not burn when they were peeled, and thus made perfect skewers for our stolen "mickies." We played tag in the abandoned buildings, tearing the plaster off the walls, tearing the wire lath off the wooden slats, tearing the wooden slats themselves, good for fires, for kites, for sword fighting. We ran up and down the fire escapes playing tag and over and across many rooftops. The war ended and the heavy Puerto Rican migration began. The Irish and the Jews disappeared from the neighborhood. The Italians tried to consolidate east of Third Avenue. . . .

Dick and Jane were dead, man. Education collapsed. Every classroom had ten kids who spoke no English. Black, Italian, Puerto Rican relations in the classroom were good, but we all knew we couldn't visit one another's neighborhoods. Sometimes we could not move too freely within our own blocks. On 109th, from the lamp post west, the Latin Aces, and from the lamp post east, the Senecas, the "club" I belonged to. The kids who spoke no English became known as Marine Tigers, picked up from a popular Spanish song. (The *Marine Tiger* and the *Marine Shark* were two ships that sailed from San Juan to New York and brought over many, many migrants from the island.)

The neighborhood had its boundaries. Third Avenue and east, Italian. Fifth Avenue and west, black. South, there was a hill on 103rd Street known locally as Cooney's Hill. When you got to the top of the hill, something strange happened: America began, because from the hill south was where the "Americans" lived. Dick and Jane were not dead; they were alive and well in a better neighborhood.

When, as a group of Puerto Rican kids, we decided to go swimming to Jefferson Park Pool, we knew we risked a fight and a beating from the Italians. And when we went to La Milagrosa Church in Harlem, we knew we risked a fight and a beating from the blacks. But when we went over Cooney's Hill, we risked dirty looks, disapproving looks, and questions from the police like, "What are you doing in this neighborhood?" and "Why don't you kids go back where you belong?"

Where we belonged! Man, I had written compositions about America. Didn't I belong on the Central Park tennis courts, even if I didn't know how to play? Couldn't I watch Dick play? Weren't these policemen working for me too?

– Jack Agueros
"Halfway to Dick and Jane"

◇◇◇◇◇

2

Before eighteen, the motto is loud and clear: "I have to get away from my parents." But the words are seldom connected to action. Generally still safely part of our families, even if away at school, we feel our autonomy to be subject to erosion from moment to moment.

After eighteen, we begin Pulling Up Roots in earnest. College, military service, and short-term travels are all customary vehicles our society provides for the first round trips between family and a base of one's own. In the attempt to separate our view of the world from our family's view, despite vigorous protestations to the contrary — "I know exactly what I want!" — we cast about for any beliefs we can call our own. And in the process of testing those beliefs we are often drawn to fads, preferably those most mysterious and inaccessible to our parents.

Whatever tentative memberships we try out in the world, the fear haunts us that we are really kids who cannot take care of ourselves. We cover that fear with acts of defiance and mimicked confidence. For allies to replace our parents, we turn to our contemporaries. They become conspirators. So long as their perspective meshes with our own, they are able to substitute for the sanctuary of the family. But that doesn't last very long. And the instant they diverge from the shaky ideals of "our group," they are seen as betrayers. Rebounds to the family are common between the ages of eighteen and twenty-two.

The tasks of this passage are to locate ourselves in a peer group role, a sex role, an anticipated occupation, an ideology or worldview. As a result, we gather the impetus to leave home physically and the identity to *begin* leaving home emotionally.

Even as one part of us seeks to be an individual, another part longs to restore the safety and comfort of merging with another. Thus one of the most popular myths of this passage is: We can piggyback our development by attaching to a Stronger One. But people who marry during this time often prolong financial and emotional ties to the family and relatives that impede them from becoming self-sufficient.

A stormy passage through the Pulling Up Roots years will probably facilitate the normal progression of the adult life cycle. If one doesn't have an identity crisis at this point, it will erupt during a later transition, when the penalties may be harder to bear.

— Gail Sheehy
Passages

◇—◇—◇—◇—◇

3

In 1971 I made a lecture tour of Italy, talking (at the request of my Italian hosts) about "contemporary American life." Everywhere I went, from Turin to Palermo, Italian students were interested in just one question: Was it really true that young people in America, no older than themselves, actually left home and lived communally according to their own rules and created their own dress styles and vocabulary and had free sex and took dope? They were talking, of course, about the hippie or psychedelic movement that had begun flowering about 1965. What fascinated them the most, however, was the first item on the list: that the hippies *actually left home and lived communally according to their own rules*.

To Italian students this seemed positively amazing. Several of the students I met lived wild enough lives during daylight hours. They were in radical organizations and had fought pitched battles with police, *on the barricades*, as it were. But by 8:30 P.M. they were back home, obediently washing their hands before dinner with Mom and Dad and Buddy and Sis and the Maiden Aunt. When they left home for good, it was likely to be via the only admissible ticket: marriage. Unmarried sons of thirty-eight and thirty-nine would still be sitting around the same old table, morosely munching the gnocchi. . . .

That people so young could go off on their own, without taking jobs, and live a life completely of their own design — to Europeans it was astounding.

– Tom Wolfe
Mauve Gloves & Madmen, Clutter & Vine

◇—◇—◇—◇—◇

4

Several years ago, my family gathered on Cape Cod for a weekend. My parents were there, my sister and her daughter, too, two cousins and, of course, my wife, my son, and me. We ate at one of those restaurants where the menu is scrawled on a blackboard held by a chummy waiter and had a wonderful time. With dinner concluded, the waiter set the check down in the middle of the table. That's when it happened. My father did not reach for the check.

In fact, my father did nothing. Conversation continued. Finally, it dawned on me. Me! I was supposed to pick up the check. After all these years, after hundreds of restaurant meals with my parents, after a lifetime of thinking of my father as the one with the bucks, it had all changed. I reached for the check and whipped out my American Express card. My view of myself was suddenly altered. With a stroke of the pen, I was suddenly an adult.

> – Richard Cohen
> "Suddenly I'm the Adult?"
> *Psychology Today*

◇—◇—◇—◇—◇

5

If you had lived at a different time in history, your relationship with your mother would have been different. You would have done what your mother did, in an actual succession. But this generation has split off not only from what their mothers did, but from their mothers themselves. It's as if you can't love and respect your mother and still live your own life — a nonsensical idea based on current notions about autonomy. . . .

In adolescence you don't split from your mother because you want to catapult into the outside world, the father's world, in which competitiveness and ambition and making it are the big things. In adolescence you *have* to split off; otherwise, you feel too dependent, too cozy, too loved, too comfortable. It's a search for your own voice. But now the struggle extends far beyond adolescence: it's a mass rejection of a whole generation of women by a younger generation of women. The younger women are often denying the feminine voice, and yet they can't take on the masculine voice either. This has led to tremendous difficulties in marriages — trying to find a new way to be in a relationship that's not the way it was, but has not yet evolved into something different.

Things are beginning to turn around as thinking women, writing women, are asking, "What are we giving up by moving into the male place in the world?" It's such a sad and empty place. So there's the beginning of a new sort of affirmation about what's good about being a woman and what's important about relationships, about nurturing, about caring, about worrying about one another, about being closer. That brings us back to our mothers: these were important things we learned from our mothers. If we lose our relationship with our mothers, we lose a very important part of what it is to be human. . . .

We all, men and women, marry some version of our mothers. That is your primary intense relationship, the one you spend the rest of your life trying to resolve through other relationships. It's the one that we're always trying to redo, to undo. That's why it's so important to resolve it.

                            – Olga Silverstein
                            "The Good Mother: An Interview
                            with Olga Silverstein"
                            Vogue

NATHALIE SARRAUTE

My First Sorrow

French novelist Nathalie Sarraute was born Nathalie Ilyanova Tcherniak in Russia in 1900. She arrived in France at the age of two. Educated at the Sorbonne and the University of Paris, she published her first book, *Tropisms,* in 1939. Sarraute was a pioneer of the *nouveau roman* ("new novel," or "antinovel") in postwar France; her books have been translated into twenty-four languages and are published in twenty-five countries. Her six plays have been performed on more than a hundred radio programs as well as in many theaters. "My First Sorrow" is from her book *Childhood* (1983), translated from the French by Barbara Wright.

When her teacher assigned a composition called "My First Sorrow," Sarraute could have chosen one of many from her own life. Her parents divorced when she was very young. Nathalie/Natasha remained close both to her mother and stepfather, with whom she lived in Paris, and to her father, with whom she exchanged visits in her Russian hometown of Ivanovo. Then her mother and stepfather returned to Russia, while her father moved to Paris and remarried. At the age of eight Nathalie spent the summer with her father and his young wife, Vera, and never went home: Her mother refused to come from St. Petersburg to fetch her. Friction between Nathalie and Vera grew when Vera had a daughter of her own. Thus the "Papa" and "Mama" in this essay, the brothers and sisters, the grandparents with their beautiful home, and the beloved little dog are all wistful figments of young Nathalie's imagination.

"My First Sorrow," like a number of Sarraute's writings, takes the form of an inner dialogue: One self recalls, another questions and interprets.

"Describe your first sorrow. 'My First Sorrow' is the title of your next French essay."

— Didn't they rather call it "composition" in primary schools?

— Perhaps . . . at all events, that particular French composition, or essay, stands out from the rest. From the moment the mistress told us to write in our notebooks "My First Sorrow," it's impossible that I didn't have a presentiment . . . I wasn't often wrong . . . that this subject was

a golden opportunity . . . I must have seen nuggets sparkling in a far-off
mist . . . the promise of treasures . . .

I imagine that as soon as I could, I set off in search of them. I had   4
no need to hurry, I had plenty of time, and yet I couldn't wait to find
. . . everything would depend on it . . . What sorrow? . . .

— You didn't start by trying, searching through your own sorrows . . .

— To find one of my own sorrows? Of course not, goodness, what
are you thinking about? One of my own real sorrows? that I had actually
experienced . . . and besides, what could I call by that name? And which
had been the first? I hadn't the slightest desire to ask myself . . . what I
needed was a sorrow outside my own life, that I could consider while
keeping myself at a safe distance . . . this would give me a sensation that
I couldn't name, but I can feel it now just as I did then . . . a feeling . . .

— Of dignity, perhaps . . . that's what it might be called today . . .
and also of domination, of power . . .

— And of liberty . . . I keep myself in the background, out of reach,   8
I don't reveal anything that belongs only to me . . . but I prepare for
other people something that I consider to be good for them, I choose
what they like, what they might expect, one of those sorrows that suit
them . . .

— And it was then that you were lucky enough to glimpse . . . Where
did you get it from?

— I have no idea, but the moment it appeared I felt a certainty, a
satisfaction . . . I couldn't hope to find a nicer, more suitable sorrow
. . . more presentable, more fascinating . . . the very model of a real
first sorrow of a real child . . . the death of my little dog . . . what could
be more imbued with childish purity, with innocence.

As improbable as it may seem, I did feel all that . . .

— But is it so improbable for a child of eleven, almost twelve . . .   12
you were in the school leaving certificate class.

— This subject gave rise, as I expected, to a host of images, still
succinct and vague, brief sketches . . . but which promised to become

real beauties as they developed . . . On my birthday, oh what a surprise, I jump up and down and clap my hands, I throw myself on Papa's, on Mama's neck, a white ball in a basket, I press it to my heart, then our games, where though? but in a beautiful big garden, flowering meadows, lawns, it belongs to my grandparents, where my parents and my brothers and sisters spend their holidays . . . and then, the horror that will come . . . the white ball goes off towards the pond . . .

— The pond you had seen in a picture, bordered with rushes, covered with water lilies . . .

— It has to be admitted that that is tempting, but here is something even more promising . . . the railway line . . . we're going for a walk near it, the little dog climbs up the embankment, I run after him, I call him, then here comes the train at full speed, the enormous, terrifying locomotive . . . this is a chance for splendors to be deployed . . .

The moment has come now . . . I keep delaying it . . . I'm afraid of   16
starting off on the wrong foot, of not taking a proper run up to it . . . I start by writing the title . . . "My First Sorrow" . . . that might get me going . . .

The words I have settled on are not my everyday words, grayish words, barely visible, rather slovenly . . . *these* words are, as it were, beautifully dressed in their best clothes . . . most of them have come from places where good manners and brilliance are required . . . they have come from my anthologies, from dictations and also . . .

— Were they from books by René Boylesve, by André Theuriet, or was it already Pierre Loti?

— In any case, they are words whose origin guarantees elegance, grace, beauty . . . I enjoy their company, I have all the respect for them that they deserve, I see to it that nothing disfigures them . . . If I feel that something is spoiling their appearance, I immediately consult my Larousse, no nasty spelling mistake, no hideous pimple must blemish them. And to connect them together, strict rules exist which you have to abide by . . . if I can't find them in my grammar book, if there is the slightest lingering doubt, it's better not to touch those words, to look for others which I can put in another phrase where they will be in their proper place, in their appropriate role. Even my own words, the ones I ordinarily use without really seeing them, when they have to come in here they acquire a respectable air, good manners, on contact with the others. Sometimes I slip in a rare word here or there, an ornament which will highlight the brilliance of the ensemble.

Often, the words guide me in my choice . . . thus, in this first sorrow,   20
the "crisp rustle" of the autumn leaves that we crushed as we ran or as we rolled over on them — my little dog and I — had, after some hesitation, made me choose the autumn rather than the spring for our games in my grandparents' garden.

— And yet "the tender shoots and the downy buds" were pretty appealing . . .

— The autumn prevailed, and I didn't regret it . . . didn't I find there "the mellowness of the rays of a pale sun, the gold and purple leaves of the trees" . . .

Behind the closed door of my room, I am engaged in the most normal, the most legitimate, the most praiseworthy activity in the world, I am doing my homework. At this moment, it happens to be a French essay. I didn't choose the subject, it was given to me, even imposed on me, it's a subject made for me, within the capabilities of a child of my age . . . I am allowed to frolic within its limits, on a well-prepared, well-laid out ground, just as I am in the school playground or even, since these frolics are accompanied by great efforts, in the gymnasium.

Now the moment has come to concentrate all my forces for the great   24
leap forward . . . the arrival of the train, its din, its scalding steam, its enormous, blazing eyes. And then, when the train has passed, between the rails the tuft of white hairs, the pool of blood . . .

But I won't let myself touch that yet, I want to let the words take their time, choose their moment, I know I can rely on them . . . the last words always make their appearance as if propelled by all the preceding ones . . .

In the darkness of the cinema in the rue d'Alésia, while I am watching goodness knows what silent film, accompanied by pleasant, exciting music, I call them up, or rather, I call them back, they have already come before, but I want to see them again . . . it's an opportune moment . . . I make them reverberate . . . should I change the place of that one? . . . I listen once again . . . really, the sentence they make unfolds and falls into place very nicely . . . still just a slight rearrangement perhaps . . . and then I must stop examining it, I might easily spoil it . . . I must just try to keep it as it is, word for word, until the moment comes to write it in my fair copy, beginning a new paragraph to make it stand out properly in all its beauty, and following it with the final full stop.

All I shall have to do then, is to judge the right distance underneath it and draw a nice straight line with my very clean pen and my ruler.

— Never, in the whole of your life, has any text you have written 28
given you such a feeling of satisfaction, of well-being . . .

EXPLORATIONS

1. When assigned to write about "My First Sorrow," Sarraute speaks of "a presentiment . . . that this subject was a golden opportunity." A golden opportunity for what? At the time, what was young Nathalie aware of accomplishing with her essay? Looking back on the experience as an adult, what is she aware of having accomplished?

2. Sarraute describes in detail the kinds of words she chose for her primary-school essay, and she gives several examples. How has her attitude toward words changed since then? Notice particularly her adjectives. For what purposes does the child Nathalie use adjectives? For what purposes does the adult Nathalie use them?

3. What advantages does Sarraute gain from using two voices in "My First Sorrow"? What are the disadvantages of this device? What other changes would Sarraute need to make in her essay if she wrote it as a continuous reminiscence in one voice?

CONNECTIONS

1. In her *Observation*, Gail Sheehy writes: "Before eighteen, the motto is loud and clear: 'I have to get away from my parents.' But the words are seldom connected to action." How do these statements apply to young Nathalie's essay on the subject "My First Sorrow"?

2. Look back at Wole Soyinka's "Nigerian Childhood" (p. 66). What can you discern about the role in each culture of imagination and make-believe? How

did Soyinka's mother react to his story of seeing the dead Bishop Crowther? How do you expect Nathalie Sarraute's teacher would have reacted to her essay if the teacher had known it was fictional?

ELABORATIONS

1. In describing her discovery of creative writing, Sarraute tells us a great deal about herself, but she does it with the indirection and subtlety of an experienced author. What can you deduce from "My First Sorrow" about eleven-year-old Nathalie's view of herself? her family? her life? Based on this essay and the biographical notes that precede it, write an essay about why Sarraute became a professional writer.

2. Think back to your childhood, and write your own essay entitled "My First Sorrow." In depicting your younger self, try to be conscious (as Sarraute is) of ways in which your perceptions, responses, and judgment as a child differed from your present attitudes.

MISHIMA YUKIO

The Boy Who Wrote Poetry

The Japanese novelist, playwright, and essayist Mishima Yukio was born in 1925 in Tokyo as Hiraoka Kimitake (to follow the Japanese custom of putting family name before given name). Disguise permeates Mishima's work: His first great literary success was the autobiographical novel *Confessions of a Mask* (1949). This followed his graduation at the top of his class from the Peers' School, his study of law at Tokyo University, and his short-lived job at the Ministry of Finance. Mishima also practiced kendo (fencing with bamboo swords) and karate, sang, modeled, acted in films, traveled, married (and stayed married), organized his own army, and designed its uniforms, among other activities.

"The Boy Who Wrote Poetry" has been described by Japanese literature scholar Howard Hibbett as "a miniature portrait of the artist, an exception to his rule of keeping a strict separation between literature and life." In this story we can see the roots of Mishima's "rule of separation" and also of his dramatic ritual suicide (seppuku) in 1970.

"The Boy Who Wrote Poetry" ("*Shi o kaku shōnen*," 1954) was translated from the Japanese by Ian H. Levy.

Poem after poem flowed with complete ease from his pen. In no time he would use up the thirty pages in one of his Peers' School notebooks. How was it possible, the boy wondered, that he could write two or three poems a day? When he was sick in bed for a week he put together *One Week: An Anthology*. He cut an oval out of the cover of his notebook to reveal the word "Poesies" on the title page. Below it, in English, he wrote "12th–18th May 1940."

His poems were attracting the notice of upperclassmen. It's all nonsense, he thought. They're making a fuss just because I'm fifteen.

But the boy was confident of his genius. He began to address his seniors with a decided impudence. He wanted to stop using phrases like "It seems to be." In all matters he would have to take care to say "It is."

Too much masturbating had made him anemic. But his own ugliness 4 had hardly begun to bother him. Poetry was a thing apart from such physical feelings of revulsion. Poetry was apart from everything. From the subtle lies in a poem he learned the art of subtle lying. All that mattered was that the words be beautiful. Every day he pored over the dictionary.

Whenever the boy felt ecstatic, a world of metaphor materialized before his eyes. Caterpillars made lace of cherry leaves; a pebble flung past shimmering oaks soared off to the sea. Cranes ripped into the crumpled sheet of the overcast sea to search below for the drowned. Peaches surrounded by whirling gold bugs were lightly powdered with makeup; the air, like an arc of flames behind a statue, swirled and twisted around scampering people. Sunset was an omen of evil; it ran in deep tinctures of iodine. The winter trees thrust their wooden legs at the sky. And a girl lay nude by a stove, her body like a burning rose. He walked up to the window, only to find an artificial flower. Her skin, goose-pimpled in the cold, became one frayed petal of a velvet flower.

It was when the world was transformed in this way that he knew bliss. The boy wasn't surprised that the birth of a poem would bring him this kind of bliss. He knew, in his head, that a poem is brought forth from sadness, malediction, or despair, from the exact center of solitude. Yet for that to be the case with him, he would need a deeper interest in himself, some problem to tax himself with. Although he was convinced of his genius, he was curiously without interest in himself. He found the outside world more fascinating. It would be more precise to say that in those moments when, for no apparent reason, he himself was happy, the world unresistingly assumed the forms he would have it take.

Did poetry come to him to guarantee his moments of happiness, or was happiness made possible by the birth of his poems? He wasn't sure. All he knew was that this happiness was of a different order from the kind he felt when his parents bought him something he had wanted for a long time or took him on a trip, and that this was a happiness known to him alone.

The boy had no taste for sustained, intent scrutiny of either the outer world or his inner self. If the object catching his attention was not at once transformed into some image — if in May at noon the white glimmer of young leaves did not become the dark sheen of night cherry blossoms — he would quickly grow bored and stop looking. Substantial, uncongenial objects that could not be transformed he dismissed coldly: "There's no poetry in that."

One morning, having anticipated the questions on a test, he hurried through the answers, placed his answer sheet on the teacher's desk without bothering to look it over, and left the room before any of his classmates. As he was crossing the deserted grounds toward the school gate his eye caught the glimmer of the golden ball at the top of the flagpole. He was seized with an ineffable feeling of happiness. The flag was down. It wasn't a holiday. But he felt that the day was a holiday for his own spirit, and that the glimmer of that ball was celebrating it. The boy's mind slipped easily away, and turned to poetry. The ecstasy of this moment. The fullness of this solitude. The extraordinary lightness. Lucid intoxication in every corner of his being. The harmony between the outer world and his inner self . . .

When this state failed to come naturally, he would try to use something around him to force the same intoxication. Holding a cigarette case of striped tortoise shell to the light and peering through it at his room. Shaking his mother's cosmetics bottle, and watching the tumultuous dance of powder leave the clear surface of the liquid and quietly settle to the bottom.

Without the slightest emotion he used words like "supplication," "malediction," and "disdain."

The boy was in the Literature Club. One of the committee members 12 had lent him a key, enabling him to get into the clubhouse alone any time he wanted to immerse himself in his favorite dictionaries. He liked the pages about the romantic poets in the *Dictionary of World Literature*: in their portraits they didn't have shaggy old beards, but were all young and beautiful.

He was interested in the brevity of the poets' lives. Poets must die young. Even a premature death was far off for one only fifteen; from this arithmetical security the boy was able to consider premature death without feeling troubled.

He liked Wilde's sonnet, "The Grave of Keats":

> Taken from life when life and love were new
> The youngest of the martyrs here is lain

The youngest of the martyrs here is lain. There was something astonishing about how actual disasters befell these poets like benefactions. He believed in preordained harmony. The preordained harmony in a poet's biography. Believing this was one and the same as believing in his own genius.

It gave him pleasure to imagine long elegies to him, posthumous fame. But to imagine his own corpse made him feel a little awkward. Ardently he thought, Let me live like a skyrocket. With my whole being let me paint the night sky for a moment, then instantly burn out. He considered all sorts of ways to live, and could think of no other for him.

But suicide was repulsive. Preordained harmony would find a more satisfactory way to kill him.

Poetry was beginning to make him lazy in spirit. If he had been more   16 diligent he would have thought more passionately of suicide.

At morning assembly the student monitor called his name. That meant a more severe reprimand than being summoned to the teacher's office. "You *know* what's the matter," his friends said intimidatingly. His face went white, and his hands shook.

The monitor, as he waited for the boy, was writing something with a steel tong in the dead ashes of the hibachi. When the boy went in, the monitor said gently: "Sit down." There was no chiding. He said he had read the boy's poems in the alumni magazine. He proceeded to ask him many questions about poetry and about his home life. Finally he said, "There are two types, Schilla and Goethe. You know Schilla, don't you?"

"You mean Schiller?"

"Yes. Don't ever try to become a Schilla. Become a Goethe."   20

The boy left the monitor's room and dragged himself back to class, dissatisfied and scowling. He had never read either Goethe or Schiller. But he knew their portraits. "I don't like Goethe. He's an old man. Schiller is young. I like him better."

The chairman of the Literature Club, a youth named R who was five years the boy's senior, looked after him. He took a liking to R too, because R clearly believed himself an unrecognized genius, and acknowledged the boy's genius without the least regard to the difference in their age. Geniuses should be friends.

R was the son of a peer. He affected the airs of a Villiers de l'Isle-Adam, was proud of his family's noble lineage, and infused his works with a decadent nostalgia for the tradition of aristocratic letters. R also had published a private edition of his own poems and essays. This made the boy envious.

Every day they exchanged long letters. They enjoyed this routine.   24 Almost every morning a letter from R came to the boy's house in a Western-style envelope the color of apricots. No matter how long the letters were, they could only be so heavy; it was their curiously bulky lightness, the feeling that they were stuffed with buoyancy, that delighted the boy. At the end of the letter could be inscribed a recent poem, often written that very day, or if there wasn't time, an older poem.

The letters were trivial in content. They began with criticism of the poem each had sent in the letter before, and proceeded into an endless banter, in which each related the music he had heard, daily episodes in his family, impressions of girls he found beautiful, reports of books he had read, poetic experiences in which worlds would be revealed from single words, and so on. Neither the twenty-year-old youth nor the fifteen-year-old boy tired of this habit.

But the boy recognized in R's letters a faint melancholy, the shadow of some slight unease that he knew was never present in his own. An apprehension about reality, an anxiety about something that he would soon have to face gave R's letters a certain quality of loneliness and pain. The untroubled boy perceived this quality as an irrelevant shadow that would never fall on him.

Will I ever awaken to ugliness? The boy never considered such problems; he never even anticipated them. Old age, for example, which finally assailed Goethe and which he had to endure for many years. Such a thing as old age would never come to him. Even the prime of youth, which some call beautiful and others ugly, was still far away. Whatever ugliness he discovered in himself, he forgot.

The boy was captive to that illusion which confuses art and artist, the illusion which naïve and pampered girls all project on the artist. He had no interest in the analysis and study of the being that was himself, yet he always had dreams for himself. He belonged to the world of metaphor, the endless kaleidoscope in which that girl's nakedness became an artificial flower. One who makes beautiful things cannot be ugly. The thought was stubbornly embedded in the boy's mind, but somehow that most important question behind it never occurred to him: Was it necessary for one who is beautiful to make beautiful things?

Necessary? The boy would have laughed at the word. For his poems were not born from necessity. They came naturally; even if he tried to deny them, the poems themselves moved his hand and made him write. Necessity assumed some lack. There was nothing he could construe as a lack. First of all, he reduced all the sources of his poetry to the single word "genius," and he couldn't believe that there might be some deep lack inside himself that he was unconscious of. Even if he did believe it, rather than express it with the word "lack," he preferred to call it "genius."

Not that the boy was incapable of criticizing his own poems. For example, there was one four-line poem that his seniors praised lavishly; he thought it frivolous and was embarrassed by it. It was a poem to this effect: just as the cut edge of such transparent glass as this is tinted blue, so your limpid eyes may be hiding a measure of love.

Of course the praise of others delighted the boy, but his arrogance kept him from drowning in it. The truth was that he was not even very impressed with R's talent. R certainly had enough talent to stand out among the upperclassmen in the Literature Club, but that meant nothing. There was a frigid spot in the boy's heart. If R had not so exhausted his verbal treasury to praise the boy's poetic talent, the boy would probably have made no effort to recognize R's.

He was well aware that the price for his occasional taste of that quiet   32 pleasure was the absence of any rough, boyish excitability. There was a baseball series called the "League Games" played twice a year, in the spring and fall, between the middle grades of the Peers' School and the middle schools affiliated with it. When the Peers' School suffered a defeat, the juniors who had cheered the players gathered around them after the game and joined in their sobbing. He never cried. He was never in the least sad.

"What's there to get so sad about, just because we lost a baseball game?" He wondered about these crying faces, so alien to him. The boy knew that he felt things easily, but his sensitivity lay in a direction different from everyone else's. Things that brought others to tears failed to echo at all in his heart.

The boy began to turn more and more to love as the material for his poetry. He had never been in love. But he was bored with basing his poetry only on the transformations within nature, and he turned to singing of metamorphoses occurring from moment to moment in the soul. He had no qualms about singing of things he had yet to experience himself. There was something in him that had always believed art to be exactly this. He did not at all lament his lack of experience. There was neither opposition nor tension between the world he had yet to experience and the world inside himself. Thus there was no need for him to go out of his way to believe in the superiority of his own inner world; a sort of unreasonable confidence even enabled him to believe that there was not one emotion in this world he had yet to feel. For the boy thought that to a spirit as keenly sensitive as his own, the archetypes of all emotion were already apprehended, though sometimes only as premonitions, and rehearsed, and that all experience could be constructed with the appropriate combinations of these basic elements of emotion. And what were the elements of emotion? He had his own arbitrary definition: "Words."

Not that the boy had attained a usage of words that was genuinely his own. But he thought that the very universality of many of those words he found in the dictionary made them varied in meaning and diverse in content, and therefore available for use in a personal, unique way by an individual. It didn't necessarily occur to him that only experience could bring words to creative fruition and lend them color.

The first encounter between our inner world and language brings   36 something entirely individual into contact with something universal. It is also the occasion when the individual, refined by the universal, comes into its own for the first time. The fifteen-year-old boy was more than adequately familiar with this indescribable inner experience. For the disharmony he felt when he encountered a new word also led him to experience an emotion previously unknown to him. And it also helped him maintain an outward calmness incompatible with his youth. When assaulted by a certain emotion, the disharmony elicited in him would lead him to recall elements of the disharmony he had felt before a word. He would remember the word, and use it to fit a name to the emotion before him. The boy became practiced at taking care of emotion in this way. Thus he came to know all things: "humiliation," "agony," "despair," "execration," "the joy of love," "the sorrow of love's loss."

It would have been easy to call this imagination. But the boy hesitated to do so. Imagination requires the kind of empathy in which the self feels pain in imagining the pain of others. The boy in his coldness never felt the pain of others. Without feeling the slightest pain he would whisper to himself: "That's pain. That's something I know."

It was a sunny afternoon in May. Classes were out. The boy was walking toward the Literature Club room to see if there was someone he might have a talk with before going home. On the way he ran into R, who said: "I was hoping I'd find you. Let's talk."

They entered the barracklike structure where old classrooms had been divided up with plywood walls to house various clubs. The Literature Club was in a corner of the dark first floor. From the Sports Club they could hear noises and laughing voices and the school song, from the Music Club the distant echo of a piano. R slipped his key into the keyhole in the dirty wooden door. It was a door that, unlocked, still wouldn't open until he threw his body against it.

The room was empty. Inside was the familiar smell of dust. R went   40 in and opened the window, slapped his dust-covered hands together, and sat down on a broken chair.

As soon as they had settled down the boy began to talk. "I saw a dream in color last night. I was going to write you about it as soon as I got home." (The boy fancied dreams in color to be the special prerogative of the poet.) "There's a hill of red earth. The red earth is very bright, and the sunset is shining a brilliant red, so the color of the earth is even more striking. And then from the right comes a man dragging a long chain. A peacock four or five times bigger than the man is tied to the end of the chain, and the peacock's feathers are all folded in as he's slowly dragged along, there in front of my eyes. The peacock is bright green. His whole body is green, and the green is glittering beautifully. I kept my eyes on that peacock as it was dragged into the distance, until it was dragged out of sight . . . It was a fantastic dream. My dreams are so vivid when they're in color, almost too vivid. I wonder what a green peacock would mean to Freud."

"I wonder."

R sounded only half-interested. He was not his usual self. His paleness was the same, but he lacked the familiar quiet fever in his voice, the passionate response. Apparently he had been listening to the boy's monologue with indifference. No, he hadn't been listening at all.

The foppishly high collar of R's student uniform was sprinkled lightly   44
with dandruff. The dark light made his golden Cherry Blossom badge glow, and magnified his somewhat prominent nose. His nose was handsomely shaped if a bit too large; now it wore an unmistakable expression of anxiety. R's distress seemed to have become manifest in his nose.

On the desk were scattered old dust-covered proof sheets, rulers, red pencils lacking lead, bound volumes of the alumni magazine, manuscript paper on which someone had begun to write. The boy loved this literary confusion. R shuffled the ancient proof sheets as if forlornly putting things in their place, and got his slender white fingers dusty. The boy grinned. But R clicked his tongue in annoyance, slapped the dust from his hands, and said:

"The truth is, there was something I wanted to talk to you about today."

"What is it?"

"The truth is," R faltered, then spat the words out. "I'm suffering.   48
Something unbearable has happened."

"Are you in love?" the boy inquired coolly.

"Yes."

R explained the circumstances. He was in love with someone else's young wife, had been discovered by his father, and forced to stop seeing her.

The boy's eyes opened wide, and he stared at R. "Here's someone in   52
love. For the first time I'm seeing love right in front of my eyes." It was

not a very beautiful sight. In fact, it was rather unpleasant. R's usual vitality was gone; he was crestfallen. He looked morose. The boy had often seen this kind of expression on the faces of people who had lost something or missed a train.

Still, being taken into confidence by a senior did tickle the boy's vanity. He was not unhappy. He made a valiant effort to assume a look of melancholy. But the banality of the appearance of a person in love was a little hard to bear.

Finally he found some words of consolation.

"That's terrible. But I'm sure a good poem will come out of it all."

Limply, R replied: "This is no time for poetry." 56

"But isn't poetry salvation at a time like this?"

The happiness lent by a poem's creation flashed through the boy's mind. He thought any sorrow or agony could be struck away with the power of that happiness.

"It doesn't work like that. You don't understand yet."

The utterance wounded the boy's self-esteem. His heart chilled, and 60 he plotted a revenge.

"But if you were a real poet, a genius, wouldn't poetry save you at such a time?"

"Goethe wrote *Werther*," R answered, "and saved himself from suicide. But he was able to write it only because, deep in his heart, Goethe knew that nothing, not poetry or anything else, could save him, and that the only thing left was suicide."

"Then why didn't Goethe commit suicide? If writing and suicide are the same thing, then why didn't he choose suicide? Because he was a coward? Or because he was a genius?"

"Because he was a genius." 64

"Then . . ."

The boy was going to press one more question, but he didn't understand it himself. The idea rose vaguely in his mind that what had saved Goethe from suicide was his egotism. He was seized with the desire to use this notion to defend himself.

R's utterance "You don't understand yet" had wounded him deeply. At his age, nothing was stronger than feelings of inferiority about age. Although he didn't come out and speak it, a logic most aptly derisive of R was born in the boy's mind: "He's no genius. Why, he falls in love."

R's love was certainly a true one. It was the kind of love a genius must 68 never have. R took the love of Fujitsubo and Genji, the love of Pelléas and Mélisande, the love of Tristan and Isolde, the love of the Princess de Clèves and the Duc de Nemours as illustrations of illicit love to ornament his distress.

As the boy listened, he was shocked that there wasn't one element in R's confession he didn't already know. All had been written, all had been anticipated, all had been rehearsed. The love written in books was more vital than this. The love sung in poems was more beautiful. He couldn't comprehend why R would go to reality for dreams more sublime. He didn't understand where this craving for the mediocre came from.

R seemed to have been soothed by his own words, and he now began an endless recounting of his girl's beauty. She must have been an extraordinary beauty, but the boy couldn't see a single image of her. "Next time I'll show you a picture," R said. Then, a little embarrassed, he wound up dramatically:

"She told me I have a really handsome forehead."

The boy looked at the forehead below R's combed-back hair. The skin   72
on his prominent brow glimmered faintly in the dim light coming through the doorway; it looked as if two fistlike bumps were jutting out on his forehead.

What a beetle brow, the boy thought. He didn't have the slightest feeling it was handsome. Mine bulges too, he told himself. Having a beetle brow and being handsome are not the same thing.

It was then that the boy awoke to something. He had seen the ridiculous impurity that always works its way into an awareness of love or life, that ridiculous impurity without which we cannot survive in either: namely, the conviction that your beetle brow is handsome.

The boy felt that he too, if in a more intellectual way, might have been making his way through life on a similar kind of conviction. Something in the thought made him shudder. "What are you thinking about?" R asked in his usual gentle tone.

The boy bit his lip and smiled. It was slowly getting dark outside. He   76
could hear shouts from where the Baseball Club was practicing. As a ball struck by a bat shot into the sky, there was a dry, lucid echo.

Someday maybe I'll stop writing poetry too, the boy thought for the first time in his life. But he was yet to learn that he had never been a poet.

EXPLORATIONS

1. "Poets must die young," thinks Mishima's central character. What reasons are given in the story — directly or indirectly, reasonable or not — for this assumption?

2. None of the characters in "The Boy Who Wrote Poetry" have names. What are the effects of this choice by Mishima? What comments in the story suggest a positive attitude on the author's part toward his central character? What comments suggest a negative attitude? Which attitude do you think comes through more strongly, and why?

3. The title of Mishima's story is "The Boy Who Wrote Poetry." His closing sentence is "But he was yet to learn that he had never been a poet." What does Mishima mean by this apparent contradiction? How do you think Mishima would define a poet? What kind of further revelation would the boy have to go through to become one?

CONNECTIONS

1. Mishima, like Nathalie Sarraute, writes about a young writer discovering the pleasure and power of words. In what ways are eleven-year-old Nathalie and Mishima's fifteen-year-old central character alike? What are the key differences between them as writers?

2. How does the childhood of Mishima's narrator resemble that described by Jack Agueros in his *Observation*? In the awakening each writer recounts, how are the central characters' situations and their reactions similar and different?

ELABORATIONS

1. Mishima explores several intriguing ideas in "The Boy Who Wrote Poetry": How can poetry (or art in general) help its creator through crises, and what are its limits? What difficulties and dangers are created by the fact that emotional upheavals often seem trite to those who are not experiencing them? What are the relationships between beauty, genius, and suicide? Choose one of these ideas, and write an essay presenting your position on it.

2. Mishima depicts the boy and his friend R as opposites, representing alternative attitudes toward the problem of being a poet and a human being simultaneously. Yet both characters are creations of the same man, whose solution

to this dilemma was suicide. Nathalie Sarraute also uses two voices to examine the writer's dilemma, but her conclusions are quite different. Looking back at "My First Sorrow," consider how you think Sarraute would respond to Mishima's story. Write an imaginary dialogue between Mishima and Sarraute in which the two argue about the role of writing in a writer's life.

SOPHRONIA LIU

So Tsi-fai

Born in Hong Kong in 1953, Sophronia Liu came to the United States to study at the age of twenty. Some of her family are still in Hong Kong; others now live here, in Canada, and in England. Liu received a bachelor's degree in English and French, and a master's degree in English, from the University of South Dakota. Currently a teaching assistant in composition at the University of Minnesota, she is working toward her Ph.D. in English and advanced feminist studies. Liu intends to return to Hong Kong eventually to pursue her writing, which thus far has been mainly autobiographical. "So Tsi-fai" was written in response to a class assignment and originally appeared in the Minnesota feminist publication *Hurricane Alice.*

Hong Kong, where Liu attended The Little Flower's School with So Tsi-fai, is a British Crown Colony at the mouth of China's Canton River. Its nucleus is Hong Kong Island, which Britain acquired from China in 1841. Most of the colony's 409 square miles consist of other Chinese territory held by Britain on a ninety-nine year lease. Hong Kong's population of over five million includes fewer than 20,000 British; it absorbed more than a million Chinese refugees after Mao's Communists won the mainland in 1949. In 1985 China and Britain agreed that Hong Kong will revert to China in 1997, when the lease expires, but will be allowed to keep its capitalist system for fifty years after that.

Voices, images, scenes from the past — twenty-three years ago, when I was in sixth grade:

"Let us bow our heads in silent prayer for the soul of So Tsi-fai. Let us pray for God's forgiveness for this boy's rash taking of his own life . . ." Sister Marie (Mung Gu-liang). My sixth-grade English teacher. Missionary nun from Paris. Principal of The Little Flower's School. Disciplinarian, perfectionist, authority figure: awesome and awful in my ten-year-old eyes.

"I don't need any supper. I have drunk enough insecticide." So Tsi-fai. My fourteen-year-old classmate. Daredevil; good-for-nothing lazy-bones (according to Mung Gu-liang). Bright black eyes, disheveled hair, defiant sneer, creased and greasy uniform, dirty hands, careless walk, shuffling feet. Standing in the corner for being late, for forgetting his homework, for talking in class, for using foul language. ("Shame on you! Go wash your mouth with soap!" Mung Gu-liang's sharp command. He did, and came back with a grin.) So Tsi-fai: Sticking his tongue out behind Mung Gu-liang's back, passing secret notes to his friends, kept behind after school, sent to the Principal's office for repeated offense. So Tsi-fai: incorrigible, hopeless, and without hope.

It was a Monday in late November when we heard of his death,   4
returning to school after the weekend with our parents' signatures on our midterm reports. So Tsi-fai also showed his report to his father, we were told later. He flunked three out of the fourteen subjects: English Grammar, Arithmetic, and Chinese Dictation. He missed each one by one to three marks. That wasn't so bad. But he was a hopeless case. Overaged, stubborn, and uncooperative; a repeated offender of school rules, scourge of all teachers; who was going to give him a lenient passing grade? Besides, being a few months over the maximum age — fourteen — for sixth graders, he wasn't even allowed to sit for the Secondary School Entrance Exam.

All sixth graders in Hong Kong had to pass the SSE before they could obtain a seat in secondary school. In 1964 when I took the exam, there were more than twenty thousand candidates. About seven thousand of us passed: four thousand were sent to government and subsidized schools, the other three thousand to private and grant-in-aid schools. I came in around no. 2000; I was lucky. Without the public exam, there would be no secondary school for So Tsi-fai. His future was sealed.

Looking at the report card with three red marks on it, his father was furious. So Tsi-fai was the oldest son. There were three younger children. His father was a vegetable farmer with a few plots of land in Wong Juk-hang, by the sea. His mother worked in a local factory. So Tsi-fai helped in the fields, cooked for the family, and washed his own clothes. ("Filthy, dirty boy!" gasped Mung Gu-liang. "Grime behind the ears, black rims on the fingernails, dirty collar, crumpled shirt. Why doesn't your mother iron your shirt?") Both his parents were illiterate. So Tsi-fai was their biggest hope: He made it to the sixth grade.

Who woke him up for school every morning and had breakfast waiting for him? Nobody. ("Time for school! Get up! Eat your rice!" Ma nagged and screamed. The aroma of steamed rice and Chinese sausages spread all over the house. "Drink your tea! Eat your oranges! Wash your face! And remember to wash behind your ears!") And who helped So Tsi-fai do his homework? Nobody. Did he have older brothers like mine who knew all about the arithmetic of rowing a boat against the currents or with the currents, how to count the feet of chickens and rabbits in the same cage, the present perfect continuous tense of "to live" and the future perfect tense of "to succeed"? None. Nil. So Tsi-fai was a lost cause.

I came first in both terms that year, the star pupil. So Tsi-fai was one 8 of the last in the class: He was lazy; he didn't care. Or did he?

When his father scolded him, So Tsi-fai left the house. When he showed up again, late for supper, he announced, "I don't need any supper. I have drunk enough insecticide." Just like another one of his practical jokes. The insecticide was stored in the field for his father's vegetables. He was rushed to the hospital; dead upon arrival.

"He gulped for a last breath and was gone," an uncle told us at the funeral. "But his eyes wouldn't shut. So I said in his ear, 'You go now and rest in peace.' And I smoothed my hand over his eyelids. His face was all purple."

His face was still purple when we saw him in his coffin. Eyes shut tight, nostrils dilated and white as if fire and anger might shoot out, any minute.

In class that Monday morning, Sister Marie led us in prayer. "Let us 12 pray that God will forgive him for his sins." We said the Lord's Prayer and the Hail Mary. We bowed our heads. I sat in my chair, frozen and dazed, thinking of the deadly chill in the morgue, the smell of disinfectant, ether, and dead flesh.

"Bang!" went a gust of wind, forcing open a leaf of the double door leading to the back balcony. "Flap, flap, flap." The door swung in the wind. We could see the treetops by the hillside rustling to and fro against a pale blue sky. An imperceptible presence had drifted in with the wind. The same careless walk and shuffling feet, the same daredevil air — except that the eyes were lusterless, dripping blood; the tongue hanging out, gasping for air. As usual, he was late. But he had come back to claim his place.

"I died a tragic death," his voice said. "I have as much right as you to be here. This is my seat." We heard him; we knew he was back.

. . . So Tsi-fai: Standing in the corner for being late, for forgetting his homework, for talking in class, for using foul language. So Tsi-fai: Palm outstretched, chest sticking out, holding his breath: "Tat. Tat. Tat." Down came the teacher's wooden ruler, twenty times on each hand. Never batting an eyelash: then back to facing the wall in the corner by the door. So Tsi-fai: grimy shirt, disheveled hair, defiant sneer. So Tsi-fai. Incorrigible, hopeless, and without hope.

The girls in front gasped and shrank back in their chairs. Mung Gu-   16
liang went to the door, held the doorknob in one hand, poked her head
out, and peered into the empty balcony. Then, with a determined jerk,
she pulled the door shut. Quickly crossing herself, she returned to the
teacher's desk. Her black cross swung upon the front of her gray habit as
she hurried across the room. "Don't be silly!" she scolded the frightened
girls in the front row.

What really happened? After all these years, my mind is still haunted
by this scene. What happened to So Tsi-fai? What happened to me?
What happened to all of us that year in sixth grade, when we were green
and young and ready to fling our arms out for the world? All of a sudden,
death claimed one of us and he was gone.

Who arbitrates between life and death? Who decides which life is
worth preserving and prospering, and which to nip in its bud? How did
it happen that I, at ten, turned out to be the star pupil, the lucky one,
while my friend, a peasant's son, was shoveled under the heap and lost
forever? How could it happen that this world would close off a young
boy's life at fourteen just because he was poor, undisciplined, and lacked
the training and support to pass his exams? What really happened?

Today, twenty-three years later, So Tsi-fai's ghost still haunts me. "I
died a tragic death. I have as much right as you to be here. This is my
seat." The voice I heard twenty-three years ago in my sixth-grade classroom follows me in my dreams. Is there anything I can do to lay it to
rest?

EXPLORATIONS

1. How do you think Liu regarded So Tsi-fai before his death? How did her
   view change after his suicide? How can you tell? What other attitudes did
   Liu evidently reexamine and alter at that point?

2. Whom and what does Liu blame for So Tsi-fai's suicide? What preventive
   measures does her story suggest to protect other students from a similar fate?
   Judging from Liu's narrative, what changes in Hong Kong's social and educational institutions do you think would help students like So Tsi-fai?

3. Liu's first three paragraphs consist almost entirely of incomplete sentences.
   How does she use these sentence fragments to establish her essay's central
   conflict? At what points does she use complete sentences? What is their effect?

CONNECTIONS

1. "So Tsi-fai," like Mishima Yukio's "The Boy Who Wrote Poetry," has two main characters who represent opposite poles. In each story, which character represents innocence and idealism, and which one represents experience and disillusion? What does each author view as the advantages of experience? of innocence?

2. Look back at Wole Soyinka's "Nigerian Childhood" (p. 66). Both Soyinka and Liu describe encounters with ghosts. What role does each ghost play in the narrative? How are their dramatic functions different? What cultural similarities do they suggest between Nigeria and Hong Kong?

3. "Education collapsed," writes Jack Agueros in his *Observation*. How were Agueros's prospects at that point similar to So Tsi-fai's? How did each boy respond to his situation? What factors do you think steered them in different directions?

ELABORATIONS

1. What is the role of Mung Gu-liang/Sister Marie in "So Tsi-fai"? Do you think the nun would agree with Liu's assessment of what happened? How might her memory and interpretation of these events differ from Liu's? Write a version of So Tsi-fai's story from Mung Gu-liang's point of view.

2. When you were in elementary school, who were the outcasts in your class, and why? If you recall one student in particular who was regarded as "different," write an essay describing him or her and narrating some of the incidents that set him or her apart. If your class consisted of two or more distinct groups, write an essay classifying these groups according to their special characteristics and their behavior toward each other. In either case, how has your attitude toward the "outcasts" changed?

LILIANA HEKER

The Stolen Party

Argentine writer Liliana Heker published her highly regarded first volume of short stories, *Those Who Beheld the Burning Bush,* while still in her teens. As editor in chief of the literary magazine *El Ornitorrinco* (*The Platypus*), Heker kept open a national forum for writers throughout the years of Argentina's chaotic and bloody military dictatorships. In its pages she debated with Julio Cortázar (see p. 436) about the proper role of a writer in a strife-torn, oppressed society: Cortázar, living in Paris, defended his role as a writer in exile, while Heker took a position similar to Nadine Gordimer's in South Africa (see p. 465): "To be heard, we must shout from within."

Four times the size of Texas, Argentina occupies most of South America's southern tip. When the first Spanish settlers appeared in the early 1500s, nomadic Indians roamed the pampas. By the late 1800s nearly all of them had been killed, making room for the influx of Europeans who today comprise 97 percent of the population. Argentina had won independence from Spain in 1819; by the century's end it was the most prosperous, educated, and industrialized Latin American nation. Military dictatorships and coups have dominated this century, however. Aside from General Juan Perón, elected president from 1946 to 1955 and again in 1973, most regimes have been nasty, brutish, and short-lived. Argentina's failed attempt to take the Islas Malvinas (Falkland Islands) from Great Britain in 1982 led to the first general election since Perón's, which put President Raúl Alfonsín at the head of a country with a democratic government and a beleaguered economy.

"The Stolen Party," first published in 1982, was translated from the Spanish by Alberto Manguel for his anthology *Other Fires* (1985).

As soon as she arrived she went straight to the kitchen to see if the monkey was there. It was: what a relief! She wouldn't have liked to admit that her mother had been right. *Monkeys at a birthday?* her mother had sneered. *Get away with you, believing any nonsense you're told!* She was cross, but not because of the monkey, the girl thought; it's just because of the party.

"I don't like you going," she told her. "It's a rich people's party."

"Rich people go to Heaven too," said the girl, who studied religion at school.

"Get away with Heaven," said the mother. "The problem with you,   4
young lady, is that you like to fart higher than your ass."

The girl didn't approve of the way her mother spoke. She was barely nine, and one of the best in her class.

"I'm going because I've been invited," she said. "And I've been invited because Luciana is my friend. So there."

"Ah yes, your friend," her mother grumbled. She paused. "Listen, Rosaura," she said at last. "That one's not your friend. You know what you are to them? The maid's daughter, that's what."

Rosaura blinked hard: she wasn't going to cry. Then she yelled: "Shut   8
up! You know nothing about being friends!"

Every afternoon she used to go to Luciana's house and they would both finish their homework while Rosaura's mother did the cleaning. They had their tea in the kitchen and they told each other secrets. Rosaura loved everything in the big house, and she also loved the people who lived there.

"I'm going because it will be the most lovely party in the whole world, Luciana told me it would. There will be a magician, and he will bring a monkey and everything."

The mother swung around to take a good look at her child, and pompously put her hands on her hips.

"Monkeys at a birthday?" she said. "Get away with you, believing any   12
nonsense you're told!"

Rosaura was deeply offended. She thought it unfair of her mother to accuse other people of being liars simply because they were rich. Rosaura too wanted to be rich, of course. If one day she managed to live in a beautiful palace, would her mother stop loving her? She felt very sad. She wanted to go to that party more than anything else in the world.

"I'll die if I don't go," she whispered, almost without moving her lips.

And she wasn't sure whether she had been heard, but on the morning of the party she discovered that her mother had starched her Christmas dress. And in the afternoon, after washing her hair, her mother rinsed it in apple vinegar so that it would be all nice and shiny. Before going out, Rosaura admired herself in the mirror, with her white dress and glossy hair, and thought she looked terribly pretty.

Señora Ines also seemed to notice. As soon as she saw her, she said: 16
"How lovely you look today, Rosaura."

Rosaura gave her starched skirt a slight toss with her hands and walked into the party with a firm step. She said hello to Luciana and asked about the monkey. Luciana put on a secretive look and whispered into Rosaura's ear: "He's in the kitchen. But don't tell anyone, because it's a surprise."

Rosaura wanted to make sure. Carefully she entered the kitchen and there she saw it: deep in thought, inside its cage. It looked so funny that the girl stood there for a while, watching it, and later, every so often, she would slip out of the party unseen and go and admire it. Rosaura was the only one allowed into the kitchen. Señora Ines had said: "You yes, but not the others, they're much too boisterous, they might break something." Rosaura had never broken anything. She even managed the jug of orange juice, carrying it from the kitchen into the dining room. She held it carefully and didn't spill a single drop. And Señora Ines had said: "Are you sure you can manage a jug as big as that?" Of course she could manage. She wasn't a butterfingers, like the others. Like that blonde girl with the bow in her hair. As soon as she saw Rosaura, the girl with the bow had said:

"And you? Who are you?"   20

"I'm a friend of Luciana," said Rosaura.

"No," said the girl with the bow, "you are not a friend of Luciana because I'm her cousin and I know all her friends. And I don't know you."

"So what," said Rosaura. "I come here every afternoon with my mother and we do our homework together."

"You and your mother do your homework together?" asked the girl,   24 laughing.

"I and Luciana do our homework together," said Rosaura, very seriously.

The girl with the bow shrugged her shoulders.

"That's not being friends," she said. "Do you go to school together?"

"No."   28

"So where do you know her from?" said the girl, getting impatient.

Rosaura remembered her mother's words perfectly. She took a deep breath.

"I'm the daughter of the employee," she said.

Her mother had said very clearly: "If someone asks, you say you're the   32 daughter of the employee; that's all." She also told her to add: "And proud of it." But Rosaura thought that never in her life would she dare say something of the sort.

"What employee?" said the girl with the bow. "Employee in a shop?"

"No," said Rosaura angrily. "My mother doesn't sell anything in any shop, so there."

"So how come she's an employee?" said the girl with the bow.

Just then Señora Ines arrived saying *shh shh,* and asked Rosaura if she wouldn't mind helping serve out the hotdogs, as she knew the house so much better than the others. 36

"See?" said Rosaura to the girl with the bow, and when no one was looking she kicked her in the shin.

Apart from the girl with the bow, all the others were delightful. The one she liked best was Luciana, with her golden birthday crown; and then the boys. Rosaura won the sack race, and nobody managed to catch her when they played tag. When they split into two teams to play charades, all the boys wanted her for their side. Rosaura felt she had never been so happy in all her life.

But the best was still to come. The best came after Luciana blew out the candles. First the cake. Señora Ines had asked her to help pass the cake around, and Rosaura had enjoyed the task immensely, because everyone called out to her, shouting "Me, me!" Rosaura remembered a story in which there was a queen who had the power of life or death over her subjects. She had always loved that, having the power of life or death. To Luciana and the boys she gave the largest pieces, and to the girl with the bow she gave a slice so thin one could see through it.

After the cake came the magician, tall and bony, with a fine red cape. 40 A true magician: he could untie handkerchiefs by blowing on them and make a chain with links that had no openings. He could guess what cards were pulled out from a pack, and the monkey was his assistant. He called the monkey "partner." "Let's see here, partner," he would say, "turn over a card." And, "Don't run away, partner: time to work now."

The final trick was wonderful. One of the children had to hold the monkey in his arms and the magician said he would make him disappear.

"What, the boy?" they all shouted.

"No, the monkey!" shouted back the magician.

Rosaura thought that this was truly the most amusing party in the whole world. 44

The magician asked a small fat boy to come and help, but the small fat boy got frightened almost at once and dropped the monkey on the floor. The magician picked him up carefully, whispered something in his ear, and the monkey nodded almost as if he understood.

"You mustn't be so unmanly, my friend," the magician said to the fat boy.

"What's unmanly?" said the fat boy.

The magician turned around as if to look for spies.   48

"A sissy," said the magician. "Go sit down."

Then he stared at all the faces, one by one. Rosaura felt her heart tremble.

"You, with the Spanish eyes," said the magician. And everyone saw that he was pointing at her.

She wasn't afraid. Neither holding the monkey, nor when the magician   52
made him vanish; not even when, at the end, the magician flung his red cape over Rosaura's head and uttered a few magic words . . . and the monkey reappeared, chattering happily, in her arms. The children clapped furiously. And before Rosaura returned to her seat, the magician said:

"Thank you very much, my little countess."

She was so pleased with the compliment that a while later, when her mother came to fetch her, that was the first thing she told her.

"I helped the magician and he said to me, 'Thank you very much, my little countess.'"

It was strange because up to then Rosaura had thought that she was   56
angry with her mother. All along Rosaura had imagined that she would say to her: "See that the monkey wasn't a lie?" But instead she was so thrilled that she told her mother all about the wonderful magician.

Her mother tapped her on the head and said: "So now we're a countess!"

But one could see that she was beaming.

And now they both stood in the entrance, because a moment ago Señora Ines, smiling, had said: "Please wait here a second."

Her mother suddenly seemed worried.   60

"What is it?" she asked Rosaura.

"What is what?" said Rosaura. "It's nothing; she just wants to get the presents for those who are leaving, see?"

She pointed at the fat boy and at a girl with pigtails who were also waiting there, next to their mothers. And she explained about the presents. She knew, because she had been watching those who left before her. When one of the girls was about to leave, Señora Ines would give her a bracelet. When a boy left, Señora Ines gave him a yo-yo. Rosaura preferred the yo-yo because it sparkled, but she didn't mention that to her mother. Her mother might have said: "So why don't you ask for one, you blockhead?" That's what her mother was like. Rosaura didn't feel like explaining that she'd be horribly ashamed to be the odd one out. Instead she said:

"I was the best-behaved at the party."   64

And she said no more because Señora Ines came out into the hall with two bags, one pink and one blue.

First she went up to the fat boy, gave him a yo-yo out of the blue bag, and the fat boy left with his mother. Then she went up to the girl and gave her a bracelet out of the pink bag, and the girl with the pigtails left as well.

Finally she came up to Rosaura and her mother. She had a big smile on her face and Rosaura liked that. Señora Ines looked down at her, then looked up at her mother, and then said something that made Rosaura proud:

"What a marvelous daughter you have, Herminia."   68

For an instant, Rosaura thought that she'd give her two presents: the bracelet and the yo-yo. Señora Ines bent down as if about to look for something. Rosaura also leaned forward, stretching out her arm. But she never completed the movement.

Señora Ines didn't look in the pink bag. Nor did she look in the blue bag. Instead she rummaged in her purse. In her hand appeared two bills.

"You really and truly earned this," she said handing them over. "Thank you for all your help, my pet."

Rosaura felt her arms stiffen, stick close to her body, and then she   72
noticed her mother's hand on her shoulder. Instinctively she pressed herself against her mother's body. That was all. Except her eyes. Rosaura's eyes had a cold, clear look that fixed itself on Señora Ines's face.

Señora Ines, motionless, stood there with her hand outstretched. As if she didn't dare draw it back. As if the slightest change might shatter an infinitely delicate balance.

EXPLORATIONS

1. What central conflict does Heker establish in her opening paragraph? What conflict does she introduce in her second paragraph? How would the story's balance change if Heker started with the second paragraph, leaving the monkey question until its chronological place?

2. At the end of "The Stolen Party," what is the intended message of Señora Ines's gift to Rosaura? What message does Rosaura draw from the gift? What

changes occur in the characters' perceptions of each other, and of themselves, in the story's last two paragraphs?

3. Rosaura has a number of standards for judging people — more specifically, for measuring herself against others. For example, in paragraph 5: "The girl didn't approve of the way her mother spoke. She was barely nine, and one of the best in her class." Find at least four other points in the story when Rosaura makes a comparative judgment. How well does she fare in her own estimation? What do you learn about Rosaura as a character from these judgments?

CONNECTIONS

1. Both "The Stolen Party" and Sophronia Liu's "So Tsi-fai" focus on young people who represent, to themselves or their families or both, ambitions higher than their present circumstances. What disadvantages do Rosaura and So Tsi-fai share? Why does Rosaura appear likely to succeed where So Tsi-fai fails?

2. "The Stolen Party," like Nathalie Sarraute's "My First Sorrow," is the story of a bright, imaginative child whose fantasies place her in a luxurious home filled with amusements. What phrases in each narrative reveal the fragility of this dream world? What rituals does each character use to protect her dream? What do these rituals tell us about Nathalie's and Rosaura's attitudes toward their real situations?

3. Look back at Jack Agueros's *Observation*. Who represents "Dick and Jane" to Rosaura in Heker's story? How are Rosaura's circumstances different from Agueros's? Which child do you think has better prospects, and why?

ELABORATIONS

1. The characters in "The Stolen Party" — particularly the two mother-daughter pairs — all have different concepts of the extent to which they control their own destinies. Write an essay classifying these concepts: Describe each mother's and daughter's sense of herself as a social actor; identify the factors she views as conferring or limiting her power, such as age, intelligence, and social class; and cite the evidence in the story that supports your conclusions.

2. In "The Stolen Party," Mishima Yukio's "The Boy Who Wrote Poetry," and Nathalie Sarraute's "My First Sorrow," the central character's innocence is an important factor. In what ways does each character's youthful ignorance of the adult world work for or against her or him? Write an essay comparing Sarraute's, Mishima's, and Heker's views of the pros and cons of innocence.

VLADIMIR NABOKOV

From *Speak, Memory*

Vladimir Nabokov was born into an aristocratic Russian family in St. Petersburg in 1899. His father, a leader of a liberal democratic party in czarist Russia, took the family to Berlin in 1922 after the Revolution; there he was assassinated while shielding another man. Young Vladimir studied in England, where he began writing in English, and lived for the next eighteen years in Germany and France. From poetry he expanded to drama and screenplays, settling on fiction as his preferred form. His first short story was published in Berlin in 1924, his first novel in 1926 (*Mashenka;* in English *Mary,* 1970). He and his wife and son lived in happy poverty while Nabokov hunted butterflies, produced scientific papers on insects, and created increasingly intricate and unorthodox novels in both Russian and English. In 1945 he became an American citizen; ten years later he published his first best-seller, *Lolita*. Controversial, idiosyncratic, and brilliant, Nabokov died in Montreux, Switzerland, in 1977. This essay comes from his autobiography *Speak, Memory* (1967).

Nabokov's birthplace of St. Petersburg, Russia, became Leningrad in the Union of Soviet Socialist Republics after the 1917 Revolution. Vladimir Ilyich Lenin substituted Communism for both the church that produced St. Peter and the dynasty that produced Czar Peter the Great. Peter's ancestor Ivan the Terrible had proclaimed himself the first czar (a title derived from the Roman *Caesar*) in 1547. Western ideas and modernization spread across Russia during the nineteenth and twentieth centuries, but the political system remained feudal. The czars' downfall was triggered by losses in Russia's 1904 war with Japan, and climaxed when workers' strikes in 1917 escalated into revolution. "When, at the end of the year, Lenin took over, the Bolsheviks immediately subordinated everything to the retention of power," writes Nabokov in *Speak, Memory,* "and a regime of bloodshed, concentration camps, and hostages entered upon its stupendous career."

(For more background on the Soviet Union, see pp. 48, 213, and 649.)

The reactionary press never ceased to attack my father's party, and I had got quite used to the more or less vulgar cartoons which appeared from time to time — my father and Milyukov handing over Saint Russia on a plate to World Jewry and that sort of thing. But one day, in the winter of 1911 I believe, the most powerful of the Rightist newspapers employed a shady journalist to concoct a scurrilous piece containing insinuations that my father could not let pass. Since the well-known rascality of the actual author of the article made him "non-duelable" (*neduelesposobnïy,* as the Russian dueling code had it), my father called out the somewhat less disreputable editor of the paper in which the article had appeared.

A Russian duel was a much more serious affair than the conventional Parisian variety. It took the editor several days to make up his mind whether or not to accept the challenge. On the last of these days, a Monday, I went, as usual, to school. In consequence of my not reading the newspapers, I was absolutely ignorant of the whole thing. Sometime during the day I became aware that a magazine opened at a certain page was passing from hand to hand and causing titters. A well-timed swoop put me in possession of what proved to be the latest copy of a cheap weekly containing a lurid account of my father's challenge, with idiotic comments on the choice of weapons he had offered his foe. Sly digs were taken at his having reverted to a feudal custom that he had criticized in his own writings. There was also a good deal about the number of his servants and the number of his suits. I found out that he had chosen for second his brother-in-law, Admiral Kolomeytsev, a hero of the Japanese war. During the battle of Tsushima, this uncle of mine, then holding the rank of captain, had managed to bring his destroyer alongside the burning flagship and save the naval commander-in-chief.

After classes, I ascertained that the magazine belonged to one of my best friends. I charged him with betrayal and mockery. In the ensuing fight, he crashed backward into a desk, catching his foot in a joint and breaking his ankle. He was laid up for a month, but gallantly concealed from his family and from our teachers my share in the matter.

The pang of seeing him carried downstairs was lost in my general 4 misery. For some reason or other, no car came to fetch me that day, and during the cold, dreary, incredibly slow drive home in a hired sleigh I had ample time to think matters over. Now I understood why, the day before, my mother had been so little with me and had not come down to dinner. I also understood what special coaching Thernant, a still finer *maître d'armes* than Loustalot, had of late been giving my father. What would his adversary choose, I kept asking myself — the blade or the bullet? Or had the choice already been made? Carefully, I took the beloved, the familiar, the richly alive image of my father at fencing and tried to transfer the image, minus the mask and the padding, to the dueling ground, in some barn or riding school. I visualized him and his adversary, both bare-chested, black-trousered, in furious battle, their energetic movements marked by that strange awkwardness which even the most elegant swordsmen cannot avoid in a real encounter. The picture was so repulsive, so vividly did I feel the ripeness and nakedness of a madly pulsating heart about to be pierced, that I found myself hoping for what seemed momentarily a more abstract weapon. But soon I was in even deeper distress.

As the sleigh crept along Nevski Avenue, where blurry lights swam in the gathering dusk, I thought of the heavy black Browning my father kept in the upper right-hand drawer of his desk. I knew that pistol as well as I knew all the other, more salient, things in his study; the *objets d'art* of crystal or veined stone, fashionable in those days; the glinting family photographs; the huge, mellowly illumined Perugino; the small, honey-bright Dutch oils; and, right over the desk, the rose-and-haze pastel portrait of my mother by Bakst: the artist had drawn her face in three-quarter view, wonderfully bringing out its delicate features — the upward sweep of the ash-colored hair (it had grayed when she was in her twenties), the pure curve of the forehead, the dove-blue eyes, the graceful line of the neck.

When I urged the old, rag-doll-like driver to go faster, he would merely lean to one side with a special half-circular movement of his arm, so as to make his horse believe he was about to produce the short whip he kept in the leg of his right felt boot; and that would be sufficient for the shaggy little hack to make as vague a show of speeding up as the driver had made of getting out his *knutishko*. In the almost hallucinatory state that our snow-muffled ride engendered, I refought all the famous duels a Russian boy knew so well. I saw Pushkin, mortally wounded at the first fire, grimly sit up to discharge his pistol at d'Anthès. I saw Lermontov smile as he faced Martïnov. I saw stout Sobinov in the part of Lenski crash down and send his weapon flying into the orchestra. No Russian writer of any repute had failed to describe *une rencontre*, a hostile meeting, always of course of the classical *duel à volonté* type (not the ludicrous back-to-back-march-face-about-bang-bang performance of movie and cartoon fame). Among several prominent families, there had been tragic deaths on the dueling ground in more or less recent years. Slowly my dreamy sleigh drove up Morskaya Street, and slowly dim silhouettes of duelists advanced upon each other and leveled their pistols and fired — at the crack of dawn, in damp glades of old country estates, on bleak military training grounds, or in the driving snow between two rows of fir trees.

And behind it all there was yet a very special emotional abyss that I was desperately trying to skirt, lest I burst into a tempest of tears, and this was the tender friendship underlying my respect for my father; the charm of our perfect accord; the Wimbledon matches we followed in the London papers; the chess problems we solved; the Pushkin iambics that rolled off his tongue so triumphantly whenever I mentioned some minor poet of the day. Our relationship was marked by that habitual exchange of homespun nonsense, comically garbled words, proposed imitations of supposed intonations, and all those private jokes which is the secret code of happy families. With all that he was extremely strict in matters of conduct and given to biting remarks when cross with a child or a servant, but his inherent humanity was too great to allow his rebuke to Osip for laying out the wrong shirt to be really offensive, just as a first-hand knowledge of a boy's pride tempered the harshness of reproval and resulted in sudden forgiveness. Thus I was more puzzled than pleased one day when upon learning that I had deliberately slashed my leg just above the knee with a razor (I still bear the scar) in order to avoid a recitation in class for which I was unprepared, he seemed unable to work up any real wrath; and his subsequent admission of a parallel transgression in his own boyhood rewarded me for not withholding the truth.

I remembered that summer afternoon (which already then seemed   8
long ago although actually only four or five years had passed) when he had burst into my room, grabbed my net, shot down the veranda steps — and presently was strolling back holding between finger and thumb the rare and magnificent female of the Russian Poplar Admirable that he had seen basking on an aspen leaf from the balcony of his study. I remembered our long bicycle rides along the smooth Luga highway and the efficient way in which — mighty-calved, knickerbockered, tweed-coated, checker-capped — he would accomplish the mounting of his high-saddled "Dux," which his valet would bring up to the porch as if it were a palfrey. Surveying the state of its polish, my father would pull on his suede gloves and test under Osip's anxious eye whether the tires were sufficiently tight. Then he would grip the handlebars, place his left foot on a metallic peg jutting at the rear end of the frame, push off with his right foot on the other side of the hind wheel and after three or four such propelments (with the bicycle now set in motion), leisurely translate his right leg into pedal position, move up his left, and settle down on the saddle.

At last I was home, and immediately upon entering the vestibule I became aware of loud, cheerful voices. With the opportuneness of dream arrangements, my uncle the Admiral was coming downstairs. From the red-carpeted landing above, where an armless Greek woman of marble presided over a malachite bowl for visiting cards, my parents were still speaking to him, and as he came down the steps, he looked up with a laugh and slapped the balustrade with the gloves he had in his hand. I knew at once that there would be no duel, that the challenge had been met by an apology, that all was right. I brushed past my uncle and reached the landing. I saw my mother's serene everyday face, but I could not look at my father. And then it happened: my heart welled in me like that wave on which the *Buynïy* rose when her captain brought her alongside the burning *Suvorov*, and I had no handkerchief, and ten years were to pass before a certain night in 1922, at a public lecture in Berlin, when my father shielded the lecturer (his old friend Milyukov) from the bullets of two Russian Fascists and, while vigorously knocking down one of the assassins, was fatally shot by the other. But no shadow was cast by that future event upon the bright stairs of our St. Petersburg house; the large, cool hand resting on my head did not quaver, and several lines of play in a difficult chess composition were not blended yet on the board.

EXPLORATIONS

1. What is Nabokov's central realization during his sleigh ride home from school? What does he realize when he arrives home? What phrases in the last paragraph reveal his response to these realizations?

2. What does Nabokov learn about life and about himself between the beginning and end of the selection? What additional insights are contributed by his adult self as narrator?

3. Nabokov's central metaphor — the duel faced by his father — is echoed throughout his essay. What examples can you find of combat between two opponents? of duel-related imagery?

4. What does Nabokov mean by his final clause: "and several lines of play in a difficult chess composition were not blended yet on the board"?

CONNECTIONS

1. Both Liliana Heker's "The Stolen Party" and Nabokov's essay feature wealthy families. What evidence in Heker's story characterizes Luciana as a spoiled child? What evidence in Nabokov's narrative characterizes him as spoiled? What does Heker perceive as the disadvantages to children of having wealthy parents? Aside from material comforts, what does Nabokov perceive as the advantages?

2. Look at the description in Olga Silverstein's *Observation* of the father's world versus the mother's, from an adolescent's point of view. What details in Nabokov's experience conform to Silverstein's picture? What details conflict with it? What factors do you think are responsible for the differences between Silverstein's view and Nabokov's?

3. Richard Cohen's *Observation*, like Nabokov's essay, is about a son's change in consciousness brought on by an act of his father's. How is Cohen's tone different from Nabokov's? How are the two writers' intentions similar, and how are they different?

ELABORATIONS

1. Both Nabokov's essay and Sophronia Liu's "So Tsi-fai" involve an untimely death. Write an essay comparing the uses these writers make of death in their narratives. How do their purposes appear to be the same and different? How would the impact of Nabokov's reminiscences change if he structured his essay more like Liu's? What does he gain or lose (or both) by focusing on a near miss rather than the more dramatic death that followed it a decade later?

2. In Nabokov's second paragraph, he shifts from exposition (explaining what circumstances drew his father into a duel) to narrative (telling how he found out about it). With typical unconventionality, Nabokov peppers the active part of his story with inactive verbs: some of them passive ("digs were taken") and some intransitive ("a magazine . . . was passing from hand to hand"). Why do writers usually prefer action-oriented verbs for a narrative scene? What does Nabokov convey by his verb choices? Rewrite the narrative section of this paragraph, from "Sometime during the day" to "number of his suits," using stronger, more active verbs. (For example: "A well-timed swoop put me in possession of" might become "I grabbed.") Then write a paragraph evaluating the scene's change in impact.

MARIO VARGAS LLOSA

Sunday, Sunday

Novelist, playwright, and essayist Mario Vargas Llosa was born in
Arequipa, Peru, in 1936. After an early education in Bolivia, where his
grandfather was the Peruvian consul, he studied at various schools and
universities in his native country. His first novel, *La ciudad y los perros*
("The City and the Dogs," 1963; published in English as *Time of the
Hero,* 1966) is set at the Lima military school he attended. Vargas Llosa
edited two literary journals and worked as a journalist and broadcaster.
Since receiving his doctorate from the University of Madrid, he has lived
in Paris, London, and Barcelona and has lectured and taught throughout
the West. In addition to numerous novels, plays, and stories, Vargas
Llosa is the author of *Gabriel García Márquez: Historia de un deicidio*
(1972) and critical studies of the French writers Flaubert, Sartre, and
Camus. "Sunday, Sunday" ("*Día domingo*") first appeared in *Los jefes;*
the following translation from the Spanish is by Alastair Reid.

Peru, an arid coastal strip north of Chile along the Pacific Ocean, was
the heart of South America's ancient Inca empire. Spaniards led by
Francisco Pizarro conquered the region in 1532, reducing the Indians to
serfdom. Peru regained its independence almost three hundred years later
as part of the general liberation movement among Spain's South American
colonies, led by rebels including Simón Bolívar and the Argentine José
de San Martín, who took Lima — Peru's capital — in 1821. The present
population is 45 percent Indian, 37 percent mestizo (mixed Spanish and
Indian), 15 percent white, and the rest black and Asian. Over 90 percent
of Peruvians are Roman Catholic; Spanish and Quechua are both official
languages. After a succession of civilian and military governments, a
constitutional republic was established in 1980.

He held his breath an instant, dug his nails into the palms of his
hands, and said quickly: "I'm in love with you." He saw her redden
suddenly, as if someone had slapped her cheeks, which had a smooth
and pale sheen to them. Terrified, he felt confusion rising and petrifying
his tongue. He wanted to run off, be done with it; in the still winter
morning, he felt the surge of that inner weakness which always overcame

him at decisive moments. A few moments before, among the vivid, smiling throng in the Parque Central in Miraflores, Miguel was still saying to himself: "Now. When we get to Avenida Pardo. I'll take a chance. Ah, Rubén, if you knew how I hate you!" And even earlier, in church, looking for Flora, he spotted her at the foot of a column and, elbowing his way brusquely through the jostling women, he managed to get close to her and greet her in a low voice, repeating tersely to himself, as he had done that morning, stretched on his bed watching the first light: "Nothing else for it. I must do it today, this morning. Rubén, you'll pay for this." And the previous night he had wept for the first time in many years, realizing that the wretched trap lay in wait for him. The crowd had gone on into the park and the Avenida Pardo was left empty. They walked on along the avenue, under the rubber trees with their high, dense foliage. "I have to hurry," Miguel thought, "or else I'll be in trouble." He glanced sideways, round about him. There was nobody; he could try it. Slowly he moved his left hand until it touched hers. The sudden contact told her what was happening. He longed for a miracle to happen, to put an end to that humiliation. "Tell her, tell her," he thought. She stopped, withdrawing her hand, and he felt himself abandoned and foolish. All the glowing phrases prepared passionately the night before had blown away like soap bubbles.

"Flora," he stammered, "I've waited a long time for this moment. Since I've known you, I think only of you. I'm in love for the first time, truly. I've never known a girl like you."

Once again a total blankness in his mind, emptiness. The pressure was extreme. His skin was limp and rubbery and his nails dug into the bone. Even so, he went on speaking painfully, with long pauses, overcoming his stammer, trying to describe his rash, consuming passion, till he found with relief that they had reached the first oval on the Avenida Pardo, and he fell silent. Flora lived between the second and third tree after the oval. They stopped and looked at one another. Flora by now was quite agitated, which lent a bright sheen to her eyes. In despair, Miguel told himself that she had never looked so beautiful. A blue ribbon bound her hair, and he could see where her neck rose, and her ears, two small and perfect question marks.

"Please, Miguel." Her voice was smooth, musical, steady. "I can't 4 answer you now. Besides, my mother doesn't want me to go out with boys until I finish school."

"All mothers say that, Flora," Miguel insisted. "How will she know? We'll meet when you say so, even if it's only Sundays."

"I'll give you an answer, only I have to think first," Flora said, lowering her eyes. And after a moment, she added, "Forgive me, but I have to go. It's late."

Miguel experienced a deep weariness, a feeling which spread through his whole body, relaxing it.

"You're not angry with me, Flora?" he asked, feebly.   8

"Don't be an idiot," she answered brightly. "I'm not angry."

"I'll wait as long as you want," said Miguel. "But we'll go on seeing each other, won't we? We can go to the movies this afternoon, can't we?"

"I can't this afternoon," she said softly. "Martha's invited me to her house."

A warm flush swept violently through him and he felt himself lacer-   12
ated, stunned, at the reply he had expected, which now seemed to him torture. So it was true what Melanés has whispered fiercely in his ear on Saturday afternoon. Martha would leave them alone; it was the usual trick. Later, Rubén would tell the gang how he and his brother had planned the setup, the place, and the time. In payment, Martha had claimed the privilege of spying from behind the curtain. His hands were suddenly wet with anger.

"Don't Flora. We'll go to the matinee as usual. I won't speak about this. I promise."

"No, I really can't," said Flora. "I've got to go to Martha's. She came to my house yesterday to invite me. But afterwards I'll go with her to the Parque Salazar."

Not even in those final words did he feel any hope. A moment later, he was brooding on the spot where the slight blue figure had disappeared, under the majestic arch of the rubber trees of the avenue. It was possible to take on a simple adversary, but not Rubén. He remembered the names of the girls invited by Martha, one Sunday afternoon. He could do nothing now; he was beaten. Once more there arose that fantasy which always saved him in moments of frustration: against a distant background of clouds swollen with black smoke, at the head of a company of cadets from the Naval Academy, he approached a saluting base set up in the park; distinguished people in formal dress, top hats in hand, and ladies with glittering jewels, all applauded him. Thick on the sidewalks, a crowd in which the faces of his friends and enemies stood out, watched him in awe, murmuring his name. Dressed in blue, a broad cape flowing from his shoulders, Miguel marched at the head, gazing off to the horizon. He raised his sword; his head described a half circle in the air. There, in the center of the stand, was Flora, smiling. In one corner, ragged and ashamed, he noticed Rubén. He confined himself to a brief, contemptuous glance. He went on marching; he disappeared amid cheers.

Like steam wiped off a mirror, the image disappeared. He was in the   16
doorway of his house, hating the whole world, hating himself. He entered and went straight up to his room. He threw himself face down on the bed. In the half-dark under his eyelids appeared the girl's face. "I love you, Flora," he said out loud — and then came the face of Rubén, with his insolent jaw and his mocking smile. The faces were side by side, coming closer. Rubén's eyes turned to mock him while his mouth approached Flora.

He jumped up from his bed. The wardrobe mirror gave him back a face both ravaged and livid. I won't allow it, he decided. He can't do that, I won't let him pull that on me.

The Avenida Pardo was still empty. Increasing his pace, he walked on till it crossed Avenida Grau; there he hesitated. He felt the cold — he had left his jacket in his room and his shirt alone was not enough to protect him from the wind which came from the sea and which combed the dense foliage of the rubber trees in a steady swish. The dreaded image of Flora and Rubén together gave him courage and he went on walking. From the door of the bar beside the Montecarlo cinema, he saw them at their usual table, occupying the corner formed by the far and left-hand walls. Francisco, Melanés, Tobías, the Scholar, they noticed him and, after a second's surprise, they turned toward Rubén, their faces wicked and excited. He recovered himself at once — in front of men he certainly knew how to behave.

"Hello," he said, approaching. "What's new?"

"Sit." The Scholar drew up a chair. "What miracle brings you here?"   20
"It's a century since you've been this way," said Francisco.

"I was keen to see you," Miguel said warmly. "I knew you'd be here. What are you so surprised about? Or am I no longer a Buzzard?" He took a seat between Melanés and Tobías. Rubén was opposite him.

"Cuncho!" called the Scholar. "Bring another glass. Not too dirty a one." When he brought the glass and the Scholar filled it with beer, Miguel toasted "To the Buzzards!" and drank it down.

"You'd have the glass as well!" said Francisco. "What a thirst!"   24
"I bet you went to one o'clock Mass," said Melanés, winking one eye in satisfaction, as he always did when he was up to something. "Right?"

"Yes, I went," said Miguel, unperturbed. "But only to see a chick, nothing more."

He looked at Rubén with a challenge in his eyes, but Rubén paid no attention. He was drumming on the table with his fingers and, the point of his tongue between his teeth, he whistled softly "La Niña Popoff."

"Great," Melanés applauded. "Great, Don Juan. Tell us, which chick?"   28

"That's a secret."

"Among the Buzzards, there are no secrets," Tobías reminded him. "Have you forgotten? Come on, who was it?"

"What's it to you?" said Miguel.

"A lot," said Tobías. "I have to know who you go with to know who   32 you are."

"There you are!" said Melanés to Miguel. "One to zero."

"I'll bet I can guess who it is," said Francisco. "Can't you?"

"I know," said Tobías.

"Me too," said Melanés. He turned to Rubén, his eyes and voice all   36 innocence. "And you, brother, can you guess? Who is it?"

"No," said Rubén coldly. "And I couldn't care less."

"My stomach's on fire," said the Scholar. "Is nobody going to order a beer?"

Melanés drew a pathetic finger across his throat. "I have not money, darling," he said in English.

"I'll buy a bottle," Tobías announced with a grand gesture. "Who'll   40 follow me? We have to quench this moron's fire."

"Cuncho, bring a half dozen Cristals," said Miguel. Cries of enthusiasm, exclamations.

"You're a real Buzzard," Francisco affirmed.

"Crazy, crazy," added Melanés. "Yes sir, a Top Buzzard."

Cuncho brought the beers. They drank. They listened to Melanés tell   44 dirty stories, crude, exaggerated, and lushed-up, and a bitter argument on football broke out between Tobías and Francisco. The Scholar told a story. He was coming from Lima to Miraflores on a bus. The other passengers got off at the Avenida Arequipa. At the top of Javier Prado, Tomasso got on, the one they call the White Whale, that giant albino who's still in the first grade, lives in Quebrada, get it? — pretending to be interested in the bus, he began to ask the driver questions, leaning over the seat from behind, at the same time slicing the cloth of the seat back systematically with a knife.

"He did it because I was there," the Scholar said. "He wanted to show off."

"He's a mental degenerate," said Francisco. "You do things like that when you're ten. At his age it isn't funny."

"The funny thing is what happened next," laughed the Scholar.

"'Listen, driver, don't you know that that monster is destroying your bus?'"

"What's that?" said the driver, braking suddenly. Ears flaming, eyes   48
wide with fright, Tomasso the Whale forced his way out the door.

"With his knife," the Scholar said. "Imagine the state he left the seat in."

The Whale finally managed to get out of the bus. He set off at a run down the Avenida Arequipa. The driver ran after him shouting: "Grab that creep!"

"He got him?" Melanés asked.

"I don't know. I got out. And I took the ignition key as a souvenir.   52
Here it is."

He took a little silver key from his pocket and placed it on the table. The bottles were empty. Rubén looked at his watch and stood up.

"I'm off," he said. "See you."

"Don't go," said Miguel. "Today I'm rich. I invite you all to eat."

A shower of hands clapped him on the back; the Buzzards thanked   56
him noisily, cheered him.

"I can't," said Rubén. "I have things to do."

"All right then, go, my boy," Tobías said. "Say hello to Martha for me."

"We'll be thinking about you, brother," said Melanés.

"No," Miguel shot out. "I'm inviting everybody or nobody. If Rubén   60
goes, it's off."

"You hear him Buzzard Rubén?" said Francisco. "You've got to stay."

"You've got to stay," said Melanés, "no question."

"I'm going," said Rubén.

"The thing is that you're drunk," said Miguel. "You're going because   64
your're afraid of screwing up in front of us, that's all."

"How many times have I taken you home nearly passed out?" said Rubén. "How many times have I helped you up the railing so your father wouldn't catch you? I can hold ten times more than you."

"You could," said Miguel. "Now it'd be difficult. Want to try?"

"With pleasure," said Rubén. "We'll meet tonight, here?"

"No. Right now." Miguel turned to the others, arms open. "Buzzards,   68
I'm making a challenge."

Fortunately, the old formula still worked. In the midst of the noisy excitement he had provoked, he saw Rubén sit down, pale.

"Cuncho!" shouted Tobías. "The menu. And two baths of beer. A Buzzard has just made a challenge."

They ordered steaks *a la chorrillana* and a dozen beers. Tobías put three bottles in front of each of the competitors. The others had the rest. They ate, scarcely speaking. Miguel drank after each mouthful and tried to show some zest, but the fear of not being able to hold the beer grew in proportion to the acid taste in his throat. They finished the six bottles just after Cuncho had taken the plates away.

"You order," said Miguel to Rubén.   72

"Three more each."

After the first glass of the new round, Miguel felt a buzzing in his ears. His head was spinning slowly; everything was moving.

"I need to piss," he said. "I'm going to the john." The Buzzards laughed.

"Give up?" asked Rubén.   76

"I'm going to piss," shouted Miguel. "Have them bring more if you want."

In the lavatory, he vomited. Then he washed his face thoroughly, trying to remove every revealing sign. His watch said half past four. In spite of the overwhelming sick feeling, he felt happy. Rubén could do nothing. He went back to the others.

"*Salud!*" said Rubén, raising his glass.

He's furious, Miguel thought. But I've stopped him now.   80

"There's corpse smell," said Melanés. "Someone here's dying on us."

"I'm like new," affirmed Miguel, trying to overcome both his disgust and his sickness.

"*Salud!*" repeated Rubén.

When they had finished the last beer, his stomach felt leaden; the   84 voices of the others reached him as a confused mixture of sounds. A hand appeared suddenly under his eyes, white and large-fingered, took him by the chin and forced him to raise his head. Rubén's face had grown. He was comical, all tousled and angry.

"Give up, kid?"

Miguel pulled himself together suddenly and pushed Rubén, but before the gesture could be followed up, the Scholar intervened.

"Buzzards never fight," he said, making them sit down. "They're both drunk. It's all over. Vote."

Melanés, Francisco, and Tobías agreed, grumblingly, to declare a   88 draw.

"I already had it won," said Rubén. "This one's incapable. Look at him."

Indeed, Miguel's eyes were glassy, his mouth hung open, and a thread of saliva ran from his tongue.

"Shut up," said the Scholar. "You are no champion, as we say, at beer-swilling."

"You're not beer-drinking champion," added Melanés. "You're only   92 the swimming champion, the scourge of the swimming pools."

"Better keep quiet," said Rubén. "Can't you see you're eaten up with envy?"

"Long live the Esther Williams of Miraflores," said Melanés.

"Over the hill already and you hardly know how to swim," said Rubén. "Don't you want me to give you lessons?"

"Now we know it all, champ," said the Scholar. "You've won a   96 swimming championship. And all the chicks are dying over you. The little champ."

"Champion of nothing," said Miguel with difficulty. "He's a phony."

"You're about to pass out," said Rubén. "Will I take you home, girl?"

"I'm not drunk," Miguel insisted. "And you're a phony."

"You're pissed off because I'm going to see Flora," said Rubén. "You're   100 dying of jealousy. Do you think I don't catch on to things?"

"Phony," said Miguel. "You won because your father is Federation President. Everybody knows that he pulled a fast one, just so you would win."

"And you most of all," said Rubén, "you can't even surf."

"You swim no better than anyone else," said Miguel. "Anybody could leave you silly."

"Anybody," said Melanés. "Even Miguel, who is a creep."   104

"Permit me to smile," said Rubén.

"We permit you," said Tobías. "That's all we need."

"You're getting at me because it's winter," said Rubén. "If it weren't, I'd challenge you all to go to the beach to see if you'd be so cocky in the water."

"You won the championship because of your father," said Miguel.   108 "You're a phony. When you want to take me on swimming, just let me know, that's all. On the beach, in Terrazas, where you like."

"On the beach," said Rubén. "Right now."

"You're a phony," said Miguel.

"If you win," said Rubén, "I promise I won't see Flora. And if I win, you can go sing somewhere else."

"Who do you think you are?" stammered Miguel. "Bastard, just who   112 do you think you are?"

"Buzzards," said Rubén, spreading his arms, "I'm offering a challenge."

"Miguel's not in shape now," said the Scholar. "Why don't you just toss for Flora?"

"You keep out of it," said Miguel. "I accept. Let's go to the beach."

"They're crazy," said Francisco. "I'm not going to the beach in this 116 cold. Make a different bet."

"He's acccptcd," said Rubén. "Lct's go."

"When a Buzzard makes a challenge, everyone holds his tongue," said Melanés. "Let's go to the beach. And if they're scared to go in, we'll throw them in ourselves."

"They're both drunk," the Scholar insisted. "The challenge doesn't stand."

"Shut up, Scholar," roared Miguel. "I'm a big boy. I don't need you 120 to look after me."

"All right," said the Scholar, shrugging his shoulders. "Suit yourself, then."

They went out. Outside, a quiet grayness hung in wait for them. Miguel took deep breaths; he felt better. Francisco, Melanés, and Rubén walked ahead, Miguel and the Scholar behind. There were a few idlers on the Avenida Grau, mostly maids dressed up, out on their free day. Gray-looking men, with long lank hair, followed them and watched them greedily. They laughed, showing gold teeth. The Buzzards paid no attention. They walked with long strides, excitement slowly growing in them.

"Feeling better?" said the Scholar.

"Yes," replied Miguel. "The fresh air's done me good."   124

At the corner of Avenida Pardo, they turned. They walked, deployed like a squadron, in the same line, under the rubber trees of the walk, over the flagstones bulged from time to time by huge tree roots which occasionally broke through the surface like great hooks. Going down Diagonal, they passed two girls. Rubén bowed to them, very formally.

"Hello, Rubén," they sang out together.

Tobías imitated them, fluting his voice.

"Hello, Prince Rubén."   128

The Avenida Diagonal gave out on a short bend which forked; in one direction wound the Malecón, paved and shining; in the other, there was an incline which followed the downward slope and reached the sea. It is called the "bathers' descent" and its surface is smooth and shines from the polish of car tires and the feet of bathers from many summers.

"Let's give off some heat, champs," shouted Melanés, breaking into a run. The others followed him.

They ran against the wind and the thin fog which came up from the beach, caught up in a whirlwind of feeling. Through ears, mouth, and nostrils, the air came in, into their lungs, and a feeling of relief and clearheadedness spread through their bodies as the slope steepened and suddenly their feet obeyed only a mysterious force which seemed to come from deep in the earth. Arms whirling like propellers, a salty tang on their tongues, the Buzzards ran down in full cry to the circular platform over the bathing huts. The sea disappeared some fifty meters from the shore, in a thick cloud which seemed ready to charge against the cliffs, the high dark bulk of which spread all along the bay.

"Let's go back," said Francisco. "I'm frozen."   132

At the edge of the platform there was a banister stained here and there with moss. An opening in it indicated the head of the almost vertical ladder which led down to the bench. The Buzzards looked down from there at a short strip of clear water, its surface unbroken, frothing where the fog seemed to join with the foam from the waves.

"I'll leave if this one gives up," said Rubén.

"Who's talking about giving up?" retorted Miguel. "Who do you think you are?"

Rubén went down the ladder three rungs at a time, unbuttoning his 136 shirt as he did so.

"Rubén!" shouted the Scholar. "Are you crazy? Come back!"

But Miguel and the others also went down, and the Scholar followed them.

From the terrace of the long, wide building backed against the cliff, which contains the changing rooms, down to the curving edge of the sea, there is a stretch of smooth stones where, in summer, people took the sun. The small beach hummed with life then, from early morning until twilight. Now the water was well up the slope, there were no brightly colored umbrellas, no elastic girls with bronzed bodies, no melodramatic screams of children and women when a wave succeeded in splashing them before receding backward over the groaning stones and pebbles, there was not a strip of beach to be seen under the flooding current which went up as far as the dark narrow space under the columns which held up the building; and in the surge of the tide, it was difficult to make out the wooden ladders and the cement supports, hung with stalactites and seaweed.

"You can't see the surf," said Rubén. "How will we do it?"   140

They were in the left-hand gallery, the women's section; their faces were serious.

"Wait until tomorrow," said the Scholar. "At noon it will be clear. Then you can judge it."

"Now that we've come all the way, let it be now," said Melanés. "They can judge it themselves."

"All right by me," said Rubén. "You?"

144

"Fine," said Miguel.

When they had undressed, Tobías joked about the veins which spread across Miguel's smooth stomach. They went down. The wood of the steps, steadily worn for months by the water, was slippery and very smooth. Holding the iron rail so as not to fall, Miguel felt a shiver run from the soles of his feet to his brain. He figured that, in some ways, the mist and the cold were in his favor, that success would depend not so much on skill as on endurance, and Rubén's skin was already purple, risen all over in gooseflesh. One rung lower, Rubén's neat body bent forward. Tensed, he waited for the ebb and the arrival of the next wave, which came evenly, lightly, leading with a flying crest of foam. When the top of the wave was two meters from the ladder, Rubén leaped. His arms stretched like arrows, his hair streaming with the dive, his body cut the air cleanly, and fell without bending, his head not dropping, his knees straight, he entered the foam, hardly going down at all, and immediately, making use of the tide, he glided forward; his arms appeared and disappeared in a frenzy of bubbles, and his feet were leaving behind a steady, flying wake. Miguel in turn climbed down one rung and waited for the next wave. He knew that the bottom there was shallow, that he would have to dive like a board, hard and rigid, without moving, or he would scrape the stones. He closed his eyes and dived; he did not touch bottom but his body was lacerated from forehead to knees, and he stung all over as he swam with all his strength to bring back to his limbs the warmth which the water had suddenly drained away. In that stretch of sea beside the Miraflores beach, the waves and undertow meet, there are whirlpools and conflicting currents, and last summer was so far away that Miguel had forgotten how to ride the water without using force. He did not remember that you had to go limp, let go, let yourself be carried with the ebb, submitting, swimming only when a wave gets up and you are on the crest, on that shelf of water where the foam is, which runs on top of the water. He forgot that it is better to suffer with patience and a certain resistance that first contact with the sea ebbing from the beach, which tumbles the limbs and makes water stream from eyes and mouth, not to resist, to be a cork, to gulp air, nothing more, every time a wave comes in without force, or through the bottom of the wave if the breaking crest is close — to cling to a rock and wait out patiently the deafening thunder of its passing, to push out sharply and keep forging ahead, furtively, with the arms, until the next obstacle, and then to go limp, not struggling against the undertow but moving slowly and deliberately in a widening spiral and suddenly escaping, at the right moment, in a single burst. Farther out, the surface is unexpectedly calm, the movement of surf small; the water is clear and level, and at some points you can make out dark, underwater rocks.

After fighting his way through the rough water, Miguel stopped, exhausted, and gulped air. He saw Rubén not far away, looking at him. His hair fell in curls on his forehead; his teeth were bared.

"Let's go."   148

"Okay."

After swimming a few moments, Miguel felt the cold, which had momentarily gone, surge back, and he stepped up his kick, for it was in the legs, above all in the calves, where the water had most effect, numbing them first and then stiffening them. He was swimming with his face in the water, and every time his right arm came out of the water, he turned his head to get rid of his held breath and to breathe again, immediately dipping his forehead and chin, lightly, so as not to check his forward motion, and to make instead a prow which parted the water, the easier to slip through. At each stroke he would see Rubén with one eye, swimming smoothly on the surface, not exerting himself, scarcely raising a wash, with the ease and delicacy of a gliding gull. Miguel tried to forget Rubén and the sea and the surf (which must still have been some distance away, for the water was clear, calm, and crossed only by small, spontaneous waves). He wanted to keep in mind only Flora's face, the down on her arms which on sunny days gleamed like a small forest of gold thread, but he could not prevent the girl's face from being succeeded by another image, shrouded, dominant, thunderous, which tumbled over Flora and hid her, the image of a mountain of tormented water, not exactly the surf (they had once reached the surf, two summers ago, with its thundering waves and greenish-black foam, for out there, more or less, the rocks ended and gave way to mud, which the waves brought to the surface and stirred up with clumps of seaweed, staining the water), instead a sea on its own wracked by internal storms, in which rose up enormous waves which could have lifted up a whole ship and upset it quickly and easily, scattering passengers, lifeboats, masts, sails, buoys, sailors, bull's-eyes, and flags.

He stopped swimming, his body sinking until it was vertical. He raised his head and saw Rubén drawing away. He thought of calling to him on some pretext, of shouting for example, "Why don't we rest a moment?" but he refrained. All the cold in his body seemed to be concentrated in his calves; he felt the muscles growing numb, the skin tightening, his heartbeat accelerating. He moved his legs weakly. He was in the center of a circle of dark water, enclosed by the fog. He tried to make out the beach, or at least the shadow of the cliffs, but the fog which appeared to dissolve as he penetrated it was deceptive, and not in the least transparent. He saw only a short stretch of sea surface, blackish, green, and the shrouding clouds, flush with the water. At that point he felt fear. The memory of the beer he had drunk came back and he thought "That could have weakened me, I suppose." Suddenly it seemed that his arms and legs had disappeared. He decided to go back, but after a few strokes in the direction of the beach, he turned and swam as easily as he could. "I won't make the beach alone," he thought: "Better to be close to Rubén. If I poop out I'll tell him he's won but we'll get back." Now he was swimming carelessly, his head up, swallowing water, stiff-armed, his eyes fixed on the imperturbable shape ahead of him.

The activity and the energy relaxed his legs, and his body recovered 152 some warmth. The distance between him and Rubén has lessened and that calmed him. Shortly after, he caught him up; flinging out an arm, he touched one of Rubén's feet. Immediately the other stopped. Rubén's eyes were very red, his mouth open.

"I think we've gone off course," said Miguel. "We seem to be swimming sideways on to the beach."

His teeth were chattering, but his voice was firm. Rubén looked all around him. Miguel watched him, tense.

"You can't see the beach any more," said Rubén.

"Not for some time," said Miguel. "There's a lot of fog."   156

"We haven't gone off," said Rubén. "Look. There's the surf."

Actually, some waves were reaching them with a fringe of foam which dissolved and suddenly formed again. They looked at them in silence.

"Then we're close to the surf," Miguel said, finally.

"Sure. We've been swimming fast."   160

"I've never seen so much fog."

"Are you very tired?" asked Rubén.

"Me? You're crazy. Let's go."

He immediately regretted that reply, but it was now too late. Rubén 164 had already said, "Okay, let's go."

He had counted twenty strokes before he decided that he could not go on. He was hardly moving forward; his right leg was semiparalyzed by cold, his arms felt limp and heavy. Panting, he called out, "Rubén!" The other one kept on swimming. "Rubén, Rubén!" He turned and began to swim toward the beach, or to splash, rather, in desperation; and suddenly he was praying to God to save him, he would be good in the future, he would obey his parents, he would not miss Sunday mass, and then he remembered having confessed to the Buzzards, "I go to church only to see a chick," and he was struck by the certainty that God was going to punish him by drowning him in those troubled waters which he was desperately battling, waters beneath which a terrible death was awaiting him and, beyond that, possibly Hell itself. Into his distress there suddenly swam up a phrase used occasionally by Father Alberto in his religion class, that divine mercy knows no limits, and while he flailed at the water with his arms — his legs were hanging down like lead weights — moving his lips, he prayed to God to be good to him, he was so young, and he swore that he would become a priest if saved, but a second later he corrected that quickly and promised that instead of becoming a priest he would offer up sacrifices and other things and dispense charity, and then he realized that hesitation and bargaining at so desperate a time could prove fatal, and suddenly he heard, quite close, wild shouts coming from Rubén, and, turning his head, he saw him, some ten meters away, his face half submerged, waving an arm, pleading:

"Miguel, friend Miguel, come, I'm drowning. Don't go!"

He remained rigid a moment, puzzled, and then it was as if Rubén's desperation stifled his own, for he felt his courage and strength return, and the tightness in his legs relax.

"I have a stomach cramp," Rubén hissed out. "I can't go on, Miguel. 168 Save me, whatever you do, don't leave me, pal."

He floated toward Rubén and was about to go to him when he remembered that drowning men always manage to hang on like leeches to their rescuers, drowning them with them, and he kept his distance, but the cries frightened him and he realized that if Rubén drowned, he would not reach the beach either, and he went back. Two meters from Rubén, a white shriveled mass which sank and then rose, he shouted: "Don't move, Rubén. I'm going to pull you by the head, but don't try to hang on to me. If you hang on we'll both drown. Rubén, you're going to keep still, pal. I'm going to pull you by the head but don't touch me." He kept a safe distance, stretching out a hand until he grasped Rubén's hair. He began to swim with his free arm, doing all he could to help himself along with his legs. Progress was slow and painful. He concentrated all his efforts and scarcely heard Rubén's steady groaning, or the sudden terrible cries of "I'm going to die; save me, Miguel!" or the retching that convulsed him. He was exhausted when he stopped. He supported Rubén with one hand, making a circular sweep on the surface with the other. He breathed deeply through his mouth. Rubén's face was twisted in pain, his lips drawn back in a strange grimace.

"Friend Rubén," gasped Miguel, "there's not far to go. Have a shot at it. Answer me, Rubén. Shout. Don't stay like that."

He slapped him sharply, and Rubén opened his eyes; he moved his head weakly.

"Shout, pal," Miguel repeated. "Try to move yourself. I'm going to massage your stomach. It's not far now. Don't give up." 172

His hands went underwater and found the tightness of Rubén's stomach muscles, spreading over his belly. He rubbed them several times, slowly at first, and then strongly, and Rubén shouted, "I don't want to die, Miguel; save me!"

He began to swim again, this time pulling Rubén by his chin. Each time a wave caught up with them, Rubén choked, and Miguel shouted at him to spit out. And he kept swimming, not resting a moment, closing his eyes at times, in good spirits because a kind of confidence had sprung up in his heart, a warm, proud, stimulating feeling which protected him against the cold and fatigue. A stone scraped one of his feet, and he shouted aloud, and hurried. A moment later he was able to stand up, and he reached out his arms to support Rubén. Holding him against himself, feeling his head leaning on one of his shoulders, he rested a long time. Then he helped Rubén to move and loosen his shoulders, and supporting him on his forearms, he made him move his knees. He massaged his stomach until the tightness began to yield. Rubén had stopped shouting and was doing all he could to get moving again, massaging himself with his own hands.

"Better?"

"Yes, pal. I'm fine. Let's go." 176

An inexpressible joy filled them as they made their way over the stones, leaning forward against the undertow, oblivious of sea urchins. Soon they caught sight of the groins of the cliffs, the bathing house, and finally, close to the water's edge by now, the Buzzards, standing in the women's gallery, looking out.

"Listen," Rubén said.

"Yes."

"Don't say anything to them. Please don't tell them I was crying for 180
help. We've always been good friends, Miguel. Don't do that to me."

"Think I'm a creep?" said Miguel. "I won't say a thing, don't worry."

They came out shivering. They sat down on the foot of the ladder,
with the Buzzards buzzing around them.

"We were ready to send out condolences to your families," said Tobías.

"You've been in over an hour," said the Scholar. "Tell us, how did it 184
come out?"

Speaking steadily, drying his body with his shirt, Rubén explained:
"Nothing at all. We got to the surf and then we came back. That's how
the Buzzards do things. Miguel beat me. By nothing more than a hand's
reach. If it had been in a pool, of course, I'd have made him look silly."

A rain of congratulatory handclaps fell on the shoulders of Miguel,
who had dressed without drying himself.

"Why, you're becoming a man," Melanés said to him.

Miguel, did not reply. Smiling, he thought that that very evening he 188
would go to the Parque Salazar. All Miraflores would know, thanks to
Melanés's ready mouth, of the heroic trials he had come through and
Flora would be waiting for him with shining eyes. Before him was
opening a golden future.

EXPLORATIONS

1. In the first paragraph of "Sunday, Sunday," why does Miguel think, "Ah,
   Rubén, if you knew how I hate you!" and "Rubén, you'll pay for this"? What
   has apparently been the relationship between Miguel and Flora up until now?
   between Miguel and Rubén?

2. When Miguel and Rubén stagger onto the shore, why are they filled with "an
   inexpressible joy?" What has Miguel learned from his swimming contest with
   Rubén?

3. What are Flora's dramatic functions in "Sunday, Sunday"? What information
   does Vargas Llosa give us about the kind of person she is? What seem to be
   Miguel's and Rubén's reasons for vying for her? How much control does
   Flora have over her role in this drama?

CONNECTIONS

1. What common elements are shared by the coming-of-age experiences described in "Sunday, Sunday" and Vladimir Nabokov's selection "From *Speak, Memory*"? What important step toward maturity is taken by Miguel and not Nabokov? by Nabokov and not Miguel?

2. Mishima Yukio's "boy who wrote poetry" is repelled by the lack of poetry in his friend R's real-life love affair. What role does poetic language play in the encounter between Miguel and Flora in "Sunday, Sunday"? What role does it play in Vargas Llosa's account of that meeting?

3. "Whatever tentative memberships we try out in the world, the fear haunts us that we are really kids who cannot take care of ourselves," writes Gail Sheehy in her *Observation*. What statements and acts in "Sunday, Sunday" are examples of Sheehy's observations?

ELABORATIONS

1. In "Sunday, Sunday," Miguel's feelings about Flora strongly affect his feelings about Rubén, and vice versa. What do you think are the likely advantages and disadvantages of this two-way influence? Write an essay comparing and contrasting the importance of opposite-sex relationships and same-sex relationships to someone moving, like Miguel, from youth into adulthood.

2. Look closely at Vargas Llosa's description of the swimming match between Miguel and Rubén. What passages in this long description could apply to either or both of the relationships in which Miguel is floundering? Write an essay examining the parallels between the literal sea and the sea of human drama in this story.

VED MEHTA

Pom's Engagement

Completely blind since the age of three, Ved Mehta is the author of more than a dozen books of autobiography, Indian social and political history, and interviews with international historians, philosophers, and theologians. His screenplay *Chachaji, My Poor Relation* airs periodically on public television. Mehta's family was instrumental in his success: He was sent away (briefly) to a school in Bombay when he was five and to the Arkansas State School for the Blind at age fifteen. He went on to graduate Phi Beta Kappa from Pomona College in California, received a master's degree from Harvard University, won a scholarship at Balliol College of Oxford University, and now works as a staff writer for *The New Yorker* magazine. "Pom's Engagement" comes from his 1984 autobiography *The Ledge between the Streams*.

Born in 1934, Mehta grew up in the Punjab, a large plain formed by five rivers in northwestern India and northeastern Pakistan. Here the earliest Indian civilization flourished thousands of years ago. Mussoorie is a hill station — a former British summer resort — to the east; a journey to Dehra Dun, a city in the same region, would have meant an over-500-mile round trip from the Mehta home in Lahore.

The Indian caste system is an ancient hereditary class structure that operated to preserve the status quo. The four principal castes are the Brahman (priests and scholars), the Kshatriya (warriors and rulers), the Vaisya (farmers and merchants), and the Sudra (peasants and laborers). Below all these were the now illegal caste of Untouchables or Panchamas, who performed the most menial tasks.

(For more background on India, see p. 28.)

Before we moved to Lahore, Daddyji had gone to Mussoorie, a hill station in the United Provinces, without telling us why he was going out of the Punjab. Now, several months after he made that trip, he gathered us around him in the drawing room at 11 Temple Road while Mamaji mysteriously hurried Sister Pom upstairs. He started talking as if we were all very small and he were conducting one of our "dinner-table-school" discussions. He said that by right and tradition the oldest daughter had to be given in marriage first, and that the ripe age for marriage was nineteen. He said that when a girl approached that age her parents, who had to take the initiative, made many inquiries and followed many leads.

They investigated each young man and his family background, his relatives, his friends, his classmates, because it was important to know what kind of family the girl would be marrying into, what kind of company she would be expected to keep. If the girl's parents decided that a particular young man was suitable, then his people also had to make their investigations, but, however favorable their findings, their decision was unpredictable, because good, well-settled boys were in great demand and could afford to be choosy. All this took a lot of time. "That's why I said nothing to you children about why I went to Mussoorie," he concluded. "I went to see a young man for Pom. She's already nineteen."

We were stunned. We have never really faced the idea that Sister Pom might get married and suddenly leave, I thought.

"We won't lose Pom, we'll get a new family member," Daddyji said, as if reading my thoughts.

Then all of us started talking at once. We wanted to know if Sister   4
Pom had been told; if she'd agreed; whom she'd be marrying.

"Your mother has just taken Pom up to tell her," Daddyji said. "But she's a good girl. She will agree." He added, "The young man in question is twenty-eight years old. He's a dentist, and so has a profession."

"Did you get a dentist because Sister Pom has bad teeth?" Usha asked. Sister Pom had always been held up to us as an example of someone who, as a child, had spurned greens and had therefore grown up with a mouthful of poor teeth.

Daddyji laughed. "I confess I didn't think of anyone's teeth when I chose the young man in question."

"What is he like?" I asked. "What are we to call him?"   8

"He's a little bit on the short side, but he has a happy-go-lucky nature, like Nimi's. He doesn't drink, but, unfortunately, he does smoke. His father died at an early age of a heart attack, but he has a nice mother, who will not give Pom any trouble. It seems that everyone calls him Kakaji."

We all laughed. Kakaji, or "youngster," was what very small boys were called.

"That's what he must have been called when he was small, and the name stuck," Daddyji said.

In spite of myself, I pictured a boy smaller than I was and imagined   12
him taking Sister Pom away, and then I imagined her having to keep his pocket money, to arrange his clothes in the cupboards, to comb his hair. My mouth felt dry.

"What will Kakaji call Sister Pom?" I asked.

"Pom, silly — what else?" Sister Umi said.

Mamaji and Sister Pom walked into the room. Daddyji made a place for Sister Pom next to him and said, "Now, now, now, no reason to cry. Is it to be yes?"

"Whatever you say," Sister Pom said in a small voice, between sobs.   16

"Pom, how can you say that? You've never seen him," Sister Umi said.

"Kakaji's uncle, Dr. Prakash Mehrotra, himself a dentist, has known our family from his student days in Lahore," Daddyji said. "As a student dentist, he used to be welcomed in Babuji's Shahalmi Gate house. He would come and go as he pleased. He has known for a long time what kind of people we are. He remembered seeing you, Pom, when we went to Mussoorie on holiday. He said yes immediately, and his approval seemed to be enough for Kakaji."

"You promised me you wouldn't cry again," Mamaji said to Sister Pom, patting her on the back, and then, to Daddyji, "She's agreed."

Daddyji said much else, sometimes talking just for the sake of talking,   20
sometimes laughing at us because we were sniffling, and all the time trying to make us believe that this was a happy occasion. First, Sister Umi took issue with him: parents had no business arranging marriages; if she were Pom she would run away. Then Sister Nimi: all her life she had heard him say to us children, "Think for yourself — be independent," and here he was not allowing Pom to think for herself. Brother Om took Daddyji's part: girls who didn't get married became a burden on their parents, and Daddyji had four daughters to marry off, and would be retiring in a few years. Sisters Nimi and Umi retorted: they hadn't gone to college to get married off, to have some young man following them around like a leech. Daddyji just laughed. I thought he was so wise, and right.

"Go and bless your big sister," Mamaji said, pushing me in the direction of Sister Pom.

"I don't want to," I said. "I don't know him."

"What'll happen to Sister Pom's room?" Usha asked. She and Ashok didn't have rooms of their own. They slept in Mamaji's room.

"Pom's room will remain empty, so that any time she likes she can   24
come and stay in her room with Kakaji," Daddyji said.

The thought that a man I never met would sleep in Pom's room with Sister Pom there made my heart race. A sob shook me. I ran outside.

The whole house seemed to be in an uproar. Mamaji was shouting at

Gian Chand, Gian Chand was shouting at the bearer, the bearer was shouting at the sweeper. There were the sounds of the kitchen fire being stoked, of the drain being washed out, of water running in bathrooms. From behind whichever door I passed came the rustle of saris, salwars, and kemises. The house smelled of fresh flowers, but it had a ghostly chill. I would climb to the landing of Sister Pom's room and thump down the stairs two at a time. Brother Om would shout up at me, "Stop it!" Sister Umi would shout down at me, "Don't you have anything better to do?" Sister Nimi would call to me from somewhere, "You're giving Pom a headache." I wouldn't heed any of them. As soon as I had thumped down, I would clatter to the top and thump my way down again.

Daddyji went past on the back veranda. "Who's coming with Kakaji?" I asked. Kakaji was in Lahore to buy some dental equipment, and in a few minutes he was expected for tea, to meet Sister Pom and the family.

"He's coming alone," Daddyji said, over his shoulder. "He's come 28 from very far away." I had somehow imagined that Kakaji would come with at least as many people as we had in our family, because I had started thinking of the tea as a kind of cricket match — the elevens facing off.

I followed Daddyji into the drawing room. "Will he come alone for his wedding, too?"

"No. Then he'll come with the bridegroom's party."

We were joined by everyone except Mamaji and Sister Pom, who from the moment we got the news of Sister Pom's marriage had become inseparable.

Gian Chand came in, the tea things rattling on his tray. 32

Later, I couldn't remember exactly how Kakaji had arrived, but I remember noticing that his footfall was heavy, that his greeting was affectionate, and that his voice seemed to float up with laughter. I don't know what I'd expected, but I imagined that if I had been in his place I would have skulked in the *gulli*, and perhaps changed my mind and not entered at all.

"Better to have ventured and lost than never to have ventured at all," Daddyji was saying to Kakaji about life's battles.

"Yes, Daddyji, just so," he said, with a little laugh. I had never heard anybody outside our family call my father Daddyji. It sounded odd.

Sister Pom was sent for, and she came in with Mamaji. Her footsteps 36 were shy, and the rustle of her sari around her feet was slow, as if she felt too conscious of the noise she was making just in walking. Daddyji made some complimentary remark about the silver border on her sari,

and told her to sit next to Kakaji. Kakaji and Sister Pom exchanged a
few words about a family group photograph on the mantelpiece, and
about her studies. There was the clink of china as Sister Pom served
Kakaji tea.

"Won't you have some tea yourself?" Kakaji asked Sister Pom.

Sister Pom's sari rustled over her shoulder as she turned to Daddyji.

"Kakaji, none of my children have ever tasted tea or coffee," Daddyji
said. "We consider both to be bad habits. My children have been brought
up on hot milk, and lately Pom has been taking a little ghi in her milk
at bedtime, for health reasons."

We all protested at Daddyji's broadcasting family matters.   40

Kakaji tactfully turned the conversation to a visit to Mussoorie that
our family was planning.

Mamaji offered him onion, potato, and cauliflower pakoras. He accepted, remarking how hot and crisp they were.

"Where will Sister Pom live?" Usha asked.

"In the summer, my practice is in Mussoorie," Kakaji said, "but in   44
the winter it's in Dehra Dun."

It struck me for the first time that after Sister Pom got married people
we didn't know, people she didn't know, would become more important
to her than we were.

Kakaji had left without formally committing himself. Then, four days
later, when we were all sitting in the drawing room, a servant brought a
letter to Mamaji. She told us that it was from Kakaji's mother, and that
it asked if Sister Pom might be engaged to Kakaji. "She even wants to
know if Pom can be married in April or May," Mamaji said excitedly.
"How propitious! That'll be the fifth wedding in the family in those two
months." Cousins Prakash and Dev, Cousin Pushpa (Bhaji Ganga Ram's
adopted daughter), and Auntie Vimla were all due to be married in
Lahore then.

"You still have time to change your mind," Daddyji said to Sister
Pom. "What do you really think of him?"

Sister Pom wouldn't say anything.   48

"How do you expect her to know what her mind is when all that the
two talked about was a picture and her bachelor's exam in May?" Sister
Umi demanded. "Could she have fallen in love already?"

"Love, Umi, means something very different from 'falling in love,'"
Daddyji said. "It's not an act but a lifelong process. The best we can do
as Pom's parents is to give her love every opportunity to grow."

"But doesn't your 'every opportunity' include knowing the person better than over a cup of tea, or whatever?" Sister Umi persisted.

"Yes, of course it does. But what we are discussing here is a simple   52
matter of choice — not love," Daddyji said. "To know a person, to love a person, takes years of living together."

"Do you mean, then, that knowing a person and loving a person are the same thing?" Sister Umi asked.

"Not quite, but understanding and respect are essential to love, and that cannot come from talking together, even over a period of days or months. That can come only in good time, through years of experience. It is only when Pom and Kakaji learn to consider each other's problems as one and the same that they will find love."

"But, Daddyji, look at the risk you're taking, the risk you're making Pom take," Sister Nimi said.

"We are trying to minimize the risk as much as we can by finding   56
Pom a family that is like ours," Daddyji said. "Kakaji is a dentist, I am a doctor. His life and way of thinking will be similar to mine. We are from the same caste, and Kakaji's family originally came from the Punjab. They eat meat and eggs, and they take religion in their stride, and don't pray every day and go to temples, like Brahmans. Kakaji knows how I walk into a club and how I am greeted there. The atmosphere in Pom's new home will be very much the same as the atmosphere here. Now, if I were to give Pom in marriage to a Brahman he'd expect Pom to live as he did. That would really be gambling."

"Then what you're doing is perpetuating the caste system," Sister Nimi said. She was the political rebel in the family. "You seem to presuppose that a Kshatriya should marry only a Kshatriya, that a Brahman should marry only a Brahman. I would just as soon marry a shopkeeper from the Bania caste or an Untouchable, and help to break down caste barriers."

"That day might come," Daddyji said. "But you will admit, Nimi, that by doing that you'd be increasing the odds."

"But for a cause I believe in," Sister Nimi said.

"Yes, but that's a whole other issue," Daddyji said.   60

"Daddyji, you say that understanding and respect are necessary for love," Sister Umi said. "I don't see why you would respect a person more because you lived with him and shared his problems."

"In our society, we think of understanding and respect as coming only through sacrifice," Daddyji said.

"Then you're advocating the subservience of women," Sister Nimi said, "because it's not Kakaji who will be expected to sacrifice — it's Pom. That's not fair."

"And why do you think that Pom will learn to respect Kakaji because   64
she sacrifices for him?" Sister Umi said, pressing her point.

"No, Umi, it is the other way around," Daddyji said. "It is Kakaji who will respect Pom because she sacrifices for him."

"But that doesn't mean that Pom will respect Kakaji," Sister Umi persisted.

"But if Kakaji is moved by Pom's sacrifices he will show more consideration for her. He will grow to love her. I know in my own case I was moved to the depths to see Shanti suffer so because she was so ill-prepared to be my wife. It took me long enough — too long, I believe — to reach that understanding, perhaps because I had broken away from the old traditions and had given in to Western influences."

"So you admit that Pom will have to suffer for years," Sister Umi said.   68

"Perhaps," Daddyji said. "But all that time she will be striving for ultimate happiness and love. Those are precious gifts that can only be cultivated in time."

"You haven't told us what this ultimate happiness is," Sister Umi said. "I don't really understand it."

"It is a uniting of ideals and purposes, and a merging of them. This is the tradition of our society, and it is the means we have adopted to make our marriages successful and beautiful. It works because we believe in the goodness of the individuals going into the marriage and rely on the strength of the sacred bond."

"But my ideal is to be independent," Sister Nimi said. "As you say,   72
'Think for yourself.'"

"But often you have to choose among ideals," Daddyji said. "You may have to choose between being independent and being married."

"But aren't you struck by the fact that all the suffering is going to be on Pom's part? Shouldn't Kakaji be required to sacrifice for their happiness, too?" Sister Nimi said, reverting to the old theme.

"There has to be a start," Daddyji said. "Remember, in our tradition it's her life that is joined with his; it is she who will forsake her past to build a new future with him. If both Pom and Kakaji were to be obstinate, were to compete with each other about who would sacrifice first, who would sacrifice more, what hope would there be of their ever getting on together, of their ever finding love?"

"Daddyji, you're evading the issue," Sister Nimi said. "Why shouldn't   76
he take the initiative in this business of sacrifice?"

"He would perhaps be expected to if Pom were working, too, as in the West, and, though married, leading a whole different life from his. I suppose more than this I really can't say, and there may be some injustice in our system, at that. In the West, they go in for romantic love, which is unknown among us. I'm not sure that that method works any better than our method does."

Then Daddyji said to Sister Pom, "I have done my best. Even after you marry Kakaji, my responsibility for you will not be over. I will always be there in the background if you should need me."

"I respect your judgment, Daddyji," Sister Pom said obediently. "I'll do what you say."

Mamaji consulted Shambu Pandit. He compared the horoscopes of   80
Sister Pom and Kakaji and set the date of the marriage for the eleventh of May. . . . "That's just three days after she finishes her B.A. finals!" we cried. "When will she study? You are sacrificing her education to some silly superstition."

But Shambu Pandit would not be budged from the date. "I am only going by the horoscopes of the couple," he said. "You might as well protest to the stars."

We appealed to Daddyji, but he said that he didn't want to interfere, because such matters were up to Mamaji. That was as much as to say that Shambu Pandit's date was a settled thing.

I recall that at about that time there was an engagement ceremony. We all — Daddyji, Mamaji, Sister Pom, many of our Mehta and Mehra relatives — sat cross-legged on the floor of the front veranda around Shambu Pandit. He recited the Gayatri Mantra, the simple prayer he used to tell us to say before we went to sleep, and made a thank offering of incense and ghi to a fire in a brazier, much as Mamaji did — behind Daddyji's back — when one of us was going on a trip or had recovered from a bout of illness. Servants passed around a platter heaped up with crumbly sweet balls. I heard Kakaji's sister, Billo, saying something to Sister Pom; she had just come from Dehra Dun bearing a sari, a veil, and the engagement ring for Sister Pom, after Romesh Chachaji, one of Daddyji's brothers, had gone to Dehra Dun bearing some money, a silver platter and silver bowls, and sweetmeats for Kakaji. It was the first time that I was able to think of Kakaji both as a remote and frightening dentist who was going to take Sister Pom away and as someone ordinary like us, who had his own family. At some point, Mamaji prodded me, and I scooted forward, crab fashion, to embrace Sister Pom. I felt her hand on my neck. It had something cold and metallic on it, which sent a shiver through me. I realized that she was wearing her engagement ring, and that until then Mamaji was the only one in our family who had worn a ring.

In the evening, the women relatives closeted themselves in the drawing   84 room with Sister Pom for the engagement singsong. I crouched outside with my ear to the door. The door pulsated with the beat of a barrel drum. The pulse in my forehead throbbed in sympathy with the beat as I caught snatches of songs about bedsheets and henna, along with explosions of laughter, the songs themselves rising and falling like the cooing of the doves that nested under the eaves of the veranda. I thought that a couple of years earlier I would have been playing somewhere outside on such an occasion, without knowing what I was missing, or been in the drawing room clapping and singing, but now I was crouching by the door like a thief, and was feeling ashamed even as I was captivated.

EXPLORATIONS

1. When Daddyji makes his opening announcement, Mehta writes, "We were stunned. We have never really faced the idea that Sister Pom might get married and suddenly leave, I thought." What other evidence in Mehta's narrative indicates that Pom has been treated as a child until a husband is found for her?

2. Judging from "Pom's Engagement," how is the traditional Indian concept of coming of age different for a woman and a man? What are the responsibilities of an adult woman? an adult man?

3. At what points and in what ways does Mehta reveal his feelings about his sister's change in status? What other clues suggest that Pom's engagement marks a coming of age for all the Mehta children?

4. Reading "Pom's Engagement" it is easy to forget that the author is blind. What sensory impressions does Mehta describe where a sighted writer might focus on what he or she sees? Give at least five examples.

CONNECTIONS

1. Compare Pom's social life in "Pom's Engagement" with Miguel's in Mario Vargas Llosa's "Sunday, Sunday." How are the limits on contact between young men and women different in India and Peru? How are each country's social restrictions different for males (Kakaji and Miguel) and for females (Pom and Flora)?

2. "Pom's Engagement" and Vladimir Nabokov's essay "From *Speak, Memory*" both show that the prospect of losing a family member can be deeply disturbing, whether the cause is a sister's marriage or a father's brush with death. What are Mehta's and Nabokov's central emotions when faced with such a loss? How does each author convey his response to his readers?

3. In her *Observation*, Olga Silverstein writes: "In adolescence you *have* to split off [from your mother]; otherwise, you feel too dependent, too cozy, too loved, too comfortable." How do you think Mehta would react to this statement with regard to his family? According to "Pom's Engagement," how is the mother-daughter split handled in India?

ELABORATIONS

1. Look back at Gyanranjan's "Our Side of the Fence and Theirs" (p. 28). Judging from that story and "Pom's Engagement," how do Indian assumptions about the role of marriage in a woman's (or man's) life differ from ours? Given Indian values and priorities, what are the advantages of their system of arranged marriages? What benefits might such a system have in the United States, with its high divorce rate and disintegrating nuclear family? Write an essay exploring one or more of these questions.

2. "Even as one part of us seeks to be an individual, another part longs to restore the safety and comfort of merging with another," writes Gail Sheehy of the years from age eighteen to twenty-two. "But people who marry during this time often prolong financial and emotional ties to the family and relatives that impede them from becoming self-sufficient." After reading "Pom's Engagement," how do you think Daddyji would respond to these statements? Write an essay comparing the balance between self-sufficiency and prolonged family ties in Indian and in American culture.

MARJORIE SHOSTAK

Nisa's Marriage

"Nisa's Marriage" comes from Marjorie Shostak's 1983 book *Nisa: The Life and Words of a !Kung Woman,* based on Shostak's two and a half years among the !Kung San of Botswana. (The *!* indicates a clicking sound.) At the time she was a research assistant on the Harvard Kalahari Desert Project, having previously received a bachelor's degree in English literature from Brooklyn College. Shostak, born in 1945, now teaches anthropology at Emory University in Atlanta. Among her current projects is a book tentatively titled *The Paleolithic Prescription: A Program of Diet and Exercise and a Design for Living.*

In her introduction Shostak writes: "Nisa is a member of one of the last remaining traditional gatherer-hunter societies, a group calling themselves the *Zhun/twasi,* the "real people," who currently live in isolated areas of Botswana, Angola, and Namibia. . . . They are also known as the !Kung Bushmen, the !Kung San, or simply the !Kung. They are short — averaging about five feet in height — lean, muscular, and, for Africa, light-skinned. They have high cheekbones and rather Oriental-looking eyes." Population biologists call these people Khoisan, from *Khoi,* the group previously known as Hottentots, and *San,* the group known as Bushmen, who together were the original inhabitants of South Africa (see p. 58).

Shostak describes meeting Nisa, who was then close to fifty years old: "Nisa wore an old blanket loosely draped over the remnants of a faded, flower-print dress, sizes too big. . . . [She] was all activity: constantly in motion, her face expressive, she spoke fast and was at once strong and surprisingly coquettish." In the following excerpt, the events Nisa describes took place more than thirty-five years earlier, just as she entered puberty.

The day of the wedding, everyone was there. All of Tashay's friends were sitting around, laughing and laughing. His younger brother said, "Tashay, you're too old. Get out of the way so I can marry her. Give her to me." And his nephew said, "Uncle, you're already old. Now, let *me* marry her." They were all sitting around, talking like that. They all wanted me.

I went to my mother's hut and sat there. I was wearing lots of beads and my hair was completely covered and full with ornaments.

That night there was another dance. We danced, and some people fell asleep and others kept dancing. In the early morning, Tashay and his relatives went back to their camp; we went into our huts to sleep. When morning was late in the sky, they came back. They stayed around and then his parents said, "Because we are only staying a short while — tomorrow, let's start building the marriage hut."

The next day they started. There were lots of people there — Tashay's   4
mother, my mother, and my aunt worked on the hut; everyone else sat around, talking. Late in the day, the young men went and brought Tashay to the finished hut. They set him down beside it and stayed there with him, sitting around the fire.

I was still at my mother's hut. I heard them tell two of my friends to go and bring me to the hut. I thought, "Oohh . . . I'll run away." When they came for me, they couldn't find me. They said, "Where did Nisa go? Did she run away? It's getting dark. Doesn't she know that things may bite and kill her?" My father said, "Go tell Nisa that if this is what she's going to do, I'll hit her and she won't run away again. What made her want to run away, anyway?

I was already far off in the bush. They came looking for me. I heard them calling, "Nisa . . . Nisa . . ." I sat down at the base of a tree. Then I heard Nukha, "Nisa . . . Nisao . . . my friend . . . a hyena's out there . . . things will bite and kill you . . . come back . . . Nisa . . . Nisao . . ."

When Nukha finally saw me, I started to run. She ran after me, chasing me and finally caught me. She called out to the others, "Hey! Nisa's here! Everyone, come! Help me! Take Nisa, she's here!"

They came and brought me back. Then they laid me down inside the   8
hut. I cried and cried. People told me, "A man is not something that kills you; he is someone who marries you, who becomes like your father or your older brother. He kills animals and gives you things to eat. Even tomorrow, while you are crying, Tashay may kill an animal. But when he returns, he won't give you any meat; only he will eat. Beads, too. He will get beads but he won't give them to you. Why are you so afraid of your husband and what are you crying about?"

I listened and was quiet. Later, we went to sleep. Tashay lay down beside the opening of the hut, near the fire, and I lay down inside; he thought I might try and run away again. He covered himself with a blanket and slept.

While it was dark, I woke up. I sat up. I thought, "How am I going to jump over him? How can I get out and go to mother's hut to sleep beside her?" I looked at him sleeping. Then came other thoughts, other thoughts in the middle of the night, "Eh . . . this person has just married me . . ." and I lay down again. But I kept thinking, "Why did people give me this man in marriage? The older people say he is a good person, yet . . ."

I lay there and didn't move. The rain came beating down. It fell steadily and kept falling. Finally, I slept. Much later dawn broke.

In the morning, Tashay got up and sat by the fire. I was so frightened   12
I just lay there, waiting for him to leave. When he went to urinate, I went and sat down inside my mother's hut.

That day, all his relatives came to our new hut — his mother, his father, his brothers . . . everyone! They all came. They said, "Go tell Nisa she should come and her in-laws will put the marriage oil on her. Can you see her sitting over there? Why isn't she coming so we can put the oil on her in her new hut?"

I refused to go. They kept calling for me until finally, my older brother said, "Uhn uhn. Nisa, if you act like this, I'll hit you. Now, get up and go over there. Sit over there so they can put the oil on you."

I still refused and just sat there. My older brother grabbed a switch from a nearby tree and started coming toward me. I got up. I was afraid. I followed him to where the others were sitting. Tashay's mother rubbed the oil on me and my aunt rubbed it on Tashay.

Then they left and it was just Tashay and me. . . .   16

That Zhun/twa, that Tashay, he really caused me pain.

Soon after we were married, he took me from my parents' village to live at his parents' village. At first my family came and lived with us, but then one day they left, left me with Tashay and his parents. That's when I started to cry. Tashay said, "Before your mother left, you weren't crying. Why didn't you tell me you wanted to go with them? We could have followed along." I said, "I was afraid of you. That's why I didn't tell you."

But I still wanted to be with my mother, so later that day, I ran away. I ran as fast as I could until I finally caught up with them. When my mother saw me she said, "Someday a hyena is going to kill this child in the bush. She's followed us. Here she is!" I walked with them back to their village and lived with them a while.

A long time passed. One day Tashay left and came to us. When I   20
saw him, I started to cry. He said, "Get up. We're going back." I said, "Why does this person keep following me? Do I own him that he fol-

lows me everywhere?" My father said, "You're crazy. A woman follows her husband when he comes for her. What are you just sitting here for?"

Tashay took me with him and I didn't really refuse. We continued to live at his village and then we all went and lived at another water hole. By then, I knew that I was no longer living with my mother. I had left my family to follow my husband.

We lived and lived and then, one day, my heart started to throb and my head hurt; I was very sick. My father came to visit and went into a medicinal trance to try and cure me. When I was better, he left and I stayed behind.

After Tashay and I had been living together for a long time, we started to like each other with our hearts and began living nicely together. It was really only after we had lived together for a long time that he touched my genitals. By then, my breasts were already big.

We were staying in my parents' village the night he first had sex with   24
me and I didn't really refuse. I agreed, just a little, and he lay with me. But the next morning, I was sore. I took some leaves and wound them around my waist, but I continued to feel pain. I thought, "Ooo . . . what has he done to my insides that they feel this way?"

I went over to my mother and said, "That person, last night . . . I'm only a child, but last night he had sex with me. Move over and let me eat with you. We'll eat and then we'll move away. Mother . . . mother . . ."

My mother turned to my father and said, "Get up, get a switch and hit this child. She's ruining us. Get up and find something to hit her with." I thought, "What? Did I say something wrong?"

My father went to find a switch. I got up and ran to my aunt's hut. I sat there and thought, "What was so bad? How come I talked about something yet . . . is that something so terrible?"

My father said to my aunt, "Tell Nisa to come back here so I can beat   28
her. The things this young girl talks about could crack open the insides of her ears."

My mother said, "This child, her talk is terrible. As I am now, I would stick myself with a poison arrow; but my skin itself fears and that's why I won't do it. But if she continues to talk like that, I will!"

They wanted me to like my husband and not to refuse him. My mother told me that when a man sleeps with his wife, she doesn't tell; it's a private thing.

I got up and walked away from them. I was trembling, "Ehn . . . nn
. . . nn . . ." I looked at my genitals and thought, "Oh, this person
. . . yesterday he took me and now my genitals are ruined!" I took some
water and washed my genitals, washed and washed.

Because, when my genitals first started to develop, I was afraid. I'd   32
look at them and cry and think something was wrong with them. But
people told me, "Nothing's wrong. That's what you yourself are like."

I also thought that an older person, an adult like my husband, would
tear me apart, that his penis would be so big that he would hurt me.
Because I hadn't known older men. I had only played sex play with little
boys. Then, when Tashay did sleep with me and it hurt, that's when I
refused. That's also when I told. But people didn't yell at him, they only
yelled at me, and I was ashamed.

That evening, we lay down again. But this time, before he came in,
I took a leather strap, held my leather apron tightly against my legs, tied
the strap around my genitals, and then tied it to the hut's frame. I was
afraid he'd tear me open and I didn't want him to take me again.

The two of us lay there and after a long time, he touched me. When
he touched my stomach, he felt the leather strap. He felt around to see
what it was. He said, "What is this woman doing? Last night she lay with
me so nicely when I came to her. Why has she tied her genitals up this
way? What is she refusing to give me?"

He sat me up and said, "Nisa . . . Nisa . . . what happened? Why   36
are you doing this?" I didn't answer. He said, "What are you so afraid of
that you had to tie up your genitals?" I said, "Uhn, uhn. I'm not afraid
of anything." He said, "No, now tell me. In the name of what you did,
I'm asking you."

Then he said, "What do you think you're doing when you do something like this? When you lie down with me, a Zhun/twa like yourself,
it's as though you were lying with another, a stranger. We are both Zhun/
twasi, yet you tied yourself up!"

I said, "I refuse to lie down with anyone who wants to take my genitals.
Last night you had sex with me and today my insides hurt. That's why
I've tied myself up and that's why you won't take me again."

He said, "Untie the strap. Do you see me as someone who kills people?
Am I going to eat you? No, I'm not going to kill you, but I have married
you and want to make love to you. Do you think I married you thinking
I wouldn't make love to you? Did you think we would just live beside
each other? Do you know any man who has married a woman and who
just lives beside her without having sex with her?"

I said, "I don't care. I don't want sex. Today my insides hurt and I   40
refuse." He said, "Mm, today you will just lie there, but tomorrow, I
will take you. If you refuse, I'll pry your legs open and take you by force."

He untied the strap and said, "If this is what use you put this to, I'm
going to destroy it." He took his knife and cut it into small pieces. Then
he put me down beside him. He didn't touch me; he knew I was afraid.
Then we went to sleep.

The next day we got up, did things, and ate things. When we returned
to our hut that night, we lay down again. That's when he forced himself
on me. He held my legs and I struggled against him. But I knew he
would have sex with me and I thought, "This isn't helping me at all.
This man, if he takes me by force, he'll really hurt me. So I'll just lie
here, lie still and let him look for the food he wants. But I still don't
know what kind of food I have because even if he eats he won't be full."[1]

So I stopped fighting and just lay there. He did his work and that time
it didn't hurt so much. Then he lay down and slept.

After that, we just lived. I began to like him and he didn't bother me   44
again, he didn't try to have sex with me. Many months passed — those
of the rainy season, those of the winter season, and those of the hot
season. He just left me alone and I grew up and started to understand about things. Because before that, I hadn't really known about
men. . . .

We continued to live and it was as if I was already an adult. Because,
beginning to menstruate makes you think about things. Only then did I
bring myself to understand, only then did I begin to be a woman.

When Tashay wanted to lie with me, I no longer refused. We just
had sex together, one day and then another. In the morning, I'd get up
and sit beside our hut and I wouldn't tell. I'd think, "My husband is
indeed my husband now. What people told me, that my husband is
mine, is true."

We lived and lived, the two of us, together, and after a while I started
to really like him and then, to love him. I had finally grown up and had
learned how to love. I thought, "A man has sex with you. Yes, that's
what a man does. I had thought that perhaps he didn't."

We lived on and I loved him and he loved me. I loved him the way   48

---

[1]Food and eating are universally used by the !Kung as metaphors for sex. However, they
claim no knowledge or practice of oral-genital contact.

a young adult knows how to love; I just *loved* him. Whenever he went away and I stayed behind, I'd miss him. I'd think, "Oh, when is my husband ever coming home? How come he's been gone so long?" I'd miss him and want him. When he'd come back my heart would be happy, "Eh, hey! My husband left and once again has come back."

We lived and when he wanted me, I didn't refuse; he just lay with me. I thought, "Why had I been so concerned about my genitals? They aren't that important, after all. So why was I refusing them?"

I thought that and gave myself to him, gave and gave. We lay with each other and my breasts were very large. I was becoming a woman.

EXPLORATIONS

1. What are Nisa's responses to her wedding? to being married? What events in her narrative play the most important role in her formal social transition from childhood to adulthood? in her personal psychological transition?

2. Judging from "Nisa's Marriage," what specific rituals are part of a Zhun/twasi wedding? What is the practical or symbolic (or both) purpose of each ritual?

3. What facts can you glean about the Zhun/twasi way of life from "Nisa's Marriage"? What appears to be the group's main food source? What dangers do they fear? What metaphoric examples can you find of these basic elements of their existence in their speech?

4. When Nisa runs home to her mother after having sex with her husband, her mother says, "As I am now, I would stick myself with a poison arrow; but my skin itself fears and that's why I won't do it. But if she continues to talk like that, I will!" What does she mean? How might an American mother express the same sentiments?

CONNECTIONS

1. What common rituals and related features appear in Ved Mehta's "Pom's Engagement" and in "Nisa's Marriage"? What can you deduce from these two accounts about the universal functions of marriage as a social institution?

2. What attitudes toward marriage do Pom and Nisa share? When, how, and why does each girl resist her parents' plans for her? Why do you think both Pom and Nisa ultimately yield to their parents' wishes?

3. By the end of her narrative, how does Nisa feel about moving from childhood

to womanhood? What statements in Mario Vargas Llosa's "Sunday, Sunday" indicate a comparable response by Miguel? Look back at Gail Sheehy's *Observation*. In Sheehy's terms, what do Nisa and Miguel evidently believe they have achieved?

ELABORATIONS

1. Reread Olga Silverstein's *Observation* on the separation between mother and daughter, and Gail Sheehy's on pulling up roots. Write an essay using Silverstein's and Sheehy's ideas to identify Nisa's feelings and explain her behavior in "Nisa's Marriage."

2. Nisa resists being thrown out of the parental nest, but finally she capitulates. Write an essay in which you either classify the tactics her old and new families use to push her into adulthood, or compare the Zhun/twasi tactics with your own family's at some point when you faced a new and scary experience.

AMOS OZ

If There Is Justice

Born Amos Klausner in Jerusalem in 1939, Amos Oz belongs to the first generation of Israeli writers who are sabras (native born). His grandfather had fled anti-Semitism in Russia and Poland to help build an ideal Jewish state in Palestine. As a schoolchild Oz filled sandbags after the British departure in 1948. Four years later, as the fledgling state of Israel struggled to accommodate over a million refugees, Oz's mother committed suicide. Her son cast off his father's scholarly right-wing Zionism to become a peasant-soldier on Kibbutz Hulda, midway between Jerusalem (then half in Israel and half in Jordan) and Tel Aviv to the north. There Oz took his new last name, which means "strength" in Hebrew; worked in the cotton fields; studied socialism; and eventually was sent to Hebrew University in Jerusalem for his bachelor's degree. On his return he adopted the routine he still follows: teaching in the high school, doing assigned chores, and writing stories and novels involving kibbutz life and ideals. Except for fellowships at Oxford and Hebrew Universities, and a lecture tour of United States campuses, Oz (who has won several international literary awards) continues to live with his wife and three children at Kibbutz Hulda.

"If There Is Justice" was translated from the Hebrew by Nicholas de Lange with assistance from the author. It comes from Oz's novel *Elsewhere, Perhaps,* which was published in Israel shortly before the Six-Day War in 1967. Oz served with Israeli armored divisions in that war, which ended in Israel's almost doubling its roughly 8000-square-mile territory by occupying Syria's Golan Heights to the north, Jordan's West Bank to the east (including Jerusalem), and the Gaza Strip, formerly administered by Egypt, to the southeast. The conflict between Jews and Arabs in this region is more than 3000 years old (human habitation dates back at least 100,000 years), and it has shaped not only Oz's writing but his homeland.

(For more background on Israel, see p. 14.)

Rami Rimon came home for the weekend on leave.

His face was thinner. His skin had shrunk a little. His jaws seemed more prominent. The lines on his face were sharper. His mother's face struggling to get out. Fine creases ringed his mouth. The sun had etched wrinkles round his eyes. Twin furrows ran from his nose to the corners of his mouth.

He was wearing an impeccable greenish uniform, with his beret tucked in his pocket. His stout boots were shod with steel at toe and heel. His sleeves were rolled up to reveal hairy forearms, and his hands were covered with little scars. He was conscious of his manly appearance as he strode slowly across the yard with an air of studied indifference. The men and women he met greeted him warmly. He responded with an offhand nod. There were traces of gun grease under his fingernails, and his left elbow was dressed with a grubby bandage.

When the first tumult of hugs and kisses, received by Rami with a   4
wavering smile, had died down, Fruma said:

"Well, you won't believe it, but I was just thinking of you the moment before you turned up. Mother's intuition."

Rami thought there was nothing strange in that. He had said in his letter that he would come on Friday afternoon, and she knew perfectly well what time the bus came. As he spoke, he put down his shabby kit bag, pulled his shirt outside his trousers, lit a cigarette, and laid a heavy hand on Fruma's shoulder.

"It's good to see you, Mom. I wanted to tell you that I'm really glad to see you again."

Fruma glanced at his dusty boots and said: 8

"You've lost so much weight."

Rami drew on his cigarette and asked about her health.

"Come inside and have a shower before dinner. You're all sweaty. Would you like a cold drink first? No. A warm drink would be better for you. Wait, though, the first thing is to take you along to the surgery. I want the nurse to have a look at your elbow."

Rami started to explain about the wound. It happened during a bayonet   12 practice; the clumsy oaf of a section commander . . . but Fruma did not let him finish the story.

"There you go dropping your ash on the floor. I've just washed it in your honor. There are four ash trays in the house, and you . . ."

Rami sat down in his filthy clothes on the clean white bedspread and kicked off his boots. Fruma rushed to fetch her husband's old slippers. Her eyes were dry, but she tried to turn her face away from her son to hide the look he disliked so much. Rami, however, pretended not to have seen that strained look, as of a dam about to burst. He lay back on the bed, looked up at the ceiling, drew the ash tray that Fruma had put in his hand closer to him, and blew out a puff of smoke.

"The day before yesterday we crossed a river on a rope bridge. Two ropes stretched one above the other, one to walk on and the other to hold. With all our stuff on our backs, spade, blankets, gun, ammunition, the lot. Now, who do you suppose it was who lost his balance and fell in the water? The section commander! We all . . ."

Fruma eyed her son and exclaimed: 16

"You've lost at least ten pounds. Have you had any lunch? Where? No, you haven't. I'll dash across to the hall and get you something to eat. Just a snack — I'll make you a proper meal when you've had a rest. How about some raw carrot? It's very good for you. Are you sure? I can't force you. All right, then, have a shower and go to sleep. You can eat when you wake up. But perhaps I'd better take you to the surgery right away. Wait a minute. Here's a nice glass of orange juice. Don't argue, drink it."

"I jumped in the water and fished him out," Rami continued. "Then I had to dive in again to look for his rifle. Poor wretch! It was hilarious. It wasn't his first accident, though. Once, on an exercise . . ."

"You need some new socks. They're all falling apart," Fruma remarked as she pulled his dirty laundry out of the kit bag.

"Once, on an exercise, he fired his submachine gun by accident.   20
Nearly killed the battalion commander. He's the clumsiest fool you can imagine. You can tell what he's like from his name. He's called Zalman Zulman. I've written a song about him, and we sing it all day long. Listen."

"But they don't feed you there. And you didn't write every other day, as you promised. But I saw in the letter box that you wrote to Noga Harish. That's life. Your mother works her fingers to the bone, and some child comes and collects the honey. It doesn't matter now. There's something I must know: Did she answer your letter? No? Just as I thought. You don't know what she's like. It was just as well you ditched her. Everybody knows what she is. The mistress of a man who's old enough to be her grandfather. It's disgusting. Disgusting. Have you got enough razor blades? It's disgusting, I tell you."

"Is it true they're starting to work the Camel's Field? That's going to cause a flare-up, all right. Provided, of course, the powers that be don't get cold feet. You know, Jewish sentimentality and all that. My buddies say . . ."

"Go and have a shower. The water's just right now. No, I heard every word. Test me. 'Jewish sentimentality.' There aren't many boys of your age with such an independent way of thinking. After your shower you can have a nap. Meanwhile, I'll ask the nurse to come here. That wound looks very nasty. You've got to have it seen to."

"By the way, Mom, did you just say that she . . ."   24

"Yes, son?"

"All right. Never mind. It doesn't matter now."

"Tell me, tell me what you need. I'm not tired. I can do anything
you want me to."

"No, thanks, I don't need anything. I just wanted to say something,   28
but it's not important. It's irrelevant. I've forgotten. Stop running around.
I can't bear it. We'll talk this evening. Meanwhile, you must have a rest,
too."

"Me! I'll rest in my grave. I don't need to rest. I'm not tired. When
you were a baby, you had something wrong with your ears. A chronic
infection. There weren't any antibiotics then. You cried all night, night
after night. You were in pain. And you've always been a sensitive boy. I
rocked your cradle all night, night after night, and sang you songs. One
does everything for children, without counting the cost. You won't repay
me. You'll repay it to your own children. I won't be here any more, but
you'll be a good father, because you're so sensitive. You don't think about
rest when you're doing something for your children. How old were you
then? You've forgotten all about it. It was the time when Yoash started
going to school, so it must have been when you were eighteen months
old. You were always a delicate child. Here am I rambling on, and you
need to sleep. Go to sleep now."

"By the way, Mom, if you're going to the surgery could you bring me
some corn ointment. You won't forget, will you?"

At five o'clock Rami woke up, put on a clean white shirt and gray
trousers, quietly helped himself to a snack, and then went to the basketball
field. On the way he met Einav, limping awkwardly. She asked how he
was. He said he was fine. She asked if it was a hard life. He said he was
ready to face any hardship. She asked if his mother was pleased with him
and answered her own question:

"Of course Fruma's pleased with you. You're so bronzed and hand-   32
some."

The field was floodlit, but the light was not noticeable in the bright
twilight. The only living souls there were Oren's gang. Rami put his
hands in his pockets and stood for a while without doing or saying
anything. The Sabbath will go by. Empty. Without anything happening.
With mother. Sticky. What do I need? A cigarette. That thin boy playing
by himself over there in the corner is called Ido Zohar. Once I caught

him sitting in the common room at night writing a poem. What was I saying? A cigarette.

Rami put the cigarette to his mouth and two planes roared by, shattering the Sabbatical calm, hidden in the twilight glow. The dying sun struck sparks off their fuselage. The metal shone back dazzlingly. In a flash Rami realized that they were not our planes. They had the enemy's markings on their wings. An excited shout burst from his throat.

"Theirs!"

Instinctively he looked down, just long enough to hear Oren's confused   36
cry, but by the time he looked up again the drama was almost over. The enemy planes had turned tail and were fleeing from other planes that were approaching powerfully from the southwest, evidently trying to block their escape. Instantly, dark shapes fell through the air toward the orchards to the north. Both planes had jettisoned the spare fuel tanks fixed to their wings to speed their flight. Rami clenched his fists and growled through his teeth, "Let them have it." Before he had finished there was an answering burst of gunfire. Lightning flashed. After what seemed a long interval, there came a dull roll of thunder. The fate of the raid was settled in an instant. The enemy planes disappeared over the mountains, one of them trailing a cloud of white smoke mixed with gray. Their pursuers paused, circled the valley twice like angry hounds, then vanished into the darkening sky.

Oren shouted jubilantly:

"We hit one! We smashed one! We brought one down!"

And Rami Rimon, like a child, not like a soldier, hugged Oren Geva and exclaimed:

"I hope they burn! I hope they burn to death!"   40

He pounded Oren's ribs exultantly with his fists until Oren drew away groaning with pain. Rami was seized by demented joy.

His joy accompanied him to the dining hall, where a spirit of noisy excitement reigned. He made his way among the tables to where Noga Harish stood in her best dress, looking at the notice board. He put his hands on her shoulders and whispered in her ear:

"Well, silly girl, did you see or didn't you?"

Noga turned to face him with a condescending smile.   44

"Good Sabbath, Rami. You're very brown. It suits you. You look happy."

"I . . . I saw it all. From beginning to end. I was up at the basketball field. Suddenly I heard a noise to the east, and I realized at once that . . ."

"You're like my little brother. You're cute. You're happy."

These remarks encouraged Rami. He spoke up boldly: 48

"Shall we go outside? Will you come outside with me?"

Noga thought for a moment. Then she smiled inwardly, with her eyes, not with her mouth.

"Why not?" she said.

"Come on then," said Rami, and took hold of her arm. Almost at   52 once he let it go.

When they were outside the dining hall, Noga said:

"Where shall we go?"

Strangely enough, at that moment Noga remembered something she had forgotten: Rami's full name was Avraham. Avraham Rominov.

"Anywhere," Rami said. "Let's go."   56

Noga suggested they sit down on the yellow bench, facing the door of the dining hall. Rami was embarrassed. People would see them there, he said. And stare at them. And talk.

Noga smiled again, and again she asked calmly, "Why not?"

Rami could find no answer to her question. He crossed his legs, took a cigarette out of his shirt pocket, tapped it three times on his matchbox, stuck in in the corner of his mouth, struck a match, shielded the flame with both hands even though there was no wind, inhaled deeply with half-closed eyes, blew out a long stream of smoke, and when all this was done, lowered his eyes to the ground once more. Finally, he gave her a sidelong glance and began:

"Well? What have you got to say for yourself?"   60

Noga replied that she hadn't been going to say anything. On the contrary, she thought it was he who was going to do the talking.

"Oh, nothing special. Just . . . What do you expect me to do?" he suddenly burst out violently. "Spend the whole evening, the whole Sabbath, my whole leave with my mother, like some mother's darling?"

"Why not? She's missed you badly."

"Why not? Because . . . All right. I can see I bore you. Don't think   64 I can't live without you. I can get on quite well without you. Do you think I can't?"

Noga said she was sure he could manage perfectly well without her.

They fell silent.

Hasia Ramigolski and Esther Klieger-Isarov came toward them, chatting in Yiddish and laughing. When they caught sight of Noga and Rami their conversation stopped dead. As they walked past, Hasia said:

"Good evening. Shabbat Shalom." She dwelt suggestively on the   68
stressed syllables.

Rami grunted, but Noga smiled and said gently:

"A very good evening to you both."

Rami said nothing for a while. Then he murmured:

"Well?"   72

"I'm listening."

"I hear they're going to start working on the hill," Rami said. "There's going to be trouble."

"It's so pointless."

Rami quickly changed the subject. He told the story of his section 76
commander who had fallen in the water trying to demonstrate how to cross a river on a rope bridge. He went on to say that it wasn't the poor fool's first accident. "Once, on an exercise, he accidently fired his submachine gun and nearly killed the battalion commander. You can tell what he's like from his name. He's called Zalman Zulman, of all things. I've written a rhyme about him:

> "Zalman Zulman's full of fun,
> Always letting off his gun.
> Zalman Zulman lost his grip,
> Took an unexpected dip.
> Zalman Zulman . . ."

"Just a minute. Does he play an instrument?"

"Who?"

"Zalman. The man you were talking about. What's the matter with your elbow?"

"What's that got to do with it?" Rami asked indignantly.   80

"With what?"

"With what we were talking about."

"You were telling me about someone called Zalman. I asked if he played an instrument. You haven't answered my question."

"But I don't see what . . ."   84

"You're very brown. It suits you."

"It's hardly surprising. We train all day in the sun. Of course we get brown. Listen: we went on a fifty-mile route march, with all the kit, gun, pack, spade, and all at the trot. Eight of the people in my squad . . ."

"Chilly, don't you think?"

". . . collapsed on the way. And we had to carry them on stretchers.   88 I . . ."

"I'm cold. Couldn't you finish the story tomorrow? If you don't mind terribly."

"What's the matter?" Rami considered, and then asked thickly, "What's up? Is somebody waiting for you? Are you rushing off to . . . to keep an appointment?"

"Yes, I've got to take my father his dinner. He isn't well."

"What, again?" Rami asked absently. Noga explained that he had a   92 pain in his chest and the doctor had ordered him to go to bed.

"Next week he's got to go and have an examination. That's all. Shall we meet here again tomorrow afternoon?"

Rami did not answer. He lit another cigarette and threw the lighted match away behind the bench. Noga said good night and started to go. Then she stopped, turned, and said:

"Don't smoke too much."

At that moment five steps separated them. Rami asked irritably why   96 she should care whether he smoked a lot or a little. Noga ignored his question and said:

"You're very brown. It suits you. Good night."

Rami said nothing. He sat alone on the bench until the dancing started in the square, as it did every Friday night at a quarter past nine.

When it was over, shortly before midnight, he set off for his mother's room. He changed his course, however, because he met Dafna Isarov, who asked him if he was going home to bed already, and Rami thought he detected a sneer in her voice. So he turned off the path. His feet guided him toward the cow shed, where he had worked before he was called up. And as he walked he talked to himself.

This could never have happened to Yoash. It's happened to me,   100 though. Women understand only one language, brute force. But, as mother said, I was always a delicate child. Hell. Now they're laughing. Everybody wants something bad to happen to someone else so as to make life more interesting. It's like that everywhere; it's like that on the kibbutz and it's even like that in the army. You're a child you're a child you're a child. You're like my little brother. Maybe being brown does suit me, but it hasn't got me anywhere. She didn't insult me for once. She didn't even call me a horse. What did she do to me tonight, how did she make fun of me? My Rami is a delicate, sensitive boy. I wish I could die. That'd show them. I can bend this sprinkler with my bare hands. That'll drive Theodor Herzl Goldring mad. I've got stronger hands than Yoash. If only he weren't dead, I'd show him. Where am I going? Walking around like some Jack looking for his Jill. Leaping on the mountains, skipping in the hills, as that filthy old lecher would say. People like that ought to be put down. Like Arabs. Punch him in the face, he raises his hands to protect himself, you hit him in the stomach and give him a kick for good measure. All over. Here we are at the cow shed. Hey, Titan, good bull. Are you awake? Bulls sleep standing up because they can't lie down because of the iron ring. If they come to slaughter you, Titan, don't let them. Don't give in. Show your mettle. Don't be a ghetto bull. Give them a *corrida*. We mustn't give in without a struggle. We must be strong and quick and light and violent like a jet fighter. Swoop and dart and turn and soar like a knife flashing through the sky like a fighter. A fighter is such a powerful thing. I could have been a pilot, but Mother.

Strange that the moon is shining. The moon does strange things. Changes things strangely. Changes the colors of things. Silver. My Rami is a delicate sensitive child Rami writes poems like Izo Zohar he loves nature hell he loves plants and animals hope they burn to death. Her father has a pain in his chest. It's because of old Berger. Dirty old man. Her father taught us a poem by Bialik once, called "The Slaughter," where it says that there is no justice in this world. It's true. It's a ghetto poem, but it's true. He's lived his life, he's got grown-up children, he's found his niche. Why did he steal her from me? What have I done to him? And she said I was brown and handsome. If I'm brown and handsome, and he's old and fat, then why.

When I die, she'll know. It'll shatter her. The moon colors everything white. Silver. Listen, Noga, listen. I've also got a pain in my chest, I'm also in pain, so why don't you. I make fun of Zalman Zulman, she makes fun of me, they all make fun of me. It shows there isn't any justice in the world, only slaughter, Titan, worse than anything the Devil could invent. That's from the same poem. The man who's being slaughtered starts thinking about justice. The man who's slaughtering him thinks only about violence. My mistake was not to use force on her. Why, Titan, why didn't I use force, do you know why? I'll tell you. Because my Rami is a delicate boy curse them he loves nature hope they burn

he loves plants and animals filthy whores. That sounds like planes over-
head. It's after midnight. I love these planes, roaring along without lights.
There's going to be a big war. I'll die. Then they'll know.

The fish ponds. A light in Grisha's hut. A pressure lamp. I can hear
Grisha's voice. In the boat. Shouting to his fishermen. He's been in three
wars and he's come out alive.

Maybe Dafna, his daughter. Ridiculous. They'd laugh. What's in this 104
filthy shed? Barrels. Sacks of fish food. The fishermen's supper. If they
find me here. Grisha's belt. A pistol. It's a revolver. Fancy leaving a
revolver in an empty shed. They'll be coming back to eat soon. They'll
laugh, they'll laugh. They'll say I went for a walk to look for inspiration.
I know how it works. It has a revolving drum with six chambers. You
put a bullet in each chamber. After each shot the drum revolves and
brings another bullet in line with the barrel. That's how the revolver
works. Now let's see how Rami Rimon works. A trial. Without a judge.
I'm the judge. Now let's begin.

Rami takes a bullet out of the leather holster, a yellow metal case
containing a little brown metal projectile. First of all, he puts the bullet
in his mouth. A sharp, metallic taste. Then he puts the bullet in one of
the chambers. He spins the drum without looking, because luck must be
blind. He puts the gun to his temple. The chances are five to one. He
squeezes the trigger. A dry thud. Rami inserts a second bullet. Spins the
blind drum. Four to two. Gun to temple. Squeezes. Dry thud. Maybe
I'm being silly. We'll soon know, Judge. I'm not trying to kill myself. It's
only an experiment. Up to five. A delicate sensitive child couldn't do
this. A third bullet. Blind spin. Cold damp hand. I've touched something
damp. If I can do this, I'm not a delicate sensitive child. Up to five. Gun
to temple. Squeeze the trigger. Dry thud. I'm past halfway. Two more
tries. Fourth bullet. Now the odds are against me. Now comes the test.
Watch carefully, Judge. Spin. Slowly. The drum, slowly. Without looking. Slowly. Temple. You're crazy. But you're no coward. Slowly
squeeze. It's cold here.

Now the fifth. Last one. Like an injection. Delicate sensitive child's
trembling. Why? Nothing will happen because nothing's happened so
far, even though according to the odds I should have died with the fourth
bullet. Don't tremble, dear little delicate child who cried all night with
earache, don't tremble, think of Grisha Isarov who's come out of three
wars alive. Yoash wouldn't have trembled, because he was Yoash. Little
ghetto boy, with a little cap and a gray coat and side curls. I want to

know how many I. Not to kill myself. Four. That's enough. Madness to
go on. No, we said five — five let it be. Don't change your mind,
coward, don't lie, you said five, not four. Five let it be. Put the gun to
your temple. Now squeeze, horse, squeeze, you're a ghetto child, you're
a little boy, you're my little brother, squeeze. Wait a moment. I'm allowed
to think first. Suppose I die here. She'll know. She'll know I wasn't
joking. But they'll say "broken heart" they'll say "unrequited love" they'll
say "emotional crisis." Sticky, very sticky. Hell. Squeeze. You won't feel
a thing. A bullet in the brain is instant death. No time for pain. And
afterward? Like plunging through the sky. An invisible fighter. It doesn't
hurt. Perhaps I've already pressed the trigger and died perhaps when you
die nothing changes. Other people see a corpse blood bones and you
carry on as usual. I can try again. If I press the trigger, it's a sign I'm still
alive. Afterward everything will be black and warm. When you die it's
warm even though the body gets cold. Warm and safe like under a
blanket in winter. And quiet. Squeeze. You've got a chance. Like when
we used to play dice when I was little and sometimes I wanted very badly
to throw a six and I threw a six. Now I want very badly to press the
trigger but my finger won't press. Trembling. Careful you don't press it
accidentally. Everything is different when the moon shines yellow. Can
hear Grisha cursing next week we're going to the firing range that'll be
interesting I'll be top of the class I'm an excellent shot now count up to
three and shoot. Eyes open. No. Eyes closed. No. One, two, th- no. Up
to ten. One, two, three, four, five, six, seven, eight, nine, t-.

But Rami Rimon did not try his luck the fifth time. He put down the
revolver and went out into the fields and wandered about till his feet
guided him back to the cow shed. Grisha won't notice. And if he does,
he'll have a shock. I forget to check the most important thing. I didn't
look inside the gun to see what would have happened if I'd pressed the
fifth time. Better not to know. Some things are better left undone.

A new thought occurred to Rami. It soothed him like a gentle caress. 108
Not all men are born to be heroes. Maybe I wasn't born to be a hero.
But in every man there's something special, something that isn't in other
men. In my nature, for instance, there's a certain sensitivity. A capacity
to suffer and feel pain. Perhaps I was born to be an artist, or even a
doctor. Some women go for doctors and others go for artists. Men aren't
all cast in the same mold. It's true. I'm not Yoash. But Yoash wasn't
me. I've got some things he didn't have. A painter, perhaps.

It'll be morning soon. Planes in the sky. Sad Zalman Zulman's full of fun, always letting off his gun. Zalman Zulman lost his grip, took an unexpected dip. Zalman Zulman, whore like me, looking for justice in the w.c. Zalman Zulman go to bed, time to rest your weary head.

I composed the poem. I can abolish it. It's an abolished poem.

EXPLORATIONS

1. Who is Yoash? What can you tell about him from the story? What is his current significance to Rami? to Fruma?

2. How does Rami feel about his mother's view of him as a "delicate sensitive child"? What kind of person does he want to be, and what kind of person does he think he is?

3. How has Rami's self-image — the qualities he sees as desirable and undesirable in himself — evidently been affected by his role as a soldier? by living in a close-knit, war-oriented community?

4. What does Rami learn from his game of Russian roulette? Why does he start it? Why does he stop?

CONNECTIONS

1. Like Nisa in Marjorie Shostak's "Nisa's Marriage," Rami Rimon fills a dual social position: part child, part adult. How do the Israeli and Zhun/twasi cultures apparently differ in their definition of adulthood? What larger contrasts in values and priorities are reflected by these differences?

2. Rami's dilemma in "If There Is Justice" bears several resemblances to Miguel's dilemma in Mario Vargas Llosa's "Sunday, Sunday." What is the role in each story of religion? attraction to the opposite sex? loyalty and conflict between male friends? What similar revelations mark the end of each story?

3. Compare the coming-of-age rituals described by Amos Oz in "If There Is Justice," Marjorie Shostak in "Nisa's Marriage," Ved Mehta in "Pom's Engagement," and Mario Vargas Llosa in "Sunday, Sunday." How do these rituals differ for boys and girls, and why?

ELABORATIONS

1. Write an essay explaining Oz's story title, "If There Is Justice." What theme(s) does the title reflect? How do specific incidents, such as Rami Rimon's game of Russian roulette, exemplify or illuminate the story's larger theme(s)?

2. In "Why Kibbutzim?" (p. 14), Bruno Bettelheim discusses how and why the kibbutzniks' child-rearing system evolved. In "If There Is Justice," Amos Oz focuses on a young man whose home is a kibbutz. Based on Bettelheim's essay and Oz's story, write an essay comparing the kibbutz way of life with the traditional social structure it supplanted.

PART THREE

WOMEN AND MEN

Images of the Opposite Sex

OBSERVATIONS:
LOOKING AT OURSELVES

Adam Smith, Dena Justin, Joe Kane,
Gloria Steinem, Susan Brownmiller, Gayle Early,
David Owen, Amy Gross, Anne Roiphe

<><><><><>

Isak Dinesen, *From "Daguerreotypes"* (DENMARK)

Santha Rama Rau, *Boris's Romance* (SOVIET UNION)

Beverley Hooper, *Falling in Love with Love* (CHINA)

Octavio Paz, *My Life with the Wave* (MEXICO)

Simone de Beauvoir, *Woman as Other* (FRANCE)

Alberto Moravia, *The Chase* (ITALY)

Naila Minai, *Women in Early Islam* (ISLAMIC WORLD)

Cherry Lindholm and Charles Lindholm, *Life Behind the Veil*
(PAKISTAN)

Yashar Kemal, *A Dirty Story* (TURKEY)

ESSENTIAL TO THE SURVIVAL OF HUMANITY IS THE BOND BETWEEN A woman and a man. Recognizing its importance, nearly every culture creates a social structure of rules, expectations, ideals, and rituals around this central relationship. Yet perhaps in no other aspect of existence is the contrast between cultures so striking. We differ not only in our courtship and marriage customs, but in our basic assumptions about what love is, what constitutes a good reason for two (or more) people to marry or divorce, and even how women and men are fundamentally different.

It is this last subject — the variety of ways men and women perceive each other — on which we focus here. *Observations: Looking at Ourselves* are diverse: Adam Smith on updated fairy tales, Dena Justin on witches and wizards, and Joe Kane on competition over power. Gloria Steinem praises positive thinking about womanhood; Susan Brownmiller examines femininity; Gayle Early outlines the John Wayne image; David Owen covets a "work wife"; Amy Gross appreciates androgynous men; and Anne Roiphe confesses female chauvinism.

Moving abroad, in "From 'Daguerreotypes,'" Danish writer Isak Dinesen sets the stage for current sexual stereotypes by describing ideal gentlemen and women of the past. In "Boris's Romance," Santha Rama Rau interviews a dreamy young Russian about the practical problems of courtship under Communism. Beverley Hooper finds a curious mixture of tradition and modernity in China. Perhaps the ultimate romance is the one depicted by Mexican poet Octavio Paz in his short story "My Life with the Wave," a tempestuous tale of passion between a man and an ocean wave.

To French feminist Simone de Beauvoir, Paz's mismatched lovers are no odder than most: In "Woman as Other" she asserts that the central obstacle to woman's fulfillment is man's tendency to view her as alien and therefore threatening. Alberto Moravia shows that male tendency in a different light with his short story "The Chase," in which an Italian husband gains a new appreciation for his wife's unpredictability.

The gender gap widens in the Islamic Middle East. Naila Minai's "Women in Early Islam" explains how Muhammad created a religion meant to safeguard women. Cherry Lindholm and Charles Lindholm, visiting Pakistan's Swat Valley in "Life Behind the Veil," find evidence that Muhammad's plan has gone awry: Women are viewed as too potent and treacherous to leave their homes or even show their faces without male permission. Sexual prejudice turns violent in Yashar Kemal's "A Dirty Story," where the citizens of a fictional Turkish village turn a victim into a villain. ❖

OBSERVATIONS:
LOOKING AT OURSELVES

1

You want quiet, passive women? Look at Sleeping Beauty and poor old Snow White. Talkative, clever women must be witches. It takes a handsome prince to wake up Snow White. But while the German Cinderella of the Brothers Grimm is quite passive, the American Cinderella develops a spunkiness of her own. Told she has no clothes to go to the ball, she says, "I'll make them"; told she is dirty, she says, "I'll wash." That is why I have always liked James Thurber's version of Little Red Riding Hood. Told to approach a little closer to the wicked wolf, the wise little girl pulls out an automatic and shoots the wolf dead, and the moral of the story is, *It is not so easy to fool little girls nowadays as it used to be.*

> – Adam Smith
> "The Myth, Fable, and
> Reality of the Working Woman"
> *Esquire*

◇◇◇◇◇

2

Although the witch, incarnate or in surrogate mother disguise, remains a universal bogey, pejorative aspects of the wizard, her masculine counterpart, have vanished over the patriarchal centuries. The term *wizard* has acquired reverential status — wizard of finance, wizard of diplomacy, wizard of science.

> – Dena Justin
> "From Mother Goddess to Dishwasher"
> *Natural History*

◇◇◇◇◇

3

For all the supposed enlightenment of the last decade, there is still no accepted place in our culture for the man whose mate is a more powerful figure than he is.

Women have begun to ascend — *have* ascended — into roles of power and prestige once reserved for men. No corresponding change in acceptable roles has occurred for men. . . .

Come on, admit it: When you meet an ambitious, successful woman, and the man in her life is not an achiever of equal note, you figure him for a wimp, don't you? And your judgment of him is far more severe than your judgment of her would be if the situation were reversed. If there is no new role for men in a world where women are rising, men will just be that much more reluctant to give up the roles they already have.

> – Joe Kane
> "Star Wars: How Men Are Coping with Female Success"
> *Ms.*

◇◇◇◇◇

4

Living in India made me understand that a white minority of the world has spent centuries conning us into thinking a white skin makes people superior, even though the only thing it really does is make them more subject to ultraviolet rays and wrinkles.

Reading Freud made me just as skeptical about penis envy. The power of giving birth makes "womb envy" more logical, and an organ as external and unprotected as the penis makes men very vulnerable indeed.

But listening recently to a woman describe the unexpected arrival of her menstrual period (a red stain had spread on her dress as she argued heatedly on the public stage) still made me cringe with embarrassment. That is, until she explained that, when finally informed in whispers of the obvious event, she had said to the all-male audience, "and you should be *proud* to have a menstruating woman on your stage. It's probably the first real thing that's happened to this group in years!"

Laughter. Relief. She had turned a negative into a positive. Somehow her story merged with India and Freud to make me finally understand the power of positive thinking. Whatever a "superior" group has will be used to justify its superiority, and whatever an "inferior" group has will be used to justify its plight. Black men were given poorly paid jobs because they were said to be "stronger" than white men, while all women were relegated to poorly paid jobs because they were said to be "weaker." As the little boy said when asked if he wanted to be a lawyer like his mother, "Oh no, that's women's work." Logic has nothing to do with oppression.

> – Gloria Steinem
> *Outrageous Acts and Everyday Rebellions*

❖❖❖❖❖

5

The world smiles favorably on the feminine woman: It extends little courtesies and minor privilege. Yet the nature of this competitive edge is ironic, at best, for one works at femininity by accepting restrictions, by limiting one's sights, by choosing an indirect route, by scattering concentration and not giving one's all as a man would to his own, certifiably masculine, interests. It does not require a great leap of imagination for a woman to understand the feminine principle as a grand collection of compromises, large and small, that she simply must make in order to render herself a successful woman. If she has difficulty in satisfying femininity's demands, if its illusions go against her grain, or if she is criticized for her shortcomings and imperfections, the more she will see femininity as a desperate strategy of appeasement, a strategy she may not have the wish or the courage to abandon, for failure looms in either direction. . . .

Femininity pleases men because it makes them appear more masculine by contrast; and, in truth, conferring an extra portion of unearned gender distinction on men, an unchallenged space in which to breathe freely and feel stronger, wiser, more competent, is femininity's special gift. One could say that masculinity is often an effort to please women, but masculinity is known to please by displays of mastery and competence while femininity pleases by suggesting that these concerns, except in small matters, are beyond its intent. Whimsy, unpredictability, and patterns of thinking and behavior that are dominated by emotion, such as tearful expressions of sentiment and fear, are thought to be feminine precisely because they lie outside the established route to success. . . .

A sociological fact of the 1980s is that female competition for two scarce resources — men and jobs — is especially fierce.

So it is not surprising that we are currently witnessing a renewed interest in femininity and an unabashed indulgence in feminine pursuits. Femininity serves to reassure men that women need them and care about them enormously. By incorporating the decorative and the frivolous into its definition of style, femininity functions as an effective antidote to the unrelieved seriousness, the pressure of making one's way in a harsh, difficult world. In its mandate to avoid direct confrontation and to smooth over the fissures of conflict, femininity operates as a value system of niceness, a code of thoughtfulness and sensitivity that in modern society is sadly in short supply.

— Susan Brownmiller
Femininity

<><><><><>

6

It used to be that males could model themselves after that all-American hero, John Wayne. He was tough, rugged, and plenty adventurous. Problems were solved in a gunslinging match or a fistfight, whichever came first.

But in today's society the John Wayne image is being shot down. Important categories of traditional male work like the cowboy or lawman are being ambushed by the advent of automated equipment and the emergence of women in traditionally male jobs.

Warren Farrell, author of *The Liberated Man*, calls John Wayne the "Moses of Masculinity," and pictures him complete with a tablet on which are written the "Ten Commandments" of traditional maledom:

1. Thou shalt not cry or expose other feelings of emotion, fear, weakness, sympathy, empathy, or involvement before thy neighbor.
2. Thou shalt not be vulnerable, but honor and respect the "logical," "practical," or "intellectual" — as thou definest them.
3. Thou shalt not listen except to find fault.
4. Thou shalt condescend to women in the smallest and biggest of ways.
5. Thou shalt control thy wife's body.
6. Thou shalt have no other egos before thee.
7. Thou shalt have no other breadwinners before thee.
8. Thou shalt not be responsible for housework — before anybody.
9. Thou shalt honor and obey the straight-and-narrow pathway to success: job specialization.
10. Thou shalt have an answer to all problems at all times.

But the problems associated with "old male" socialization are reflected in men's health statistics:

men live, on the average, almost 10 years less than women;
males commit suicide 300 percent more often;
all the major diseases leading to death show significantly higher rates for males;

men have higher murder, assault, and battery rates; and
men show a significantly higher rate of drug and alcohol abuse.

> – Gayle Early
> "The Hazards of Being Male"
> *Chico News & Review*

◇–◇–◇–◇–◇

7

I don't work in an office, so I miss out on a lot of things that people who do don't, such as a new pen whenever I want one, coffee breaks, comical stories about my dumb boss, the concept of the weekend, lunchtime jazzercise with my coworkers, a mysteriously burgeoning colony of Sweet 'N Low packets in my desk, nice clothes for daytime wear, and work marriage.

Work marriage is a relationship that exists between certain people of the opposite sex who work at the same place. For example, let's suppose that you, like me, are a man. In that case your work wife would be the woman in your office who

a. as you walk past her desk on your way to a big meeting, tells you that you have dried shaving cream behind your ear
b. has lunch with you pretty often
c. returns stuff she borrows from your desk
d. tells you things about her other (home) husband that he wouldn't want you to know
e. waits for you to finish up so you can go down in the elevator together
f. complains to you without embarrassment about an uncomfortable undergarment
g. expects you to tell her the truth, more or less, about the thing she has done to her hair
h. doesn't comment on how much you eat, drink, and smoke
i. knows at least one thing about you — such as the fact that you can do a pretty good imitation of Liza Minnelli — that your home wife doesn't know.

Work marriage is, in some ways, better than home marriage. For example, your work wife would never ask you why you don't just put your dishes right into the dishwasher instead of leaving them in the sink — she doesn't know you do it! Also, she would never get your car wedged between two other cars in the parking lot at Bradlees, sign you up to be the pie auctioneer at a church bazaar, or grab hold of your stomach and ask, "What's this? Blubber?" She knows you only as you appear between nine and five: recently bathed, fully dressed, largely awake, and in control of your life.

My wife and I both work at home. In that sense, I guess, my home wife is also my work wife. And yet this cannot be. Our argument about whether rapidly changing channels hurts the TV does not disappear at nine o'clock on Monday morning. Like many other self-employed (and thus work-single) people, I am forced to content myself with fleeting and ultimately unsatisfying pseudowork marriages, such as my relationship with a checkout girl at the grocery store. She has a pretty good idea of what I like to eat, and I help her out sometimes by doing my own bagging, but that is about as far as it goes. (Perhaps I have merely discovered a new, less committed type of relationship: store dating.)

The only way to have a real work marriage is, sadly, to work. Sure, I'd like a work wife someday — *someday*. But I'm not willing, right now, to get a regular job in order to have one. There are just too many things about offices (no dogs or children, no nap whenever you want one, parking problems) that rub me the wrong way.

Meanwhile, my home wife and I keep trying to work out our differences. There are some indications that we are making progress. The other day she borrowed the ruler–alarm clock–thermometer that I use to hold down the pile of papers on my desk. This morning, without any hint from me, she brought it back. Next week maybe I'll return her scissors.

– David Owen
"Work Marriage"
Atlantic Monthly

◇◇◇◇◇

8

James Dean was my first androgynous man. I figured I could talk to him. He was anguished and I was twelve, so we had a lot in common. With only a few exceptions, all the men I have liked or loved have been a certain kind of man: a kind who doesn't play football or watch the games on Sunday, who doesn't tell dirty jokes featuring broads or chicks, who is not contemptuous of conversations that are philosophically speculative, introspective, or otherwise foolish according to the other kind of man. He is more self-amused, less inflated, more quirky, vulnerable, and responsive than the other sort (the other sort, I'm visualizing as the guys on TV who advertise deodorant in the locker room). He is more like me than the other sort. He is what social scientists and feminists would call androgynous: having the characteristics of both male and female.

Now the first thing I want you to know about the androgynous man is that he is neither effeminate nor hermaphroditic. All his primary and secondary sexual characteristics are in order and I would say he's all-man, but that is just what he is not. He is more than all-man.

The merely all-man man, for one thing, never walks to the grocery store unless the little woman is away visiting her mother with the kids, or is in the hospital having a kid, or there is no little woman. All-men men don't know how to shop in a grocery store unless it is to buy a six-pack and some pretzels. Their ideas of nutrition expand beyond a six-pack and pretzels only to take in steak, potatoes, scotch or rye whiskey, and maybe a wad of cake or apple pie. All-men men have absolutely no taste in food, art, books, movies, theater, dance, how to live, what are good questions, what is funny, or anything else I care about. . . .

Male chauvinism is an irritation, but the real problem I have with the all-man man is that it's hard for me to talk to him. He's alien to me, and for this I'm at least half to blame. As his interests have not carried him into the sissy, mine have never taken me very far into the typically masculine terrains of sports, business and finance, politics, cars, boats, and machines. But blame or no blame, the reality is that it is almost as difficult for me to connect with him as it would be to link up with an Arab shepherd or Bolivian sandalmaker. There's a similar culture gap.

– Amy Gross
"The Appeal of the Androgynous Man"
Mademoiselle

◇◇◇◇◇

9

The women's movement cannot remake consciousness, or reshape the future, without acknowledging and shedding all the unnecessary and ugly baggage of the past. It's easy enough now to see where men have kept us out of clubs, baseball games, graduate schools; it's easy enough to recognize the hidden directions that limit Sis to cake baking and Junior to bridge building; it's now possible for even Miss America herself to identify what *they* have done to us, and, of course, *they* have and *they* did and *they* are. . . . But along the way we also developed our own hidden prejudices, class assumptions, and an antimale humor and collection of expectations that gave us, like all oppressed groups, a secret sense of superiority (coexisting with a poor self-image — it's not news that people can believe two contradictory things at once). . . .

Why are there laws insisting on alimony and child support? Well, everyone knows that men don't have an instinct to protect their young and, given half a chance, with the moon in the right phase, they will run off and disappear. Everyone assumes a mother will not let her child starve, yet it is necessary to legislate that a father must not do so. We are taught to accept the idea that men are less than decent; their charms may be manifold but their characters are riddled with faults. To this day I never blink if I hear that a man has gone to find his fortune in South America, having left his pregnant wife, his blind mother, and taken the family car. I still gasp in horror when I hear of a woman leaving her asthmatic infant for a rock group in Taos because I can't seem to avoid the assumption that men are naturally heels and women the ordained carriers of what little is moral in our dubious civilization. . . .

I remember shivering in the cold vestibule of a famous men's athletic club. Women and girls are not permitted inside the club's door. What are they doing in there, I asked? They're naked, said my mother, they're sweating, jumping up and down a lot, telling each other dirty jokes, and bragging about their stock market exploits. Why can't we go in? I asked. Well, my mother told me, they're afraid we'd laugh at them.

The prejudices of childhood are hard to outgrow. I confess that every time my business takes me past that club, I shudder. Images of large bellies resting on massage tables and flaccid penises rising and falling with the Dow Jones average flash through my head. There it is, chauvinism waving its cancerous tentacles from the depths of my psyche.

Minorities automatically feel superior to the oppressor because, after all, they are not hurting anybody. In fact, they feel morally better. The old canard that women need love, men need sex — believed for too long by both sexes — attributes moral and spiritual superiority to women and makes of men beasts whose urges send them prowling into the night. This false division of good and bad, placing deforming pressures on everyone, doesn't have to contaminate the future. We know that the assumptions we make about each other become a part of the cultural air we breathe and, in fact, become social truths. Women who want equality must be prepared to give it and to believe in it, and in order to do that it is not enough to state that you are as good as any man, but also it must be stated that he is as good as you and both will be humans together. If we want men to share in the care of the family in a new way, we must assume them as capable of consistent loving tenderness as we.

— Anne Roiphe
"Confessions of a Female Chauvinist Sow"
New York

ISAK DINESEN

From "Daguerreotypes"

Isak Dinesen was born Karen Christentze Dinesen in Denmark in 1885. She studied painting in the Danish capital of Copenhagen and in Paris, then married the Baron Blixen and moved to Kenya. Her adventures there — chronicled in such books as *Out of Africa* (1937) — included running a coffee plantation, divorcing, and falling in love with the Englishman Denys Finch-Hatton. Her farm's failure and her lover's death forced her back to Europe, where she took up writing in her forties to make a living. Dinesen wrote in English out of loyalty to Finch-Hatton, and — following in the footsteps of such women writers as George Eliot in England and George Sand in France — took a male pseudonym: *Isak*, "the one who laughs." This essay, from *Daguerreotypes and Other Essays* (1979), was originally published in 1951. Isak Dinesen/Karen Blixen died in 1962 at Rungstedlund, her Danish home.

The kingdom of Denmark occupies most of the Jutland Peninsula plus a number of islands in northern Europe. Denmark is surrounded by water except for its southern border with Germany; its neighbors across the sea are Norway to the north, Sweden to the east, and Scotland to the west.

One hundred years ago a gentleman's education was an elaborate and costly matter. He was produced through specially predetermined, dignified, and complicated processes. And it is difficult at the present day fully to understand how many of these were intended to give him the proper feeling for women's nobility and the correct attitude towards it. A true gentleman was known primarily by his position on this matter. "Yes, he drinks too much," women could say about him. "He never pays his tailor. We know well he can be brutal." Yet if he was irreproachable in the first article of faith, they would conclude, "But he's a real gentleman." In the English officers' messes it was forbidden under any circumstances whatsoever to mention a lady's name. To break this law was a greater breach of the gentleman ideal than any other.

It will be still more difficult to explain today how the skirt — the long garment — had become such a significant, indeed decisive, symbol of women's nobility and her legs the one sacrosanct taboo. Women of those days were not reticent about displaying their physical charms above the belt. But from the waist to the ground there were mysteries, holy secrets.

Personally, I imagine the explanation to be that trousers are in reality a dubious item of clothing, an item without dignity — even for men they were called "unmentionables" in the days of the daguerreotypes — or that in reality it is a debatable matter whether a dressed person should have two legs. It is often said that trousers are not suitable for women, and I agree, but I must add that they are not suitable for men either. When I think of the robes my friends among the Arabs and Somalis wore, and of the dignity and expressiveness which robes communicated to the movements of their slim figures, I deplore our European men in their sheathings. In Berlin I saw a King Lear appear on the stage in tight-fitting trousers and I understood at once that the garment made it impossible for the actor to play the great, mad king's role, in which the folds of clothing must respond to the mighty outbursts of human passion, and to the gestures. The great dramatic scenes of antiquity — Socrates' death, the murder of Caesar at the Capitol — are incompatible with any image of trousers. Moses in trousers could never have brought forth water from a rock.

In any case, that was the way it was. Long skirts were the most sacred attribute of womanly nobility. . . .

4

In trying to explain this matter, it has seemed to me as if the men of that older generation viewed women from three points of view or as three groups — that is to say, viewed or judged them officially in such a manner (but that is a point to which I shall return). Women were for them either guardian angels or housewives or, in a third group, what the Swedish poet Viktor Rydberg calls the priestesses of pleasure, the dancers, and what I here, to use a nice word — for there are a good many that are not so nice — shall call the bayadères.

The ideal woman of real life was a mixture of guardian angel and housewife. In art the most admired and most popular ideal was a mixture of angel and bayadère. We know that from *La Dame aux camélias* and a long series of later novels and plays, right down to *Trilby*.

The guardian angel — unadulterated — shed a heavenly light at a man's side and protected him against the power of darkness. Bjørnson depicts her in a poem in which he describes how a youth "is wounded deep by Eden's serpent and doubts"; he continues:

> And on the sunny height
> with bridal wreath his childhood dream:
> in love's eyes bright,
> faith's heav'nly dream.
> As from his mother's arms he came
> and stammering Jehovah's name,
> he kneels and prays
> and weeps.

This angelic ideal of woman was probably more generally accepted in Germany and Scandinavia than among the Latins, who are more practically inclined. Goldschmidt relates in a letter from Paris his astonishment that there a young suitor did not look upon his beloved as a heavenly creation and adds, "Not that our young Scandinavian suitor always or unconditionally views his beloved as such a creation — but we assume he does." It is plain that a guardian angel is surrounded by a mystical aura, and where she is envisaged in long white garments, hovering, it would certainly be profane or actually precluded to direct attention to her legs.

The housewife — whether she is the mistress of a castle or of a manse   8
or is a farmer's wife — is naturally more tangible. But she nevertheless wears decent long garments. In the nineteenth century — in any case in the country, for I believe in the cities thing were somewhat different — the religion and poetry of everyday existence belonged to woman's domain. Though the children and servants in the household would risk a strong reprimand if they made fun of the master of the house, that did not mean they were lost souls. But to scoff at the mother or mistress of the household was a sacrilege. "Invisible," wrote Jonas Lie, "invisible yet ever present like the good spirit of the house — isn't that the best thing one can say about a woman?" The housewife didn't have legs either.

An anecdote will serve to throw light on the relationship. At the end of the nineteenth century in Jutland there was a local prefect who had a wife of the unadulterated housewife type and also a gardener named Larsen. One day Larsen came to the prefect's house and asked to speak to him in private. "I feel I must tell the prefect something," he said. "I dreamed last night that I saw the prefect's wife in the nude." The prefect was just as embarrassed to receive this confession as Larsen was to make it. What he replied is not known for certain, but the story goes that he said, "It is quite proper of you, Larsen, to tell me about this. But it must not happen again." If one imagines one's self in the position of the prefect, one will understand it would have been easier if the prefect's wife had been more of a guardian angel or bayadère type.

And now the bayadère. Yes, she did have legs to be sure, and this fact gave her almost her greatest significance. But the fact in no way negates the holy taboo; in reality it reinforces it: it is the same taboo expressed in a different mode.

Here the taboo may be defined in figures, and in figures which will seem incomprehensibly large to your time. One might say that in this matter the true gentleman's loyalty vis-à-vis the dignity of woman found expression in the sums he was willing to pay to see the bayadère's legs.

My old friend Mr. Bulpett, who with a clear conscience had ruined   12
himself for the sake of a bayadère — La Belle Otéro — has many times told me about the grand courtesans who played a rôle in France during the Second Empire and up to the turn of the century. Millions passed through their hands every year. Like Zola's Nana, they drove to the races in a four-in-hand; their jewels outshone those of the guardian angels as well as those of the housewife. Gaby Deslys, he said, had been the last of the really great courtesans. When I asked him the reasons they were no longer in the picture, he answered after reflection, "There are too many amateurs these days." In his capacity as a real sporting man, he was incidentally displeased to see the borderline erased between amateurs and professionals. I remember I once told him something I had read in a fashion journal from home, that the fan was about to make a comeback. He was so pleased by this piece of news that he rubbed his hands together, and when I asked the reason for his satisfaction he answered, somewhat surprised at my ignorance, that it was perfectly clear. A fan was the only gift, save for a bouquet of flowers, which a gentleman could allow himself to give a lady *comme il faut*. For that matter it could be very expensive. "It will," he said, "fill a long-felt need, since you women have not used fans for a long time."

The guardian angel and the housewife could not possibly sanction the existence of the bayadère. Nevertheless there must have been a certain satisfaction for them to have, in the bayadère, on paper and in definite figures, so to speak, a kind of proof of what their own womanly stake was worth.

In reality it was worth more than could be put on paper, for the bayadère, with her four-in-hand and her jewels, was an outcast of society — if not also of Paradise.

I have said that the men of the nineteenth century viewed their women from these points of view, or in three groups, officially. I use the word "officially" because in reality they had in their consciousness still another type of woman which for all of them was very much alive and present but was not mentioned or recognized by the light of day.

The guardian angel, the housewife, and the bayadère — each had her   16 calling, her justification, and her importance in relationship to man. They saved and guided him, or they took care of his well-being and reputation, or they enraptured and transported him. Eve was created from Adam's rib; it was for man's sake that woman existed and Søren Kierkegaard defined a woman's being as "existence for something else."

But there was a woman who, long before the words "emancipation of women" came into use, existed independently of a man and had her own center of gravity. She was the witch.

The witch has played a greater or lesser rôle in various eras but she has never entirely disappeared. One may suppose that for most men the explanation is, that a woman who can exist without a man certainly also can exist without God, or that a woman who does not want to be possessed by a man necessarily must be possessed by the devil. The witch had absolutely no scruples about showing her legs; she sat quite unconstrained astride her broomstick and took off.

And still — despite all the sinister atmosphere and abandon which surrounded her — the witch cannot be said to have renounced or to have betrayed the dignity of woman. She confirmed — in demonic fashion but with gravity — the fundamental dogma that that secret of woman's power is suggestion.

The judges at the witch trials who used every means to procure the   20 witch's confession that on the island of Samsö she had worked magic which kept Princess Anne from her journey to her bridegroom, James VI of Scotland, refrained from acquiring the magic recipe itself from her.

In Africa it is assumed that all old women can practice sorcery. More than that: that they turn into hyenas at night and run around, laughing, on the veldt looking for corpses. I once saw this quite seriously expounded in a book by an important English traveler. I told my brother, who had been on a safari in Somaliland, about it. He grew silent, but told me later that one night — in order to chase hyenas away from the "kill" on which he hoped to shoot a lion or leopard — he had fired a couple of shots and unwittingly hit a hyena. It could not be found in the morning; he could follow the trail of its blood for a way, but then the trail ceased.

When he went home to the Somali village, he heard weeping and wailing from far off. A respected old lady, a grandmother and a great-grand-mother, had inexplicably lost her life during the night.

I once — also in Africa — had a conversation on this subject with a French-born friend. She expressed her unshakable conviction that all men without exception believed in witches. They only differed in the degree they feared them. "The more a man is a man, my dear," she said, "the more openly will he admit to believing in witches, but he will correspondingly hate or fear them less. Sailors are willing to admit they have made the acquaintance of more than one witch in their lifetime, but towards them they are rather kindly disposed, and will even admit from time to time that they owe them a debt of gratitude. Men of learning are not ready to admit the existence of witches, but the fear of a witch is in their blood. And those men who themselves dress in long robes — the clergy — they hate and fear a witch more than they hate and fear her lord and master."

"Even though the witch is a lonely figure," said my friend, "she has a good relationship with her sister witches. She is a black guardian angel, a bat on a dark night filled with Northern lights as a flickering reflection from the time that Lucifer was the morning star. She is a housewife to the hilt: fire and fireplace are precious to her and the caldron is indispensable. She is a bayadère and a seductress even as a Sibyl or a mummy:

> black from Phoebus's pinch of love
> and wrinkled deep by time . . .

And if the learned gentlemen feel their masculine dignity is affronted by the thought that she prefers the devil to a man, then the layman and outdoorsman find some compensation in another remark: the basis, in-deed the prerequisite for the witch's entire activity is the circumstance that the devil is masculine."

The old lady continued, "We women, my child, are often very simple.   24 But that any female would lack reason to such a degree that she would start reasoning with a man — that is beyond my comprehension! She has lost the battle, my dear child, she has lost the battle before it began! No, if a woman will have her way with a man she must look him square in the eye and say something of which it is impossible for him to make any sense whatsoever and to which he is at a loss to reply. He is defeated at once."

She supported her theory with examples from history. Englishwomen, she said, had for a long time tried to obtain the franchise, and their arguments and rationalism had failed to budge the resistance of the English MP's.[1] Then around the turn of the century the "suffragettes" began their maneuvers illegally and quite irrationally — they climbed up on rooftops, stretched ropes across highways, and threw themselves in front of the winning horse at the Derby — then the gentlemen in Parliament were overcome by fright; their old convictions began to creak at the joints. And a short time later women had the franchise.

"And I can assure you," said Lady Colville, "that women's societies and women's organizations could achieve far more, indeed would make shortcuts directly to their goals if, instead of forming committees, making speeches, and writing articles — all tame and simple imitations of men — they would let it be known the country over that they would meet on the heath and on the commons under a waning moon."

My young female listeners who have had the patience to follow me to this point will perhaps turn towards me and declare, "But we don't want to be mysterious at all. We are and want to be part of reality. We renounce all our secret power!"

I have already said that the views which I am presenting here are not   28 my own, and that I cannot be held responsible for them. I myself — many years ago, in Africa — had my reservations about Lady Colville's creed.

But when my old friend and teacher in the art of witchcraft had reflected upon my protest, she replied,

"It is of course up to you, *ma jolie*,[2] to make your own choice. I wish only in this connection to tell you a little story.

"As a young girl, my sister returned home from a trip to Italy and declared at a family gathering, 'I wouldn't give five francs for all the paintings in the Uffizi.' My half-grown brother cried out at once, 'For heaven's sakes, Marie-Louise, keep your opinion to yourself; you reveal a complete lack of business acumen!'"

---

[1]Members of Parliament. — ED.
[2]My pretty. — ED.

EXPLORATIONS

1. What clues in her essay reveal Dinesen's opinion of the social attitudes she is summarizing? What is the effect of her attributing these attitudes to a specific small group — nineteenth-century gentlemen — rather than to a larger group or to society as a whole? How might her essay gain or lose impact if Dinesen expressed her opinion of these gentlemanly attitudes outright?

2. What is the joke in the "little story" that ends this essay? What is the serious point behind the joke? Where else does Dinesen make her point by humor rather than by stating explicitly what she means?

3. In the process of describing how nineteenth-century gentlemen viewed women, Dinesen says a good deal about how men were viewed as well. What qualities did men value in each other? What qualities did women value in men? What undesirable male behavior might be excused, and what behavior was unforgivable?

4. The ideas Dinesen presents tend to be abstract and metaphorical: "A guardian angel is surrounded by a mystical aura"; "The religion and poetry of everyday existence belonged to woman's domain." What types of evidence does she use to back up her statements? What supporting role(s) does she herself play within the essay?

CONNECTIONS

1. What ideas about male and female roles are expressed both by Dinesen and by Susan Brownmiller in her *Observation*? How do these two writers differ in their evaluation of the pros and cons of femininity?

2. Look back at Ved Mehta's "Pom's Engagement" (p. 162). What evidence do you find in Mehta's India of the female ideals that Dinesen describes? Which of Dinesen's categories best fits the role(s) Pom is expected to play as a daughter and as a wife?

ELABORATIONS

1. Dinesen begins her essay by describing a male stereotype. Do twentieth-century Americans idealize gentlemen as nineteenth-century Danes did? Referring to Gayle Early's and other *Observations*, write an essay either defining a gentleman in the contemporary United States or classifying current stereotyped male roles.

2. Do the female stereotypes described in Dinesen's essay exist in the United States today? What confirmation (or not) of Dinesen's ideas do you find in the *Observations: Looking at Ourselves*? Write an essay either classifying the categories into which modern Americans (male and/or female) divide women or evaluating the changes time has wrought in Dinesen's guardian angel, housewife, bayadère, and witch.

SANTHA RAMA RAU

Boris's Romance

Santha Rama Rau's background is international: She was born in Madras, India, in 1923, went to school in England, attended college in America, and has lived and traveled in diverse parts of the world. At present she lives outside New York City with her husband, Gurdon Wattles (retired from the United Nations), but she does not think of any one country as exclusively home. Rama Rau has written several books of fiction and nonfiction, as well as the film script on which the 1984 screenplay for *A Passage to India* was based. She is currently working on a plan to televise the story of the Indian Mutiny of 1857, known in the West as the Sepoy Mutiny and in India as the First War of Independence. "Boris's Romance" comes from Rama Rau's 1958 book *My Russian Journey,* based on her travels in the Soviet Union with her then husband, Faubion Bowers.

At the time Rama Rau wrote "Boris's Romance," the late Communist dictator Joseph Stalin was a recent and vivid memory for Russians. Premier Nikita Khrushchev had replaced Stalin in 1953 as political leader of the world's largest country (the Soviet Union is nearly two and a half times the size of the United States); already he had done much to discredit Stalin's regime of mass executions, exiles, and "purge" trials. Khrushchev's triumph would be short lived, however: He was deposed in 1964, two years after withdrawing Soviet missiles from Cuba during a confrontation with U.S. President John F. Kennedy.

While it was still warm enough to sit outdoors, Faubion and I frequently returned to Gorki Park and often met Boris there, sometimes by appointment and sometimes by accident, seeing his untidy blond head and purposeful walk between the trees and waving to him to come over. There we would sit sipping our drinks, nibbling on fruit or sandwiches or candy, and we would talk. Bit by bit we learned a good deal about Boris, that he was considered a very good student and received a relatively large government stipend because of his high grades, that he was a serious worker in his Young Communist League group, that he was ambitious, that . . . he was not particularly interested in sights and monuments and visual art, but preferred reading and had devoured any novel in English that he could find. But he was reticent about his home life, and it was

only after a rather unexpected conversation one day in the park that we
began to know more of how he lived, the moment, really, that we began
to be friends.

It was a pleasantly mild, sunny afternoon at the moment just before
evening when the sun is slanting low between the trees. We were all
sitting at our usual place and looking around at the other people making
the most of the short season. Autumn is, in any case, a sentimental time
of year, and as we watched the couples strolling along the paths or sitting
on the park benches under the yellowing leaves of the trees, eating ice
cream, smiling, talking to each other in low voices, I asked Boris, "Tell
me, have you equivalents in Russian for a saying like 'All the world loves
a lover,' or 'All's fair in love and war,' or 'It's love that makes the world
go round'?"

Boris thought for a moment. "Sometimes we say, 'Love is not a potato,
do not throw it out the window.' Ah, yes, and — this is very difficult of
translation — 'Love is so — so,'" he thumped his head with his fist in
exasperation, "'so cruel-and-stubborn, you can even fall in love with a
mountain goat.'"

"Those don't sound very romantic," I said.   4

Boris looked astonished. With a characteristic gesture he pushed his
blond hair back from his forehead, which only made it messier, and said
very seriously, "But we are the most romantic people in the world! We
— especially students — think of it all the time. Often it interferes with
our study — "

"Are there many college romances?"

"Of course, many."

"With girls that you meet in class?"   8

"In class, or at a *vecherinka*" (any evening party, sometimes given by
schools or clubs or the Young Communist League), "or, if he has a job
in the vacation, then in the office can also be. But really, it is time for
the boy to fall in love — he is in love even before he speaks to the girl."

"And then he makes a date with her?"

"So quick? No. He sees her at an evening party, in school, in the
office. He is too shy to dance with her. His friend urges him, but he
says, 'No, no! Never with no one!'" (Boris never grasped the principle of
the double negative — in Russian it is a perfectly reasonable construction.) "He will perhaps be braver on the phone, but still so shy that he
is rude — abrupt? — and she is very annoyed. 'Who is this boy? He is
very uncultured.'" Boris made a face of extreme scorn. "At last he has
the courage to ask her to the cinema. He is certain she will not come.

He waits in front of the cinema watching every person getting off at the bus stop. Perhaps she has decided to come by métro? He runs to the corner to watch the métro entrance. He runs back to find her waiting in the lobby. Will she forgive him for not reaching there first? He is so proud to buy her ticket, he thinks that even the woman in the *kassa* — what is *kassa*?"

"Box office."   12

"So. Box office. Even the box-office woman notices him with his girl." Boris sat back in his chair looking vaguely at the golden leaves above us. "After this he *knows* he is in love. He cannot concentrate. He walks about the streets in a dream. He sees the flower seller on the corner. He stops to stare at the flowers — the raindrops are still on them — they look so fresh, they remind him of his girl, and he buys some for her."

Boris's words immediately brought to mind the scene I had often noticed on Moscow streets, of an elderly Russian woman in her knitted shawl and shabby jacket from a man's suit worn over a black dress, sitting on a folding stool, hip-deep in flowers. Stiff bunches of chrysanthemums and snapdragons stuck into tall tin cans all around her on the sidewalk. She always caused a small eddy in the stream of pedestrians hurrying back from work in the early evening — she used to make me stop too whenever I passed her. I liked the sudden sight of the massed reds and yellows and purples against the sober coloring of Moscow's streets and, besides, she seemed to me such an odd reminder of pre-Revolutionary life in Russia — the bright flowers and the dingy clothes — in my mind I had peopled the street corners of old Russian novels with women like her.

"At last the day comes," Boris was saying, "when the girl invites him to meet her parents. Terrible! He has too many feet. He falls over the furniture. He does not dare to pick up his tea glass for fear it spills. When he has gone, her parents say, 'How can you go out with such a clumsy boy, an educated girl like you? Whatever else, we have always had good manners in this house.' Then she goes to meet his parents and is so shy that she cannot talk. Afterwards they say, 'She may be a sweet girl, but evidently she is too dull even to speak.' The young people decide that their parents do not understand them. They are old-fashioned and have forgotten what it is to be in love. From then on they meet in public places."

As you live in Moscow you learn that there are a number of popular   16 rendezvous places — the steps of the Bolshoi or the porch of the Lenin Museum right next to Red Square — but the favorite one, the equivalent of under-the-clock-at-the-Biltmore, is the statue of Pushkin. There are always flowers on its pedestal or its steps, and always a few impatient young men pacing about nearby, glancing up occasionally at the sad, dark face with its curly hair and long sideburns, then looking quickly back at each girl that crosses the square. If a young man has brought flowers for his girl, she will certainly pull one out of the bunch and throw it to join the others on the steps before she turns away and takes her escort's arm.

"And then what do they do?" I asked Boris. "Since they can't go home, I mean."

"In any case they cannot go home," he said casually. And I realized a bit guiltily that I should have known that privacy must be one of the biggest problems that young couples have to cope with. Conditions at home are almost always, in Boris's phrase, "somewhat crowded." On the whole, you are lucky if your family has an apartment to itself and does not share at least the kitchen or the bath with other families. Even then it is very unlikely that such an apartment would have a separate living room. If a married couple has a grown son they are usually entitled to an extra room for him; often there is only a flimsy partition between the two rooms, or simply a curtained glass door. If they have two sons, of course the boys share the second room. And then (again if they are fortunate and the kitchen is large enough) the kitchen becomes the dining room as well, and one of the bedrooms doubles as a living room. In these circumstances it is quite understandable that romantic exchanges are impossible at home. Besides, private automobiles are extremely rare, so access to the family car is no solution.

"So they just walk about the streets together?" I asked Boris.

"Or the parks," he said. "Everything else costs money."   20

Apparently, if they can't afford the theater or a movie, they wander about the city. Often they can be seen standing close together against the first chill of the late evening, in plazas and some of the wide sidewalks, listening to the recorded music pouring from outdoor loudspeakers, perhaps the clear brilliance of Oistrakh's violin mixing strangely with the sound of traffic. Russians seem to enjoy listening to music in the open air — even in cold weather — and for the young people street concerts have the added advantage of costing nothing.

Somewhere in this conversation I began to realize that Boris was telling us about himself, and I listened carefully, picturing him in the middle of a romance, while he told us how young Russians love to take long walks along the Moscow River, under the walls of the Kremlin, sometimes crossing one of the big bridges to the island in the middle of the river, pausing on the bridge to watch the water and the boats go by. Often they sit by the river and read poetry aloud to each other. "To a girl at one time I read *Eugene Onegin* by Pushkin. She was very moved. She determined to learn it all by heart."

"But it's immensely long."

"Of course. Nearly as a novel. The boys and girls are always very 24 serious," Boris assured us. It was easy to believe, for frivolity is, in any case, strikingly absent in Russian life.

"Also," Boris continued, "they have long conversations. They criticize each other. He says, 'You should study harder. It is as important for a girl to be intellectual as a man.' She says, 'You have no sense of money. You spend too much on me — on everything — you must save.'"

In extreme cases, if being in love is clearly interfering with a student's work, if he is spending too much time on romance and his grades are getting low, then a friend — or sometimes even his girl — can report him to the local head of the Young Communist League, who will reprimand him, and this can well mean a black mark on his record.

"That doesn't sound very nice," I said carefully. "What business is it of his?"

"It is a good thing," Boris said with emphasis. "A Komsomol leader 28 must know that the members of his group are reliable and serious."

"I see. Well, how do they prove that? By getting married?"

"Perhaps. If they are really in love. They decide to get married." This time when they meet each other's parents things are very different. "They show their maturity. Now they have confidence," Now the young man will not only pick up his girl from her apartment whenever they have a date, and drop her home every evening (instead of leaving her at the street corner), he will also be expected to spend a short while with her parents before they go out and will often come to meals at her home. He will, in fact, behave like a fiancé rather than a beau, even though he will not give her an engagement ring or make any formal declaration of their intention to marry.

Their wedding is a simple, unromantic signing of forms at the marriage registration office. Usually there is no fuss beforehand and possibly only a celebration party for a few friends that evening. The parents, even if they disapprove of the match, have to take an accepting attitude. They can express their displeasure, of course, but can do very little about enforcing their wishes. A father cannot, for instance, cut his daughter off without a penny. If she is a student she is, in any case, receiving a government stipend to cover both her tuition and her living expenses. If she is a very good student she may receive as much as 800 rubles ($80) a month, though the stipend varies according to her grades and capabilities. This amount, combined with her husband's allowance, will give them enough to live on.

"But sometimes," Boris said consideringly, "they are not really in love.   32
They do not get married." During the time of their courtship perhaps another man has come along, and "the girl realizes that the other was only a friend, or because he was the first she had no judgment," and mistook a passing fancy for love. They break each other's hearts, they are miserable. They talk together for hours about how they can't bear to hurt each other. "Then the girl marries the second man. At least," Boris finished abruptly, "that is how it was with me."

"Cheer up, Boris," I said. "There are other girls, and one day you'll be glad you didn't marry the first."

"But I *am* married," Boris replied.

"Oh." I paused to work out the situation. "So you were the second man?"

He smiled. "To *her* I was the second man."   36

He appeared to feel that this rather cryptic remark needed no explanation, so rather timidly I asked, "But to some other girl you were the first?"

"Ah," he said, "that is the difficulty."

EXPLORATIONS

1. In form, how does Rama Rau's narrative resemble a short story? What specific techniques does the author use to help her readers see, hear, and sympathize with Boris's world? How does she create suspense about the outcome of his romance?

2. Early in this essay Boris quotes two Russian proverbs about love. What does each one mean? What attitudes and behavior do you think Boris is referring to when he says, "But we [Russians] are the most romantic people in the world!"

3. Why do you think Rama Rau and Boris react differently to Boris's proverbs? What other observations by Rama Rau indicate contrasting attitudes on her part and Boris's?

CONNECTIONS

1. Boris's description of a Russian romance contains some evidence of the female stereotypes proposed by Isak Dinesen. Which stereotype best fits the girl in Boris's story? In whose eyes does she play that role? Which stereotype best fits the sweethearts' mothers? To what extent do you think they share their children's view of them?

2. In paragraphs 11–13, Boris describes a boy's first date with the girl he admires, in which they go to the cinema together. Look back at Ved Mehta's description of Pom's first meeting with Kakaji in "Pom's Engagement" (p. 162). Which couple is outwardly more uncomfortable? Which couple is inwardly more uncomfortable? What social goals is each system of courtship designed to accomplish, and how is the system tailored to meet those goals?

3. Rama Rau writes as a quasi-insider rather than a researcher or reporter. What differences in approach do you notice between (a) Rama Rau's interview with Boris and (b) Ruth Sidel's "The Liu Family" (p. 21) and Vincent Crapanzano's "Growing Up White in South Africa" (p. 58)? In writing up their interviews, how do these authors differ in their use of quotation, paraphrase, and summary?

ELABORATIONS

1. What changes would Rama Rau have to make in order to shift "Boris's Romance" from a narrative essay about one individual to an expository essay about Soviet courtship customs? Make an outline of the informative facts that would go into such an essay. Then write your own expository version of "Boris's Romance."

2. What impact is added to Rama Rau's essay by character details such as Boris's tousled hair and sketchy English? Why is it useful for Boris to be visually more vivid than the author, and for his voice as main character to contrast with hers as narrator? Think of a story you have been told by a friend, as Rama Rau is told Boris's story. Write a narrative essay with your friend's story as its main thread. Around this thread create a portrait of the person telling it, using his or her voice (style of speaking), description, and gestures as well as the story's content. You may also want to break in, as Rama Rau does, with background information in your own authorial voice.

BEVERLEY HOOPER

Falling in Love with Love

Beverley Hooper grew up in Tasmania, an island off Australia's southeast tip, where she was born in 1940. She left school at sixteen, took a secretarial course, and then set off to see the world. After working in Europe and at the Australian embassy in Moscow, Hooper returned to Australia, where she studied at the University of Tasmania and the Australian National University. Learning Russian and Chinese paved her way to a scholarship to Peking from 1975 to 1977 and other research visits to China. Now a research fellow in history at the University of Western Australia, Hooper has written extensively about contemporary China, including her book *Youth in China* (1985), in which the chapter "Falling in Love with Love" appears.

Hooper's observations were made at a time of upheaval in China, in attitudes toward not only love but the rigid political, economic, and social systems created during Mao Zedong's regime. The takeover of China in 1949 by Mao and his Communist cohorts marked the climax of a long push to modernize this ancient empire. While Mao's government achieved much progress and won wide popular support, its methods included periodic crackdowns on ideological foes — real or imagined. One such violent wave of oppression was the Cultural Revolution of 1966, masterminded partly by Mao's wife, Jiang Qing. When Mao died in 1976, backlash against the Cultural Revolution swept Jiang Qing and her three top comrades — the "Gang of Four" — out of power into prison. China's new leader, Deng Xiaoping, recognizes the country's need for intellectuals as well as workers, peasants, and soldiers. He has also opened China to the outside world, countering Mao's dogmatic socialism with remarks like "Black cat, white cat — it's a good cat if it catches mice."

(For more background on China, see pp. 450 and 635.)

"I have this feeling, here in my heart. I've never had it before. Is it love?" The earnest inquirer was twenty-two-year-old Cao Wenyuan, a good-looking bright-eyed young man working in Harbin's International Hotel.

Cao explained his predicament. Six months earlier he had met Wang Xilei, a twenty-one-year-old Hong Kong girl who was visiting relatives in China and had spent ten days in Harbin. Cao had shown her round the city when he wasn't working and they had been to the cinema. The evening before she left Harbin he had kissed her at the door of the hotel.

"I realized then she was something special," Cao said blushing. "We promised to write to each other." They had been exchanging letters ever since, he added, producing a color photo she had enclosed with her last letter. A pretty girl in white fitted trousers and a reasonably low-cut pink cotton shirt, she was perched on a bed in her family's small Hong Kong apartment.

"This must be very significant," the young man pontificated. "Sitting   4
on a bed? I think she's trying to tell me something."

It sounds like the naive romantic stuff of which many a Hong Kong or Taiwanese film is made. But Cao, who has spent his entire life under the rigid socialist moral code, was deadly serious.

Could there by any future in their relationship, he wondered. After all, she lived in Hong Kong and, even as an office worker, earned about six times what he did. Surely she would not be prepared to live in China, especially not married to an ordinary hotel employee. Even though Cao was a senior high school graduate and studied English conscientiously, he had little chance of improving his job. And he had heard about Hong Kong's strict immigration laws. He might not be able to go there even if he received official approval to leave China.

Like most young people in love, Cao was not particularly impressed by the obvious solution: that he forget Wang Xilei and meet a nice local girl. "But I don't want a local girl. I want Wang Xilei."

Cao's feeling in his heart, as he called it, reflects the new infatuation   8
with romantic love in contemporary China. As an elderly man in Harbin put it: "Falling in love is the thing for young people to do these days — for the first time in the People's Republic."

When the Communists came to power in 1949, they attempted to define "love" in socialist terms, denouncing what they described as bourgeois love as individualistic and self-centered. Socialist love, they said, must not be based on strange feelings in one's heart or flights of passion but on common political attitudes and interests. And personal feelings must always be subordinated to the development of socialist new China, even if this meant separation from the man or woman one loved.

Still, love was allowed to exist and even to be written about, albeit in the socialist realist boy-loves-girl-loves-tractor style characteristic of the Soviet Union. It was only during the Cultural Revolution that all mention of love disappeared from the face of China, condemned as an undesirable manifestation of bourgeois decadent thought: vulgar, cheap, and even obscene.

"We're not supposed to talk or even think about love," my roommate at Peking University had responded when I queried her on the subject in 1976. "We're only supposed to think about class struggle and continuing the revolution."

Soon after Mao's death love began making a tentative reappearance,   12 initiated by the more adventurous writers and poets and flourishing in the short-lived new realism literature of 1979–80. There was Zhang Jie's moving short story "Love Must Not Be Forgotten," a tale of romantic but chaste love between two officials who were married to other people. Zhang Xian's story "The Corner Forsaken by Love" took love beyond the romantic into the realms of passion. And Shu Ting's love poem "Longing" dealt with inner feelings in a more direct manner than almost any poetry had done in the history of Communist China: "O in the vistas of the heart, in the depths of the soul."

The revival of traditional Chinese culture, with its human emotions and love intrigues, placed the new attitudes firmly in a historical framework. In late 1978 the famous traditional Peking opera *The Tale of the White Snake* was featured on stage and television. It was all there: the beautiful maiden falling in love, her victimization and her imprisonment by a wicked abbot, her eventual rescue by her lover and his army. New films, such as the production of Lao She's novel *Rickshaw Boy*, temporarily brought audiences into contact with flesh-and-blood individuals instead of bland class stereotypes.

By the early 1980s love had gained a secure foothold in China. Indeed writers and magazine publishers soon realized their readers were no different from people elsewhere in the world in enjoying the titillation of personal love stories and romantic dramas. One tabloid entitled *Story*, filled with traditional fables about concubines and libertines, attracted some 2 million readers across the country. Regular subscribers reportedly included 700 of the 800 students at one Shanghai high school.

Young people's selective access to Western culture only heightened their interest in romantic love as they came into contact, not with the sexual revolution and the permissive society but with the Brontës[1] and the Hollywood era of the 1930s and 1940s. For the most part, it was an

---

[1]The Brontë sisters, Emily (1818–1848) and Charlotte (1816–1855), respectively, authors of *Wuthering Heights* and *Jane Eyre*. — ED.

image of handsome men and beautiful women falling in love, tender but chaste embraces in the moonlight, and couples living happily ever after.

The new atmosphere was soon reflected in young people's attitudes 16 towards one another. Of course, love and romance — even illicit sex — had never been completely eradicated from China. A wander through the more deserted spots of a public park in the mid-1970s was bound to bring glimpses of young men and women holding hands and even having a quick embrace in the bushes, completely oblivious to passers-by.

But it was furtive and even guilt-ridden.

"A few years ago love seemed to me something vulgar, a petty-bourgeois sentiment," one young man told a Chinese magazine in 1979. "And once when I did love someone, I didn't dare acknowledge it even to myself." . . .

Nowadays, young couples who a few years ago would have met secretly at the back of Peking's Summer Palace — if they had been brave enough to meet at all — wander along the main streets hand in hand. The quick hug or kiss in public is still considered rather brazen, just as it is in Hong Kong or Taiwan, and used to be in the West. Still, there is a new naturalness in male-female relations that was entirely absent ten years ago.

But love and romance are not always clear sailing for young Chinese. 20 Newspapers and magazines now have special advice columns, such as *Chinese Women*'s "Window on Love," to deal with their anxieties. The columns are headed with romantic line drawings: a young man and woman silhouetted against a moonlit sky; a young woman staring wistfully at a sky filled with hearts and flowers.

"I'm madly in love with a young man in the same workshop," wrote one female factory worker. "I don't know how to express my feelings to him. I'm afraid he'll reject me. I'd be so embarrassed. What should I do?"

"I think I'm in love with two men at the same time," wrote another young woman. "I've been going out with both of them and they both say they love me. I can't decide between them and I'm worried that, if I do choose one of them, the other one will be very upset. I'm hopelessly confused. Can you help me?"

The replies are invariably models of common sense, similar to those in traditional women's magazines in the West. The young factory worker was advised to strike up a conversation with the young man, maybe at lunchtime or when they left work, and perhaps even suggest that they go skating or see a film. The young woman in love with the two men was sternly told that it was unfair to lead them both on. She had to make up her mind and tell the young man who had missed out, even if he was upset at the time.

Like other letter writers, these young people were also told that they   24 should not become obsessed with their personal problems and allow their work or studies to suffer. "Love must be kept in its proper place," declares many an editorial article, reflecting the government's alarm at the somewhat overenthusiastic public response to its slightly liberalized attitudes towards personal relations. Cartoons in newspapers and magazines ridicule the alleged surfeit of love being fed to young people on television and in novels and films. In one cartoon, a disappointed nine-year-old girl and her grandfather stand in front of a theater marquee advertising nothing but plays about love.

Official commentators warn writers and film and television producers not to refer to love excessively. "Love is only part of real life," declared the national newspaper *Guangming Daily*, accusing some writers of "seeking love themes like a swarm of bees alighting on one flower." When love is portrayed, it should not "emphasize wooing, embracing, and kissing. Rather it should conform with reality, national customs, communist morality, and the socialist legal system — especially the Marriage Law."

Love, then, is directly related to marriage, at least as the Chinese Communists see it. This connection is emphasized in the huge number of advice books bearing such titles as *Love and Marriage*, *Young People and Falling in Love*, and *Correspondence on Love*. Even ostensibly academic books treat the two subjects as one. "The outcome of young people falling in love is marriage," the book *Youth Psychology* declared categorically.

With the Chinese authorities encouraging young people not to marry until around their midtwenties, the teenage years are considered too early to be thinking about love. Magazine editors offer little sympathy to lovesick high school students.

"I'm a sixteen-year-old male student," wrote one correspondent to a   28 women's magazine. "Recently I've had strong feelings about a classmate. Sometimes our eyes meet and we gaze at each other. When I get home I think of her all the time."

"One day I admired my male classmate's bookmark," said a female student. "That evening when I arrived home I found he'd put it in my schoolbag. I can't really give it back to him. Nor can I keep it. All my friends would know. What will I do?"

These and similar letters, published under the heading "The Secrets of My Heart," provoked a stern response from the editor of the column. "Separating off and pairing up is not right," she stated. "Nor is talking and thinking about love. How can you establish genuine friendships if you behave in this way?"

But the admonitions have little effect. A recent academic work on youth issues complained that Chinese boys and girls, influenced by films and television, are thinking about love at a younger and younger age. "Even third and fourth year primary school pupils talk about falling in love," it revealed.

For all the obsession with love and romance in present-day China, there is still little idea of Western-style dating and going out with a variety of members of the opposite sex before deciding on a marriage partner. The traditional segregation of the sexes is still strong, especially in rural areas. Most young men and women in their teens and even early twenties spend their spare time with members of their own sex, whether going to the cinema, shopping, or strolling in the park.   32

Even on university campuses there is little of the "coed" atmosphere characteristic of most Western universities. While male and female students attend the same classes, they usually sit in separate groups. In a discussion with thirty or so English-language students at the Canton Foreign Language Institute, for example, the girls sat on chairs lining the left side of the room, the boys on the right side. In between was a no man's land of empty seats.

"It's the custom," is the invariable response to queries about the high degree of sexual segregation. "If a young man sat with the women, or a young woman with the men, they would be considered very forward and rather strange. We're more used to being with the members of our own sex."

To a Westerner, the sight of young Chinese women — and sometimes young men — wandering around arm in arm, even hand in hand, can be somewhat disarming. "What a great place to be a homosexual," commented an Australian friend. "No one would even look at you."

Some Westerners interpret physical contact between members of the same sex in China as a sign of latent homosexuality, or perhaps as a sublimation of heterosexual drives. But this behavior is also common in many countries in Asia and elsewhere in the world where it is customary for young men and women to socialize mainly with members of their own sex.   36

Living in a virtually single-sex subculture does, though, reinforce sex-stereotyped characteristics: men tend to talk about football, women about clothes and knitting. It also makes some young people rather awkward, even tongue-tied, in their limited contacts with the opposite sex. "I always blush when a young man comes up and talks to me," confessed one twenty-year-old. "I know it's silly, but I can't help it. And everyone looks at you."

Once young men and women are seen spending any time together they are normally assumed to have entered the stage of "going steady." Some people working or studying together complain that they are unable to have a casual friendship with a member of the opposite sex without being teased and labeled as boyfriend and girlfriend. "Xiao Wang and I work in the same section of the factory," said a young woman in Shanghai. "We share a number of interests and enjoy talking to each other. People assume there is something personal between us. But there isn't. Can't young men and women just be friends?"

The countryside is even more tradition bound, as many a young rural dweller grumbles. One twenty-year-old told a youth advice column that after a village film show he had merely walked home with a young woman who was his neighbor and former classmate. The gossip spread round the village that the two young people were now "in love." "This is the 1980s," protested the young man. "Do we really still adhere to the old ideas? I'm too young to think about such things."

What things? Marriage. Once a young man and woman are assumed   40
to be boyfriend and girlfriend, they are also assumed to have embarked on the road towards matrimony. "Not everyone marries their first boyfriend or girlfriend," commented a teacher in Peking. "But many do. Young people get a bad reputation if they take up with different people and then discard them."

If love has its proper place in China, so has sex: not mentioned publicly and confined within marriage. The Chinese Communists have never had any time for the early Soviet ideas on free love expounded by feminists including Aleksandra Kollontai who argued that the sexual act was no more significant than drinking a glass of water. Rather they took up Lenin's puritanical idea that "dissoluteness in sexual life is bourgeois. . . . Self-control, self-discipline is not slavery, not even in love." Although the private behavior of some members of the Chinese Communist leadership has not always been exemplary — Mao himself discarded a sick wife to take up with young actress Jiang Qing — the Party has imposed a rigid code of moral behavior on the Chinese people.

"Before they marry, young people in love must protect their bodies like jade and not rashly lose their virtue," declared the book *Youth Psychology*. "Premarital sex is contrary to the principles of social ethics. It can produce psychological conflict and affect physical and mental health."

Letters of anguish involving sexual matters receive rather less sympathy from magazine editors than those about romantic love. One villager said her boyfriend had visited her house one evening with the present of a woolen sweater, a conventional symbol of intended matrimony. He told her they would be together forever.

"I had faith in him — and I gave myself to him," she confessed. "Who was to know that three months later he would go off to the city to work and that our relationship would cool? I've heard he's already got a new girlfriend at the factory. I'm a girl who's lost her virtue. What am I worth now? I feel desperate. Please help me." 44

Instead of receiving understanding, the young woman was subjected to a stern lecture. "Sexual relations are lawful only after marriage. You have therefore indulged in unlawful behavior."

Nor does the Chinese government have any time for the argument put forward by Western feminists that sexual freedom is vital to male-female equality. Another young woman who had forsaken her chastity wondered whether it was really so important. "Losing one's chastity is no great thing in the West," she declared. "Isn't our attitude rather feudal?" "No, it is not a feudal attitude," was the solemn response. "It is a socialist attitude. Dissolute behavior between the sexes is a phenomenon of capitalist society."

If official admonitions do not always deter young people from engaging in sexual relations, sheer logistics often do. Finding a place to be alone in Chinese cities and towns can be a formidable challenge. The cramped housing conditions are hardly conducive to intimacy for married couples, let alone for young people wanting to indulge in what is considered unlawful behavior. "We can't wait to get our own flat," one recently married young woman told me in Peking, blushing as she did so. "It's very difficult for couples when they have to share tiny flats with relatives — often just one room with a partition."

Young people living away from home, whether in a university or factory dormitory, are often faced with six or more roommates. And the buildings are usually sex segregated. "You can't get much privacy when 48 you go out either," complained a university student. Broad daylight is a deterrent to all but the most adventurous and park gates are usually securely locked at sunset. Bicycles are no substitute for the West's cars and panel vans.

But China is not the puritanical wonderland some officials would have one believe. Despite the greater conservatism of the countryside, the opportunities for privacy probably result in a higher level of sexual activity among young rural dwellers than their urban brothers and sisters. Even young urban couples manage, in the words of a favorite Communist expression, to "overcome difficulties." A symposium held in Peking in mid-1982 by the Society for Marriage and the Family expressed concern that cases of pregnancy before marriage were on the increase. And a survey of abortions carried out at one hospital revealed that over half involved unmarried women. "Some young people these days are adopting a rather casual attitude towards sex," a women's magazine complained in mid-1983.

Although the Communist authorities and even social scientists vehemently denounce premarital sex, they do not deny the existence of youthful sex instincts and passions. The basic responsibility for keeping these instincts under control until marriage is laid squarely on young women, just as it was in traditional China. "It is a small matter to die of starvation, but a grave matter to lose one's chastity," was one of many common sayings firmly imprinted on young women's minds over the centuries.

Recent comments in the Chinese media sound familiar not just to women who grew up in prerevolutionary China but also to anyone who was a teenager in the West in the 1950s or earlier. "One must make girls understand that they should hold fast to their morals," declared one article in *Chinese Women*. "If your boyfriend makes excessive demands, you must calmly and graciously decline," urged another.

This might not always be easy, the magazine acknowledged when it 52 cited the case of one Xiao Dan and her persuasive boyfriend. "If you refuse me, it shows you don't really love me, and we might as well break up," her boyfriend had told her. Afraid of losing him, Xiao Dan had succumbed to his advances — several times. To her dismay, the young man did not marry her, as he had promised, but moved on to another young woman to whom he made similar promises and advances.

"Sexual desire and love are not the same thing," concluded the article. "Young people must be careful to distinguish between the two."

When the inevitable does happen, the traditional Hollywood-style scenario is also rather familiar; the young man stirred by the sight of a female body and the young woman, against all her better judgment and sense of morality, succumbing to sheer physical passion. Such a scenario takes place in the short story "The Corner Forsaken by Love" which describes a relationship — not in traditional China but in the late 1970s — between two young peasants. Fairly astounding even in China's new realism literature, it is probably the closest to a sex scene that has yet appeared in contemporary Chinese literature.

> That instant Xiao Baozi froze as if electrified. He stared blankly, his breath stopped — and a gush of warm blood rushed to his head. It was because when the young woman took off her sweater, her shirt was pulled up, exposing half of a pale, full, and bouncing breast.
>
> Like a leopard springing from its cave, Xiao Baozi leaped forward. He embraced her tightly as if he had completely lost his senses. Startled, the young woman tried to lift her arm to block him. But when his burning, quivering lips touched her own moist lips, she was overcome with a mysterious dizziness. Her eyes closed and her outstretched arms were paralyzed. All her intentions to resist disappeared instantly. A kind of primitive reflex burned like a fierce flame in the blood of this pair of materially poor, spiritually barren, but physically robust young people. Traditional morality, rational dignity, the danger of breaking the law, the shame in a young woman's heart — all of these, everything, in a moment were burnt to ashes.

Their punishment was not long in coming. Found out by the villagers, they were abused and beaten for their illicit behavior. The young woman, Shen Cunni, was so completely overcome by the shame and disgrace she had brought on herself and her family that she took the traditional Chinese way out, drowning herself in the village pond.

The theme in this and similar stories is that of the universal "fallen woman," irretrievably soiled and spoiled for any other man. Losing one's chastity might no longer be a graver matter than dying of starvation, but it is very serious — if one is female. For all the official assertions of male-female equality, the double standard is still alive and well in contemporary China. And it is only reinforced by the expounders of so-called socialist morality.

In a discussion of youth issues at the Chinese Academy of Social Sciences, I mentioned that some young people in the West live together without being married. Although the idea initially met with puzzlement, some of the researchers seemed reasonably responsive.

"It's quite a good idea in the West considering the high divorce rate," one ventured.

"What about in China?"

"Oh, it wouldn't work in China. If the couple broke up, the woman   60
would have great difficulty finding another man to marry her. Chinese women are expected to be virgins when they marry."

"What about men?"

"That's not so important."

The young woman who succumbs to her boyfriend's advances finds herself in a highly vulnerable position, especially if he decides not to marry her. Unless she can hide her past misdemeanors, which can be difficult in a society with little physical mobility, she has placed her marriage prospects in serious jeopardy. "I'm feeling desperate," a young woman in Heilongjiang province wrote to an advice column. "My boyfriend and I had been planning to get married for some time. Suddenly he told me that we were breaking up. Why? When I saw his cold expression, I knew he'd found out that I had had sexual relations with a former boyfriend."

No mention was made in her letter, or in the predictably unsympa-   64
thetic reply, of whether or not her husband-to-be had also had a previous sexual relationship.

The lack of formal sex education for young people until they are about to get married, together with the difficulty of obtaining contraceptives, means that quite a few young women face an even more traumatic situation: the discovery that they are pregnant. The stereotyped raging father in the West is a mild character compared with his Chinese counterpart, especially in the countryside. Threatened with family shame and disgrace, he may well beat his daughter and then, accompanied by other male family members, go and beat up the young man and even his family.

"It can cause complete uproar in a village when a girl gets pregnant," confirmed one former rural resident. "It's bad enough when a young couple are caught having a sexual relationship — or even assumed to be having one."

But even in China raging fathers are quick to face reality. "What usually happens in the case of pregnancy is that a speedy marriage takes place," a Women's Federation official told me in Harbin. "If the couple are not old enough to get married officially, then the young woman will probably have an abortion at the local clinic. In the countryside, the young couple might just have a traditional marriage ceremony and live together. They'll probably register the marriage when they reach the official minimum marriage age — twenty-two for men and twenty for women."

In 1981, almost 400,000 babies — one in every 50 newborns in China — were born to women nineteen years old or under. 68

"Can a woman have and keep a baby if she's not living in an official or traditional marriage relationship?" I asked.

"I've heard that quite a few women become single mothers in the West," the Women's Federation official replied. "But in China it's against both traditional morality and socialist ethics — as well as the present policy of one child per *couple*. It happens occasionally, of course, and illegitimate children have the same formal rights as other children. But the woman would be regarded as something of a social outcast, as well as bringing disgrace to her family. And she would probably be resigning herself to a life without a husband. No man is likely to want to marry a woman who already has a child, not just because of her reputation but because of the one-child policy. He'd want to have his own child, not bring up someone else's."

The single mother would also face severe practical difficulties unless she had her family's close support and financial backing. Without formal marriage registration, a woman is not entitled to paid maternity leave or subsidized hospital costs and child care. And while the father is legally responsible for part of the cost of the child's upbringing and education, he is no more likely to acknowledge paternity than many men in similar circumstances in the West.

If possible rejection by a boyfriend, pregnancy, parental rage, and 72 abortion are not sufficiently traumatic, the young woman discovered having a sexual relationship also has to face official censure. If she is still at high school, she might well find herself spending a year or two in reform school to ponder the error of her ways. If she is lucky, she will only be subjected to criticism and a substantial burst of ideological education about correct socialist morality.

"We classify sexual relations in the category of behavior liable to expulsion," one university administrator told me. "It depends to some extent on the attitude and behavior of the person concerned. If she is repentant and promises to behave in future, we'll usually give her a second chance. But repeated behavior of this sort cannot be tolerated. It has a corrupting influence on others."

In one recent case, he told me, a young woman who became pregnant was suspended from the university for one year as punishment.

What about the young man? I asked.

"We criticized him."   76

EXPLORATIONS

1. What types of source has Hooper used as the basis for "Falling in Love with Love"? Which of these sources provide the most credible support for her conclusions about romantic love in contemporary China? Which sources provide the most vivid and detailed picture of the new national attitudes? What is the effect of Hooper's including some of her own questions to interview subjects as well as their responses?

2. In keeping with her subject, Hooper uses a number of expressions that convey emotion. What quoted words and phrases in "Falling in Love with Love" show that love is as confusing and highly charged for young Chinese as for men and women in any other culture? Which of the author's own words and phrases highlight her subjects' emotional turmoil?

3. Hooper writes, "Young people's selective access to Western culture only heightened their interest in romantic love as they came into contact, not with the sexual revolution and the permissive society but with the Brontës and the Hollywood era of the 1930s and 1940s. For the most part, it was an image of handsome men and beautiful women falling in love, tender but chaste embraces in the moonlight, and couples living happily ever after." In what specific ways does this Western image of romance suit the interests of the Communist state? What statements later in Hooper's essay, regarding sex roles, the Marriage Law, and other Chinese practices under Communism, suggest reasons why the government gave its citizens access to that particular segment of Western culture?

CONNECTIONS

1. The Chinese Communist attitude toward romance described by Hooper contains parallels with the Soviet Communist attitude described by Santha Rama Rau in "Boris's Romance." What are the main similarities? What important differences do you notice? In what ways are courtship customs in each country affected by unromantic factors, such as housing and transportation?

2. Beginning in paragraph 50, Hooper discusses sex-role stereotypes in contemporary China. Which of the four female stereotypes described by Isak Dinesen apparently prevail in China? Which ones would the Chinese probably deny

or condemn? Which one do you think Chinese officials probably would view as the greatest threat to the Communist social order, and why?

3. Ruth Sidel's "The Liu Family" (p. 21) describes China as it was in the early 1970s. What does Hooper — writing more than a decade later — tell us about the place of love in Chinese culture back then? On the basis of these two essays, why do you think "love began making a tentative reappearance" after Mao's death? What steps did the post-Mao regime take, according to Hooper, to control the influence of love on its citizens?

ELABORATIONS

1. Hooper suggests that the Chinese government considers itself both able and entitled to regulate its citizens' love life. Our Declaration of Independence takes a contrary view, insisting on the individual's right to pursue happiness and to "alter or to abolish" any government that infringes that right. Using "Falling in Love with Love" as a source, write an essay comparing and contrasting the Chinese and American concepts of the role of the state. Focus not only on describing but on interpreting: How does each system meet (and/ or fail to meet) the needs of those who live with it?

2. Ruth Sidel's "The Liu Family" (p. 21) and Hooper's "Falling in Love with Love" together create an intriguing portrait of a culture in transition. From the information in these two essays (and their headnotes), write your own essay about the recent history of romance in China. Potential themes include the loosening of government control from Mao's era to the present, the parallel rise of individual freedom, and the shift in Chinese perceptions of the West that has accompanied the new attitude toward love.

OCTAVIO PAZ

My Life with the Wave

Although Octavio Paz is represented in this book by a short story, he is best known for his poetry. Paz was born in Mexico City in 1914. Educated at a Roman Catholic school and the National University of Mexico, he published his first book of poems at nineteen. Four years later he went to Europe, where he supported the Republican side in the Spanish Civil War, established himself as a writer with another book of poems, and met prominent Surrealist poets in Paris. Back in Mexico he founded and edited several literary reviews and produced his famous study of Mexican character and culture, "The Labyrinth of Solitude" (1950). Paz served as Mexico's ambassador to India from 1962 to 1968, resigning over Mexico's brutal treatment of student radicals. He has also lived in England, France, and the United States, where he spent most of the 1970s at Harvard University.

The United States' neighbor to the south has been populated since around 21,000 B.C. The great Olmec, Toltec, Mayan, and Aztec civilizations arose between A.D. 100 and A.D. 900. When Hernán Cortés and other explorers arrived from Spain in the 1500s, they conquered the ruling Aztecs and made Mexico a heavily exploited colony until a series of rebellions achieved independence in 1823. While democracy has persisted, reform has progressed haltingly. After an oil boom in the 1970s, Mexico's economy declined; most of the rural and much of the urban population remains poor, so many workers seek jobs across the northern border. Both folk art and fine art have burgeoned, however: writers such as Paz and Carlos Fuentes are internationally regarded, as are a number of Mexican painters, composers, and other artists.

"My Life with the Wave" first appeared in *Arenas movedizas* (1949); the translation from the Spanish is by Eliot Weinberger from *Eagle or Sun?* (1970; *¿Águila o sol?* 1951).

When I left that sea, a wave moved ahead of the others. She was tall and light. In spite of the shouts of the others who grabbed her by her floating clothes, she clutched my arm and went off with me leaping. I didn't want to say anything to her, because it hurt me to shame her in front of her friends. Besides, the furious stares of the elders paralyzed me. When we got to town, I explained to her that it was impossible, that life in the city was not what she had been able to imagine with the ingenuity of a wave that had never left the sea. She watched me gravely:

234

"No, your decision is made. You can't go back." I tried sweetness, hardness, irony. She cried, screamed, hugged, threatened. I had to apologize.

The next day my troubles began. How could we get on the train without being seen by the conductor, the passengers, the police? Certainly the rules say nothing in respect to the transport of waves on the railroad, but this same reserve was an indication of the severity with which our act would be judged. After much thought I arrived at the station an hour before departure, took my seat, and, when no one was looking, emptied the water tank for the passengers; then, carefully, poured in my friend.

The first incident came about when the children of a nearby couple declared their noisy thirst. I stopped them and promised them refreshments and lemonade. They were at the point of accepting when another thirsty passenger approached. I was about to invite her also, but the stare of her companion stopped me. The lady took a paper cup, approached the tank, and turned the faucet. Her cup was barely half full when I leaped between the woman and my friend. She looked at me astonished. While I apologized, one of the children turned the faucet again. I closed it violently. The lady brought the cup to her lips:

"Agh, this water is salty."   4

The boy echoed her. Various passengers rose. The husband called the conductor:

"This man put salt in the water."

The conductor called the Inspector:

"So you put substances in the water?"   8

The Inspector in turn called the police:

"So you poisoned the water?"

The police in turn called the Captain:

"So you're the poisoner?"   12

The Captain called three agents. The agents took me to an empty car, amid the stares and whispers of the passengers. At the next station they took me off and pushed and dragged me to the jail. For days no one spoke to me, except during the long interrogations. When I explained my story no one believed me, not even the jailer, who shook his head, saying: "The case is grave, truly grave. You didn't want to poison the children?" One day they brought me before the Magistrate.

"Your case is difficult," he repeated. "I will assign you to the Penal Judge."

A year passed. Finally they judged me. As there were no victims, my sentence was light. After a short time, my day of liberty arrived.

The Chief of the Prison called me in: 16

"Well, now you're free. You were lucky. Lucky there were no victims. But don't do it again, because the next time won't be so short . . . "

And he stared at me with the same grave stare with which everyone watched me.

The same afternoon I took the train and after hours of uncomfortable traveling arrived in Mexico City. I took a cab home. At the door of my apartment I heard laughter and singing. I felt a pain in my chest, like the smack of a wave of surprise when surprise smacks us across the chest: my friend was there, singing and laughing as always.

"How did you get back?"   20

"Simple: in the train. Someone, after making sure that I was only salt water, poured me in the engine. It was a rough trip: soon I was a white plume of vapor, soon I fell in a fine rain on the machine. I thinned out a lot. I lost many drops."

Her presence changed my life. The house of dark corridors and dusty furniture was filled with air, with sun, with sounds and green and blue reflections, a numerous and happy populace of reverberations and echoes. How many waves is one wave, and how it can make a beach or a rock or jetty out of a wall, a chest, a forehead that it crowns with foam! Even the abandoned corners, the abject corners of dust and debris were touched by her light hands. Everything began to laugh and everywhere shined with teeth. The sun entered the old rooms with pleasure and stayed in my house for hours, abandoning the other houses, the district, the city, the country. And some nights, very late, the scandalized stars watched it sneak from my house.

Love was a game, a perpetual creation. All was beach, sand, a bed of sheets that were always fresh. If I embraced her, she swelled with pride, incredibly tall, like the liquid stalk of a poplar; and soon that thinness flowered into a fountain of white feathers, into a plume of smiles that fell over my head and back and covered me with whiteness. Or she stretched out in front of me, infinite as the horizon, until I too became horizon and silence. Full and sinuous, it enveloped me like music or some giant lips. Her presence was a going and coming of caresses, of murmurs, of kisses. Entered in her waters, I was drenched to the socks and in a wink of an eye I found myself up above, at the height of vertigo, mysteriously suspended, to fall like a stone and feel myself gently deposited on the dryness, like a feather. Nothing is comparable to sleeping in those waters, to wake pounded by a thousand happy light lashes, by a thousand assaults that withdrew laughing.

But never did I reach the center of her being. Never did I touch the   24 nakedness of pain and of death. Perhaps it does not exist in waves, that secret site that renders a woman vulnerable and mortal, that electric button where all interlocks, twitches, and straightens out to then swoon. Her sensibility, like that of women, spread in ripples, only they weren't concentric ripples, but rather excentric, spreading each time farther, until they touched other galaxies. To love her was to extend to remote contacts, to vibrate with far-off stars we never suspected. But her center . . . no, she had no center, just an emptiness as in a whirlwind, that sucked me in and smothered me.

Stretched out side by side, we exchanged confidences, whispers, smiles. Curled up, she fell on my chest and there unfolded like a vegetation of murmurs. She sang in my ear, a little snail. She became humble and transparent, clutching my feet like a small animal, calm water. She was so clear I could read all of her thoughts. Certain nights her skin was covered with phosphorescence and to embrace her was to embrace a piece of night tattooed with fire. But she also became black and bitter. At unexpected hours she roared, moaned, twisted. Her groans woke the neighbors. Upon hearing her, the sea wind would scratch at the door of the house or rave in a loud voice on the roof. Cloudy days irritated her; she broke furniture, said bad words, covered me with insults and green and gray foam. She spit, cried, swore, prophesied. Subject to the moon, to the stars, to the influence of the light of other worlds, she changed her moods and appearance in a way that I thought fantastic, but it was as fatal as the tide.

She began to miss solitude. The house was full of snails and conches, of small sailboats that in her fury she had shipwrecked (together with the others, laden with images, that each night left my forehead and sank in her ferocious or pleasant whirlwinds). How many little treasures were lost in that time! But my boats and the silent song of the snails was not enough. I had to install in the house a colony of fish. I confess that it was not without jealousy that I watched them swimming in my friend, caressing her breasts, sleeping between her legs, adorning her hair with light flashes of color.

Among all those fish there were a few particularly repulsive and ferocious ones, little tigers from the aquarium, with large fixed eyes and jagged and bloodthirsty mouths. I don't know by what aberration my friend delighted in playing with them, shamelessly showing them a preference whose significance I preferred to ignore. She passed long hours confined with those horrible creatures. One day I couldn't stand it any more; I threw open the door and launched after them. Agile and ghostly they escaped my hands while she laughed and pounded me until I fell. I thought I was drowning. And when I was at the point of death, and purple, she deposited me on the bank and began to kiss me, saying I don't know what things. I felt very weak, fatigued and humiliated. And at the same time her voluptuousness made me close my eyes, because her voice was sweet and she spoke to me of the delicious death of the drowned. When I recovered, I began to fear and hate her.

I had neglected my affairs. Now I began to visit friends and renew old and dear relations. I met an old girlfriend. Making her swear to keep my secret, I told her of my life with the wave. Nothing moves women so much as the possibility of saving a man. My redeemer employed all of her arts, but what could a woman, master of a limited number of souls and bodies, do in front of my friend who was always changing — and always identical to herself in her incessant metamorphoses. 28

Winter came. The sky turned gray. Fog fell on the city. Frozen drizzle rained. My friend cried every night. During the day she isolated herself, quiet and sinister, stuttering a single syllable, like an old woman who grumbles in a corner. She became cold; to sleep with her was to shiver all night and to feel freeze, little by little, the blood, the bones, the thoughts. She turned deep, impenetrable, restless. I left frequently and my absences were each time more prolonged. She, in her corner, howled loudly. With teeth like steel and a corrosive tongue she gnawed the walls, crumbled them. She passed the nights in mourning, reproaching me. She had nightmares, deliriums of the sun, of warm beaches. She dreamt of the pole and of changing into a great block of ice, sailing beneath black skies in nights long as months. She insulted me. She cursed and laughed; filled the house with guffaws and phantoms. She called up the monsters of the depths, blind ones, quick ones, blunt. Charged with electricity, she carbonized all she touched; full of acid, she dissolved whatever she brushed against. Her sweet embraces became knotty cords that strangled me. And her body, greenish and elastic, was an implacable whip that lashed, lashed, lashed. I fled. The horrible fish laughed with ferocious smiles.

There in the mountains, among the tall pines and precipices, I breathed the cold thin air like a thought of liberty. At the end of a month I returned. I had decided. It had been so cold that over the marble of the chimney, next to the extinct fire, I found a statue of ice. I was unmoved by her weary beauty. I put her in a big canvas sack and went out to the streets with the sleeper on my shoulders. In a restaurant in the outskirts I sold her to a waiter friend who immediately began to chop her into little pieces, which he carefully deposited in the buckets where bottles are chilled.

EXPLORATIONS

1. What problems does Paz's narrator face in his romance with a wave which he might also face in a romance with a women? What problems occur purely because his lover is a wave? What additional kinds of human interaction are illuminated by the narrator's wave-specific problems? (See, for example, the scene on the train.)
2. What attractive qualities does the wave share with human women? What parts of the story seem to represent a man's fantasies about a woman, either positive or negative, rather than qualities that a real woman might have?
3. What points does Paz make in "My Life with the Wave" about men in love? about women in love? about relationships between men and women? How would the story's impact change if its female character were a woman instead of a wave?

CONNECTIONS

1. In "Falling in Love with Love," Beverley Hooper mentions the Soviet feminist Aleksandra Kollontai, "who argued that the sexual act was no more significant than drinking a glass of water." How do you think Paz would respond to Kollontai's assertion? What view of sex does Paz express in "My Life with the Wave"?
2. In Santha Rama Rau's "Boris's Romance," Boris quotes a Russian proverb: "Love is so cruel-and-stubborn, you can even fall in love with a mountain goat." How does Paz's story illustrate this proverb? What specific observations and incidents in "My Life with the Wave" show the cruel and stubborn aspects of loving someone in spite of oneself?
3. Which of the female stereotypes described by Isak Dinesen apply to Paz's wave? Which comments about the wave show what images Paz's narrator has of her?

ELABORATIONS

1. Choose one of the three main sections of "My Life with the Wave": the train incident (paragraphs 2–13), love in bloom (paragraphs 19–25), or the end of love (paragraphs 25–30). What points is Paz making in this section, and what techniques does he use to make them? Rewrite the section in your own words, following Paz's structure and underlying intentions but replacing the wave with a human lover. (If you wish, you may replace the wave with a man and the narrator with a woman.)

2. Like Mario Vargas Llosa in "Sunday, Sunday" (p. 145), Paz uses the sea as the central metaphor in his story. Write an essay comparing and contrasting the sea's role in these two stories. For example: What emotional reality does the sea represent in each story? Is the author's description highly visual? tactile? aromatic? Does he emphasize how the sea appears or what it does? What parts of speech (nouns, verbs, adjectives, adverbs) are most important and effective in linking the sea with the story's characters and theme?

SIMONE DE BEAUVOIR

Woman as Other

Simone de Beauvoir, born in Paris in 1908, was best known for her feminist fiction and nonfiction and for her lifelong relationship with the existentialist philosopher and writer Jean-Paul Sartre. De Beauvoir was twenty when she met Sartre while studying at the Sorbonne. The two never married, lived together, or viewed their liaison as exclusive, but they worked closely together and kept apartments in the same building until Sartre's death in 1980. De Beauvoir's several memoirs chronicle her social and political development; her novels examine existentialist ideas and sometimes their proponents as well. *The Mandarins* (1954), based on her affair with American novelist Nelson Algren, won the prestigious Prix Goncourt. De Beauvoir's most famous work is the international best-seller *The Second Sex* (1952; *Le Deuxième Sexe,* 1949), translated from the French by H. M. Parshley, from which "Woman as Other" is taken. A vigorous champion of antiestablishment causes, de Beauvoir died in Paris in 1986.

What is a woman?

To state the question is, to me, to suggest, at once, a preliminary answer. The fact that I ask it is in itself significant. A man would never get the notion of writing a book on the peculiar situation of the human male. But if I wish to define myself, I must first of all say: "I am a woman"; on this truth must be based all further discussion. A man never begins by presenting himself as an individual of a certain sex; it goes without saying that he is a man. The terms *masculine* and *feminine* are used symmetrically only as a matter of form, as on legal papers. In actuality the relation of the two sexes is not quite like that of two electrical poles, for man represents both the positive and the neutral, as is indicated by the common use of *man* to designate human beings in general; whereas woman represents only the negative, defined by limiting criteria, without reciprocity. In the midst of an abstract discussion it is vexing to hear a man say: "You think thus and so because you are a woman"; but I know that my only defense is to reply: "I think thus and so because it is true," thereby removing my subjective self from the argument. It would be out of the question to reply: "And you think the contrary because you are a man," for it is understood that the fact of being a man is no peculiarity.

A man is in the right in being a man; it is the woman who is in the wrong. It amounts to this: just as for the ancients there was an absolute vertical with reference to which the oblique was defined, so there is an absolute human type, the masculine. Woman has ovaries, a uterus; these peculiarities imprison her in her subjectivity, circumscribe her within the limits of her own nature. It is often said that she thinks with her glands. Man superbly ignores the fact that his anatomy also includes glands, such as the testicles, and that they secrete hormones. He thinks of his body as a direct and normal connection with the world, which he believes he apprehends objectively, whereas he regards the body of woman as a hindrance, a prison, weighed down by everything peculiar to it. "The female is a female by virtue of a certain *lack* of qualities," said Aristotle; "we should regard the female nature as afflicted with a natural defectiveness." And St. Thomas for his part pronounced women to be an "imperfect man," an "incidental" being. This is symbolized in Genesis where Eve is depicted as made from what Bossuet called "a supernumerary bone" of Adam.

Thus humanity is male and man defines woman not in herself but as relative to him; she is not regarded as an autonomous being. Michelet writes: "Woman, the relative being. . . ." And Benda is most positive in his *Rapport d'Uriel*: "The body of man makes sense in itself quite apart from that of woman, whereas the latter seems wanting in significance by itself. . . . Man can think of himself without woman. She cannot think of herself without man." And she is simply what man decrees; thus she is called "the sex," by which is meant that she appears essentially to the male as a sexual being. For him she is sex — absolute sex, no less. She is defined and differentiated with reference to man and not he with reference to her; she is the incidental, the inessential as opposed to the essential. He is the Subject, he is the Absolute — she is the Other.

The category of the *Other* is as primordial as consciousness itself. In [4] the most primitive societies, in the most ancient mythologies, one finds the expression of a duality — that of the Self and the Other. This duality was not originally attached to the division of the sexes; it was not dependent upon any empirical facts. It is revealed in such works as that of Granet on Chinese thought and those of Dumézil on the East Indies and Rome. The feminine element was at first no more involved in such pairs as Varuna-Mitra, Uranus-Zeus, Sun-Moon, and Day-Night than it was in the contrasts between Good and Evil, lucky and unlucky auspices, right and left, God and Lucifer. Otherness is a fundamental category of human thought.

Thus it is that no group ever sets itself up as the One without at once setting up the Other over against itself. If three travelers chance to occupy the same compartment, that is enough to make vaguely hostile "others" out of all the rest of the passengers on the train. In small-town eyes all persons not belonging to the village are "strangers" and suspect; to the native of a country all who inhabit other countries are "foreigners"; Jews are "different" for the anti-Semite, Negroes are "inferior" for American racists, aborigines are "natives" for colonists, proletarians are the "lower class" for the privileged.

Lévi-Strauss, at the end of a profound work on the various forms of primitive societies, reaches the following conclusion: "Passage from the state of Nature to the state of Culture is marked by man's ability to view biological relations as a series of contrasts; duality, alternation, opposition, and symmetry, whether under definite or vague forms, constitute not so much phenomena to be explained as fundamental and immediately given data of social reality." These phenomena would be incomprehensible if in fact human society were simply a *Mitsein* or fellowship based on solidarity and friendliness. Things become clear, on the contrary, if, following Hegel, we find in consciousness itself a fundamental hostility toward every other consciousness; the subject can be posed only in being opposed — he sets himself up as the essential, as opposed to the other, the inessential, the object.

But the other consciousness, the other ego, sets up a reciprocal claim. The native traveling abroad is shocked to find himself in turn regarded as a "stranger" by the natives of neighboring countries. As a matter of fact, wars, festivals, trading, treaties, and contests among tribes, nations, and classes tend to deprive the concept *Other* of its absolute sense and to make manifest its relativity; willy-nilly, individuals and groups are forced to realize the reciprocity of their relations. How is it, then, that this reciprocity has not been recognized between the sexes, that one of the contrasting terms is set up as the sole essential, denying any relativity in regard to its correlative and defining the latter as pure otherness? Why is it that women do not dispute male sovereignty? No subject will readily volunteer to become the object, the inessential; it is not the Other who, in defining himself as the Other, establishes the One. The Other is posed as such by the One in defining himself as the One. But if the Other is not to regain the status of being the One, he must be submissive enough to accept this alien point of view. Whence comes this submission in the case of woman?

There are, to be sure, other cases in which a certain category has been 8 able to dominate another completely for a time. Very often this privilege depends upon inequality of numbers — the majority imposes its rule upon the minority or persecutes it. But women are not a minority, like the American Negroes or the Jews; there are as many women as men on earth. Again, the two groups concerned have often been originally independent; they may have been formerly unaware of each other's existence, or perhaps they recognized each other's autonomy. But a historical event has resulted in the subjugation of the weaker by the stronger. The scattering of the Jews, the introduction of slavery into America, the conquests of imperialism are examples in point. In these cases the oppressed retained at least the memory of former days; they possessed in common a past, a tradition, sometimes a religion or a culture.

The parallel drawn by Bebel between women and the proletariat is valid in that neither ever formed a minority or a separate collective unit of mankind. And instead of a single historical event it is in both cases a historical development that explains their status as a class and accounts for the membership of *particular individuals* in that class. But proletarians have not always existed, whereas there have always been women. They are women in virtue of their anatomy and physiology. Throughout history they have always been subordinated to men, and hence their dependency is not the result of a historical event or a social change — it was not something that *occurred*. The reason why otherness in this case seems to be an absolute is in part that it lacks the contingent or incidental nature of historical facts. A condition brought about at a certain time can be abolished at some other time, as the Negroes of Haiti and others have proved; but it might seem that a natural condition is beyond the possibility of change. In truth, however, the nature of things is no more immutably given, once for all, than is historical reality. If woman seems to be the inessential which never becomes the essential, it is because she herself fails to bring about this change. Proletarians say "We"; Negroes also. Regarding themselves as subjects, they transform the bourgeois, the whites, into "others." But women do not say "We," except at some congress of feminists of similar formal demonstration; men say "women," and women use the same word in referring to themselves. They do not authentically assume a subjective attitude. The proletarians have accomplished the revolution in Russia, the Negroes in Haiti, the Indochinese are battling for it in Indochina; but the women's effort has never been anything more than a symbolic agitation. They have gained only what men have been willing to grant; they have taken nothing, they have only received.

The reason for this is that women lack concrete means for organizing themselves into a unit which can stand face to face with the correlative unit. They have no past, no history, no religion of their own; and they have no such solidarity of work and interest as that of the proletariat. They are not even promiscuously herded together in the way that creates community feeling among the American Negroes, the ghetto Jews, the workers of Saint-Denis, or the factory hands of Renault. They live dispersed among the males, attached through residence, housework, economic condition, and social standing to certain men — fathers or husbands — more firmly than they are to other women. If they belong to the bourgeoisie, they feel solidarity with men of that class, not with proletarian women; if they are white, their allegiance is to white men, not to Negro women. The proletariat can propose to massacre the ruling class, and a sufficiently fanatical Jew or Negro might dream of getting sole possession of the atomic bomb and making humanity wholly Jewish or black; but woman cannot even dream of exterminating the males. The bond that unites her to her oppressors is not comparable to any other. The division of the sexes is a biological fact, not an event in human history. Male and female stand opposed within a primordial *Mitsein*, and woman has not broken it. The couple is a fundamental unity with its two halves riveted together, and the cleavage of society along the line of sex is impossible. Here is to be found the basic trait of woman: she is the Other in a totality of which the two components are necessary to one another.

One could suppose that this reciprocity might have facilitated the liberation of woman. When Hercules sat at the feet of Omphale and helped with her spinning, his desire for her held him captive; but why did she fail to gain a lasting power? To revenge herself on Jason, Medea killed their children; and this grim legend would seem to suggest that she might have obtained a formidable influence over him through his love for his offspring. In *Lysistrata* Aristophanes gaily depicts a band of women who joined forces to gain social ends through the sexual needs of their men; but this is only a play. In the legend of the Sabine women, the latter soon abandoned their plan of remaining sterile to punish their ravishers. In truth woman has not been socially emancipated through man's need — sexual desire and the desire for offspring — which makes the male dependent for satisfaction upon the female.

Master and slave, also, are united by a reciprocal need, in this case 12 economic, which does not liberate the slave. In the relation of master to slave the master does not make a point of the need that he has for the other; he has in his grasp the power of satisfying this need through his own action; whereas the slave, in his dependent condition, his hope and fear, is quite conscious of the need he has for his master. Even if the need is at bottom equally urgent for both, it always works in favor of the oppressor and against the oppressed. That is why the liberation of the working class, for example, has been slow.

Now, woman has always been man's dependent, if not his slave; the two sexes have never shared the world in equality. And even today woman is heavily handicapped, though her situation is beginning to change. Almost nowhere is her legal status the same as man's, and frequently it is much to her disadvantage. Even when her rights are legally recognized in the abstract, long-standing custom prevents their full expression in the mores. In the economic sphere men and women can almost be said to make up two castes; other things being equal, the former hold the better jobs, get higher wages, and have more opportunity for success than their new competitors. In industry and politics men have a great many more positions and they monopolize the most important posts. In addition to all this, they enjoy a traditional prestige that the education of children tends in every way to support, for the present enshrines the past — and in the past all history has been made by men. At the present time, when women are beginning to take part in the affairs of the world, it is still a world that belongs to men — they have no doubt of it at all and women have scarcely any. To decline to be the Other, to refuse to be a party to the deal — this would be for women to renounce all the advantages conferred upon them by their alliance with the superior caste. Man-the-sovereign will provide woman-the-liege with material protection and will undertake the moral justification of her existence; thus she can evade at once both economic risk and the metaphysical risk of a liberty in which ends and aims must be contrived without assistance. Indeed, along with the ethical urge of each individual to affirm his subjective existence, there is also the temptation to forgo liberty and become a thing. This is an inauspicious road, for he who takes it — passive, lost, ruined — becomes henceforth the creature of another's will, frustrated in his transcendence and deprived of every value. But it is an easy road; on it one avoids the strain involved in undertaking an authentic existence. When man makes of woman the *Other*, he may, then, expect her to manifest deep-seated tendencies toward complicity. Thus, woman may fail to lay claim to the status of subject because she lacks definite resources, because she feels the necessary bond that ties her to man regardless of reciprocity, and because she is often very well pleased with her role as the *Other*.

EXPLORATIONS

1. "Woman as Other" was originally published as part of *The Second Sex* in 1949. Which, if any, of de Beauvoir's observations about women's status have been invalidated since then by political and social changes? Which of her then radical ideas have gained acceptance?

2. Which of the problems mentioned by de Beauvoir are live issues in our society today? Which (if any) of her statements do you disagree with, and why?

3. What emotionally loaded words, phrases, and sentences indicate that de Beauvoir is presenting an argument in "Woman as Other"? Who is her intended audience? To what extent, and for what reasons, do you think she expects part or all of her audience to resist the case she is making?

4. What types of sources does de Beauvoir cite? In what ways would her essay gain or lose impact if she included quotations from interviews with individual women and men? In what ways would it gain or lose impact if she cut all references to outside sources?

CONNECTIONS

1. De Beauvoir and Isak Dinesen wrote at approximately the same time about some of the same issues. What ideas do they have in common? How are de Beauvoir's purposes different from Dinesen's? How do the two authors' tones differ? Are they fundamentally in agreement or disagreement about the social roles of women and men?

2. In what ways does Boris's narrative in Santha Rama Rau's "Boris's Romance" confirm de Beauvoir's theory about the way men regard women? What additional interactions described by Boris show one person or group treating itself as subject and treating some other person or group as object? What aspects of these interactions contradict or complicate de Beauvoir's generalizations about men and women, the One and the Other?

3. Which of the *Observations* on pages 195–203 show men viewing women as "Other"? Which ones show women viewing men as "Other"? What recommendations do the American authors make about overcoming the problems de Beauvoir describes?

ELABORATIONS

1. In "My Life with the Wave," Octavio Paz takes to a logical extreme de
   Beauvoir's idea that men regard women as the Other. Does Paz agree with
   de Beauvoir about the implications of this male attitude? Go through his story
   and her essay carefully, listing the main points each author makes. Then
   write an essay using "My Life with the Wave" to illustrate — or refute —
   arguments presented in "Women as Other."

2. "What is a woman?" asks de Beauvoir. She goes on: "If I wish to define
   myself, I must first of all say: 'I am a woman.'" Already she is letting her
   readers know that her choice of *definition* as the form for her inquiry has a
   political as well as a rhetorical basis. That is, she is not simply defining
   woman, as her opening question implies; she is examining a definition of
   woman imposed by men. The same tactic can be applied to any issue in
   which a preexisting definition is crucial to the argument. Choose such an
   issue that interests you — for instance, What is a drug? or What is the
   Strategic Defense Initiative? Write a definition essay exploring the issue by
   examining the tacit definitions that underlie it.

ALBERTO MORAVIA

The Chase

Alberto Moravia has been called the first existential novelist in Italy — a forerunner of Sartre and Camus in France. Moravia is best known in the United States for the films that have been based on his work: Michelangelo Antonioni's *L'Avventura* (1961), Jean-Luc Godard's *Le Mépris (Contempt,* 1965), and Bernardo Bertolucci's *The Conformist* (1970). The film of *Conjugal Love* (1949) was directed by Moravia's wife, Dacia Maraini. Born Alberto Pincherle in Rome in 1907, Moravia had little formal schooling but was taught to read English, French, and German by governesses and earned a high-school diploma. He began his first novel at age sixteen while in a sanatorium for the tuberculosis he had contracted when he was nine; he considers his long illness a major influence on his career. Moravia's novels, stories, and scripts are too numerous to list. Many of them are available in English. "The Chase," translated from the Italian in 1969 by Angus Davidson, is from the story collection *Command, and I Will Obey You.*

Italy, Moravia's homeland and the setting of this story, is a boot-shaped European peninsula across the Mediterranean Sea from Libya. Occupied since the Stone Age, it had its political heyday during the Roman Empire, which by A.D. 180 ruled from Britain to Africa to Persia (now Iran). The Roman civilization fell to barbarian invaders in the fourth and fifth centuries but left as a legacy its alphabet, roads, laws, and arts. Italy remained politically fragmented until the 1860s, when it united under a parliament and king. In 1922 Fascist dictator Benito Mussolini took over the government, proclaiming Victor Emmanuel III emperor and subsequently joining Germany in World War II. After Fascism was overthrown in 1943, Italy declared war on Germany and Japan. Mussolini was killed in 1946, and the king was voted out the next year. Despite economic growth, recent governments have been short-lived, and terrorism is on the increase.

I have never been a sportsman — or, rather, I have been a sportsman only once, and that was the first and last time. I was a child, and one day, for some reason or other, I found myself together with my father, who was holding a gun in his hand, behind a bush, watching a bird that had perched on a branch not very far away. It was a large, gray bird — or perhaps it was brown — with a long — or perhaps a short — beak; I

249

don't remember. I only remember what I felt at that moment as I looked at it. It was like watching an animal whose vitality was rendered more intense by the very fact of my watching it and of the animal's not knowing that I was watching it.

At that moment, I say, the notion of wildness entered my mind, never again to leave it: everything is wild which is autonomous and unpredictable and does not depend upon us. Then all of a sudden there was an explosion; I could no longer see the bird and I thought it had flown away. But my father was leading the way, walking in front of me through the undergrowth. Finally he stooped down, picked up something, and put it in my hand. I was aware of something warm and soft and I lowered my eyes: there was the bird in the palm of my hand, its dangling, shattered head crowned with a plume of already-thickening blood. I burst into tears and dropped the corpse on the ground, and that was the end of my shooting experience.

I thought again of this remote episode in my life this very day after watching my wife, for the first and also the last time, as she was walking through the streets of the city. But let us take things in order.

What had my wife been like; what was she like now? She once had   4 been, to put it briefly, "wild" — that is, entirely autonomous and unpredictable; latterly she had become "tame" — that is, predictable and dependent. For a long time she had been like the bird that, on that far-off morning in my childhood, I had seen perching on the bough; latterly, I am sorry to say, she had become like a hen about which one knows everything in advance — how it moves, how it eats, how it lays eggs, how it sleeps, and so on.

Nevertheless I would not wish anyone to think that my wife's wildness consisted of an uncouth, rough, rebellious character. Apart from being extremely beautiful, she is the gentlest, politest, most discreet person in the world. Rather her wildness consisted of the air of charming unpredictability, of independence in her way of living, with which during the first years of our marriage she acted in my presence, both at home and abroad. Wildness signified intimacy, privacy, secrecy. Yes, my wife as she sat in front of her dressing table, her eyes fixed on the looking glass, passing the hairbrush with a repeated motion over her long, loose hair, was just as wild as the solitary quail hopping forward along a sun-filled furrow or the furtive fox coming out into a clearing and stopping to look around before running on. She was wild because I, as I looked at her, could never manage to foresee when she would give a last stroke with the hairbrush and rise and come toward me; wild to such a degree that sometimes when I went into our bedroom the smell of her, floating in the air, would have something of the acrid quality of a wild beast's lair.

Gradually she became less wild, tamer. I had had a fox, a quail, in the house, as I have said; then one day I realized that I had a hen. What effect does a hen have on someone who watches it? It has the effect of being, so to speak, an automaton in the form of a bird; automatic are the brief, rapid steps with which it moves about; automatic its hard, terse pecking; automatic the glance of the round eyes in its head that nods and turns; automatic its ready crouching down under the cock; automatic the dropping of the egg wherever it may be and the cry with which it announces that the egg has been laid. Good-by to the fox; good-by to the quail. And her smell — this no longer brought to my mind, in any way, the innocent odor of a wild animal; rather I detected in it the chemical suavity of some ordinary French perfume.

Our flat is on the first floor of a big building in a modern quarter of the town; our windows look out on a square in which there is a small public garden, the haunt of nurses and children and dogs. One day I was standing at the window, looking in a melancholy way at the garden. My wife, shortly before, had dressed to go out; and once again, watching her, I had noticed the irrevocable and, so to speak, invisible character of her gestures and personality: something which gave one the feeling of a thing already seen and already done and which therefore evaded even the most determined observation. And now, as I stood looking at the garden and at the same time wondering why the adorable wildness of former times had so completely disappeared, suddenly my wife came into my range of vision as she walked quickly across the garden in the direction of the bus stop. I watched her and then I almost jumped for joy; in a movement she was making to pull down a fold of her narrow skirt and smooth it over her thigh with the tips of her long, sharp nails, in this movement I recognized the wildness that in the past had made me love her. It was only an instant, but in that instant I said to myself: She's become wild again because she's convinced that I am not there and am not watching her. Then I left the window and rushed out.

But I did not join her at the bus stop; I felt that I must not allow   8
myself to be seen. Instead I hurried to my car, which was standing nearby, got in, and waited. A bus came and she got in together with some other people; the bus started off again and I began following it. Then there came back to me the memory of that one shooting expedition in which I had taken part as a child, and I saw that the bus was the undergrowth

with its bushes and trees, my wife the bird perching on the bough while I, unseen, watched it living before my eyes. And the whole town, during this pursuit, became, as though by magic, a fact of nature like the countryside: the houses were hills, the streets valleys, the vehicles hedges and woods, and even the passersby on the pavements had something unpredictable and autonomous — that is, wild — about them. And in my mouth, behind my clenched teeth, there was the acrid, metallic taste of gunfire; and my eyes, usually listless and wandering, had become sharp, watchful, attentive.

These eyes were fixed intently upon the exit door when the bus came to the end of its run. A number of people got out, and then I saw my wife getting out. Once again I recognized, in the manner in which she broke free of the crowd and started off toward a neighboring street, the wildness that pleased me so much. I jumped out of the car and started following her.

She was walking in front of me, ignorant of my presence, a tall woman with an elegant figure, long-legged, narrow-hipped, broad-backed, her brown hair falling on her shoulders.

Men turned around as she went past; perhaps they were aware of what I myself was now sensing with an intensity that quickened the beating of my heart and took my breath away: the unrestricted, steadily increasing, irresistible character of her mysterious wildness.

She walked hurriedly, having evidently some purpose in view, and even the fact that she had a purpose of which I was ignorant added to her wildness; I did not know where she was going, just as on that far-off morning I had not known what the bird perching on the bough was about to do. Moreover I thought the gradual, steady increase in this quality of wildness came partly from the fact that as she drew nearer to the object of this mysterious walk there was an increase in her — how shall I express it? — of biological tension, of existential excitement, of vital effervescence. Then, unexpectedly, with the suddenness of a film, her purpose was revealed.

A fair-haired young man in a leather jacket and a pair of corduroy trousers was leaning against the wall of a house in that ancient, narrow street. He was idly smoking as he looked in front of him. But as my wife passed close to him, he threw away his cigarette with a decisive gesture, took a step forward, and seized her arm. I was expecting her to rebuff him, to move away from him, but nothing happened: evidently obeying the rules of some kind of erotic ritual, she went on walking beside the young man. Then after a few steps, with a movement that confirmed

her own complicity, she put her arm around her companion's waist and
he put his around her.

I understood then that this unknown man who took such liberties with
my wife was also attracted by wildness. And so, instead of making a
conventional appointment with her, instead of meeting in a café with a
handshake, a falsely friendly and respectful welcome, he had preferred,
by agreement with her, to take her by surprise — or, rather, to pretend
to do so — while she was apparently taking a walk on her own account.
All this I perceived by intuition, noticing that at the very moment when
he stepped forward and took her arm her wildness had, so to speak, given
an upward bound. It was years since I had seen my wife so alive, but
alas, the source of this life could not be traced to me.

They walked on thus entwined and then, without any preliminaries,
just like two wild animals, they did an unexpected thing: they went into
one of the dark doorways in order to kiss. I stopped and watched them
from a distance, peering into the darkness of the entrance. My wife was
turned away from me and was bending back with the pressure of his
body, her hair hanging free. I looked at that long, thick mane of brown
hair, which as she leaned back fell free of her shoulders, and I felt at
that moment her vitality reached its diapason, just as happens with wild
animals when they couple and their customary wildness is redoubled by
the violence of love. I watched for a long time and then, since the kiss
went on and on and in fact seemed to be prolonged beyond the limits of
my power of endurance, I saw that I would have to intervene.

I would have to go forward, seize my wife by the arm — or actually   16
by that hair, which hung down and conveyed so well the feeling of
feminine passivity — then hurl myself with clenched fists upon the blond
young man. After this encounter I would carry off my wife, weeping,
mortified, ashamed, while I was raging and brokenhearted, upbraiding
her and pouring scorn upon her.

But what else would this intervention amount to but the shot my father
fired at that free, unknowing bird as it perched on the bough? The
disorder and confusion, the mortification, the shame, that would follow
would irreparably destroy the rare and precious moment of wildness that
I was witnessing inside the dark doorway. It was true that this wildness
was directed against me; but I had to remember that wildness, always
and everywhere, is directed against everything and everybody. After the
scene of my intervention it might be possible for me to regain control of

my wife, but I should find her shattered and lifeless in my arms like the bird that my father placed in my hand so that I might throw it into the shooting bag.

The kiss went on and on: well, it was a kiss of passion — that could not be denied. I waited until they finished, until they came out of the doorway, until they walked on again still linked together. Then I turned back.

EXPLORATIONS

1. What are the functions of the long opening section of "The Chase"? What role does the narrator assign himself here in relation to the adult male world? How would the story's impact change without this section?

2. At what point(s) in "The Chase" does the narrator recall his childhood hunting incident again? How is his role different now from the first time he mentioned the incident? How does the narrator vacillate between roles at the end of the story, and what role does he finally choose for himself?

3. Reread Moravia's last sentence; then look back at his third paragraph. What do you conclude that the narrator has done, and intends to do, after the point when the story ends? In what way is he himself adopting qualities he prizes in his wife? What effects does he apparently expect this behavior to have on his marriage?

CONNECTIONS

1. What evidence in "The Chase" confirms Simone de Beauvoir's contention that men perceive women as Other? How does Moravia differ from de Beauvoir regarding the advantages and/or disadvantages of this perception? How does Moravia's narrator feel about his wife's "otherness"? What can you deduce from the story about his wife's view of their situation?

2. Compare the narrator of "The Chase" with the narrator of Octavio Paz's "My Life with the Wave." What attitudes do the two men share? In what ways is each of these characters similar to, and different from, the nineteenth-century gentleman described by Isak Dinesen? Which of Dinesen's four roles does each man seem to want his wife to play?

3. What qualities does Moravia's narrator share with the traditional macho male

described in Gayle Early's *Observation*? What qualities does he share with the androgynous male described in Amy Gross's *Observation*? By the story's end, what kind of man does the narrator evidently want to be, and why?

ELABORATIONS

1. Moravia's narrator might be said to have the opposite problem from Boris in Santha Rama Rau's "Boris's Romance" and the Chinese interviewees in Beverley Hooper's "Falling in Love with Love": With few restrictions on his romance, the chase loses its thrill. What are the main problems faced by lovers in the capitalist societies depicted in "The Chase" and Paz's "My Life with the Wave"? How do they differ from the problems of Communist Soviet and Chinese lovers? Write an essay comparing the obstacles to romantic happiness in these capitalist and Communist societies.

2. In the first section of "The Chase," Moravia's narrator speaks as if he knows his wife as completely as a farmer knows his hens. In the second section, he discovers that he does not know her so well after all. Think of a situation in which you based your expectations about another person on an image — perhaps an idealized social role, such as mother, grandfather, friend, or fiancé. How did you come to realize that the person was not as predictable as you thought? Write a narrative essay about the incident(s) that changed your attitude.

NAILA MINAI

Women in Early Islam

Naila Minai was born in Japan and grew up in Turkey and many other countries of the Middle East. "My Turkish-Tatar grandmother was tutored at home, married a polygamous man, and has never discarded her head veil," she writes. "My mother never wore the veil, studied in schools close to home, and settled down as a housewife in a monogamous marriage. I left my family as a teenager to study in the United States and Europe, where I hitchhiked from country to country . . . eventually making a solo trip across the Sahara." Minai's flight took her to the Sorbonne in Paris and the University of California at Berkeley, where she received her degree in literature and biology. She has worked as a United Nations correspondent and has continued to travel widely as a free-lance journalist. She currently divides her time between the United States and her extended family in the Middle and Far East.

The city of Mecca, where Islam originated, lies near the Red Sea in what is now Saudi Arabia; Medina is north of Mecca. Arabia — the peninsula divided from Africa by the Red Sea and from Iran by the Persian Gulf — currently comprises Saudi Arabia, Yemen, Southern Yemen, Oman, the United Arab Emirates, Qatar, Kuwait, Bahrain, and several neutral zones. North of the Arabian peninsula, and among the members of the Arab League, are the Islamic nations of Jordan, Syria, Lebanon, and Iraq. Iran to the east and Turkey to the north are also Islamic by religion but have ethnically distinct populations from Arabia (see pp. 76 and 279). Egypt, Sudan, Libya, Tunisia, Algeria, and Morocco in northern Africa belong to the Arab League as well, are predominantly Islamic, and generally are counted as Arab nations. Israel, surrounded by Islamic Arabs, is a Jewish nation (see p. 180).

Khadija, an attractive forty-year-old Arabian widow, ran a flourishing caravan business in Mecca in the seventh century A.D., and was courted by the most eligible men of her society. But she had eyes only for an intelligent and hardworking twenty-five-year-old in her employ named Muhammad. "What does she see in a penniless ex-shepherd?" her scandalized aristocratic family whispered among themselves. Accustomed to having her way, however, Khadija proposed to Muhammad and married him. Until her death some twenty-five years later, her marriage was much more than the conventional Cinderella story in reverse, for Khadija not only bore six children while comanaging her business with her husband, but also advised and financed him in his struggle to found Islam, which grew to be one of the major religions of the world.

It was a religion that concerned itself heavily with women's rights, in a surprisingly contemporary manner. A woman was to be educated and allowed to earn and manage her income. She was to be recognized as legal heir to her father's property along with her brother. Her rights in marriage were also clearly spelled out: she was entitled to sexual satisfaction as well as economic support. Nor was divorce to consist any longer of merely throwing the wife out of the house without paying her financial compensation.

This feminist bill of rights filled an urgent need. Meccans in the seventh century were in transition from a tribal to an urban way of life. As their town grew into a cosmopolitan center of trade, kinship solidarity had deteriorated, but municipal laws had not yet been fully established to protect the citizens. Women were particularly vulnerable, their rights closely linked with the tribal way of life their people had known before renouncing nomadism to settle in Mecca around A.D. 400. In nomadic communities of the desert a woman was not equal to a man. During famine a female could be killed at birth to increase her brother's food supply. However, if she managed to reach adulthood she had a better status in the desert than in the city, largely because her labors were indispensable to her clan's survival in the harsh environment. While the men protected the encampment and engaged in trade, she looked after the herds and produced the items to be traded — meat, wool, yogurt, and cheese, all of which bought weapons and grains as well as other essentials. As a breadwinner the tribal woman enjoyed considerable political clout. Even if she did not always participate in council meetings, she made her views known. Only a fool refused to heed his womenfolk and risked antagonizing a good half of his tribe, with whom he had to live in the close confines of the camp and caravan.

If tribal discord was uncomfortable in the best of circumstances, it was   4
catastrophic during the battles that broke out frequently among the clans over pasture and watering rights or to avenge heroes slain by the enemy. With the battlefront so close to home, a woman was needed as a nurse, cheerleader, and even soldier. She was sometimes captured and ransomed or sold into slavery. If her tribesmen could not pay her captors the required number of camels in ransom, they valiantly stormed the enemy's camp to rescue her. These were men brought up on recitations of epic poems

about brave warriors who rescued fair damsels in distress. Poets and poetesses of the tribe kept chivalry alive, constantly singing praises of heroism among their people and condemning cowardliness and disloyalty. No one who wanted a respectable place in his tribe could afford to ignore the ubiquitous "Greek chorus," for life without honor was worse than death to a nomad, who could not survive as an outcast in the desert.

Marriage customs varied from tribe to tribe, but the most popular were those that tended to maintain the woman's independence, if only incidentally, by having her remain within her family circle after marriage. If the husband was a close relative, the couple set up a conjugal tent near both of their parents. A husband who was not kin merely visited her at her home. In some clans women could be married to several visiting husbands at the same time. When the wife bore a child, she simply summoned her husbands and announced which of them she believed to be the child's father. Her decision was law. Actually, it did not matter greatly who the biological father was, since children of such unions belonged to the matrilineal family and were supported by communal property administered by her brothers or maternal uncles.

Life in the desert was so hard and precarious that some of the most impoverished tribes renounced nomadism to submit to a less independent existence in towns. Muhammad's ancestors, a segment of the Kinanah tribe, were among them. They settled down at the crossroads of important caravan routes in the place which is now Mecca, and prospered as middlemen under the new name of Quraysh. Their great wealth and power undoubtedly helped their deities extend their spiritual influence far beyond Mecca's boundaries and make Kaaba, their sanctuary, the most important shrine in central Arabia. As keepers of the shrine the leading Quraysh families grew immeasurably rich, but the wealth was not equitably distributed. As survival no longer depended on communal sharing and on women's contributing equally to the family budget, Meccans became more interested in lucrative business connections than in kinship ties. Glaring socioeconomic differences — unknown among nomads — emerged. Women lost their rights and their security.

If brothers went their separate ways, their sister who continued to live with them after marriage lost her home unless one of them took her and her children under his protection. A woman could not automatically count on her brothers to assume this duty, for with the rise of individualism the patrilineal form of marriage, which had coexisted with other marital arrangements in seventh-century Mecca, was gaining popularity. A self-made man tended to prefer leaving his property to his own sons, which sharpened his interest in ensuring that his wife bore only his children. The best ways to guarantee this was to have her live under close supervision in his house. The woman thus lost her personal freedom, but the security she gained from the marital arrangement was precarious at best in the absence of protective state laws. Not only did she have to live at her in-laws' mercy, she could be thrown out of the house on her husband's whim. Khadija escaped such a fate because she was independently wealthy and belonged to one of the most powerful families of the Quraysh — a fact that must have helped her significantly to multiply her fortune.

It was against such a backdrop of urban problems that Islam was born.   8
Even though Muhammad lived happily and comfortably with his rich wife, he continued to identify with the poor and the dispossessed of Mecca, pondering the conditions that spawned them. He himself had been orphaned in early childhood and passed on from one relative to another. Since his guardians were from the poor and neglected branch of the Quraysh, Muhammad earned his keep as a shepherd from a very early age. But he was luckier than other orphans, for he at least had a place in loving homes and eventually got a good job with Khadija's caravan, which allowed him to travel widely in the Middle East.

These journeys had a direct bearing on his spiritual growth and gave focus to his social concerns by exposing him to Christian monks and well-educated Jewish merchants. They intrigued him, for they seemed to have put into practice a monotheistic faith which a few Meccans of the educated circles were beginning to discuss. How did the Christian God inspire such diverse nationalities to worship Him alone? How did the Judaic God manage to unite widely dispersed Semitic groups under one set of laws which provided for the protection of women and children even in large cities? The astral deities that Muhammad's people inherited from their nomadic ancestors demanded offerings but gave nothing in return. After discussions with people of various faiths, Muhammad sought the ultimate solution to his community's problems in the solitude of a cave on Mount Hiraa overlooking Mecca, where he often retreated in his spare moments, with Khadija or by himself.

While meditating alone one day in the cave, Muhammad heard a voice which he believed to be the angel Gabriel's. "Proclaim in the name of thy Lord and Cherisher who created, created man out of a clot of congealed blood" (Quran, surah [chapter] 96, verses 1–2), it said, pointing out that there was only one God and that man must serve Him alone. When Muhammad recovered from his ecstasy, he ran back, shaken, and described his experience to his wife. Having shared his spiritual struggles, Khadija understood that her husband had received a call to serve the one God whom the Christians and the Jews also worshiped. Bewildered and confused, Muhammad went on with his daily work in the city and occasional meditations on Mount Hiraa. Again the voice commanded him to tell his people about the one omnipotent God, who would welcome believers into heaven and cast wicked people into hell. With Khadija's repeated encouragement, Muhammad finally accepted his prophetic call and devoted the rest of his life to preaching God's word as the new religion of Islam (which means *submission [to the will of God]*). Converts to it were called Muslims (*those who submit*). They were not to be called Muhammadans, because they did not worship Muhammad, who was merely a human messenger for the one God. Though invisible and immortal, this God was named Allah after the Zeus of the old Meccan pantheon.

Numerous revelations that Muhammad received from Allah throughout his life were compiled shortly after his death into the Muslim bible, named the Quran, which formed the basis for the Shariah, or Islamic law. A supplement to it was provided by the Hadith, or Muhammad's words, which were recorded over many years as his survivors and their descendants remembered them. Despite the exotic Arabic words in which it is couched, Islam's message is similar in its essentials to the one promulgated by Judaism and Christianity, and can be summed up by the Ten Commandments. *Allah*, after all, is but the Arabic name for the God worshiped by both Jews and Christians. But the rituals differed. Muhammad required his followers to obey the commandments through the practice of five specific rituals, called the pillars of Islam. A Muslim must (1) profess faith in one God; (2) pray to Him; (3) give alms to the poor; (4) fast during Ramadan, the month in the lunar calendar during which Muhammad received his first revelation; and (5) go on a pilgrimage to Mecca at least once in his lifetime (if he can afford to do so) to pay respects to the birthplace of Islam and reinforce the spirit of fellowship with Muslims from all over the world. Although these laws preached fairness and charity among all mankind, God — through Muhammad — preferred to establish specific guidelines to protect the interests of women.

Once he had united enough people under Allah to make a viable community, Muhammad devoted an impressive number of his sermons to women's rights. In doing so, however, he did not attempt to fight the irreversible tide of urbanization. Nor did he condemn the trend toward patrimonial families, although they often abused women. Too shrewd a politician to antagonize Mecca's powerful patriarchs, he introduced a bill of rights for women which would not only ensure their protection under patriarchy but also reinforce the system itself so that it would stand as a minitribe against the rest of the world.

He did this mainly by providing for women's economic rights in marriage in such a way that they had a financial stake in the system which constantly threatened to erode their independence. Upon marriage a man had to pay his bride a dowry, which was to be her nest egg against divorce or widowhood. While married to him, she could manage the dowry and all other personal income in any way that she pleased, exclusively for her own benefit, and will them to her children and husband upon her death. In her lifetime she did not have to spend her money on herself, or her children for that matter, since only the man was responsibile for supporting his family. If the woman stayed married to her husband until his death, she also inherited part of his property. While her share was less than her children's, she was assured of being supported by her sons in widowhood. By the same line of reasoning, her inheritance from her father was half that of her brother's: her husband supported her, whereas her brother had to support his wife. The daughter's right to inherit tended to divide the patriarch's wealth, but the problem was customarily solved by having her marry a paternal first cousin. Failing that, the inheritance became a part of yet another Muslim family in the same tribe of Islam, united through faith rather than kinship. In either case, a Muslim woman with neither a paid occupation nor an inheritance enjoyed a modicum of financial independence, at the price of her submission to a patriarchal form of marriage.

But she was to be allowed to choose her own spouse, according to the Hadith: "None, not even the father or the sovereign, can lawfully contract in marriage an adult woman of sound mind without her permission, whether she be a virgin or not." This freedom was to be assured by a law that required the dowry to be paid to the bride herself. Since the parents were not to pocket it, as they often did before Islam, they were presumably above being "bought." But the brides' freedom remained largely theoretical, since most of them were barely ten years old when engaged to be married for the first time. Aysha, whom Muhammad married after Khadija's death, was only about six or seven years old when she was betrothed and about ten when she moved into her husband's house with her toys. Muhammad was not playing legal tricks on women, however. He did revoke the parents' choice of mate when their daughters complained to

him about it. Although parents were to be honored and obeyed, he made
it clear that the grown-up daughter was to be respected as an individual
— so much so that the marriage contract could be tailored to her specific
needs: the bride could impose conditions on her contract. A cooperative
wife, he pointed out, was the best foundation for a stable marriage.

Though Muhammad repeatedly preached compassion and love as the
most important bonds of marriage, he also gave men financial entice-
ments to keep the family together. The husband was allowed to pay only
a part of the dowry upon marriage, with the balance payable upon
divorce. If the dowry was large enough, the arrangement deterred the
husband from throwing out his wife without substantial cause. In fact,
under Islam he could no longer just throw her out. He had to pay her
not only the balance of the dowry but also "maintenance on a reasonable
scale" (Quran 2:241). He was also to support her through the ensuing
idda, the three months of chastity which the Shariah asked her to observe
in order to determine whether she was carrying his child. If pregnant,
she was to be helped until she delivered and had nursed the infant to the
point where he could be cared for by the husband's family. All of her
children remained under the paternal roof. In a patriarchal society where
men were not eager to support others' children or to provide employment
for women, the child custody law assured children a decent home and
enabled the divorcée to remarry more easily, but even an independently
wealthy woman was forbidden to walk out of her husband's home with
her children.

Any sexual behavior that would weaken the patriarchal system was   16
strongly discouraged or made illegal. If the custom of taking a visiting
husband was frowned upon, her taking more than one at a time was
condemned as adultery, which was punishable by whipping. Although
men were also forbidden to sow wild oats, they could marry up to four
wives and have as many concubines as they could afford. This law may
have been partly a concession by Muhammad to the widely accepted
custom among wealthy urban men, but he also saw it as a way to attach
surplus women to the men's households for their own protection as well
as to maintain social order. Due to frequent intertribal warfare and attacks
on the merchants' caravans, women always outnumbered men. The
conflict became increasingly serious as Muhammad's following grew large
enough to threaten the purse and the prestige of the families who amassed
fortunes from pilgrims to the Kaaba. So vicious were the attacks that in
A.D. 622, after Khadija died, Muhammad moved his budding Muslim
community to Medina, an agricultural community without important

shrines that would be threatened by Allah. Moreover, the perpetually quarreling clans of Medina welcomed Muhammad because of his reputation as a just man and a skillful arbitrator.

Muhammad succeeded brilliantly in settling the clan's differences and won a prominent place in Medina. This made Meccans even more determined to destroy him before he built up an alliance against them. Violent battles between the Muslims and the Meccans followed. Alliances and betrayals by various tribal factions during each battle engendered more battles, which decimated the Muslim community. The number of widows mounted to such catastrophic proportions after the battle fought at Uhud, near Medina, that God sent a message officially condoning polygamy: "Marry women of your choice, two, or three, or four." But He added, "If you fear that you cannot treat them equitably, marry only one" (3:3). A polygamous husband was required to distribute not only material goods but also sexual attention equally among his wives, for sexual satisfaction, according to Muhammad, was every woman's conjugal right. Besides, a sexually unsatisfied wife was believed to be a threat to her family's stability, as she was likely to seek satisfaction elsewhere.

Unmarried men and women also posed a threat to Muhammad's scheme of social order, which may be one reason why he frowned upon monasticism. Sexual instincts were natural, he reasoned, and therefore would eventually seek fulfillment in adultery[1] unless channeled into legitimate marriage. Wives and husbands were thus necessary for each other's spiritual salvation. "The curse of God be upon those women who remain unwed and say they will never marry," he said, "and a man who does not marry is none of mine."

Though the Quran abolished the ancient custom of stoning adulteresses to death and called instead for public whipping — a hundred lashes administered to male and female offenders alike — Muhammad knew that the sexual double standard would single out women as targets of slander. After a bitter personal experience, he hastened to build safety features into his antiadultery and antifornication laws.

One day Aysha was left behind inadvertently by Muhammad's caravan   20 when she stepped away to look for a necklace that she had lost. She was brought back to the caravan the following morning by a man many years younger than her middle-aged husband, which set tongues wagging. Even Ali, Muhammad's trusted cousin and son-in-law, cast doubt on her

---

[1]Here *adultery* refers to premarital as well as extramarital sex.

reputation. The Prophet's faith in his wife was severely shaken. Aysha was finally saved when her husband fell into a trance, which indicated that he was receiving a message from God. Relief spread over his face. God had vouched for her innocence. The "affair of the slander," as it came to be known, was closed. Four witnesses were henceforth required to condemn women of adultery, as against only two for business transactions and murder cases. Moreover, false witnesses were to be whipped publicly.

Other than false witnesses, violators of women's rights were not punished on this earth. The law would catch up with them in the next world, where they would be cast into the fire (an idea borrowed from the Christians). The good, on the other hand, would reside forever in a heavenly oasis with cool springs in shady palm groves where their every whim would be served by lovely dark-eyed houris. Like the Christian preachers who promised believers a heaven with pearly gates and haloed creatures floating about on white clouds, Muhammad merely presented images that would spell bliss to the common man. Though he did not specify who was going to serve the deserving women, probably for fear of offending their husbands, Muhammad guaranteed a place for them in paradise. Women had the same religious duties as men, and their souls were absolutely equal in God's eyes, with not even the responsibility for original sin weighing upon them. Islam rejects the idea of original sin altogether, claiming that every child is born pure. Nor does the Quran single out Eve as the cause of man's fall (though folklore in various parts of the Middle East does condemn her). According to the Quran, Allah tells both Adam and Eve not to eat the apple. "Then did Satan make them slip from the Garden" (2:36). Allah scolds them both equally, but promises mercy and guidance when they repent.

Muhammad's decision to rely on each man's conscience to fulfill his Islamic obligation toward women reflected a realistic approach to legislation. He seems to have recognized how far he could carry his reforms without losing his constituents' support. In a city where woman had neither economic nor political weight, men would take only so much earthly punishment for disregarding her rights. By the same token, they would not entirely give up their old prerogative of divorcing their wives for any cause without answering to a third party, or pay them more than comfortably affordable compensation. Muhammad therefore struck a compromise in his laws, but repeatedly emphasized the spirit of kindness and respect for women which was implied in them. . . .

The unspecified rights that women had enjoyed during Muhammad's time were chipped away gradually. But the meticulously detailed laws on marital and financial rights were too specific to be ignored entirely, and gave women a modicum of security and independence in the patriarchal family, which survived as a minitribe in the sprawling empire. Within the family circle women exerted considerable influence, not only on their men but also on the blossoming of Arab culture in the Middle Ages. An exceptional few followed Aysha's example and ruled the caliphs and their empire, which spread Islam to lands and peoples far beyond the Arabian peninsula.

EXPLORATIONS

1. According to Minai, what were the main responsibilities, privileges, and dangers of being female in a nomadic tribe?
2. Why did Khadija's and Muhammad's Quraysh ancestors gain by giving up their nomadic existence? In what ways did the urbanization of Mecca pave the way for a monotheistic religion? for a social code ensuring protection for women?
3. How did Muhammad's marriage to Khadija contribute to the founding of Islam? How did his marriage to Aysha contribute to the religion's rules?
4. What is the effect of Minai's opening her essay with a romantic anecdote? What elements in this first paragraph were presumably added by the author rather than drawn from source documents? How would you evaluate the balance she has struck between human interest and historical accuracy?

CONNECTIONS

1. "Other than false witnesses," writes Minai, "violators of women's rights were not punished on this earth. The law would catch up with them in the next world, where they would be cast into the fire." How is this Arabian system for ensuring women's rights similar to the system described by Isak Dinesen in Denmark over a thousand years later? What are the advantages to women of being protected by a moral rather than a legal code? What are the disadvantages?
2. Muhammad's founding of Islam, like the Communists' takeover of China, put an extensive set of new rules into place within a short time. Looking back

at Beverley Hooper's "Falling in Love with Love," what resemblances, if any, can you find between Islamic and Communist policies on male-female relations? What similar social goals appear to have influenced both new behavioral codes?

3. Look back at Ved Mehta's "Pom's Engagement" (p. 162). In what ways do the Hindu concepts of male and female rights and responsibilities resemble those of Islam? What aspects of both cultures' definition of sex roles illustrate points made by Simone de Beauvoir in "Woman as Other"?

ELABORATIONS

1. Minai undertook a delicate task in deciding to write about a religion and its founder. What different viewpoints toward Islam do you think she anticipated among her audience? What concessions, if any, does her writing show to Muslims? to members of other religions? Having looked at Minai's tactics for handling a sensitive subject, write an essay about the history of a social phenomenon with which you are familiar. For example, you might compare attitudes toward marriage in your parents' generation, your grandparents' generation, and your own; or you might describe changes in your church that have resulted from social developments in the past decade. Shape your essay, as Minai does, for a potentially diverse audience.

2. When Muhammad went home after hearing God's message from the angel Gabriel, writes Minai, "Khadija understood that her husband had received a call to serve the one God." In our culture people who report receiving messages from God are seldom believed (an irony, given the centrality of such messages in our Judeo-Christian religions). Yet our tabloids, magazines, and films are full of alleged encounters between an ordinary person and God, or extraterrestrials, or time travelers. Why do you think Americans are so fascinated with a subject that so few of us believe in? — or why are we so skeptical about a subject we find so intriguing? Write an essay classifying or explaining the role(s) in our culture of meetings with the supernatural.

CHERRY LINDHOLM and CHARLES LINDHOLM

Life Behind the Veil

Cherry Lindholm was born in 1942 in Hull, England. After graduating with a degree in fine arts from Durham University in Durham, England, she received a master's of education in counseling psychology from Columbia University. Her current main pursuit is painting. Charles Lindholm was born in 1946 in Minnesota and holds four degrees in anthropology from Columbia University. He currently teaches at Harvard University and is working on a book on charisma. "Life Behind the Veil" originally appeared in *Science Digest* in 1980, preceding the book *Generosity and Jealousy: The Swat Pakhtun of Northern Pakistan* (1982). The authors' purpose, says Charles Lindholm, was to "look beneath the things that seem to us to be exotic, strange, alienating, and try to understand the milieu that makes those things make sense. We're trying to break through the veil of custom to touch the people beneath, to achieve some empathy with those people."

Pakistan came into existence the year after Charles Lindholm was born. Conflict between Hindus and Muslims spurred the British (who then controlled the region) to divide Islamic Pakistan from Hindu India. Both countries remained British protectorates. Pakistan — consisting of two separate sections on opposite sides of India — became an independent republic within the British Commonwealth in 1956. In 1971 East Pakistan split from West Pakistan, taking the name of Bangladesh. The Swat Valley visited by Cherry and Charles Lindholm lies in northern Pakistan, near Peshawar and the Afghanistan border (see Doris Lessing's "The Afghan Resistance," p. 519).

The bazaar teems with activity. Pedestrians throng the narrow streets, wending past donkey carts, cyclists, and overloaded vehicles. Vendors haggle in the dark doorways of their shops. Pitiful beggars shuffle among the crowds, while bearded religious mendicants wander about, their eyes fixed on a distant world.

Drifting among the mobs of men are, here and there, anonymous figures hidden beneath voluminous folds of material, who float along like ships in full sail, graceful, mysterious, faceless, instilling in the observer a sense both of awe and of curiosity. These are the Moslem women of the Middle East. Their dress is the customary *chador*, which they wear when obliged to leave the privacy of their homes. The *chador* is but one means by which women maintain their *purdah*, the institution of female seclusion, which requires that women should remain unseen by men who are not close relatives and strikes Westerners as so totally foreign and incomprehensible.

Sometimes the alien aspect is tempered with a touch of Western familiarity. A pair of plastic sunglasses may gleam from behind the lace that covers the eyes, or a platform shoe might peep forth from beneath the hem of the flowing *chador*. Nevertheless, the overall presence remains one of inscrutability and is perhaps the most striking image of Middle Eastern societies.

We spent nine months in one of the most strict of all the *purdah*   4 societies, the Yusufzai Pakhtun of the Swat Valley in the North-West Frontier Province of Pakistan. ("Pakhtun" is the designation preferred by the tribesmen, who were generally called Pathans in the days of the British *raj*.)

We had come to the Swat Valley after a hair-raising ride on a rickety bus from Peshawar over the 10,280-foot Malakand Pass. Winston Churchill came this way as a young war correspondent attached to the Malakand Field Force in 1897. As we came into the valley, about half the size of Connecticut, we passed a sign that said WELCOME TO SWAT. We were fortunate to have entrée into the community through a Swati friend we had made eight years before. In Swat, women are secluded inside the domestic compound except for family rituals, such as marriage, circumcision, and funerals, or visits to saints' tombs. A woman must always be in the protective company of other women and is never allowed out alone. It tells a great deal about the community that the word for husband in Pakhto, the language of the Pakhtun, is *khawund*, which also means God.

However, as everywhere, rules are sometimes broken or, more frequently, cleverly manipulated. Our Pakhtun host's stepmother, Bibi, an intelligent and forceful woman, was renowned for her tactics. Once, when all the females of the household had been forbidden to leave the compound to receive cholera inoculations at the temporary clinic next door, Bibi respectfully bowed her head and assured the men they could visit the mosque with easy minds. Once the men had gone, she promptly climbed the ladder to the flat roof and summoned the doctor to the door of her compound. One by one, the women extended their bare arms through the doorway and received their shots. Later, Bibi could honestly swear that no woman had set foot outside the compound walls.

Despite such circumventions, *purdah* is of paramount importance in Swat. As one Pakhtun proverb succinctly states: "The woman's place is in the home or the grave." Years ago in Swat, if a woman broke her *purdah*, her husband might kill her or cut off her nose as punishment and as a means of cleansing his honor. If a woman is caught alone with an unrelated man, it will always be assumed that the liaison is sexual, and public opinion will oblige her husband to shoot her, even if he does not desire her death; to go unavenged is to be known henceforth as *begherata*, or man without honor. As such, he would no longer have the right to call himself Pakhtun.

A shameless woman is a threat to the whole society. Our host remembered witnessing, thirty years ago when he was a child, the entire village stoning an adulteress. This punishment is prescribed by Islamic law, though the law requires there be four witnesses to the sexual act itself to establish guilt. Nowadays, punishments for wifely misdemeanors have become less harsh, though adulterous wives are still killed.

In the rural areas, poorer families generally cannot maintain *purdah* as rigorously as their wealthier neighbors, for often the wife must help her husband in the fields or become a servant. Nevertheless, she is required to keep her hair covered at all times and to interact with men to a minimum. Here again, the rules are sometimes flouted, and a poor woman might entice a man with her eyes or even, according to village men who claimed personal experiences, become more aggressive in her seductive attempts and actually seize a man in a deserted alleyway and lure him into her house. Often, the man is persuaded. Such a woman will accept money from her lover, who is usually a man from a wealthy family. Her husband is then a *begherata*, but some men acquiesce to the situation because of the money the wife is earning or because of fear of the wife's socially superior and more powerful lover. But most poor men, and certainly all of the elite, keep their women under strict control.

In the Islamic Middle East, women are viewed as powerful and dangerous beings, highly sexual and lacking in personal discipline and discrimination. In Middle Eastern thought, sexual intercourse itself, though polluting, lacks the same negative connotations it has in the West. It has always been believed that women have sexual climaxes, and there is no notion of female frigidity. Male impotence, however, is well-documented, and some middle-aged and even young men admitted to us that they had lost their interest in women. Sometimes, though rarely, a young bride-groom will find himself incapable of consummating his marriage, either because he finds his bride unattractive or because he has been previously enchanted by a male lover and has become impotent in a heterosexual relationship. Homosexuality has never been seen as aberrant in the Middle East. As a famous Afghan saying humorously declares: "A woman is for bearing children, a boy is for pleasure, but ecstasy is a ripe water-melon!" However, with Western influence, homosexuality in the Middle East is now less overt. But even when it was common and open, the man was still expected to marry and produce children.

Men must marry, though women are regarded as a chaotic and an-archic force. They are believed to possess many times the sexual desire of men and constitute a potential threat to the family and the family's honor, which is based in large measure on the possession and control of women and their excessive and dangerous sexuality.

Among the Pakhtun of Swat, where the male-female relation is one   12 of the most hostile in the Middle East, the man avoids showing affection to his wife, for fear she will become too self-confident and will begin to assert herself in ways that insult his position and honor. She may start by leaving the compound without his permission and, if unchecked, may end by bringing outside men into the house for sexual encounters, secure in the knowledge that her husband, weakened by his affection for her, will not take action. This course of events is considered inevitable by men and women alike and was illustrated by a few actual cases in the village where we lived.

Women are therefore much feared, despite the pronouncements of male supremacy. They must be controlled, in order to prevent their alarming basic natures from coming to the fore and causing dishonor to their own lineages. *Purdah* is generally described as a system that serves to protect the woman, but implicitly it protects the men and society in general from the potentially disruptive actions of the powerful female sex.

Changes are occurring, however, particularly in the modern urban centers. The educated urban woman often dispenses with the *chador,* replacing it with a simple length of veiling draped over the head or across the shoulders; she may even decide to adopt modest Western dress. The extent of this transformation will depend partly upon the attitude of the community in which she lives.

In the urban centers of the stricter *purdah* regions the public display of *purdah* is scrupulous, sometimes even more striking than that of the tribal village. Behind the scenes, though, the city-dwelling woman does have more freedom than she would have in the village. She will be able to visit not only relatives but friends without specific permission from her husband, who is out at work all day. She may, suitably veiled, go shopping in the bazaar, a chore her husband would have undertaken in the village. On the whole, the city woman will have a great deal more independence, and city men sometimes lament this weakening of traditional male domination.

The urbanized male may speak of the custom-bound tribesmen (such   16 as the Swat Pakhtun, the Bedouin nomads of Saudi Arabia or the Qashqai herdsmen of Iran) as country bumpkins, yet he still considers their central values, their sense of personal pride, honor, and autonomy, as cultural ideals and views the tribesmen, in a very real way, as exemplars of the proper mode of life. Elite families in the cities proudly emphasize their tribal heritage and sometimes send their sons to live for a year or so with distant tribal cousins, in order to expose them to the tribesman's integrity and moral code. The tribesman, on the other hand, views his urbanized relatives as weak and womanly, especially with reference to the slackening of *purdah* in the cities. Though the *purdah* female, both in the cities and in the tribal areas, rarely personifies the ideal virtues of silence, submission, and obedience, the concept of *purdah* and male supremacy remains central to the male identity and to the ideology of the culture as a whole.

The dynamic beneath the notion of male supremacy, the institution of *purdah*, and the ideology of women's sexual power becomes apparent when one takes an overall view of the social structure. The family in the Middle East, particularly in the tribal regions, is not an isolated element; kinship and marriage are the underlying principles that structure action and thought. Individuals interact not so much according to personal preference as according to kinship.

The Middle Eastern kinship system is known to anthropologists as a segmentary-lineage organization; the basic idea is that kinship is traced through one line only. In the Middle East, the system is patrilineal, which means that the male line is followed, and all the links through women are ignored. An individual can therefore trace his relationship to any other individual in the society and know the exact genealogical distance between them; i.e., the distance that must be traced to reach a common male ancestor. The system obliges men to defend their patrilineal relatives if they are attacked, but if there is no external force threatening the lineage, then men struggle against one another according to the principle of genealogical distance. This principle is nicely stated in a famous Middle Eastern proverb: "I against my brothers; my brothers and I against my cousins; my cousins, my brothers, and I against the world." The cousins in question are of course patrilineal.

Within this system, women appear to have no role, though they are the units of reproduction, the mothers of the sons who will carry on the patriline. Strange as it may seem, this is the core contradiction of the society: The "pure" patriline itself is actually descended from a woman. This helps explain the exaggerated fear of women's promiscuity and supposedly voracious sexuality. In order to protect the patriline, women must be isolated and guarded. Their sexuality, which threatens the integrity of the patriline, must be made the exclusive property of their husbands. Women, while being absolutely necessary for the perpetuation of the social order, are simultaneously the greatest threat to it.

The persistent denigration of women is explained by this core contra-   20
diction. Moslem society considers women naturally inferior in intelligence and ability — childlike, incapable of discernment, incompetent to testify in court, prey to whims and fancies. In tribal areas, women are prohibited from inheritance, despite a Koranic injunction, and in marriage they are purchased from their fathers like a commodity. Were women not feared, these denials of her personhood would be unnecessary.

Another unique element of Middle Eastern culture is the prevalence of marriage with the father's brother's daughter. In many areas, in fact, this marriage is so favored that a boy must give explicit permission to allow his patrilineal female cousin to marry elsewhere. This peculiar marriage form, which is found nowhere else in the world, also serves to negate the woman by merging her lineage with that of her husband, since both are members of the same patriline (indeed, are the offspring of brothers). No new blood enters, and the sanctity of the patriline is steadily maintained.

However, this ploy gives rise to other problems: Cousin marriage often divides the brothers rather than uniting them. Although the bride-price is usually reduced in such marriages, it is always demanded, thus turning the brothers into opponents in a business negotiation. Furthermore, giving a woman in Swat carries an implication of inferiority; historically, victors in war took women from the vanquished. Cousin marriage thus renders the brothers' equality questionable. Finally, the young couple's fights will further alienate the brothers, especially since such marriages are notoriously contentious. This is because patrilineal male cousins are rivals for the common grandfather's inheritance (in fact, the Swati term for father's brother's son is *tarbur*, which also means enemy), and a man who marries his patrilineal cousin is marrying the sister of his lifelong opponent. Her loyalty is with her brother, and this is bound to cause frequent disputes.

Though the girl is treated like goods, she does not see herself as such. The fundamental premise of tribal life is the equality of the various landed families. There are very few hierarchies in these societies, and even the leaders are often no more than first among equals. Within this system, which has been described as a nearly perfect democracy, each *khan* (which means landowner and literally translates as king) family sees itself as superior to all others. The girls of the household feel the same pride in their lineage as their brothers and cannot help but regard their husbands' families through jaundiced eyes. The new bride is prepared to defend the honor of her family, even though they have partially repudiated her by negotiating the marriage. Her identity, like that of a man, rests on her lineage pride, which she will fight to uphold. The husband, meanwhile, is determined to demonstrate his domination and mastery, since control of women is the nexus of a man's sense of self-respect.

Hostility is thus built into marriage by the very structure of the society,   24 which pits every lineage against every other in a never-ending contest to maintain an equilibrium of power within this markedly egalitarian culture. The hostility of the marriage bond is evident from its beginnings. The reluctant bride is torn from her cot in her family's house and ensconced on a palanquin that strongly resembles a bier. The war drums that announce the marriage procession indicate the nature of the tie, as does the stoning of the palanquin by the small boys of the village as it is carried through the dusty streets. When the bride arrives at her new husband's house, his family triumphantly fires their rifles into the air. They have taken a woman! The young wife cowers in her veils as she is prodded and poked curiously by the females of the husband's house who try to persuade her to show her face. The groom himself is nowhere to be seen, having retreated to the men's house in shame. In three days, he will creep to her room and consummate the marriage. Taking the virginity of the bride is a highly charged symbolic act, and in some areas of the Middle East the display of the bloody nuptial sheet to the public is a vital part of the wedding rite. Breaking the hymen demonstrates the husband's possession of his wife's sexuality. She then becomes the most junior adult in the household, subordinate to everyone, but, most especially, under the heavy thumb of her mother-in-law.

The household the bride enters will be that of her husband's father, since the system, as well as being patrilineal, is also patrilocal. She will be surrounded by his relatives and will be alone with her husband only at night. During the day he will pay no attention to her, for it is considered shameful for a man to take note of his wife in front of others, particularly his father and mother. Within the compound walls, which shield the household from the rest of the world, she is at the mercy of her new family.

Life within the compound is hardly peaceful. Wives squabble among themselves, and wives who have built a power base by having sons even quarrel with the old matriarch, their mother-in-law. This is usually a prelude to a couple moving out of the house into their own compound, and husbands always blame their wives for the breakup of the extended family, even though they, too, will be glad to become the masters of their own homes and households.

But the worst fights among women are the fights between women married to the same man. Islam permits polygamous marriage, and legally a man may have four wives. Not all men are financially able to take more than one wife, but most men dream of marrying again, despite the Swati proverb that says, "I may be a fool, but not so much of a fool as the man with two wives." Men who can afford it often do take a second wife. The reason is not sexual desire, for wives do not mind if their husbands have liaisons with prostitutes or promiscuous poor women. Rather, the second wife is brought in to humiliate an overly assertive first wife. Bringing in a second wife is a terrible insult; it is an expression of contempt for the first wife and her entire lineage. The insult is especially cutting in Swat, where divorce is prohibited (though it is permitted in the Koran) and where a disliked wife must either endure her lot or retreat to her family's house and a life of celibacy. Small wonder then that households with two wives are pits of intrigue, vituperation, and magical incantation, as each wife seeks to expel the other. The Koran says a man should only practice polygamy if he is sure he can treat each wife equally; the only man we met who was able to approximate this ideal was a man who never went home. He spent his time in the men's house, talking with his cronies and having his meals sent to him.

The men's house is the best-built structure in any village, along with the mosque, which is also prohibited to women. It is a meeting place for the clan, the center for hospitality and refuge, and the arena for political manipulation. This is where the visitor will be received, surrounded by men who gossip, doze, or clean their rifles. Here, the guest might well imagine that women do not even exist. Only the tea and food that is sent over from the compound nearby tell him of the women working behind the walls.

Formerly, in Swat, most men slept in the men's house, visiting their wives secretly late at night and returning before daybreak. But now only a few elders and some ne'er-do-well youths live permanently in the elegant, aging buildings. Sometimes, however, a man may be obliged to move to the men's house for a few days if his wife makes his home too uncomfortable, for women too have their own weapons in the household battles. Arguments may flare up over almost anything: the husband buying a rotten piece of meat or forgetting to bring home a length of material, the wife ruining some curd or gossiping too much with a neighbor. The wife may then angrily refuse to cook, obliging the husband to retreat to the men's house for food. The man's weapon in fights is violence, while the woman can withdraw domestic services at will.

In the early days of a marriage, when the bride is new to the household and surrounded by her husband's people, she may be fairly meek. But when her status has improved as a result of producing sons, she will become more aggressive. Her lacerating tongue is renowned, and she will also begin to fight back physically as well as verbally. Finally, her exasperated husband may silence her with a blow from a heavy stick he keeps for that purpose. No shame is attached to beating one's wife, and men laugh about beatings they have administered. The women themselves, though they decry their men's brutality, proudly display their scars and bruises, characterizing a neighbor who is relatively gentle to his wife as "a man with no penis."

The older a woman gets, the more powerful and fearless she becomes. She is aided by her sons who, though respecting their father, regard him as an obstacle to their gaining rights in land. The old man, who gains his stature from his landholding, is always reluctant to allot shares to his grown sons. Furthermore, the sons' ties of affection are much stronger with the mother. The elderly father, who is generally ten or fifteen years older than his wife, is thus surrounded by animosity in his own house. The situation of the earlier years has reversed itself, and the wife, who began alone and friendless, gains allies in her old age, while the husband becomes isolated. Ghani Khan, a modern Pakhtun writer, has described the situation well: "The Pakhtun thinks he is as good as anyone else and his father rolled into one and is fool enough to try this even with his wife. She pays for it in her youth, and he in his old age."

But many women do not live to see their triumph. In northern Swat,   32 for every 100 women over the age of sixty there are 149 men, compared to the more equal 100 to 108 ratio below sixty. The women are worn out by continual childbearing, breast feeding, and a lack of protein. Though fertile in places, the Swat valley is heavily overpopulated with an estimated 1 million people, and survival is always difficult. The diet consists chiefly of bread, rice, seasonal vegetables, and some dairy products. Meat is a rarity and goes to the men and boys as a matter of course. They perpetuate the patrilineal clan and must survive, while women can always be replaced. The lives of men are hard, but the lives of women are harder, as witnessed by their early deaths.

In this environment, people must learn to be tough, just as they must learn to fit the structure of the patrilineal system. Child rearing serves both functions.

The birth of a boy in Swat is greeted by rejoicing, while the birth of a girl is an occasion for gloom. But the first few years for both sexes are virtually identical. Like most Middle Easterners, the Swatis practice swaddling, binding the baby tightly so that it is immobilized. Ostensibly, this is to help the baby sleep and prevent it from blinding itself with its flailing hands, but anthropologists have hypothesized that swaddling actually serves to develop a certain character type: a type which can withstand great restraint but which also tends to uncontrolled bursts of temper. This hypothesis fits Swat, where privation and the exigencies of the social structure demand stoicism, but where violent temper is also useful. We often saw Swati children of all ages lose themselves in tantrums to coerce their parents, and such coercion was usually successful. Grown men and women as well are prone to fits of temper, and this dangerous aspect makes their enemies leery of pressing them too hard.

Both sexes are indoctrinated in the virtues of their family and its lineage. In marital fights this training is obvious, as both partners heatedly assert, "Your ancestor was nothing, and mine was great!" At a man's death his sister, not his wife, is his chief mourner. And if a woman is killed it is her brother, not her husband, who avenges her.

Child training in Swat produces strong characters. When they give 36 affection, they give it wholeheartedly, and when they hate, they hate bitterly. The conditions under which they live are cruel and cramped, and they respond with cruelty and rigidity in order to survive. But at the same time, the people are able to bear their hard lives with pride and dignity.

EXPLORATIONS

1. On what types of evidence do the Lindholms base their generalizations about Swat? What information in their essay, if any, appears to have come from outside sources rather than from their visit to the valley?

2. What use do the Lindholms make of direct quotation? How would the essay's effect change if the authors quoted local people more extensively?

3. What statements in "Life Behind the Veil" reflect value judgments by the Lindholms? What emotionally weighted words and phrases (for example, "The *reluctant* bride is *torn from* her cot") show the authors' feelings about the customs they describe? What is the positive or negative impact (or both) of the authors' revealing their reactions to the Pakhtun?

CONNECTIONS

1. According to Naila Minai in "Women in Early Islam," what concept did seventh-century Meccans hold of female sexuality? How did the prevailing customs of betrothal and marriage create a balance between women's right to sexual satisfaction and men's desire to support only their own children? What concept of female sexuality dominates the Swat Pakhtun today?

2. Look again at Minai's "Women in Early Islam": How do the Pakhtun customs of betrothal, marriage, and divorce coincide and conflict with those outlined by Muhammad? Why do you think Muhammad's ideas, as described by Minai, have not been more strictly followed in this Islamic culture?

3. What beliefs and practices among the Pakhtun confirm Simone de Beauvoir's contention that men perceive women as Other? How do Pakhtun customs bear out de Beauvoir's explanation of why men hold this perception, and why women cooperate with it? What considerations not mentioned by de Beauvoir have evidently influenced Pakhtun sex roles?

4. Beverley Hooper's "Falling in Love with Love" and "Life Behind the Veil" both examine attitudes toward male-female relations. In what ways are these two essays' purposes different? How do the writing strategies of each author reflect her or his particular purposes?

ELABORATIONS

1. Minai's "Women in Early Islam" shows how Islam came into being; "Life Behind the Veil" shows how it affects one culture today. Which of Muhammad's hopes for his religion, as described by Minai, are fulfilled in modern Swat? What Islamic principles cited by Minai are violated by the Swat Pakhtun? What rules aimed at protecting women, according to Minai, have been twisted over time by the Pakhtun into means of oppression? Write an essay comparing and contrasting Islam 1400 years ago in Arabia with Islam today in the Swat Valley, based on Minai's and the Lindholms' accounts.

2. According to the Lindholms, a Pakhtun wife's place in her home changes dramatically from her wedding day to her old age; so does her husband's. In what ways does the role of a wife or husband in the United States change over time? Based on your family's experience, interviews you conduct, or both, write an essay defining the different parts played by an American man or woman from courtship through retirement.

YASHAR KEMAL

A Dirty Story

Yashar Kemal, a Nobel Prize candidate, is widely considered Turkey's greatest living writer. Born in 1922 as Yashar Kemal Gokceli, he grew up among the desperately poor Anatolian peasants, whose plight became a central theme of his writing and his life. At the age of five he saw his father murdered in a mosque; after two years of secondary school he went to work in the Turkish cotton fields and factories. Kemal held a variety of jobs before his arrest in 1950 for alleged Communist propaganda (he was later acquitted). Moving to Istanbul, he dropped his surname, became a journalist, and rose to the post of Anatolian bureau chief of the daily paper *Cumhuriyet*. His 1955 novel *Ince Memed*, translated into more than fifteen languages, reached the English-speaking world in two parts: *Memed My Hawk* (1961) and *They Burn the Thistles* (1977). Other fiction, nonfiction, and plays have followed. "A Dirty Story" comes from *Anatolian Tales* (*Butun hikayeler*, 1967) and was translated from the Turkish by the author's wife, Thilda Kemal. Kemal is a member of the Turkish Workers' Party, which he considers the most compassionate and sensible political movement in Turkey. He now lives in Istanbul.

The Islamic nation of Turkey consists of a European section and an Asian section separated by water. European Turkey borders Greece and Bulgaria and includes Istanbul. Asian Turkey, or Anatolia, is many times larger; it borders Syria, Iraq, Iran, and the Soviet Union and includes the capital city of Ankara. Human habitation there dates back to the Stone Age, at least 7000 B.C. The Ottoman Empire, which in the sixteenth century ruled much of Europe, the Middle East, and North Africa, began in Anatolia and lasted through World War I. The Young Turk movement started a revolt in 1908 which culminated in Turkey's becoming a republic under President Kemal Ataturk in 1923. As Yashar Kemal's story suggests, however, the economy remains agrarian, and many of the Turkish people must eke out a living under unfavorable conditions.

The three of them were sitting on the damp earth, their backs against the dung-daubed brush wall and their knees drawn up th their chests, when another man walked up and crouched beside them.

"Have you heard?" said one of them excitedly. "Broken-Nose Jabbar's done it again! You know Jabbar, the fellow who brings all those women

from the mountain villages and sells them in the plain? Well, this time
he's come down with a couple of real beauties. The lads of Misdik have
got together and bought one of them on the spot, and now they're having
fun and making her dance and all that . . . It's unbelievable! Where
does the fellow find so many women? How does he get them to come
with him? He's the devil's own son, he is . . ."

"Well, that's how he makes a living," commented one of the men.
"Ever since I can remember, this Jabbar's been peddling women for the
villagers of the Chukurova plain. Allah provides for all and sundry . . ."

"He's still got the other one," said the newcomer, "and he's ready to   4
give her away for a hundred liras."

"He'll find a customer soon enough," put in another man whose head
was hunched between his shoulders. "A good woman's worth more than
a team of oxen, at least, in the Chukurova plain she is. You can always
put her to the plow and, come summer, she'll bind and carry the sheaves,
hoe, do anything. What's a hundred liras? Why, a woman brings in that
much in one single summer. In the fields, at home, in bed. There's
nothing like a woman. What's a hundred liras?"

Just then, Hollow Osman came up mumbling to himself and flopped
down beside them without a word of greeting. He was a tall, broad-
shouldered man with a rather shapeless potbellied body. His lips drooped
foolishly and his eyes had an odd squintlike gaze.

"Hey, Osman," the man who had been talking addressed him. "Broken-Nose Jabbar's got a woman for sale again. Only a hundred liras. Tell
Mistress Huru to buy her for you and have done with living alone and
sleeping in barns like a dog."

Osman shrugged his shoulders doubtfully.   8

"Look here, man," pursued the other, "this is a chance in a million.
What's a hundred liras? You've been slaving for that Huru since you
dropped out of your mother's womb and she's never paid you a lira. She
owes you this. And anyway she'll get back her money's worth in just one
summer. A woman's good for everything, in the house, in the fields, in
bed . . ."

Osman rose abruptly.

"I'll ask the Mistress," he said. "How should I know? . . ."

A couple of days later, a short, broad-hipped girl with blue beads   12
strung into her plaited hair was seen at the door of Huru's barn in which
Hollow Osman always slept. She was staring out with huge wondering
eyes.

A month passed. Two months . . . And passersby grew familiar with the sight of the strange wide-eyed girl at the barn door.

One day, a small dark boy with a face the size of a hand was seen pelting through the village. He rushed up to his mother where she sat on the threshold of her hut gossiping with Seedy Doneh.

"Mother," he screeched, "I've seen them! It's the truth, I swear it is. Uncle Osman's wife with . . . May my eyes drop out right here if I'm telling a lie."

Seedy Doneh turned to him sharply.

"What?" she cried. "Say it again. What's that about Fadik?"

"She was with the Agha's son. I saw them with my own eyes. He went into the barn with her. They couldn't see me where I was hiding. Then he took off his boots, you know the shiny yellow boots he wears . . . And then they lay down and . . . Let my two eyes drop out if . . ."

"I knew it!" crowed Seedy Doneh. "I knew it would turn out this way."

"Hollow Osman never had any manhood in him anyway," said the child's mother. "Always under that viper-tongued Huru's petticoats . . ."

"Didn't I tell you, Ansha, the very first day she came here that this would happen?" said Doneh. "I said this girl's ready to play around. Pretending she was too bashful to speak to anyone. Ah, still waters run deep . . ."

She rose quickly and hurried off to spread the news.

"Have you heard? Just as I foretold . . . Still waters . . . The Agha's son . . . Fadik . . ."

In a trice all the neighboring women had crowded at Ansha's door, trying to squeeze the last drop of information out of the child.

"Come on, tell us," urged one of the women for perhaps the hundredth time. "How did you see them?"

"Let my two eyes drop out right here if I'm lying," the child repeated again and again with unabated excitement. "The Agha's son came in, and then they lay down, both of them, and did things . . . I was watching through a chink in the wall. Uncle Osman's wife, you know, was crying. I can't do it, she was saying, and she was sobbing away all the time. Then the Agha's son pulled off those shiny yellow boots of his . . . Then I ran right here to tell Mother."

The news spread through the village like wildfire. People could talk about nothing else. Seedy Doneh, for one, seemed to have made it her job to leave no man or woman uninformed. As she scoured the village for new listeners, she chanced upon Osman himself.

"Haven't you heard what's come upon you?" she said, drawing him aside behind the wall of a hut. "You're disgraced, you jackass. The Agha's son has got his fingers up your wife's skirt. Try and clear your good name now if you can!"

Osman did not seem to understand.

"I don't know . . ." he murmured, shrugging his shoulders. "I'll have to ask the Mistress. What would the Agha's son want with my wife?"

Doneh was incensed.

"What would he want with her, blockhead?" she screamed. "Damn   32 you, your wife's become a whore, that's what! She's turned your home into a brothel. Anyone can come in and have her." She flounced off still screaming. "I spit on you! I spit on your manhood . . ."

Osman was upset.

"What are you shouting for, woman?" he called after her. "People will think something's wrong. I have to ask the Mistress. She knows every- thing. How should I know?"

He started walking home, his long arms dangling at his sides as though they had been hitched to his shoulders as an afterthought, his fingers sticking out wide apart as was his habit. This time he was waylaid by their next-door neighbor, Zeynep, who planted herself before him and tackled him at the top of her voice.

"Ah Osman! You'd be better off dead! Why don't you go and bury   36 yourself? The whole village knows about it. Your wife . . . The Agha's son . . . Ah Osman, how could you have brought such a woman into your home? Where's your honor now? Disgraced . . . Ah Osman!"

He stared at her in bewilderment.

"How should I know?" he stammered, his huge hands opening out like pitchforks. "The Mistress knows all about such things. I'll go and ask her."

Zeynep turned her back on him in exasperation, her large skirt bal- looning about her legs.

"Go bury yourself, Osman! I hope I see you dead after this."   40

A group of children were playing tipcat nearby. Suddenly one of them broke into a chant.

"Go bury yourself, Osman . . . See you dead, Osman . . ."

The other children joined in mechanically without interrupting their game.

Osman stared at them and turned away.   44

"How should I know?" he muttered. "I must go to the Mistress."

He found Huru sitting at her spinning wheel. Fadik was there too, squatting near the hearth and listlessly chewing mastic gum.

"Mistress," said Osman, "have you heard what Seedy Doneh's saying? She's saying I'm disgraced . . ."

Huru stepped on the pedal forcefully and brought the wheel to a stop.   48 "What's that?" she said. "What about Seedy Doneh?"

"I don't know . . . She said Fadik . . ."

"Look here," said Huru, "you mustn't believe those lying bitches. You've got a good wife. Where would you find such a woman?"

"I don't know. Go bury yourself, they said. The children too . . ."   52

"Shut up," cried Huru, annoyed. "People always gossip about a beautiful woman. They go looking for the mote in their neighbor's eye without seeing the beam in their own. They'd better hold their peace because I've got a tongue in my head too . . ."

Osman smiled with relief.

"How could I know?" he said.

Down in the villages of the Chukurova plain, a sure sign of oncoming   56 spring is when the women are seen with their heads on one another's lap, picking the lice out of one another's hair. So it was, on one of the first warm days of the year. A balmy sun shone caressingly down on the fields and village, and not a leaf stirred. A group of women were sitting before their huts on the dusty ground, busy with the lice and wagging their tongues for all they were worth. An acrid odor of sweat hung about the group. Seedy Doneh was rummaging in the hair of a large woman who was stretched full length on the ground. She decided that she had been silent long enough.

"No," she declared suddenly, "it's not as you say, sister! He didn't force her or any such thing. She simply fell for him the minute she saw those shiny yellow boots. If you're going to believe Huru! . . . She's got to deny it, of course."

"That Huru was born with a silver spoon in her mouth," said white-haired, toothless old Zala, wiping her bloodstained fingers on her ragged skirt. "Hollow Osman's been slaving for her like twenty men ever since she took him in, a kid the size of your hand! And all for a mere pittance of food. And now there's the woman too. Tell me, what's there left for Huru to do?"

"Ah," sighed another woman, "fortune has smiled on Huru, she has indeed! She's got two people serving her now."

"And both for nothing," old Zala reminded her.   60

"What it amounts to," said Seedy Doneh spitefully, "is that Huru used to have one wife and now she's got two. Osman was always a woman, and as for Fadik she's a real woman. He-he!"

"That she is, a real woman!" the others agreed.

"Huru says the Agha's son took her by force," pursued Doneh. "All right, but what about the others? What about those lining up at her door all through the night, eh? She never says no to any one of them, does she? She takes in everyone, young and old."

"The Lady Bountiful, that's what she is," said Elif. "And do you know 64
something? Now that Fadik's here, the young men are leaving Omarja's yellow bitch in peace . . ."

"They've got somewhere better to go!" cackled the others.

Omarja's dumpy wife jumped up from where she was sitting on the edge of the group.

"Now look here, Elif!" she cried. "What's all this about our yellow dog? Stop blackening people's characters, will you?"

"Well, it's no lie, is it?" Doneh challenged her. "When was that bitch 68
ever at your door where she should be all night? No, instead, there she came trotting up a-mornings with a rope dangling from her neck!"

"Don't go slandering our dog," protested Omarja's wife. "Why, if Omarja hears this, he'll kill the poor creature. Upon my word he will!"

"Go on!" said Doneh derisively. "Don't you come telling me that Omarja doesn't know his yellow bitch is the paramour of all the village youths! What about that time when Stumpy Veli caught some of them down by the river, all taking it in turns over her? Is there anyone in this village who didn't hear of that? It's no use trying to whitewash your bitch to us!"

Omarja's wife was alarmed.

"Don't, sister," she pleaded. "Omarja'll shoot the dog, that's sure . . ." 72

"Well, I'm not to blame for that, sister," retorted Doneh tartly. "Anyway, the bitch'll be all right now that Fadik's around. And so will Kurdish Velo's donkey . . ."

Kurdish Velo's wife began to fidget nervously.

"Not our fault," she blurted out in her broken Turkish. "We lock our donkey in, but they come and break the door! Velo furious. Velo say people round here savage. He say, with an animal deadly sin! He say he kill someone. Then he complain to the Headman. Velo going sell this donkey."

"You know what I think?" interposed Seedy Doneh. "They're going to 76
make it hot for her in this village. Yes, they'll do what they did to Esheh."

"Poor Esheh," sighed old Zala. "What a woman she was before her man got thrown into prison! She would never have come to that, but she had no one to protect her. May they rot in hell, those that forced her into it! But she is dead and gone, poor thing."

"Eh!" said Doneh. "How could she be otherwise after the youths of five villages had done with her?" She straightened up. "Look here, sister," she said to the woman whose head was on her lap, "I couldn't get through your lice in days! They say the Government's invented some medicine for lice which they call Dee-Dee. Ah, if only we had a spoonful of that . . . Do you know, women, that Huru keeps watch over Fadik at night? She tells the youths when to come in and then drives them out with a stick. Ha-ha, and she wants us to believe in Fadik's virtue . . ."

"That's because it suits her. Where will she find people who'll work for nothing like those two?"

"Well, the lads are well provided for this year," snickered Doneh.   80 "Who knows but that Huru may hop in and help Fadik out!"

Just then, Huru loomed up from behind a hut. She was a large woman with a sharp chin and a wrinkled face. Her graying hair was always carefully dyed with henna.

"Whores!" she shouted at the top of her voice, as she bore down upon them with arms akimbo. "City trollops! You get hold of a poor fellow's wife and let your tongues go wagging away. Tell me, are you any better than she? What do you want of this harmless mountain girl?" She pounced on Doneh who cringed back. "As for you, you filthy shitty-assed bitch, you'll shut your mouth or I'll start telling the truth about you and that husband of yours who pretends he's a man. You know me, don't you?"

Doneh blenched.

"Me, sister?" she stammered. "Me? I never . . . Other people's good   84 name . . ."

The women were dispersing hastily. Only Kurdish Velo's wife, unaware of what was going on, continued picking lice out of her companion's hair.

"Velo says in our country women like this burnt alive. He says there no virtue in this Chukurova. No honor . . ."

The eastern sky had only just begun to pale as, with a great hullabaloo and calls and cries, the women and children drove the cattle out to pasture. Before their houses, red-aproned matrons were busy at the churns beating yogurt. The damp air smelled of spring.

Osman had long ago yoked the oxen and was waiting at Huru's door.   88

She appeared in the doorway.

"Osman, my lion," she said, "you're not to come back until you've plowed through the whole field. The girl Aysheh will look after your food and get you some bedding. Mind you do the sowing properly, my child. Husneh's hard pressed this year. And there's your wife to feed too now . . ."

Husneh was Huru's only child, whom in a moment of aberration she had given in marriage to Ali Efendi, a low-salaried tax collector. All the product of her land, everything Huru had, was for this daughter.

Osman did not move or say a word. He stood there in the half-light, a large black shadow near the yoked oxen whose tails were flapping their legs in slow rhythm. 92

Huru stepped up to him.

"What's the matter with you, Osman, my child," she said anxiously. "Is anything wrong?"

"Mistress," whispered Osman, "it's what Seedy Doneh's saying. And Zeynep too . . . That my house . . . I don't know . . ."

Huru flared up. 96

"Shut up, you spineless dolt," she cried. "Don't you come babbling to me about the filthy inventions of those city trollops. I paid that broken-nosed thief a hundred good bank notes for the girl, didn't I? Did I ask you for as much as a lira? You listen to me. You can find fault with pure gold, but not with Fadik. Don't let me hear such nonsense from you again!"

Osman hesitated.

"I don't know . . ." he murmured, as he turned at last and drove the oxen off before him.

It was midmorning. A bright sun glowed over the sparkling fields. 100

Osman was struggling with the lean, emaciated oxen, which after plowing through only one acre had stretched themselves on the ground and simply refused to budge. Flushed and breathless, he let himself drop onto a mound and took his head in his hands. After a while, he rose and tried pulling the animals up by the tail.

"Accursed beasts," he muttered. "The Mistress says Husneh's in need this year. Get up this minute, accursed beasts!"

He pushed and heaved, but to no avail. Suddenly in a burst of fury, he flung himself on the black ox, dug his teeth into its nose, and shook it with all his might. Then he straightened up and looked about him sheepishly.

"If anyone saw me . . ." He swore as he spat out blood. "What can I do? Husneh's in need and there's Fadik to feed too. And now these heathen beasts . . . I don't know." 104

It was in this state of perplexity that Stumpy Veli found him when he strolled over from a neighboring field.

"So the team's collapsed, eh?" he commented. "Well, it was to be expected. Look at how their ribs are sticking out. You won't be able to get anything out of them."

"I don't know," muttered Osman faintly. "Husneh's in a bad way and I got married . . ."

"And a fine mess that's landed you in," burst out Veli angrily. "You'd 108 have been better off dead!"

"I don't know," said Osman. "The Mistress paid a hundred liras for her . . ."

Stumpy Veli took hold of his arm and made him sit down.

"Look, Osman," he said, "the villagers told me to talk to you. They say you're giving the village a bad name. Ever since the Agha's son took up with your wife, all the other youths have followed suit and your house is just like a brothel now. The villagers say you've got to repudiate her. If you don't, they'll drive you both out. The honor of the whole village is at stake, and you know honor doesn't grow on trees . . ."

Osman, his head hanging down, was as still as a statue. A stray ant 112 had caught his eye.

What's this ant doing around here at this time of day, he wondered to himself. Where can its nest be?

Veli nudged him sharply.

"Damn you, man!" he cried. "Think what'll happen if the police get wind of this. She hasn't got any papers. Why, if the gendarmes once lay their hands on her, you know how it'll be. They'll play around with her for months, poor creature."

Osman started as though an electric current had been sent through 116 his large frame.

"I haven't got any papers either," he whispered.

Veli drew nearer. Their shoulders touched. Osman's were trembling fitfully.

"Papers are the business of the Government," Veli said. "You and me, we can't understand such things. If we did, then what would we need a Government for? Now, listen to me. If the gendarmes get hold of her, we'll be the laughingstock of villages for miles around. We'll never be able to hold up our heads again in the Chukurova. You mustn't trifle

with the honor of the whole village. Get rid of her before she drags you
into more trouble."

"But where will I be without her?" protested Osman. "I'll die, that's 120
all. Who'll do my washing? Who'll cook bulgur pilaf for me? I'll starve
to death if I have to eat gruel again every day. I just can't do without
her."

"The villagers will buy you another woman," said Veli. "We'll collect
the money among us. A better woman, an honorable one, and beautiful
too . . . I'll go up into the mountain villages and pick one for you myself.
Just you pack this one off quickly . . ."

"I don't know," said Osman. "It's the Mistress knows about these
things."

Veli was exasperated.

"Damn the Mistress!" he shouted. "It's up to you, you idiot!"   124

Then he softened. He tried persuasion again. He talked and talked.
He talked himself hoarse, but Osman sat there immovable as a rock, his
mouth clamped tight. Finally Veli spat in his face and stalked off.

It was well on in the afternoon when it occurred to Osman to unyoke
the team. He had not stirred since Veli's departure. As for the oxen, they
had just lain there placidly chewing the cud. He managed to get them
to their feet and let them wander about the field, while he walked back
to the village. He made straight for the Agha's house and waited in the
yard, not speaking to anyone, until he saw the Agha's son riding in, the
bridle of his horse lathered with sweat.

The Agha's son was taken aback. He dismounted quickly, but Osman
waylaid him.

"Listen," he pleaded, "you're the son of our all-powerful Agha. What 128
do you want with my wife?"

The Agha's son became the color of his famous boots. He hastily
pulled a five-lira note out of his pocket and thrust it into Osman's hand.

"Take this," he mumbled and hurried away.

"But you're a great big Agha's son!" cried Osman after him. "Why do
you want to drive her away? What harm has she done you? You're a
great big . . ."

He was crushed. He stumbled away towards Huru's house, the five- 132
lira note still in his hand.

At the sight of Osman, Huru blew her top.

"What are you doing here, you feebleminded ass?" she shouted.
"Didn't I tell you not to come back until you'd finished all the plowing?
Do you want to ruin me, you idiot?"

"Wait, Mistress," stammered Osman. "Listen . . ."

"Listen, he says! Damn the fool!"   136

"Mistress," he pleaded, "let me explain . . ."

Huru glared at him.

"Mistress, you haven't heard. You don't know what the villagers are going to do to me. They're going to throw me out of this village. Stumpy Veli said so. He said the police . . . He said papers . . . We haven't got any papers. Fadik hasn't and I haven't either. He said the gendarmes would carry Fadik away and do things to her. He said I must repudiate her because my house is a brothel. That's what he said. I said the Mistress knows these things . . . She paid the hundred liras . . ."

Huru was dancing with fury. She rushed out into the village square   140 and began howling at the top of her voice.

"Bastards! So she's a thorn in your flesh, this poor fellow's wife! If you want to drive whores out of this village why don't you start with your own wives and daughters? You'd better look for whores in your own homes, pimps that you are, all of you! And tell your sons to leave poor folks' women alone . . ."

Then she turned to Osman and gave him a push.

"Off you go! To the fields! No one's going to do anything to your wife. Not while I'm alive."

The villagers had gathered in the square and had heard Huru out in   144 profound silence. As soon as she was gone, though, they started muttering among themselves.

"Who does that bitch think she is, abusing the whole village like that? . . ."

The Agha, Wolf Mahmut, had heard her too.

"You just wait, Huru," he said grinding his teeth. "If you think you're going to get away with this . . ."

The night was dark, a thick damp darkness that seemed to cling to the   148 face and hands. Huru had been waiting for some time now, concealed in the blackest shadow of the barn, when suddenly she perceived a stirring in the darkness, and a voice was calling softly at the door.

"Fadik! Open up, girl. It's me . . ."

The door creaked open and a shadow glided in. An uncontrollable trembling seized Huru. She gripped her stick and flung herself on the door. It was unbolted and went crashing back against the wall. As she stood there trying to pierce the darkness, a few vague figures hustled by and made their escape. Taken by surprise, she hurled out a vitriolic oath and started groping about until she discovered Fadik crouching in a corner. She seized her by the hair and began to beat her with the stick.

"Bitch!" she hissed. "To think I was standing up for you . . ."

Fadik did not utter a sound as the blows rained down on her. At last 152 Huru, exhausted, let go of her.

"Get up," she ordered, "and light some kindling."

Fadik raked out the dying embers and with much puffing and blowing managed to light a stick of torchwood. A pale honeyed light fell dimly over the stacked hay. There was an old pallet in one corner and a few kitchen utensils, but nothing else to show that the place was lived in.

Huru took Fadik's hand and looked at her sternly.

"Didn't you promise me, girl, that you'd never do it again?" 156

Fadik's head hung low.

"Do you know, you bitch," continued Huru, "what the villagers are going to do? They're going to kick you out of the village. Do you hear me?"

Fadik stirred a little. "Mistress, I swear I didn't go after them! They just came in spite of everything."

"Listen to me, girl," said Huru. "Do you know what happened to 160 Esheh? That's what you'll come to if you're not careful. They're like ravening wolves, these men. If you fall into their clutches, they'll tear you to shreds. To shreds, I tell you!"

"But Mistress, I swear I never did anything to — "

"You must bolt your door because they'll be after you whether you do anything or not, and their pimps of fathers will put the blame on me. It's my hundred liras they can't swallow. They're dying to see it go to pot . . . Just like Esheh you'll be. They had no one in the world, she and her man, and when Ali was thrown into jail she was left all alone. He'd lifted a sheep from the Agha's flock and bought clothes and shoes for their son. A lovely child he was, three years old . . . Ali doted on him. But there he was in jail, and that yellow-booted good-for-nothing was soon after Esheh like the plague. She kept him at arm's length for as long as she could, poor Esheh, but he got what he wanted in the end. Then he turned her over to those ravening wolves . . . They dragged her about from village to village, from mountain to mountain. Twenty, thirty good-for-nothings . . . Her child was left among strangers, the little boy she had loved so. He died . . . Those who saw her said she was like a consumptive, thin and gray, but still they wouldn't let her go, those scoundrels. Then one day the village dogs came in all smeared with blood, and an eagle was circling over the plain. So the men went to look, and they found Esheh, her body half devoured by the dogs . . . They'd made her dance naked for them . . . They'd done all sorts of things to her. Yes, they as good as killed her. That's what the police said when they came up from the town. And when Ali heard of it, he died of grief in jail. Yes, my girl, you've got Esheh's fate before you. It isn't my hundred liras that I care for, it's you. As for Osman, I can always find another woman for him. Now I've warned you. Just call me if they come again. Esheh was all alone in the world. You've got me, at least. Do you swear to do as I'm telling you?"

"I swear it, Mistress," said Fadik.

Huru was suddenly very tired.   ·   164

"Well, I'm going. You'll call me, won't you?"

As soon as she was gone, the youths crept out of the darkness and sneaked into the barn again.

"Hey, Fadik," they whispered. "Huru was lying to you, girl. Esheh just killed herself . . ."

There was a stretch of grass in front of the Agha's house, and on one 168 side of it dung had been heaped to the size of a small hillock. The dung steamed in the early morning sun and not a breath stirred the warm air. A cock climbed to the top of the heap. It scraped the dung, stretched its neck, and crowed triumphantly, flapping its wings.

The group of villagers squatting about on the grass silently eyed the angry Agha. Wolf Mahmut was a huge man whose shadow when he was sitting was as large as that of an average man standing up. He was never seen without a frayed, checked overcoat, the only one in the village, that he had been wearing for years now.

He was toying irritably with his metal-framed glasses when Stumpy Veli, who had been sent for a while ago, made his appearance. The Agha glared at him.

"Is this the way you get things done, you fraud?" he expostulated. "So you'd have Hollow Osman eating out of your hand in no time, eh?"

Stumpy Veli seemed to shrink to half his size. 172

"Agha," he said, "I tried everything. I talked and talked. I told him the villagers would drive them both out. I warned him of the gendarmes. All right, he said, I'll send her away. And then he didn't . . . If you ask me, Huru's at the bottom of it all."

The others stirred. "That she is!" they agreed.

Mahmut Agha jumped up. "I'll get even with her," he growled.

"That, you will, Agha," they assented. "But . . ." 176

"We've put up with that old whore long enough," continued the Agha, sitting down again.

"Yes, Agha," said Stumpy Veli, "but, you see, she relies on her son-in-law Ali, the tax collector. They'd better stop treading on my toes, she said, or I'll have Ali strip this village bare . . ."

"He can't do anything," said the Agha. "I don't owe the Government a bean."

"But we do, Agha," interposed one of the men. "He can come here 180 and take away our blankets and rugs, whatever we have . . ."

"It's because of Huru that he hasn't fleeced this village up to now," said another. "We owe a lot of money, Agha."

"Well, what are we to do then?" cried Mahmut Agha angrily. "All our youths have left the plow and the fields and are after the woman night and day like rutting bulls. At this rate, the whole village'll starve this year."

An old man spoke up in a tremulous voice. "I'm dead, for one," he wailed. "That woman's ruined my hearth. High morning it is already. Go to the plow, my son, I beg the boy. We'll starve if you don't plow. But he won't listen. He's always after that woman. I've lost my son because of that whore. I'm too old to plow any more. I'll starve this year. I'll go and throw myself at Huru's feet. There's nothing else to do . . ."

The Agha rose abruptly. "That Huru!" He gritted his teeth. "I'll settle 184 her account."

He strode away.

The villagers looked up hopefully. "Mahmut Agha'll settle her account," they muttered. "He'll find a way . . ."

The Agha heard them and swelled with pride. "Yes, Mahmut Agha'll settle her account," he repeated grimly to himself.

He stopped before a hut and called out.   188
"Hatije Woman! Hatije!"

A middle-aged woman rushed out wiping her hands on her apron.

"Mahmut Agha!" she cried. "Welcome to our home. You never visit us these days." Then she whirled back. "Get up, you damned lazybones," she shouted angrily. "It's high morning, and look who's here."

Mahmut Agha followed her inside.   192

"Look, Agha," she complained, pointing to her son, "it's high morning and Halil still abed!"

Startled at the sight of the Agha, Halil sprang up and drew on his black *shalvar* trousers shamefacedly, while his mother continued with her lamentations.

"Ah, Mahmut Agha, you don't know what's befallen us! You don't know, may I kiss your feet, my Agha, or you wouldn't have us on your land any longer . . . Ah, Mahmut Agha! This accursed son of mine . . . I would have seen him dead and buried, yes, buried in this black earth before . . ."

"What are you cursing the lad for?" Mahmut Agha interrupted her. 196 "Wait, just tell me first."

"Ah, Agha, if you knew! It was full day when he came home this night. And it's the same every night, the same ever since Hollow Osman's woman came to the village. He lies abed all through the livelong day. Who'll do the plowing, I ask you? We'll starve this year. Ah, Mahmut Agha, do something! Please do something . . ."

"You go outside a little, will you, Hatije," said the Agha. Then he turned to Halil, stretching out his long, wrinkled neck which had become as red as a turkey's. "Listen to me, my boy, this has got to end. You must get this whore out of our village and give her to the youths of another village, any village. She's got to go and you'll do it. It's an order. Do you hear me?"

"Why, Agha!" Halil said ingratiatingly. "Is that what's worrying you? I'll get hold of her this very night and turn her over to Jelil from Ortakli village. You can count on me."

The Agha's spirits rose. 200

"Hatije," he called out, "come in here. See how I'm getting you out of this mess? And all the village too . . . Let that Huru know who she's dealing with in the future. They call me Wolf Mahmut and I know how to put her nose out of joint."

Long before dawn, piercing shrieks startled the echoes in the village.

"Bastards! Pimps!" Huru was howling. "You won't get away with this, not on your life you won't. My hundred liras were too much for you to swallow, eh, you fiends? You were jealous of this poor fellow's wife, eh? But you just wait and see, Wolf Mahmut! I'll set the tax collector after you all in no time. I'll get even with you if I have to spend my last penny! I'll bribe the Mudir, the Kaymakam, all the officials. I'll send telegrams to Ankara, to Ismet Pasha, to the head of the Democrats. I'll have you all dragged into court, rotting away in police stations. I'll get my own back on you for Fadik's sake."

She paused to get her breath and was off again even louder than 204 before.

Fadik had disappeared, that was the long and the short of it. Huru soon found out that someone else was missing too. Huseyin's half-witted son, The Tick.

"Impossible," she said. "The Tick ravishing women? Not to save his life, he couldn't! This is just another trick of those good-for-nothings . . ."

"But really, Huru," the villagers tried to persuade her, "he was after her all the time. Don't you know he gathered white snails in the hills, threaded them into a necklace, and offered it to Fadik, and she hung it up on her wall as a keepsake? That's the plain truth, Huru."

"I don't believe it." Huru said stubbornly. "I wouldn't even if I saw 208 them together with my own eyes . . ."

The next day it started raining, that sheer, plumb-line torrent which sets in over the Chukurova for days. The minute the bad news had reached him, Osman had abandoned his plow and had rushed back to the village. He was standing now motionless at Huru's door, the peak of his cap drooping over his eyes. His wet clothes clung to his flesh, glistening darkly, and his rawhide boots were clogged with mud.

"Come in out of the rain, Osman, do!" Huru kept urging him.

"I can't. I don't know . . ." was all he could say.

"Now, look here, Osman," said Huru. "She's gone, so what? Let them 212 have that bitch. I'll find you a good woman, my Osman. Never mind the money. I'll spend twice as much on a new wife for you. Just you come in out of the rain."

Osman never moved.

"Listen, Osman. I've sent word to Ali. Come and levy the taxes at once, I said. Have no mercy on these ungrateful wretches. If you don't fleece them to their last rag, I said, you needn't count on me as a mother again. You'll see what I'm going to do to them, my Osman. You just come inside . . ."

The rain poured down straight and thick as the warp in a loom, and Osman still stood there, his chin resting on his staff, like a thick tree whose branches have been lopped off.

Huru appealed to the neighbors. Two men came and pulled and 216 pushed, but he seemed nailed to the ground. It was well in the afternoon when he stirred and began to pace the village from one end to the other,

his head sunk between his shoulders and the rain streaming down his
body.

"Poor fellow, he's gone mad," opined the villagers.

A few strong men finally carried him home. They undressed him and
put him to bed.

Huru sat down beside him. "Look, Osman, I'll get you a new woman
even if it costs me a thousand liras. You mustn't distress yourself so. Just
for a woman . . ."

The next morning he was more his normal self, but no amount of 220
reasoning or pleading from Huru could induce him to go back to the
field. He left the house and resumed his pacing up and down.

The villagers had really begun to feel sorry for him now.

"Alas, poor Osman!" they murmured as he passed between the huts.

Osman heard them and heaved deep, heartrending sighs. And still he
roamed aimlessly round and round.

Wolf Mahmut should have known better. Why, the whole village saw 224
with half an eye what a rascal Halil was! How could he be trusted to give
up a woman once he had got her into his hands? He had indeed got
Fadik out of the way, but what he had done was to shut her up in one
of the empty sheep pens in the hills beyond the village, and there he had
posted The Tick to guard her.

"Play around with her if you like," he had told him contemptuously.
"But if you let her give you the slip — " and he had seized The Tick's
wrist and squeezed it until it hurt — "you're as good as dead."

Though twenty years old, The Tick was so scraggy and undersized
that at first glance people would take him to be only ten. His arms and
legs were as thin as matchsticks and he walked sideways like a crab. He
had always had a way of clinging tenaciously to people or objects he took
a fancy to, which even as a child had earned him his nickname. No one
had ever called him by his real name and it looked as though his own
mother had forgotten it too . . .

Halil would come every evening bringing food for Fadik and The
Tick, and he would leave again just before dawn. But it was not three
days before the village youths found out what was going on. After that
there was a long queue every night outside the sheep pen. They would
take it in turns, heedless of Fadik's tears and howls, and at daybreak,
singing and firing their guns as though in a wedding procession, they
would make their way back to the village.

Night was falling and Fadik began to tremble like a leaf. They would 228
not be long now. They would come again and torture her. She was weak
with fear and exhaustion. For the past two days, her gorge had risen at
the very sight of food, and she lay there on the dirt floor, hardly able to
move, her whole body covered with bruises and wounds.

The Tick was dozing away near the door of the pen.

Fadik tried to plead with him. "Let me go, brother," she begged. "I'll
die if I have to bear another night of this."

The Tick half-opened his eyes. "I can't," he replied.

"But if I die, it'll be your fault. Before God it will . . . Please let me 232
go."

"Why should it be my fault?" said The Tick. "I didn't bring you here,
did I?"

"They'll never know. You'll say you fell asleep. I'll go off and hide
somewhere. I'll go back to my mother . . ."

"I can't," said The Tick. "Halil would kill me if I let you go."

"But I want to go to my mother," she cried desperately. "You must let 236
me go. Please let me go . . ."

It was dark now and the sound of singing drifted up from the village.

Fadik was seized with a violent fit of trembling. "They're coming,"
she said. "Let me get away now, brother. Save me! If you save me, I'll
be your woman. I'll do anything . . ."

But The Tick had not been nicknamed for nothing.

"They'd kill me," he said. "Why should I die because of you? And 240
Halil's promised to buy me a pair of shoes, too. I'm not going to go
without shoes because of you."

Fadik broke into wild sobbing. There was no hope now.

"Oh, God," she wept, "what shall I do now? Oh, Mother, why was I
ever born?"

They lined up as usual at the entrance to the pen. The first one went
in and a nerve-racking scream rose from Fadik, a scream that would have
moved the most hardened of hearts. But the youths were deaf to everything. In they went, one after the other, and soon Fadik's screams died
down. Not even a moan came out of her.

There were traces of blood on the ground at the back of the sheep 244
pen. Halil and the Agha's son had had a fight the night before and the
Agha's son had split open Halil's head.

"The woman's mine," Halil had insisted. "I've a right to go in first."

"No, you haven't," the Agha's son had contended. "I'm going to be the first."

The other youths had taken sides and joined the fray which had lasted most of the night, and it was a bedraggled band that wended back to the village that night.

Bowed down with grief, Hatije Woman came weeping to the Muhtar.   248

"My son is dying," she cried. "He's at his last gasp, my poor Halil, and it's the Agha's son who did it, all because of that whore of Huru's. Ah, Muhtar, if my son dies what's to become of me? There he lies struggling for life, the only hope of my hearth. But I won't let the Agha get away with this. I'll go to the Government. An old woman's only prop, I'll say . . ."

The Muhtar had great difficulty in talking Hatije out of her purpose.

"You go back home, Hatije Woman," he said when she had calmed down a little, "and don't worry. I'll deal with this business."

He summoned the Agha and the elders, and a long discussion ensued.   252
It would not do to hand over the woman to the police station. These rapacious gendarmes! . . . The honor of the whole village was at stake. And if they passed her on to the youths of another village, Huru was sure to find out and bring her back. She would not rest until she did.

After long deliberation, they came to a decision at last. The woman would be returned to Osman, but on one condition. He would take himself off with her to some distant place and never appear in the village again. They had no doubt that Osman, grateful to have Fadik back to himself, would accept. And that would cook Huru's goose too. She would lose both the woman and Osman. It would teach her to insult a whole village!

A couple of men went to find Osman and brought him back with them to the Muhtar's house.

"Sit down," they urged him, but he just stood there grasping his staff, staring about him with bloodshot eyes. His clothes hung down torn and crumpled and stained yellow from his lying all wet on the hay. His hair was a tangled, clotted mass and bits of straw clung to the stubble on his chin.

Wolf Mahmut took off his glasses and fidgeted with them.   256

"Osman, my lad," he remonstrated, "what's this state you're in? And all for a woman! Does a man let himself break down like this just for a woman? You'll die if you go on like this . . ."

"I don't know," said Osman. "I'll die . . ."

"See here, Osman," said the Agha. "We're here to help you. We'll get your woman back for you from out of those rascals' hands. Then you'll take her and go. You'll both get away from here, as far as possible. But you're not to tell Huru. She mustn't know where you are."

"You see, Osman," said Stumpy Veli, "how good the Agha's being to 260 you. Your own father wouldn't have done more."

"But you're not to tell Huru," the Agha insisted. "If you do, she'll never let you go away. And then the youths will come and take your woman away from you again. And how will you ever get yourself another woman?"

"And who'll wash your clothes then?" added Stumpy Veli. "Who'll cook your bulgur pilaf for you? You mustn't breathe a word to Huru. Just take Fadik and go off to the villages around Antep. Once there, you'll be sure to get a job on a farm. You'll be much better off than you ever were with Huru, and you'll have your woman with you too . . ."

"But how can I do that?" protested Osman. "The Mistress paid a hundred liras for Fadik."

"We'll collect that much among us," the Agha assured him. "Don't 264 you worry about that. We'll see that Huru gets her money back. You just take the woman and go."

"I don't know," said Osman. His eyes filled with tears and he swallowed. "The Mistress has always been so good to me . . . How can I . . . Just for a woman . . ."

"If you tell Huru, you're lost," said the Agha. "Is Huru the only mistress in the world? Aren't there other villages in this country? Take the woman and go. You'll never find another woman like Fadik. Listen, Veli'll tell you where she is and tomorrow you'll take her and go."

Osman bowed his head. He thought for a long time. Then he looked up at them.

"I won't tell her," he said at last. "Why should I want to stay here? 268 There are other villages . . ."

Before dawn the next day, he set out for the sheep pen which Stumpy Veli had indicated.

"I don't know . . ." he hesitated at the door. "I don't know . . ." Then he called out softly, "Fadik? Fadik, girl . . ."

There was no answer. Trembling with hope and fear, he stepped in, then stopped aghast. Fadik was lying there on the dirt floor with only a few tatters left to cover her naked body. Her huge eyes were fixed vacantly on the branches that roofed the pen.

He stood frozen, his eyes filling with tears. Then he bent his large   272
body over her.

"Fadik," he whispered, "are you all right?"

Her answering moan shook him to the core. He slipped off his shirt
and helped her into it. Then he noticed The Tick who had shrunk back
into a corner, trying to make himself invisible. Osman moved on him
threateningly.

"Uncle Osman," cried The Tick shaking with fear, "I didn't do it. It
was Halil. He said he'd buy me a pair of shoes . . . And Fadik would
have died if I hadn't been here . . ."

Osman turned away, heaved Fadik onto his back swiftly, and threw   276
himself out of the pen.

The mountain peaks were pale and the sun was about to rise. A few
white clouds floated in the sky and a cool breeze caressed his face. The
earth was wet with dew.

The Tick was scurrying off towards the village.

"Brother," Osman called after him, "go to the Mistress and tell her I
thank her for all she's done for me, but I have to go. Tell her to forgive
me . . ."

He set out in the opposite direction with Fadik on his back. He walked   280
without a break until the sun was up the height of two minarets. Then
he lowered Fadik to the ground and sat down opposite her. They looked
at each other for a long while without speaking.

"Tell me," said Osman. "Where shall we go now? I don't know . . ."

Fadik moaned.

The air smelled of spring and the earth steamed under the sun.

EXPLORATIONS

1. In what ways is "A Dirty Story" an appropriate title for Kemal's narrative?
   What people or factors does Kemal blame for Fadik's fate? What remedies, if
   any, does he recommend?

2. Reread the opening scene of "A Dirty Story" (paragraphs 1–11). What concept
   of women's role is presented here? Who holds this concept? How do we as
   readers learn it? How would the story's impact change if Kemal had written
   this scene as an expository paragraph from the author's point of view?

3. According to Kemal, by what qualities are men in this culture judged as
   successful or unsuccessful by other men? by women? How does women's
   concept of their own social role differ from men's concept?

4. The third scene in "A Dirty Story" (paragraphs 56–86) takes place among the village women. How do they interpret the situation between Fadik, Huru, and the local youths? How do their comments about Omarja's dog and Velo's donkey suggest that the situation is not really as the women depict it? What do you think is actually going on between Fadik, the youths, Osman, and Huru at this point in the story? What other clues in this scene help you to guess what is happening?

CONNECTIONS

1. Like Cherry and Charles Lindholm's "Life Behind the Veil," Kemal's "A Dirty Story" examines sex roles and stereotypes in a poor rural Eastern culture. How are women's and men's social roles in the Swat Valley of Pakistan similar to those in the fictional Turkish village of Chukurova? What views do men in both cultures share of women, and what views do women share of men, which the opposite sex would dispute?

2. Look again at the Lindholms' "Life Behind the Veil." What role is played in that essay and in Kemal's short story by government? by religion? What is the Lindholms' view, as visiting scientists, of the Islamic custom of purdah for women? How do you think Kemal, writing as an insider, would agree and disagree with their view?

3. In "Woman as Other" Simone de Beauvoir gives several reasons why women collaborate with men's perception and treatment of them as Other. What evidence of those reasons can you find in "A Dirty Story"? Why do you think the women of Chukurova show so little inclination to protect or even stand up for Fadik?

4. Gayle Early's *Observation* describes "the John Wayne image" of manhood. What qualities do the men of Chukurova share with this American image? Which of Early's "problems associated with 'old male' socialization" do they appear to share as well? From your reading in Part Three of this book, what possible cause-and-effect links can you propose between the image and the problems?

ELABORATIONS

1. Kemal avoids editorializing in "A Dirty Story"; he simply narrates and trusts his audience to draw their own conclusions. In so doing he follows the time-honored writers' rule of "*show* rather than *tell*." Readers of such a narrative often learn more from it than they realize. For example, Kemal weaves into

his story a vivid description of his native Anatolia. Go through "A Dirty Story" and pick out passages about its setting. Then write an imaginary travel article for a magazine in which you describe this region of Turkey as it would appear to a Western visitor.

2. Kemal also applies a strategy of "show rather than tell" to his characters' weaknesses. How would the story's impact change if he stated their faults and mistakes explicitly? Think of a dramatic incident in your experience in which one person or group caused harm to another without acknowledging that they were behaving badly. An example might be schoolmates bullying a weakling, an older sibling teasing a younger, or an employer or landlord discriminating on the basis of race or sex. Write a narrative essay about the incident in which you let the characters' actions speak for them, as Kemal does.

3. Does economics affect — or determine — sex roles? Naila Minai, Cherry and Charles Lindholm, and Kemal all describe Islamic attitudes toward male and female roles. All also focus on the poverty, lack of technology, and subsistence-farming economy that many Islamic communities have in common. On the basis of these three selections, write an essay examining the relation between male-female roles and nontechnological agrarian economies.

PART FOUR

WORKING

We Are What We Do

OBSERVATIONS:
LOOKING AT OURSELVES

Alice Walker, Mario Puzo, Richard Rodriguez,
Elliot Liebow, Bruce Weber, Marge Piercy,
Russell Baker, Betty Friedan, Studs Terkel

<><><><><>

Andrew H. Malcolm, *Snowbird* (CANADA)

Zhang Xinxin and Sang Ye, *The Hunter* (CHINA)

R. K. Narayan, *Trail of the Green Blazer* (INDIA)

Shiva Naipaul, *The Palmers* (KENYA)

Ezekiel Mphahlele, *Tradition and the African Writer*
(SOUTH AFRICA)

David Plath, *Tomoko on Her Television Career* (JAPAN)

Satoshi Kamata, *Six Months at Toyota* (JAPAN)

Hedrick Smith, *Skoro Budet — It'll Be Here Soon*
(SOVIET UNION)

Jill Gay, *Patriotic Prostitutes* (THAILAND, SOUTH KOREA,
PHILIPPINES)

Thelma Forshaw, *The Demo* (AUSTRALIA)

WE IDENTIFY OURSELVES AND RECOGNIZE EACH OTHER BY WHAT WE do. People's work varies from plowing fields to judging disputes, from teaching children to leading armies, from feeding chickens to programming computers. For some of us, work is a burden; for some, a pleasure; and for some, a source of pride. How we feel about our work both affects and is affected by how we feel about ourselves.

Observations: Looking at Ourselves start with Alice Walker on the healing power of writing. Mario Puzo recalls his own and his mother's goals for him, and Richard Rodriguez notes the irony of escaping from his parents' limited sphere with their help. Elliot Liebow compares insider and outsider views of unskilled workers; Bruce Weber is surprised by the ambitions of current college students; Marge Piercy comments on being a "professional"; Russell Baker sympathizes with children who wonder what Daddy does. Betty Friedan quotes a lawyer about to become a mother, and Studs Terkel presents an organizer's views on his work with and for other workers.

Crossing the border into Canada, we share Andrew Malcolm's dogsled trek through frozen woods with "Snowbird." Zhang Xinxin and Sang Ye interview "The Hunter," He Guangwei, a captor of leopards, tigers, and other wild beasts of China. A hunter of another sort is the Indian pickpocket Raju in R. K. Narayan's short story "Trail of the Green Blazer." On the opposite end of the social scale are "The Palmers," a British-minded tea grower and his wife visited on their Kenya plantation by Shiva Naipaul. The South African writer Ezekiel Mphahlele offers a contrasting view of the postcolonial dilemma in "Tradition and the African Writer," in which he cites the effects of a dual heritage on himself and his compatriots.

Tomoko, a Japanese producer, talks about the challenges of being a wife, mother, and professional in David Plath's "Tomoko on Her Television Career." Shifting to Japan's much-discussed auto factories, we follow Satoshi Kamata through a grueling "Six Months at Toyota." Factory workers in the Soviet Union tell Hedrick Smith about their monthly custom of storming in *Skoro Budet* — It'll Be Here Soon."

For southeast Asian women of Thailand, South Korea, and the Philippines in need of a job, reports Jill Gay in "Patriotic Prostitutes," sometimes the only practical option is selling sex — with the government's enthusiastic encouragement. Still farther south, Thelma Forshaw's short story "The Demo" follows an Australian immigrant from Eastern Europe through a harrowing day at his milk bar, where a threat to his shop is a threat to his soul. ◆

OBSERVATIONS:
LOOKING AT OURSELVES

1

I think writing really helps you heal yourself. . . . I think if you write long enough, you will be a healthy person. That is, if you write what you need to write, as opposed to what will make money, or what will make fame.

– Alice Walker
"Telling the Black Woman's Story"
New York Times Magazine

◇◇◇◇◇

2

As a child I had the usual dreams. I wanted to be handsome, specifically as cowboy stars in movies were handsome. I wanted to be a killer hero in a worldwide war. Or if no wars came along (our teachers told us another was impossible), I wanted at the very least to be a footloose adventurer. Then I branched out and thought of being a great artist, and then, getting ever more sophisticated, a great criminal.

My mother, however, wanted me to be a railroad clerk. And that was her *highest* ambition; she would have settled for less. At the age of sixteen when I let everybody know that I was going to be a great writer, my friends and family took the news quite calmly, my mother included. She did not become angry. She quite simply assumed that I had gone off my nut. She was illiterate and her peasant life in Italy made her believe that only a son of the nobility could possibly be a writer. Artistic beauty after all could spring only from the seedbed of fine clothes, fine food, luxurious living. So then how was it possible for a son of hers to be an artist? She was not too convinced she was wrong even after my first two books were published many years later. It was only after the commercial success of my third novel that she gave me the title of poet.

– Mario Puzo
"Choosing a Dream:
Italians in Hell's Kitchen"

◇◇◇◇◇

3

"Your parents must be very proud of you." People began to say that to me about the time I was in sixth grade. To answer affirmatively, I'd smile. Shyly I'd smile, never betraying my sense of the irony: I was not proud of my mother and father. I was embarrassed by their lack of education. It was not that I ever thought they were stupid, though stupidly I took for granted their enormous native intelligence. Simply, what mattered to me was that they were not like my teachers. . . .

Tightening the irony into a knot was the knowledge that my parents were always behind me. They made success possible. They evened the path. They sent their children to parochial schools because the nuns "teach better." They paid a tuition they couldn't afford. They spoke English to us.

 For their children my parents wanted chances they never had — an easier way. It saddened my mother to learn that some relatives forced their children to start working right after high school. To *her* children she would say, "Get all the education you can." In schooling she recognized the key to job advancement. . . .

When I was in high school, I admitted to my mother that I planned to become a teacher someday. That seemed to please her. But I never tried to explain that it was not the occupation of teaching I yearned for as much as it was something more elusive: I wanted to *be* like my teachers, to possess their knowledge, to assume their authority, their confidence, even to assume a teacher's persona.

– Richard Rodriguez
Hunger of Memory

◇◇◇◇◇

4

Menial jobs are not, by and large, the starting point of a track system which leads to even better jobs for those who are able and willing to do them. The busboy or dishwasher in a restaurant is not on a job track which, if negotiated skillfully, leads to chef or manager of the restaurant. The busboy or dishwasher who works hard becomes, simply, a hard-working busboy or dishwasher. Neither hard work nor perseverance can conceivably carry the janitor to a sit-down job in the office building he cleans up. And it is the apprentice who becomes the journeyman electrician, plumber, steamfitter, or bricklayer, not the common unskilled Negro laborer.

Thus, the job is not a stepping-stone to something better. It is a dead end. It promises to deliver no more tomorrow, next month, or next year than it does today.

Delivering little, and promising no more, the job is "no big thing."
The man appears to treat the job in a cavalier fashion, working and not
working as the spirit moves him, as if all that matters is the immediate
satisfaction of his present appetites, the surrender to present moods, and
the indulgence of whims with no thought for the cost, the consequences,
the future. To the middle-class observer, this behavior reflects a "present-
time orientation" — an "inability to defer gratification." It is this "present-
time" orientation — as against the "future orientation" of the middle-
class person — that "explains" to the outsider why Leroy chooses to spend
the day at the Carry-out rather than report to work; why Richard, who
was paid Friday, was drunk Saturday and Sunday and penniless Monday;
why Sweets quit his job today because the boss looked at him "funny"
yesterday.

But from the inside looking out, what appears as a "present-time"
orientation to the outside observer is, to the man experiencing it, as much
a future orientation as that of his middle-class counterpart. The difference
between the two men lies not so much in their different orientations to
time as in their different orientations to future time or, more specifically,
to their different futures.

> — Elliot Liebow
> *Talley's Corner: A Study of*
> *Negro Streetcorner Men*

◇◇◇◇◇◇

5

According to annual surveys of 300,000 college freshmen conducted
by the Higher Education Research Institute at the Graduate School of
Education of the University of California at Los Angeles, young people
today, by the time they *enter* college, are more inclined to express
concrete life objectives than they've been for many years. Of those surveyed last fall, 73.2 percent cited being "very well off financially" as an
essential or very important objective. That's up from 63.3 percent in
1980, 49.5 percent in 1975. Other objectives that the survey shows have
risen in importance include "obtain recognition from colleagues for con-
tributions to my special field"; "have administrative responsibility for the
work of others"; "be successful in my own business"; and "raise a family."
At the same time, the percentage of freshmen who consider it important
to "develop a meaningful philosophy of life" has declined from 64.2
percent in 1975 to 40.6 percent last year.

Many of the people I spoke to feel the pressure of peer scrutiny. A status thing has evolved, to which many seem to have regretfully succumbed. Several expressed a weariness with meeting someone new and having to present themselves by their credentials. Yet, overwhelmingly, asked what they're looking for in a romantic partner, they responded first with phrases such as "an educated professional" and "someone with direction." They've conceded, more or less consciously, that unenlightened and exclusionary as it is, it's very uncool not to know what you want and not to be already chasing it.

> – Bruce Weber
> "Alone Together: The Unromantic Generation"
> *New York Times Magazine*

◇–◇–◇–◇–◇

6

One trouble: to be a professional anything in the United States is to think of oneself as an expert and one's ideas as semisacred, and to treat others in a certain way — professionally.

> – Marge Piercy
> "The Grand Coolie Damn"

◇–◇–◇–◇–◇

7

It is not surprising that modern children tend to look blank and dispirited when informed that they will someday have to "go to work and make a living." The problem is that they cannot visualize what work is in corporate America.

Not so long ago, when a parent said he was off to work, the child knew very well what was about to happen. His parent was going to make something or fix something. The parent could take his offspring to his place of business and let him watch while he repaired a buggy or built a table.

When a child asked, "What kind of work do you do, Daddy?" his father could answer in terms that a child could come to grips with. "I fix steam engines." "I make horse collars."

Well, a few fathers still fix engines and build things, but most do not. Nowadays, most fathers sit in glass buildings performing tasks that are absolutely incomprehensible to children. The answers they give when asked, "What kind of work do you do, Daddy?" are likely to be utterly mystifying to a child.

"I sell space." "I do market research." "I am a data processor." "I am in public relations." "I am a systems analyst." Such explanations must seem nonsense to a child. How can he possibly envision anyone analyzing a system or researching a market?

– Russell Baker
Poor Russell's Almanac

◇◇◇◇◇

8

In a fascinating study of women at the huge Government-sponsored National Women's Conference in Houston in 1977, the eminent sociologist Alice Rossi found that feminists who were involved mainly in sexual politics did not show a general increase in political competence or self-confidence sufficient to risk mainstream politics. This was not the case for feminists involved in the battle for equal opportunity and changing women's condition in society. But actual experience in the professional work world or the mainstream political world — as one's own person, not as wife — brought the greatest increase in that competence, which is, of course, both political and personal.

A young Wall Street lawyer, deciding finally to have a baby, described her personal evolution in this way:

> I never had any confidence in myself before I practiced law. I think the women's movement not only gave me those opportunities — it helped me respect women a lot more — and respect myself as a woman. I like the self-confidence, the ability as a problem solver and the courage to speak out that I got in law. I've lost a vague, tentative, ethereal quality I used to have. But my style in work is not like a man's. I'm very determined but I'm not aggressive. I'm not put off by a blowhard. I let them rant and rave, then quietly handle their points, one by one. It works every time. The men in my firm go for the jugular, take every punch, always on the aggressive. I was put off by that, I wasn't sure I could be that aggressive. It seemed to be the only way, at first, but it's just not me.
>
> When I began to handle my own cases, I began to find my own style. I think there is a difference between men and women. I don't try to rant and rave in court like the men.
>
> A few years ago, when I was pregnant, I felt having a baby would interfere with my career. I had an abortion. Today, I go into court and

see a lot of women in their thirties with pregnant bellies way out to here. And I think they look just beautiful, handling their cases with confidence and professional skill and confident enough to have the baby too.

– Betty Friedan
The Second Stage

◇–◇–◇–◇–◇

9

My work is trying to change this country. This is the job I've chosen. When people ask me, "Why are you doing this?" it's like asking what kind of sickness you got. I don't feel sick. I think this country is sick. The daily injustices just gnaw on me a little harder than they do on other people.

I try to bring people together who are being put down by the system, left out. You try to build an organization that will give them power to make the changes. Everybody's at the bottom of the barrel at this point. Ten years ago one could say the poor people suffered and the middle class got by. That's not true any more. . . .

I put together a fairly solid organization of Appalachian people in Pike County [Kentucky]. It's a single industry area, coal. You either work for the coal company or you don't work. Sixty percent of its people live on incomes lower than the government's guidelines for rural areas.

I was brought in to teach other organizers how to do it. I spent my first three months at it. I decided these middle-class kids from Harvard and Columbia were too busy telling everybody else what they should be doing. The only thing to do was to organize the local people. . . .

The word organizer has been romanticized. You get the vision of a mystical being doing magical things. An organizer is a guy who brings in new members. I don't feel I've had a good day unless I've talked with at least one new person. We have a meeting, make space for new people to come in. The organizer sits next to the new guy, so everybody has to take the new guy as an equal. You do that a couple of times and the guy's got strength enough to become part of the group.

You must listen to them and tell them again and again they are important, that they have the stuff to do the job. They don't have to shuck themselves about not being good enough, not worthy. Most people were raised to think they are not worthy. School is a process of taking beautiful kids who are filled with life and beating them into happy slavery.

That's as true of a twenty-five-thousand-dollar-a-year executive as it is for the poorest.

You don't find allies on the basis of the brotherhood of man. People are tied into their immediate problems. They have a difficult time worrying about other people's. Our society is so structured that everybody is supposed to be selfish as hell and screw the other guy. Christian brotherhood is enlightened self-interest. Most sins committed on poor people are by people who've come to help them.

I came as a stranger but I came with credentials. There are people who know and trust me, who say so to the others. So what I'm saying is verifiable. It's possible to win, to take an outfit like Bethlehem Steel and lick 'em. Most people in their guts don't really believe it. Gee, it's great when all of a sudden they realize it's possible. They become alive.

Nobody believed PCCA [Pike County Citizens' Association] could stop Bethlehem from strip mining. Ten miles away was a hillside being stripped. Ten miles away is like ten million light years away. What they wanted was a park, a place for their kids. Bethlehem said, "Go to hell. You're just a bunch of crummy Appalachians. We're not gonna give you a damn thing." If I could get that park for them, they would believe it's possible to do other things.

They really needed a victory. They had lost over and over again, day after day. So I got together twenty, thirty people I saw as leaders. I said, "Let's get that park." They said, "We can't." I said, "We can. If we let all the big wheels around the country know — the National Council of Churches and everybody start calling up, writing, and hounding Bethlehem, they'll have to give us the park." That's exactly what happened. Bethlehem thought: This is getting to be a pain in the ass. We'll give 'em the park and they'll shut up about strip mining. We haven't shut up on strip mining, but we got the park. Four thousand people from Pike County drove up and watched those bulldozers grading down that park. It was an incredible victory.

Twenty or thirty people realized we could win. Four thousand people understood there was a victory. They didn't know how it happened, but a few of 'em got curious. The twenty or thirty are now in their own communities trying to turn people on. . . .

I work all the way from two in the morning until two the next morning seven days a week. (Laughs.) I'm not a martyr. I'm one of the few people I know who was lucky in life to find out what he really wanted to do. I'm just havin' a ball, the time of my life. I feel sorry for all these people

I run across all the time who aren't doing what they want to do. Their lives are hell. I think everybody ought to quit their job and do what they want to do. You've got one life. You've got, say, sixty-five years. How on earth can you blow forty-five years of that doing something you hate?

I have a wife and three children. I've managed to support them for six years doing this kind of work. We don't live fat. I have enough money to buy books and records. The kids have as good an education as anybody in this country. Their range of friends runs from millionaires in San Francisco to black prostitutes in Lexington. They're comfortable with all these people. My kids know the name of the game: living your life up to the end.

All human recorded history is about five thousand years old. How many people in all that time have made an overwhelming difference? Twenty? Thirty? Most of us spend our lives trying to achieve some things. But we're not going to make an overwhelming difference. We do the best we can. That's enough.

The problem with history is that it's written by college professors about great men. That's not what history is. History's a hell of a lot of little people getting together and deciding they want a better life for themselves and their kids.

I have a goal. I want to end my life in a home for the aged that's run by the state — organizing people to fight 'em because they're not running it right. (Laughs.)

– Studs Terkel
Bill Talcott in *Working*

ANDREW H. MALCOLM

Snowbird

Born in 1943, the only child of Canadian parents, Andrew H. Malcolm has described himself as "the first American in the family." His parents had crossed the border into the United States for his father's job; their son grew up in both countries during the 1940s and 1950s. Malcolm went on to become a journalist, traveling around the world to report for the *New York Times* from Indochina, Japan, Korea, New York, and San Francisco. He has won four major awards for national reporting. A generation after leaving Canada, he returned as Toronto bureau chief for the *Times.* "Snowbird" is an excerpt from *The Canadians* (1985), the story of his four-year exploration of the country. Malcolm and his wife and three children currently live in Connecticut, where he is First Assistant National Editor for the *Times.*

The world's second largest country (after the Soviet Union), Canada extends from the Atlantic to the Pacific Ocean and from the North Pole to the U.S. border. Fort Chipewyan, where the Malcolms and Snowbird began their trek, lies on roughly the same latitude as Juneau, Alaska. Canada was settled and explored around the same times as the United States. The French were the first Europeans to live there, establishing Quebec City and Montreal in the 1600s. Britain won control shortly before the American Revolution but agreed to respect the French Canadians' language, religion, and civil law. Various British colonies united as the Dominion of Canada in 1867, which became a self-governing dominion within the British Empire in 1931. Canada achieved complete legislative independence in 1982.

The most memorable Canadian for me is a man named Napoleon Snowbird Martin. He was seventy-seven when my son Spencer, then seven, and I met him early on a bright March morning on the outskirts of Fort Chipewyan. Fort Chip, as it is known, is the oldest community in Alberta, a gathering of 1,400 souls around a Hudson's Bay trading post in northeastern Alberta hard by the Northwest Territories. It is 800 miles by frozen trail from the outside world. The barges come regularly on the Athabasca River in summer. The planes come a couple of times a week, weather permitting.

Snowbird (he never uses any other name; everyone in his world knows who he is) came to town reluctantly that winter. His wife was ill. Physically he stood about five feet tall in his caribou-skin boots. His hands were dark and wide, the skin thick like leather, showing, as I remember my grandfather's hands had shown, the collected strength and scars of many years in the open. Snowbird's face, heavily lined, was free of expression as it peered from under the peak of a battered baseball cap. It was a sport he had never heard of. But the old eyes, even behind bifocals, were sharp and clear. Snowbird has lived in the Canadian bush, in cabins, behind lean-tos, on mattresses of boughs, and under buffalo robe blankets and the crisp stars ever since Theodore Roosevelt was President of the United States. Snowbird is unable to read words on paper. But he can read tracks and blood in the snow and branches broken certain ways, and sounds in the air. He knows the colors of good clouds and bad clouds and the sunsets and different winds that presage tomorrow's weather. He knows tales as timeless as their morals. He has some theories on modern problems. And he can speak four languages — Cree, English, Chipewyan, and dog — sometimes in the same sentence. "I'm seventy-seven years old," he told us. "I'm just beginning to grow."

Through that special invisible bond that links the very old and the very young, my son Spencer knew instantly about Snowbird. "He's neat," he said. It took me, stymied by the old man's initial silence, an hour longer to fall under his spell. And by the end of our first day on the trail with him, when the wind was banging the tent walls and the dogs were howling back at a wolf they would never see, the two city residents who had come to discover dogsleds and the Canadian wilderness were also discovering the unusually strong presence of a man who is old only in terms of years.

Snowbird is one of a few Canadian natives who still run dogs. Most   4
have changed to modern snowmobiles, which can go farther faster across the frozen lakes, down the frozen rivers, and through the frigid forests of their countryside. Snowmobiles don't get sick with worms or fight each other, but snowmobile spark plugs can easily foul a very long way from help. And there aren't too many gas stations in the woods. Snowbird's sled dogs, no purebreds they, have never let him down, never turned on him, never even nipped him. All they want are a couple of frozen fish a day to crunch up whole, frequent mouthfuls of snow along the route, and the chance to hear through much of the day his reassuring tone of voice behind them as the wooden sled whispers its way across the snow.

As a married couple after years of living together come to read each other's moods and meanings through little signs, movements, and inflec-

tions, Snowbird reads his dogs. He knows their tail signals, what a cocked
ear or wiggled nose means, the instincts behind certain howls or growls,
when a fight is about to erupt. "Dogs can't live without love," according
to Snowbird's philosophy. "All my dogs are friendly, except that last one.
He's borrowed and doesn't know my rules yet."

In turn the animals, all males with no names, learn Snowbird's little
signals — what "click-click," "hup," and "jah" mean; when and where
they can expect to eat. They know that two or three of them trying to
grab a mouthful of snow on the run prompts Snowbird to call a rest stop
for a longer "drink" of snow. They know it means trouble when Snowbird
breaks off a handy branch and strides forward, muttering. But they read,
too, the abiding affection in Snowbird's voice, regardless of the words.
"This dog something you call dumb," he said, smiling, as he lifted one
misplaced leg back into harness. The dog gave Snowbird a lick of appreciation.

"Okay, boys," he said, "click-click hup now jah" (translation: "let's go,
get going now to the left"). Even when the trail is obvious down a frozen
riverbed, Snowbird continues a nonstop bilingual banter. "They like to
hear me here," he said, omitting how much he liked it, too. Then,
addressing the dogs, he whistled and said, "Hapsiko hup chee chee let's
go, don't get crazy, boys, watch out I kill you and eat you click keep
quiet you." We were to spend many hours like this, my son in my lap,
half sitting atop the soft sleeping bags, feeling the gentle nonrhythmic
rocking of the oaken sled bending its way over hills and mounds and
through woods. The six animals had their accustomed trotting pace,
hauling their 600-pound sled along at four or five miles an hour, softly
panting while turning their heads to the right and left and waving their
snouts about in olfactory observations of the surrounding wilds. Canine
chaos erupted one time when a tiny field mouse darted across the trail
beneath the padding feet of our band of dogs. Instantly six mouths reached
for the intruder, and, for a moment, running and the sled were forgotten.
It took several minutes to untangle twenty-four feet and a thirty-seven-
foot-long leather harness and proceed on our way.

The warming March sun tanned our faces inside parka hoods while   8
Snowbird addressed the dogs and us, sometimes in the same breath,
issuing orders or observations or memories or tidbits of bush knowledge.
"See that Y-shaped birch?" he said once. "That makes a good natural
vice."

"A wolf came through here last night. A big one."

"And that blood over there was his breakfast. It was deer."

"I wish I keep you one month in the bush. Boy, I show you how to live pretty good for sure."

The old man took little Spencer in tow, dubbing him Little Snowbird, assigning him camp chores and lessons, and seemingly inadvertently giving little lectures, passing on the same knowledge he had heard from his father seven decades before. "Animals are like garden," the veteran trapper told the wide-eyed boy. "You treat them right, and they grow right. You treat them bad, and they don't grow right." One time Spencer stepped off the trail of packed snow and promptly sank up to his waist in powder. Snowbird strapped a pair of snowshoes on the boy, and the youngster ker-flumfed off across the drifts. He taught us how to harness the dogs, how to feed them (whole frozen fish tossed from a distance), and how to start morning fires when the wood is damp ("pinecones always stay dry"), and he passed on a modicum of Cree vocabulary: *dahnsi* ("hello"), *atim* ("dog"), *peahtik* ("look out"), *hay-hay* ("yes"), *nehmoyeh* ("no"), *kaynana-skoh-mitten* ("thank you"), *etahtomskahgan* ("good-bye"), and, Snowbird's favorite phrase, *aygotah* ("right on, brother").

The voyage into the northern wilderness with Snowbird is one of a growing number of such excursions organized by Canadian groups to utilize their wilderness resource and to pump needed money into the native economy there. It is not a luxury trip where guests are pampered or waited on. There is wood to be cut, snow to be melted for tea, food to be prepared, and countless other chores. The bathroom is the great outdoors. There are no such things as showers. We spent two nights on cabin floors and one in a tent. The temperature was around 20 below, Fahrenheit. Usually we were up by 7:00 A.M., and the sled was under way a couple of hours later. We stopped for lunch at midafternoon, when the spring sun starts to make the snow sticky for sleds, then resumed our travels by 5:00, when the night chill has tightened the snow and made the pull easier for the dogs.

The dogs seemed to love their work, as long as the temperature didn't climb too close to freezing, when the "heat" starts to affect them. They would jump up and down and bark excitedly every morning as we emerged to start our day's travels. The alleged objective of visitors to that backcountry is a tour through the Wood Buffalo National Park; at 17,000 square miles of woods, swamp, and lake, it is North America's largest park. It is also the wild home for nesting whooping cranes in summer and, all year, for around 5,500 wood buffalo, the larger, shaggier cousins of the American Plains buffalo. . . .

12

In this life, mechanical timepieces strike Snowbird as unnecessary, just as newly arrived visitors find it hard to comprehend the need for eight Indian words for different kinds of ice. Thus, the first day Spencer and Snowbird and I were to have begun our trip from Fort Chipewyan at 8:00 A.M., we actually left at 12:30 P.M. And the first afternoon Snowbird, the man now in charge of everything, including our lives, asked me, "How long we stay out?"

"Uh," I replied, about to escalate my level of concern, "until Friday."   16

"Okay," he said cheerily. "Today Monday, right?"

"No, it's Tuesday."

"Okay."

Except for the last night, when we got in trouble, we stopped for the   20
night around seven. Snowbird has an aversion to dogsledding in the dark, having once helplessly watched a traveling companion die after spearing himself on a protruding branch. Being his latest traveling companions, we were willing to avoid that fate, too.

The tasty meals were prepared in wood stoves by oil lanterns. We had snacked all day on chunks of dried caribou in a paper bag and impromptu sandwiches at a rest stop. But at night there was duck, rabbit, and buffalo with instant potatoes, powdered drinks, and muffins. In March, food is kept frozen by being put just outside the door. After dinner Snowbird would scratch his head through his green cap and inevitably comment, "Good food. Now I have power for two days."

These were also the times when Snowbird, if coaxed, would sit on the buffalo robes that made his bed, sip his tea, and talk a little about his life on the land. He talked of simple joys like muskrats. "You trap some rats," he said, "and skin them and build a little fire and roast the rats. It's nice, I tell you." He talked about his personal philosophy of life, although he would never package it that grandly. It is more a collection of observations on life that he would pass down to his children, an amalgam of thought from his elders plus what he himself had seen. He believes the important elements of life include respect for nature, for being part of nature, not an intruder. He will cut down a tree for wood and hunt animals for food, but never for fun. Having a wife is important, and picking the right one is even more so. Snowbird had moved into Fort Chipewyan (population 1,400) that winter for the first time because he had to, but he didn't like it. "Too many people," he said. If he were hunting for a wife now, Snowbird said, he would go to a city. Women seem more adventurous nowadays, he said. And of course, mothers must nurse their babies naturally. He has seen too many sad cases of children and animals that were not nursed by their mothers and then grew up to be plain, mean creatures.

He remembers when he and his friends spent all summer getting ready for winter and all winter trapping and hunting and cutting wood to earn money and food to spend all summer getting ready for winter and all winter trapping and hunting and cutting wood. "In old days," he said as we crunched along a frozen river in our sled, "people live all down this river in sheds and tents. They fish and hunt and trap. All Cree. Now all gone. They don't move to town. They move down into ground. All dead. Some sick. Some get funny, you know. Some just die. I sick once. They say flu, something like that. Long time ago. I don't remember what time that is."

But things have changed in the wild now. "Today," said Snowbird,   24 "young people go in bush, they get lost. They don't listen to fathers, and fathers don't try teach. Always drinking and stuff like that. Now buy everything from store. I don't know why — crazy or lazy, I guess." As one example, he told us about an older friend who had left the bush to move near town. They had found him two days before our visit out on the lake ice, a solid frozen block, the victim likely of a meandering drunken stroll at midnight. Snowbird's point was that this would never have happened in the bush, where everyone knew the rules and watched over each other.

Then, as the fire died down and the dogs outside noisily chewed on some bones they had discovered, he told us a tale that Cree grandfathers have told for the 9,000 years since the glaciers left those northern boreal plains pocked and open as one of the world's richest fur grounds. It is the story of an old Indian, blind and unable to hunt for his own food, a terrible fate. He was sitting sadly by the lake when a loon approached. "'Hang onto my neck like this and come swim with me,'" Snowbird said the bird said. And the old man did. Three times the bird dived under the water. And three times the man opened his eyes there. And when they surfaced the third time, the Canadian waters had done their healing job, and the forces of nature, the hunter and the hunted, were back in balance. The man could see. "He could hunt once more his own food," said Snowbird. "It is a true story." And he got no contradictions from either of his wide-eyed listeners.

EXPLORATIONS

1. What aspects of his work does Snowbird evidently enjoy most? How does Snowbird's view of his work differ from Malcolm's view of it? In what ways is each man's idea of Snowbird's work colored by the professional relationship between them?

2. This excerpt from Malcolm's book *The Canadians* centers on the character of Snowbird. Suppose Malcolm had written the story of his trip for an adventure magazine instead, or for a book about father-son relationships. How might he have changed his focus in each case? What elements in the narrative would receive more emphasis? What anecdotes and information would probably be left out?

3. When a field mouse distracts Snowbird's dogs, Malcolm writes, "Instantly six mouths reached for the intruder. . . . It took several minutes to untangle twenty-four feet and a thirty-seven-foot-long leather harness and proceed on our way." How would the incident's impact change if the numbers were omitted? What other types of specific detail does Malcolm use? Why is emphasis on detail a good stylistic tactic for this particular essay?

CONNECTIONS

1. In his *Observation*, Elliot Liebow writes, "What appears as a 'present-time' orientation to the outside observer is, to the man experiencing it, as much a future orientation as that of his middle-class counterpart." How does Snowbird's work situation resemble that of the laborers Liebow is describing? How is it different?

2. Which of the attitudes toward work described in the *Observations* is closest to Snowbird's? How and why are they similar?

ELABORATIONS

1. As Snowbird guides his dogs through the snow, he points out sights that are likely to interest his companions. To them these facts are exotic; to Snowbird they are threads in the fabric of daily life. If Snowbird wrote (or dictated) an account of this trek, how would it differ from Malcolm's? What do you think Snowbird perceives as interesting? boring? amusing? Put yourself in his place, and write an essay about your job as a wilderness guide, using the Malcolms' trip as a source of examples.

2. Suppose you were guiding visitors through a place that is familiar to you but not to them — a park or woods in your neighborhood; a church, museum, town hall, or subway station. Following Malcolm's model, write an essay focusing on the points of interest, and the facts you know about them, that are most likely to fascinate and educate your audience.

ZHANG XINXIN
and SANG YE

The Hunter

Zhang Xinxin was born in 1954 in Nanjing, a Chinese city northwest of Shanghai and due west of both Nagasaki, Japan, and San Diego, California. A graduate of the Central Drama Institute, she began to write in 1978 and published her first story a year later. Since then Zhang has published a number of critically acclaimed short stories and essays and become a member of the Chinese Writers' Association. Sang Ye was born in 1955 in the Chinese capital of Beijing, which lies on the same latitude as Philadelphia. She has been a journalist since the late 1970s and is also a researcher in modern Chinese history.

"The Hunter" comes from *Chinese Profiles* (1986), a collection of interviews with ordinary Chinese citizens conducted by Zhang and Sang during a year on the road. Begun as a regular feature for a New York Chinese newspaper, these interviews were quickly picked up by literary magazines in China. One hundred of the best were published in book form; thirty-nine of these have been translated from the Chinese into English as *Chinese Profiles.* The translator of "The Hunter" was Geremie Barmé. Its subject, He Guangwei, is a seventy-six-year-old member of the People's Political Consultative Conference of Hunan Province.

I can't really say I'm much good at anything apart from hunting. I'm all at sea when it comes to meetings like this; but the government's thought enough of me to make me a member of the conference, so it's only proper that I should come along and do my share in ruling the country. The only problem is that food they feed us. No, I can't quite put my finger on it. Seems a bit off, you know; none too fresh. Maybe it's because it's high-class tucker.

I live at Wu Family Bridge, it's due north of the Meng County Seat. There's a story connected with the place that says it's the place where Wu Song was banished and had that drunken spree in Jiang Menshen. (A delegate at a neighboring table breaks in: "The people where he comes from say Comrade He is a reincarnation of Wu Song. No, really. But he has a more impressive record than Wu Song: over the last sixty years he's killed or captured seven tigers and over 330 leopards with his bare hands, not to say anything of the 2000 or so wolves and wild boars he's hunted. Wu Song would've been no match for him, believe you me.") Thanks very much all the same, but you're laying it on a bit thick. I'm a hunter pure and simple, it's my job.

Who do you reckon's the king of the mountains? The tiger? You're way off, it's man; man's the real king. Say when you're after a leopard, all you need is the right method, the strength and enough pluck and you'll be able to do the job. Leopards don't go for people, they try and run away the moment they catch sight of a human being. But you've got to stick with him, rile him. You keep at him until he turns on you in anger, then you stand your ground and wait for him to come at you and you aim a solid blow at his snout. That'll knock the wind out of his sails. There's 200 catties behind him; add the same again for your strength, and that means he takes 400 catties on the snout. He'll be so dazed he'll forget all about biting you. It's when he's panting and wiping away the tears that you have to go straight up, grab him by the head with one hand and by the tail with the other, using your legs to scissor his head, and press down on his pelvis. Then you wait for the cage you've made to be brought along. And there you have it: catching a leopard is no harder or simpler than that.

They're funny things, leopards; they care more about eating than staying free. They're not like other wild animals that refuse to feed in captivity. You hold him down and make him eat a bit of meat and once he has he'll be as good as gold. You have to tie him proper around the legs and he's ready for the cage. You take him down the mountain in a small cage and put him in a larger one later. You have to drug him to prevent shock. Leopards are easier to keep alive and transport since we started using sedatives.

What's the key you say? Well, the thing you have to watch out for is flies. Every creature has its natural enemy, and leopards don't take to flies at all. Now if a fly fouls his eye then he'll be sure to get sick. And once they get sick they're as good as done for. What are you laughing about? It's true. Forget that stuff you've read, that's just the way it is.

Originally I'm from Hejiapaifang, southeast of the county seat of Suxian in Anhui. I finally settled in Mengxian County. My dad was drowned by a landlord's lackeys when I was only ten. After that I was forced to go to work for a landlord too. He was all smiles on the surface — they're the worst kind. He was scared I'd steal from him and so one night he spread some coppers in the courtyard and waited to see whether I picked them up. I did because I thought I could use them to pay for a doctor to see my gran. But then I reckoned I'd sooner starve than steal from someone so I put the damned lot down on his doorstep. We've been submissive villagers, my family, for generations.

During the autumn wheat harvest of the year I turned fifteen I got news from the village that both my brothers were dead. The elder one had been sold to be a soldier by the village head and had died on the way to Suzhou. My other brother hung himself after he was caught stealing some wheat stalks and beaten. You couldn't even eat wheat stalks; people used them for kindling. The landlords couldn't use them for anything. My second brother was only nine when he died. I had a dream in which my father and brothers said to me, "Don't work for the landlord any more, break away and make a life for yourself." I hugged them and cried, "The world is a large place, there must be somewhere for me. I'll go and learn a trade and when I'm rich I'll be a good man and show them all."

I went to a fortune-teller who said to me, "It's a wide world and there's no end of places where you can settle down and make a life for yourself. Go out and make your own way." He wrote the words "He Guangwei will prosper anywhere" on my waistband. He was very kind and refused to accept any money. "You can make a donation to me when you've become a rich man, that'll satisfy me."

I met Master Wang in Luohe. He was a short man with very smooth skin, something feminine about him. But you couldn't let that fool you, he was a talent. He had a reputation all over the place as a "two-in-one": small like Wu Dalang, but as deadly as Wu Erlang. His specialty was tigers; he caught them unarmed.

He wouldn't take me on as a disciple, though I approached him twice. He refused to teach me, but I pestered him so much that in the end he offered me money to go away. "I know all you want is enough money to feed your family. Well, here, take this." I knelt down in front of him and pleaded, "I'm the only family I have left. All I want is to learn something to keep myself going. I have nothing to live for." When he heard that he decided to take me on. "It's not that I didn't want to accept you," he explained, "but you have to understand that whoever lives by catching tigers will one day be killed by a tiger. I've got a bad back and it's getting worse all the time. I don't even have a son who can keep my name alive when I'm gone. But the reason I never got married was that I didn't want my son to follow in my footsteps. Now I'll take you on as a disciple on the condition that you're only to stay with me for three months."

For the first two months I studied eagle kung fu, then pushing techniques and the use of fists and legs. Finally my master took me out into the hills. He showed me how to catch a tiger in the Dabie Mountains. I remember it was snowing that day and what seemed like a whirlwind came rushing up out of a hollow. My master shouted, "He's coming," and pushed me aside with the words, "Watch me carefully." He crouched down in the eagle position, straightened his shoulders, using his left hand to block the sun out of his eyes and his right fist was clenched and raised to protect his chest. He let out a mighty yell and knocked the tiger down with one blow. Then he called me over to help tie the beast up and take it out of the mountains. We sold it for over 100 yuan and we split the money between us. My master said to me, "Here, take this money; this is the end of our acquaintance. I've taught you everything I know. You can only expect your children to be yours for life; disciples always leave you sooner or later. I'm nearly done for, and you've got a long way ahead of you. Let's call it quits now. If you ever think of me go into the hills and call out; I'll hear you whether I'm in this world or the next." I searched for him for years after that, but never got any news. I don't know if he was killed by a tiger, or maybe he died in a fall in the mountains. Possibly he was shot by stray soldiers. I guess I'll never know.

After that I caught five tigers in Hunan. The first was in Changde.   12
But once I became famous things became very sticky — bandit gangs were always after the tiger bones and leopard skins I had; the KMT[1] people had an eye on the money I made; and the girls kept chasing me, too. For a while there it was so easy to get into trouble that I gave up hunting altogether. Since I was out of work I learned to make "refugee cigarettes." I started out in Dong'an and Quanzhou, then I moved on to the Talisman Cigarette Factory in Guilin. The cigarettes we made were a local version of Manila cigars. That's right, cheap cigars; they stunk.

I got married in Quanzhou, though I was introduced to my wife in Dong'an. I don't want to go into any of that if you don't mind. But there is one thing about that first meeting I should tell you. I ate a whole bucket of rice at her parents' place and two huge bowls of pork gelatin. I've always been a big eater and I'm not the type to pretend I'm full when I'm not. I could tell they were shocked at how much I ate and so I figured it was a lost cause. That afternoon I gave the matchmaker some

---

[1]Kuomintang, the main non-Communist political party in China from before World War I until after World War II, when its supporters were forced from the mainland to the island of Taiwan by the Communist takeover. — ED.

money for the parents — I hadn't gone there just to get a free meal. Then I left for Quanzhou. It was the last thing I thought'd happen, but she followed me there and we got married. Know what she said to me? "The spirit in my dreams told me it's my fate to cook for a big eater." Dreams and all; sure, whatever you say.

We spent time in Guangxi during the War of Resistance Against Japan. The KMT came along with all that stuff about taking a sidetrack to achieving national salvation. They screwed up the locals something terrible. We were running from the Japanese all the way to Guilin. Our first boy died not long after he learnt to walk. We had another one but he died too. God, we were poor, and things were really hard for us. There was no way we could keep the little ones alive, and it wasn't safe to stay in Guilin so we moved on to Panxian County where we had a little girl. At the age of three she fell into the wok when she was crawling around the stove looking for food — scalded to death. . . . I got blind drunk and jumped into the pond and started drinking the mud. Then I turned a gun on myself, just wanted to end it all. But I used too much strength and the barrel slipped over my shoulder. Didn't shoot myself but I did get the house. . . . My father, two brothers, then my own two sons and my daughter. Six lives. Then there was my master and my friend, a guy who worked with me in the tobacco factory in Guilin. He was a Communist and the KMT killed him. Eight people in all. The world was a rotten place, and I didn't want to live any more.

I went hunting all over the country — Yunnan, Sichuan, Hunan, and finally ended up in Mengxian County. That was after Liberation.

I've caught over three hundred leopards in the past sixty years. I remember this really wild fella in Shanxi — he used to chase trucks on the road. He ran after the mail truck once and forced it right off the road on a corner. Then he'd scamper away to make trouble somewhere else. But I took care of him, sent him packing. Off to a big place where he'd see lots of action: the zoo.

They've got my leopards in zoos in Shanghai, Qingdao, Jiaozuo, and Anyang. Sure. Why, just before this conference started a fellow from Xinjiang came to see me. Said he wanted me to capture a snow leopard for their zoo. I told him to hang on till the conference is over. This is important to me; anyway, Xinjiang's a long way away.

Sometimes I do make a slip. Once I came a real shocker. It was over in Hongdong County in Shanxi. There was this leopard there, you see, a real brute. They got me in to trap him. I knew it wasn't going to be an easy job as the locals had spoiled him rotten, feeding him like a prince for years. Every time he came out of the hills he'd walk straight into someone's place and make off with a pig or a dog. The locals would just stand by and watch. I put up at an old boy's place in a village. Boy, his daughter-in-law sure had a mean mouth on her. The very first night she came out with something incredible while we were having dinner. "Sure you're still up to catching leopards at your age? Better watch out or the leopard will end up catching you." There's lots of superstitions attached to catching animals in the hills, and one of them is that you shouldn't jinx a person by saying things like that. Puts a fella right off. I was feeling edgy all night. First thing the following morning she had another go at me, "You really should take care, you know. The leopard made short work of Shuanquan from over the back yard just a while ago." That really knocked the wind out of me. Then on the way into the mountains I kept coming across snakes, rabbits, and such. That decided it; I wasn't in the mood, so I turned back.

I started back up. I reckoned the locals would all laugh at me for being a coward; then if I went on would I come across more bad omens? I ended up going on. I caught the leopard and my son came up with the cage. We'd just got his head inside it when things went wrong. As I was holding him someone came up behind me and tapped me on the shoulder, "Hey, so this is the old man-eater, isn't it?" That gave me such a start — I'd told them to make sure no one followed me. So what was this guy doing there? The shock made me loosen my grip for just a second and that wily old leopard slipped away from me and went straight for the guy who'd tapped me on the shoulder. I grabbed hold of his tail just in time and swung him over a cliff that was a dozen or so feet off. It took every ounce of strength I had to do it.

Now I just had to cage him. He'd had a narrow escape and it'd be   20 hard to get close to him again. If he went free he really would be a wild man-eater. So I jumped down to see where he'd landed; he was stunned but the moment I went to grab him he came to and got up on his hind legs and hugged me. We ended up rolling around on the ground for a while but I eventually got the better of him. I'd captured him alive, but it was a first for me: I spent nine days flat on my back in a hospital. They gave me injections, medicines, the lot. I'd been wounded in over ten different places. Oh, him? The guy who patted me on the shoulder was the head of their production brigade. Bit of a slacker. But I wasn't meant to die in Hongdong County.

I make enemies easily. The government put out a new regulation about not killing river deer, red deer, wild bulls, and tigers, so I refuse to. Even in the case of leopards I make sure I catch them alive. I know it's all got to do with ecology and making sure there'll be wild animals around for our grandchildren. I've studied all about it like everyone else, so we don't shoot protected animals even if they're staring straight into our guns. But there's some local bigwigs — blokes on the county or commune level who rule the roost — and they want to show off a bit by getting their own tiger skin and they try and force me to shoot protected animals. I refuse and that makes me enemies. They foul-mouth me behind my back.

And there's catching monkeys. Nothing to it really; once you've got the knack you can catch them by the dozen. But it's prohibited. People who want monkeys come after me offering money and just won't leave me alone. It's a real pain in the neck. And there was this time in Linfen when I caught a leopard for the people at Luoyang. A group of locals took it off me on the spot and wouldn't give it back until they'd held an exhibition in the county township for three days. They said they could get two cents a head and at least 10,000 people would come to see it. They even promised me all the takings. But the weather was boiling hot, don't you think it would have been damned cruel on the animal? So I refused. I told them the heat would kill her. They wouldn't give in, so I told them just what I thought of them. "Look, I'll pay you if you'll only let us go, all right?" Acting like that doesn't make you any friends.

The zoos can upset you at times, too. You hand over a leopard that's pregnant and warn them that whatever they do not to watch it when it's giving birth. Then they go and ignore your advice because they're curious. And it's a loss to the state when the mother gets all riled and kills its cub. And everyone knows you shouldn't separate a pair, but they go sending the male off to Anyang and the female is sold off to Qingdao. I tell them, "You can't do that. They care for each other, go on, get her back from Qingdao." The zoo keeper only says, "Come on, old man, why all the fuss. If they don't have cubs it'll mean all the more business for you." Now that really got my back up; I was furious. "If that's how I wanted it then I wouldn't waste my time coming here to Anyang." In the end they took my advice. Good thing, too.

A man's integrity is more important than money. You've got to have 24 a heart. It's just not right to be too carried away by money.

I've got three sons. The eldest is called Zhenqian 'cause he was born in Guizhou. The second is Zhenxiang: he was born in Hunan; and the youngest was born in 1949 so we called him Zhenqi. They got it wrong on his birth certificate though. The wife of the eldest boy is a kind lass and she's in complete charge of the kitchen. The other is a hard worker, good as a man, and she comes hunting every time we go out — a regular Mu Guiying or Sister Gu.[2] The wife of my youngest son is clever and pretty. My three boys are good workers and big eaters — they can polish off eight or nine catties of rice a day, even when they don't go hunting.

Now that I'm well-off I reckon it's my turn to do my bit for others and work for the common good. You've got to do what you feel is right. The Communist Party has been good to me, they've treated me with respect; so I figure I owe them.

Problems? Sure I've got problems. You're from Beijing; do you have any friends who have contacts with the Minister of Forestry? My permit to go into the mountains has expired, can you pass the word on for me? To get some things done you have to go straight to the top man. The local authorities are useless. Oh, and there's another thing. Nowadays it's real important to develop transportation; you can't do a thing without vehicles. If you have any connections ask around for me whether I can buy a motorbike in Beijing. I want a three-wheeler, one of those jobs with two wheels on the back. Yes, got two. Money? No problem.

We've been written up by lots of people. Just about have to get 'em   28 to line up. And how they fight over whether a story or a photograph is real. But all in all I'm nothing more than a hunter, so don't go getting carried away. Otherwise people will think I've been bullshitting.

Sure could. Use it to record a sheep and then turn it on in the woods. Ba-a-a, ba-a-a. The leopards an' all would be out in a flash. . . .

EXPLORATIONS

1. Why did He Guangwei become a hunter? What aspects of his job does he seem to find most satisfying? What aspects are most frustrating to him?

2. Judging from He's account, what traits, skills, and attitudes are essential for a successful hunter? How does he indicate these qualities to his listeners? How do you think He would define success?

3. Zhang Xinxin writes in her introduction: "We had never wanted to use a tape recorder. . . . Write down in a notebook the main points, figures, the actual words the narrator uses at critical moments. . . . Or else write nothing down,

---

[2]Two heroines in ancient China.

just listen, ask, and listen again. Sometimes it feels like sketching, trying to form a mental picture of your subject in a momentary but significant attitude." What are the advantages of this approach? Why do you think Zhang and Sang did wind up using a tape recorder?

CONNECTIONS

1. How is He's work as a hunter similar to and different from Snowbird's work as a wilderness guide? What attitudes toward work do these two men share?

2. In response to readers' comparisons of *Chinese Profiles* with American interviews conducted by Studs Terkel, Sang mentions a Chinese "group consciousness which needs no explanations that makes the oral narratives of the speakers in *Chinese Profiles* different from those in Terkel's books." Look back at Ruth Sidel's "The Liu Family" (p. 21) and Beverley Hooper's "Falling in Love with Love" (p. 220). Compare these accounts and "The Hunter" with Studs Terkel's *Observation*. What evidence do you find in the Chinese selections of a group consciousness that contrasts with the more individual consciousness of Americans such as Terkel's Bill Talcott?

3. He Guangwei states: "My other brother hung himself after he was caught stealing some wheat stalks and beaten. . . . [He] was only nine when he died." Look back at Sophronia Liu's "So Tsi-fai" (p. 127). Why did He's brother commit suicide? Why did So Tsi-fai? What is each author's attitude toward the suicide she or he describes?

ELABORATIONS

1. In commenting on the parallels between *Chinese Profiles* and Studs Terkel's interviews of Americans, Sang writes: "There is hardly a single person in [our] book who shows the Western spirit of starting out by saying they want this and that, or of following up the failure of an old dream by dreaming a new one, even if that too is going to end in failure." In "The Hunter," where and how does He Guangwei talk about his desires or dreams? How is his attitude similar to and different from Bill Talcott's in Studs Terkel's *Observation*? Write an essay comparing and contrasting these two working men's dreams, their attitudes toward their dreams, and the apparent reasons for their differences.

2. Paragraphs 3–5 of "The Hunter" constitute a brief process-analysis essay which might be titled "How to Handle a Leopard." Most of us have confronted an

animal at one time or another that was temporarily or permanently wild. (Recall the lobster scene, or the spider scene, in Woody Allen's film *Annie Hall*.) Look closely at how He Guangwei gives his instructions, and then write your own essay — serious or humorous — on how to handle some type of out-of-control animal.

R. K. NARAYAN

Trail of the Green Blazer

R. K. Narayan was born in Madras, India, in 1906. Best known for his fiction, he has written thirteen novels, over two hundred short stories, a memoir, and retellings of classic Indian epics. In 1958 Narayan's novel *The Guide* received the National Prize of the Indian Literary Academy, his country's highest literary honor. Since 1959 he has lived on and off in New York City for months at a time; in 1981 he was made an honorary member of the prestigious American Academy and Institute of Arts and Letters. Now back at home in Mysore, India, Narayan became a member of the Indian parliament in 1986.

The setting for "Trail of the Green Blazer," as for most of Narayan's novels and stories, is the fictional town of Malgudi. Malgudi is said to be a composite of Madras, the author's birthplace on India's southeast coast, and Mysore, farther west, where he has spent most of his life. Like William Faulkner's Yoknapatawpha County, Narayan's Malgudi has been praised for the vivid sense of place it conveys and the intimate details of its characters' daily life. Narayan writes in English but not with a Western audience in mind; his work is deeply and distinctively Indian.

(For more background on India, see p. 28.)

The Green Blazer stood out prominently under the bright sun and blue sky. In all that jostling crowd one could not help noticing it. Villagers in shirts and turbans, townsmen in coats and caps, beggars bare-bodied and women in multicolored saris were thronging the narrow passage between the stalls and moving in great confused masses, but still the Green Blazer could not be missed. The jabber and babble of the marketplace was there, as people harangued, disputed prices, haggled, or greeted each other; over it all boomed the voice of a Bible-preacher, and when he paused for breath, from another corner the loudspeaker of a health van amplified on malaria and tuberculosis. Over and above it all the Green Blazer seemed to cry out an invitation. Raju could not ignore it. It was not in his nature to ignore such a persistent invitation. He kept himself half-aloof from the crowd; he could not afford to remain completely aloof or keep himself in it too conspicuously. Wherever he might be, he was harrowed by the fear of being spotted by a policeman; today he wore a loincloth and was bare-bodied, and had wound an enormous turban over his head, which overshadowed his face completely, and he hoped that he would be taken for a peasant from a village.

He sat on a stack of cast-off banana stalks beside a shop awning and watched the crowd. When he watched a crowd he did it with concentration. It was his professional occupation. Constitutionally he was an idler and had just the amount of energy to watch in a crowd and put his hand into another person's pocket. It was a gamble, of course. Sometimes he got nothing out of a venture, counting himself lucky if he came out with his fingers intact. Sometimes he picked up a fountain pen, and the "receiver" behind the Municipal Office would not offer even four annas for it, and there was always the danger of being traced through it. Raju promised himself that someday he would leave fountain pens alone; he wouldn't touch one even if it were presented to him on a plate; they were too much bother — inky, leaky, and next to worthless if one could believe what the receiver said about them. Watches were in the same category, too.

What Raju loved most was a nice, bulging purse. If he saw one he picked it up with the greatest deftness. He took the cash in it, flung it far away, and went home with the satisfaction that he had done his day's job well. He splashed a little water over his face and hair and tidied himself up before walking down the street again as a normal citizen. He bought sweets, books, and slates for his children, and occasionally a jacket piece for his wife, too. He was not always easy in mind about his wife. When he went home with too much cash, he had always to take care to hide it in an envelope and shove it under a roof tile. Otherwise she asked too many questions and made herself miserable. She liked to believe that he was reformed and earned the cash he showed her as commission; she never bothered to ask what the commissions were for: a commission seemed to her something absolute.

Raju jumped down from the banana stack and followed the Green   4
Blazer, always keeping himself three steps behind. It was a nicely calculated distance, acquired by intuition and practice. The distance must not be so much as to obscure the movement of the other's hand to and from his purse, nor so close as to become a nuisance and create suspicion. It had to be finely balanced and calculated — the same sort of calculations as carry a *shikari*[1] through his tracking of game and see him safely home

---

[1]Professional hunter. — ED.

again. Only this hunter's task was more complicated. The hunter in the forest could count his day a success if he laid his quarry flat; but here one had to extract the heart out of the quarry without injuring it.

Raju waited patiently, pretending to be examining some rolls of rush mat, while the Green Blazer spent a considerable length of time drinking a coconut at a nearby booth. It looked as though he would not move again at all. After sucking all the milk in the coconut, he seemed to wait interminably for the nut to be split and the soft white kernel scooped out with a knife. The sight of the white kernel scooped and disappearing into the other's mouth made Raju, too, crave for it. But he suppressed the thought: it would be inept to be spending one's time drinking and eating while one was professionally occupied; the other might slip away and be lost forever. . . . Raju saw the other take out his black purse and start a debate with the coconut seller over the price of coconuts. He had a thick, sawing voice which disconcerted Raju. It sounded like the growl of a tiger, but what jungle-hardened hunter ever took a step back because a tiger's growl sent his heart racing involuntarily! The way the other haggled didn't appeal to Raju either; it showed a mean and petty temperament . . . too much fondness for money. Those were the narrow-minded troublemakers who made endless fuss when a purse was lost. . . . The Green Blazer moved after all. He stopped before a stall flying colored balloons. He bought a balloon after an endless argument with the shop-man — a further demonstration of his meanness. He said, "This is for a motherless boy. I have promised it him. If it bursts or gets lost before I go home, he will cry all night, and I wouldn't like it at all."

Raju got his chance when the other passed through a narrow stile, where people were passing four-thick in order to see a wax model of Mahatma Gandhi reading a newspaper.

Fifteen minutes later Raju was examining the contents of the purse. He went away to a secluded spot, behind a disused well. Its crumbling parapet seemed to offer an ideal screen for his activities. The purse contained ten rupees in coins and twenty in currency notes and a few annas in nickel. Raju tucked the annas at his waist in his loincloth. "Must give them to some beggars," he reflected generously. There was a blind fellow yelling his life out at the entrance to the fair and nobody seemed to care. People seemed to have lost all sense of sympathy these days. The thirty rupees he bundled into a knot at the end of his turban and wrapped this again round his head. It would see him through the rest of the month. He could lead a clean life for at least a fortnight and take his wife and children to a picture.

Now the purse lay limp within the hollow of his hand. It was only 8 left for him to fling it into the well and dust off his hand and then he might walk among princes with equal pride at heart. He peeped into the well. It had a little shallow water at the bottom. The purse might float, and a floating purse could cause the worst troubles on earth. He opened the flap of the purse in order to fill it up with pebbles before drowning it. Now, through the slit at its side, he saw a balloon folded and tucked away. "Oh, this he bought. . . ." He remembered the other's talk about the motherless child. "What a fool to keep this in the purse," Raju reflected. "It is the carelessness of parents that makes young ones suffer," he ruminated angrily. For a moment he paused over a picture of the growling father returning home and the motherless one waiting at the door for the promised balloon, and this growling man feeling for his purse . . . and, oh! it was too painful!

Raju almost sobbed at the thought of the disappointed child — the motherless boy. There was no one to comfort him. Perhaps this ruffian would beat him if he cried too long. The Green Blazer did not look like one who knew the language of children. Raju was filled with pity at the thought of the young child — perhaps of the same age as his second son. Suppose his wife were dead . . . (personally it might make things easier for him, he need not conceal his cash under the roof); he overcame this thought as an unworthy side issue. If his wife should die it would make him very sad indeed and tax all his ingenuity to keep his young ones quiet. . . . That motherless boy must have his balloon at any cost, Raju decided. But how? He peeped over the parapet across the intervening space at the far-off crowd. The balloon could not be handed back. The thing to do would be to put it back into the empty purse and slip it into the other's pocket.

The Green Blazer was watching the heckling that was going on as the Bible-preacher warmed up to his subject. A semicircle was asking, "Where is your God?" There was a hubbub. Raju sidled up to the Green Blazer. The purse with the balloon (only) tucked into it was in his palm. He'd slip it back into the other's pocket.

Raju realized his mistake in a moment. The Green Blazer caught hold of his arm and cried, "Pickpocket!" The hecklers lost interest in the Bible and turned their attention to Raju, who tried to look appropriately outraged. He cried, "Let me go." The other, without giving a clue to what he proposed, shot out his arm and hit him on the cheek. It almost blinded him. For a fraction of a second Raju lost his awareness of where and even who he was. When the dark mist lifted and he was able to regain his vision, the first figure he noticed in the foreground was the Green Blazer, looming, as it seemed, over the whole landscape. His arms were raised ready to strike again. Raju cowered at the sight. He said, "I . . . I was trying to put back your purse." The other gritted his teeth in fiendish merriment and crushed the bones of his arm. The crowd roared with laughter and badgered him. Somebody hit him again on the head.

Even before the Magistrate Raju kept saying, "I was only trying to put   12 back the purse." And everyone laughed. It became a stock joke in the police world. Raju's wife came to see him in jail and said, "You have brought shame on us," and wept.

Raju replied indignantly, "Why? I was only trying to put it back."

He served his term of eighteen months and came back into the world — not quite decided what he should do with himself. He told himself, "If ever I pick up something again, I shall make sure I don't have to put it back." For now he believed God had gifted the likes of him with only one-way deftness. Those fingers were not meant to put anything back.

EXPLORATIONS

1. Why is the ending of "Trail of the Green Blazer" ironic? What resolution for the future do Raju's wife and others want him to make after his experience with the Green Blazer? What conclusion does Raju draw instead, and why?

2. Look closely at the story's first paragraph. How does Narayan put us as readers in sympathy with Raju? What specific phrases or sentences suggest that the Green Blazer really is more at fault than Raju? How would the story's impact change if the Green Blazer were described as a person rather than a garment?

3. Elsewhere in the story, what specific actions on Raju's part, and what descriptive words on Narayan's part, show Raju as having admirable qualities? In what ways does the author depict his main character as a victim of circumstances? What are Raju's negative qualities? How would the story's effect be different if Raju were portrayed as purely admirable?

CONNECTIONS

1. Raju the pickpocket, like He Guangwei in Zhang Xinxin and Sang Ye's "The Hunter," sees himself as a skilled professional. What similar views do Raju and He hold about hunting as an occupation? What similar observations do they make about human nature and life?

2. Narayan's "Trail of the Green Blazer," like Gholam-Hossein Sa'edi's "The Game Is Over" (p. 76), shows a character brought to justice for doing wrong. In each story, why does the pivotal character commit the act that causes his downfall? What conflict exists in each story between justice and fairness?

3. In his *Observation*, Mario Puzo writes, "I wanted to be a killer hero in a worldwide war . . . [or] a footloose adventurer. Then I branched out and thought of being a great artist, and then, getting ever more sophisticated, a great criminal." How does Raju's vision of criminality as a profession differ from Puzo's?

ELABORATIONS

1. Narayan presents enough evidence on both sides to convince a jury that Raju is either a victim or a villain. What are the arguments for each view? Which position do you think is stronger? Choose a side, and write an essay that both makes your case and rebuts the opposing view.

2. "Trail of the Green Blazer" shares a central metaphor with Alberto Moravia's "The Chase" (p. 249): In each story, the main character sees himself as a hunter tracking a quarry. The contrast in these two authors' use of the same image shows how flexible the image is. Having read "The Hunter" by Zhang Xinxin and Sang Ye, what additional ways can you imagine using the hunting metaphor? Write a narrative essay about an adventure of your own which could be viewed as a hunt. Be sure to show, as Narayan and Moravia do, what this metaphor implies about the hunter, the quarry, and the social relationship between them.

SHIVA NAIPAUL

The Palmers

Shiva Naipaul was born in 1945 in Port of Spain, Trinidad. He attended college in Trinidad, then won a scholarship to Oxford University, where he studied Chinese. His first novel, *Fireflies* (1970), won four literary prizes; his second novel, *The Chip-Chip Gatherers* (1973), won the Whitbread Award. Though less well known than his brother, novelist V. S. Naipaul (see "Entering the New World," p. 606), Shiva Naipaul was highly regarded for his fiction, journalism, and travel writing, which often probed social problems of the Third World. He was living in London with his wife and son when he died of a heart attack in 1985.

"The Palmers" comes from *North of South: An African Journey* (1979). Naipaul met the Palmers in Kenya, which — as his book title implies — is north of southern Africa, on the east coast of the continent between Somalia and Tanzania. The first Europeans to appear there were German missionaries in the early nineteenth century. At that time the dominant inhabitants were the Kikuyu and Masai tribes. First the Germans and then the British took political control, making Kenya a British protectorate in 1890 and a Crown colony in 1920. In the 1950s the Kikuyus rose up in the so-called Mau Mau Rebellion, prompting the British to declare a state of emergency which lasted until the early 1960s. In 1963 Kenya became independent. Its first president was Jomo Kenyatta, who served until his death in 1978 (see pp. 419–420). Today the Republic of Kenya comprises about seventy different ethnic groups; the official languages are English and Swahili. Around four-fifths of the work force is employed in agricultural enterprises like the Palmers' tea plantation.

The ridges of the Kikuyu country stretched away on all sides, wave upon wave sweeping toward the horizon. Where the land was cut away to accommodate the passage of the road, its red heart was startlingly exposed to view. Looking at that bloody redness one sensed not only the richness of the land but — more disturbingly — its visceral appeal. It seemed to symbolize the Kikuyu's fierce attachment to it, the unity of soil and tribe. In *Facing Mount Kenya* (first published in 1938), [Jomo] Kenyatta expressed his tribe's attitude toward the land they considered peculiarly theirs. "The Gikuyu," he wrote, "consider the earth as the 'mother' of the tribe. It is the soil that feeds the child through lifetime;

and again after death it is the soil that nurses the spirits of the dead for eternity. Thus the earth is the most sacred thing above all that dwell in or on it . . . an everlasting oath is to swear by the earth." Those oaths were to surface, in a more murderous form, during the Mau Mau insurrection.

The road, which to begin with had been wide enough for two cars, narrowed to a single land. We left behind the forest reserve through which we had been traveling and entered the coffee belt, the leaves of the neatly staked-out shrubs glistening in the soupy sunlight. "Kenya is lucky," my companion said, gesturing at the plantations on either side of us. "The Brazilian crop has been hit by frost this year."

We passed through a straggling township replete with the usual beer parlors and "ration" shops and unsightly hoardings advertising detergents, refrigerators, and vacuum cleaners. The air was noisy with jukebox music. A roadside market was in progress. Long strips of colorfully dyed cloth were spread out on the ground. Young boys danced out in front of the car flourishing fruit and vegetables. Beyond the township was typical *shamba* country: small plots planted with corn; foraging goats and cows and pigs and chickens. This, even in colonial days, had been a "native" area, and it clung tenaciously to its traditional character. The coffee plantations reappeared. A veil of pearly mist obscured the more distant reaches of the open, undulating landscape. Its "English" character was emphasized by the scattered condensations of color created by stands of trees set amid the acres of coffee. The tarmac ended. Clouds of red dust billowed in our wake. We were climbing now, and after a time, the coffee country gave way to tea country. The tea gardens, emerald green, even-topped, forming an unbroken wave of cultivation, were like a scaly sheath thrown over the land.

It was almost noon when we reached the Palmers' farm. Mrs. Palmer, 4 jovial and red-faced, her hair bunched in a scarf, greeted us amiably. It was cool enough for a sweater. The day was autumnal. Gray cloud hid the sun, and there was a vapor of blue mist in the shallow valleys. A chill, clammy wind blew. The Palmers' house — a modest-sized brick bungalow — was finely situated on a rising piece of ground. We stood for a while on the well-kept lawn surrounding it, admiring the extensive views. "In good weather," our hostess said, "you can see Kilimanjaro." We gazed in the direction she indicated, paying the invisible mountain ritual homage. Then we went inside.

A fire was going in the brick fireplace; an Alsatian was stretched out on the rug in front of it. Two high-backed armchairs with chintz coverings were drawn up in front of the fireplace. Ancestral photographs lined the walls. A piano, piled with papers, occupied a corner. Next to it was a large, brass-studded chest. Agricultural journals, old copies of *The Times*, and some back numbers of the *Illustrated London News* were distributed in neat piles on a low table in the center of the room. A complete set of *Chambers' Encyclopedia* filled a small bookshelf. I noticed no other books apart from those. The wooden floor gleamed. There was not a speck of dust to be seen. It was a forbiddingly hygienic room. I felt that nothing new had happened here for a long time — just endless dusting, cleaning, preserving.

"I hear it's been a lovely summer in England," Mrs. Palmer said. "We've been reading all about it." She nodded at the pile of newspapers. "Now here you are on the Equator — and sitting in front of a fire. It must seem strange."

She rang a bell. A barefooted "boy" appeared. She ordered him to bring ice and glasses. "And Simon . . ." Simon, who had started to leave, paused but did not turn around. Mrs. Palmer smiled. " . . . when you put the ice in the glasses, do please remember to use the tongs and not your fingers. That's what the tongs are *for*. Now off you go."

Simon disappeared into the kitchen.   8

Mrs. Palmer was still smiling when she turned to face us. "Simon seems to have a block about using those tongs. I can't understand it. I've told him so many times. Still, Simon has one great virtue. He hasn't been *spoiled*. Not as yet, anyway. I'm keeping my fingers crossed. It's amazing how quickly they do get spoiled, though. There used to be an old saying in this country: put a native in shoes and that's the end of him. Nowadays, of course, they've all got shoes and we aren't even allowed to call them natives." Mrs. Palmer sighed, staring out the window toward invisible Kilimanjaro. Taking a key from the pocket of her dress, she unlocked the liquor cabinet. "I'm sorry to seem so jailerlike," she said, "but pilfering, I'm afraid, is a big problem. I have to keep everything under lock and key. They take the oddest things sometimes, things they can't possibly have any use for. The other day my shower cap disappeared." She peered at the ranks of bottles. "I close my eyes to the sugar and flour they take from the larder — but I *do* draw the line at our precious Scotch. Simon is still fairly trustworthy. But you can never be sure. Leaving bottles of Scotch hanging about the place is more than a temptation. It's an invitation. And once they get a taste for alcohol, that's the end."

"Worse even than putting them into shoes," my companion said.

"*Much* worse," Mrs. Palmer replied, not catching the irony. "In the old days people used to say that to give a native alcohol was like putting a loaded gun in the hands of a child. In my opinion that's still true. But . . ." She sighed again.

She extracted bottles of whiskey, gin, and sherry.   12

Simon came in carrying a bowl of ice in one hand and three glasses in the other.

"Simon . . . Simon . . ." Mrs. Palmer wagged her head.

Simon looked at her expressionlessly.

"Why didn't you use the tray, Simon?" Mrs. Palmer relieved him of   16 his burdens. "You can carry several things at once on a tray. That's what a tray is *for*."

My eyes strayed to Simon's bare, uncorrupted feet.

"You see what I mean," Mrs. Palmer said when Simon had left the room. "The tray is another of his peculiar blocks." She poured generous measures of whiskey into our glasses.

The Alsatian sprang up, barking loudly: Mr. Palmer had arrived. He came in chattering apologies for his late arrival. He was dressed in khaki — short-sleeved khaki shirt tucked into short khaki trousers, matching knee-high socks and thick-soled brown shoes; a lean, wiry man of medium height, probably in his midfifties. He fondled and pummeled the fawning dog.

"Awfully sorry about the weather," he said. "Wish we could have put   20 on a better show for you. On a fine day you can see Kili."

The tea gardens — the Palmers had about three hundred acres under tea — began not many yards beyond the lawn surrounding the house. The day's work was drawing to a close, and the pluckers, bent under leaf-filled nets slung from their shoulders, were filing down the aisles between the rows of bushes, slowly making their way to the weighing shed. The afternoon had become colder and gloomier. Thickening mists obscured the summits of neighboring ridges. The wind was cutting. Smoke rose from a group of huts clustered together on the shallow slope of a nearby depression. A moorland bleakness overhung the scene. The pluckers — men, women, and children — crept like an army of subdued ghosts through the premature twilight, the sharp odor of the raw leaf they carried tanging the chill air. A muted murmur of conversation rose among them as they waited for the product of their day's labor to be weighed. All were equipped with shining aprons, reaching from neck to knee, made of vinyl.

"I supply the aprons myself," Mr. Palmer said. "They are very appreciative. It reduces the wear and tear on their clothing."

"They like the bright colors," Mrs. Palmer said. "They are very fond of bright colors."

The estate employed roughly two hundred people. Most of them had 24 been brought in from outside the district   or had migrated of their own accord in search of work. The local people were not particularly interested in agricultural labor of the type offered by the Palmers. Nairobi, less than a hundred miles away, was a powerful magnet.

"The local people have been spoiled," Mrs. Palmer said. "Many actually prefer to be beggars and prostitutes in Nairobi than to earn an honest living from the soil. They consider it to be beneath their dignity." She pursed her lips.

The pluckers smiled and saluted as they shuffled past with their loads. Mrs. Palmer's scarf snapped like a flag as she surveyed the beasts of burden who marched past her. They could, with luck, earn up to a pound a day.

"I know it sounds appallingly little by English standards," Mr. Palmer said. "But by *their* standards it's a good wage. *They* don't complain. *They* are grateful that they can actually work and earn something. It's only certain left-wing journalists looking for a sensational story who come here and weep crocodile tears on their behalf."

Mr. Palmer stooped, picked up a tea leaf from the ground, and stared 28 at it critically.

"These people," he went on, "are simple, hardworking folk. They're not spoiled . . ."

"Not as yet," Mrs. Palmer put in grimly. Her scarf fluttered and snapped.

"Their needs are basic," Mr. Palmer said. "They want to have food in their bellies, to be warm, to have a roof over their heads. *I* supply those basic needs. Many of them, you know, prefer to work for us whites than to work for their own people. Their own people often treat them like slaves. They don't pay them properly, they offer no medical facilities, they house them in atrocious conditions. Paternalism like mine has something to be said for it, don't you think?" He grinned at me.

He beckoned over a boy of about ten. "Have a look at this *toto*." He 32 squeezed the boy's arms and legs, lifted up his shirt and exhibited the well-fleshed diaphragm. "Six months ago Sammy was skeletal, covered with sores, had a bad cough. He's all right now, though. Aren't you, Sammy?" He chucked the boy under the chin. The boy, not knowing what was happening to him, gazed at us with wild, frightened eyes. His mother watched from a distance, obviously pleased to see her son the focus of her master's attention.

"In the old days we used to have an estate shop," Mrs. Palmer said. "That way you made sure they got reasonably fed. Now they spend their money how and where they like." She laughed grimly. "Maize meal isn't good enough for them these days. They want rice."

"Rice is more nutritious than maize meal," Mr. Palmer said.

"But more expensive."

"It's their money."   36

Mrs. Palmer sighed. We returned to the house for lunch.

EXPLORATIONS

1. What is Mrs. Palmer's work, and what are its components? What does she perceive as the obstacles to her success? What is Mr. Palmer's work, and what are its components? What does he perceive as the obstacles to his success?

2. As tea planters the Palmers employ roughly two hundred people. What do Mrs. and Mr. Palmer consider to be the rewards and frustrations of their employees' jobs? What clues in his narrative suggest points on which Naipaul disagrees?

3. What are the sources of the Palmers' attitudes toward work? What are the sources of their employees' attitudes toward work? Look back at the biographical notes on Naipaul. In what ways is he qualified to write about both groups?

CONNECTIONS

1. Like R. K. Narayan's "Trail of the Green Blazer," Naipaul's "The Palmers" contrasts wealthy and poor characters. From whose point of view does Narayan tell his story? From whose point of view does Naipaul present the Palmers and their employees? Which characters in each narrative are most and least sympathetic, and why?

2. Look back at Vincent Crapanzano's "Growing Up White in South Africa" (p. 58). South Africa is at the other end of the continent from Kenya. Judging from Crapanzano's and Naipaul's essays, what characteristics do both countries share? What attitudes do Hennie and the Palmers have in common, and why? Why do you think Hennie's view of himself as an African has changed over time, whereas the Palmers' views have stayed the same?

3. Compare the Palmers' comments about Simon and their other black employees with Elliot Liebow's *Observation* about unskilled black workers. How do you think Liebow would reply to the Palmers? How do you think the Palmers would reply to Liebow?

ELABORATIONS

1. According to Naipaul, what is the attitude of black Kenyans toward their land? What is the Palmers' attitude toward the same land? Write an essay comparing and contrasting the ways these two groups think about land: What do they see when they look at it? What do they value most about it? How do they perceive their relationship to it? What are some likely reasons why many native Kenyans choose to leave their farms for Nairobi?

2. Isak Dinesen was one of Kenya's first coffee planters. On the basis of her comments in "From 'Daguerreotypes'" (p. 204), how do you think Dinesen would describe Mrs. Palmer? Mr. Palmer? Write an essay defining the transplanted English lady and gentleman in Africa, using the Palmers' attitudes, decor, and so forth to create the kind of archetypes Dinesen creates in her essay.

EZEKIEL MPHAHLELE

Tradition and the African Writer

Born in South Africa in 1919, Ezekiel Mphahlele grew up in the capital city of Pretoria and became a writer in exile in 1957. He received his Ph.D. from the University of Denver in 1968 and taught in the English department there; he also lived in Kenya, Nigeria, and France. Only recently has he returned to South Africa. Mphahlele has published three story collections, several works of criticism, and an autobiography; his essays have appeared in numerous journals. His novel *The Wanderers* won the first prize for Best African Novel of the year 1968–69. "Tradition and the African Writer" comes from his essay "African Literature: What Tradition?" which originally appeared in the *Denver Quarterly.*

Many of Mphahlele's works are concerned — directly or indirectly — with the racial and political conflicts in his homeland. The Dutch and British who vied for power in South Africa two centuries ago displaced native Khoisan and Bantu tribes (see p. 58). Conflict intensified when diamonds and gold were discovered in the late 1800s. The ensuing Anglo-Boer (British versus Dutch) War was won by the British, who created the Union of South Africa in 1910. The "white is right" policy of apartheid — racially separate development and residential areas — had existed for some time; in 1948 it became official. In 1961, with only whites allowed to vote, South African voters withdrew their nation from the British Commonwealth. Recently a limited vote has been extended to Asians and Coloureds, and laws banning interracial marriage have been repealed. However, the black majority remains shut out of government as well as most desirable jobs and housing.

(For more background on South Africa, see p. 58.)

It all started when Africa was shanghaied into the history of the West in the late nineteenth century. What were we coming into? — a long line of continuity going back some 9000 years since the civilizations of the great river valleys of the Nile, the Tigris and Euphrates, the Indus, and the Hwang-ho had launched man on a long intellectual quest. We had been discovered by an aggressive Western culture which was never going to let us be. Nor could we cease following the neon lights — or has it been a will o' the wisp? Time will tell. Perhaps Hegelian historical determinism will have it that it is as it should be: how could Africa be left out of it all indefinitely?

And so here I am, an ambivalent character. But I'm nothing of the oversimplified and sensationalized Hollywood version of a man of two worlds. It is not as if I were pinned on a rock, my legs stretched in opposite directions. Education sets up conflicts but also reconciles them in degrees that depend on the subject's innate personality equipment. It seems to me a writer in an African setting must possess this equipment and must strive toward some workable reconciliation inside himself. It is an agonizing journey. It can also be humiliating to feel that one has continually to be reassessing oneself with reference to the long line of tradition he has entered — the tradition of the West. How else? I have assimilated the only education the West had to offer me. I was brought up on European history and literature and religion and made to identify with European heroes while African heroes were being discredited, except those that became Christians or signed away their land and freedom, and African gods were being smoked out. I later rejected Christianity. And yet I could not return to ancestral worship in any overt way. But this does not invalidate my ancestors for me. Deep down there inside my agnostic self, I feel a reverence for them.

The majority of writers in Africa, I venture to say, are attached in a detached manner to one indigenous religion or another. They are not involved in its ritual, but they look at it with reverence. When, in their full consciousness, they have found themselves Christian — which can often just mean baptized — they have not adopted churchianity. Because our whole education system in Africa has been mission-ridden right from the beginning, and the white minister was supposed by the government or commercial or school-board employer to know the "native," you had always to produce a testimonial signed by a white church minister when you were applying for a job. Not even black ministers could speak for you. If you wanted to go out for further studies, you knew where to find St. Peter. The black minister himself required testimonials from one of his white brethren, never from another black minister. So we called ourselves Christians; we entered "Christian" on the line against an item that asked for it on all the multiplicity of forms, just in order to save ourselves the trouble of explaining and therefore failing to go through the gates. In independent Africa, we are luckily able to trust fellow blacks who vouch for us and others. And you can almost see the Christian veneer peeling off because it has nothing to do with conscience.

The Negro sculptor in Africa south of the Sahara (one must always   4
make a distinction between this and North Africa with its predominantly Muslim culture) has always felt the tug of tradition acutely. It will be a tribal or ethnic tradition, not an all-African one. Sculpture has always been related in some subtle way to the handicrafts — all three-dimensional products. Like handicrafts, sculpture, mostly in wood, was a utility article. Wooden carvings have been used as shrines. They were practically all the same within groups. There would seem to have been little or no individuality in the works, because they had to conform to ritual. But then the African artist enjoyed the creative moment in itself, even if it produced the same kind of article over and over again. The figures at the shrine might rot or break, and similar ones would be made. And there have always been so many ideas to be expressed around any particular cult that a great variety of figures emerged. Again, others worked in metal they cast themselves. The close tie with tradition is only natural when one considers the sculptural medium itself.

In a story of his childhood, *The Dark Child*, Camara Laye of Guinea describes a scene in which he is watching his father, a goldsmith, melting his metal. As the boy sits looking on, he realizes that gold smelting in his father's workshop is a magical operation that "the guiding spirits could look upon with favor or disfavor." It is a traditional ceremony or a shorter version of one. All the apprentices present stand or sit motionless. Only when the gold is a fluid can the silence be broken. His father's lips move all the time, uttering secret incantations, which is why the goldsmith would rather perform the operations himself instead of the equally efficient apprentices. A black serpent that moves in and out of the workshop always comes and coils itself up under a sheepskin during the preparatory stages.

It is the custom, he reports, "to keep apart from the working of gold all influences outside those of the jeweler himself." Because "the working of gold, besides being a task of the greatest skill, is a matter of confidence, of conscience, a task which is not undertaken excepting after due reflection and experiment." "I believe my father," Laye proceeds, "never entered his workshop except in a state of ritual purity." After the preliminaries, he then begins to beat out his trinkets.

In one novel, Camara Laye tells of a blacksmith who attached the same spiritual value to his axe making as the author's father did to his craft. It didn't matter how many axes he turned out; what did matter was the whole creative process. . . .

By far the larger part of Africa is still traditionally minded in varying degrees. The whole dialogue around tradition is an intellectual one. The parents of people of my generation, although they may be urbanized, are still close to tradition. They worry a great deal about the way in which we break loose at one point and ignore some elements of tradition. Each time an African mother sends a child to high school, it is like giving birth to him all over again. She knows she is yielding something. Dialogue between her and the child decreases and eventually stays on the level of basic essentials: our needs, our family relations, family life, which must continue more or less normally, whatever else around us may progressively be reduced to abstractions or gadgets. It is no less excruciating for the young man who stands in this kind of relationship with his parents. But he can reconcile himself to it — the very educational process that wrenches him from his moorings helps him to arrange a harmonization within himself.

The parent will often moan and complain to him about the awkward distance he has reached away from tradition. But it is never a reprimand; it is an indulgent complaint. Because, I think, the parents are always aware that this whole business of education does not of itself engage you in an activity that expressly subverts the morals of the family, the clan, or of the tribe. They are aware of the many situations around them that require an education to cope with them. The benefits of tradition are abstract, and the parents' own thinking has not been stagnant while the whole landscape around them has been changing, while the white man's government has been impinging on their way of life over several decades. And the benefits of a modern education are tangible, real.

I have always asked myself what it is in one's formal education that leads to the rupture, to the ever widening gulf between one and one's parents and one's community. You recognize the alphabet, then words, and then you can extract meaning from many sentences in a row. With that shock of recognition, words leap into life in front of you. They set your mind on fire; longings and desires you would never have known are released and seem to whirl around in currents that explode into other currents: something like what you see in a glass flask of water that you have on a naked flame to observe the movement of heat in liquid. From then on, one must not stop. Yet it is not something one can take for granted in an African context, because to start at all is not inevitable: education is not compulsory, and the financial cost of it is immense.

In your higher education, you assimilate patterns of thought, argument, and so on from an alien culture in an alien language; they become your own. Of course you cannot help using your African setting as your field of reference; you cannot help going out of the queue of Western orientation now and again to consult those of your people who are not physically in it. You try to express their philosophy in a European language whose allegory, metaphor, and so on are alien to the spirit of that philosophy: something that can best be understood in terms of allegory and metaphor that are centered heavily on human relationships and external nature. All the same, you are in the queue, and you belong not only to an African community but also to a worldwide intellectual or worldwide economic community, or both. This is why communication becomes difficult, sometimes impossible between your people who are still not tuned into Western intellectual systems and yourself. Your mind operates in a foreign language, even while you are actually talking your mother tongue, at the moment you are engaged in your profession. You try hard to find correspondences and you realize there are only a few superficial ones: you have to try to *make* most of them. In the pure sciences, which are universally applicable, the correspondences are numerous; there is no problem.

Indigenous languages that have only recently become literary, that is,   12
only since the church missions established presses in Africa, seem to have relied more and more heavily on the spoken word, so that gesture, facial expression, inflection of voice became vital equipment in communication. Language became almost a ritual in itself, and metaphor and symbol became a matter of art and device. Metaphor became a sacred thing if it had descended from usage in earlier times; when an elder, in a traditional court case, prefaced a proverb or aphorism or metaphor by saying, "Our elders say . . ." his audience listened with profound reverence. Notice the present tense in "our elders *say.* . . ." Because his elders would be the ancestors, who are still present with us in spirit. You can imagine what confusion prevails in a modern law court when a witness or the accused operate in metaphor and glory in the sensuousness of the spoken word quite irrelevant to the argument at hand. Ask any magistrate or prosecutor or lawyer in a differentiated Western-type society whether they find a court trial a sensuous activity, and hear what they say. Even the rhetoric that a lawyer may indulge in is primarily a thing of the brain rather than of the heart. In African

languages, activities overlap a great deal, and there are no sharp dividing lines between various functions.

All that I have said so far has been an attempt to indicate the relative distances between tradition and the present — some shifting, others freezing, some thawing, others again presenting formidable barriers. And we are living in a situation in which the past and the present live side by side, because the past is not just a segment in time to think *back* upon: we can see it in living communities. We need to appreciate these distances if we are to understand what the African writer is about. He is part of the whole pattern.

EXPLORATIONS

1. As an African writer, what are the "two worlds" to which Mphahlele belongs? What choices does his dual heritage force him and other African artists to make?

2. Why does Mphahlele perceive education as so crucial an issue for African writers? What price do they pay for it? What happens if they refuse to pay that price?

3. "The whole dialogue around tradition is an intellectual one," writes Mphahlele. Cite three or four passages that show him to be part of the Western intellectual tradition. What passages show that he also belongs to the African tradition in which speakers "operate in metaphor and glory in the sensuousness of the spoken word"?

4. In keeping with his theme, Mphahlele writes in all the persons and numbers available in English: the first-person singular *I*, the first-person plural *we*, the second-person singular and plural *you*, the third-person singular *he*, and the third-person plural *they*. Whom does he evidently mean when he refers to "you"? to "we"? to "they"?

CONNECTIONS

1. Sang Ye commented on the interviews she and Zhang Xinxin did with Chinese citizens such as "The Hunter": "The inner riches of our nation, like some grammatical usages of the spoken language, are hard to convey fully in writing." What observations by Mphahlele suggest that African writers face a similar problem? What point do both authors seem to be making about written language?

2. "I have always asked myself," writes Mphahlele, "what it is in one's formal education that leads to the rupture, to the ever widening gulf between one and one's parents and one's community." Look back at Nathalie Sarraute's "My First Sorrow" (p. 109). What signs does Sarraute give of perceiving a similar gulf? What possible reasons for it does her essay suggest? How is her case like and unlike Mphahlele's?

3. In his *Observation*, Richard Rodriguez describes the dilemma of education and separation from parents for a fledgling Hispanic-American writer. What common responses are voiced by Rodriguez and Mphahlele? Why do you think these two writers on opposite sides of the world, from contrasting heritages, face the same problems?

ELABORATIONS

1. In "Nigerian Childhood" (p. 66), Wole Soyinka describes his early years in a former British African colony. What evidence in his essay suggests that he shares Mphahlele's sense of embodying two distinct traditions? How has Soyinka made use of both traditions? Is he writing as "an ambivalent character . . . a man of two worlds" (Mphahlele's self-description), or as someone who has reconciled his dual heritage? Write an essay comparing and contrasting Mphahlele and Soyinka as examples of Mphahlele's theses in "Tradition and the African Writer."

2. "The benefits of tradition are abstract," writes Mphahlele. "The benefits of a modern education are tangible, real." What does he mean? Looking at your own role in the world as an adult, what have you gained (or do you hope to gain) from your education? from the tradition(s) in which you grew up? Write an essay classifying the abstract and tangible benefits to you of your education and heritage.

DAVID PLATH

Tomoko on Her Television Career

David Plath was born in 1930 in Elgin, Illinois. He received a degree in journalism from Northwestern University and did graduate work at Sophia University in Tokyo, Japan, the University of Michigan, and Harvard University. During this period he returned to Japan. Plath has written four books as well as numerous articles, essays, and reviews, and has received a number of awards and fellowships. He now teaches anthropology and Asian studies at the University of Illinois. "Tomoko on Her Television Career" is excerpted from his 1980 book *Long Engagements: Maturity in Modern Japan.*

Japan's interaction with the United States began in 1854 with U.S. Commodore Matthew C. Perry's opening of trade to the islands (see p. 36). The breakdown of geographic isolation did not end Japan's ethnic isolation: 99.4 percent of the population remains racially Japanese. (Other groups may enter the country, but they are not assimilated.) Japan gained a small but significant Korean population after it annexed Korea in 1910 — having previously fought China and gained Taiwan, and fought Russia and got half of Sakhalin Island. (In Russia this defeat triggered the Czar's downfall; see p. 139). The Japanese attitude toward the rest of the world remained superior and belligerent through World War I, when Japan took over Germany's Pacific Islands and then Manchuria, starting a new war with China. The tide turned in World War II, when Japan attacked the United States at Pearl Harbor, Hawaii, in 1941. After the atomic bombing of Hiroshima and Nagasaki, Japan surrendered in 1945 and was administered by the United States until 1952. During that period Japan switched from military to technological adventures. By the time the last Japanese islands under American control were returned in 1972, Japan had established itself as a major economic power, with the highest growth rate in the industrialized world.

Tomoko is a product of Japan's new age. She is a television producer, described by Plath as "a confident woman of thirty-eight, dressed well but without flair." She lives with her husband and son in her husband's parents' house in the southern Japanese city of Osaka. "She is intrigued by the reversal of roles, by being on the receiving end of an interview for a change," reports Plath. "Her opinions come into words easily, though she does not appear opinionated. . . . But she does like to emphasize the contrast she sees between herself and most Japanese women." Tomoko has nicknamed her father "my Education Papa," because of his unusual insistence on a strong education for his daughter.

I knew I had to have a career. In high school I became a celibatarian. I was not going to marry; I would dedicate myself to my profession. Then I began to think about what I would lose by going through life as an old maid. When I was even younger than that, I had wanted to become a concert pianist. I had been taking lessons ever since primary school. When it came time for high school, I asked people if I should go to a music academy. After all, you have to have the talent. I wasn't sure I did. The piano teacher said, well, as a music student your horizons would become very narrow, that after all I had taken up the piano as a hobby originally. So I dropped the idea of a career in it, and went to an academic high school.

After that I began to think about a career in the mass media — in publishing, newspapers, radio, it didn't much matter. I really knew little or nothing about how the media function, had only a few foggy notions. What I'm saying is that my ambitions were not well focused then, but I knew that as a celibatarian I was going to have to earn my own living.

My Education Papa had been warning me not to pin any hopes on becoming a pianist. He wanted me to concentrate on getting into a good university. So in high school I quit taking lessons and used the time instead to study for exams. I didn't touch the keyboard very often. Dad and I even argued over whether to lock it up. The first time around, I failed the exams magnificently. So I had to cram for them for another year, and that time got accepted into Osaka National University.

That was one of the most important watersheds in my life. It gave me   4
the confidence that I can accomplish what I'm determined to do. Remember that in those days in a national university there might be three or four women to a hundred men. And it wasn't exactly easy for us to find jobs, either, after graduation. In the late '50s, good jobs still were scarce. Of forty-five women in my graduating class, only ten of us found work, and the other nine were hired as schoolteachers. Hundreds of people applied to the network that year. When they picked me, I felt as if I had won a lottery.

The network has a training institute in Tokyo now, and new employees go there first. But when I joined the Osaka studio, TV was still a new idea. There were not many hours of broadcasting, and relatively few people had sets. You just trailed after an experienced producer and learned by imitating him.

I've changed since I first began working, and the change has its good and bad sides. In my student days I had been uncritical. I thought my professors were brilliant. I majored in German and took little else, nothing broadening, just narrow specialty courses. But my kind of work is broad ranging and I find myself asking, "What makes society tick?" and "Is an enemy obstructing our way of life?"

Most men seem to be going in the opposite direction. Maybe it's just that work and family are too heavy a burden for them, but whatever the reason they tend to withdraw, it seems to me. Possibly I'm too harsh on those who do that, but I get to feeling pity for them. And when a man is in a crunch, his wife not only fails to comfort him, she pokes him in the posterior. "Why aren't you being promoted faster?" Wives have got to become more independent.

People had told me that the private networks are more liberal than the public one. But along about the fourth year here, I began to be aware of what a feudalistic place ours is. They don't do a thing to help a woman develop her abilities. Some programs are utterly routine; on others you can take your time, spend money freely, do it the way you want it done. The men angle to be assigned to the good programs. And though I'm itching to take a shot at one, in more than a dozen years in the studio I've never once been given the chance. Women are stuck with the ordinary little daily programs, the ones the men don't want. And the promotions somehow come your way just a little more slowly. 8

Not that we stiff-upper-lip it all the time. I am no great admirer of the women in the studio, but it's a fact that they are better at their work than most of the men are. So when I see a man promoted early, even though he has just been mumbling around and not paying any attention to the world outside, I get sore. We complain, but there are so few of us we can be ignored. The administrators are transferred in and out so often that we can't get results by complaining. Three years and there's a complete turnover in the station administrative staff. No continuity.

I've avoided taking administrative positions though they might give me more influence over policy than I have as a producer. As an administrator, you never know where you might be transferred next. You're a tool. You have to change your personality, and the tensions mount. All the men seem eager to go that route. But soon they look so awfully haggard and worn. Administrative work is sheer mental agony. You have no time to learn anything new. You die soon after you retire, or end up as another old dodderer.

Only about 10 percent of the professional staff are female now. There were more in the past, but they quit for various reasons and were replaced by men. The Fukuoka station is the worst: not even one woman on their staff any more on the broadcast side. Like it or not, the men there have to handle the Tea-and-flowers programs.

If I could start over again, I would take it from high school. I might not have been able to pass the exams for the college of science, but it may have been a mistake to have gone to the college of literature as I did. I wonder if I've gone into the wrong line of work? What I'm doing now probably could be done by just about anyone. Maybe I should have become a doctor or a judge.

Not that my work is uninteresting, but I find myself in something of a dilemma. I've begun to have doubts about the network. Lately I've begun to wonder whether the very existence of such vast organizations is contrary to the well-being of society, because of the authoritarianism (or whatever you want to call it) built into the very structure of such an institution. And yet here I am working in such a place. I'd been with the network for ten years before I began to think about it all.

Nothing would be solved by my quitting and going elsewhere. And the pay is not the point. I honestly did not expect a white-collar professional to be so hedged in by restrictions, but there is an invisible framework that you can't budge. For example, broadcasters are not to comment on the behavior of members of the Imperial Household. Senior men in the studio take that for granted, and if you try to insert anything about the Imperial Household into a program script, they clamp down on you without thinking. The three great taboos are the Emperor, the new religions, and sex. And for sure the network will not offer air time to a leftist or to anybody they think would have the nerve to denounce the very existence of the network itself.

When I'm putting together a program, if I think they might clamp down on me, I make a pitch at the planning conference and try for their approval. But I'm often left with the feeling that the people I pick for my programs are just barely acceptable. The network's rule is to not air anybody who is known to be strongly biased in any direction, which is why you end up with nothing but dullards. What I'm saying is that I'm beginning to reconsider the role of the networks in society. The union pays attention only to the positive side of the role: the cultural and informational functions. That's no threat.

Ours is a closed shop; we're obligated to join the union. I took no interest in it when I first joined the network. The union itself was feeble then, though it has gained a little strength since. But in this line of work, you don't ordinarily think of yourself as a laborer, so most people are smugly indifferent to the union. Nobody wants to run for office, not even the men. I suspect that it's because as an officer you have to do battle with the establishment, and most men don't like to do that.

I was shop vice-chairperson for one term. Part of the reason why I agreed to do it was that I knew rather little about the union and wanted to learn, and part of the reason is that I apparently don't have the high professional pride the others have. While they're working they gripe and gripe. Then the minute an administrator turns up, they button lip. I hoped I could help make the atmosphere more open, that we wouldn't be so afraid to stand up for our point of view as workers. Well, I tried. . . .

If they ever fired me, I would go right out and get another job. I'd prefer one in the media, though in Japan it is just about impossible to find a position with any large organization once you are in midcareer. So it might mean I would have to free-lance. For the present, however, I'm doing my work for the studio peacefully and don't really want to leave it, for better or worse. I know I could get along as a free-lance commentator on women's affairs; offers come in frequently. Though I'm not certain I'd be really good at it. . . .

My life has gone along pretty much as I had hoped. I'm the stubborn kind: when a roadblock looms up in front of me, I blast my way through it. Not that adults didn't try to change my mind, when I was younger. When I was taking exams for the university, they said I should consider a woman's college instead. When I wanted to get married, both my parents were absolutely dead set against it. Dad warned me that the man I wanted to marry was the same age as me, that we were both in college, and it's a mistake to marry a man until you know for sure how he'll turn out. It's best to be five years younger than your husband, he said. Because when a woman marries a man her age she starts looking older sooner, and eventually he'll leave her.

Ours is far and away a better marriage than my parents'. But then, they were pressured into marrying each other. I don't regard that as marriage in the true sense of the word. That's where the fault lies, for Mom and Dad did not have a very happy relationship. I used to blame them for it, but over the years I've come to find a little sympathy for them. Otherwise, I suspect I would never have been willing to get married myself.

But from high school onward, I warned them that I had no intention of going into an arranged marriage. Mom was adamantly opposed to the idea of marrying for love, absolutely against it until the day she died.

She had a fantastic sense of family pride. For that reason her death was a blessing — she died of cancer at forty-two. She'd have exploded if I had so much as ever hinted that I was fond of any particular man.

And she was uncompromising about ideas of liberation. She could very well accept the idea of a woman wanting a career. But as for marriage, she told me, if I would not agree to an arranged marriage, then I would have to stay single.

Your first year in college, suddenly you have much more freedom than you did in high school, and we hung around with boys pretty often. That made my mother furious. Called me a slut. If I would quit seeing boys, she said, I could trust her to find me a good man. But I told her that no matter how hard she searched, if he didn't appeal to me I would never marry him, so why not forget the whole thing. At times like that she would — how should I put it — become *very* worked up. "There you go, playing around the opposite sex just like your father!" she'd bellow. We'd battle. And it would leave me feeling victimized.

After all, I had been attending coed schools from the beginning. I was   24
only being friendly with boys in the usual ways. But Mom could not understand that, our idea of friendship. We often sent letters to each other, and when Mom found out about it, she would get all emotional.

My first impressions of my husband were not exactly favorable, at that. Takeo seemed, oh, call it fragile, womanish. I had this feeling of Hmmmm — so there are men like this in the world, too? By fragile I mean delicate and slender, willowy, weak-looking. Not masculine. This is not the type for me, I said to myself.

We were in the same German class in college. Takeo was a science major. Now he's a research chemist for a pharmaceutical company. Little by little, I began to see his good points. He was kind to everybody, not blunt the way I am. I admired the way he had of always doing the right thing. He was nothing like my brothers, who are hard-boiled types. It occurred to me that he and I could help each other, that we might get along very well indeed. And I found that I was intrigued by a man who would be continuing his studies even after he left college.

We were married two years after graduation. By then I was working, of course, but Takeo was still in graduate school. Most of our friends also married somebody they met in college, and in many of the couples both parties have careers. Among them, our dual-career marriage is nothing out of the ordinary. . . .

And he still surprises me. The network has a male-female talk show,   28
and one night the topic was sex discrimination at retirement age. The

two of us were watching. I got peeved because it was such a cheap imitation of a broadcast, but he was guffawing and getting a kick out of it. As far as I was concerned, they were not really facing up to the discrimination issue, they had turned it into a question of women's abilities. Somebody had stacked the panel, and the men were getting away with heaping scorn on women in biological terms. It made my blood boil, but Takeo said, "So what, it's a fun show." He believes that men and women are unquestionably different. Intellectually he can accept the idea that it is a result of different life experiences, but he can't accept it emotionally. Men must protect women, in his view. . . .

I do have friends among male colleagues at the station. I see eye to eye with a couple of them and enjoy talking to them. I like the way one of them thinks — he has such a fresh point of view on so many topics. And he's one of those rare individuals who doesn't brownnose the bosses. He's a good drinker, and I enjoy drinking with him when we're out on trips to gather material for a program. We've taken care not to become involved with each other — though of course the gossips in the studio say we are. I expect they're jealous. I see nothing wrong with that kind of friendship; a man and a woman can be good friends without its having to be an affair. I know that there are young women in the lab where Takeo works, and that they work on projects together. That doesn't upset me. But I've learned not to say anything about my friendships to him. He can't accept the idea.

In a sense, my husband is my best friend. We're trying to sustain a mutual understanding. Others tell me he is a very simpatico guy. And there is no question that I owe him a great deal. Without him I would not be able to have both a family and a career.

I would not protest if he accepted a position elsewhere, but it doesn't seem likely to happen. He isn't interested in the idea. If he did, however, I would not just give up my career to move with him. I believe that we could continue as a married couple even though we were living apart, but he detests the very thought of it. "What kind of life would that be?" he says. I sure don't go for the idea either. Sometimes I wonder if I'm not acting too much as if I don't need my family. He's even been going out and buying his breakfast on his way to work. . . .

Ours was the first generation that came of age under postwar democracy, and many of us women wanted to work. The present generation seems to be moving backwards, with fewer and fewer women pursuing careers. My husband says that if a woman must work, then she needs a special skill so that she doesn't end up just pouring tea for the men. If it's a flunky job that anybody could do, then she is better off staying home and taking care of her family. Most men seem to feel that it's all right for a woman to work if she has talent, but that if it's only for the money it's a loss of face for her husband. Japanese are peculiar that way, not wanting to admit that they're doing anything for the money.

EXPLORATIONS

1. What are Tomoko's dissatisfactions with her job as a television producer? Which of these dissatisfactions appear to relate mainly to the network, and which ones relate to customs in Japanese society?

2. What kinds of programs are broadcast by Tomoko's network? How does Tomoko define the network's ideal role and its actual role in Japanese society? How is the Japanese media's attitude toward newsworthy people and events different from that of the American media?

3. Tomoko comments: "My husband says that if a woman must work, then she needs a special skill so that she doesn't end up just pouring tea for the men. If it's a flunky job that anybody could do, then she is better off staying home and taking care of her family." What statements by Tomoko elsewhere in her interview suggest that she agrees with her husband's opinion? What statements suggest that she disagrees?

CONNECTIONS

1. Ezekiel Mphahlele comments on the widening gulf between child and parents when the child's education takes him or her out of the parents' tradition-oriented sphere. How do Mphahlele's observations apply to Tomoko? How has her education affected her relationship with her parents, and vice versa?

2. Like Pom's parents in "Pom's Engagement" by Ved Mehta (p. 162), Tomoko's parents — particularly her mother — wanted to follow the custom of choosing their daughter's husband. What contrasts in Pom's and Tomoko's cultural and personal backgrounds do you think made Pom accept her parents' wishes while Tomoko rebelled? In what ways is Tomoko better equipped than Pom to choose her own husband? How does her having a career affect the chances that her parents could have placed her in a successful marriage?

3. What values and attitudes toward work does Tomoko as a union member share with Bill Talcott in Studs Terkel's *Observation*? How do their ideas

differ? Which differences appear to relate to contrasts between Japan and the United States? to contrasts in social and professional class? to personal contrasts between Tomoko and Talcott?

ELABORATIONS

1. In his *Observation*, Bruce Weber says of current college students: "It's very uncool not to know what you want and not to be already chasing it." In making the decisions that have shaped her life — on education, career, marriage, and family — has Tomoko been guided by consistent long-range goals? When and how have her goals directed her choices, and when has that relationship been reversed? Write an essay examining the strategies behind Tomoko's life choices, her degree of satisfaction with the results, and the probable reasons for her decision-making methods.

2. Betty Friedan's *Observation* quotes a woman who, like Tomoko, sees herself both as a mother and as a worker. Carola Hansson and Karin Lidén's "Liza and Family" (p. 48) also features a working mother. What contrasting conclusions have these three women reached about themselves as workers, mothers, and wives, and why? What self-concepts and views of the world do all three women share that differ from those of working fathers, such as Snowbird in Andrew Malcolm's selection, He Guangwei in Zhang Xinxin and Sang Ye's selection, and Bill Talcott in Studs Terkel's *Observation*? Choose one of these questions, and write an essay investigating it.

SATOSHI KAMATA

Six Months at Toyota

"Six Months at Toyota" comes from Satoshi Kamata's book *Japan in the Passing Lane*. Born in 1938, Kamata graduated from Waseda University in 1964. After working briefly for a trade paper in the steel industry and as an editor for a popular general magazine, he became a full-time free-lance reporter. He continues to write frequently about Japanese industry and labor.

The book's translator, Tatsuru Akimoto, writes: "The impetus for *Japan in the Passing Lane,* Kamata's third book, came in large part from conversations with a friend who had been a seasonal worker for several years at Honda manufacturing plants. . . . Kamata wanted to experience the situation firsthand and chose Toyota because he had heard that the working conditions there were much harsher than at other automobile plants in Japan. Kamata stayed at Toyota for the full term of his six-month contract, and the diary he kept there forms the basis of this book. Kamata was married, and while he worked at Toyota his wife and two small children lived at home a few hundred miles away." *Japan in the Passing Lane* was first published in Japan in 1973 and updated in 1980; it appeared in the United States in 1982.

(For more background on Japan, see pp. 36 and 351.)

Monday, September 18

My first workday. Up at 5:00 A.M. It's still dark when I go out. The eastern mountains are glowing faintly, but I can still see the stars shining brightly in the sky. The street is lit by a few scattered lamps. It's a forty-minute walk to the factory. Unfortunately, the plant I have to work in is at the farthest corner of the factory compound. I can't find the canteen and miss breakfast.

I have really been fooled by the seeming slowness of the conveyor belt. No one can understand how it works without experiencing it. Almost as soon as I begin, I am dripping with sweat. Somehow, I learn the order of the work motions, but I'm totally unable to keep up with the speed of the line. My work gloves make it difficult to grab as many tiny bolts as I need, and how many precious seconds do I waste doing just that? I do my best, but I can barely finish one gear box out of three within the fixed length of time. If a different-model transmission comes along, it's simply beyond my capacity. Some skill is needed, and a new hand like me can't do it alone. I'm thirsty as hell, but workers can neither smoke nor drink water. Going to the toilet is out of the question. Who could have invented a system like this? It's designed to make workers do nothing *but* work and to prevent any kind of rest. Yet the man beside me the other day deftly handled his hammer, put the bolts into their grooves with both hands, and fastened them with a nut runner (a power screwdriver that can tighten six bolts simultaneously), seemingly with no difficulty.

The conveyor starts at 6:00 A.M. and doesn't stop until 11:00 A.M. One box of transmissions arrives on the conveyor belt every minute and twenty seconds with unerring precision. When the line stops at eleven o'clock, we tear off our gloves and leave our positions as quickly as we can. We wash our greasy hands and run to the toilet, then rush to the canteen about a hundred yards away where we wait in another line to get our food. After standing five hours, my legs are numb and stiff. My new safety shoes are so heavy that I feel I can barely move. I put my ticket into a box, take an aluminum tray, a pair of chopsticks, a plate of food, a tea cup, and a bowl of rice. I'm still unfamiliar with the routine and have a hard time finding a seat at one of the long tables. Finally, just as I'm settling down to eat, I have the sensation that the trays on the table are moving slowly sideways as if they're on a conveyor belt! At 11:45, the line starts again. There's not much time to rest since ten minutes before work starts we have to begin preparing a large enough supply of parts for the afternoon assemblage.

Above the line, a little to my right, there's a big electric display panel. Under the words "Transmission Assembly Conveyor," there are numbers from 1 to 15. When it is absolutely impossible to catch up with the conveyor, you have to push a button under the belt. This lights up your number in yellow on the board. To halt the line in an emergency, you have to push another button, which triggers a red light and stops the line. Although there are fifteen buttons on the line, there are now only eight workers. To increase production, Toyota decided to use two shifts starting this month. September is the beginning of the high-demand season, and I'm in the first group of seasonal workers hired under this new schedule.

The first shift ends at 2:15 P.M. Already, the man on the next shift is standing beside me, waiting for me to finish. As soon as I put my hammer down on the belt, he picks it up and begins precisely where I left off. A baton pass, and neatly done, too.

Still, it turns out I'm not finished! I have to spend thirty more minutes replenishing the supply parts for the afternoon shift. I also have to pick up the parts I've scattered on the floor. Damn! My legs ache the entire forty-minute walk back to the dorm. I'm bone tired. Is this the life for a worker in a great enterprise, a famous auto company, proud of being tops in Japan and the third in the world? Somehow I'll have to get used to it.

Tonight Kudo, who had left at eight in the morning, comes back a little after seven. He also had to work two hours overtime. For some reason, the lights in the dorms have gone out. It's really depressing to return to a dark room after walking all the way from the plant.

Kudo is lying spread-eagled on the mat floor. "I didn't quite expect the work to be so hard," he says. Still, he tells me somewhat proudly that he's made 400 pieces today. I don't know how many I made myself, or for that matter, don't really know what I was making. Exactly what part of the gear box were they? I was much too busy to look at the other guys' operations. I didn't even have time to look at my watch. After a while, I felt like I was making some part of a child's plastic toy. What was I really doing? The sign in my shop has a word for it — "Assembly"!

Tonight, I'm too tired to sleep and awfully nervous about having to get up early tomorrow. I get up and go out to buy a can of beer. A picture of Ken Takakura, a famous actor, smiles down at me from the vending machine. Even beer is sold by machines. . . .

Thursday, September 28

I went to take a bath downstairs this morning. When I came out, my wooden clogs were gone. You're not often robbed these days, even in public baths. When I went to the dining room, there was nothing left to eat. Here every day is a small war.

There is a Safety First meeting ten minutes before the shift begins. It's not fair for management to force a meeting on the workers during their off time, but no one protests.

There are some complaints among the workers. When the company declared an increase in output, it promised that ten workers from another plant would be sent here as reinforcements. In the end, only eight came.

The only way not to hold up the line was to offset the labor shortage by working overtime. Workers are angry.

"What we can't do, we can't do," one worker says. "The company should be satisfied."

"If we really care about Safety First," another says, "why don't they hire more workers? That's top priority."

But still, when the time comes, we all return to work without protest. By 10:00 P.M. everyone is exhausted. It is all I can do to keep my hands in motion on the line. But strangely, time passes and the line moves on, and somehow each day's work ends.

I'm responsible for assembling two kinds of truck transmissions, and   16 by now I can do about 90 percent of the required work. I'd give anything just to keep up with the murderous conveyor. I hate having to push the button to call the team chief and reveal my incompetence again and again.

Takeda, whose position is next to mine, helps me sometimes by rushing through his own work to give me a whole minute of his precious time. "Tell me how to do it and I'll help you. My job is simple. I can spare the minute."

I know he really can't spare the minute. Nobody on the line can afford the luxury of helping others. I am touched.

But there's another side to Takeda's generosity. He's dying from the monotony of his own work. I'm thankful for his help, of course, but Takeda also wants to try something new and strange, something that breaks the deadly boredom, the relentless repetition of the assembly line. There, where no amount of intelligence, creativity, or freedom is permitted, he can release some tension and refresh his energy by helping me, and that helps him get through the day.

Almost all the workers here are hardworking. In most factories, there   20 are those who work very hard and those who don't. But here, the conveyor-belt system makes everyone work at exactly the same pace. Even off the line, we all begin preparing parts even before our shift starts, time which is still our supper break, for without this preparation we'd never get the work done.

It is raining when work finishes. I am depressed, already worrying if I will make it through to next February, when my contract expires. Takeda asks Yoshizaki, who happens to live near my dorm, to give me a lift.

The joint at the base of my right third finger is numb. I can't bend it at all. . . .

Thursday, October 5

A meeting after work. Mostly, we talk about our section manager's new order to check the tightness of all six bolts in the transmission. It's impossible for us to add one more operation. We're already too pressed for time. The team chief tries to force it on us, using the oldest excuse in the world:

"It's an order from the section manager."   24

One worker answers coldly, "Well, if it's an order, it's an order. But the line's going to stop."

"I don't care. Let it stop."

"You say you don't care? But the people on the second shift will have to work overtime to make up for us."

Another worker exclaims, "They'll have to work until two or three   28 o'clock in the morning! That's impossible. What sort of people do the management think we are?"

Everybody starts complaining all at once. Finally, the general foreman, a stout man with a white cap, proposes a compromise: "Well, we'll try measuring at only one point. I'll ask the management about it."

"One place is plenty!" someone shouts in disgust.

Suddenly the section manager, who issued the order, comes in. He's still young, about forty. The general foreman tells us rather ceremoniously, "Please pay special attention to safety." Then he stands and leaves in spite of our anger. The meeting has "ended." We also stand and leave the narrow locker room. As we're filing out, someone tells the section manager, "You've got to think more about us," but the words no longer have an icy edge. They're more like a joke. Even the experienced workers are getting upset. I'm relieved to know that others are as discontented as I am. . . .

Thursday, January 11

When I went to work last night, I knew immediately something was   32 wrong. The team chief on the other shift stood there rather uneasily, and the workers who had just arrived surrounded him. I asked Miura, who works with me, if there had been an accident. He said that Kawamura, a seasonal worker, had been severely shocked. Kawamura is a young man from Hokkaido, where he worked as a carpenter. They carried him to the Toyota Hospital, and he'll probably be there for more than a week.

Before work started, the general foreman made one of his little speeches: "Kawamura's biorhythm chart shows that today is his worst day. Looks like the chart was right!"

The workers knew the real story. Going to get some parts he needed, Kawamura crossed over two small conveyor belts and touched a machine. But the machine (a parts feeder that fits washers in bolts) was so old that some of a 200-volt electric cord was frayed. And his gloves were wet. He received a severe shock and fell to the floor. He suffered a concussion and lost consciousness. Luckily the current passed through the base of his finger. If it had gone near his heart, he would have been killed instantly.

On the day of the accident, his team was short of workers, since two people hadn't showed up and one seasonal worker had quit. Superficially, the cause of the accident was that he took a shortcut to get the parts, but the real cause was the short circuit in the old machine, and also, the fact that there was no bridge over the line. But according to the general foreman (who's also a member of the union!), the problem was in the worker's biorhythm, and the key to safety is for all of us to be careful when our own biorhythms are bad.

This year's new slogan is written on the company's blackboard: "Whatever you do, be prepared to take responsibility for it." . . . 36

Thursday, January 18

They say we made 425 boxes today. Though we have no time to count, our production has increased by 25 boxes a day. Soon we'll be making 450 boxes a day. When I get back tonight, I find Kudo still there.

"Aren't you going to work?"

"No, not today. Not tomorrow, either."

"Are you feeling bad?" 40

"I'm leaving. Today I fell on the floor unconscious," he says, looking at me weakly.

Last night he worked the night shift, but as soon as he started, he felt sick. He tried to keep on working. When he checked the clock, it was 12:50 A.M. Ten minutes to go until the break for the midnight meal. When he looked at the clock again, three minutes had passed. Seven more minutes, he thought, and then he fell on the floor. When he came to he was lying on a bench, covered with the coat he had just bought. Someone must have opened his locker and put it over him. The foreman, who was standing beside him, told him that right after he fell, they had carried him to the Toyota Hospital, just outside the factory grounds. They had given him an injection, and then he had been transferred to the infirmary inside the factory. It was already morning when he came to. Why hadn't they left him to sleep in a soft hospital bed?

When he was carried to the hospital again, Kudo told them about the traffic accident he'd had before. The general foreman told Kudo, "Once you fall, you can't work any more. I'll see that your account is settled. Rest well at home, and then come and see us again." That was all; he was fired.

"At least I'm glad I'm alive," Kudo adds. "Well, I won't worry. Anyway,   44 they need someone at home to shovel the snow off the roof. It's only forty-six days till the end of my contract, though. Then I could have gotten my bonus." His voice becomes choked with emotion and he can't talk any more.

I recall how he worked from eight to eight, but he reported to the shop an hour early to prepare for work, wash parts, and melt wax. He wasn't paid for these jobs, but without doing them he wouldn't have been able to keep up with his work. He's a real craftsman. He wants to do his job well. Both of us just sit looking at each other for a while, and finally he speaks: "I'm feeling much better. I could go to work right now." . . .

Sunday, February 4

I rarely have time to sit and talk with the others in my team. But when we do talk over a glass of sake, they speak frankly of their discontent, even to a seasonal worker like me.

Worker A's story:

"Now the work is nearly three times tougher than when I came here   48 six or seven years ago. Around 1965, they measured our work by stop-watch. Since then it's been getting tougher. But until a couple of years ago we still had enough workers, and the line used to stop ten minutes before finishing time. After the Tsutsumi plant was built in December 1970, everything really got worse. They changed from the daytime single shift to the two-consecutive-shift system, and now we've got day and night split shifts with time between shifts. And they keep speeding up the line. The faster the line gets, the harder we work to catch up, because we want to go home quickly. But when we finally get used to the speed, then they make it even faster. Right now it's a minute and fourteen seconds per unit, but I bet they'll speed it up. The new guys can't handle it any more. You read in the newspapers that Toyota workers are quick and active. We're not quick. We're forced to work quickly. It's the ones up there who benefit by exploiting us down here. I'm sure the section managers know very well how hard a time we're having. And the union, they're supported by our money, but they only work for the company. You can't expect anything from them because the leaders are all general foremen and foremen. They change every year, so nobody has enough time to get into the job seriously. If you complain to them, they just tell you to 'cooperate' and say, 'Unless you produce more your salary will not go up.'

"Two years ago we talked about ending overtime, but we realized that we couldn't make ends meet without it, so nothing changed. Personally, I enjoy physical labor. I like to work with my hands. But here, it's just too fast. I guess I can put up with the hard pace, but the trouble is I never know when I can go home. When I come home all I do is take a bath, have something to eat, and go to bed. I don't have more than an hour to talk with my wife. Nowadays I vomit whenever I'm not feeling well, and if I go see a doctor at Toyota Hospital, he just tells me to get back to work."

B's Story:

"You know Yamashita lost his finger, don't you? Or was that before you came? Anyway, during the break — we were on the second shift — the section manager came and made a speech on safety for about thirty minutes. So we were late for supper, and there were no noodles left at the canteen. We had some rice, but we all like to have a bowl of noodles at the end of the meal, you know. Afterwards we complained about this to the section manager. Then he took ten dollars out of his pocket and gave it to us. We handed it to our foreman, and he went out on his bicycle to buy some bread and ice cream. When he came back we stopped the line and sat around and ate. I was impressed. It was an amazing thing. I've decided to work for this section manager, and as long as he's here, I won't take any days off. I may be a fool, but I've never heard of anything like that happening at Toyota. Nobody would spend ten dollars out of his pocket for us. The section managers all think they have nothing to do with us.

"When I first came here the job was so tough I thought of quitting. I remember one morning I woke up and discovered I couldn't move my wrist. I wondered why I had to do work like this. And then I thought, once I've mastered the job it'll be a lot easier, and this idea kept me going. The people who stay here are the ones who have no other place to go and who like to endure pain. But in the end, we'll all be crushed by Toyota. There's hardly anyone at Toyota I can trust.

"The union? I hear they buy it off with women. I don't know if it's true or not, but I can't think of any other way. We all want to go home earlier. If you ask anybody, they'll say 'We don't want any more money, but let us go home without overtime.' When we come home late after overtime, we hardly have time to look at our wives, and they complain. That adds insult to injury. But they don't know what we go through. And I guess they'd better not find out. If they did, they'd tell us to quit. I don't want my wife to see what I'm doing here — it would make me feel even worse. I work for the sake of my children, and my only enjoyment here is having a good laugh over dumb jokes during the lunch break. Other than that, I don't have any hopes for this job.

"If you quit, Kamata, another guy'll take your place. With a new worker, the line'll stop again, and we won't be able to go home until we finish the day's quota. We'll be up shit creek."

Toyota's current slogan is "Toyota . . . Cars to Love, the World Over." On television, a charming film star, Sayuri Yoshinaga, smiles and says, "It's the car with distinction, the car for someone special." The people who buy the cars never realize that they were made, quite literally, over the dead and mutilated bodies of workers who were given no "distinction" at all. . . .

Thursday, February 15

I wake up around five this morning and hear the clatter of empty cans   56 echoing coldly on concrete as someone sorts them out of the trash cans. At 6:45 the sound of the morning chimes blares over the loudspeaker. Soon, I hear car engines warming up in the parking lot below my window. Then the clatter and hiss and banging of the heating system being turned on. Bright sunshine falls in through the cracks of my curtains. Fine weather. I couldn't sleep last night and stayed up until one. I was excited and nervous wondering if I could hold out one more day . . .

At the end of the morning meeting, the foreman orders me to stand beside him in the center of a circle and says, "Thank you very much for working with us for such a long time." He seems sincere. During the lunch break, as I walk to the canteen, a regular worker joins me.

"Finally finishing, aren't you?"

"Yeah, I'm getting out of this prison."

"Us regulars are condemned to life imprisonment, I guess," he says, 60 looking at the ground.

During the break, a guy I've never had a chance to talk to comes up to me at the locker-room bench.

"You've only got three-and-a-half hours to go, haven't you? I wish I did, too. I've got to stay here for life. And no matter how hard I try, I doubt if I'll ever be able to wear a white general foreman's cap."

"Hey, you better not get too excited yet," someone else says. "I know a guy, a seasonal, who drank the night he left and went walking with a girl and got run over by a car."

"Maybe that was the best thing that could've happened," another guy 64 says. "Better to die happy than be killed little by little in this goddamn factory."

Finally, it's time to go. Shimoyama, who works two positions ahead of me on the line, keeps coming over to tease me.

"You'll be hit by the impactor at the last second," he says.

"Only thirty minutes left!"

At 4:27 the foreman comes over to take my place. He smiles and says 68 simply, "OK. That's all. You need time to change." Somehow, it is all too simple. I feel strange, as if resigning means simply changing places with somebody. I go around the line and say good-bye to everyone. Shimoyama holds out his hand. Takeda says with a big smile, "Thanks for everything." One worker says, "If you come back, you'd better get a softer job in one of the subcontracting companies." The line doesn't let us stop and talk. The team chief and the deputy section manager in the office look at me as if I don't exist. I go to the personnel office to get my pay and pick up some papers for unemployment insurance. My wages for twelve days' work, including basic pay, overtime, night work, and other fringe allowances together with the final bonus of $43, come to $197.40. Net pay: $185.08. As he hands me the money the clerk says, "Mr. Kamata, you earned it." He knows how it is. "Isn't there anyone else finishing today?" I ask. "There was one in December." Only two completed their contracts at the main plant — only Yamamoto and I. Two! At first I can't believe it. After I get my money, I take a last slow walk around the place. It all seems so simple and matter-of-fact, putting an end to such hard work just like that. It isn't so much a feeling of liberation as of weariness and emptiness. I have a dull pain in my right wrist; my right fingers are stiff; my palms have shreds of metal in them; my back is sore all over; I feel continually nauseated. These are the only things I can take with me.

I return to my room and find Hamada still in bed. I show him my pay slip and tell him how to read it. He looks at it closely and says, "I'll try hard to complete my contract." I go to the dormitory office and return my key, name tag, and bedding. The clerk glances at me, but doesn't say anything, not even thank you. I'm still nothing more to them than a thing. My neighbor Miyamoto drives me to the nearest train station. As soon as I sit down I'm overcome by fatigue, cold, and a deep desire to sleep. . . .

When I left Toyota in February 1973, assembly time at the Main Plant for transmissions was one minute and fourteen seconds. This had been shortened by six seconds in the six months since I had begun, while production had been increased by 100 to 415 units. Now, seven years later, the assembly time is forty-five seconds and the production is 690 units. This increase was achieved solely through accelerating the work pace. Knockdown part packing at the Takaoka plant needed sixty minutes for a set (which includes 20 cars) three years ago. Today it takes twelve minutes, and still the manpower has been reduced from 50 to 40. Before, workers stood in front of conveyors; now they rush around from one part to another, pushing mobile work desks with wheels.

At the assembly lines for passenger cars, parts have become larger and have increased in number, owing to exhaust-emission control. In addition, parts for various models come down the line all mixed together because of the simultaneous production of many models. Nevertheless, the speed of the conveyor belts only accelerates. The Tahara plant on the Chita Peninsula, which started its operation in January 1979, recently completed arrangements to produce 5000 small trucks and 5000 Corollas. To fill its manpower needs, many workers were taken from the other Toyota plants. Despite this loss, conveyor belts at each plant are running as if nothing had happened. Many workers have been moved onto the assembly line as "reinforcements." Workers are forced to work on Sundays and holidays. The reinforcement work and Sunday-holiday work are a lubricant without which the conveyors could not run.

At the management-union convention mentioned above, Executive 72 Director Yoshiaki Yamamoto said: "In this day and age of uncertainty and severe competition, we must and shall concentrate our production on popular models and adjust the imbalance of work loads among shops. So please be cooperative in establishing flexible shop arrangements that will be able to respond quickly to requests for help."

Reinforcement work is feared by workers who have had no work experience on conveyor lines. Most workers begin losing weight within a few days. Even without the everyday work they're expected to do, inexperienced reinforcement workers would be exhausted by such difficult labor in a totally unfamiliar environment. A directive to management ("On Accepting Reinforcement Workers: Daily Guidance and Management") from the Takaoka plant personnel division shows that reinforcement workers have many complaints and dissatisfactions, more than half of which pertain to safety issues. But the guidance policy goes no farther than the following:

> Management personnel and the longtime workers in the shop should "say hello and a few words" to reinforcement workers at least once a day, and unit members should make an effort to create a congenial atmosphere so that the management and senior workers can easily "say hello and a few words." . . . It is not easy for reinforcement workers to speak out.

One evening, I met with workers from various plants. I wanted to know the facts behind Toyota's remarkable production records. What the workers counted on their fingers was the number of suicides — more than twenty in the past year. These were only cases that they remembered at that moment. They told me that in June there were three suicides within a couple of days. There was a twenty-seven-year-old worker at the Takaoka plant who reported to work and then disappeared; he had thrown himself into the sea. A team leader at the same plant drove his car into a reservoir. These were the only cases reported in the newspapers. The other cases were all related by those who had been close to the suicides. There are no statistics.

The number, they said, is particularly high at the Takaoka plant, whose products are popular and whose production cannot keep pace with demand. On June 28, a forty-five-year-old worker at the Tsutsumi plant hanged himself in his company-rented apartment. Around the same time, a Takaoka plant reinforcement worker from the Tsutsumi plant committed suicide in his dormitory by taking sleeping pills. He was depressed after having been blamed by the team leader for his tardiness and forced to "apologize to his fellow workers for the inconvenience he caused." Also around the same time, a team leader of the Maintenance Department in the Head Office hanged himself. A body found at the Takaoka plant dormitory was taken away by a member of the Security Division staff. Afterwards he complained that while playing pinball, he imagined he saw the suicide's face in the glass of the pinball machine. The workers who met with me that evening talked endlessly of similar cases. I had heard rumors of mentally disturbed workers and suicides many times while I worked at Toyota. But the rapid increase in their numbers is frightening.

EXPLORATIONS

1. What are the Toyota factory workers' general and specific complaints about their jobs? What are their sources of job satisfaction? If you were a manager at this plant, what change would be your top priority?

2. What passages on Kamata's first and last days at Toyota suggest that he viewed himself then more as a writer than as a factory worker? What passages in the rest of his narrative show him perceiving himself as a factory worker? How would his experience have been different if he had thought of himself as a writer throughout?

3. At several points Kamata quotes speeches by workers or managers. Why do you, or don't you, believe that these are exact quotations? How would the narrative's effect change if Kamata reported the gist of other people's comments instead of presenting them as dialogue?

CONNECTIONS

1. In David Plath's selection, Tomoko, as a television producer, works in a completely different stratum from Kamata and his fellow Toyota employees. What attitudes toward work do Tomoko and Kamata share? What job complaints do they share? What other similarities in their accounts reflect the fact that Japan is a small country with a relatively homogeneous culture?

2. How do you think the physical toll on Toyota workers compares with the toll on He Guangwei in Zhang Xinxin and Sang Ye's "The Hunter"? How do Kamata's and He's attitudes toward stress and injuries differ? What are the probable reasons for this difference?

3. "I think everybody ought to quit their job and do what they want to do," says Bill Talcott in Studs Terkel's *Observation*. What reasons do the Japanese

Toyota workers give for not doing this? What other reasons does Kamata suggest, especially in his description of his last day on the job, for why quitting is difficult? To what extent do these same reasons apply to American workers?

ELABORATIONS

1. Imagine that you are an organizer who has come to the Toyota plant to help employees win better working conditions. Write a memo to the section manager describing the problems you think are most urgent, recommending changes, and making a case for the changes you suggest. (Take into account the management attitudes described by Kamata.)

2. Do you think American workers would put up with the conditions Kamata describes? What specific incidents in Kamata's account would draw a different response from Americans than they do from Japanese? Using "Six Months at Toyota," David Plath's "Tomoko on Her Television Career," and Terkel's and other *Observations* as references, write an essay comparing and contrasting the attitudes toward management of American and Japanese workers. (You may also use excerpts from these selections as examples.)

HEDRICK SMITH

Skoro Budet — *It'll Be Here Soon*

Born in Scotland in 1933, Hedrick Smith graduated from Williams
College in Massachusetts and studied at Balliol College at Oxford University on a Fulbright scholarship. Smith started his journalism career as
a reporter for United Press International in Tennessee. Since 1962 he has
worked for the *New York Times,* reporting from Saigon, Cairo, and
Washington. From 1971 to 1974 he was *Times* bureau chief in Moscow;
he prepared for the trip at Harvard University as a Neiman fellow. The
author of several books and many magazine articles, Smith received the
Pulitzer Prize for international reporting in 1974, two years after his work
at the *Times* helped that paper win the Pulitzer Prize for public service.
Since 1976 Smith has been chief *Times* Washington correspondent.
"*Skoro Budet* — It'll Be Here Soon" comes from his 1975 book *The
Russians,* based on his years in the Soviet Union.

The "Plan" Smith refers to is a central component in the Soviets'
effort to modernize their economy, which was virtually feudal until this
century. "It is the Five-Year Plans, launched in 1928 by Stalin to force
the pace of industrialization, that are officially credited with multiplying
Soviet output fiftyfold from 1913 to 1973 and building the backbone of
the Soviet economy," writes Smith. "The Plan comes close to being the
fundamental law of the land . . . treated with almost mystical venera-
tion." Because most enterprises in the Soviet Union are state owned, the
Plan is extremely comprehensive — it is as if the U.S. government set
production goals for every corporation in the country.

(For more background on the Soviet Union, see pp. 48, 139, 213,
and 649.)

"The tempo of work is different for each ten-day period of the month,"
said Rashid, a stocky, honey-colored factory foreman from Uzbekistan,
who was explaining what work was like at the Tashkent Tractor Parts
Factory. "Do you know the words — *spyachka, goryachka,* and *likhor-
adka?*"

Literally, I knew they meant something like hibernation, hot time,
and feverish frenzy, but I did not immediately associate them with his
factory, so I shook my head. Rashid smiled at my innocence and rubbed
a calloused hand across his cheek.

"Those are the nicknames we give the 'decades,' the ten-day periods into which each month is divided," he said. "The first decade is the sleeper time, the second decade is for hot work, and the third decade is like fever." He paused to let me absorb that and went on. "The tempo of work also depends on payday. Normally, we have two paydays a month: one between the fifteenth and twentieth and the other, in the first days of the next month. Two or three days before payday, there is a preholiday feeling and no one is in the mood for working. And two or three days afterward, people are practically sick from drinking and they have to drink off their hangovers."

With variations and embellishments, it was a story repeated by others including Yosif, a tall, slender, middle-aged engineer from a big city in southern Russia who chain-smoked as he talked about the plants where he had worked. To hear his description of Soviet factories that made air-conditioning and refrigeration units was to pass through a Soviet looking glass and to discover a world inside Soviet industry that seemed almost a travesty of the Command Economy imagined in the West to be functioning with monopolistic harmony and monolithic discipline.

"Storming" is what Rashid and Yosif were describing. It is a practice so endemic and essential to the Soviet system that Russians have coined the fancy word *shturmovshchina* to denote the entire national phenomenon of crash programs and the wildly erratic work rhythm of Soviet factories, large and small, civilian and military. Storming to fulfill the monthly, quarterly, or annual Plan turns every month into a sort of crazy industrial pregnancy, sluggish in gestation and frenzied at the finish.

"Usually, at the start of the month an enterprise is virtually paralyzed after the storming in the final days of the preceding month," Yosif explained. By his account, the work force was in a state of exhaustion not only because of drinking but because so many skilled workers had been pressed into long overtime shifts during the storming campaign. "A lot have to put in two shifts a day during storming," he said. "They work all day both Saturdays and Sundays, their normal days off. Management doesn't have the right [to pay them for overtime] because it has a ceiling on its payroll and financial inspection organs check on that. Sometimes if a worker is badly needed, he can get time-and-a-half or double time off to compensate for his overtime. But whether or not they get time off, workers have to put in those extra days [Black Saturdays, they are universally called] without extra pay. So usually there are a lot of workers off at the start of the month and the enterprise is in a state of paralysis."

"Plants couldn't operate at normal capacity anyway because they do not have a lot of the materials and components needed for operation," Yosif went on. "In spite of the Plan and seemingly definite delivery deadlines, suppliers don't fulfill the Plan or meet delivery schedules. So manufacturing plants cannot work rhythmically. Normally, not enough parts and components are available until about the tenth or twelfth of the month. Some items can be assembled almost completely, but they lack certain parts. A large number of items cannot be shipped out and accumulate in storerooms. They are held as late as the twentieth of the month because parts aren't ready or certain components are missing. Finally comes the third decade (twentieth to thirtieth). It's a good month if absolutely everything required is actually on hand by the twentieth. When everything has finally been received, the storming of the Plan can begin. Immediately work starts in many sections simultaneously."

Yosif spoke about it matter-of-factly, making clear this was a normal   8 state of affairs for Soviet industry, not some aberration peculiar to factories where he worked or to particular seasons of the year, though December, being the end of the year, is worse than other months.

"In other countries, production normally goes on throughout the month," Yosif observed, "but here, it can only begin on the fourteenth or twentieth when all materials have been received. So factories must fulfill about eighty percent of the Plan [quotas] in the last ten to fifteen days. No one cares any longer about quality. Volume is the main thing. Some workers are sent to finish the items that were partly assembled and kept in storerooms. Some of the production is no longer finished in factory conditions but often in the open air. Water, dirt, and dust can fall in the equipment which, of course, lowers its quality and cuts down its life span.

"The whole population knows all about this because everyone works," Yosif commented. "So normally, when someone buys a household appliance, he tries to buy one with a certificate saying that it was produced before the fifteenth of the month and not after the fifteenth. [Soviet goods carry tags with production dates.] If the item was made before the fifteenth, obviously it was not made in a rush and the customer thinks, 'maybe it will work.' If it was made after the fifteenth, there's a good chance it will stop working pretty quickly."

Other Russians with whom I talked were more flexible than Yosif who, as a technical man, may have had higher standards than most. They reckoned it was not too great a risk to buy something made as late as the twentieth. But no matter what the object, the candid advice of one middle-aged Moscow woman, echoed by others was: "Don't buy if it was made after the twentieth."

Her husband nodded in agreement and with a typical Russian laughter-   12
through-tears sense of humor launched into his favorite joke about storming. It concerned a hapless Soviet worker who died and found himself in purgatory confronted by an official who addressed him in the stilted, condescending rhetoric of Soviet bureaucrats: "According to your moral qualities, you will not be permitted to enter heaven. Your papers are not in good enough order to be accepted. You may only enter hell. My duty is to warn you that there are two sections of hell — capitalist hell and socialist hell. You have a choice."

The worker inquired about the difference.

"In the capitalist hell, they will drive a nail into your butt every day all month long," the official said curtly.

"And does the same thing go on in the socialist hell, too?"

"The socialist hell is different, comrade," the functionary advised.   16
"There, the Devil gets drunk a lot and there is a chronic shortage of nails."

"Well, in that case," said the newcomer, brightening, "I'll take the socialist hell."

"All right, that is your choice," the official acknowledged, "but it is my duty to warn you that all the same they'll drive those thirty nails into your butt in the last five days of the month."

That irreverent view of the workings of the Soviet economy has the kind of insight into Russian reality that prompted Dostoyevski to describe his native land as a sublime, universal, ordered chaos. It is a far cry, however, from the picture that Western visitors derive from officially guided tours through spruced-up Soviet industrial installations, from the image of technological prowess given by live television coverage of the Soviet *Soyuz* spacecraft docking with an American *Apollo*, or from the impression projected to the world at large by the Kremlin's perennial boasting about overfulfilling its Five-Year Plans. . . .

The mechanistic Soviet Economic Plan seems to cut against the grain   20
of Russian nature. In the world at large, Russians have a reputation for discipline because of their seemingly docile obedience to authority. But this is a discipline imposed from outside. Left to their own devices, Russians are generally an easygoing, disorderly, pleasantly disorganized, and not very efficient people. (Significantly, the Russian language had

no word for efficiency and had to borrow one from English.) The typical Soviet office, often unseen by foreign visitors, is a supercrowded, disorderly muddle with a little propaganda corner and not enough desks to go around for everyone, I was told by Moscow friends. Factories through which I was taken were usually neat, though I was struck by the terrible din of machinery and by how few industrial safety signs there were. But Soviet friends insisted these were *pokazukha* factories, spruced up for show, and that the run-of-the-mill Soviet factory was "a bordello," as more than one put it.

Moreover, the foreigner can tour plenty of installations and stare at machinery without learning about "storming" or understanding that the Russian sense of time is at once enchantingly and frustratingly loose or nonexistent. It bears little relation to time in a commercial society. Most tourists learn to their consternation that just ordering dinner in a restaurant can require an hour or more. A one-hour press conference begins nearly an hour late and runs for two more; a short answer can take forty-five minutes; a ten-minute drop-in with friends invariably stretches to three or four hours; staying late, until 2:00 or 3:00 A.M., is one of the more attractive Russian vices; a week's job takes three weeks; elevators break down and stay out of order for a fortnight or more; other repair work consumes unpredictable gobs of time; construction timetables nationwide run years behind. Russians are genuinely put off by the impatience of Westerners, especially Americans, who go up the wall with frustration at the dawdling uncertainties of Russian life. The innocent Western visitor, assuming that the Soviet Union is an advanced society, is often bruised when he first bumps against the essentially underdeveloped tempo of most Soviet commerce. It takes a while to learn that *skoro budet*, literally, "It'll be here soon," is really *mañana*[1] stretched to eternity. For procrastination is built into the Russian temperament. Perhaps that's the main reason for constant propaganda hounding Russians to finish the Plan on time.

Although Russians are capable of great exertion if pressed to produce, sustained hard work is not a national characteristic. They do not have the work ethic of Americans, Germans, or Japanese. "Americans work hard, put in long hours, get ahead, and also get ulcers," was the comment of a Soviet editor who admitted that he rarely strained on his job. "Russians don't work very hard or try very hard. And we live more relaxed

---

[1]Spanish for "tomorrow." — Ed.

lives." A schoolteacher told Ann that she considered her job the best part of her life "because no one pushes me there." Martic Martentz, an Armenian-American Communist who voluntarily returned from New York to try living in the Soviet Union, told me he was astonished at the Soviet image of Americans. "They think everyone [in America] is rich," he gasped. "They don't realize how hard people have to work in America."

A movie script writer suggested that one reason many Russians don't work harder is that generally it doesn't pay enough. If one doctor in a polyclinic gets a reputation for good, conscientious work, she winds up with extra patients and a lot of overtime work but she cannot be paid for overtime, the writer said, whereas those who get ahead are usually doctors who speak up in Party meetings and curry favor with Party officials. Another reason, Russian friends reminded me, is that the Soviet Union is still not as money oriented as Western societies. "Money alone is not enough, you have to have something to spend it on," remarked a young scientist. "Connections matter more than money. With connections you can find the deficit goods and spend the money. Without them, it's not worth the effort."

Playing hooky from work is a national pastime so common that Arkady 　24 Raikin, the comedian, has gotten censors to approve several skits on that theme. In one, he plays an engineer who lolls all day on a bed the size of a putting green and rationalizes skipping work by recalling how little he does on the job. "I'm doing them a favor by staying away," he quips. In another, three men sneak out during working hours to the barbershop but get lousy service because the barbers themselves are trying to sneak away. One barber wants to buy oranges, another, to get some gadget repaired, and the third, to visit the dentist. The barbers return defeated, only to discover that the grocer, repairman, and dentist are the three customers sitting in their chairs. "That's just what happens," a Russian confessed to me during intermission. "My wife goes out shopping during working hours. It's the only way, because after work the crowds in the stores and the lines are simply terrible. Everybody does it." A linguist told me her friends would duck out of work just to pay social calls or see a movie.

If part-time hooky is a pervasive problem among white-collar workers, full-scale absenteeism among blue-collar workers reaches such disaster proportions, especially around paydays, that the Kremlin leadership and Soviet press periodically inveigh against "slackers" and "bad labor discipline." The Moscow manager for a Western airline told me his Soviet ground crews were so unreliable that his Western technical chief had to check personally that fuel was available, ground service ready, and deicing and other equipment prepared for their incoming flights. On the days that their planes came in, the technical chief would pick up his Soviet mechanics and workmen at home to insure they would be on the job.

Soviet managers have a great deal of trouble disciplining factory workers not only because it is almost impossible to fire them but also because labor is generally short and a disgruntled worker knows he can quit and find another job easily. Theoretically, Soviet Marxism holds that workers are not alienated under socialism because they enjoy the full fruits of their labor, and Soviet propagandists seek to maintain this fiction. But occasional sociological studies and press items revealing that 2.8 million workers changed jobs in the Russian Republic alone in 1973 undercut that contention. Poor working conditions and lack of side benefits, such as housing, rather than pay are cited by workers as reasons for dissatisfaction. . . .

In an effort to increase output the Communist Party resorts to various moral inducements, from special awards to model workers, to "socialist competition" between work brigades or factories, to the perennial technique of "socialist obligations." Before every great holiday, work collectives across the country take upon themselves obligations to exceed their work norms. They solemnly pledge to implement Party decisions, to "increase their ideological level," and to raise their output. Steel mills promise to roll out 110 percent of their quota of steel, candy factories vow to produce a year's output of sweets in just eleven months, and libraries take an oath to insure that an unprecedented number of books by or about Lenin will be read in the next three months.

Another favorite gimmick of Soviet propagandists is the *vstrechny plan*, 28 literally, the Counter Plan, or the Plan the workers themselves put forward to meet, match, and exceed the official Plan fixed for them. Theoretically, it is spontaneously offered. But the entire ritual is widely viewed as such cynical humbug that factory workers have contrived their own raunchy put-down of the *vstrechny plan*. According to this joke, a factory worker arrives home late one evening and to protect himself from his wife's scolding, he explains that he was delayed by a long factory meeting on the *vstrechny plan*.

"What is this *vstrechny plan*?" asks his skeptical spouse.

"Well," he says, "it's as if I proposed that we screw twice tonight and you come back and propose we screw three times when both of us know damned well we couldn't do it more than once."

The two young Russians who told me this joke as we walked along a

Moscow boulevard broke into loud guffaws and were disappointed that I was not similarly moved by their earthy humor. "At least you get the idea about the *vstrechny plan*?" one asked. I nodded.

EXPLORATIONS

1. What is storming, and when does it occur? According to Smith, what happens at a Soviet factory during each decade of the month?

2. What aspects of the Russian temperament does Smith believe help to explain workers' and consumers' acceptance of storming? What evidence does he give to support his theories, and how convincing is it?

3. At two points in *"Skoro Budet — It'll Be Here Soon,"* Smith gives examples of Russian humor. What effect do these jokes have on the essay's interest level? What facts does each joke enable Smith to introduce or emphasize about Russian workers?

CONNECTIONS

1. Judging from Smith's description, what is the top-priority goal of Soviet factories? Judging from Satoshi Kamata's "Six Months at Toyota," what is the top-priority goal of Japanese factories? What secondary goals does each management group consider important and not so important?

2. Smith and Shiva Naipaul are both foreigners in the countries they are writing about. How are their journalistic goals similar and different? What types of source does each author use to give his report the weight of inside information?

3. How do the Russians in *"Skoro Budet — It'll Be Here Soon"* describe American attitudes toward work? How do you think Bill Talcott in Studs Terkel's *Observation* would agree and disagree? What does Smith see as the main contrasts in attitude between American and Soviet workers? Do you think Talcott would agree? Why or why not?

ELABORATIONS

1. The current Soviet leadership, headed by Mikhail Gorbachev, has begun taking steps to raise the quality of Soviet-produced goods within the Communist framework. Based on *"Skoro Budet — It'll Be Here Soon,"* what do you think are the main problems Gorbachev's administration will have to

address? From your other reading in Part Four, Working, and from your own experience, what changes would you recommend in the way Soviet factories and workers are currently managed? Write an essay proposing your suggestions.

2. "Theoretically, Soviet Marxism holds that workers are not alienated under socialism because they enjoy the full fruits of their labor," writes Smith. Theoretically, why does our American capitalist system claim to be the best one for workers? Using *"Skoro Budet* — It'll Be Here Soon," Kamata's "Six Months at Toyota," and the *Observations* on pages 305–312 as sources, write an essay discussing the practical problems that get in the way of both the Communist and the capitalist ideals.

JILL GAY

Patriotic Prostitutes

Jill Gay was born in New York in 1951 but grew up in Venezuela and Spain. She now lives in Maryland, near Washington, D.C., where she is a consultant at the Institute of Medicine at the National Academy of Sciences. She also serves on the board of the Third World Women's Project at the Institute for Policy Studies. Gay spent 1971 in Israel, studied in Peru in 1972, graduated from Barnard College, and received her master's degree in international affairs from Columbia University in 1978. She has traveled through Western Europe, Latin America, Japan, and South Korea. The author of more than a dozen articles for various magazines, she has also coedited a book on Third World women. "Patriotic Prostitutes" is excerpted from an article that appeared in *The Progressive* (Feb. 1985).

Gay quotes *World View 1984*: "Between 70 and 80 percent of male tourists who travel from Japan, the United States, Australia, and Western Europe to Asia do so solely for the purpose of sexual entertainment." Of the roughly two dozen Asian countries, she focuses on three as providers of sex for hire: Thailand, South Korea, and the Philippines. All three are ancient nations with distinct ethnic and cultural heritages, altered dramatically by contact with the West.

Thailand lies between Burma and Laos on a peninsula across the Bay of Bengal from India. Inhabited for the last 20,000 years, it is the only Southeast Asian country never to have been taken over by a European power. King Mongkut and his son Chulalongkorn, who reigned from 1851 to 1910, modernized Thailand (then Siam); signed trade treaties with both Britain and France; ceded Laos and Cambodia to France; and hired the English teacher Anna Leonowens, from whose memoirs came *The King and I*. A coup in 1932 limited the monarchy and let in military control, which has persisted off and on to the present. Disrupted by Japanese occupation in World War II, surrounded by conflict in Vietnam, Laos, and Cambodia, inundated with foreign soldiers and refugees, Thailand has undergone more than two dozen coups in half a century.

Farther east is the Philippines, a republic of more than 7000 islands extending northward from Malaysia and Indonesia off the coast of Vietnam. After Ferdinand Magellan brought the Philippines to Europe's attention in 1521, Spain took control of the archipelago, forcing a mass conversion to Roman Catholicism. Following the Spanish-American War of 1898, Spain ceded the islands to the United States, which proclaimed

their independence on July 4, 1946. The present government is modeled
on that of the United States; English as well as Pilipino is an official
language. From 1965 to 1986 (and at the time this article first appeared)
the Philippine president was Ferdinand Marcos, whose dictatorial regime
had U.S. support until the assassination of opposition leader Benigno
Aquino swept Aquino's widow, Corazón, into office (see "The Philippine
Election," p. 422.)

Due north of the Philippines is Korea, a peninsula jutting southward
from China toward Japan. Annexed by Japan in 1910, Korea was divided
after World War II into the northern, Soviet-controlled Democratic People's Republic of Korea and the southern, U.S.-controlled Republic of
Korea. Although both powers soon withdrew, efforts at reunification
failed. In 1950 North Korean troops invaded the South, pitting their
Chinese backers against United Nations troops (mostly from the United
States) who supported South Korea. The Korean War ended with an
armistice in 1953. Currently two-thirds of the population lives in South
Korea, which has been tightly controlled by its presidents since the
republic was established in 1948.

Germany's Rosie Travel sells sex tours to Thailand. "Anything goes in
this exotic country," says the company's brochure. "Especially when it
comes to girls. Still, it appears to be a problem for visitors to Thailand
to find the right places where they can indulge in unknown pleasures.
. . . Rosie has done something about this. . . . You can book a trip to
Thailand with erotic pleasures included in the price."

Japan Air Lines (JAL) is a little more subtle. "In order to embellish
and relish better the nights of Korea," its brochure advises, "you must
start above all else with a Kisaeng party." In South Korea, Kisaeng women
were traditionally hired to sing and dance at parties; today, however, the
word is synonymous with prostitute. "A night spent with a consummate
Kisaeng girl dressed in a gorgeous Korean blouse and skirt is just perfect,"
continues the JAL pamphlet. Kisaeng parties, it adds, have "become one
of the nation's most charming attractions."

"I felt I was picking out a slave girl at a slave market," says one
Japanese tourist about his visit to Korea.

The international sex trade has reached shocking proportions. Between   4
70 and 80 percent of male tourists who travel from Japan, the United
States, Australia, and Western Europe to Asia do so solely for the purpose
of sexual entertainment, according to *World View 1984*, a French political almanac. The Thai police estimated in 1982 that there were 700,000

prostitutes in the country — about 10 percent of all Thai women between the ages of fifteen and thirty. A 1982 International Labor Organization (ILO) study found some 500,000 prostitutes in Bangkok alone. In the Philippines, an estimated 200,000 prostitutes operate; in South Korea, 260,000.

But far from being alarmed by these figures, leaders of the affected countries are spurring the trade along. "Within the next two years, we are going to need money," said Thailand's vice premier, talking to a meeting of provincial governors in 1980. "Therefore, I ask of all governors to consider the natural scenery in your provinces, together with some forms of entertainment that some of you might consider disgusting and shameful because they are forms of sexual entertainment that attract tourists.

"Such forms of entertainment should not be prohibited . . . because you are morally fastidious. . . . We must do this because we have to consider the jobs that will be created for the people."

In South Korea, the government sponsors an "orientation program" where prostitutes are issued identification cards that serve as hotel passes.

"You girls must take pride in your devotion to your country," the 8 women are told at the orientation sessions. "Your carnal conversations with foreign tourists do not prostitute either yourself or the nation, but express your heroic patriotism."

Though prostitution is called the world's oldest profession, the boom in Southeast Asia started with the U.S. presence in Vietnam. There were 20,000 prostitutes in Thailand in 1957; by 1964, after the United States established seven bases in the country, that number had skyrocketed to 400,000. Throughout the war, Bangkok was a favorite "rest-and-recreation" (R&R) spot for GIs. Similarly, the number of R&R centers in the Philippines increased from 20 to 600. And in South Vietnam itself, there were about 400,000 prostitutes at the height of the war — almost one for every GI.

"Saigon has become an American brothel," Senator J. William Fulbright notes. And the South Vietnamese government didn't seem to mind. "The Americans need girls; we need dollars," one official said. "Why should we refrain from the exchange? It's an inexhaustible source of U.S. dollars for the State."

When the American soldiers left in the mid-1970s, "the post-Vietnam slack was picked up by tourism," says an activist with Friends of Women, an organization based in Bangkok. The area around the U.S. military base at Subic Bay and the R&R center in Olongapo — both in the

Philippines — are the largest bases for prostitution in Asia. But something more than the presence of soldiers accounts for the flourishing business.

"Sex tourism in the Philippines really took off during the period after   12
1972 when martial law was declared, and the government gave priority to export promotion," says Irene Santiago, a Filipina community organizer. "We needed a lot of dollars in order to pay off the foreign debt, so tourism was a major thrust for dollar earning. And with that, came the sex tourists — mainly from Japan." Currently, as the economy of the Philippines deteriorates, "the government feels there is a more urgent need to earn foreign exchange," adds Santiago, "so there's been a proliferation of prostitutes now."

The Manila Midtown Ramada Inn hands out a printed sheet "to our Japanese guests with ladies" that lists the charges for taking a woman to a room. One source reported in 1979 that the Manila Ramada made 40 percent of its income from extra fees for prostitutes.

In South Korea, massive investments have been made in resort areas for the sex trade, and the government is counting on billions of dollars in tourism revenues to help cover a foreign debt that exceeds $20 billion.

The sex trade has also figured in Thailand's economic development strategy, which calls for reducing investment in agriculture and aggressively pushing the export of goods produced in the cities. In a typical village in the north, as many as one-third of the families have no land, and three-quarters have less than the two acres needed for subsistence. Many send their daughters to Bangkok to work as prostitutes.

And some women opt for the profession because they don't care to   16
work in the hazardous export-oriented plants. "You get cancer working in factories, we get abortion and VD working as prostitutes," one woman says. Prostitution now vies with sugar as Thailand's second largest producer of foreign exchange.

Taew grew up as one of eight children in northern Thailand. Her two elder sisters worked as prostitutes to American GIs at the base at Udon. When the U.S. Air Force left in 1975, her sisters came back to farm the land. But the soil was too poor to support them, so they went back to work as prostitutes in the cities. Then they got married, and the family lost its major source of income.

So Taew was sent to Bangkok to find work. She made $1.50 a day mixing cement and steel, then $20 a month as a housemaid. Later she tried waitressing. Still struggling, she was finally persuaded to sell her virginity for $400, of which she received $100. Taew sent her earnings home so her family could build a well for drinking water.

After her parents kept writing letters asking for more money, Taew went back to work as a prostitute, frequenting the Grace Hotel.

The Grace Hotel does not employ prostitutes, but it makes its coffee   20
shop available as a marketplace. The owner charges an entrance fee of $2. Women who come to the Grace Hotel are usually on the way down in the market. They are not so attractive, having lost the sweet and innocent look, and are heavily made up. Men who come to the Grace Hotel are searching for specific styles of sex that they have difficulty finding elsewhere. They bargain. In the lounge of the hotel, men in their sixties can be seen propositioning girls in their teens.

Taew's story is not an aberration. Indeed, the ILO study found that of fifty prostitutes interviewed, all but four mail money home. Most sent one-third to one-half of their earnings, sums essential to their rural families' survival.

Pasuk Phongpaichit, author of the ILO study, says she first met a woman named Lek in a so-called massage parlor, which was actually a brothel. "She still had the look of a little girl, and her figure was not fully developed," recalls Phongpaichit. "When asked if she liked the job, she said she did not. She would like to go home."

But she couldn't go home. Lek's employer had lent her parents some money; it was up to Lek to work for the employer as repayment for the loan. She figured she would have to work 150 hours more, but then her parents took out another loan to pay for her grandparents' medical bills. Lek was their only source of income.

Many times, the prostitutes' earnings are meager. Airlines, travel agen-   24
cies, hotels, madams, pimps — all take a chunk of the prostitutes' earnings. Korea Church Women United estimates that prostitutes receive less than one-thirtieth of the fees their patrons pay.

But the hazards of the business are borne by the prostitutes alone. "After having my body ravaged by several customers in a row, I just get too tired to move my limbs," one prostitute says. "At times like this, a shot of heroin is needed. This enables me to handle five or six men in a single night. I can't help but take the drug in order to keep myself in working condition."

The United Nations Fund for Population Activities disclosed that out of 1000 prostitutes studied in Thailand, one-quarter were regular users of drugs, particularly speed, barbiturates, and heroin; 41 percent of the prostitutes had venereal disease, and 19 percent had undergone abortions, which are prohibited by law in Thailand (and therefore often hazardous).

Suicides are not uncommon. One woman killed herself after observing her own naked body in a mirror. It was covered with scars inflicted by a man who used lit cigarettes. Another woman, as recounted in a Korean newspaper story a few years ago, tried unsuccessfully to escape, but failed.

"At one o'clock every night, a guard locked the door of my room and   28 took away the key," the woman said. "In the daytime, a receptionist kept a constant watch over the entrance. Since all ground-floor windows were covered with iron grids, it was impossible to think of escaping through them. Even when I went to the bathhouse, someone was sent along to guard me." So she jumped out of a second-story window — and now is paralyzed from the waist down.

Women's groups around the world have begun to mobilize against the international big business of prostitution. In 1982, Dutch women held a protest at the Amsterdam airport near a departing plane to Bangkok, dubbed the "gonorrhea express." When the jet landed in Bangkok, it was greeted by another demonstration, held by Friends of Women and other Thai feminists.

In the Philippines as well, women have protested the sex trade. When then–Prime Minister Zenko Suzuki of Japan visited the Philippines in 1981, "the Japanese women's groups were able to link up with Philippine women's groups," recalls Irene Santiago. The protest was coordinated by the Filipina Organization, Third World Movement Against the Exploitation of Women, and it "really embarrassed the Prime Minister on his state visit," Santiago says. "They presented him with a letter of protest saying that this is a shame on the Japanese people, and that he should put a stop to the whole thing. That really got the attention of the press. And it actually stopped Japanese sex tours for a while."

Currently, the Catholic Women's League, other church groups, and even the mayor have been holding rallies against sex tourism in the Philippines town of Sebu, a new center of the trade.

Such demonstrations are essential if the sex trade is to come to a halt.   32 But they are not likely to succeed unless there are more profound changes, both in the presence of the U.S. military and in the export-oriented development strategies of Asian countries that depend on foreign exchange — at the expense of their most impoverished women.

EXPLORATIONS

1. According to Gay, why do so many Asian women become prostitutes? What positive and negative factors keep women in the job once they start it?
2. What are the reasons for a government to encourage prostitution? How do the countries involved benefit from the sex trade? What reasons exist for these countries to discourage prostitution?
3. In countries that promote prostitution, how does the government encourage women to participate? In what ways do you think the government's encouragement helps to maintain the supply of prostitutes?

CONNECTIONS

1. How is the situation of the prostitutes described by Gay similar to that of the factory workers described by Hedrick Smith and Satoshi Kamata? What attitudes by government, and toward government, are noted by both Gay and Smith? What causes for despair among workers are cited by both Gay and Kamata?
2. In Shiva Naipaul's "The Palmers," Mrs. Palmer says of the local workers: "Many actually prefer to be beggars and prostitutes in Nairobi than to earn an honest living from the soil." After reading "Patriotic Prostitutes," how do you think Gay would answer Mrs. Palmer?
3. Look back at two or more of the following pieces: Sri Delima's "Black-and-White Amah" (p. 9), John David Morley's "Acquiring a Japanese Family" (p. 36), Ved Mehta's "Pom's Engagement" (p. 162), and David Plath's "Tomoko on Her Television Career." (You may also want to refer to Isak Dinesen's "From 'Daguerreotypes,'" p. 204.) In the Asian cultures you have read about, what qualities are highly valued in women? In what ways do the governmental attitudes toward prostitution described by Gay reflect a traditional view of women's role in society? In what ways are these governmental attitudes aimed at overcoming traditional Asian views of women?

ELABORATIONS

1. After seeing *Jaws*, in which a shark terrorizes a New England seaside town, Cuba's Premier Fidel Castro is said to have applauded the film's splendid socialist message: The town officials' refusal to close their beaches (said Castro) show that capitalists value a chance to make money more than human life and safety. How do you think Castro — an advocate of women's rights — would evaluate the Asian sex trade? Write an essay criticizing prostitution in Asia from a socialist's point of view. Or write an essay from a capitalist's point of view rebutting the socialist argument.

2. In his *Observation*, Elliot Liebow writes about unskilled workers and their middle-class critics. How does Liebow's analysis apply to the women in "Patriotic Prostitutes"? What problems do these women share with Fadik in Yashar Kemal's "A Dirty Story" (p. 279)? Write an essay on the clash between morality and practicality for people at the bottom of the economic ladder: What can and should they do for themselves? What can and should others (such as the government and private employers) do to help, deter, or punish them?

THELMA FORSHAW

The Demo

Thelma Forshaw was born in Sydney, Australia's largest city, in 1923. She began writing at the age of ten; at eleven she became editor of the children's page of the local newspaper. At eighteen she published her first short story and joined the Women's Auxiliary Australian Air Force which she left a year later because of a nervous breakdown: "Regimental life did not suit me." Forshaw worked as a private secretary during and after World War II and later became a publicity writer at the advertising firm of J. Walter Thompson. She married George Korting, a Viennese refugee, in 1948; they have a son and a daughter. Forshaw has published many short stories in the press, in literary magazines such as *Meanjin, Overland, Southerly,* and *Quadrant,* and in foreign countries including Denmark, Hungary, England, China, and the United States. Some of her stories — including "The Demo" — were collected in the 1967 book *An Affair of Clowns.* Since 1962 Forshaw has been a book reviewer for three leading Australian newspapers and a columnist for *The Australian.* She currently writes a column for *Quadrant* and is working on a radio play and a new short story.

Australia, with an area of almost 3 million square miles, is the world's smallest continent and sixth largest country. It lies south of Indonesia (and Vietnam), across the Indian Ocean from southern Africa, and across the Pacific from South America. The native Aborigines may have migrated there from Southeast Asia as long as 40,000 years ago. By 1770, when Captain James Cook claimed Australia for Britain, the Aborigines numbered around 300,000. The British settled their new domain with shiploads of transported convicts. Gold and copper were discovered, and sheep ranches were established, spurring economic growth but displacing the Aborigines. Australia became a commonwealth in 1901 and gained full independence in 1975. Since World War II its ties with Britain have weakened in favor of the United States. Australian troops joined Americans in the Vietnam War (1965–1971), fighting on the side of non-Communist South Vietnam along with Air Vice-Marshal Ky — the target of the demonstration, or "demo," in Forshaw's story.

The morning of the demonstration nobody could be bothered with the Odd Bod who came into the milk bar the moment it opened at seven o'clock and asked did they sell French letters.[1] He was always asking — could they sell him a comb, postage stamps, rosary beads, porridge — everything, in fact, which a milk bar did not stock.

Mr. Hele Ganor, half wild with nervousness, could not face the regular encounter with the Odd Bod, when he would utter his usual protesting howl: "You're in the way! You've been sittink there for hours!" or "If you don't want to buy anythink — buzz off! Buzz off!"

These peremptory outbursts unleashed Mr. Ganor's accent at full blast, and the overlay of Australian idiom built up over twenty years cracked and was swallowed up in a veritable eruption of foreignness. He turned now, gnashing, on the Odd Bod.

"I have no time! I have worries! Why must you come today? You   4
must wait till the chemist opens for your bloody French letters. What you think I am, eh? A bloody peddler, maybe. Buzz off! Buzz off!"

The Odd Bod, his youthful face emaciated and unshaven, slunk into a chair at one of the tables and ordered tea and toast.

"Too early! Too early!" Mr. Ganor cried hoarsely. "The girls have not come yet. No tea and toasts. I have my hands full and today a demo. Maybe my shop will be smashed. How do I know? I have worries and you come here and make me mad, mad!" He struck his own brow with a clenched fist, since he could not strike the Odd Bod.

"A milk shake, then," said the Odd Bod immovably. He had a penchant for Mr. Ganor's milk bar and came there almost daily with his irrelevant requests — perhaps conversation starters, for when refused these absurd things he made no attempt to find them elsewhere. Mostly he sat for hours, watching people coming and going, making an occasional abortive attempt to chat with the staff, lapsing into silence, but in some way comforted by the atmosphere of burring milk shake mixers, the clash of the till, the laughter and chiacking of the girls behind the counter.

He had been a divinity student who had suffered a nervous breakdown,   8
and only five weeks ago two passing strangers had prevented him from leaping off the Harbour Bridge. Mr. Ganor viewed him with distaste and uncomprehension, but could find no way to banish him from his shop, short of calling his darlings the police and charging the Odd Bod with vagrancy or loitering. That, however, he stopped short of.

As the girls arrived, Mr. Ganor flew at them gabbling: "The demo,

---

[1]Condoms. — ED.

the demo! My Christ, what a terrible thing! Twenty years in Australia and now this. We're not safe any more. Give them what they want. Don't argue. We want no donnybrook. Jesus, my shop! What if they smash my shop!"

May yawned. "Oh boy, talk about a heavy night at the South Sydney Leagues — we hit a jackpot and then it was on! Let me take you one night Mr. Gay. Hell, don't tell me the Odd Bod's turned up already."

Cheryl tied her pink overall sullenly, "I should be studying this morning, instead of coming here to help you out." She was a veterinary science student.

Mr. Ganor could not make his girls understand. They were completely unperturbed by the demonstration which was to take place just down the street from his shop when Air Vice-Marshal Ky of Vietnam arrived at Admiralty House. They grumbled only at the prospect of the heavy work. They did not understand Mr. Ganor's conflicting terror and exhilaration. Nor did they believe in violence as Mr. Ganor believed in it. He remembered election days in his native European city, the killings, the armed police; above all he remembered the Second World War when Hitler's gangs roamed the streets, enforcing, terrorizing. Today he was filled with both elation and fear. Elation because of the prospect of big takings for his milk bar — and fear of riots in which maybe his car would be overturned, bottles broken, and biscuits stolen from the display stand near the door.

For twenty years he had lived in Australia and found them a quiet if skeptical and sardonic people. They were not the demo type. Hadn't he seen them laughing and ridiculing the rebels and rabble-rousers who shouted their views in the Sydney Domain on Sundays? He could not believe in an Australia seething with protest and violence. Twenty years and now a demo on the very doorstep of his milk bar. His heart beat hard with apprehension and dread, then skipped with hope, his sallow face strained, tensely lined as if he were enduring great inner pressures.

Mr. Ganor's business both masked and compensated what would have been loneliness, a lack of social ease as a foreigner, and every kind of personal failure, for he was either suspicious or envious of his own countrymen and avoided them. The shop flowed into all his voids and filled them. He was full of love for the money it brought him, he had the girls and the customers as company without need of the graces and social techniques he lacked. The shop *was* Mr. Ganor. Like an artist he made it, and like the artist's work it made him.

Therefore any threat to it endangered not merely glass and chromium and money, but a solid edifice which had become himself. Strip the shop from Mr. Ganor and there would have been left a naked, empty, lonely, and loveless exile. The shop protected Mr. Ganor from the modern malady of alienation. In his shop he was marvelously in touch with life. He knew nothing of alienation. At the first chill breath, instinct had swiftly created a protective carapace, and it was for this carapace he feared.

And so today was not a day like any other when he cuffed the heads   16
of rowdy schoolboys, or cursed the Odd Bod for "smelling up" his shop with fish and chips. Today he could not sing with passionate fervor:

> *Pale hands I loved beside the Shalimar-ar,*
> *Where are you now, who lies beneath your spell?*
> *I would have ra-ather felt them round my thro-oat*
> *Crrrrrushing out life than waving me farewe-ell,*
> *Crrrrrushing out li-i-i-i-fe than waving me-ee farewe-e-ell.*

It was unnerving to hear Mr. Ganor bellowing out "Pale Hands I Loved" while he shook all over. May said it was the hands pushing money across the counter that *he* loved — never mind about beside the Shalimar. Bloody money-grubber.

The song could never have referred to Mr. Ganor's ex-wife whose hands had been blotched by hard work and who, on no account, however romantic, would he have suffered to strangle him rather than depart. He had in fact accepted her farewell with relief rather than regret. She had found a less obsessed man with time for her kind of love. Mr. Ganor sang with frightening intensity, and confounded those who speculated on his sexual proclivities by preferring the song to a mistress's obstructing reality. We all have some unlived life in us, and so we sing, or recite, or savagely dream. Mr. Ganor sang his unrealizable romance. But not today.

His pallor, the lines of suffering in his face were a source of amusement to the girls, who had never experienced, never ever thought about, nor some so much as read of the outbreaks of violence in other countries. They viewed the demo with amusement and the demonstrators were dismissed as "a pack of nuts." Even the patrolling police, though disgruntled at being deprived of their weekend leave, wore deprecating grins, and were lavish with winks.

As the time of the demonstration approached, Mr. Ganor ran down   20
the street to see if he could assess the situation and found the way lined with an unprecedented number of police — "Just like a foreign country,"

he said with agitation. He seriously thought of shutting the shop — an unheard-of procedure, for Mr. Ganor's shop was open all the year round, every day of the week, including Good Friday and Christmas Day. He was torn in two. He suffered all the torments of the schizoid — his heart bounding with exultation at the prospect of a good day, yet unable to shake off a sense of terror and foreboding. He wrestled with himself . . . and wrestled. In the end . . . He would stay open.

Courage is as relative as anything else. For Mr. Ganor to keep the shop open in the face of possible rioting by the demonstrators was an act of courage. That his motive was greed for extra profits and that this motive proved stronger than his terror did not make his stand less courageous. He would risk life and limb by keeping his shop open in the face of what he saw as the onslaught of ravening hordes who would either make or break him.

As he saw the crowds passing on their way to watch the demonstration or join it, Mr. Ganor's bowels moved frequently and ever and anon as he fled, his anguished cry: "May, watch the shop — I must *go*!" became the object of indelicate jokes between the girls.

"He's got the runs because of the demo," May jeered, then, wheeling swiftly, in a lilting voice: "Yes, sir, what can I get you?" as a customer breasted the counter.

In his extremity — perhaps inspired by his own discomfort — Mr.   24
Ganor had an hysterical vision in which he saw the demonstrators effectively deactivated. He tested this vision on his girls. "I tell you what I do — I go to the chemist and buy cascara and put it in their drinks when they come here — ha, ha, you laugh, eh? — Good idea? Then they think of nothing but shitting."

The girls doubled up with laughter, catching underlips between their teeth as a sketchy gesture of modesty, for Mr. Ganor always used the crudest words in English with the abandon of one who does not fully feel their impact in the adopted language.

Outside, shouts and chanting had begun and grew stronger and more impassioned, indicating that the Vietnamese Premier had arrived. Peering from the doorway, Mr. Ganor saw at the bottom of the street hundreds of people surging forward against the linked hands of the police. The fire brigade stood by with hoses at the ready. He withdrew, trembling. Just like a foreign country. What was happening to his haven, quiet Australia? When would it be guns instead of fire hoses?

Standing like a sentinel behind his counter, brave as could be, he served the numerous people who strayed in off the streets, many of whom he knew, who grinned and winked and referred to the demonstrators as a "bunch of fanatics" or a "pack of crackpots," and he felt comforted by these Australians who had not changed.

He dreaded the mood of the demonstrators if the police thwarted their will to protest. He understood perfectly well the expression "pecking order." He had been a victim of it often enough. Frustrates, foiled of their original target, who came into the milk bar and made trouble, abusing and threatening him, calling him a "wog," "a dago," "a bloody foreigner." Yes, he knew all about pecking order. And he had a Caesar's enthusiasm for festivals, carnivals, and fêtes of all kinds — a Caesar's shrewd dread of the people's mood and a desire to see it deflected into pleasurable activities. He would have approved of the arenas of ancient Rome. He wanted to get on with what he was doing and not be troubled by the fury of a populace desperate for emotional outlets. Mr. Ganor was neither a Freudian nor a politician but, as a dedicated shopkeeper — a man, therefore, with a purpose — he dreaded everything that conflicted with his purpose: to be left to make money in peace.

The Odd Bod, who had been meditating ever since his thwarted attempt to leap from the Harbour Bridge, chose this moment, while the roaring and chanting of the demonstrators rose like a wild surf outside, to communicate the result of his meditations. He stood up and said quietly and firmly: "The Hound of Heaven is on my trail. He wants me."

"Yeah, and He's about all that *does* want you." May grinned, as she wiped his table. "Look, love, clear out, will yuh — you're gonna be in the way."

Several customers stared and smiled and turned back to their drinks. The poor crazy nut.

The Odd Bod approached Mr. Ganor confidently. "You have read, of course, "The Hound of Heaven" by Francis Thompson," he asked, surely not unreasonably.

Mr. Ganor did not look at him blankly, because you only look at people blankly when you wish you knew what on earth they meant. Mr. Ganor did not give a rap for anything he did not know. Frightened people can barely contend with what they already know. Any more may shake — even destroy — the crude or elaborate fortifications they erect to defend themselves. Mr. Ganor's identity was well sandbagged against mysticism.

"I have been waiting for grace," explained the ex-divinity student. What was so irrational about that?

"She is not here, so wait for her somewhere else," Mr. Ganor retorted, supremely unaware that he had been witty, even when a customer, standing near by, laughed aloud. Mr. Ganor had felt many things, but never embarrassment.

"You see, I have been fleeing the Hound of Heaven," the Odd Bod 36 pointed out. Mr. Ganor, who understood pecking order so well did not, however, disdain its practice himself.

"For Christ's sake," he cried with unwitting aptness, "go, go with your Hound of Heaven. You have bought nothing for two hours."

"He wants me," said the Odd Bod out of his obsessed dream, at the same time slapping down twenty cents for the chocolate bar which would buy him another two hours in Mr. Ganor's milk bar. He looked triumphant.

Mr. Ganor interpreted the triumph as directed towards himself and pushed away the twenty cents. "I sell you nothing. Buzz off. I will need all the tables when *they* come."

The Odd Bod knew a thing or two. "You can't refuse to sell me a bar 40 of chocolate."

In the end he got it and went back to his table.

And now they came — the demonstrators and their amused or sympathetic observers, streaming up the street, the sound of their voices, their footsteps, causing Mr. Ganor to flex and tremble. The demos, oh God, the demos. What would be their mood? If the police had suppressed them would they take it out on *him*? The window of the shop darkened as a mass of figures surged towards the milk bar doorway. Young men came carrying placards with the flaring legend KILLER KY looking, Mr. Ganor thought, themselves like killers. Numerous Save Our Sons ladies bustled in, taking over tables and chairs as if they owned the place, ordering tea and sandwiches. Mr. Ganor was offended by what he saw as high-handedness and aggression. They were only women. His voice hoarse and wavering he shouted, "No tea and sandwiches. Not enough staff." It was *his* shop and he would declare his rules if they killed him for it — these — these *untypical* Australians. He confronted the annoyed women, trembling, but with his sense of possession stiffening him to anger. They were only women.

Just then half a dozen huge policemen entered, towering over the heads of the crowd in the shop. An expression of deep content erased the lines of strain from Mr. Ganor's face. Here were his protectors against all unruliness and disorder. Lovingly, he cried, "Officers, what do you wish?"

"Can you do tea and sandwiches for six?" 44

"Certainly, officers, certainly."

Several demonstrators protested: "Thought you said the tea and sand-wiches were off."

"Yes — off. Off!" Mr. Ganor said with open hostility. Hadn't they scared the living daylights out of him?

"How come they're on for the coppers?"   48

Loudly Mr. Ganor said, "A very special favor for the officers."

"That's not fair!"

At that moment the demonstrators saw no difference at all between the police and themselves — only outside in the street earlier, chanting, and straining against the linked beefy hands. Inside Mr. Ganor's shop all men were equal. Not so. In Mr. Ganor's shop the police were more equal than others. The police who would protect his beloved property. No one could be *more* equal than the police. In a low caressing voice Mr. Ganor added: "It's on the house, officers."

When he refused tea and sandwiches to the demonstrators he was   52 punishing them for the terror they had aroused in him and at the same time literally curtsying to the police — as ostentatiously flattering as a mayor's wife greeting royalty. Had the police been more popular they could have afforded to despise Mr. Ganor's petty bribery — his effort to keep them in his shop as long as the demonstrators were still at large. But beggars can't be choosers and their smiles were gratified as trays of tea and sandwiches were borne under the very noses of the hungry demonstrators to the tables of the favored. What Mr. Ganor knew of men was what he knew of himself, which was, so to speak, brief and to the point. Quite a number of people had agreed to "play ball" with Mr. Ganor after a carton of cigarettes or a box of chocolates had been pressed into their hands. It was said he had a local M.P. on lay-by. Mr. Ganor, a foreigner and a charmless man, believed that people would do nothing for him out of sweet Christian charity. It was all very much a bargain-basement affair, a sort of minipolitics. The grand scale was not Mr. Ganor's. Free tea and sandwiches for the police would gain him what he wanted.

For a moment there was restiveness among the demonstrators; some stormed out, but the rest remained, discontentedly accepting the drinks and chocolate which was all Mr. Ganor vouchsafed them — so long as six policemen sat at his tables. Everyone clamored to be served and now they were served with a will.

Mixing drinks, selling bottles of cordial, slapping down cigarettes and sweets, running, bustling his girls, breathing fast as a lover, now Mr.

Ganor flew on the wings of delectable exertions, while the cash register chimed like a carillon. The shop seethed and swarmed as people came and went, or clustered together talking, groups surged in and struggled out pushing their way past the packed shoulders of others. The cash register chimed continually, Mr. Ganor whirled like a prima ballerina from customer to customer, while his girls flagged and began to complain of feet, varicose veins, headaches.

Eventually the tempo slowed, the shop began to empty. The police rose, winking here and there at those they knew, and departed with a now-we're-square nod to Mr. Ganor. The musical clamor of the cash register became no more than occasional hiccuping. The girls drew off their clammy overalls, eager to leave and soak their feet in a Radox or salt bath.

"Oh, Christ!" glowed Mr. Ganor with heartfelt religiosity. "What a bloody lovely day!" *His* feet might never have touched the cement floor.   56

Serious but exhilarated, lives bursting with meaning, the demonstrators trailed off home, and Mr. Ganor began to count the day's takings. The Odd Bod loped away, happily pursued by the Hounds of Heaven, telling it to himself:

> *Now of that long pursuit*
> *Comes on at hand the bruit,*
> *That voice is round me like a bursting sea . . .*
> something something something
> *Lo, all things fly thee, for thou fliest Me!*

. . . Oh, yes, God, oh, Yes!"

In the milk bar, Mr. Ganor indulged himself in a little well-earned passion as he wrapped his multitudinous coins for banking. His voice soared tremulous:

> *Pale hands I loved, beside the Shalimar-ar,*
> *Where are you now,*
> *Where are-are you no-o-owwwwwww?*

EXPLORATIONS

1. From what questions and challenges is Mr. Ganor shielded by his milk bar? What personal issues would he have to face if his "protective carapace" were removed? What would he stand to lose, and to gain?

2. To what extent do Mr. Ganor's eccentricities reflect his foreign background, and to what extent are they individual quirks? How would Mr. Ganor's character change if Forshaw had made him an Australian? if she had named his native country?

3. In what ways is the Odd Bod more of a foreigner than Mr. Ganor? What effect does this customer have on the relationships between Mr. Ganor and "his girls"? How would the story's impact change without the Odd Bod?

CONNECTIONS

1. In "Patriotic Prostitutes," Jill Gay writes about the pressures that encourage some women to become prostitutes. What differences between those women's situation and that of the girls in Mr. Ganor's milk bar do you think are responsible for their contrasting choice of jobs?

2. What similarities can you identify between Mr. Ganor's attitude toward his milk bar and the Palmers' attitude toward their tea plantation in Shiva Naipaul's "The Palmers"? What clues suggest that both Mr. Ganor and the Palmers have strong but mixed feelings about the people who work for them? What are these feelings, and what are their sources?

3. People in the United States like to think of our country as the land of opportunity. What statements and incidents in the *Observations*, pages 305–312, reflect this view? What statements and incidents in "The Demo" echo those in the *Observations*, suggesting that Australians (including Forshaw) regard their country as a land of opportunity?

ELABORATIONS

1. In "The Demo," Forshaw does not limit her viewpoint to one character; instead she shows us each character from the inside and out. How would the story's emphasis change if it were a first-person narrative by Mr. Ganor? May or Cheryl? the Odd Bod? one of the policemen who come in for tea and sandwiches? Choose two of these characters whose viewpoints contrast. Write a short first-person description through each one's eyes of the day of the demo.

2. Over and over in "The Demo," a potential clash between characters fails to materialize. How would the story's impact change if the Odd Bod had a second nervous breakdown in Mr. Ganor's milk bar? if Mr. Ganor tried to throw him out? if the demonstrators attacked the police? if they attacked Mr. Ganor (or his shop) for his refusal to feed them? Choose a plot twist that would transform "The Demo" into a story about a dramatic turning point in Mr. Ganor's life. Write a scene of at least one page depicting that dramatic moment. (You may want to refer to Part Two, Coming of Age, for ideas on how to handle your scene.)

PART FIVE

CITIZENS

*Government For and
Against the People*

OBSERVATIONS:
LOOKING AT OURSELVES

Frank Trippett, Vicki Williams, William Least Heat Moon,
John Kenneth Galbraith, Robert Nisbet, Annie Dillard

❖❖❖❖❖

David Lamb, *The New African Chiefs* (ZAIRE)

James Fenton, *The Philippine Election* (PHILIPPINES)

Julio Cortázar, *Regarding the Eradication of Crocodiles
from Auvergne* (FRANCE)

Germaine Greer, *In Cuba* (CUBA)

Liang Heng and Judith Shapiro, *Chairman Mao's
Good Little Boy* (CHINA)

Nadine Gordimer, *Africa Emergent* (SOUTH AFRICA)

Guzel Amalrik, *A Visit with Andrei at the Labor Camp*
(SOVIET UNION)

Janine Wedel, *Polish Line Committees* (POLAND)

Gabriel García Márquez, *Death Constant Beyond Love*
(COLOMBIA)

OUR SOCIETY, LIKE MOST OF THOSE WE DEAL WITH, ACCEPTS THE theory of the social contract: Members agree to collaborate for mutual protection and other benefits, ceding in return some personal freedom. We gain such advantages as security (provided by institutions including the military, the justice system, and health-care networks); the price we pay ranges from the literal cost of taxes to the threat of arrest if we violate the laws passed by our representatives. Many of us in the United States are typically unaware from day to day of the benefits and costs of our particular social contract. Yet nearly every aspect of our lives is affected by the democratic government our founders established.

Observations: Looking at Ourselves focus on some overt contracts between citizens and government in the United States. Frank Trippett comments on microphilia in state legislatures; Vicki Williams complains about representatives who put words into her mouth. William Least Heat Moon talks with blacks on Martin Luther King, Jr., Drive in Selma, Alabama. John Kenneth Galbraith warns of a switch in the relationship between our democracy and its military forces; Robert Nisbet casts the state as a predator on society. Annie Dillard relates a comic exchange between an American and a Chinese writer at Disneyland.

In Zaire and other postcolonial African nations, David Lamb reports an obsession with glory among "The New African Chiefs." James Fenton chronicles the surprise overthrow of glitzy President Ferdinand Marcos by People Power in "The Philippine Election." Argentine writer Julio Cortázar's "Regarding the Eradication of Crocodiles from Auvergne" pokes fun at bureaucrats in France and everywhere. An encouraging report on the Western Hemisphere's first Communist republic is Germaine Greer's "In Cuba." Chinese Communism receives a darker assessment from Liang Heng and Judith Shapiro, who describe Liang's shattered childhood in "Chairman Mao's Good Little Boy." Nadine Gordimer's short story "Africa Emergent" depicts the no-win situation created for both whites and blacks by apartheid in South Africa, where a man's honor is vindicated by his arrest. Guzel Amalrik describes a Soviet prison from the inside in "A Visit with Andrei at the Labor Camp." In Poland, Janine Wedel finds consumers responding creatively to state-created shortages with "Polish Line Committees." A close-up on a disillusioned South American legislator is offered by Gabriel García Márquez's "Death Constant Beyond Love," an ironic short story about one bleak stop on the campaign trail. ◈

OBSERVATIONS:
LOOKING AT OURSELVES

1

This is the homestretch of the silly season, when state legislatures across the land seem to vie for the imaginary Golden Nit. There is nothing imaginary, though, about the time, effort, and deliberation they customarily devote to the trivial, the insignificant, the utterly negligible. Nebraska's legislature, for example, has just dealt with a bill to add, as consumer representatives, two corpses to the state anatomical board: that passes for humor in Lincoln. Rhode Island's senators breezily adopted a resolution praising the hairdo of a female legislator, but the house turned aside a proposal to decree ricotta the State Cheese. In Florida, the legislature recently indulged in boisterous repartee over a measure that would have made it a crime to molest the "skunk ape," a mythical critter occasionally sighted around the state that is said to stand 7 feet tall, weigh 700 pounds, and smell like swamp gas.

This legislative preoccupation with the trivial, which is confirmed in almost every state capital, goes by the term *microphilia*. Though the ailment was named only a few years ago (by a justly obscure political diagnostician), it has been in evidence as long as state legislatures have existed — though sometimes upstaged by more dramatic defects such as procrastination, carelessness, and venality. These larger historic faults were undoubtedly in the mind of John Burns when he wrote in *The Sometime Governments* (1970): "We expect very little of our legislatures, and they continually live up to our expectations." In fact, many state legislatures have improved in some respects over the past two decades, attracting members of higher caliber, for example, and tightening up their staffs and internal organization. But their fascination with trivia has, if anything, got worse; microphilia has become chronic and endemic in the statehouses. . . .

While the outcroppings of microphilia are plain to see, the cause of the condition is not so conspicuous. Actually, the legislative obsession with trivia is best understood in the same way a psychologist understands the compulsive quirks and tics of an individual — as a signal of unresolved inner frustrations. The main one of several unresolved twists in the legislative psyche is a baffled, often stifled, creative urge; thus action on trivia becomes a substitute for action on substantial matters. Viewed just so, microphilia can be seen as a symptom of the legislatures' historic and persisting aversion for using their powers, a trait, students of the species have long noted, that accounts for the fact that state government is the weakest link in the chain of American federalism. The same institutional frustration underlies many of the other dubious but widespread legislative characteristics that have put state legislatures right where University of Pittsburgh Professor William Keefe once located them: "On the outskirts of public esteem and affection."

– Frank Trippett
"The Trivial State of the States"
Time

◇◇◇◇◇

2

I consider myself the classic "poor overburdened taxpayer" that you hear so much about these days. I work for an electronics company and make $6.58 an hour which translates into $204 per week after deductions, $30.21 of which are federal withholding taxes. I have a husband, laid off, whose unemployment compensation has run out, and a thirteen-year-old son who thinks he should have a leather coat, a P. K. Ripper motocross bike, a Pioneer stereo, and an Asteroids game. It bothers me a lot that I can't afford to buy him any of these things. It also bothers me that I'm not sure how we're going to fill up the fuel tank often enough to stay warm this winter.

There is something else that bothers me, though not to the same extent as my son's unfulfilled desires or the ever-hungry fuel tank, and that is that every single politician and editorialist is positive he knows exactly what I think. Everyone seems to be wildly anxious to be my spokesman. Yet these people don't know a damn thing about how the "poor overburdened taxpayer" thinks or lives. I imagine it's been quite some time since most politicians or well-known journalists lived on $204 per week, though I've read plenty of complaints from congressmen about their meager salaries. One even said he had to sleep in his office because he couldn't afford to buy a house. Do you know how much pity I can spare for a senator who can't live on $60,000 a year?

I know I'm not as articulate as the people who write the editorials for newspapers and the speeches for politicians, but just once I'd like to have on the record the thoughts of an average taxpayer. I'm tired of these people putting their words in my mouth and their thoughts in my head.

One of the statements I read and hear most often is how fed up I'm supposed to be with the amount of my taxes that goes toward welfare, food stamps, programs for the elderly, subsidized school lunches, and other supportive social services. Wrong! What the people "up there" don't understand is that I identify with the beneficiaries of these programs much more than I do with the politicians and the media people. "There, but for the grace of God, go I." So far, I have never had to rely on welfare, free lunches, or Medicaid, but I very well might someday. When I was divorced, I could have qualified for welfare. Fortunately, I had parents who were in a position to help, but if I hadn't, you can believe I would have swallowed my pride rather than watch my son go hungry. People like me, who live only a hairbreadth from economic disaster, are glad those programs are out there, though we pray we'll never have to use them. We feel sympathy for the ones who do.

In 1977 my sister-in-law was abandoned by her husband. Her health did not permit her to work full-time, so she drew $194 per month from the welfare department to support herself and her child. I doubt that anyone can think she lived extravagantly on $194 per month.

I think it's possible that at least one of the very same politicians who are now complaining about welfare recipients might have taken a political junket during one of the months that my sister-in-law and her son lived on $194. Believe me, I resent that junket at my expense much, much more than I resent helping an ADC [Aid to Dependent Children] mother, or buying eyeglasses for an elderly person or free lunches for a ghetto child.

To me, Reaganomics is cruel and self-serving. Reagan seems to be telling us that the United States is a sinking ship and that if we harden our hearts and throw a few people overboard, we can lighten the load. Then, possibly, the Ship of State can sail back to shore. I don't see my country quite that way. The philosophy behind the original structure of the United States is that we are a people who sink or swim together. We don't make human sacrifices.

> – Vicki Williams
> "The View from $204 a Week"
> *Newsweek*

<>&<>&<>&<>&<>

3

Martin Luther King, Jr., Drive used to be Sylvan Street. Some whites in Selma still called it Sylvan Street. It's the main route through the so-called project — a typical federally sponsored housing district — and the street the Southern Christian Leadership Conference assembled the marchers on, using the block under the high steeple of Brown's Chapel as the starting point. The first marchers walked down Sylvan (as it was then), up Water Avenue, turned left, and started across Pettus Bridge. About half a mile. At the other end of the bridge, deputies and troopers, shouting to the people they had no permit to march, forced them back to Water Street. But for once, chants and signs and feet were better weapons than anything the state could summon. Whitman, the egalitarian, said it a century before:

> I will make a song for the ears of the President, full of weapons
>   with menacing points,
> And behind the weapons countless dissatisfied faces.

When King assembled the marchers again two weeks later, he had not only a permit, he had also the protection — albeit spotty — of federal troops called out by President Johnson, the man with the big ears. People gathered at Brown's Chapel and walked fifty miles to Montgomery. The two marches roused Washington as none of the other SCLC confrontations had, and a few months later the Congress passed the Federal Voting Rights Act.

It was dark and moonless when I started looking for Brown's Chapel. I planned just to drive by, but I stopped near a big brick church that fit the description to ask a black man if it was the chapel. "That's it," he said. "What difference does it make?"

Without knowing it, he had asked me the question I'd come to Selma to answer. "Isn't this where King started the march?"

"What they say. So who cares?"

I stood on the step of the van. "I'm trying to find out if things have changed since the march."

"Tell you in three words. *Ain't nothin' changed.*"

"Let me ask another question. Could you get a drink in Mickey's tonight?"

"Go ask me if I *want* in there, because I'll tell you they don't gotta keep this man out because he don't want in."

"I hear you, but *could* you?"

"Minute I do it's membership time."

"I just went in and nobody said anything about membership."

"Your membership's got a way of standin' out — just like mine."

Several teenagers gathered around. I was the wrong color on the wrong street, but no one said anything. The man talking to me was James Walker, born and raised in the Selma project and just discharged from four years in the Air Force. "Been almost ten years to the day since King got shot," he said, "and the movement's been dead that long. Things slippin'. Black man's losin' ground again. My momma's afraid to talk to a white, and my grandmomma don't care. She just worries about the kids."

"Didn't the march do anything you can see?"

"Say what? Last week I went to get my driver's licence. Twelve-thirty. Lunchtime. Sign on the door says they open again at one. I wanted to wait inside, so I pulled on the door. Trooper comes out and says, 'What's wrong, fool? Cain't read? Get off that door less you want me next time comin' out shootin'.' There's your change."

"Where?"

"Ten years ago he woulda come out shootin' the first time."

– William Least Heat Moon
Blue Highways: A Journey into America

⬦⬦⬦⬦

4

In the United States, the first source of the military's power is the belief that all government instruments are subject to the democratic process. This belief is strong in our rhetoric; it is what our children are still taught in school. But it is, in fact, something that no fully informed citizen can believe. The modern military establishment extensively controls the democratic process. In the organization it possesses, the money it deploys, the captive politicians it commands, the scientific community it subsidizes, the military has become a force in its own right. It employs 4.5 million people and last year generated over $146 billion in business for private enterprise. The military now has in its embrace the civilian authority to which legally and constitutionally it is presumed to be subject. . . .

The rise and awesome triumph of this military power have profoundly altered our society. The most significant effect arises from the need of any military power for an enemy — a plausible enemy. In the absence of such, a military's influence and, more pertinently, its financial support are gravely at risk.

The United States in the last century and again in the years between the world wars had no plausible military adversary. As a result, the American military establishment had negligible power and resources — our army in that period was on a par with that of Portugal. This condition has been remedied. In recent years enemies have been manifestly more available — or have been made so. China, until it was promoted to its current role as an honorary bastion of free enterprise, for a time so served: the atomic yellow peril. North Vietnam, Cuba, and Nicaragua have functioned as enemies. We also have Colonel Quaddafi. But overwhelmingly and durably, the plausible enemy has been the Soviet Union.

The Soviet Union is indispensable to the military power in the United States. Tension in our relations with the Russians directly and overtly serves that power, and any relaxation of tension would diminish the resources it commands. Military appropriations were once made in response to external threat. But let us not now be in doubt: Action and response have been reversed. External threat is now in the service of military appropriations and weapons development.

– John Kenneth Galbraith
"The Military: A Loose Cannon?"

⬦⬦⬦⬦⬦

5

The chief prey of political power is not the individual but society. It is the war between state and society that has overriding political and social consequences in the West.

By society I mean nothing supraindividual; nothing large, abstract, or remote. I use the word to mean all the ordinary relationships that bind human beings together and separate them from the horde. Family, neighborhood, and religion, each of which long antedates the political state, are society's molecular elements. To these ancient unities have been added over the centuries the more complex elements of society: towns, cities, monasteries, schools, universities, business enterprises, hospitals, and professions. These are all social inventions, created by the same combination of perceived need and ingenuity that spurred the invention of clocks, mills, steam engines, art forms, and games.

The political state is an institution that is very much a part of society, especially in the modern world. But there is one great difference between the state and all other associations: It alone possesses sovereignty — power backed by military force. By its nature, the state reaches all individuals. In the process it necessarily impinges upon the social groups that come between it and the individual. . . .

Consider the state's forays into the slums in the name of urban renewal. Years ago the brilliant city planner Jane Jacobs pointed out the seeming inability of the state to avoid bulldozing entire neighborhoods along with the dilapidated buildings of condemned urban areas. A sense of community can keep crime rates low no matter how squalid the physical appearance of a neighborhood may be. But the state can no more create a sense of neighborhood or community than it can create love or friendship.

The war between state and society can also be seen in much of what the state is pleased to call affirmative action programs. The state's declared objective is to rescue the powerless individual from the social forces that oppress him. I readily concede that there are times when the state is obligated to do so. After all, the Thirteenth Amendment trespassed on the rights of slaveholders. But busing schoolchildren many miles in order to meet some bureaucrat's arbitrary standard for the proper integration of the races grievously flouts the will of the community. From all we hear, these children are no happier about their new "rights" than are their parents.

Of all the wars waged by the state, the most important is the war against the family — taking the family in its fullest sense to include clan and kindred. We can observe that war in the state's recent involvement in the traditional patient-physician relationship. Here the individual being "liberated" by state action is Baby Doe. To protect the baby against her parents and their doctor the state has set up a so-called hot line in Washington, D.C., and proclaimed it the right, nay the duty, of hospital personnel to report any abuses of a handicapped infant's civil rights to the government. The question cannot be avoided: Is the possible benefit — if that is the proper word — to Baby Doe worth the damage to family autonomy? Can the remote, inquisitorial, adversarial court system be relied on for justice? Or are the hard decisions in cases such as Baby Doe's best left to the family and its physician?

Consider, too, the university. Many will remember the determination with which the academic community fought the efforts of state legislatures in the 1940s and 1950s to circumscribe its right to supervise student admissions, determine curricula, and appoint faculty members. But today universities submit to demands that were not even dreamed of two generations ago. The requirements of affirmative action have sanctioned a degree of federal scrutiny of university affairs more intrusive than the old inquisition against supposedly disloyal professors. A faculty member at the University of Georgia was jailed for contempt after refusing to reveal to a court his vote (*pace* democracy) on another faculty member's promotion. But no scholars departed the institution, and the American Association of University Professors did not bother to protest. This is how far universities have moved from the autonomy they once knew and valued.

– Robert Nisbet
"Besieged by the State"

<><><><><>

6

It is a sunny September morning in Disneyland. Bands are playing; people are walking with their children and pushing empty strollers; couples are taking pictures. There is a good proportion of people, buildings, and trees.

The Chinese writers, the UCLA conference hosts, Allen Ginsberg, and I have all just seen a movie, *America the Beautiful*, put out by Bell Laboratories in the fifties. On seven big screens the movie showed highlights of U.S. tourism: the Liberty Bell, the Lincoln Memorial, the Rocky Mountains, Savannah, Big Sur. It also showed long, cheerfully filmed segments of U.S. militarism: tanks rolling on parade, soldiers firing salutes, cadets training with weapons at Annapolis and West Point — all to swelling music and rising choruses.

We have emerged, blinking, from this movie and entered the bright Disneyland streets. The Chinese writers seem content to be here. They are familiar with Disney paraphernalia. In China you can buy Donald Duck on pink thermos bottles, Mickey Mouse and Goofy on yellow cotton handkerchiefs. Filmed Disney cartoons are widely known.

A sophisticated and cosmopolitan Chinese writer named Liu Binyan is strolling down the street with Allen Ginsberg. At home in Beijing, Liu Binyan is a muckraking journalist. The target of his muckraking is corruption in high places; it is astonishing that he is free to travel. He is in the United States on a six months' visit. He speaks English, as well as Russian, Japanese, and Chinese.

Liu Binyan's upright, forceful carriage enhances the grandeur of his leonine head with its curved forehead, wide cheekbones, and strong jaw. He is young; he is at home in the world; his dark suit, remarkably, fits him. For twenty-two years in China he was not permitted to write; he worked at forced labor. Now he is in Disneyland.

Allen Ginsberg, beside Liu Binyan, is walking with his head down. He is sensibly dressed for a hot September day in a short-sleeved white shirt and green chinos. The spectacle of the movie we have just seen has made him gloomy. He says he considers all that military emphasis in the film to be Mickey Mouse.

Liu Binyan, walking so erectly in his fine suit, cocks an ear and says, "Mickey Mouse?"

"You know," Ginsberg says. He is preoccupied. "Mickey Mouse. With the ears?" He wags his fingers desolately over his head. "A little mouse?"

Liu Binyan stands on his dignity. "Yes," he says slowly, in his careful English, "I know Mickey Mouse. Yes. But the film?"

Ginsberg is emphatic. "That was a Mickey Mouse film."

It is all breaking down for Liu Binyan. He has probably seen dozens of Mickey Mouse films. Incredulity raises his voice: "The film we just saw was a Mickey Mouse film?"

Ginsberg, still shaking his head over the film, chooses another tack. "You know," he explains. "Hallucinatory. Delusional."

Liu Binyan slowly lights a cigarette and lets the subject go.

– Annie Dillard
Encounters with Chinese Writers

DAVID LAMB

The New African Chiefs

David Lamb was born in Boston in 1940. After graduating from the University of Maine, he served briefly in the army, emerging as a lieutenant. Lamb joined the *Los Angeles Times* in 1970 and has reported from more than a hundred countries on all seven continents. He served as *Times* bureau chief in Australia, a battlefield reporter in Vietnam for United Press International, and *Times* correspondent in Nairobi, Kenya. After four years of roaming around sub-Saharan Africa, he wrote *The Africans* (1982), from which "The New African Chiefs" is excerpted. Lamb has been a Nieman fellow at Harvard and an Alicia Patterson fellow; he has received six nominations for the Pulitzer Prize. He was *Times* bureau chief in Cairo for three and a half years, ending in 1985; his latest book is *The Arabs: Journey Beyond the Mirage* (1987).

In "The New African Chiefs" Lamb focuses on Zaire, Africa's third-largest country, which lies on the Equator and occupies most of the eastern Congo River basin. Zaire's capital is Kinshasa; its four national languages are Swahili, Tshiluba (Kiluba), Lingala, and Kikongo. The country's official language of business, administration, and international communications, however, is French. Belgium occupied the Congo basin in the late 1800s, ruling it as the Congo Free State under King Leopold II. Exploitation and abuses drew international criticism and forced King Leopold to grant a colonial charter in 1908 to the Belgian Congo. Though ill prepared for self-government, the Congo became independent in 1960. Widespread violence ensued, causing Europeans to flee and the United Nations to send in troops. A 1965 coup by General Joseph Mobutu (later President Mobutu Sese Seko) brought some political stability; however, as Lamb relates, the price was high and prosperity short-lived.

The television screen fills with an image of heavenly clouds. A choir of voices swells in the background. The music grows louder, and as the clouds drift apart there emerges the face of a man, dark and handsome, a leopard-skin cap perched jauntily on his head. His gaze is steady and the faintest trace of a smile crosses his lips. The camera zooms in and holds for what seems like a very long time on the face. It speaks of strength, compassion, wisdom, though no words are uttered. What the viewer knows immediately is that this is no mere mortal. No indeed. It is Mobutu Sese Seko, a political survivor whose name translates roughly as "the all-powerful warrior who, by his endurance and will to win, goes from contest to contest, leaving fire in his wake." And this is the start of the eight o'clock TV news in Kinshasa.

Mobutu became president of Zaire in 1965, and though lurching from crisis to crisis, has managed to hold together his huge country with its 200 tribes and bloody history of instability. Like most African presidents, he rules as half-god, half-chieftain, combining the techniques of twentieth-century communication with ancient tribal symbolism. By his own decree he has become the embodiment of a homespun philosophy and a national symbol above criticism. He has caused his people great suffering, but at his command they turn out by the tens of thousands to line the parade routes and fill the stadiums and sing his praises. In short, Mobutu is more than a president. He is a cult.

His teachings — called Mobutism — have, by his order, become the national philosophy. His portrait is the only picture allowed in public places; it even hangs in hotel elevators. His people wear Mobutu badges, pinned over their hearts, and T-shirts bearing his likeness, and Mao-style attire known as a Mobutu shirt. They sing his name in popular songs and recite his sayings ("It is better to die of hunger than to be rich and a slave to colonialism") in schools and factories. None of this, though, means that Mobutu's 26 million people have any great fondness for him. They are only doing what they are told to do and paying homage to their chief as they are expected to do. One day, when Mobutu is overthrown, they will tear down his statues, burn his pictures, curse his name, and pay allegiance to a new chief.

Although Mobutu's excesses are extravagant even by African standards, the man himself is not an aberration among his presidential peers. He is but one in a fraternity whose members command respect by words, not deeds. These men represent a curious mixture of European influence and African tradition, and their power is absolute. Their overseas bank accounts are stuffed with pilfered funds, and their loyalties and concerns are distinctly self-centered, often having little to do with national advancement.

Mobutu is, in fact, more a creation of Western capitalism than he is of African custom. Like Africa's other second-generation presidents, he is the symbol of his country's sickness, not the sole cause of it. After independence the inherited European systems soon ceased to work and the substitute African systems broke down. Men like Mobutu were left to rule by experiment. They became, in effect, neocolonial governors, operating and living much in the style of their former white masters. The welfare of the African people is generally not much more important to them than it was to the colonial governors.

When Mobutu came to power, Zaire (formerly the Belgian Congo) was a country on the move. Rich copper mines stood ready for exploring, fertile fields for tilling. By the early 1970s, with copper bringing record prices on the world market, Mobutu, a former journalist and one-time army sergeant, found himself presiding over an unprecedented economic boom. His response was to go on a spending orgy that made economists' heads whirl. But his priorities were sadly confused; what he sought was not national development, but personal prestige and national grandeur.

He built palaces, eleven in all, and linked some of them to the capital with four-lane highways. He dedicated monuments to himself and constructed stadiums in which to address his people. He visited New York, admired the World Trade Center, and had a small-scale duplication of the buildings constructed in Kinshasa. He bought off his enemies and turned his friends — most of them from his own Gbande tribe — into overnight millionaires. He redesigned the main street of Kinshasa and cut down the lovely old trees in the center divider so the boulevard could accommodate more military vehicles for a parade. He spent $15 million sponsoring the Muhammad Ali–George Foreman world championship fight in 1974. Said Ali: "Zaire's gotta be great. I never seen so many Mercedes." And as for himself — well, Mobutu was hardly the penniless army sergeant of a decade ago. He was now one of the world's wealthiest men, with assets conservatively estimated by Western intelligence sources at more than $3 billion. Mobutu, incidentally, did not have enough faith in his country's economic future to invest at home; like other African presidents, his fortune was in European banks and European real estate.

Of every dollar coming into Zaire, whether it was in the form of a foreign aid grant or a business contract, Zairian officials took twenty cents off the top for their personal cut. In 1977 Zaire's coffee crop was valued at $400 million. Because of smuggling and underinvoicing, only $120 million was returned to Zaire's treasury. The rest ended up in foreign bank accounts held by Mobutu and his Gbande colleagues. Everyone was on the take, and in Zaire you needed to know only two things to survive or prosper: Whom do I see and how much will it cost?

Not surprisingly, from the very beginning Mobutu and his pals were about the only ones excited over the course of developments in Zaire. So, trying to drum up some national spirit, Mobutu launched what he called an African "authenticity" program. "We are resorting to this authenticity," he said, "in order to rediscover our soul, which colonization had almost erased from our memories and which we are seeking in the tradition of our ancestors."

He ordered all Zairians to replace their Christian names with African ones, and set the example himself by dropping his first and middle names (Joseph Desiré) in favor of Sese Seko. He changed the Congo's name to Zaire (meaning "river"), forbade the wearing of Western attire, designed a national uniform that looks like a Mao suit, canceled Christmas, and put up his portrait in the churches.

Carrying his zeal a step further, he expropriated $500 million in foreign enterprises and expelled the Asian merchants who had kept the economy running. Most of the Belgian plantation owners, technicians, and businessmen were forced out, too. Mobutu awarded the confiscated businesses to his friends. In many cases the new operators merely sold the merchandise still in stock and closed up shop.

The Zairian people whispered about Mobutu's misdeeds, but only   12 quietly because his secret police had permeated every level of society. In the U.S. Congress there were debates about Washington's cozy alliance with the Kinshasa government, but the official line was that Zaire was economically and strategically important, that it was a counterbalance to growing Soviet influence in central Africa, and that Mobutu, a staunch anti-Communist, should be supported regardless of his shortcomings. As a result, Zaire in the late 1970s was receiving nearly half of all the aid money the Carter Administration allocated for black Africa. But Washington wasn't helping a country develop; it was merely buying the loyalty of a chieftain, much in the same way Europe did during the colonial era. It was encouraging the very conditions that could lead to revolution and expanded Soviet influence.

Zaire paid a heavy price for Mobutu's shortsightedness. Copper prices plunged and the boom of the seventies quickly became the bust of the eighties. Zaire became an economic cripple and a social misfit, and by 1980 Mobutu was experiencing the ultimate humiliation for a black African leader: he turned the running of his country over to foreigners. He invited back the Belgian businessmen whose firms he had expropriated in the 1970s. He brought in Moroccan guards to provide his security. The International Monetary Fund was running the central bank, and Belgian specialists were operating the customs department. Other Europeans were moving into the finance ministry, the taxation office, and the transportation system. Mobutu called this new experiment for economic recovery the Mobutu Plan. It was well named because it was an attempt to save Mobutu, not Zaire.

By the time I made my last visit to Zaire — the country V. S. Naipaul described so vividly in A *Bend in the River* — it seemed to be rapidly disintegrating in spite of the Mobutu Plan. At Mama Yemo General Hospital (named for Mobutu's mother) unattended patients were dying because there were no bandages, no sterilization equipment, no oxygen, no film for X-ray machines. The dead often remained for hours in the intensive care unit before being removed because there was no room for extra bodies in the morgue.

The health clinics at the university campuses in Kinshasa and Lubumbashi had shut down because the medicines intended for use there had been diverted to the black market. The university cafeterias were closed for the simple reason that there was no food. With inflation running at over 100 percent, a bag of cornmeal needed to feed a family of six for a month cost $130, twice a laborer's monthly salary. In the rural areas people were reverting from cash-crop to subsistence farming because the transportation system had broken down and the food they had intended to sell at market lay rotting on the ground. (Zaire had 31,000 miles of main roads at independence in 1960; twenty years later only 3,700 miles of usable roads remained.)

Zaire's debt to foreign banks and governments soared to $4 billion in 1980, and shortages of food and spare parts became critical. The government's news agency closed down for lack of paper, 360 abandoned buses stood rusting near the airport, and the national airline, Air Zaire, could afford only enough fuel to operate one of every four domestic flights each day. Its Boeing 747 and Douglas DC-10 were repossessed. Through it all, Mobutu kept insisting that Zaire and its people were doing fine; the problems Western journalists wrote about, he said, were illusionary ones that merely underscored the media's bias against Africa. 16

President cultism is hardly unique to Africa. In the United States, after all, John F. Kennedy became a cult figure, in death perhaps more than in life. But what African leaders have managed to do is mold cultism into a fine art. They have bestowed upon themselves godlike qualities and the unquestioned authority of the most powerful chieftain. Most, however, are not leaders in the true sense; they are images, the creations of a sort of African-style public relations campaign. As peculiar as the phenomenon may seem to a Westerner, it makes sense in Africa, where the uneducated masses respond to strong central authority. They do not want to be bullied by their governments but they do expect their presidents to exercise the same kind of authoritarian control that tribal chiefs and colonial governors used. Anything less is considered a sign of weakness.

Mobutu may have carried cultism to the extreme, but almost every black African president is, in varying degrees, a cult figure who has adopted a nickname to convey a desired image. Mobutu and President Etienne Eyadéma of Togo both like to be referred to as "the Guide." Jomo Kenyatta, the late Kenyan president, was known as Mzee, the Swahili word for "Wise Old Man." Julius Nyerere of Tanzania is known as "the Teacher"; Hastings Kamuzu Banda of Malawi as "the Chief of Chiefs"; Félix Houphouët-Boigny of the Ivory Coast as "the No. 1 Peasant"; and the late Macias Nguema Biyogo of Equatorial Guinea as "the National Miracle." Uganda's former president Idi Amin Dada used to refer to himself, only half in jest, as "the Conquerer of the British Empire."

Togo's Eyadéma has a presidential cheering section consisting of a thousand women and he wouldn't think of making a public appearance without it. The women's prime responsibility is to perform traditional dances and lavish their president with songs of praise — a ritual that Eyadéma says helps build a national spirit and identity. For $20, Togolese can buy wristwatches on whose face the illuminated portrait of Eyadéma fades and reappears every fifteen seconds. Eyadéma also has built a huge bronze statue of himself in the downtown square of Lomé, and commissioned an Eyadéma comic book in which he plays a Superman-type character.

In Malawi, everything from university dormitories to highways is 20 named for President Banda, and women wear dresses embroidered with Banda's portrait. The mildest criticism of Banda guarantees a stretch in jail. "They say my people love me," observes President-for-Life Banda, "and I would be naive to deny it."

The lead item on most radio newscasts in black Africa seldom covers the major news story of the day; instead it deals with what the country's president said or did that day, however routine or mundane. "President Daniel arap Moi said today that Kenya is a friend to all people of the world," reports the Voice of Kenya. Or: "President Daniel arap Moi has called on leaders in the country to refrain from spreading malicious rumors among *wananchi* [the masses]." In Jomo Kenyatta's final days, when he was a senile and largely incapacitated man of eighty-six years withering away in State House, the Voice of Kenya reported daily that he was on "a busy working tour of the coast provinces." The two daily newspapers were required to run the usual page-one photograph of Kenyatta conducting that day's affairs of state — even though they had to dig old pictures out of their files. The premise was that the people wouldn't know the difference. But they did, of course, and no one was surprised when the Voice of Kenya suddenly started playing funeral music without any announcement one day in August 1978. Kenyatta had gone on his last "busy working tour."

Moi, Kenyatta's vice-president, allowed only a respectful period before he started taking down Kenyatta's pictures and putting up his own. Moi's words soon became the headline item on each newscast and the *wananchi* were soon urged to turn out and cheer their president each time he left State House. One cult — a legitimate one, given Kenyatta's great charisma and early influence in the anticolonialist movements — had ended and another one of questionable authenticity had begun. (Quite deservedly, Kenyatta remains a legendary figure in Africa.)

The honeymoon for Moi did not last long. In short order he turned Kenya into a one-party state and started arresting dissidents and journalists. As Kenya's economy deteriorated in the worldwide recession, Moi, a former schoolteacher, and his band of ruling elite grew richer by the day through various business deals. The inevitable happened early one morning in August 1982: a group of air force men seized the radio station and announced that they had overthrown the government. Before forces loyal to Moi could put down the attempted coup, more than 120 people had died and soldiers had gone on a rampage in Nairobi, looting, raping, and shooting. Moi closed down the university and disbanded the air force. But the cancer had already started to spread. At best, Moi was now fighting a delaying action.

Like Moi, few African presidents would consider taking a trip without 24 summoning the full diplomatic corps to the airport or ordering the masses to line the route from State House to the terminal. I always found it a rather sad spectacle to watch thousands of Africans waving banners that they could not read and obediently applauding some man who demanded — but had not necessarily earned — their allegiance, respect, and love. True, they didn't have many other opportunities to show they really did belong to a nation, but the prime purpose of the exercise was designed to pamper the egos of insecure men needing acceptance and authenticity.

EXPLORATIONS

1. What reasons does Lamb give for Zaire's financial problems under Mobutu? What does he cite as Mobutu's two explanations for these problems?
2. What was the United States' response to Zaire's economic difficulties in the 1970s? Why does Lamb accuse Washington of "encouraging the very conditions that could lead to revolution and expanded Soviet influence"?
3. Which of the gestures mentioned by Lamb indicate African leaders' desire to be superior to everyone they rule? Which gestures indicate a desire for solidarity with the citizenry? How would you summarize these leaders' attitude toward their people?

CONNECTIONS

1. Shiva Naipaul's "The Palmers" (p. 337) suggests that white landowners in black Africa share some attitudes with African rulers like Mobutu Sese Seko. How does each group regard the other? How does each group regard its employees or subjects.
2. Look back at Ruth Sidel's "The Liu Family" (p. 21). What resemblances do you notice between the cults of Mobutu and Mao? From the standpoint of the Chinese and Zairians, what are the key differences?

ELABORATIONS

1. In his *Observation*, John Kenneth Galbraith talks about the military's need for an enemy to maintain its credibility and power. How do Galbraith's comments help to explain Mobutu's early success as a nationalistic native president in Zaire? What specific tactics show Mobutu using an enemy for his regime's benefit? Write an essay describing Mobutu's strategy as Galbraith might assess it, identifying its pros and cons as a way to run a country.
2. In "Tradition and the African Writer" (p. 344), Ezekiel Mphahlele talks about the psychological conflict of having roots in two different cultures. What two cultures influenced Mobutu Sese Seko? What impact did each one have on him? What efforts has he made to reconcile that conflict for himself and his country? Write an essay on "tradition and the African ruler" in which you use Mphahlele's ideas to explain Mobutu's (and his fellow second-generation presidents') behavior.

JAMES FENTON

The Philippine Election

The English poet and critic James Fenton was born in 1949. His first literary success came when he was nineteen: Critics acclaimed his sonnet sequence *Our Western Furniture,* on Commodore Matthew Perry's forced opening of Japan to trade (see p. 36). In addition to political poetry, Fenton writes "found poetry" and light verse. His first poetry collection was *Terminal Moraine* (1972); his most recent is the retrospective *Children in Exile* (1983), an expansion of *The Memory of War* (1982). Between *Terminal Moraine* and *The Memory of War* Fenton worked as a journalist, traveling extensively in Germany and Indochina; between 1973 and 1975 he spent a total of eighteen months in Vietnam, Cambodia, Laos, and Thailand. Fenton is currently the theater critic for London's *Sunday Times*; his reviews have been collected in *You Were Marvellous* (1983).

In "The Philippine Election," excerpted from an issue of *Granta* entitled "The Snap Revolution," Fenton explains why and how he got caught up in the popular overthrow of President Ferdinand Marcos. Marcos first took office in 1965, two decades after the United States (which had won the Philippines from Spain) granted the islands independence. Manila, the capital, is on the large northern island of Luzon; at the southern end of the archipelago is Mindanao, once a Muslim bastion against Spanish rule and Roman Catholicism. President Marcos ruled — with U.S. support — from Malacañang Palace in Manila. After achieving early reforms, his regime eroded into a dictatorship maintained by ruthless greed and deceit. When exiled opposition leader Benigno Aquino landed at Manila airport in 1983, he was shot. Judges (appointed by Marcos) acquitted the suspects, but a fact-finding panel concluded differently, citing General Fabian Ver — Marcos's armed forces chief of staff — for covering up the murder. As popular outrage grew, Aquino's widow, Corazón (Cory), announced her candidacy in the forthcoming presidential elections. Senator Salvador Laurel, another opposition leader and candidate, became her running mate.

After the events narrated by Fenton, Marcos and his wife, Imelda, fled to Hawaii, while Aquino and Laurel triumphantly took office. Laurel has since split with Aquino, whose government faces an uphill battle to make People Power a working reality.

(For more background on the Philippines, see p. 383.)

A man sets light to himself, promising his followers that he will rise again in three hours. When the time has elapsed, the police clear away the remains. Another man, a half-caste, has himself crucified every year — he has made a vow to do this until God puts him in touch with his American father. A third unfortunate, who has lost his mother, stands rigid at the gate of his house and has been there, the paper tells us, for the last fourteen years, "gazing into an empty rubber plantation."

I don't know when it was that I began noticing stories like these, or began to think that the Philippines must be a strange and fascinating place. Pirates came from there last year to attack a city in Borneo. Ships sank with catastrophic loss of lives. People came from all over the world to have psychosurgeons rummage through their guts — their wounds opened and closed in a trice. There was a Holy War in Mindanao. There was a communist insurgency. Political dialogue was conducted by murderers. Manila was a brothel.

It was the Cuba of the future. It was going the way of Iran. It was another Nicaragua, another Cambodia, another Vietnam. But all these places, awesome in their histories, are so different from each other that one couldn't help thinking: this kind of talk was a shorthand for a confusion. All that was being said was that something was happening in the Philippines. Or more plausibly: a lot of different things were happening in the Philippines. And a lot of people were feeling obliged to speak out about it.

But still at this stage, although the tantalizing little items were appearing daily in the English press, I had not seen any very ambitious account of what was going on. This fact pleased me. I thought that if I planned well in advance, engineered a decent holiday, and went off to Manila, I would have the place to myself, as it were. I would have leisure and space enough to work away at my own pace, not running after a story, not hunting with the pack of journalists. I would watch, and wait, and observe. I would control my project rather than have it control me.

But I had reckoned without the Reagan administration and the whims of a dictator. Washington began sending urgent and rather public envoys to Manila, calling for reforms and declaring that time was running out. There was something suspicious in all this. It looked as if they were trying to fix a deal with Marcos — for if they weren't trying to fix things the alternative view must be that they were destabilizing the dictatorship, and this seemed out of character. Then Marcos went on American television and announced a snap election. And this too smelled fishy. I couldn't imagine that he would have made such a move had he not been certain of the outcome. For a while it was uncertain whether the snap election could or would be held, for the terms which the dictator offered to his people appeared unconstitutional. The constitution required that Marcos resign before running again for office. But Marcos would not resign: he would offer a post-dated resignation letter only, and he would fight the presidential election in his role as president.

In other words, the deal was: Marcos would remain president but would hold a fair election to reassure his American critics that he still had the support of his people; if, by some fluke, it turned out that he did not have this support, the world had his word of honor that he would step down and let somebody else be president. And this somebody else, in all probability, would be the woman who was accusing Marcos of having murdered her husband. So if he stepped down, Marcos would very likely be tried for murder.

It didn't sound as if it was going to be much of an election.

What's more, it was going to wreck my dream of having Manila all   8
to myself. Indeed, my project was already in ruins. By now everybody in the world seemed to have noticed what an interesting place the Philippines was. There would be a massive press corps running after every politician and diplomat. There would be a deluge of background articles in the press. People would start getting sick of the subject well before I had had the chance to put pen to paper.

I toyed with the idea of ignoring the election altogether. It was a sham and a fake. It would be a "breaking story." If I stuck to my original plan, I would wait till Easter, which is when they normally hold the crucifixions. I wasn't going to be panicked into joining the herd.

Then I panicked and changed all my plans. Contrary to some expectations, the opposition had united behind Corazón Aquino, the widow of the national hero Benigno "Ninoy" Aquino. She was supposedly an unwilling candidate, and supposedly a completely inexperienced politician. But she was immensely popular — unwillingness and inexperience, it appeared, made a refreshing change. The assassination of her husband in 1983, as he stepped off the plane in Manila airport, was a matter that had never been cleared up. So there was a highly personal, as well as political, clash ahead. . . .

It wasn't hard to tell which areas were going to vote for Marcos and which for Cory. In the Cory areas people were out on the road, cheering and waving and making the Laban sign.[1] In the Marcos areas there was an atmosphere of quiet tension. The crowd, such as it was, did not speak freely. There was a spokesman who explained calmly and simply that Marcos had done so much for this village that there was no support for the opposition. As we could see, the explanation continued, there was no intimidation or harassment. People were voting according to their own free will. They all supported Marcos.

It was only out of earshot of this spokesman that members of my group   12 were told *sotto voce* that they had been threatened with eviction if they voted the wrong way. Even so, some people said, they were not going to be coerced.

We drove to Tadeco, the huge banana plantation run by Antonio Florendo, one of the chief Marcos cronies. The Cory campaigners were hoping to get the votes from this area disqualified, as the register apparently featured far more names than Mr. Florendo employed. He had something like 6,000 workers, many of whom were prisoners. But the register had been wildly padded.

The polling station was at the center of Mr. Florendo's domain. Rows and rows of trucks were lined up, and a vast crowd was milling around, waiting to vote. At the gates, a couple of disconsolate observers from NAMFREL, the National Movement for a Free Election, complained that they had been excluded from the station on the grounds that their papers lacked the requisite signatures. In fact the signatures were there and in order, but the people on the gate insisted this was not so. A sinister "journalist" began inquiring who I was, and writing down my particulars. "Oh, you come from England," he said menacingly. "Well, that may be useful if we all have to flee the country." Whenever I tried to speak to somebody, this man shoved his microphone under my nose.

We asked to speak to Mr. Florendo, and to our surprise he appeared, with an angry, wiry little lawyer at his side. The lawyer was trying to explain to us why the NAMFREL people should not be allowed in. He had a sheaf of papers to support his case. We introduced ourselves to Mr. Florendo, who looked like a character from *Dynasty* or *Dallas* — Texan hat, distinguished white hair, all smiles and public relations. He was a model employer. Everything here was above board. No, the register had not been padded — we could come in and see for ourselves. We asked him why the NAMFREL people had been excluded. He turned to his

---

[1]An L made with the thumb and first finger; the sign for Aquino's campaign. *Laban* means "fight" in Tagalog, a Philippine language. — ED.

lawyer and said: "Is this so? Let them in, by all means." The lawyer expostulated and pointed to his sheaf of papers. Mr. Florendo waved him aside. Of course the NAMFREL people could come in. There was nothing to hide.

(One of the things they might have hidden better, which my compan-   16
ions noticed, was a group of voters lining up with ink on their fingers: they had already been through at least once.)

We asked if we could take Mr. Florendo's picture. "Oh," he said, "you must photograph my son, Tony-Boy — he's the handsome one." And he called to Tony-Boy, a languid and peculiarly hideous youth. Mr. Florendo thought that Tony-Boy could be a Hollywood star. I thought not. Mr. Florendo invited us to lunch. I thought not again. Mr. Florendo was overwhelming us with his honesty and generosity. He asked the crowd whether he was not a model employer, always available to his workers, and they all agreed that he was indeed a model employer. . . .

Now the returns began to be announced over the NAMFREL radio. The idea was to do a quick count, so that the possibilities of tampering would be kept to a minimum. In precinct after precinct the results were showing Cory winning by a landslide. Around Davao alone they had expected her to get 70 percent of the vote. And this indeed seemed possible. It all depended on what went on in the outlying areas such as Mr. Florendo's fief. NAMFREL could not observe everywhere. They simply didn't have enough people. But if they could monitor enough returns fast enough, they might be able to keep cheating to a minimum.

Davao, which features in stories as being one of the murder capitals of the world, had had a quiet day. I think only two people had been killed. The NPA-dominated[2] quarter called Agpao, and nicknamed Nicaragpao, had voted for Cory, although it was plastered with boycott posters, including one which showed the people taking to the mountains.

As the radio continued to announce Cory wins, Jojo came up with an   20
idea. The votes could be converted into different currencies. Cory gets 10 million votes, and these are expressed as rupees. Marcos gets 5 million, but these are dollars. So Marcos wins after all.

Certainly some kind of device was going to be needed.

In the hotel lobby, a desk had been set up to coordinate the results. The blackboard showed Cory with a healthy lead.

---

[2]NPA is the Communist guerrilla fighting force in the Philippines. It opposed the Marcos government but has continued its attacks since Aquino's election; Aquino has created controversy by offering to negotiate with the NPA rather than trying to defeat it. — Ed.

On the television, it appeared that far fewer of the results had so far been added up. Marcos was doing okay.

The figures in the lobby came from NAMFREL, which was the 24 citizens' arm of the official tabulating organization, COMELEC. In the end it would be the COMELEC figures which counted. But the sources of both figures were the same certified returns. Something very odd was happening.

The head of NAMFREL was called Joe Concepción. The head of COMELEC was Jaime Opinión. The television told us to trust Mr. Opinión; the radio, Mr. Concepción.

Late that night, the COMELEC count ground to a complete halt. Something had gone wrong — and it was perfectly obvious what.

There were several ways of fixing the election, all of which Marcos tried. The first was to strike names off the electoral register in areas of solid Cory support, and to pad out other registers with fictional names for the flying voters. You could bribe the voters with money and sacks of rice, or, aboveboard and publicly, with election promises. You could intimidate the solid areas. You could bribe the tellers. You could have fake ballot papers (a franking machine for these had gone missing for a whole week before the election). You could put carbon paper under the ballot form, to make sure that an individual had voted the right way before you paid him off. You could print money for his payoff, and if you printed the money with the same serial numbers there would be no record of how much you had printed. You could force the early closure of polling stations in hostile areas. You could do all these things and you might, if you were Marcos, get away with it.

But what if, after all that, the early returns made it plain that you still 28 hadn't won?

Then you would have to start stealing the ballot boxes, faking the returns, losing the ballots, shaving off a bit here, padding a bit there, and slowing down the returns so that, you hoped, once the initial wave of anger had subsided, you could eventually declare yourself the winner. To explain the delays in the counting of returns, there was a formula which never failed to unconvince. You could say over and over again on Channel Four, the government broadcasting station: "What the foreign observers fail to realize is that the Philippines is a nation comprised of over 7,000 islands. It takes a long time to collect the ballot boxes. Some of them have to be brought by boat or by carabao from very remote areas." But in the meantime votes would be taking a mysteriously long time to find their way from one side of Manila to the other.

This second phase of corruption was now beginning, and the people who stood against it were the NAMFREL volunteers and the Church. There was a great deal of overlap. Outside the town halls where the ballot boxes were kept and counted stood rows of nuns chanting Hail Marys, seminarians grouped under their processional crosses, Jesuits, priests, and laypeople. Outside Pasay Town Hall in Manila, the day after the election, I asked a Jesuit whether the whole of his order had taken to the streets in this way. He said that the only ones who hadn't were the foreigners, who didn't feel they could interfere. They were manning the telephones instead. . . .

The next evening I was sitting with some Americans in the foyer of the Manila Hotel, wondering whether perhaps we might not have preferred to be in Haiti. There was after all something gripping about the way the people there had dug up Papa Doc's bones and danced on them. And what would happen to all the dictators in exile? *Rolling Stone* suggested a Dictator Theme Park, where we could all go to visit them in natural surroundings.

A chap came up to our table, hovering about three inches off the floor, his eyes dilated. He had taken some high-quality something. "Listen you guys, nobody move now because the opposition's watching. The COMELEC girls have walked out of the computer count, in protest at the cheating. The whole thing's fucked."

We got up casually, one by one, and paid our bills. The "opposition," the rival networks, were no doubt very far from deceived. At the door I bumped into Helen.

"Helen," I said, "be absolutely casual. Just turn round and come out with me. The COMELEC girls have walked out of the computer count. Let's get down there."

But Helen was bursting for a pee. I swore her to secrecy and told her again to act natural. I knew, as I waited for her, that the chances of Helen crossing the foyer of the Manila Hotel without meeting a friend were zero. I dithered, frantic with casualness, by the door.

Helen kept her word, though, and only told one other journalist.

The COMELEC count was taking place in public, in a large conference center which was one of the Marcoses' notorious extravagances. When we reached the auditorium there was nothing much to see. The girls, around thirty of them, had got up, taking their disks with them, and simply walked out of the building before anyone realized what was going on. The remaining operators were still in place, but because the girls who had walked out occupied a crucial part of the whole computer system, nothing could be done until they and their software were replaced.

A seething general, Remigio P. Octavio, was outside the auditorium. Helen asked him what had happened. Nothing had happened. "Well, General, there seem to be quite a lot of operators missing."

Nobody was missing, said Remigio. The girls had needed a rest. People in the gallery had been jeering at them, throwing stones and paper darts, and they'd gone outside for a rest. They were upset. The gallery had been full of Communists. And tomorrow, he said, he would make sure there were enough police down here to prevent a recurrence. He would bring in reinforcements.

"As for the girls," said the General, "they will be back again shortly." 40

Helen wrote all this down on her pad. When she clicks into her reportorial mode and starts firing questions, it's an impressive sight. She laces her sentences with respectful language, and makes a great show of taking down every detail and improbability. But when somebody is lying to her in the way Remigio P. was, the effect of all this is mockery. I wondered whether the general would realize he was being sent up. If I had been him, I would have shot Helen.

The girls had taken refuge in Baclaran Church, and it was there the press corps tracked them down. By now they were said to be very scared at the consequences of their walkout. They needed all the protection the church could give them, but they also perhaps needed the protection of the press. Perhaps. Perhaps not. Members of the official teams of observers arrived. There was a great sense that these girls were in extreme danger.

It was the second time that day that I had been in Baclaran Church. In the afternoon it had been jam-packed as Cardinal Sin celebrated mass. Cory had attended. The crowds had spilled out into the churchyard and the street market nearby. Cardinal Sin had preached a sermon so emphatic in its praise of NAMFREL that he had made its members seem almost saints. Depending on your point of view, they were either heroes or villains. There was no middle ground.

Now the church was about a quarter full. Those who had heard about 44 the walkout had come to express their support. To pass the time they sang *"Bayan Ko,"*[3] and when the girls finally came out in front of the high altar the audience burst into applause.

The cameras had been set up long since and there were masses of photographers angling for a shot. The girls were sobbing and terrified. I could hardly bear to watch the grilling they got. Their spokeswoman said that they would not give their names, and that it was to be understood that what they had done was not political. They were not in fact (although we called them the COMELEC girls) officials of COMELEC. They were computer operators, highly qualified, who had been engaged to perform what they had taken to be a strictly professional job. All had gone well until the night before, when they began to be instructed not to feed in certain figures, so that the tally board giving the overall position was now at odds with what they knew to be the actual total so far.

I remember the word that was used. Discrepancies. Certain discrepancies had crept in, and the girls were worried by them. Finally they had decided that they were being asked to act unprofessionally. They had come out, and they had brought printouts and disks with them, in order to prove their case.

Earlier that evening the international team of observers had given a press conference at which John Hume, from Northern Ireland, had been the spokesman. He had been adamant that there had been cheating on the part of the KBL,[4] but he had purposely left open the question of whether that cheating had been on such a scale as to alter the eventual result of the election. The reason he had done this was that people feared Marcos might declare the election null and void, using the evidence of the foreign observers. Marcos was still president. He hadn't needed to call the snap election. If he now annulled it he could, constitutionally, go on as if nothing had happened.

Now the COMELEC girls had come out with the most authoritative evidence of cheating so far. People had been killed for much, much smaller offenses. The Americans could not possibly overlook this evidence, I thought. There would be no getting around it. That was why the girls were in such danger.

One of the American reporters said to the girls that of course they were entitled to withhold their names, but that if they did so Marcos

---

[3]The national anthem of the Philippine opposition. Fenton describes Bayan as "the umbrella organization for the legal, 'cause-oriented' groups in the opposition." — ED.

[4]Ferdinand Marcos's political party. — ED.

would claim they had not come from COMELEC at all, that this was just black propaganda. For their sakes, they should tell us their names.

At which another pressman snapped, "It's not for their sakes. You just want to get a good story."

The press conference drew to a close. I was thinking: so many people have gone so far — they're so exposed — that the Cory campaign must move forward. If it grinds to a halt now, all these people are just going to be killed.

A figure came rushing into the church. It was the Jesuit from Pasay 52 Town Hall, the one who had been so entertained by Marcos. He came up through the press. "It's very important," he said, "it's very important. They *must* give their names. They *must* give their names."

But the conference was already over, and the girls had gone into hiding. . . .

When it happens, it happens so fast you can't believe it's happening, and only afterwards can you truly catch up with your perceptions and your emotions. It began on a Saturday and ended the next Tuesday, and I doubt that there was anybody in the Philippines who really felt abreast of events. I wasn't. I was in Baguio when the Minister of Defense Juan Ponce Enrile and the Chief of National Police General Fidel Ramos, having supposedly learned that they were about to be arrested, took refuge in the Ministry of Defense at Camp Aguinaldo. [They later moved across the street to Camp Crame.] And even the next morning I wasn't quite sure what to make of the news. "You see what I was saying last night," said a friend, "Enrile could be the next president." We wondered whether Philip Habib, Reagan's latest envoy to the country, had tipped him the wink.

But if it looked like a coup it also looked ominously abortive. Ramos and Enrile were holed up with a small number of men. It sounded as if they were scared as well as cornered. Ramos had said: "I am calling on the people of the world to help us restore decency, justice, freedom, and democracy in this land. There is no justice, no decency, no real freedom, much less democracy in this helpless land. Nobody has indicated any help to us. We are going to help ourselves even with our bare hands." He had fought for his country, he said: "I don't have plenty of medals but the hour of reckoning is here and now for me. When you serve your country you have to take risks. Anyway, if I die tonight or tomorrow, Mr. Marcos will also die someday. He has no immortality, but at least my heart is clean." . . .

"Marcos," said the taximan the next morning, "is in Guam."   56
"Bullshit," I replied. "I saw him on the television late last night. About one-thirty. He can't be already in Guam."
"It was probably a recording," said the taximan. He was the type I would normally have assumed to be working for the secret service.
"So where did you get this information?"
"Oh," he said conspiratorially, "military sources."   60
He tuned in to the rebel radio. Unconfirmed reports, said a voice, have it that Marcos has been seen arriving in Guam.
"I think we'd better go to Malacañang [Palace] as quickly as possible," I said. . . .

As we came through security, a voice began to speak over the public address. It was giving instructions to the military to confine itself to the use of small arms in dealing with attacks. It was outlining Marcos's supposed policy of the whole election campaign — Maximum Tolerance.
"Whose voice is that?" I asked.   64
"It's Marcos. It must be a recording."
We ran up the grand staircase and turned right into the anteroom. And there sat Marcos himself, with Imelda and the family all around him, and three or four generals to the right. They had chosen the anteroom rather than the main hall, for there were only a few journalists and cameramen, and yesterday's great array of military men was nowhere to be seen. I looked very closely at Marcos and thought: it isn't him. It looked like ectoplasm. Like the Mighty Mekon. It was talking in a precise and legalistic way, which contrived to sound both lucid and utterly nonsensical. It had its left hand under the table, and I watched the hand for a while to see whether it was being deliberately concealed. But it wasn't.
So Marcos was still hanging on. Indeed he was back in his calm, lawyer's frame of mind. I remember somebody asking him whether he was going to go ahead with his inauguration the next day, as planned. Marcos replied that it was his duty to do so, as laid down by the constitution. The inauguration had to take place ten days after the proclamation by the National Assembly. If he'd been pressed any further in the matter he would have started quoting acts and statutes. That part of his brain was functioning perfectly. The bit that wasn't functioning, it appeared, was the bit that should have told him the game was up.
At first I felt embarrassed, as if I had been caught red-handed by   68
Marcos, trespassing in the palace. Then I felt embarrassed because, there

being so few pressmen around, I might be expected to ask the president a question. And I couldn't think of a thing to ask. People hovered around the microphone, and whispered to each other, "D'you want to go next?" Very few people did. One journalist actually went to the side of the room, sat down, and buried his head in his hands, as if overwhelmed by the irreality of the occasion.

General Ver was quivering and in an evident panic. . . . He stepped forward and asked for permission to bomb Camp Crame. There were two government F-5 jets circling over it, he said. (Just outside the palace someone had told me that the crowd at Camp Crame appeared to think that these jets were on their side, for they cheered every time the aircraft came over.) Marcos told Ver they were not to be used. Ver's panic increased.

"The air force, sir, is ready to attack were the civilians to leave the vicinity of Camp Crame immediately, Mr. President. That's why I come here on your orders so we can immediately strike them. We have to immobilize the helicopters that they got." (Marcos had sent helicopter gunships against the camp, but the pilots had come out waving white flags and joined the rebels.)

Marcos broke in with tired impatience, as if this had been going on all through the night and he was sick and tired of Ver. "My order is not to attack. No, no, no. Hold on; not to attack."

Ver was going wild. "Our negotiations and our prior dialogue have   72
not succeeded, Mr. President."

Marcos: "All I can say is that we may have to reach the point we may have to employ heavy weapons, but you will use the small weapons in hand or shoulder weapons in the meantime."

Ver said: "Our attack forces are being delayed."

The *Christian Science Monitor*, at my elbow, said: "This is absurd. It's a Mutt-and-Jeff act."

Ver said: "There are many civilians near our troops, and we cannot   76
keep on withdrawing. We cannot withdraw all the time, Mr. President."

All this was being broadcast live on Channel Four, which Marcos could see on a monitor. Ver finally saluted, stepped backwards, and left with the other officers. I forget who they were, just as Marcos, when he introduced them to us, had forgotten all their names and needed prompting. Now the family withdrew as well.

An incident then occurred whose significance I didn't appreciate at the time. The television began to emit white noise. A soldier stepped forward and fiddled with the knobs. The other channels were working, but Channel Four had been knocked off the air. The rebels had taken the government station, which Marcos must have realized. But he hardly batted an eyelid. It was as if the incident were some trivial disturbance, as if the television were simply on the blink.

For me, the most sinister moment of the morning had been when Marcos said that if the rebels continued they would "be chewed up by our roaming bands of loyal troops."

Someone asked why the troops at the gate were wearing white arm- 80
bands. They had said, he told Marcos, that it meant they would surrender to the rebels.

Marcos explained that this was not so. The armbands were a countersign.

A soldier in the audience said that the countersign was red, white, and blue.

The questioner then said, "No, these were plain white armbands."

Marcos said, a trifle quickly, "The colors are changed every day." 84

Somebody asked him whether he was going to leave the country. "No," he said, "as you can see, we are all still here." And as he said these words he turned round to discover that there was absolutely nobody standing behind him.

EXPLORATIONS

1. What impression does Fenton give of the Philippines in his opening paragraphs? How is this impression confirmed or changed by the rest of "The Philippine Election"?

2. What were Fenton's original goals in going to the Philippines? How and why did his goals change once he got there?

3. What techniques did Ferdinand Marcos use to make sure of staying in power? What incidents and details described by Fenton are clues that Marcos's efforts were doomed?

4. Judging from Fenton's account, what are the reasons why a Philippine voter was likely to choose Aquino over Marcos? What would Aquino's disadvantages have been if this had been an American election? Why were these disadvantages less significant in the Philippines?

CONNECTIONS

1. What are the similarities between Ferdinand Marcos and the African leaders described by David Lamb? Having read "The New African Chiefs," what can you surmise about Marcos as a ruler beyond what Fenton has specified in "The Philippine Election"?

2. Jill Gay wrote "Patriotic Prostitutes" (p. 383) during Marcos's presidency. Putting together the information in her report and Fenton's, what kinds of changes do you think are most urgently needed in the Philippines? What problems is Aquino's administration likely to face in trying to make those changes?

ELABORATIONS

1. As a news story, "The Philippine Election" puts more than usual focus on the journalist's viewpoint and his role in the story he is covering. What did you learn from Fenton's account about the news media's impact on the Marcos-Aquino contest? Write an essay examining the role(s) the media and their representatives played over the course of the election, and assessing their influence on its outcome.

2. Fenton writes: "When it happens, it happens so fast you can't believe it's happening, and only afterwards can you truly catch up with your perceptions and your emotions." Think of an event to which you responded in this way, not fully grasping it until it was over: a national shock such as Watergate or the Iran-Contra affair, an assassination or other unexpected death. Write an essay describing your specific memories and emotions at the time, compared with your understanding now, as you look back.

JULIO CORTÁZAR

Regarding the Eradication of
Crocodiles from Auvergne

Julio Cortázar began life in Belgium and ended in it France. Born in Brussels in 1914, he returned with his Argentine parents to their homeland after World War I. There he graduated from the teachers' college in Buenos Aires, taught in Argentine secondary schools, began publishing poems and plays, and became a literary translator. Cortázar opposed the dictatorial presidency of General Juan Perón, who came to power in 1946. He moved to France in 1951 — a year which also brought literary success with his book of stories *Bestiario*. Cortázar won the Prix Medicis for his 1973 book *Libro de Manuel* (*A Manual for Manuel*, 1978) and donated the money to the United Chilean Front. In France he translated for UNESCO, wrote, and pursued his interest in the jazz trumpet, with time out for visits to Cuba and Nicaragua. He lived both in Paris and in Provence, east of the Auvergne region in southern France, and died in 1984, the year after democratic rule returned to Argentina with President Raúl Alfonsín. "Regarding the Eradication of Crocodiles from Auvergne," translated by Thomas Christensen, comes from his posthumous collection *Around the Day in Eighty Worlds* (1986).

Gabriel García Márquez (see p. 493) writes of Cortázar: "From the very first page [of *Bestiario*] I knew that he was the kind of writer I wanted to become when I was older. . . . He was the tallest man one could imagine, with the face of a wicked child, inside an endless black overcoat that looked like a priest's soutane, and his eyes were set very far apart like those of a young bull, so oblique and diaphanous that they could have been the eyes of the devil, were they not so evidently ruled by his heart."

The Auvergne, in south-central France, has been politically noteworthy since Julius Caesar's time, when the legendary chieftain Vercingetorix headed the powerful Arverni there. Hereditary aristocratic titles were established by local counts starting in 913. At different times parts of the Auvergne were controlled by the ducs de Bourbon, Louise de Savoie, Catherine de Médicis, and finally the French Crown. Today the Auvergne comprises four *départements*; its economy is mostly agricultural, with manufacturing centered in the capital of Clermont-Ferrand.

(For more background on Argentina and Cortázar, see p. 132.)

The problem of the eradication of crocodiles from Auvergne has long troubled the governors and administrators of that region, who have stumbled over all sorts of obstacles in carrying out their task and have often been on the verge of abandoning it with plausible, but clearly fallacious, pretexts.

The pretexts are plausible because, in the first place, no one has ever admitted seeing a crocodile in Auvergne, so that from the start any attempt to exterminate them is surrounded with difficulties. The most sophisticated investigations, based on the latest findings of the Butantan Institute and the FAO,[1] like similar investigations in which one never addresses the central proposition directly, instead accumulating tangential data that can, using a structuralist methodology, expose the object sought, have always resulted in complete failure. Both the police forces and the psychologists who have conducted these investigations believe that the negative responses and bewilderment of the interrogated subjects prove unequivocally the existence of vast numbers of crocodiles in Auvergne and that, given the mentality of the inhabitants of that region, there must be a tacit, ancestral understanding among them that causes them to react with wide-eyed astonishment when they are interviewed in their farms and fields and asked if they have ever seen a crocodile in the immediate vicinity, or if a crocodile has ever eaten their eggs or their children, that is, their means of existence and continuance.

There can no longer be any doubt that nearly all the inhabitants have seen crocodiles, but the belief that the first to speak out will suffer grave injury to person and property makes them bide their time in the hope that someone else, driven beyond his endurance by the devastation these pernicious animals have wrought on his fields and stables, will decide to lodge a complaint with the authorities. According to the calculations of the OMS,[2] four or five centuries have already elapsed in that expectation, and obviously the crocodiles have taken advantage of this to multiply and proliferate freely throughout Auvergne.

In recent years the authorities have managed to convince a few of the more educated and intelligent countrymen that they will not be harmed if they reveal the existence of the crocodiles, whereas their eradication will instead greatly improve the quality of life in this French province. To this end, social workers and psychologists specially sent from the urban centers have offered the strongest assurances that announcing the

4

---

[1] Food and Agriculture Organization of the United Nations. — Ed.
[2] French initials for the World Health Organization of the United Nations. — Ed.

existence of the crocodiles will not bring one any harm — certainly no one will be asked to leave his lands to repeat his testimony in Clermont Ferrand or any other city, his property will not be invaded by police, and his wells will not be poisoned. All that is needed, in fact, to launch a full-scale attack on these dangerous beasts is for one inhabitant to say the word, and the authorities will set in action a plan that has been in the works for years for the greater public good.

Nothing has come of these promises. As yet no one had admitted seeing a crocodile in Auvergne, even though our investigators possess scientific evidence showing that even very young children are perfectly aware of their existence and talk about it among themselves when they are playing or drawing, so the crocodiles continue to enjoy the malignant impunity afforded them by their spurious nonexistence. Needless to say, these circumstances make their eradication more than problematical, and the danger of swimming in the streams or walking through the fields grows greater every year. The frequent disappearance of minors, which the police are forced for statistical purposes to attribute to speleological[3] mishaps or white slavery, is undoubtedly the work of the crocodiles. Often neighboring farmers argue and even kill each other over vanished cows and sheep for which they hold each other responsible. From the obstinate silence that follows these bloody disputes, the psychologists have drawn the conclusion that the true culprits were crocodiles, and that the personal accusations came from the desire to feign an ignorance that in the end benefits no one. How else can we explain the fact that no one has ever found the skeleton of a crocodile that has died of age or illness? The region's trout fishermen could surely answer that question, but they too hold their tongues; yet it is not difficult to guess the reason for the fires frequently lit at night under the pretext of making woodash, where under thick layers of branches and trunks lie remains that would finally prove the existence of these dangerous animals.

In the hope of surprising a slip-up, an involuntary admission, or some other lucky break that will at last furnish the official proof that is required, the authorities long ago made the necessary arrangements for the eradication of the vast numbers of crocodiles that infest Auvergne. Thanks to the enlightened cooperation of UNESCO, the best African, Indian, and Thai specialists have explained methods and provided instruction that will permit the eradication of the plague within a few months. In every

---

[3]Speleology is the study or exploration of caves. — ED.

district headquarters there is an official who controls strategically situated stockpiles of arms and the most lethal poisons and has the power to execute a bold offensive against the crocodiles. Each week practice exercises are carried out in the police schools for the battle against the crocodiles and, with the coming of autumn, the season when these reptiles lay their eggs and show a greater tendency to lie in the sun and become lethargic, these forces will initiate extensive maneuvers in the rural areas, including dragging the rivers, exploring the numerous caves and pits, and systematically searching the fields and barns where the females can hide to raise their young. All of this, however, has so far assumed the guise of an ordinary campaign against annoying insects, predatory birds, and illicit hunting, because the authorities, understandably, shrink from exposing themselves to ridicule for persecuting animals whose existence is not borne out by any concrete evidence. Nonetheless, inhabitants are surely aware of the real purpose of these operations and contribute cheerfully to their execution, which will result in the obvious benefits already mentioned, since the psychologists who accompany the police on their forays have noted that any casual mention of crocodiles, made casually or to entice an unofficial statement, are greeted with signs of astonishment and hilarity, which, even if they don't fool anyone, compromise the smooth development of the operations, which demand absolute cooperation between the inhabitants and the armed forces.

In summary, though this assertion may appear a bit abstract, Auvergne may be considered effectively protected against crocodiles, whose depredations will be terminated with unusual efficiency. From a strictly theoretical and logical point of view, we can even affirm that crocodiles do not exist in Auvergne, since everything is prepared for their extinction. Unfortunately, as long as circumstances do not permit these operations to be undertaken, Auvergne will remain infested with crocodiles, which constitute a permanent threat to the economy and well-being of that lovely region of France.

EXPLORATIONS

1. From whose viewpoint is "Regarding the Eradication of Crocodiles from Auvergne" ostensibly written? What clues in the essay enable you to tell?

2. How would you describe the tone of Cortázar's essay? What seems to be the attitude of the governors and administrators of Auvergne toward their jobs? toward their constituents?

3. What evidence does Cortázar cite as proof that Auvergne is infested with crocodiles? What prejudicial words and phrases (for example, "plausible" and "there must be" in paragraph 2; "admitted" and "are forced . . . to attribute" in paragraph 5) help him make his case?

CONNECTIONS

1. What similarities exist between the administrators' strategies in "Regarding the Eradication of Crocodiles from Auvergne" and Marcos's strategies in James Fenton's "The Philippine Election"? How do the administrators and Marcos view their constituents in relation to their goals?

2. What comments in Frank Trippett's *Observation* help to explain the behavior Cortázar describes? What noteworthy differences exist between Trippett's legislators and Cortázar's administrators?

ELABORATIONS

1. Write an essay analyzing "Regarding the Eradication of Crocodiles from Auvergne" as a commentary on the role of trust in the relationship between governors and governed.

2. The history of politics, including U.S. politics, is full of governmental over-reactions to perceived threats. (A classic recent example is the Watergate incident, in which supporters of Republican President Richard Nixon broke into Democratic headquarters, although in fact Nixon's reelection was virtually certain.) "Regarding the Eradication of Crocodiles from Auvergne" dramatizes this kind of political paranoia by making the threat so farfetched that the government's reaction becomes absurd. Choose a threat to the United States, or to your town or school, that you think has been exaggerated. Write an essay in which you use satire, as Cortázar does, to dramatize your case.

GERMAINE GREER

In Cuba

Germaine Greer was born in Australia in 1939. She won scholarships first to a convent in Melbourne and then to Melbourne University, from which she graduated at age twenty. After receiving a First Class Honours master's degree from Sydney University, she taught in a girls' high school and later at the university. Greer went to England in 1964 as a Commonwealth Scholar and received her Ph.D. on Shakespeare from Cambridge University. While working on her thesis she lived in Calabria in southeastern Italy, where she was impressed by the satisfaction and prestige the local women found in a matriarchal role. (Those women feature in her 1985 book *Sex and Destiny*; her feminist interpretation *Shakespeare* appeared in 1986.) Greer went on to teach at Warwick University, simultaneously working in television and journalism, and to write her first book, *The Female Eunuch* (1971). This manifesto of the feminist movement made her a celebrity and spokeswoman, in which capacity she has continued to travel, lecture, research, and write.

The Republic of Cuba, consisting of one large and several small islands 135 miles off Florida's southern tip, is the first Communist republic in the Western Hemisphere. Cuba became a Spanish possession in 1492, when Christopher Columbus claimed it on his first voyage to the New World. By the nineteenth century its economy centered on the sugar industry. The United States, a major trading partner and investor, became involved in Cuba's struggles for independence. Following the Spanish-American War, Spain freed Cuba (1899) and the United States occupied it, withdrawing its troops in 1902 but continuing to play a dominant role in the economy. Sugar, gambling, and tourism prospered but benefited only a few Cubans. In 1958 Fidel Castro and a guerrilla army succeeded in overthrowing the government of dictator Fulgencio Batista. Allying with the Soviet Union, Castro nationalized foreign-owned businesses and instituted many Soviet-style changes. Cuba currently supports Communist revolution throughout the Third World, sending troops to Angola (see p. 576) and arms and advisers to various African and Central American countries.

I came to Cuba with my heart in my mouth. Ever since my first contact with the "Third World," in Jamaica in 1971, I had been aware how burningly important it is for the developing nations that Cuba not be a fraud or a failure. As the years passed and I wandered through slums in Bombay, past windowless huts in Morocco, Tunis, and Yucatán, through the dust of Uttar Pradesh and the infested dirt of the Brazilian northeast and the menace of Bogotá and the Guatemalan highlands, every step showed me that paternalist development aid is worse than useless. In the eighties, as the external debts of the developing countries mushroom over them while their people grow steadily poorer and the number of landless multiplies daily, the need of a genuine alternative is agonizing. If Cuba had shown me nothing but the institutionalized poverty and bureaucratic rhetoric and repression that Western megamedia taught me to expect, a brainwashed militarized population living by hypocrisy and fear, the dark future would show no sign of dawn. If Cuba's was really a revolution of the people, then even if a malignant power should blast Cuba out of the Caribbean, its people will be invincible.

My arrival coincided with the Fourth Congress of the Federation of Cuban Women, the FMC. Billboards and posters announced it all over Havana. *Toda la fuerza de la mujer en el servicio de la revolución* ("The entire women's force in the service of the revolution"). The logo was an art nouveauish montage of Kalashnikov rifles and Mariposa lilies. I was not keen on the implications of either. On the Rampa, the floodlit exhibition pavilion was turned over to the exploits of women. Banked television sets showed color videos of the history of Cuban women, and a succession of booths displayed everything from the techniques of screening for breast cancer to scent and hair curlers. Women whose bottoms threatened to burst out of their elasticized pants tottered round the exhibits on four-inch heels, clutching their *compañeros* for support. Their nails and faces were garishly painted. Their hair had been dragged over rollers, bleached, dyed, and colored. Their clothes, including their brassieres, were all two or three sizes too small and flesh bulged everywhere. Most people rushed past the educational exhibits to where a painted, conked, and corseted trio bumped and ground its way through an amorous rumba. At the sight of an unattached woman, the loose men began a psst! psst! and beckoned to me, as if I had been a dog.

The next day, my minder from the Ministry of Exterior Relations came to take me to the Palacio de Congresos for the first session of the FMC Congress. Security was tight. I was directed to a press box in the back of the vast auditorium, with no facilities for simultaneous translation. A policeman ordered me not to put my tape recorder up on the parapet. Later I discovered that one such instrument had been accidentally knocked off and narrowly missed braining a delegate seated thirty feet below, but then and there it seemed that Cuba was determined that I would see little and understand less. The whole day was taken up with the reading of the *informe central*, the 157-page official report to the congress. The reader was Vilma Espín, president of the FMC, alternate member of the Politburo, member of the Central Committee of the Communist Party, and wife of Raúl Castro, Fidel's brother. She read correctly and quietly, a calm, matronly figure hard to associate with the slender girl who had organized the medical support system during the *lucha clandestina* and joined the guerrilla fighters in the Sierra Maestra. I complained that she was hardly a charismatic speaker. "She doesn't have to impress us," answered one of the delegates. "We know her. She is our Vilma."

Alongside her, in the front row of the serried ranks of officebearers on the dais, sat Fidel Castro, quietly reading through the report. I expected him to make some formal rhetorical statement, as befits a totalitarian figurehead, putting in a token appearance for the Association of Townswomen's Guilds before leaving to take care of more pressing matters of state. To my surprise, he sat there quietly the whole day long, reading, caressing his beard, thinking, and listening. The next day he was there again. As one of the delegates waxed eloquent on discrimination against women in the workplace, a man's voice interjected. "This is the heart of the problem, isn't it? Women's access to work!" I looked about, wondering who owned these mild, slightly high-pitched tones. It was Castro, whom I soon learned to call what every Cuban calls him, Compañero Fidel. He was leaning forward earnestly, intent on participating in the debate, not leading but participating. If anything, the discussion became less formal and more spontaneous, as delegates held up their hands for recognition and described precise problems of access to work. The women claimed that they were considered more likely to absent themselves from work, because of their family responsibilities. Fidel pointed out that men still refuse to shoulder their part of the burden of housekeeping and child rearing as laid down by the Cuban Family Code. The women pointed out that in fact the absenteeism of women workers was often less than that of men, and certainly no greater. Fidel pointed out that women shoulder a double duty, which is unequal, and the women argued that they were not prepared to give it up. Sometimes when the head of state wagged his hand for recognition, the chairperson ignored him. At other times, the delegates noisily disagreed with him, crying, "No, no!" some even booing.

I had been prepared for the chants of Fidel! Fidel! but nothing had prepared me for this. I thought ruefully of Margaret Thatcher and Indira Gandhi, each incapable of listening, especially to someone who disagreed with her. And all the time Fidel made jokes, selected funny comparisons, continually pressing the delegates to give concrete, living examples. Their carefully prepared statements went all to pieces. We discovered that women did not want men to have the same leave to absent themselves from work for family reasons, because they would abuse it and use the time to visit other women — or at least the delegates thought they might — and thus one of the most fascinating contradictions in Cuban sexual politics was drawn out in a public forum of 1,400 participants. . . .

This was early days, but already I could feel something unfamiliar and very special about Cuba. The absence of theatricality that I noticed in Vilma and Fidel was part of a complex of attitudes. People did not sell themselves as they do in consumer society. Life was not soap opera, but real. There was no competition or character assassination, as people jockeyed for limelight. They spoke not to persuade or bamboozle, but to explain. They had not our prurient interest in domestic and sexual affairs. No one was quite sure how many children Fidel might have had, or, for that matter, Vilma. Public functionaires were assessed on their performance of their public duty, and did not have to drag their bed partners around with them, miming domestic bliss. Life without gossip magazines and advertising seemed wonderfully uncluttered. There was no equivalent of Princess Diana's latest outfit or Elizabeth Taylor's latest wedding or the American president's hemorrhoids. Doubtless there are some Cubans who think life would be more interesting if murder and rape were reported in the newspapers and convicted criminals were paid a working man's earnings over ten years to describe their activities in lurid detail, but most of the people I met know the other culture from glimpses of Miami television and find it crazy and perverse. The slice of American culture they get from Miami includes late-night pornographic videos, which do nothing to improve the U.S. image. Some Cubans, the ones who steal designer jeans off foreigners' clotheslines in Miramar and offer to change pesos for dollars, giving five times the official exchange rate so that they can buy ghetto blasters in the dollar shops, obviously envy the hyperstimulated life-style of capitalism, but all the Cubans I met and talked to were more interested in Ethiopia and Guatemala than in Michael Jackson.

A Chilean exile explained to me, "I could have stayed in West Germany. They were paying me a fortune, but what could I do with it? Invest in the latest parsley cutter? Life is exciting here, even if I have very little money. There is always something to do, and it's exciting. People are creating their own future. If I got sick in Germany I could lie and rot. Here, if I don't show up at the *tienda* for my rations, people are straight round to help." Her bath was kept permanently full of water to flush the lavatory, for Havana has a chronic and crippling water shortage, just another minor inconvenience that women have to deal with, but it made no dent in Elisabeth's fierce loyalty to Cuba. As we sat on her tiny balcony, drinking *añejo sobre las rocas*, while people flowed in and out of the tiny apartments above, beside, and below us, and the old red buses, affectionately known as *guaguas*, groaned and shrieked down the hill, disgorging streams of workers, she said, "It's a hard life, but a good life."

The Cubans are involved after all in a much bigger adventure than 8 sex, speed, and smack could possibly supply. Their morale is towering, even if their energy should occasionally flag, as they negotiate the daily obstacle course which is life in a poor country, cursed by an irreplaceable investment in a single crop — sugar — and strangled by the American blockade which has cut off the only cheap source of supply for all the goods a single-crop economy does not produce. Every Cuban will tell you that underdevelopment is a feature of minds and hearts as well as economies. As Cubans struggle to develop logistical and communicative skills, they encounter inefficiency and confusion at all levels of social organization. The response is not irritability and hostility, but tolerance and mutual assistance.

Because of rationing, limited supplies of essential commodities, and the unreliability of transport (given shortage of vehicles and spare parts), queuing is a way of life, but Cubans do not try to jump queues or stand guard to see that no one else does. Instead they have developed a characteristic solution to an intolerable situation. When you arrive at the *tienda*, to find fifty people already waiting for their ration of rice, beans, oil, crackers, fruit juice, or whatever other commodity is on sale that day, you simply ask who is *el último*. When another person arrives, and you are asked the same thing, you are free to go about other business and return when the queue has moved up. People less pressed chat, criticize the authorities, flirt, and clown around. When you come back the person who was behind you will call you to your place. This ad hoc system involves cooperation and a degree of awareness of other people, neither often found in rich countries. Even on my last day in Cuba, when I found a hundred people queuing at the hotel cashier's desk, I could hardly prevent myself from panicking, thinking I had no time to pack because I would be queuing for two hours or so (given the mean speed of such transactions in Cuba). However, I tried asking *el último* and went about my other chores. When I came down, the honeymooners behind me waved me to my place, by now only four from the head of the line. As I had screamed and ranted at the hotel management about their inefficiency, while they politely defended a system I condemned as hopeless, I felt truly ashamed. . . .

Outsiders may assume that Cuba is actually a dictatorship masquerading as a democratic republic and that real power is vested in the Politburo or the Central Committee of the Communist Party; such in fact is not the case. In 1976, Cubans voted in a referendum to accept a socialist constitution which enunciated the principle by which the popular assemblies became the ultimate legislative power in the land. Those of us accustomed to seeing democratic processes subverted by lobbying, patronage, and secret government would assume that the huge machinery of *Poder Popular* [People Power] could do little but rubber-stamp legislation originating in the inner recesses of the Communist Party. In fact, the grass-roots-level assemblies do originate the legislative process, follow it through, and participate actively in the drafting of legislation. For such a cumbersome system to work, the enthusiastic participation of large numbers of people for frequent and long sessions is indispensable, yet the system has produced the new housing law in Cuba, which has less to do with socialist ideology than the pragmatic expression of the people's will. Rather than nationalize housing, the Cubans have chosen to own their own homes, amid a multitude of special considerations regarding leasing, letting, and inheritance, all designed to protect the right to own one's home and prevent speculation or profiteering.

Democratic centralism, if earnestly undertaken, is the system which produces the least return for the most massive expenditure of human resources. Frequent long meetings, with the intervening struggle to study unfamiliar matters, such as housing law, contract, equity, conveyancing, and alternative administrative systems, as in the case of the 1985 *Ley de las Viviendas* (Housing Law), must arrive at unanimity, much as juries do, by long argument and counterargument. The amateur legislators — for only the full-time functionaries are paid — must struggle to keep the process under control, agreeing agendas and then following them through. The process demands what Cuban women have least of — time — yet, even so, 27 percent of delegates in *Poder Popular* are women. This is more significant than the presence of women on the Central Committee of the Communist Party; nevertheless of 119 members and 71 alternates, 27 are women, 17 of them full members. Women formed 22 percent of the delegates elected at the Second Party Congress, an increase of 50 percent over the First Party Conference. The Third Party Congress this year will probably be attended by a high proportion of women and elect more female members of the Central Committee. . . .

Perhaps the true extent of women's power in Cuba is best illustrated   12 not by quoting numbers on the Central Committee, but in a homely example which shows how important women are to Cuba. Every sexually active woman in Cuba at risk of contracting cervical cancer is given her smear test every two years. Every year hundreds of women's lives are saved by prompt treatment, while in England, Equal Opportunities Commission or no, women are dying because they have not had their smears, because they did not have them often enough, and because they were not informed when the cells were seen to be abnormal. The British health service could not cope with the demand if all the women who should ask for smear tests did, and presented themselves for further treatment. Yet little Cuba manages it. Follow-up and recall are carried out at street level by the FMC and the Committee for the Defense of the Revolution, while the state institutions supply the technical facilities. This may not be evidence of power as it is commonly perceived by capitalist societies, but access to the technology in order to save your own life is the kind of power women want. It is real power, unlike the authoritarian fantasies that pass for power in most of the world. And the women of Cuba struggled for it, defined it, and exercise it on their own behalf. It remains to be seen now whether Cuban women will raise their own standard in the world forum and show the other emergent nations how to harness the strength and tenderness of women in the remaking of our tired and guilty world. As Cuba's leaders have always realized, survival is too desperate a matter to be left to half the world's population.

EXPLORATIONS

1. What mood does Greer create with her opening sentence? What central question is posed in her first paragraph? Where and how does she answer this question? How would the essay's impact change if Greer began with her conclusions about Cuba instead of her curiosity?

2. What biases does Greer bring to her report on Cuba? How does she reveal her biases? What efforts does she make to allow for or counterbalance her biases? What evidence in her essay suggests whether and how Greer's biases affected her conclusions?

3. In describing Cuba's legislative process, Greer comments, "For such a cumbersome system to work, the enthusiastic participation of large numbers of people for frequent and long sessions is indispensable." What aspects of Cuban culture, as Greer describes it, seem likely to have influenced the country's choice of this system?

CONNECTIONS

1. What similar problems seem to have triggered "people power" in Cuba and the Philippines? What goals are shared by citizens of both countries? Which government do you think has a bigger job ahead of it, and why?

2. "She doesn't have to impress us," an FMC Congress delegate says of FMC President Vilma Espín. "We know her. She is our Vilma." What does the delegate mean? How does her attitude resemble the Filipinos' attitude toward Corazón Aquino? the Zairians' attitude toward Mobutu Sese Seko? What are the advantages and dangers of citizens' feeling a strong personal rapport with their leader?

3. Which of the concerns expressed by Vicki Williams in her *Observation* are shared by the Cubans Greer interviewed? How do Williams's assumptions and expectations about government compare with Greer's? Do you think Williams would leave the United States for Cuba? Why or why not?

ELABORATIONS

1. "The state can no more create a sense of neighborhood or community than it can create love or friendship," writes Robert Nisbet in his *Observation*. Do you think Greer would agree? Write an essay comparing and contrasting Nisbet's and Greer's views of the state's potential impact on society, drawing on your reading in this book for evidence and examples.

2. In describing Fidel Castro's participation in the FMC Congress, Greer writes, "Sometimes when the head of state wagged his hand for recognition, the chairperson ignored him. At other times, the delegates noisily disagreed with him." In "The New African Chiefs," David Lamb writes, "The mildest criticism of [Malawi's President] Banda guarantees a stretch in jail." Write an essay comparing the pros and cons of these two approaches to political power.

LIANG HENG and
JUDITH SHAPIRO

Chairman Mao's
Good Little Boy

Liang Heng was born in 1954 in Changsha, the Central Chinese city where Mao Zedong went to high school. Liang's childhood coincided with a period of violent pendulum swings in Communist Party policy. For about eight years after establishing the People's Republic of China in 1949, Chairman Mao and his cohorts enjoyed wide popular support for unifying the government and improving economic and social conditions. In the mid-1950s, however, the Party's moves to encourage criticism boomeranged into an "Anti-Rightist" campaign against the critics. "Chairman Mao's Good Little Boy" comes from the first chapter of Liang's autobiography, *Son of the Revolution* (1983), which describes the chaos and fear of those early years.

His family's victimization hardly dampened Liang's revolutionary loyalty. After the events he narrates here, Liang became a Red Guard, went on a quixotic "New Long March" during which he nearly starved and froze, traveled to Beijing to see Mao, plunged into the "black society" of teenage dropouts scrounging for a living on the streets of Changsha, and worked as a peasant on a commune. His escape route was basketball, which took him to a city job and eventually to college. Judith Shapiro was born in 1953. She met Liang at Hunan Teachers' College, where she was teaching American literature. Their secret romance culminated in marriage in 1980. They now live in New York City, where Liang is a doctoral candidate at Columbia University and Shapiro writes and works as an interpreter for the U.S. State Department.

(For more background on China, see pp. 220 and 635.)

Once when I was nearly four, I decided to escape from the child-care center. The idea of waiting through another Saturday afternoon was unbearable. I would stand with the other children in the office doorway, yelling out the names of those whose relatives we spotted coming to rescue them. I would become frantic and miserable as the possibility that I had been forgotten seemed more and more real. Then at last the frail figure of my beloved Waipo, my maternal grandmother, would appear to take me away. But this week I wouldn't have to wait. I had just discovered a doorway leading from the kitchen directly onto the Changsha streets, left ajar, perhaps, by the cooks now that the bitter winter weather had passed. So, during after-lunch nap, I crawled over the green bars of my crib and stole softly out, past the sleeping rows of my fellow inmates, past Nurse Nie dozing in her chair. I crept into the coal-dark kitchen with its silent black works. Then I exploded out the door into the dazzling light of freedom.

The child-care center was hateful. You couldn't eat sweets when you wanted to, and you had to fold your hands behind your back and sing a song before the nurses would let you eat your meals. Then, if you ate too fast, they hit you over the head with a fly swatter. The songs and dances — like "Sweeping the Floor," "Working in the Factory," and "Planting Trees in the Countryside" — were fun, but I was constantly in trouble for wanting to dance the army dance when it was time for the hoeing dance or for refusing to take the part of the landlord, the wolf, or the lazybones. I also had problems with the interminable rest periods. We weren't allowed to get up even if we weren't tired, so I had nothing to do but stare at a small mole on my leg for hours at a time.

At the time, such early education was a privilege for which only the children of cadres were eligible. Although neither of my parents' ranks was high, my father's position as reporter, editor, and founding member of the Party newspaper the *Hunan Daily*, and my mother's as a promising cadre in the Changsha Public Security Bureau were enough to qualify me. My parents were deeply involved in all the excitement of working to transform China into a great Socialist country, eager to sacrifice themselves for others. They dreamed passionately of the day when they would be deemed pure and devoted enough to be accepted into the Party. It was only natural that the family come second; Father's duties at the newspaper often kept him away for several months at a time, and my mother came home only on Sundays, if at all, for she had a room in her own unit and stayed there to attend evening meetings. So at the age of three I was sent off to the child-care center for early training in Socialist thought through collective living, far from the potentially corrupting influence of family life. My departure may have been harder for my two grandmothers, of course. They had had the major responsibility for raising the three of us children; I was the last child to go and they would miss me very much.

I had lived first with my paternal grandmother, my Nai Nai, a tall, stern, bony woman who always wore traditional black. She lived in the apartment the *Hunan Daily* had allotted to Father, two rooms on the

4

second floor of a cadres' dormitory, spacious enough but with a shared kitchen and an outhouse some distance away. She was a pious Buddhist and a vegetarian, strict with herself and everyone else but her own grandchildren.

At ten pounds, I had been the biggest baby ever recorded at Changsha's No. 1 Hospital, and Nai Nai had hired a series of seven wet nurses before she found one who could satisfy my appetite. She was a nineteen-year-old peasant girl from a town beyond the city whose own baby had died. Nai Nai told me later that she was the only one who had enough milk so that I could suck her breasts dry without throwing a tantrum immediately afterwards; I have always given credit to her for my unusual height — I am 6'1". Then after she left because she had no Changsha city residence card, Nai Nai sent me to live with my maternal grandmother, my Waipo, who lived off a winding little alleyway not far away.

It was much more crowded there, since Waipo, my Uncle Yan, and his wife and their small children made three generations in a single dark room. But I liked the place for its liveliness and because I was Waipo's favorite. She gave me candies and took me everywhere with her, even to the free market to buy from the peasants who had carried in their vegetables from the suburbs. Waipo was a tiny woman with big twisted teeth and little wrinkled hands, talkative and lively and very different from Nai Nai. Her husband had died when she was young, after only two children, whereas Nai Nai's husband had given her nine before he slipped and fell on the icy road in front of the old City Gate. In the old society, a woman couldn't remarry and remain respectable, so Waipo had supported herself and her children by making shoe soles at home. She continued to do this even after Mother and Uncle Yan were grown and had jobs, and the cloth patches she used were among my first toys.

Another reason I liked living with Waipo was that Mother often preferred to go there on Sundays rather than to our own home, where Nai Nai was, because she didn't get along well with her mother-in-law. Nai Nai sometimes carried her concern for others so far that she became a busybody. She was always the first to sweep the public stairwell or volunteer to lead neighborhood hygiene movements, and she was constantly scolding Mother for not dressing us warmly enough or not buying us more milk to drink. She was so tall that she must have been imposing for Mother to deal with, and tradition demanded that Mother obey her. So although Mother was a feisty woman, she was supposed to look on silently as Nai Nai spoiled us with candy and, in later years, did my second sister's homework for her. Father was no help, because he was bound by the same filial laws as she.

In any case, Mother's ties to her new home could not have been 8 strong ones, for she had hardly known Father before they married. Someone had introduced them as prospective mates; they had exchanged a few letters (Father was working in Guilin at the time) and decided the question soon after on the basis of their common political enthusiasm. Father was far more intellectual than she, for he had been trained by the Party as a reporter, had a wide range of literary interests, and was an accomplished poet as well as an amateur composer and conductor. Mother was capable too, of course, a strong-willed person who liked to express her opinions, and a loving mother when she had the time. Still, as I thought back on it in later years, I realized my parents were so rarely together that it was almost a marriage of convenience.

So it was Waipo's home that was my early emotional center, and it was there that I went on the fresh spring day of my flight. I had to cross a large street, but fortunately I made it from one side to the other without mishap, and ran the remaining few hundred yards to the narrow room off the little gray alley.

To my utter dismay, Waipo didn't look at all glad to see me. "Little Fatso, what are you doing here?" she cried, and with scarcely a pause grabbed my hand and pulled me the few blocks to Nai Nai's home in *Hunan Daily* compound. From there the two old ladies half lifted, half dragged me back to my confinement, ignoring my screams and tears.

The nurses had discovered my absence. Without any show of the politeness they usually maintained before their charges' relatives, they cursed and scolded me as if they would never stop. When my grandmothers had left, they locked me up in a room with two other offenders, saying, "You are not Chairman Mao's good little boy; you haven't upheld Revolutionary discipline. You can stay in there until you think things over."

My fellow captives were as miserable as I. One had stolen some candy, 12 and the other, having graduated proudly from wearing slit pants, had promptly soiled his new ones. Although it was certainly convenient to be able to squat down anywhere and do one's business, among us children the slit was an embarrassing symbol of immaturity. It had another drawback too: Nai Nai's blows still stung on my bottom. I looked at the unlucky boy with pity. He would now be doomed to at least another year of babyhood and easy spankings.

The nurses' words had another kind of sting for me, since I had been taught Chairman Mao was like the sun itself. At home, "Mao" had been my first word after "Mama," "Baba," and "Nai Nai," for I had been held up to the large framed picture Father had hung over the doorway and instructed in the sound. Later I had learned how to say "I love Chairman Mao" and "Long Live Chairman Mao." But it wasn't until I got to the child-care center that I really began to understand. He presided over our rest and play like a benevolent god, and I believed that apples, grapes, everything had been given to us because he loved us. When the nurses told me the next day that Chairman Mao had forgiven me, I was the happiest child in the world.

During the next year, my second at the child-care center, I learned how to write my first characters. The first word was made up of the four strokes in the Chairman's name. Next I learned to write the characters in my own name, and I discovered that I was not called "Little Fatso," as Waipo had proudly nicknamed me, but something quite different, with a political story behind it:

On the morning of May 2, 1954, the Vietnamese won a decisive victory over the French at Dien Bien Phu. That very afternoon my mother gave birth to me, a ten-pound baby boy, the distant sounds of drums and cymbals an accompaniment to her labors. My father, reporting the Vietnam story for the *Hunan Daily*, thought it only natural to name me Liang Dian-jie, "Liang Good News from Dien Bien Phu." He was flushed with a double victory, for at last he had a son to carry on the family line.

It wasn't the first time he had chosen a significant name for a child. 16 My eldest sister was born in 1949, so she joined the ranks of thousands of children named for the birth of New China with the name Liang Fang, "Liang Liberation." My second sister, born in 1952 when the Chinese armies were marching across the Yalu River to defend Korea against the Americans, was called Liang Wei-ping, "Liang Defender of Peace." As we grew up we discovered that you could often guess someone's age by his name, and that at times, if someone had been named at the height of some movement that was later discredited, a name could become an embarrassment, a burden, or even a reason for being attacked. My parents' own names reflected an earlier, less politicized time; my mother Yan Zhi-de was "Yan the Moral," and my father Liang Ying-qiu was "Liang Whose Requests Will Be Answered," although he usually went by his literary name, Liang Shan.

I came gradually to recognize all of these characters and more, for during the third year and final fourth year at the child-care center we began our study properly, writing "Chairman Mao is our Great Saving Star," "We are all Chairman Mao's good little children," "The Communist Party is like the sun," "When I am big I will be a worker" (or peasant or soldier). We also learned simple arithmetic, paper folding and paper cutting, and were given small responsibilities like watering the plants or cleaning the classroom.

Meanwhile, whenever I went home to Waipo's, I hoped Mother would be there, for I loved her very much despite our limited time together. But when I was about four, I began to sense there was something wrong. She would come home looking worried and she never played with me, just talked on and on with Uncle Yan in a hushed Liuyang County dialect which I couldn't understand. Finally, one Saturday afternoon it was Nai Nai who came to get me, and I was told Mother had gone away and I shouldn't go to Waipo's house anymore.

Only years later was I old enough to understand what had happened, and more than twenty years passed before anyone, including Mother herself, got the full picture. In early 1957 the "Hundred Flowers Movement" had been launched. Its official purpose was to give the Party a chance to correct its shortcomings by listening to the masses' criticisms. Father was away in the countryside reporting on something, but in the Changsha Public Security Building, meetings were held and everyone was urged to express his or her opinions freely.

Mother didn't know what to do. She really loved the Party and didn't 20 have any criticisms to make; the Party had given her a job and saved her from the most abject poverty. Still, her leaders said that everyone should participate actively in the movement, especially those who hoped someday to join the Party. Mother was already in favor; she had been given the important job of validating arrest warrants for the whole city. So, regarding it her duty to come up with something, she finally thought of three points she could make. She said that her Section Head sometimes used crude language and liked to criticize people, that he should give his housekeeper a bed to sleep on instead of making her sleep on the floor, and that sometimes when it came time to give raises, the leaders didn't listen to the masses' opinions.

But then, with utterly confusing rapidity, the "Hundred Flowers Movement" changed into the "Anti-Rightist Movement." Perhaps the Party was caught off guard by the amount of opposition and felt compelled to crack down. Or maybe, as I've heard said, the "Hundred Flowers Movement" had been a trap designed from the beginning to uncover Rightist elements. Anyway, every unit was given a quota of Rightists, and Mother's name was among those at the Public Security Bureau.

It was disastrous. When she was allowed to see her file in 1978, she found out that she had been given a Rightist's "cap" solely because of those three criticisms she had made. Perhaps her Section Head was angry at her; perhaps her unit was having trouble filling its quota. At the time she had no idea what the verdict was based on, she only knew that a terrible wrong had been done. But there was no court of appeal. Mother was sent away to the suburb of Yuan Jia Ling for labor reform. She lost her cadre's rank and her salary was cut from fifty-five to fifteen *yuan* a month. (A *yuan* is one hundred Chinese cents. . . .). My naive and trusting mother went to work as a peasant.

Just as his wife was being declared an enemy of the Party, Father was actively participating in the Anti-Rightist Movement in his own unit. Father believed in the Party with his whole heart, believed that the Party could never make a mistake or hand down a wrong verdict. It was a tortuous dilemma; Father's traditional Confucian sense of family obligation told him to support Mother while his political allegiance told him to condemn her. In the end, his commitment to the Party won out, and he denounced her. He believed that was the only course that could save the family from ruin.

I still remember the first time Mother came home for a visit. It was a   24
rainy Sunday in late autumn, and Father and Nai Nai were both out. There were footsteps on the stairs and in the corridor, but it was almost a minute before the knock came, timidly. Liang Fang opened the door.

Mother was almost unrecognizable. She was in patched blue peasant clothing, muddy up to the knees. The skin on her kind round face looked thick, leathery, and not too clean, and someone had chopped her hair off short and uneven. There was something both broader and thinner about her. "Mama!" cried Liang Fang.

Liang Wei-ping and I ran up to her too, and she was hugging us all at once, weeping, forgetting to put down her oilpaper umbrella. Then as my sisters rushed to pour tea and bring a basin of hot water for her to wash her face, she sat on the bed and held me tightly for a long time. After she had rested, she busied herself with all the housework Nai Nai couldn't do alone, sweeping, dusting, and sharpening our pencils for us, scrubbing our clothes, and cleaning the windows. She wouldn't speak of where she'd been, just asked us about our schoolwork, our health, Father's health. We were so happy. We thought Mother had come home.

She was tying bows on Liang Fang's braids when Father came back. He was astounded to see her, and not very warm. "What are you doing here?" he demanded. "Did you ask for leave?"

Mother lowered her head at his harshness. "Of course I asked for leave," she said defensively. "I can come home once a month." 28

This silenced Father for a few minutes, and he paced meditatively around the room, his tall thin frame overpowering hers as Nai Nai's used to do. Then he poured out a stream of words, political words — on the meaning of the Anti-Rightist Movement, on her obligation to recognize her faults and reform herself. It was as if he had turned into a propaganda machine. I suppose he thought it was his duty to help reeducate her.

For a while she listened in silence, her head bowed, but at last she protested. "All right, I'm a Rightist, it's all my fault. You don't have to say anything else, my head is bursting. I hear this kind of thing all day long, write self-criticisms every week, and now I come home and I have to hear it all over again."

"I don't think you recognize what you've done. You're just wasting your labor reform," he said.

"What makes you so sure?" Mother's face was white and defiant. 32

Father exploded: "Rightist element! Have some thought for your influence on the children."

It was Mother's turn to lose control. "What did I ever do wrong? The Party asked me to make suggestions, so I did. You give me one example — " But Mother stopped midsentence, for Father had struck her a ringing blow across the face.

She fell back on the bed, weeping; Father strode into the other room and slammed the door. Then slowly, painfully, she picked up her dirty jacket and umbrella as we sobbed miserably. When she was halfway out the door, Father emerged and shouted after her, "Don't come back until you've reformed yourself. The children in this house need a Revolutionary mother, not a Rightist mother." When she paused and turned her tear-streaked face to him, his voice became gentler. "It doesn't matter what you say here, I won't tell anyone. But please watch what you say at the labor camp."

Despite Father's cruelty, Mother came back every month to see us. 36 She must have missed us very much to endure Father's lectures and the inevitable fights. Sometimes she slept in Father's bed and I slept with them; she never lay still and her pillow was always wet in the morning. On other occasions the quarrel was so fierce that she left again almost as soon as she arrived. Father often warned us against her, and if we defended her he became furious, calling us ignorant children who understood nothing.

We didn't know that Father had already raised the question of divorce. He must have reasoned that all of us were doomed unless he broke off with Mother completely, for the custom in such instances was that the whole family would be considered as guilty as the single member who had committed the crime. If there were no legal separation, Father would never be allowed to join the Party, and the files that would be opened on us when we came of age for middle school would say that we came from a Rightist background. We would be branded forever as people with "questions," and it would be difficult for us to go to middle school and college, get decent jobs, or find husbands and wives. Mother's misfortune might mean the end of all of Father's dreams for himself and for his children; he must have hated her for what she had done.

Mother was a proud woman. She believed so deeply she had been wrongly accused that she told him she would divorce him only after her Rightist label was removed. Her stubbornness enraged Father, particularly because there was a secondary movement to criticize those with Rightist tendencies, and with his Rightist wife, Father was a natural target. He had to criticize Mother publicly, write reports confessing his innermost thoughts. And the pressure became even greater after what happened to Uncle Yan.

When Mother first came under attack, her older brother had been as outraged as she. He went to the Public Security Bureau to argue in her defense, and spoke for her at his own unit, the No. 1 Hospital, where he worked with the Communist Youth League. He even came to our house to urge Father to try to help her, although Father thought he was crazy to stick out his neck like that. Sure enough, Uncle Yan was punished for his family loyalties and given a Rightist "cap" of his own to wear, bringing a second black cloud to rest over Waipo's home. His experience proved that Father's sad choice had been a practical one in view of the harsh political realities; when we were old enough to understand, we could hardly blame Father for what he had done.

Nai Nai was frightened to see how easily the Rightist label could 40 spread from one member of the family to another. She had been an enthusiastic supporter of the "Get Rid of the Four Evils" hygiene movement, but where cartoons had once shown housewives sweeping away rats, flies, mosquitoes, and fleas, now they had added a fifth evil, Rightists. Nai Nai could no longer face lecturing lazy neighbors on the dangers of letting water stagnate; she could imagine what they might be saying behind her back about how she ought to get rid of that evil in her own house. When, with traditional filial deference, Father asked for her opinion on the divorce question, she agreed with relief. The family burden was too heavy for her.

Meanwhile, Mother was working hard to rid herself of her "cap." The calluses on her hands were thicker and sharper every time she came home, and her shoulders were rough where the shoulder pole rested. Her skin toasted to a rich yellow-brown. It was a hard life for a young woman who had lived between the protection of her mother's home and her Public Security Bureau office.

The Rightists at Yuan Jia Ling were all trying to prove to the political officials in charge that they had reformed themselves and were ready to leave. There were all types of people, intellectuals, high-ranking cadres, and ordinary workers, but friendships were impossible because the best strategy for gaining the officials' confidence was to report on others. Thus everyone was always watching everyone else, and a grain of rice dropped on the floor could mean an afternoon of criticism for disrespecting the labors of the peasants. Everything was fair game, even what people said in their sleep.

The second essential strategy was to write constant Thought Reports about oneself. Few of the people in the camp felt they were really Rightists, but the only thing to do was to confess one's crimes penitently, record one's lapses, and invent things to repent. Writing these reports eventually became a kind of habit, and Mother almost believed what she was saying about herself.

The last important route to freedom was hard work. One had to add 44 deliberately to one's misery in small ways, like going without a hat under the hot summer sun or continuing to work in the rain after everyone else had quit. Generally the Rightists did ordinary peasants' work, like digging fish-breeding ponds and planting fruit trees, but sometimes they were taken in trucks to special laboring areas to break and carry stones. Then they were put together with ordinary thieves, hoodlums, and Kuomintang (KMT)[1] spies. The people whose arrest warrants Mother had once been in charge of validating were now her equals; it was almost more than she could bear. Still, bear it she did, and all the rest of it, and after three long years, when she could carry more than a hundred pounds of rocks

---

[1] Non-Communist political party. — Ed.

on her back with ease, a bored-looking official summoned her and told her she was no longer a Rightist. She could go home.

She came to the house late at night, looking like a beggar traveling with her ragged belongings. But when she spoke, her voice was clear and proud. "Old Liang," she announced to Father, "I'm a person again." She told us she had been assigned to the headlight-manufacturing plant on May First Road as an ordinary worker. Her salary would be much lower than it had been at the Public Security Bureau and the loss of her cadre status would be permanent, but she was free, a normal member of society. My sisters and I thought all the trouble was over, but that night as I lay in bed with them I heard talk not of the beginning of a new family life but of how to institute divorce proceedings.

The difficulty lay in what to do with us. We were fought over like basketballs that winter, for Mother insisted that she wanted at least one of us, preferably Liang Fang, who was already eleven and understood life better than Liang Wei-ping and I. Mother was staying at Waipo's, but she came every day to the house. When I got home from the *Hunan Daily*'s Attached Primary School, she was always there, waiting.

One bitterly cold Sunday she took the three of us out to the Martyr's Park so we could talk alone. No one else was out in that weather; they were all at home huddled under their blankets or warming themselves by coal burners. We were bundled up in everything we had, and I felt as though I could have been rolled down a hill, but I was still cold. The park was desolate and beautiful, the huge monument to the dead martyrs a lonely pinnacle over the city, the pavilions gray and defenseless against the wind. We walked to the large manmade lake, the park's main attraction, and sat by the water, usually filled with rowboats but now covered with a thin layer of ice. I crawled between Mother's knees and Liang Fang and Liang Wei-ping pressed up on each side of her. She spoke to us with great emotion and tenderness.

"Your mother is an unlucky woman. When you're older, you'll understand how I've wept for all of us these three years. Now I won't be able to come see you anymore, but you can visit me at Waipo's house. Liang Fang will live with me, but I don't have enough money for all of you. . . ."   48

Liang Wei-ping and I were in tears, saying that we wanted to go with her too. Soon everyone was crying. Mother held us so tightly that I could hardly believe it was true that she would go away.

We stayed in the park for a long time, but when Mother noticed that my cheeks were chapped red, she took us home. She brought us to the stairwell and refused to come up. Her parting words were "Remember, Liang Fang, you'll come with me."

That evening Father called us into the inner room. "Children, you're still small and there are many things you don't understand," he said sadly. "If you went with your mother, your life with her would be unhappy. Look at the way your father has to criticize himself because of her. Stay here with me and Nai Nai and we'll take care of you."

Liang Fang wouldn't listen. "Mama isn't a Rightist anymore," she said. "What difference does it make who I go with? Isn't it glorious to be a worker?"   52

"Your mother's political life is over," said Father with annoyance. "Her file will always have a black mark, and the Party will never trust her again. Don't you know that if you want to go to middle school you'll be asked if your parents have made any political mistakes? If you stay with me, you won't even have to mention your mother, because there will be a legal separation. But if you go with her, you might not even get to go to middle school, to say nothing of joining the Communist Youth League or the Party. And you," he said angrily, turning to me and Liang Wei-ping. "Can't you guess why you haven't been allowed to join the Young Pioneers? Isn't it because of your mother?"

Nai Nai rushed into the room to urge him to control his temper, then she turned to us. "Children, your father is good to you, he understands the situation. Don't I wish I had a good daughter-in-law? Don't I know you need a good mother? But Fate is inevitable. Stay with us, children. It's the only way."

Ultimately, the question was decided in court. Father came home one afternoon looking exhausted and said, "It's settled, you'll all stay with me. Mother is coming in a little while to say good-bye."

We had dinner with her that night, and even Nai Nai's eyes were wet.   56
No one said anything, and no one had any appetite for the fish or the tofu soup. As Nai Nai took the dishes away and washed up, Mother went through her possessions, leaving almost everything for us. Father sat smoking furiously, as he did whenever he was upset. Finally she stood up to leave.

Then the three of us broke out of our numbness and ran to her, begging her not to go, pulling her back, wrapping ourselves around her legs so she couldn't walk. Father didn't interfere; he just let her embrace us again and again and at last shake us off and close the door firmly behind herself. We ran to the balcony and called after her until her broad square figure turned the corner and she was gone.

In fact, Father had been much too optimistic, and the divorce did nothing to rid us of having a Rightist in the family. He even forbade our having the slightest contact with Mother, thinking that if we drew a clear line of separation, things might be better. But there wasn't the slightest change in our status: in the eyes of the Party, my sisters and I were the children of a Rightist and Father had a Rightist wife. Liang Fang still had to say she had a Rightist mother on her application to go to middle school, Liang Wei-ping still found "Rightist child" written on her desk in chalk when she went to class, and I was still turned down when I asked to be allowed to join the Young Pioneers.

When I first went to the Attached Primary School in the *Hunan Daily* compound at age six, my classmates had often teased me about Mother. I had always shrugged off their taunts because I did well and achieved more than enough recognition to offset a few minor slights. I remember how pleased Father was when I started to take prizes for my paintings; my drawing of a morning glory was first in the whole primary school.

But as I got older, more and more stress was placed on the three stages 60 of Revolutionary glory: the Young Pioneers, the Communist Youth League, and the Party itself. It became clear to me that success in the political arena was a prerequisite for success in anything else, and if I had the slightest ambitions for myself I had to achieve these basic signs of social recognition. Those students who had the right to wear the Pioneer's triangular red scarf received much more praise than those who didn't, no matter what their grades; and at home Father and Nai Nai were constantly asking me if my application had been approved. But it was no use. I was rejected year after year, until I found myself in a tiny minority of outsiders whose "political performances" were the very worst in the class.

One day I was given a clue to the trouble when our teacher gave us a lecture. "We all have to join forces to oppose Capitalist thought," Teacher Luo said. "Some students want to eat well and dress well from the time they are small. This is Capitalist thought. Some students are from good worker or Revolutionary cadre backgrounds; they should be careful not to be proud of themselves. And those students from families with questions — they must be more careful to draw a clear line of separation." He looked meaningfully at me and at the other boy with a Rightist in his family. And all the other students in the classroom turned to stare at us too.

In fact, after the divorce I had continued to go secretly to see my mother despite Father's warnings that doing so would harm my future.

She was always overjoyed to see me, and, even during China's hard years, just after the breakup, she always found a way to give me a few *fen* (a *fen* is a Chinese cent . . .) or a roasted sweet potato. But after Teacher Luo's lecture, it really began to bother me when other students mocked me as a Rightist's son. And they became bolder in their mockery, as well. They would slap me, or kick me when I wasn't looking, and then pretend not to have done anything. Sometimes I would get into real fights, and then there were reprimands from Father and the teachers. The other Rightist's son was as lonely as I, but we never spoke much, for that might have made things even worse.

So perhaps inevitably, over the years, I came to resent my mother for making my life so miserable. I began to believe that she really had done something wrong. My father and teachers said so, and my classmates hated me for her supposed crimes. At last I no longer wished to visit her despite my loneliness, and when I saw her at a distance I didn't even call out to her. I cut her out of my life just as I had been told to do, and became solitary and self-reliant. But that was when I was much older, and many things happened before then.

EXPLORATIONS

1. At the time of which Liang writes, the People's Republic of China had existed for less than a decade. What details in "Chairman Mao's Good Little Boy" suggest the Chinese people had thoroughly accepted their new society's new ideas and activities? What details show leftover traces of the old China?

2. What appears to be the standard Party definition of a Rightist? of a Revolutionary? What definition of each term was in use when Liang's mother was discredited?

3. Where did the various members of Liang's family live when he was a small child? Who would have been affected, and how, if Liang's father as well as his mother had been removed from his job and sent away for rehabilitation? In what other ways did the Party use housing, work, and family ties to control behavior?

4. Look at Liang's first paragraph, particularly the last sentence. How do he and his coauthor, Shapiro, notify their readers of the point of view they intend to take? Through whose eyes is Liang's childhood depicted? Through what kind of consciousness is it interpreted? What is the significance of the paragraph's last sentence?

CONNECTIONS

1. We in the United States sometimes speak of Fidel Castro and Mao Zedong as almost identical: two Communist dictators who function as virtual demigods. Having read Germaine Greer's "In Cuba" and Liang and Shapiro's "Chairman Mao's Good Little Boy," what real similarities can you identify between Castro and Mao? What are their differences?

2. In "The New African Chiefs," David Lamb notes that Zaire's president Mobutu "designed a national uniform that looks like a Mao suit." What goals do you think Mobutu hoped to achieve with this move? What differences between his regime and Mao's may have affected his chances of success?

3. Look back at Ruth Sidel's "The Liu Family" (p. 21), which takes place twenty years after "Chairman Mao's Good Little Boy." What similarities and differences can you identify between the Liu and Liang families? Which differences do you think are due to changes in China during those two decades?

4. Having read Liang's account of life in China during Mao's regime, reread Annie Dillard's *Observation*. Aside from the obvious misunderstanding, why might it be inconceivable to Chinese writer Liu Binyan that Allen Ginsberg would publicly allude to his government's military forces as "Mickey Mouse"?

ELABORATIONS

1. At several points in Liang and Shapiro's narrative, individuals are forced to choose between traditional values and "Revolutionary discipline." What traditional Chinese customs does Liang describe which resemble "Revolutionary discipline"? How do you think these old customs affected the Chinese people's receptivity to the new ones imposed by the Party? Write an essay classifying the ways Mao's regime made use of existing foundations to build its new China. (You may refer to Ruth Sidel's "The Liu Family," p. 21, and Beverley Hooper's "Falling in Love with Love," p. 220, as well as "Chairman Mao's Good Little Boy.")

2. The *Observations* by Vicki Williams and Robert Nisbet, and the selections by Germaine Greer and Liang and Shapiro, show contrasting concepts of the role of government in a society. Choose the concept that is closest to your own idea of what government can and should do, and write an essay defining and defending it.

NADINE GORDIMER

Africa Emergent

Born in South Africa in 1923 and educated there, Nadine Gordimer is an outspoken civil libertarian who believes that change in her country's policies is best spurred from within. Her writing — much of it focusing on the impact of apartheid on South Africans — is renowned around the world. For her novel *The Conservationist* (1974) Gordimer was co-winner of the Booker McConnell Prize in England; in 1986 she received *Hudson Review*'s Bennett Award. She has contributed to many American magazines, including *The New Yorker, Harper's, Atlantic Monthly,* and *The New York Review of Books,* as well as taught creative writing at Columbia University's Graduate School of the Arts. She holds honorary degrees from Harvard and Yale universities. In 1978 she was elected an honorary member of the American Academy and Institute of Arts and Letters, whose citation read: "The brilliance with which she renders her varied characters has opened her country to passionate understandings which most of us have no other access to." Gordimer currently lives with her family in Johannesburg. She has published nine novels, the most recent being *A Sport of Nature* (1987), and eight volumes of short stories. "Africa Emergent" comes from her 1971 collection *Livingstone's Companions.*
(For background on South Africa, see pp. 58 and 344.)

He's in prison now, so I'm not going to mention his name. It mightn't be a good thing, you understand. — Perhaps you think you understand too well; but don't be quick to jump to conclusions from five or six thousand miles away: if you lived here, you'd understand something else — friends know that shows of loyalty are all right for children holding hands in the school playground; for us they're luxuries, not important and maybe dangerous. If I said, I was a friend of so-and-so, black man awaiting trial for treason, what good would it do him? And, who knows, it might draw just that decisive bit more attention to me. *He'd* be the first to agree.

Not that one feels that if they haven't got enough in my dossier already, this would make any difference; and not that he really was such a friend. But that's something else you won't understand: everything is ambiguous, here. We hardly know, by now, what we can do and what we can't do; it's difficult to say, goaded in on oneself by laws and doubts and rebellion and caution and — not least — self-disgust, what is or is not a friendship. I'm talking about black-and-white, of course. If you stay with it, boy, on the white side in the country clubs and garden suburbs if you're white, and on the black side in the locations and beer halls if you're black, none of this applies, and you can go all the way to your segregated cemetery in peace. But neither he nor I did.

I began mixing with blacks out of what is known as an outraged sense of justice, plus strong curiosity, when I was a student. There were two ways — one was through the white students' voluntary service organization, a kibbutz-type junket where white boys and girls went into rural areas and camped while they built school classrooms for African children. A few coloured and African students from their segregated universities used to come along, too, and there was the novelty, not without value, of dossing down alongside them at night, although we knew we were likely to be harboring Special Branch spies among our willing workers, and we dared not make a pass at the coloured or black girls. The other way — less hard on the hands — was to go drinking with the jazz musicians and journalists, painters and would-be poets and actors who gravitated towards whites partly because such people naturally feel they can make free of the world, and partly because they found an encouragement and appreciation there that was sweet to them. I tried the VSO briefly, but the other way suited me better; anyway, I didn't see why I should help this Government by doing the work it ought to be doing for the welfare of black children.

I'm an architect and the way I was usefully drawn into the black scene   4
was literally that: I designed sets for a mixed colour drama group got together by a white director. Perhaps there's no urban human group as intimate, in the end, as a company of this kind, and the colour problem made us even closer. I don't mean what *you* mean, the how-do-I-feelabout-that-black-skin stuff; I mean the daily exasperation of getting round, or over, or on top of the colour bar laws that plagued our productions and our lives. We had to remember to write out "passes" at night, so that our actors could get home without being arrested for being out after the curfew for blacks, we had to spend hours at the Bantu Affairs Department trying to arrange local residence permits for actors who were being "endorsed out" of town back to the villages to which, "ethnically," apparently, they belonged although they'd never set eyes on them, and we had to decide which of us could play the sycophant well enough to persuade the Bantu Commissioner to allow the show to go on the road from one Group Area, designated by colour, to another, or to talk some town clerk

into getting his council to agree to the use of a "white" public hall by a mixed cast. The black actors' lives were in our hands, because they were black and we were white, and could, must, intercede for them. Don't think this made everything love and light between us; in fact it caused endless huffs and rows. A white woman who'd worked like a slave acting as PRO cum-wardrobe-mistress hasn't spoken to me for years because I made her lend her little car to one of the chaps who'd worked until after the last train went back to the location, and then he kept it the whole weekend and she couldn't get hold of him because, of course, location houses rarely have telephones and once a black man has disappeared among those warrens you won't find him till he chooses to surface in the white town again. And when this one did surface, he was biting, to me, about white bitches' "patronage" of people they secretly still thought of as "boys." Yet our arguments, resentments, and misunderstandings were not only as much part of the intimacy of this group as the good times, the parties, and the lovemaking we had, but were more — the defining part, because we'd got close enough to admit argument, resentment, and misunderstanding between us.

He was one of this little crowd, for a time. He was a dispatch clerk and then a "manager" and chucker-out at a black dance club. In his spare time he took a small part in our productions now and then, and made himself generally handy; in the end it was discovered that what he really was good at was front-of-house arrangements. His tubby charm (he was a large young man and a cheerful dresser) was just the right thing to deal with the unexpected moods of our location audiences when we went on tour — sometimes they came stiffly encased in their churchgoing best and seemed to feel it was vulgar to laugh or respond to what was going on, on stage; in other places they rushed the doors, tried to get in without paying, and were dominated by a *tsotsi*, street urchin, element who didn't want to hear anything but themselves. He was the particular friend — the other, passive half — of a particular friend of mine, Elias Nkomo.

And here I stop short. How shall I talk about Elias? I've never even learnt, in five years, how to think about him.

Elias was a sculptor. He had one of those jobs — messenger "boy" or some such — that literate young black men can aspire to in a small gold-mining and industrial town outside Johannesburg. Somebody said he was talented, somebody sent him to me — at the beginning, the way for every black man to find himself seems inescapably to lead through a white man. Again, how can I say what his work was like? He came by train to the black people's section of Johannesburg central station, carrying a bulky object wrapped in that morning's newspaper. He was slight, roundheaded, tiny-eared, dunly dressed, and with a frown of effort between his eyes, but his face unfolded to a wide, apologetic yet confident smile when he realized that the white man in a waiting car must be me — the meeting had been arranged. I took him back to my "place" (he always called people's homes that) and he unwrapped the newspaper. What was there was nothing like the clumps of diorite or sandstone you have seen in galleries in New York, London, or Johannesburg marked "Africa Emergent," "Spirit of the Ancestors." What was there was a goat, or a goatlike creature, in the way that a centaur is a horselike, manlike creature, carved out of streaky knotted wood. It was delightful (I wanted to put out my hand to touch it), it was moving in its somehow concretized diachrony, beast-man, coarse wood–fine workmanship, and there was also something exposed about it (one would withdraw the hand, after all). I asked him whether he knew Picasso's goats? He had heard of Picasso but never seen any of his work. I showed him a photograph of the famous bronze goat in Picasso's own house; thereafter all his beasts had sex organs as joyful as Picasso's goat's udder, but that was the only "influence" that ever took, with him. As I say, a white man always intercedes in some way, with a man like Elias; mine was to keep him from those art-loving ladies with galleries who wanted to promote him, and those white painters and sculptors who were willing to have him work under their tutelage. I gave him an old garage (well, that means I took my car out of it) and left him alone, with plenty of chunks of wood.

But Elias didn't like the loneliness of work. That garage never became 8 his "place." Perhaps when you've lived in an overcrowded yard all your life the counterstimulus of distraction becomes necessary to create a tension of concentration. No — well all I really mean is that he liked company. At first he came only at weekends, and then, as he began to sell some of his work, he gave up the messenger job and moved in more or less permanently — we fixed up the "place" together, putting in a ceiling and connecting water and so on. It was illegal for him to live there in a white suburb, of course, but such laws breed complementary evasions in people like Elias and me and the white building inspector didn't turn a hair of suspicion when I said that I was converting the garage as a flat for my wife's mother. It was better for Elias once he'd moved in; there was always some friend of his sharing his bed, not to mention the girls who did; sometimes the girls were shy little things almost of the kitchen maid variety, who called my wife "madam" when they happened to bump into her, crossing the garden, sometimes they were the bewigged and painted actresses from the group who sat smoking and gossiping with my wife while she fed the baby.

And *he* was there more often than anyone — the plump and cheerful front-of-house manager; he was married, but as happens with our sex, an old friendship was a more important factor in his life than a wife and kids — if that's a characteristic of black men, then I must be black under the skin, myself. Elias had become very involved in the theater group, anyway, like *him*; Elias made some beautiful *papier-mâché* gods for a play by a Nigerian that we did — "spirits of the ancestors" at once amusing and frightening — and once when we needed a singer he surprisingly turned out to have a voice that could phrase a madrigal as easily as whatever the forerunner of Soul was called — I forget now, but it blared hour after hour from the garage when he was working. Elias seemed to like best to work when the other one was around; *he* would sit with his fat boy's legs rolled out before him, flexing his toes in his fashionable shoes, dusting down the lapels of the latest thing in jackets, as he changed the records and kept up a monologue contentedly punctuated by those soft growls and sighs of agreement, those sudden squeezes of almost silent laughter — responses possible only in an African language — that came from Elias as he chiseled and chipped. For they spoke in their own tongue, and I have never known what it was they talked about.

In spite of my efforts to let him alone, inevitably Elias was "taken up" (hadn't I started the process myself, with that garage?) and a gallery announced itself his agent. He walked about at the opening of his one-man show in a purple turtlenecked sweater I think his best friend must have made him buy, laughing a little, softly, at himself, more embarrassed than pleased. An art critic wrote about his transcendental values and plastic modality, and he said, "Christ, man, does he dig it or doesn't he?" while we toasted his success in brandy chased with beer — brandy isn't a rich man's sip in South Africa, it's made here and it's what people use to get drunk on. He earned quite a bit of money that year. Then the gallery owner and the art critic forgot him in the discovery of yet another interpreter of the African soul, and he was poor again, but he had acquired a patroness who, although she lived far away, did not forget him. She was, as you might have thought, an American lady, very old and wealthy according to South African legend but probably simply a middle-aged widow with comfortable stock holdings and a desire to get in on the cultural ground floor of some form of art collecting not yet overcrowded. She had bought some of his work while a tourist in Johannesburg. Perhaps she did have academic connections with the art world;

in any case, it was she who got a foundation to offer Elias Nkomo a scholarship to study in America.

I could understand that he wanted to go simply in order to go: to see the world outside. But I couldn't believe that at this stage he wanted or could make use of formal art school disciplines. As I said to him at the time, I'm only an architect, but I've had experience of the academic and even, God help us, the frenziedly nonacademic approach in the best schools, and it's not for people who have, to fall back on the jargon, found themselves.

I remember he said, smiling, "You think I've found myself?"   12

And I said, "But you've never been lost, man. That very first goat wrapped in newspaper was your goat."

But later, when he was refused a passport and the issue of his going abroad was much on our minds, we talked again. He wanted to go because he felt he needed some kind of general education, general cultural background that he'd missed, in his six years at the location school. "Since I've been at your place, I've been reading a lot of your books. And man, I know nothing. I'm as ignorant as that kid of yours there in the pram. Right, I've picked up a bit of politics, a few art terms here and there — I can wag my head and say 'plastic values' all right, eh? But man, what do I know about life? What do I know about how it all works? How do I know *how* I do the work I do? Why we live and die? — If I carry on here I might as well be carving walking sticks," he added. I knew what he meant: there are old men, all over Africa, who make a living squatting at a decent distance from tourist hotels, carving fancy walking sticks from local wood; only one step in sophistication below the "Africa Emergent" school of sculptors so rapturously acclaimed by gallery owners. We both laughed at this, and following the line of thought suggested to me by his question to himself: "How do I know how I do the work I do?" — although in me it was a different line of thought from his — I asked him whether in fact there was any sort of traditional skill in his family? As I imagined, there was not — he was an urban slum kid, brought up opposite a municipal beer hall among paraffin-tin utensils and abandoned motorcar bodies which, perhaps curiously, had failed to bring out a Duchamp in him but from which, on the contrary, he had sprung, full-blown, as a classical expressionist. Although there were no rural walking-stick carvers in his ancestry, he did tell me something I had no idea would have been part of the experience of a location childhood — he had been sent, in his teens, to a tribal initiation school in the bush, and been circumcised according to rite. He described the experience vividly.

Once all attempts to get him a passport had failed, Elias's desire to go to America became something else, of course: an obsessive resentment against confinement itself. Inevitably, he was given no reason for the refusal. The official answer was the usual one — that it was "not in the public interest" to reveal the reason for such things. Was it because "they" had got to know he was "living like a white man"? (Theory put to me by one of the black actors in the group.) Was it because a critic had dutifully described his work as expressive of the "agony of the emergent African soul"? Nobody knew. Nobody ever knows. It is enough to be black; blacks are meant to stay put, in their own ethnically apportioned streets in their own segregated areas, in those parts of South Africa where the government says they belong. Yet — the whole way our lives are maneuvered, as I say, is an unanswered question — Elias's best friend suddenly got a passport. I hadn't even realized that *he* had been offered a scholarship or a study grant or something, too; *he* was invited to go to New York to study production and the latest acting techniques (it was the time of the Method rather than Grotowski). And *he* got a passport, "first try" as Elias said with ungrudging pleasure and admiration; when someone black got a passport, then, there was a collective sense of pleasure in having outwitted we didn't quite know what. So they went together, *he* on his passport, and Elias Nkomo on an exit permit.

An exit permit is a one-way ticket, anyway. When you are granted   16
one at your request but at the government's pleasure, you sign an undertaking that you will never return to South Africa or its mandatory territory, South West Africa. You pledge this with signature and thumbprint. Elias Nkomo never came back. At first he wrote (and he wrote quite often) enthusiastically about the world outside that he had gained, and he seemed to be enjoying some kind of small vogue, not so much as a sculptor as a genuine, real live African Negro who was sophisticated enough to be asked to comment on this and that: the beauty of American women, life in Harlem or Watts, Black Power as seen through the eyes, etc. He sent cuttings from *Ebony* and even from the *New York Times Magazine*. He said that a girl at *Life* was trying to get them to run a piece on his work; his work? — well, he hadn't settled down to anything new, yet, but the art center was a really swinging place, Christ, the things people were doing, there! There were silences, naturally; we forgot about

him and he forgot about us for weeks on end. Then the local papers picked up the sort of news they are alert to from all over the world. Elias Nkomo had spoken at an antiapartheid rally. Elias Nkomo, in West African robes, was on the platform with Stokely Carmichael. "Well, why not? He hasn't got to worry about keeping his hands clean for the time when he comes back home, has he?" — My wife was bitter in his defense. Yes, but I was wondering about his work — "Will they leave him alone to work?" I didn't write to him, but it was as if my silence were read by him: a few months later I received a cutting from some university art magazine devoting a number to Africa, and there was a photograph of one of Elias's wood sculptures, with his handwriting along the margin of the page — *I know you don't think much of people who don't turn out new stuff but some people here seem to think this old thing of mine is good.* It was the sort of wry remark that, spoken aloud to me in the room, would have made us both laugh. I smiled, and meant to write. But within two weeks Elias was dead. He drowned himself early one morning in the river of the New England town where the art school was.

It was like the refusal of the passport; none of us knew why. In the usual arrogance one has in the face of such happenings, I even felt guilty about the letter. Perhaps, if one were thousands of miles from one's own "place," in some sort of a bad way, just a small thing like a letter, a word of encouragement from someone who had hurt by being rather niggardly with encouragement in the past . . . ? And what pathetic arrogance, at that! As if the wisp of a letter, written by someone between other preoccupations, and in substance an encouraging lie (how splendid that your old work is receiving recognition in some piddling little magazine) could be anything round which the hand of a man going down for the second time might close. Because before Elias went under in that river he must have been deep in forlorn horrors about which I knew nothing, nothing. When people commit suicide they do so apparently out of some sudden self-knowledge that those of us, the living, do not have the will to acquire. That's what's meant by despair, isn't it — what they have come to know? And that's what one means when one says in extenuation of oneself, *I knew so little about him, really.* I knew Elias only in the self that he had presented at my "place"; why, how out of place it had been, once, when he happened to mention that as a boy he had spent weeks in the bush with his circumcision group! Of course we — his friends — decided out of the facts we knew and our political and personal attitudes, why he had died: and perhaps it is true that he was sick to death, in the real sense of the phrase that has been forgotten, sick unto death with homesickness for the native land that had shut him out forever and that he was forced to conjure up for himself in the parody of "native" dress that had nothing to do with his part of the continent, and the shame that a new kind of black platform-solidarity forced him to feel for his old dependence, in South Africa, on the friendship of white people. It was the South African government who killed him, it was culture shock — but perhaps neither our political bitterness nor our glibness with fashionable phrases can come near what combination of forces, within and without, led him to the fatal baptism of that early morning. *It is not in the private interest that this should be revealed.* Elias never came home. That's all.

But his best friend did, towards the end of that year. *He* came to see me after he had been in the country some weeks — I'd heard he was back. The theater group had broken up; it seemed to be that, chiefly, he'd come to talk to me about: he wanted to know if there was any money left in the kitty for him to start up a small theatrical venture of his own, he was eager to use the know-how (his phrase) he'd learned in the States. He was really plump now and he wore the most extraordinary clothes. A Liberace jacket. Plastic boots. An Afro wig that looked as if it had been made out of a bit of karakul from South West Africa. I teased him about it — we were at least good enough friends for that — asking him if he'd really been with the guerrillas instead of Off Broadway? (There was a trial on at home, at the time, of South African political refugees who had tried to "infiltrate" through South West Africa.) And felt slightly ashamed of my patronage of his taste when he said with such good humor, "It's just a fun thing, man, isn't it great?" I was too cowardly to bring the talk round to the point: Elias. And when it couldn't be avoided I said the usual platitudes and he shook his head at them — "Hell, man," and we fell silent. Then he told me that that was how he had got back — because Elias was dead, on the unused portion of Elias's air ticket. *His* study grant hadn't included travel expenses and he'd had to pay his own way over. So he'd had only a one-way ticket, but Elias's scholarship had included a return fare to the student's place of origin. It had been difficult to get the airline to agree to the transfer; he'd had to go to the scholarship foundation people, but they'd been very decent about fixing it for him.

He had told me all this so guilelessly that I was one of the people who became angrily indignant when the rumor began to go around that he was a police agent: who else would have the cold nerve to come back on a dead man's ticket, a dead man who couldn't ever have used that portion of the ticket himself, because he had taken an exit permit? And who could believe the story, anyway? Obviously, *he* had to find some way of explaining why he, a black man like any other, could travel freely back and forth between South Africa and other countries. He had a passport, hadn't he? Well, there you were. Why should *he* get a passport? What black man these days had a passport?

Yes, I was angry, and defended him, by proof of the innocence of the   20 very naïveté with which — a black man, yes, and therefore used to the necessity of salvaging from disaster all his life, unable to afford the nice squeamishness of white men's delicacy — he took over Elias's air ticket because he was alive and needed it, as he might have taken up Elias's coat against the cold. I refused to avoid him, the way some members of the remnant of our group made it clear they did now, and I remained stony-faced outside the complicity of those knowing half-smiles that accompanied the mention of his name. We had never been close friends, of course; but he would turn up from time to time. He could not find theatrical work and had a job as a traveling salesman in the locations. He took to bringing three or four small boys along when he visited us; they were very subdued and whisperingly well-behaved and well-dressed in miniature suits — our barefoot children stared at them in awe. They were his children plus the children of the family he was living with, we gathered. He and I talked mostly about his difficulties — his old car was unreliable, his wife had left him, his commissions were low, and he could have taken up an offer to join a Chicago repertory company if he could have raised the fare to go back to America — while my wife fed ice cream and cake to the silent children, or my children dutifully placed them one by one on the garden swing. We had begun to be able to talk about Elias's death. He had told me how, in the weeks before he died, Elias would get the wrong way on the moving stairway going down in the subway in New York and keep walking, walking up. "I thought he was foolin' around, man, you know? Jus' climbin' those stairs and goin' noplace?"

He clung nostalgically to the American idiom; no African talks about "noplace" when he means "nowhere." But he had abandoned the Afro wig and when we got talking about Elias he would hold his big, well-shaped head with its fine, shaven covering of his own wool propped between his hands as if in an effort to think more clearly about something that would never come clear; I felt suddenly at one with him in that gesture, and would say, "Go on." He would remember another example of how Elias had been "acting funny" before he died. It was on one of those afternoon visits that he said, "And I don't think I ever told you about the business with the students at the college? How that last weekend — before he did it, I mean — he went around and invited everybody to a party, I dunno, a kind of feast he said it was. Some of them said he said a barbecue — you know what that is, same as a *braaivleis*, eh? But one of the others told me afterwards that he'd told them he was going to give them a real African feast, he was going to show them how the country people do it here at home when somebody gets married or there's a funeral or so. He wanted to know where he could buy a goat."

"A goat?"

"That's right. A live goat. He wanted to kill and roast a goat for them, on the campus."

It was round about this time that *he* asked me for a loan. I think that was behind the idea of bringing those pretty, dressed-up children along with him when he visited; he wanted firmly to set the background of his obligations and responsibilities before touching me for money. It was rather a substantial sum, for someone of my resources. But he couldn't carry on his job without a new car, and he'd just got the opportunity to acquire a really good secondhand buy. I gave him the money in spite of — because of, perhaps — new rumors that were going around then that, in a police raid on the house of the family with whom he had been living, every adult except himself who was present on that night had been arrested on the charge of attending a meeting of a banned political organization. His friends were acquitted on the charge simply through the defense lawyer's skill at showing the agent provocateur, on whose evidence the charge was based, to be an unreliable witness — that is to say, a liar. But the friends were promptly served with personal banning orders, anyway, which meant among other things that their movements were restricted and they were not allowed to attend gatherings.

He was the only one who remained, significantly, it seemed impossible to ignore, free. And yet his friends let him stay on in the house; it was a mystery to us whites — and some blacks, too. But then so much becomes a mystery where trust becomes a commodity on sale to the police. Whatever my little show of defiance over the loan, during the last year or two we have reached the stage where if a man is black, literate, has "political" friends and white friends, *and* a passport, he must be considered a police spy. I was sick with myself — that was why I gave him the money — but I believed it, too. There's only one way for a man like that to prove himself, so far as we're concerned: he must be in prison.

Well, *he* was at large. A little subdued over the fate of his friends, about which he talked guilelessly as he had about the appropriation of

Elias's air ticket, harassed as usual about money, poor devil, but generally cheerful. Yet our friendship, that really had begun to become one since Elias's death, waned rapidly. It was the money that did it. Of course; he was afraid I'd ask him to begin paying back and so he stopped coming to my "place," he stopped the visits with the beautifully dressed and well-behaved black infants. I received a typed letter from him, once, solemnly thanking me for my kind cooperation and, etc., as if I were some business firm, and assuring me that in a few months he hoped to be in a position, etc. I scrawled a note in reply, saying of course I darned well hoped he was going to pay the money he owed, sometime, but why, for God's sake, in the meantime, did this mean we had to carry on as if we'd quarreled? Damn it all, he didn't have to treat me as if I had some nasty disease, just because of a few rands.

But I didn't see him again. I've become too busy with my own work — the building boom of the last few years, you know; I've had the contract for several shopping malls, and a big cultural center — to do any work for the old theater group in its sporadic comings-to-life. I don't think he had much to do with it anymore, either; I heard he was doing quite well as a salesman and was thinking of marrying again. There was even a — yet another — rumor, that he was actually building a house in Dube, which is the nearest to a solid, bourgeois suburb a black can get in these black dormitories outside the white man's city, if you can be considered to be a bourgeois without having freehold. I didn't need the money, by then, but you know how it is with money — I felt faintly resentful about the debt anyway, because it looked as if now *he* could have paid it back just as well as *I* could say I didn't need it. As for the friendship; he'd shown me the worth of that. It's become something the white man must buy just as he must buy the cooperation of police stool pigeons. Elias has been dead five years; we live in our situation as of now, as the legal phrase goes; one falls back on legal phrases as other forms of expression become too risky.

And then, two hundred and seventy-seven days ago, there was a new 28 rumor, and this time it was confirmed, this time it was no rumor. *He* was fetched from his room one night and imprisoned. That's perfectly legal, here; it's the hundred-and-eighty-day Detention Act. At least, because he was something of a personality, with many friends and contacts in particular among both black and white journalists, the fact has become public. If people are humble, or of no particular interest to the small world of white liberals, they are sometimes in detention for many months before this is known outside the eyewitness of whoever happened to be standing by, in house or street, when they were taken away by the police.

But at least we all know where *he* is: in prison. They say that charges of treason are being prepared against him and various others who were detained at the same time, and still others who have been detained for even longer — three hundred and seventy-one days, three hundred and ten days — the figures, once finally released, are always as precise as this — and that soon, soon they will be brought to trial for whatever it is that we do not know they have done, for when people are imprisoned under the Detention Act no one is told why and there are no charges. There are suppositions among us, of course. Was he a double agent, as it were, using his laissez-passer as a police spy in order to further his real work as an underground African nationalist? Was he just unlucky in his choice of friends? Did he suffer from a dangerous sense of loyalty in place of any strong convictions of his own? Was it all due to some personal, unguessed-at bond it's none of our business to speculate about? Heaven knows — those police spy rumors aside — nobody could have looked more unlikely to be a political activist than that cheerful young man, second-string, always ready to jump up and turn over the record, fond of Liberace jackets and aspiring to play LeRoi Jones Off Broadway.

But as I say, we know where he is now; inside. In solitary most of the time — they say, those who've also been inside. Two hundred and seventy-seven days he's been there.

And so we white friends can purge ourselves of the shame of rumors. We can be pure again. We are satisfied at last. He's in prison. He's proved himself, hasn't he?

EXPLORATIONS

1. What facts does Gordimer tell us about her story's narrator? about the man referred to as *he*? How does her depiction of the two main protagonists bear out the narrator's comment that "everything is ambiguous, here"?

2. What impression of South Africa is created by Gordimer's first sentence? by her first two paragraphs? How would the story's impact change if she omitted these two paragraphs?

3. What conflict(s) does the sculptor Elias embody or represent? How is Elias's role in the story simpler than the roles of the two protagonists? What facets of those two characters are brought out by their involvement with Elias?

4. What laws and rules are mentioned in "Africa Emergent"? Who evidently made these laws? How are they enforced? How would the story's impact change if government officials made personal appearances in it?

CONNECTIONS

1. What aspects of the South African government as depicted by Gordimer resemble the Communist Chinese government as depicted by Liang Heng and Judith Shapiro? How does Gordimer's narrator's attitude toward the state and its demands differ from Liang and his family's attitude? What contrasts in those demands and in the nature of the government do you think account for the attitude difference?

2. Look back at Ezekiel Mphahlele's "Tradition and the African Writer" (p. 344). What comments by Mphahlele are exemplified by Elias Nkomo? Having read Mphahlele's essay, why do you think Elias committed suicide?

3. What is the literal meaning of Gordimer's title, "Africa Emergent"? On the basis of the other African writing you have read, particularly Mphahlele's "Tradition and the African Writer," how would you explain the title's deeper meaning?

4. What similar attitudes are expressed by Gordimer's characters and the black Alabamans in William Least Heat Moon's *Observation*? In each setting, does official policy or personal prejudice make a larger contribution to racial discrimination?

ELABORATIONS

1. "Everything is ambiguous, here," writes Gordimer. How might the events she narrates in "Africa Emergent" look different to different observers? Write a synopsis of these events from the viewpoint of a South African official reporting to a superior. Then summarize the same events from the viewpoint of a Western journalist hoping to sell the story to a magazine or newspaper.

2. Look back at Vincent Crapanzano's "Growing Up White in South Africa" (p. 58). Based on that account and Gordimer's, write an essay on political and social conditions in South Africa.

GUZEL AMALRIK

A Visit with Andrei
at the Labor Camp

Guzel Amalrik was born Guzel Makudinova to a poor Tatar family in Moscow in 1942. An artist by profession, she painted portraits "so far removed from Socialist Realism that she had no chance," wrote her husband, "and not even the wish, to be admitted into the Union of Artists and to receive official commissions." Guzel married Andrei Amalrik in 1965, while he was serving sixteen months in Siberian exile for writing undesirable (though unperformed) plays. Andrei had previously been expelled from Moscow University for disputing an official point of view on early Russian history. He was arrested again in 1970 for an essay entitled "Will the Soviet Union Survive Until 1984?" and sentenced to three years in a labor camp in the remote Northeast for "slander of the Soviet state and social order." Guzel and Andrei Amalrik emigrated in 1976 to the Netherlands, the United States, and later France. Andrei was killed in a car accident on his way to an East-West conference in Madrid in 1981. Guzel now lives in Utrecht, the Netherlands, where she wrote "A Visit with Andrei at the Labor Camp" in 1976, five years after the visit occurred. The essay was translated from the Russian by Alfred C. Schmidt and Tanya Schmidt.

(For more background on the Soviet Union, see pp. 48, 139, 213, and 649.)

In the summer of 1971 I received a letter from the labor camp. My husband wrote that we would be permitted to see each other in the coming winter — to spend three whole days together! All excited, I began preparing for the trip right away. There is a Russian proverb that says you should fix up your sleigh in the summer and your wagon in winter. This was the proper moment for me to heed that maxim, because in Russia you can never get what you need at the time you need it.

Winter came. A twelve-hour flight and there I was, in the dirty little airport at Magadan, only 250 kilometers away from the Talaya settlement, where my Andrei was languishing in camp. Magadan struck me as a gray and foggy place, gloomy and depressing; only the mountains surrounding the town looked beautifully majestic. The Sea of Okhotsk was frozen over, and the wind blew in powerful gusts.

Next morning I took the bus to Talaya. There was only one. Sitting in front of me was a tall thickset man, wearing a dark overcoat with the insignia of the public prosecutor on his cuffs. He exchanged glances with a young couple and frequently turned around to look at me intently. Finally he asked me if I was on my way to meet my husband. Evidently I was riding to Talaya with the public prosecutor himself!

We arrived at the settlement toward evening. In his letter, my husband 4 had given me the address of a girl who would let me stay with her. I wandered at random, lugging my huge bundles and backpack. For a while the only people I passed were military, and I could not bring myself to ask them for directions. I approached a shriveled and wrinkled old woman, who led me uphill past a lane lined with little houses and faceless concrete three-story buildings. My load was terribly heavy, but the old woman trotted on at a lively pace, until at last we reached the communal hostel on the hill. It was a long, narrow structure painted white; people who looked like workers were constantly going in and coming out. Inside the hostel was a long hall, with doors on either side opening into the rooms.

Lena greeted me cordially. Her room was sparsely furnished: two iron beds, a small table, and a slender wardrobe, plus two chairs for which there was hardly enough space. On one of the beds sat a little girl of eight or so, licking her finger and leafing through a book whose pages were already well worn. The child was Lena's little sister; their mother was dead. Lena was twenty-six and unmarried, though to me she seemed an awfully attractive blonde.

Another unmarried young woman named Masha shared the same room, together with her daughter, who was about the same age as Lena's sister. The four of them slept on those two narrow beds. An hour after I came, Masha's friend showed up. He was drunk, and he started pawing her in front of everyone. The little girls, solemn beyond their age, understood what was going on. They huddled on a corner of the bed, playing with dolls and pretending not to notice; every so often they would glance surreptitiously at the couple and whisper between themselves. Then Lena's friend appeared. He was sober. The ten square meters of living space were insufferably crowded, and it was painful to watch those unhappy children and those unfortunate women.

The next day I went to the camp, where I was told that I would not be allowed to see my husband until evening. So I decided to have a look around the village and to visit the famous health resort of Talaya, two kilometers away from the camp. The contrast was shocking. In order to build a resort around the mineral springs, they had first set up a labor camp so that the prisoners could do the construction work. Now that resort employs many of the wives of the camp supervisors. The two girls I was staying with worked there as waitresses, and brought leftover soup and meat home to feed to their children; they were even so clever as to get away with sugar and cookies. Under the clothes in their wardrobe they kept piles of sugar taken from the resort.

I was struck by the contrast between the resort buildings — gaudy palaces, full of columns and grottoes, fountains and a pond — and the pitiful houses in the village with its rough streets strewn with chunks of the local rock.

From the window of the hostel on the hill I looked down and saw an area surrounded by a high barbed-wire fence. This was a wood-processing combine where prisoners worked. They came from the camp in long rank and file with pairs of soldiers and dogs in front and in the rear; clad in quilted jackets and tarpaulin boots, they walked with heads bowed through the freezing cold. It was twenty degrees below zero centigrade — sometimes the temperature dropped to as low as minus sixty degrees. I ran out of the house and waved my scarf at the prisoners. Some of them caught sight of me, and the last man in the line waved his hand back at me. For an instant I thought it was Andrei, although I knew that he was not supposed to go out on heavy work details ever since he had come down with meningitis in prison. A guard began to poke the prisoner in the back with the butt of his rifle, prodding him to get a move on. The dogs barked loudly. Later I learned that it was not Andrei. But I think that those prisoners were pleased to see any woman wave at them from the hillside; many of them knew that Andrei was expecting a visit from his wife, and they described me to him: That is how he learned of my arrival.

As dusk fell, I put my things together and got ready for the visit. I was tremendously excited. It was almost like meeting him for the first time, when we were young. Now we had been separated for nearly a year and a half. How would he greet me? Would there be any estrangement between us? When you live together, you do not notice changes of character so readily as you do after long absence. It was with misgivings like this that I approached the wall of the camp.

First they showed me into the room of the officer on duty, took my passport and checked it for the marriage registration, then went through the entire contents of my backpack and bundles. They even cut the chocolate into bits to see whether it contained some sort of political proclamation or letters from friends; they also looked for a tape recorder or camera on me. Suppose I should take a picture of my husband, who had lost twenty kilograms, all skin and bones, and show it to the outside world! They found my little bottle of cognac and set it aside, saying that it was unauthorized. And here I had been so hoping that we might celebrate the New Year ahead of time with that token quantity of cognac.

They led me down a hall, through a door that opened and closed automatically, then down another little hall, and into a small room with two neatly made iron beds, a table, and two chairs. It resembled the girls' room at the hostel, or any room at all in some village hotel, except that here there were bars on the tiny window. And I had to pay for this room, too, as I would in a hotel.

My husband was not in the room. I was confronted, instead, by an elderly woman, all dried out, with an angry expression on her face. My escorts went away; the woman sprang at me like a panther and began to frisk me. She insisted that I undress of my own accord, as much as to say: Don't lose time, you want to see your husband in a hurry, don't you? I refused to undress. Then she simply felt me over, fingering the seams in my clothes; she grabbed my comb and jerked it through my hair, thinking that maybe I was hiding something up there. I thought I was dreaming. Like a sleepwalker, I resisted feebly; she ran the comb through one last time, and apparently convinced herself that she would find nothing of interest in my hair. When I threatened to complain, she snapped back that she was afraid of nobody, that she had been in this place for thirty years, that she knew all the rules and regulations and followed them. She tried to take away my fountain pen and even my eyebrow pencil, but I absolutely refused to give them up.

Finally the old woman left. I was upset and in tears. Expecting Andrei to appear at any moment, I slipped into a lovely French negligee, lit a candle, and spread our old red tablecloth on the table. It was our favorite, though shabby, and I had brought it with me from home. The door opened. There stood the slender figure of my husband — or rather his shadow, he was so thin. He wore a white cap like a clown's hat and gray overalls with a number sewed on. We flew into each other's arms. I had the feeling we had never been apart, but the sight of his face jolted me back to reality: He was terribly emaciated and covered with pimples from lack of vitamins.

Those three days were a dream for us. We did not want to think how quickly the time would pass. With the delicious things I had brought from Moscow I tried to fatten Andrei up a little bit. I did the cooking

12

right there in the room on an electric hot plate, but my husband was practically unable to eat. After the first supper he was so ill that the very next day the camp doctor had to be summoned to give him a shot. I will have a word to say later about that female doctor.

I was very excited. Three days was not enough time for all the news   16 we had to share. I tried to write down on paper everything important I had to tell him, and we talked under the blanket, for we knew that the room was bugged. Andrei also wrote a long letter to his Dutch friend Karel van het Rewe, describing how he had been transported across Siberia as a sick man. It would be up to me to smuggle this letter out and send it to Holland.

When we parted, I gave Andrei some warm underwear. I also wanted to leave him a pair of shorts, into the waistband of which I had sewn a few ten-ruble notes, so that he would have the means to buy smuggled-in food at the camp. But he declined to keep the shorts, explaining that when they searched him after our visit they would certainly discover the money and confiscate it.

They came and took Andrei away. I was left alone. Suddenly an officer and two women entered the room. One of them was the old woman who had searched me. She was employed at the camp as a censor, reading the prisoners' mail. The other, a younger woman, was the doctor who had examined Andrei. She wore a white smock and gynecological gloves. The officer said that these women would rapidly look through my things and then release me. He walked out. The women got busy on the clothing, checked every seam and were delighted at finding the money sewn into the shorts. The old woman, throwing hostile glances at me, turned to her partner and said: "People like this ought to be shot, nobody would miss them!" To me she added: "We work hard and never go anywhere, we make a contribution to the State, while all you do is spread slander, you anti-Soviets. Your husband is getting off light. If it were up to me, I'd let him rot here." I was silent and I gritted my teeth. Then, unable to hold back, I called her an old Fascist.

After my belongings had been inspected, the women asked me to undress, but I refused. I was not an inmate of the camp, hence not obliged to strip and be searched. The woman with the rubber gloves was ready. I began to scream at them and demanded to see the public prosecutor. Grinning insolently, they sat down at the table where my husband and I had breakfast that morning. One woman said to the other: "I feel like a cup of tea." The doctor kept her rubber gloves on while drinking her tea and even took a piece of sugar without removing them.

Two hours passed. I kept repeating that, however long they might   20
detain me, I would not allow myself to be searched and would speak
only with the prosecutor. Two more hours went by, and I was hungry. I
still had a lot of good things left to eat, because the prisoners were not
permitted to take food back with them after a visit. I ate, and the women
looked at me with envy: They drank their tea with plain dry bread. I then
dozed for a spell, which made them so furious that they began to quarrel
with each other. The doctor said crossly: "My workday is over, my son is
already back from school, and I'm not home yet!"

At that point I had to step out for a moment, but they would not let
me go. They brought a bucket, placed it in the middle of the room, and
said: "We aren't men, go ahead, don't mind us." Praying silently to all
the saints that I would not accidentally drop Andrei's papers, which I
had so carefuly hidden, I succeeded in relieving myself right under the
watchful gaze of those two pairs of eyes. The women appeared to relax
somewhat. One of them left the room and returned ten minutes later
with the public prosecutor for the Magadan region. He was the man who
had been on the bus with me, yet all the while they had been trying to
tell me that there was no prosecutor here.

The prosecutor greeted me like an old acquaintance. After listening
to me attentively, he gave the order for my release, but only on condition
that I report to the camp commander. On my way through the hall I ran
into the young couple who had also been on the bus. When they saw
me they retreated into one of the rooms. Later I learned that KGB agents
had arrived on the scene to stay for the entire length of my visit: Perhaps
these two were the agents.

The camp commander rose from his desk and walked up to me with
a smile. That surprised me. Usually the chief remains seated, eyes the
visitor with a cold stare, mutters a greeting through his teeth, and proceeds
with formal questioning. But this chief politely inquired about my meeting with my husband. I began to tell him about the six-hour search. He
asked how it happened that a pair of men's shorts was found among my
effects, with money sewn into the seam. Keeping myself under control,
I replied: "What makes you think those shorts were meant for my husband? They were not found on him. They are my shorts, and I sewed
the money in so as not to lose it while I was traveling." I doubt that he
believed me, but he did not bring up the matter again. Subsequently,
my husband submitted a complaint, and they had to return the money.

The commander asked whether I was acquainted with Solzhenitsyn   24
and why he wrote only about the horrors, painting everything black.

Don't we have our brighter side, too? I asked him if he had read Solzhenitsyn's books.

"I have only read *One Day in the Life of Ivan Denisovich*. A very interesting story."

"Then how can you say that he writes only horrible things, if all you have read is one story of his?"

"I have read the reviews in the newspaper, and I have no reason to disbelieve them."

That was the end of our discussion of Solzhenitsyn. The commander 28 stood up. Taking a fountain pen from his pocket, he said it was a Korean pen and that he was giving it to me as a present. In a fairly friendly manner he showed me to the door, smiling as before. Perhaps he was simply being clever with me, fearing that once back in Moscow I might complain about the way I was treated here; or perhaps he really sympathized with me. I had the impression that his job was beginning to be too much for him. And indeed, he was relieved of his duties shortly thereafter.

Freedom at last! It was already dark outside, and there was a moon. I was in a state of agitation. After I had walked barely three hundred meters, I instinctively turned around and went back to the camp. I walked up to the headquarters building, looked into the lighted window, and saw my husband. He was standing and arguing with the duty officer. I rapped on the window and shouted through the transom that everything was all right, that they had held me for six hours but now I was fine. "Take care of yourself, and be sure to wear the cap I brought you." Andrei was terribly happy to see me. He had been worried about me and now he felt better. We said good-bye over and over again through the window, until the officer rudely interrupted our excited cries, slammed the transom shut, and drew the curtain.

Calmly I walked back to the village. I was on my way back to Magadan and Moscow. Later I gave Andrei's letter to friends who took it to Holland, and Karel van het Rewe still has that letter in his strongbox.

EXPLORATIONS

1. How long does it take Guzel Amalrik to travel to the camp at Talaya? How long must she wait at the settlement before seeing her husband? How long are she and Andrei allowed to be together, and under what conditions?

2. What major discomforts and obstacles does Amalrik barely seem to notice? Why do you think she is able to tolerate so cheerfully conditions that would appall most Americans? What hardships seem to bother her most, and why?

3. What points does the Soviet government aim to prove by its treatment of the Amalriks? How would you describe its strategy? In what ways does this strategy succeed, and in what ways does it fail?

4. What attitude toward Guzel Amalrik and her husband is expressed by the prison censor and doctor who search her? In what other ways besides their comments do these two women reveal their attitude? How does their strategy with Amalrik mirror that of the Soviet government?

CONNECTIONS

1. What restrictions, frustrations, and dangers appear in both "A Visit with Andrei at the Labor Camp" and Nadine Gordimer's "Africa Emergent"? What group of people in each account is the target of government persecution, and why?

2. In "Chairman Mao's Good Little Boy," Liang Heng's father fears — correctly — that his wife's disgrace will taint the whole family and affect their prospects. What evidence in "A Visit with Andrei at the Labor Camp" suggests that Guzel Amalrik faces the same danger? How is her response different from Liang's, and why?

3. What similar attitude is expressed by the Soviet labor camp officials toward the Amalriks and by the Alabama police officer toward the black man in William Least Heat Moon's *Observation*? What beliefs and emotions apparently motivate each group? How is the Amalriks' response similar to and different from the black man's, and why?

ELABORATIONS

1. Look back at Julio Cortázar's "Regarding the Eradication of Crocodiles from Auvergne." What techniques does Cortázar use to make bizarre suspicions sound almost plausible? Following Cortázar's model, write a report on Guzel Amalrik's visit with Andrei at the labor camp from the viewpoint of the old woman assigned to search her before and afterward.

2. Think of a situation in which you felt highly emotional but had to accommodate other people's demands and pretend to be calm. Write an essay about the experience, including the small details (as Amalrik does) that grated on your nerves.

JANINE WEDEL

Polish Line Committees

Originally from Newton, Kansas, Janine Wedel has traveled and lived in Poland since 1977. She studied at Bethel College and Indiana University, receiving her Ph.D. in social anthropology from the University of California at Berkeley. A Fulbright scholar, Wedel has published articles in the United States, Western Europe, and Poland. In addition to living with Polish families around the country, she toured as a singer with a Polish country music group. "Polish Line Committees" is from her book *The Private Poland* (1986), based on her experiences and research there.

Wedel's most recent extended stay in Poland began just two months after the government declared martial law in December 1981. Occupied by Germany during the World War II, Poland was subsequently taken over by the Soviet Union. Strict Stalinism eventually gave way to some independence for Polish Communists. Opposition between the Party and the Roman Catholic church lessened during the 1970s. In 1979 Pope John Paul II visited his Polish homeland. The next year the illegal Solidarity union organized shipyard strikes and won concessions — including legalization — from Party leader Edward Gierek. Gierek was replaced by the defense minister, General Wojciech Jaruzelski. Solidarity and its leader, Lech Wałesa, pressed for further change, calling for a nationwide referendum on establishing a non-Communist government if their demands were not met. Fearing Soviet intervention, Jaruzelski declared martial law, outlawed the union again, and arrested hundreds. A year later martial law ended and most of the detainees were released, but struggles between Party and Solidarity supporters continue.

As a Soviet-bloc country, Poland officially has a two-tiered economy consisting of a state socialized sector and a private sector which, though smaller, is still the largest in Eastern Europe. Integrated with the official economy is a thriving informal economy of connections and influence, black-market deals and under-the-table arrangements. It is this economy that concerns Wedel in "Polish Line Committees."

Poles lead two lives, the public and the private. Stories that reach the West tend to extol Solidarity's virtues and present contemporary Poles as saints, who, in the face of incredible odds and at great personal risk, have become radical Solidarity activists. Poles tend to talk about things they think foreigners respect and omit more dubious parts foreigners may approve less of — even if they are the bane of Polish existence. Thus, Western writers did not usually learn how the Poles they interviewed obtained high-fashion French shoes or Italian boots — when the rationing system allowed each citizen one pair of Polish-made shoes per year (1982 and 1983).

In order to get by under trying economic and political conditions, Poles shape their selves to mesh with the varying demands of private and public worlds. They have developed a keen ability, not only to live with the contradictions of their society, but also to manipulate them creatively. At one and the same time, they are pulled by the cacophonous demands of individual and family needs on the one hand, and on the other hand, contemporary realities: a rigid bureaucracy, uneven market distribution, the constraints of official titles.

Poles participate in the standard rituals of public life but — literally, in order to survive in Polish society — they must continually show different sides of themselves. One moral code is reserved for the private world of family and friends, another one for the public. The Communist Party member who serves as a government advisor in the public eye, also acts as an advocate for Solidarity activists in trouble. The employee who himself "organizes" a desk, is indignant when someone "steals" the same desk from him. The policemen who try to prevent Poles from making contact with the embassy of an enemy country, go out of their way to make pleasant conversation with a citizen of that country. . . .

Exchange in Poland is generally based on individual problem-solving strategies. A striking exception to the purely individual approach is the re- frigerator "line committee," an ad hoc organization of individuals who have one thing in common — a hope to buy refrigerators and other goods. 4

Since demand for refrigerators far exceeds supply, consumers are not likely to be successful by simply arriving at a store and standing in line for a refrigerator, unless they have an unofficial exchange relationship with the store management or access to unofficial information about delivery schedules. Consumers without such privileges would have to maintain their place in line twenty-four hours a day for however long it might take for their turn to arrive — often weeks. Given these conditions, line committees have spontaneously arisen, organized and controlled solely by people who wish to buy refrigerators.

In order to get a refrigerator for the apartment he will inherit from his great aunt when she dies, Paweł voluntarily took part in a line committee.

Paweł heard about the line committee through acquaintances, so one day he simply went to the refrigerator store. People connected with the line committee congregated outside to conduct unofficial business. The main activity was the control of a list of names of individuals who wanted to buy refrigerators. The list was made up of people in the order in which they had arrived at the state store. An average list might consist of 300 names; Paweł was number 440 when he signed up.

Deliveries of refrigerators to state stores are sporadic and no information   8
on inventories or delivery schedules is publicly available. Deliveries take place from several times a week to once in six weeks. Anywhere from five to sixty refrigerators may be delivered in a given shipment.

Controlling the list requires time and cooperation from everyone whose name appears on it. Twice each day, at 10:00 A.M. and at 9:00 P.M. at Paweł's store, the roll call of all the names on the list is read off. This is called "verifying the list." People whose names appear on the list of the line committee choose the person who will read off the list for each roll call. This is usually the person who is first on the list at the moment. Of course, as soon as that person succeeds in buying his refrigerator, he is no longer on the list or a participant in the line committee.

If Paweł is unable to be present for a particular roll call, he sends a friend or family member to say, "I am here" when his name is read off. For, if no one were to speak for Paweł, his name would be automatically crossed off the list and added to the end. Missing only one roll call would cause him to lose his place.

But the line committee's work involves more than controlling the list. Even though a delivery of refrigerators arrives only every two weeks on the average, eighteen people must stand guard in front of the refrigerator store round the clock. Vigilant groups are necessary to protect the integrity of the list by preventing people from barging into the store. Store managers do not honor the list.

So, in addition to roll call twice a day, Paweł has obligatory guard   12
duty for three hours, roughly every third day. Though no information is officially available, individuals participating in the line committee do their best to find out when deliveries will arrive. They do this by developing relationships with clerks or with the store manager, who is sometimes tipped off about when deliveries will be made or how many refrigerators are scheduled to arrive. In exchange for information on delivery schedules and inventories, people connected with the line committee may tip the clerks or manager by doing favors or giving gifts such as flowers.

But the line committee is rarely privy to information that is completely reliable, and so the store must be guarded from potential line jumpers. Round the clock, day after day, people on the committee's list take turns at guard duty. Paweł was on the list for four weeks, appearing for roll call and assuming guard duty, before there were any actual deliveries of refrigerators.

Any information about timing and number of refrigerators is of vital importance, for, when an individual is in the first sixty on the list, he is wise to stay after morning roll call in case a delivery materializes that day.

If a delivery materializes, those who have numbers one through about sixty are allowed by the others on the line committee to go into the store when sales begin, in the order they appear on the list. If only twenty or thirty refrigerators are delivered, the remaining thirty or forty people will move up in the line and have more likelihood of success when the next delivery is made, perhaps in days or weeks.

Line committees have been formed not only among prospective re-   16
frigerator buyers. They also conserve time for and improve the success of prospective washing machine, sewing machine, and other household appliance consumers. Line committees tend to be found in conjunction with the purchase of commodities that are unevenly distributed and in scarce supply.

EXPLORATIONS

1. Who organizes and runs line committees in Poland? What economic conditions brought these committees into existence? What social conditions make them practical?

2. In what way(s) do line committees represent the socialist side of Poland, with its emphasis on state control? In what way(s) do they represent the country's capitalist or private-enterprise side?

3. How would the impact of Wedel's account of line committees change without Paweł as a central character? What facts about line committees would Wedel probably have been unable to learn except through a friend like Paweł?

CONNECTIONS

1. How are Polish line committees similar on a practical level and on a philosophical level to the Cuban practice of "asking *el último*" described by Germaine Greer in "In Cuba" (p. 441)?

2. What similarities do you notice between life in Poland, as described by Wedel, and life in the Soviet Union, as described by Guzel Amalrik, Hedrick Smith (p. 374), Santha Rama Rau (p. 213), and Carola Hansson and Karin Lidén (p. 48)? Taking into account that Wedel's essay describes only a small segment of Polish life, what differences do you notice from the Soviet Union?

3. Robert Nisbet's *Observation* concerns the state's encroachment on society and individual freedom. Which of Nisbet's complaints evidently apply to Poland as well as the United States? How is government encroachment fundamentally different in these two countries?

ELABORATIONS

1. As archaeologists or art historians sometimes use an object to illustrate the culture that made it, so do writers. What can we learn about state-controlled manufacturing and distribution of consumer goods by studying a refrigerator? Based on "Polish Line Committees" and Hedrick Smith's "*Skoro Budet* — It'll Be Here Soon" (p. 374), write an essay describing the life cycle of a refrigerator in a Soviet-bloc country, from the day its components begin to arrive at the manufacturing plant to the day it breaks down in someone's home.

2. Why do you think the Solidarity movement happened in Poland, where citizens already had some freedom to take part in private enterprise, instead of in the Soviet Union or some other more rigidly socialist state? Referring to your reading elsewhere in this book on the Soviet Union and other countries, write an essay suggesting some reasons why so many Poles have united behind the idea of a labor union, while Soviets have not.

GABRIEL GARCÍA MÁRQUEZ

Death Constant Beyond Love

Gabriel García Márquez was born in the declining town of Aracataca, Colombia, in 1928. Out of local myths, idiosyncrasies, and his grandmother's storytelling would later grow his fictional village of Macondo, setting for many of his stories as well as his monumental novel *Cien años de soledad* (1967; *One Hundred Years of Solitude,* 1970). Like R. K. Narayan's Indian village of Malgudi (see p. 331), Macondo has links with William Faulkner's Yoknapatawpha County. García Márquez attended the University of Bogotá in Colombia's capital; while there he became a journalist, traveling to other parts of South America, the United States, and Europe, and began to write short stories. Recognition came with his novella *No One Writes to the Colonel* (1968), during a general flowering of Latin American literature referred to as "El Boom." His fusion of naturalism and fantasy made him one of the foremost practitioners of the genre known as magic realism. After his 1975 novel *The Autumn of the Patriarch,* depicting the evils of despotism, García Márquez vowed not to release any new fiction until the fall of General Pinochet's regime in Chile. In 1982 he published the journalistic *Chronicle of a Death Foretold* and won the Nobel Prize in literature. "Death Constant Beyond Love" reached this country in 1978 as part of the collection *Innocent Erendira and Other Stories,* translated from the Spanish by Gregory Rabassa.

Colombia, the northwesternmost country in South America, was ruled by Spain as New Granada from the 1500s until its independence in 1819. Venezuela and Ecuador, also part of New Granada, broke away ten years later; Panama followed in 1903. The Republic of Colombia is currently headed by President Virgilio Barco Vargas, elected in 1986. The national language is Spanish; 97 percent of the people are Roman Catholic, while ethnically a majority are mestizos (mixed Spanish and Indian blood).

Senator Onésimo Sánchez had six months and eleven days to go before his death when he found the woman of his life. He met her in Rosal del Virrey, an illusory village which by night was the furtive wharf for smugglers' ships, and on the other hand, in broad daylight looked like the most useless inlet on the desert, facing a sea that was arid and without direction and so far from everything no one would have suspected that someone capable of changing the destiny of anyone lived there. Even its name was a kind of joke, because the only rose in that village was being worn by Senator Onésimo Sánchez himself on the same afternoon when he met Laura Farina.

It was an unavoidable stop in the electoral campaign he made every four years. The carnival wagons had arrived in the morning. Then came the trucks with the rented Indians who were carried into the towns in order to enlarge the crowds at public ceremonies. A short time before eleven o'clock, along with the music and rockets and jeeps of the retinue, the ministerial automobile, the color of strawberry soda, arrived. Senator Onésimo Sánchez was placid and weatherless inside the air-conditioned car, but as soon as he opened the door he was shaken by a gust of fire and his shirt of pure silk was soaked in a kind of light-colored soup and he felt many years older and more alone than ever. In real life he had just turned forty-two, had been graduated from Göttingen with honors as a metallurgical engineer, and was an avid reader, although without much reward, of badly translated Latin classics. He was married to a radiant German woman who had given him five children and they were all happy in their home, he the happiest of all until they told him, three months before, that he would be dead forever by next Christmas.

While the preparations for the public rally were being completed, the senator managed to have an hour alone in the house they had set aside for him to rest in. Before he lay down he put in a glass of drinking water the rose he had kept alive all across the desert, lunched on the diet cereals that he took with him so as to avoid the repeated portions of fried goat that were waiting for him during the rest of the day, and he took several analgesic pills before the time prescribed so that he would have the remedy ahead of the pain. Then he put the electric fan close to the hammock and stretched out naked for fifteen minutes in the shadow of the rose, making a great effort at mental distraction so as not to think about death while he dozed. Except for the doctors, no one knew that he had been sentenced to a fixed term, for he had decided to endure his secret all alone, with no change in his life, not because of pride but out of shame.

He felt in full control of his will when he appeared in public again at three in the afternoon, rested and clean, wearing a pair of coarse linen slacks and a floral shirt, and with his soul sustained by the antipain pills. Nevertheless, the erosion of death was much more pernicious than he had supposed, for as he went up onto the platform he felt a strange disdain for those who were fighting for the good luck to shake his hand, and he didn't feel sorry as he had at other times for the groups of barefoot

Indians who could scarcely bear the hot saltpeter coals of the sterile little square. He silenced the applause with a wave of his hand, almost with rage, and he began to speak without gestures, his eyes fixed on the sea, which was sighing with heat. His measured, deep voice had the quality of calm water, but the speech that had been memorized and ground out so many times had not occurred to him in the nature of telling the truth, but, rather, as the opposite of a fatalistic pronouncement by Marcus Aurelius in the fourth book of his *Meditations*.

"We are here for the purpose of defeating nature," he began, against all his convictions. "We will no longer be foundlings in our own country, orphans of God in a realm of thirst and bad climate, exiles in our own land. We will be different people, ladies and gentlemen, we will be a great and happy people."

There was a pattern to his circus. As he spoke his aides threw clusters of paper birds into the air and the artificial creatures took on life, flew about the platform of planks, and went out to sea. At the same time, other men took some prop trees with felt leaves out of the wagons and planted them in the saltpeter soil behind the crowd. They finished by setting up a cardboard facade with make-believe houses of red brick that had glass windows, and with it they covered the miserable real-life shacks.

The senator prolonged his speech with two quotations in Latin in order to give the farce more time. He promised rain-making machines, portable breeders for table animals, the oils of happiness which would make vegetables grow in the saltpeter and clumps of pansies in the window boxes. When he saw that his fictional world was all set up, he pointed to it. "That's the way it will be for us, ladies and gentlemen," he shouted. "Look! That's the way it will be for us."

The audience turned around. An ocean liner made of painted paper   8 was passing behind the houses and it was taller than the tallest houses in the artificial city. Only the senator himself noticed that since it had been set up and taken down and carried from one place to another the superimposed cardboard town had been eaten away by the terrible climate and that it was almost as poor and dusty as Rosal del Virrey.

For the first time in twelve years, Nelson Farina didn't go to greet the senator. He listened to the speech from his hammock amidst the remains of his siesta, under the cool bower of a house of unplaned boards which he had built with the same pharmacist's hands with which he had drawn and quartered his first wife. He had escaped from Devil's Island and appeared in Rosal del Virrey on a ship loaded with innocent macaws, with a beautiful and blasphemous black woman he had found in Paramaribo and by whom he had a daughter. The woman died of natural causes a short while later and she didn't suffer the fate of the other, whose pieces had fertilized her own cauliflower patch, but was buried whole and with her Dutch name in the local cemetery. The daughter had inherited her color and her figure along with her father's yellow and astonished eyes, and he had good reason to imagine that he was rearing the most beautiful woman in the world.

Ever since he had met Senator Onésimo Sánchez during his first electoral campaign, Nelson Farina had begged for his help in getting a false identity card which would place him beyond the reach of the law. The senator, in a friendly but firm way, had refused. Nelson Farina never gave up, and for several years, every time he found the chance, he would repeat his request with a different recourse. But this time he stayed in his hammock, condemned to rot alive in that burning den of buccaneers. When he heard the final applause, he lifted his head, and looking over the boards of the fence, he saw the back side of the farce: the props for the buildings, the framework of the trees, the hidden illusionists who were pushing the ocean liner along. He spat with rancor.

"Merde," he said. "C'est le Blacamán de la politique."[1]

After the speech, as was customary, the senator took a walk through   12
the streets of the town in the midst of the music and the rockets and was besieged by the townspeople, who told him their troubles. The senator listened to them good-naturedly and he always found some way to console everybody without having to do them any difficult favors. A woman up on the roof of a house with her six youngest children managed to make herself heard over the uproar and the fireworks.

"I'm not asking for much, Senator," she said. "Just a donkey to haul water from Hanged Man's Well."

The senator noticed the six thin children. "What became of your husband?" he asked.

"He went to find his fortune on the island of Aruba," the woman answered good-humoredly, "and what he found was a foreign woman, the kind that put diamonds on their teeth."

The answer brought on a roar of laughter.   16

"All right," the senator decided, "you'll get your donkey."

A short while later an aide of his brought a good pack donkey to the woman's house and on the rump it had a campaign slogan written in indelible paint so that no one would ever forget that it was a gift from the senator.

---

[1]"Shit. . . . It's the Blacamán of politics." — ED.

Along the short stretch of street he made other, smaller gestures, and he even gave a spoonful of medicine to a sick man who had had his bed brought to the door of his house so he could see him pass. At the last corner, through the boards of the fence, he saw Nelson Farina in his hammock, looking ashen and gloomy, but nonetheless the senator greeted him, with no show of affection.

"Hello, how are you?"   20

Nelson Farina turned in his hammock and soaked him in the sad amber of his look.

"*Moi, vous savez,*"[2] he said.

His daughter came out into the yard when she heard the greeting. She was wearing a cheap, faded Guajiro Indian robe, her head was decorated with colored bows, and her face was painted as protection against the sun, but even in that state of disrepair it was possible to imagine that there had never been another so beautiful in the whole world. The senator was left breathless. "I'll be damned!" he breathed in surprise. "The Lord does the craziest things!"

That night Nelson Farina dressed his daughter up in her best clothes   24 and sent her to the senator. Two guards armed with rifles who were nodding from the heat in the borrowed house ordered her to wait on the only chair in the vestibule.

The senator was in the next room meeting with the important people of Rosal del Virrey, whom he had gathered together in order to sing for them the truths he had left out of his speeches. They looked so much like all the ones he always met in all the towns in the desert that even the senator himself was sick and tired of that perpetual nightly session. His shirt was soaked with sweat and he was trying to dry it on his body with the hot breeze from an electric fan that was buzzing like a horsefly in the heavy heat of the room.

"We, of course, can't eat paper birds," he said. "You and I know that the day there are trees and flowers in this heap of goat dung, the day there are shad instead of worms in the water holes, that day neither you nor I will have anything to do here, do I make myself clear?"

No one answered. While he was speaking, the senator had torn a sheet off the calendar and fashioned a paper butterfly out of it with his hands. He tossed it with no particular aim into the air current coming from the fan and the butterfly flew about the room and then went out through the

---

[2]"Me, you know." — ED.

half-open door. The senator went on speaking with a control aided by the complicity of death.

"Therefore," he said, "I don't have to repeat to you what you already   28
know too well: that my reelection is a better piece of business for you than it is for me, because I'm fed up with stagnant water and Indian sweat, while you people, on the other hand, make your living from it."

Laura Farina saw the paper butterfly come out. Only she saw it because the guards in the vestibule had fallen asleep on the steps, hugging their rifles. After a few turns, the large lithographed butterfly unfolded completely, flattened against the wall, and remained stuck there. Laura Farina tried to pull it off with her nails. One of the guards, who woke up with the applause from the next room, noticed her vain attempt.

"It won't come off," he said sleepily. "It's painted on the wall."

Laura Farina sat down again when the men began to come out of the meeting. The senator stood in the doorway of the room with his hand on the latch, and he only noticed Laura Farina when the vestibule was empty.

"What are you doing here?"   32

"*C'est de la part de mon père*,"[3] she said.

The senator understood. He scrutinized the sleeping guards, then he scrutinized Laura Farina, whose unusual beauty was even more demanding than his pain, and he resolved then that death had made his decision for him.

"Come in," he told her.

Laura Farina was struck dumb standing in the doorway to the room: 36
thousands of bank notes were floating in the air, flapping like the butterfly. But the senator turned off the fan and the bills were left without air and alighted on the objects in the room.

"You see," he said, smiling, "even shit can fly."

Laura Farina sat down on a schoolboy's stool. Her skin was smooth and firm, with the same color and the same solar density as crude oil, her hair was the mane of a young mare, and her huge eyes were brighter than the light. The senator followed the thread of her look and finally found the rose, which had been tarnished by the saltpeter.

"It's a rose," he said.

"Yes," she said with a trace of perplexity. "I learned what they were   40
in Riohacha."

The senator sat down on an army cot, talking about roses as he

---

[3]"It's on behalf of my father." — ED.

unbuttoned his shirt. On the side where he imagined his heart to be inside his chest he had a corsair's tattoo of a heart pierced by an arrow. He threw the soaked shirt to the floor and asked Laura Farina to help him off with his boots.

She knelt down facing the cot. The senator continued to scrutinize her, thoughtfully, and while she was untying the laces he wondered which one of them would end up with the bad luck of that encounter.

"You're just a child," he said.

"Don't you believe it," she said. "I'll be nineteen in April."   44

The senator became interested.

"What day?"

"The eleventh," she said.

The senator felt better. "We're both Aries," he said. And smiling, he   48
added:

"It's the sign of solitude."

Laura Farina wasn't paying attention because she didn't know what to do with the boots. The senator, for his part, didn't know what to do with Laura Farina, because he wasn't used to sudden love affairs and, besides, he knew that the one at hand had its origins in indignity. Just to have some time to think, he held Laura Farina tightly between his knees, embraced her about the waist, and lay down on his back on the cot. Then he realized that she was naked under her dress, for her body gave off the dark fragrance of an animal of the woods, but her heart was frightened and her skin disturbed by a glacial sweat.

"No one loves us," he sighed.

Laura Farina tried to say something, but there was only enough air   52
for her to breathe. He laid her down beside him to help her, he put out the light and the room was in the shadow of the rose. She abandoned herself to the mercies of her fate. The senator caressed her slowly, seeking her with his hand, barely touching her, but where he expected to find her, he came across something iron that was in the way.

"What have you got there?"

"A padlock," she said.

"What in hell!" the senator said furiously and asked what he knew only too well. "Where's the key?"

Laura Farina gave a breath of relief.   56

"My papa has it," she answered. "He told me to tell you to send one of your people to get it and to send along with him a written promise that you'll straighten out his situation."

The senator grew tense. "Frog bastard," he murmured indignantly. Then he closed his eyes in order to relax and he met himself in the darkness. *Remember,* he remembered, *that whether it's you or someone else, it won't be long before you'll be dead and it won't be long before your name won't even be left.*

He waited for the shudder to pass.

"Tell me one thing," he asked then. "What have you heard about 60 me?"

"Do you want the honest-to-God truth?"

"The honest-to-God truth."

"Well," Laura Farina ventured, "they say you're worse than the rest because you're different."

The senator didn't get upset. He remained silent for a long time with 64 his eyes closed, and when he opened them again he seemed to have returned from his most hidden instincts.

"Oh, what the hell," he decided. "Tell your son of a bitch of a father that I'll straighten out his situation."

"If you want, I can go get the key myself," Laura Farina said.

The senator held her back.

"Forget about the key," he said, "and sleep awhile with me. It's good 68 to be with someone when you're so alone."

Then she laid his head on her shoulder with her eyes fixed on the rose. The senator held her about the waist, sank his face into woods-animal armpit, and gave in to terror. Six months and eleven days later he would die in that same position, debased and repudiated because of the public scandal with Laura Farina and weeping with rage at dying without her.

EXPLORATIONS

1. How is the title "Death Constant Beyond Love" appropriate to this story's plot? What does the title mean in relation to the story's underlying theme?

2. How does Senator Onésimo Sánchez define his job to the ordinary people of Rosal del Virrey? How does he define it to the town's important people? How do you think he defines it to himself?

3. The author tells us that Senator Onésimo Sánchez "had decided to endure his secret all alone, with no change in his life, not because of pride but out of shame." What reasons does Sánchez have to be proud? What reasons does he have to be ashamed? How does his pride contribute to his shame?

4. García Márquez starts a pattern of ironically juxtaposed opposites with his title, which reverses the common expression "love constant beyond death." What pair of opposites appears in the story's first sentence? What further pairs appear in the opening paragraph? What roles do these juxtaposed opposites play in the rest of García Márquez's story?

CONNECTIONS

1. In "Death Constant Beyond Love," Senator Sánchez tells his backers that if he ever kept his promises to improve the local people's lives, "that day neither you nor I will have anything to do here." What evidence in Julio Cortázar's "Regarding the Eradication of Crocodiles from Auvergne" suggests that his narrator shares that view? What ideas about political power do these two stories share? How do they differ?

2. Looking back at Jill Gay's "Patriotic Prostitutes" (p. 383), what attitude(s) do you think Nelson Farina shares with the Asian governments that encourage prostitution? What attitude(s) does Laura Farina share with the prostitutes? What clues in the story suggest García Márquez's feelings about these attitudes?

3. Raju in R. K. Narayan's "Trail of the Green Blazer" (p. 331) succeeds as a criminal but fails when he yields to a noble impulse. In what sense is this also true of Senator Sánchez? What are the significant differences in these two characters' fates? What contrast in the two stories' themes is reflected by those differences?

4. Toward the end of "Death Constant Beyond Love," García Márquez characterizes Laura Farina as "an animal of the woods." Looking back at Alberto Moravia's "The Chase" (p. 249), what effect do you think García Márquez is aiming for with this image? Which of Isak Dinesen's categories in "From 'Daguerreotypes'" (p. 204) best fit Moravia's narrator's wife and Laura Farina, as they are perceived by the men in these two stories?

ELABORATIONS

1. García Márquez has been hailed for his masterful fusion of realism with myth and fantasy, as well as for the political implications of his work. To analyze his writing is probably a task beyond the most ambitious critic, but we can gain some appreciation of his art by looking closely at his craft. What, for instance, are the functions of flying paper in "Death Constant Beyond Love"? Write an essay describing and explaining García Márquez's uses of this phenomenon.

2. "No one loves us," sighs Senator Sánchez to Laura Farina. What does he mean? Is he correct? Why or why not? Write an essay on the role and significance of love in "Death Constant Beyond Love."

PART SIX

WITNESSES
TO WAR

Soldiers and Survivors

OBSERVATIONS:
LOOKING AT OURSELVES

David Byrne, William H. Sullivan, Mark Baker,
William Broyles, Jr., George Gilder, Barbara Ehrenreich

<><><><>

Czeslaw Milosz, *American Ignorance of War* (POLAND)

Doris Lessing, *The Afghan Resistance* (AFGHANISTAN)

Roger Rosenblatt, *Children of Cambodia* (CAMBODIA)

Shelley Saywell, *Women Warriors of El Salvador* (EL SALVADOR)

Albalucía Ángel, *The Guerrillero* (COLOMBIA)

Milovan Djilas, *Ideas Against Torture* (YUGOSLAVIA)

Frank O'Connor, *Guests of the Nation* (IRELAND)

Ryszard Kapuściński, *Carlotta* (ANGOLA)

Chinua Achebe, *Civil Peace* (NIGERIA)

Günter Grass, *Resistance* (WEST GERMANY)

In our era of *Rambo* and *The A-Team*, violence appears to many as an attractively simple solution to complex national and international problems. If it is true that those who ignore history are doomed to repeat it, we owe it to our future to listen to the stories of people who have fought in, been victimized by, or witnessed war and other forms of violence around the world.

Observations: Looking at Ourselves focus primarily on the war in Vietnam that involved our country in the 1960s and 1970s. To open, David Byrne reminds us what life during wartime isn't. William H. Sullivan, retired from the U.S. Foreign Service, recalls a 1962 war game with the Joint Chiefs of Staff. Mark Baker interviews a nurse who patched up wounded soldiers in Vietnam; William Broyles, Jr., wonders why he and other veterans are nostalgic about their war experience. Economist George Gilder suggests that the United States really won the Vietnam War; and Barbara Ehrenreich asks how we can wipe out the warrior caste that seeks in each war a seed for the next.

The Polish writer Czeslaw Milosz reports despair among Europeans over the naive, bellicose optimism arising from "American Ignorance of War." In a refugee camp in Pakistan, English novelist Doris Lessing finds Mujahideen fighters of "The Afghan Resistance" eager for U.S. help to overthrow the Soviet puppet government. Roger Rosenblatt visits a Thai camp for Khmer Rouge refugees to interview "Children of Cambodia," whose idea of revenge is as unique as their ancient culture.

Canadian Shelley Saywell talks with two "Women Warriors of El Salvador," who give a passionate insiders' account of their nation's guerrilla revolution. In Colombia, Albalucía Ángel's short story "The Guerrillero" speaks for a woman about to be interrogated by the secret police. Milovan Djilas has several recommendations for torture victims in "Ideas Against Torture," based on his personal experience in Yugoslavia.

Those who kill are often victims as well, as Frank O'Connor demonstrates in "Guests of the Nation," a short story narrated by an Irishman fighting to free his country from English occupation. "Carlotta" is Ryszard Kapuściński's memoir of a hot afternoon with a Portuguese camera crew and a beautiful Angolan soldier which turned tragic. Chinua Achebe's short story "Civil Peace" depicts a Nigerian family in the aftermath of Biafra's doomed attempt at secession. Finally, Günter Grass's "Resistance" shows a novelist who turned seventeen with Hitler's army vowing to rid his nation of the means to start future wars.   ◈

OBSERVATIONS:
LOOKING AT OURSELVES

1

This ain't no party, this ain't no disco,
This ain't no fooling around.

> – David Byrne
> "Life During Wartime"

◇◇◇◇◇

2

My first serious involvement with Vietnam was in the form of a weeklong war game organized by the Joint Chiefs of Staff in 1962. In order to ensure maximum objectivity, the Chiefs had engaged the Rand Corporation to draw up the rules of the game and to act as a control team. The opposing red and blue teams were to represent all factions that would presumably be involved if the United States were to expand its role in Vietnam. The game would be played as a command post exercise; its point was to project how the Vietnam situation might unfold over a span of about ten years given certain assumptions that would be introduced into the proceedings from a script prepared by the control team. In principle, those assumptions were neutral, and their effect on the outcome of the game would be determined by the way in which the red and blue teams reacted to them.

The opposing teams were divided into two echelons. The senior group functioned on the policy level and met only sporadically during the game. The other group operated at the action level and was in session eight hours a day. The blue team's policy chief was John McCone, head of the CIA, and its action chief was an Air Force general. The red team's policy chief was General Maxwell Taylor, former chief of staff of the Army, who was then senior military adviser to President Kennedy; I was head of the red action team. On my action team there was a Marine Corps general, colonels from the Army and Air Force, a Navy captain, some senior intelligence officers, and civilians from relevant government departments and agencies.

Taylor instructed me to play the game according to the rules of guerrilla warfare, accept heavy casualties, exploit propaganda opportunities, and brazenly disregard the truth. He particularly wanted our action group to play upon any weaknesses we could find in the traditional military doctrines of our opponents as well as in the civil processes of a democracy.

He took some relish in casting himself as Ho Chi Minh and encouraged me to think of myself as General Giap, the case-hardened commander of North Vietnam's troops. We launched the game with zeal.

By the end of the week — a point that represented the winter of 1972 — the game had played itself out. The red (North Vietnamese) forces were everywhere on the map on Indochina. We had overrun most of Laos and we controlled the countryside of South Vietnam and the cordillera extending into Cambodia. We had suffered severe casualties, but our structure was still intact and we had solid support from the Soviet Union and China. We had extended and demoralized the forces of South Vietnam. Most important, 500,000 American troops had been bogged down in the quagmire of Indochina and a large portion of the U.S. Navy and Air Force had become involved. We had caused great U.S. expenditures on this feckless enterprise and had provoked great agitation and unrest in the American population, especially on university campuses. Moreover, we had all but isolated the United States in the United Nations and in world public opinion and we had driven the U.S. Congress to the brink of revolt over the seemingly endless war.

John McCone concluded that his organization ought to call it quits and cut its losses. The experience of playing that game made him a dove on Vietnam. He felt that its projections were accurate and that the shadows they cast should be heeded.

Other participants drew different conclusions. Some Air Force officers felt that the control team was unrealistic in its scoring of certain actions. . . . I specifically remember their cry of foul when my guerrillas were able to blow up a large number of U.S. aircraft at Bien Hoa airfield. I remember this so clearly because when I looked out the window of my airplane in November 1964 as I was leaving Vietnam to return to Washington to be sworn in as ambassador to Laos, I saw black smoke billowing from the airport at Bien Hoa, where a guerrilla attack had succeeded in blowing up fuel, ammunition, and a number of U.S. aircraft.

– William H. Sullivan
"Vietnam Portents"
Harper's

⬦⬦⬦⬦⬦

3

I never saw so many guys cry as I did while I was in Vietnam. Some of those corpsmen and men from the field amazed me with how gentle they were with their buddies. One of the big fears the guys had was of dying alone. A lot of guys came into the hospital really badly hurt and they did die, but their buddies stayed with them.

"Don't leave me, please don't leave me." And they didn't.

About the time I'd get fed up with being there, I'd walk into the ward and see a paraplegic who could still use his arms, feeding the guy next to him who had been blinded. I'd think to myself, "You may hate it here and you may feel like shit and look like hell and think you just can't stand another day, but at least you're not one of these guys. If that boy with no legs can get over to feed his blind friend, you can do what *you* have to do."

I went over to Vietnam thinking Army doctors were hard-asses. It's just not so. We had a Vietnamese girl on the ward. She was the same age as I was — twenty-one. She was cleaning the barracks. They used to clean the floors with kerosene or something to get the wax off. Some smart guy flipped a match on the floor while she was down there scrubbing it. *Whoosh*, she was gone in a puff of smoke.

The surgeon taking care of her was named Paul. When he got to her, she was 100 percent second- and third-degree burns. Plus she had inhaled a lot of smoke. Usually these people are going to die, so you let them. The thing was, she was still conscious and talking, and her kidneys were still working. So he had to try and save her. He started an IV on her and she came up to my ward.

Burn victims shed the inside of their lungs. It's like getting sunburned on the inside and peeling. She would cough up her lungs and she'd be bleeding and slowly choking to death. She could speak English. She would hold on to Paul and beg him not to let her die.

It was getting to the point that she was really bad and he had to make a decision. Either you trach her, so that you can clean her out and let her breathe, or you just let her die. Paul said, "I've got to think about it. I'm going to leave the ward for a while. I'll be back in an hour."

An hour went by and he didn't come back. Another hour went by and he didn't show. Finally, I went looking for him. He was in this place that was our library — it was about the size of a walk-in closet. He was in there crying his eyes out. He said, "What am I going to do? I never should have started that IV on her. I never should have put that catheter in her. But she was alive when she came in and I had to do something. I can't trach her. She'll live six weeks and then she'll die horribly. What am I going to do with her? What am I going to do?"

He didn't do anything. He was going to let her die. We had to go over and change the dressings on her. He didn't want to do it any more than I did. But he helped me. The whole time she just cried and begged him not to let her die. But it was inevitable; she was gone in another day or so.

The doctors used to help us with the dressing changes quite a bit, because they knew how ugly they were. You've got a guy and you've got to change his whole body when you change the dressing. You have to give the guy morphine just to take the edge off, because he's so badly injured. The doctors felt bad for us. There were days when there wasn't a dry eye in the house, what with the patients screaming and us crying, trying to get the job done.

> – Mark Baker
> *Nam: The Vietnam War in the Words
> of the Men and Women Who Fought
> There*

◇◇◇◇◇

4

Ask me, ask any man who has been to war about his experience, and chances are we'll say we don't want to talk about it — implying that we hated it so much, it was so terrible, that we would rather leave it buried. And it is no mystery why men hate war. War is ugly, horrible, evil, and it is reasonable for men to hate all that. But I believe that most men who have been to war would have to admit, if they are honest, that somewhere inside themselves they loved it too, loved it as much as anything that has happened to them before or since. And how do you explain that to your wife, your children, your parents, or your friends?

That's why men in their sixties and seventies sit in their dens and recreation rooms around America and know that nothing in their life will equal the day they parachuted into St.-Lô or charged the bunker on Okinawa. That's why veterans' reunions are invariably filled with boozy awkwardness, forced camaraderie ending in sadness and tears: you are together again, these are the men who were your brothers, but it's not the same, can never be the same. That's why when we returned from Vietnam we moped around, listless, not interested in anything or anyone. Something had gone out of our lives forever, and our behavior on returning was inexplicable except as the behavior of men who had lost a great — perhaps the great — love of their lives, and had no way to tell anyone about it.

In part we couldn't describe our feelings because the language failed us: the civilian-issue adjectives and nouns, verbs and adverbs, seemed made for a different universe. There were no metaphors that connected the war to everyday life. But we were also mute, I suspect, out of shame. Nothing in the way we are raised admits the possibility of loving war. It is at best a necessary evil, a patriotic duty to be discharged and then put behind us. To love war is to mock the very values we supposedly fight for. It is to be insensitive, reactionary, a brute.

But it may be more dangerous, both for men and nations, to suppress the reasons men love war than to admit them. In *Apocalypse Now* Robert Duvall, playing a brigade commander, surveys a particularly horrific combat scene and says, with great sadness, "You know, someday this war's gonna be over." He is clearly meant to be a psychopath, decorating enemy bodies with playing cards, riding to war with Wagner blaring. We laugh at him — Hey! nobody's like that! And last year in Grenada American boys charged into battle playing Wagner, a new generation aping the movies of Vietnam the way we aped the movies of World War II, learning nothing, remembering nothing.

Alfred Kazin wrote that war is the enduring condition of twentieth-century man. He was only partly right. War is the enduring condition of man, period. Men have gone to war over everything from Helen of Troy to Jenkins's ear. Two million Frenchmen and Englishmen died in muddy trenches in World War I because a student shot an archduke. The truth is, the reasons don't matter. There is a reason for every war and a war for every reason.

For centuries men have hoped that with history would come progress, and with progress, peace. But progress has simply given man the means to make war even more horrible; no wars in our savage past can begin to match the brutality of the wars spawned in this century, in the beautifully ordered, civilized landscape of Europe, where everyone is literate and classical music plays in every village café. War is not an aberration; it is part of the family, the crazy uncle we try — in vain — to keep locked in the basement.

> – William Broyles, Jr.
> "Why Men Love War"
> *Esquire*

◇◇◇◇◇

5

If we consider the economic consequences of Vietnam, I think we'll see that there's a real sense in which the United States won the Vietnam War. At least we won the one prize that was worth anything — the boat people [Southeast Asian refugees]. The boat people are now key figures in the high-tech companies in Silicon Valley and across the country, and are thus contributing substantially to American economic growth.

America's victory in Vietnam is more evident when we look at our economy's growing dominance in the world. At the end of the war, our gross domestic product was a quarter of the world's output; for 1984 it is estimated at almost a third. And the predominance of the capitalist system is nowhere more dramatic than in Asia. The communists may continue to dominate the pathetic small places, but less pathetic small places — Singapore, Hong Kong, Taiwan — are booming capitalist countries.

This massive shift in economic power from the communist world to the capitalist world, symbolized by the boat people, has been far more important than the tactical defeat the United States suffered in Vietnam. America's position in the world has steadily improved in the last decade. And it will keep improving if we continue the emancipation of our economy that President Reagan has begun — recapturing the momentum the Kennedy Administration began with its tax cut. The Vietnam War was a crucial factor in this economic development, because in the late 1960s, partly to pay for the war, the government started raising tax rates again. There was economic devastation for several years because of Vietnam. But as soon as the war was over, as soon as tax rates were cut, the United States began to demonstrate that it could again dominate the world economically — which is the way that counts.

Indeed, perhaps the most harmful consequence of Vietnam was that it helped reinforce the fallacy of geopolitics — the idea that the cold war is about real estate, that it really makes a difference to America's power that the Russians control Afghanistan or Angola or Ethiopia, all those pathetic countries you can't even visit without getting sick.

> – George Gilder
> in "What Are the Consequences of Vietnam?"
> *Harper's*

◇◇◇◇◇◇

6

When I first saw Oliver North on television, testifying — or, rather, declining to testify before the House Committee of Foreign Affairs — I was so taken by the expression on his face that I almost missed the main point. The expression was one of exaggerated attentiveness: eyebrows drawn up high into the center of his forehead, the corners of his mouth tucked down ceremoniously toward his chin. It was the kind of face you might wear for a solemn occasion where it would be tactless, if not incriminating, to break out into a grin.

The main point, however, is not that Oliver North may have enjoyed his role in Iranscam, or been amused by the feeble institution of Congress. The main point — the only real message of his silent testimony — was the uniform. This prince of Reagan's secret government had chosen to confront the public in a costume that proclaimed his license to kill — not just impersonally, as a President may by pressing a button — but, if necessary, messily and by hand. A civilian official in a civilian government, he had chosen to come as a warrior.

I think that this may be one of the more useful ways to think of North and his cabal of collaborators: as members of the oldest male elite there is, the Warrior Caste. Not that, in the crafting of Iranscam, ideology was unimportant — or profiteering, or personal neurosis, or sheer hell-raising adventurism. But the same mixed motives have inspired the warrior elite throughout history, from the sacking of Troy to the raids of Genghis Khan and the Crusades against the Muslim world. What defines the Warrior Caste, and sets it apart from the mass of average military men, is a love of war that knows no bounds, accepts no peace, and always seeks, in the ashes of the last battle, the sparks that might ignite the next. For North and many of his key collaborators, the sequence was Vietnam, then Nicaragua, with detours into war-torn Angola and prerevolutionary Iran. The end of one war demanded the creation of the next. . . .

My guess is that the historical "success" of the Warrior Caste rests on the fact that it is, in more than one sense, self-propagating. First, in a geographical sense: the existence of a warrior elite in City-State 1 called forth its creation in City-State 2 — otherwise the latter was likely to be reduced to rubble and the memories of slaves. Natural selection, as it has operated in human history, favors not only the clever but the murderous.

Second, and quite apart from ordinary biology, the Warrior Caste has the ability to reproduce itself from one generation to the next. Only women can produce children, of course; but — more to the point — only wars can produce *warriors*. One war leads to the next, in part because each war incubates the warriors who will fight the next, or, I should say, *create*, the next. The First World War engendered the warrior elite that ushered in the Third Reich, and hence the Second World War. And Vietnam created men like Oliver North, who, through subterfuge and stealth, nourished the fledgling war in Central America.

But to return to North: the real point, it occurs to me, may not have been the uniform, after all. For the key characteristic of the Warrior Caste in its modern form is that it does *not* dress up in battle costume or indulge in recreational throat slitting. The men of the true warrior elite in the United States today (and no doubt in the Soviet Union as well) wear tailored suits, kiss their wives good-bye in the morning, and spend their days at desks, plotting covert actions, megadeaths, and "low-intensity" interventions. They are peaceable, even genial, fellows, like the President himself. But still I would say, to the extent that they hoard the resources of the nation for the purposes of destruction, they live for war.

> – Barbara Ehrenreich
> "Iranscam: The Real Meaning
> of Oliver North"
> *Ms.*

CZESLAW MILOSZ

American Ignorance of War

Czeslaw Milosz (pronounced Ches-law Mec-losh) has been called Poland's greatest living poet, although his work was refused publication in Poland from 1936 until 1980, when he won the Nobel Prize in literature. Milosz was born in 1911 in Lithuania, a small Baltic country historically controlled by Poland or the Soviet Union. He began writing poetry and became active in leftist politics while studying law at the University of Vilnius. After Germany invaded Poland in 1939, he wrote, edited, and translated for the Polish resistance in Warsaw. In 1946 he entered the diplomatic service of Poland's new Communist government and was stationed at the Polish embassy in Washington until 1950. After a year as first secretary for cultural affairs in Paris, Milosz broke with the Warsaw government, feeling too restricted as a writer by its regimentation of cultural life. He now lives in Berkeley, California, where he continues to write both poetry and prose. "American Ignorance of War," translated from the Polish by Jane Zielonko, is excerpted from his first American publication, *The Captive Mind* (1953).

(For more background on Poland, see p. 488.)

"Are Americans *really* stupid?" I was asked in Warsaw. In the voice of the man who posed the question, there was despair, as well as the hope that I would contradict him. This question reveals the attitude of the average person in the people's democracies toward the West: it is despair mixed with a residue of hope.

During the last few years, the West has given these people a number of reasons to despair politically. In the case of the intellectual, other, more complicated reasons come into play. Before the countries of Central and Eastern Europe entered the sphere of the Imperium, they lived through the Second World War. That war was much more devastating there than in the countries of Western Europe. It destroyed not only their economies, but also a great many values which had seemed till then unshakable.

Man tends to regard the order he lives in as *natural*. The houses he passes on his way to work seem more like rocks rising out of the earth than like products of human hands. He considers the work he does in his office or factory as essential to the harmonious functioning of the world. The clothes he wears are exactly what they should be, and he laughs at the idea that he might equally well be wearing a Roman toga or medieval armor. He respects and envies a minister of state or a bank director, and regards the possession of a considerable amount of money as the main guarantee of peace and security. He cannot believe that one day a rider may appear on a street he knows well, where cats sleep and children play, and start catching passersby with his lasso. He is accustomed to satisfying those of his physiological needs which are considered private as discreetly as possible, without realizing that such a pattern of behavior is not common to all human societies. In a word, he behaves a little like Charlie Chaplin in *The Gold Rush*, bustling about in a shack poised precariously on the edge of a cliff.

His first stroll along a street littered with glass from bomb-shattered   4 windows shakes his faith in the "naturalness" of his world. The wind scatters papers from hastily evacuated offices, papers labeled "Confidential" or "Top Secret" that evoke visions of safes, keys, conferences, couriers, and secretaries. Now the wind blows them through the street for anyone to read; yet no one does, for each man is more urgently concerned with finding a loaf of bread. Strangely enough, the world goes on even though the offices and secret files have lost all meaning. Farther down the street, he stops before a house split in half by a bomb, the privacy of people's homes — the family smells, the warmth of the beehive life, the furniture preserving the memory of loves and hatreds — cut open to public view. The house itself, no longer a rock, but a scaffolding of plaster, concrete, and brick; and on the third floor, a solitary white bathtub, rain-rinsed of all recollection of those who once bathed in it. Its formerly influential and respected owners, now destitute, walk the fields in search of stray potatoes. Thus overnight money loses its value and becomes a meaningless mass of printed paper. His walk takes him past a little boy poking a stick into a heap of smoking ruins and whistling a song about the great leader who will preserve the nation against all enemies. The song remains, but the leader of yesterday is already part of an extinct past.

He finds he acquires new habits quickly. Once, had he stumbled upon a corpse on the street, he would have called the police. A crowd would have gathered, and much talk and comment would have ensued. Now he knows he must avoid the dark body lying in the gutter, and refrain from asking unnecessary questions. The man who fired the gun must have had his reasons; he might well have been executing an Underground sentence.

Nor is the average European accustomed to thinking of his native city as divided into segregated living areas, but a single decree can force him to this new pattern of life and thought. Quarter A may suddenly be designated for one race; B, for a second; C, for a third. As the resettlement deadline approaches, the streets become filled with long lines of wagons, carts, wheelbarrows, and people carrying bundles, beds, chests, caldrons, and bird cages. When all the moves are effected, 2,000 people may find themselves in a building that once housed 200, but each man is at last in the proper area. Then high walls are erected around quarter C, and daily a given lot of men, women, and children are loaded into wagons that take them off to specially constructed factories where they are scientifically slaughtered and their bodies burned.

And even the rider with the lasso appears, in the form of a military van waiting at the corner of a street. A man passing that corner meets a leveled rifle, raises his hands, is pushed into the van, and from that moment is lost to his family and friends. He may be sent to a concentration camp, or he may face a firing squad, his lips sealed with plaster lest he cry out against the state; but, in any case, he serves as a warning to his fellow men. Perhaps one might escape such a fate by remaining at home. But the father of a family must go out in order to provide bread and soup for his wife and children; and every night they worry about whether or not he will return. Since these conditions last for years, everyone gradually comes to look upon the city as a jungle, and upon the fate of twentieth-century man as identical with that of a caveman living in the midst of powerful monsters.

It was once thought obvious that a man bears the same name and   8 surname throughout his entire life; now it proves wiser for many reasons to change them and to memorize a new and fabricated biography. As a result, the records of the civilian state become completely confused. Everyone ceases to care about formalities, so that marriage, for example, comes to mean little more than living together.

Respectable citizens used to regard banditry as a crime. Today, bank robbers are heroes because the money they steal is destined for the Underground. Usually they are young boys, mothers' boys, but their appearance is deceiving. The killing of a man presents no great moral problem to them.

The nearness of death destroys shame. Men and women change as soon as they know that the date of their execution has been fixed by a fat little man with shiny boots and a riding crop. They copulate in public, on the small bit of ground surrounded by barbed wire — their last home

on earth. Boys and girls in their teens, about to go off to the barricades
to fight against tanks with pistols and bottles of gasoline, want to enjoy
their youth and lose their respect for standards of decency.

Which world is "natural"? That which existed before, or the world of
war? Both are natural, if both are within the realm of one's experience.
All the concepts men live by are a product of the historic formation in
which they find themselves. Fluidity and constant change are the characteristics of phenomena. And man is so plastic a being that one can
even conceive of the day when a thoroughly self-respecting citizen will
crawl on all fours, sporting a tail of brightly colored feathers as a sign of
conformity to the order he lives in.

The man of the East cannot take Americans seriously because they   12
have never undergone the experiences that teach men how relative their
judgments and thinking habits are. Their resultant lack of imagination is
appalling. Because they were born and raised in a given social order and
in a given system of values, they believe that any other order must be
"unnatural," and that it cannot last because it is incompatible with human
nature. But even they may one day know fire, hunger, and the sword.
In all probability this is what will occur; for it is hard to believe that
when one half of the world is living through terrible disasters, the other
half can continue a nineteenth-century mode of life, learning about the
distress of its distant fellow men only from movies and newspapers. Recent
examples teach us that this cannot be. An inhabitant of Warsaw or
Budapest once looked at newsreels of bombed Spain or burning Shanghai,
but in the end he learned how these and many other catastrophes appear
in actuality. He read gloomy tales of the NKVD[1] until one day he found
he himself had to deal with it. *If something exists in one place, it will
exist everywhere.* This is the conclusion he draws from his observations,
and so he has no particular faith in the momentary prosperity of America.
He suspects that the years 1933–1945 in Europe[2] prefigure what will
occur elsewhere. A hard school, where ignorance was punished not by
bad marks but by death, has taught him to think sociologically and
historically. But it has not freed him from irrational feelings. He is apt
to believe in theories that foresee violent changes in the countries of the
West, for he finds it unjust that they should escape the hardships he had
to undergo.

---

[1]The Soviet secret police, 1935–1943. — ED.
[2]Hitler's takeover of Germany through World War II. — ED.

EXPLORATIONS

1. Why does Milosz's questioner wonder, "Are Americans *really* stupid?" What is Milosz's answer?

2. What does Milosz predict will happen in the West? What aspects of the Western situation, and what beliefs of his own, are the grounds for this prediction?

3. How would the impact of Milosz's observations change if he presented them in a historical or argumentative essay instead of in narrative form? What concepts and comments in "American Ignorance of War" struck you most forcefully, and why?

CONNECTIONS

1. What statements in "American Ignorance of War" suggest that David Byrne's *Observation* is making the same point as Milosz? What changes (if any) in behavior or attitude or both are these two writers recommending to Americans, and why?

2. In "The Demo" (p. 391), Thelma Forshaw describes how the European exile Hele Ganor appears to employees in his Australian milk bar: "His pallor, the lines of suffering in his face were a source of amusement to the girls, who had never experienced, never ever thought about, nor some so much as read of the outbreaks of violence in other countries." What similarities exist between these Australians and the Americans described by Milosz? What advantages does Forshaw suggest the girls have over Mr. Ganor because of their ignorance?

3. Which characters in Amos Oz's "If There Is Justice" (p. 180) are oblivious to the military life from which Rami Rimon has just returned? What comments by Rami (and by Oz about Rami) echo comments by Milosz?

ELABORATIONS

1. Milosz describes Eastern Europeans' attitude toward the West as "despair mixed with a residue of hope." What are the reasons for their despair? for their hope? Write an essay indicating why Eastern Europeans are concerned by Americans' ignorance of war, and why you believe their attitude is or is not justified.

2. How would your life change if the United States went to war tomorrow? Imagine your school or town under attack by a foreign power. Write a letter to a friend or family member describing, as Milosz does, what you observe around you and how you respond.

DORIS LESSING

The Afghan Resistance

Doris Lessing was born in Persia (now Iran) in 1919. Her English parents soon moved the family to Rhodesia, which became the setting for several of her works; her first novel, *The Grass Is Singing* (1950), was hailed for confronting apartheid there. Lessing settled in London in 1949. Primarily a fiction writer, she has often centered her novels and stories on racism, the dilemma of modern women, or both. Her best-known work is *The Golden Notebook* (1962), an experimental novel whose form parallels the heroine's effort to integrate her fragmented life and self through art. In the 1970s Lessing shifted spheres, first to highly psychological "inner space fiction" and then to a "space fiction" series called *Canopus in Argos: Archives.* In 1983 and 1984 she published two novels under the pseudonym Jane Somers to dramatize how hard it is for an unknown writer to get into print, and to elude critics' biases about her.

"The Afghan Resistance" is excerpted from a report in *The New Yorker* entitled "The Catastrophe." Lessing visited Afghanistan as a member of the organization Afghan Relief, which invited her "to see for myself the conditions of the refugees and the Mujahideen — the 'holy warriors' of the Afghan resistance." She and her group of filmmakers and journalists landed in Peshawar, Pakistan, an over-the-border resistance center. Lessing describes Peshawar as "an enticing town born to be the setting for a Bogart movie . . . all confusion, noise, traffic — a ramshackle, haphazard place." Since 1978, when Afghan refugees began pouring across the border, Peshawar's population has almost doubled.

What Afghans call "the catastrophe" is their country's occupation by, and long-running battle with, the Soviet Union. Surrounded by Iran to the west, Pakistan to the east and south, and the U.S.S.R. to the north, Afghanistan has historically been a target for invasion. Five years after it became a republic in 1973, a bloody leftist coup brought in a pro-Soviet government. This regime was replaced three months later in a Soviet-backed coup, and again in 1986 when — despite the presence of over 100,000 Soviet troops — the government had proved unable to suppress rebel forces. As Lessing describes, the war continues.

The Mujahideen stride all over Peshawar — thousands of them. Westerners think they all look like bandits, and are either titillated or put off. The Mujahideen wear baggy pants — the coolest garb ever invented, a Westerner who has donned them tells me, with currents of air flowing around you as you move. Then a long, loose shirt to knee level and, slung over one shoulder, a blanket, which is their bedding, their covering, their tent. They sometimes wear waistcoats. (I saw one waistcoast of good-quality English tweed with the selvage "Made in Britain" used as decoration.) They wear little Afghan pillbox hats, by themselves or with a turban around them, or else wear the Afghan berets. The turbans are many and amazing. If these men are not carrying Kalashnikovs — and they are not supposed to carry them in the city — it is as if they were shouldering imaginary weapons. These fierce men may seem to have come out of another century, and in some ways they have, but they are well informed about what is going on in the world. They have no idea how to present themselves sympathetically to the Westerner, adopting instead all kinds of heroic attitudes, talking about martyrdom, dying for their faith, seeking Paradise with maidens and pretty boys and wine. When photographed, they assume warriorlike postures. They do this because they think it is what will impress. Talking ordinarily, they do not use this kind of bravado. They have that brand of sardonic humor special to people up against it: black and wry and shocking — like Jewish humor.

These warriors move in and out of Peshawar from the battles that take place all the time over the mountainous eastern part of Afghanistan. They rest and they feed themselves, give wounds time to heal, visit their families in the refugee camps. They bring letters and messages. You will see two or three Mujahideen, or a group, meeting on a street: hugs and kisses all round. They are relieved to see each other alive — these comrades whom they last saw or heard of in battle. Their comradeship is strong; it is war comradeship, quite apart from the comradeship of Islam, which is another subject. When they are thinking of how they are presenting themselves to you, the word *Jihad* is used in every sentence. This is their word for their resistance, and it does not mean simply "Holy War"; it is like the Resistance in France during the Occupation. They all intend to fight until the Russians are out of their country. They say things like "We fought the Arabs for a hundred years before they finally defeated us, and we'll fight the Russians for as long." The Mujahideen have a hard life, and often a short one. If badly wounded in battle, they do not survive: there are all those great mountains to cross to reach hospitals. The boys growing up in the camps are their replacements. Every boy you see longs to be off with his father, his brothers, but some commanders won't let a boy fight until he is sixteen. Masoud, for example, who is continually besieged by boys begging to fight, sends them back to their families. Masoud is a commander admired throughout Afghanistan, by nearly all the Mujahideen — even members of different parties. He is the nearest thing to a national leader in this war. . . .

From the moment you arrive in Peshawar, Afghanistan enfolds you — the enormity of it, the horror, the sadness. Every Afghan you meet, Mujahid or refugee, is another tragic story. Each one is an appeal: Help us, help us! We in the West are ill-informed, they say — otherwise, we would be helping them. From the start of this war, the Russians have claimed, and might even believe, that the West, mainly America, has financed the resistance in Afghanistan. Russian soldiers are told that they are going to fight against American imperialists (even American Zionist imperialists — a nice twist); the Chinese; the bandits of international capitalism. They find ragged and barefooted men with Kalashnikovs, stolen from their own troops. Some Russians defect because of this, but a Mujahid warns, "Don't exaggerate this. One percent, perhaps, are upset enought to defect to us. The rest are Soviet-minded, and they are taught to see us as animals to be hunted down and killed." Even now, after seven years, most of the Mujahideen weapons are captured from the Russians. The Mujahideen say that when officials of the United States first denied that they were sending aid they did it in such a way that it sounded as if they were in fact supplying aid but had to deny it. Now the Mujahideen say yes, aid is being sent, but what happens to it? They get very little of what is being sent. It is the major theme of every conversation with every Mujahid commander. "We are fighting for you as well as for ourselves," they say. "The Russians want what they've always wanted — to gain access to the warm-water ports and to take what is now Pakistan. Why do you not aid us? It is in your interest to do so." The theme that beats through every conversation, every interview, is this: "From the very beginning, the West has underestimated the extent of the resistance. We have been reading for years, and often from your leading journalists, that we are finished, ready to give up. This has never been true. You describe us as if we were passive under the Russians, occasionally making little hit-and-run raids, and not as we are — a nation continuously at war, with everyone involved. Would you like to see for yourselves?"

Our group sat for the whole of a morning in the headquarters of a   4
certain political party while the Mujahideen commanders from all over eastern Afghanistan, from north to south, came in, three at a time, to sit for a while, answer questions, and then make way for others. They

came from Paghman, from Baghlan and Bagram, from Kabul and Paktia; there were Turkomans from Mazar-i-Sharif, with their Chinese-warlord faces, and men from Nuristan, who sometimes look astonishingly as if they had just come from Scotland or from Kent. They have blue or green eyes, light hair, perhaps freckles.

One commander, just in from fighting near Mazar-i-Sharif, has come to get new ammunition: "It was a big battle — jets, helicopters. They come in from over the Soviet border and run away back there. They fight like cowards. They bomb us from a great height. They have burned all the crops — they waited until they were ripe, because they wanted to destroy our supply basis with the people."

Another commander, from the extreme north, tells how he and his band cut the pipelines of kerosene, gas, petrol: "We destroy them again and again. The Russians can't keep them in repair. They can guard them only in the middle of the day, for we control the night." Then he asked us, "Where are the arms? We have even been fighting with axes. We have no food — we have been chewing wool and leather. We do this until we grow weak and have to end a battle even when we're winning."

Another commander from the north says that families and dependents are living in caves in the hills with their horses and donkeys. Their villages have been razed; there's nothing left of them, and the irrigation systems have been destroyed. For each fighter, there are five dependents. The fighters take turns going into battle, in units of a hundred. "We have no medicines, no doctor, no food. Yes, we capture some from the Russians, but often the Russian medicines are things we have never seen — hypodermics and drugs. We don't know how to use them."

A commander from Kabul says, "We have two organizations — one   8 inside Kabul and one out. The one inside is a sabotage organization. Everyone in Kabul is on our side, and that is why the Russians can't catch us. The women help us — even the children. We have people in KHAD — so many that the Russians could never catch them all — and they tell us when to expect attacks, and that is why we win. The Russians cannot move more than five miles from Kabul."

And through the long morning, again and again and again, from all the commanders: it is hunger and exposure that are destroying the Mujahideen. "We have no food. We have no warm clothes. No boots, only sandals. We lose our feet and hands from frostbite. In some places, people are already starving, and it is only autumn — there is the whole of the winter to come. Send us food, send us warm clothes. If you supplied us with enough ground-to-air missiles, we would defeat the Russians. Why do you not do this?"

And, continually repeated: "The West says we are disunited, because you are seeing things through your eyes. You are always looking for a single command over all Afghanistan. That is why you are always building up Masoud or someone else, speculating whether he will become a national leader. It is not the Afghan way. We have area leaders. They respect each other and work together, but is is not likely that a national leader will evolve.". . .

Three of us — all women — were driven in a taxi out to visit the family of a Mujahid commander who had become our friend. The route took us at first through the ordinary streets of Peshawar, lined with their light, graceful brick or mud buildings, freshly whitewashed or not, sometimes stained or flaking or cracked. The big markets in Peshawar are everything you would expect a medieval Oriental market to be — mazes of little lanes and courts and booths — and the roads running out of Peshawar have these same shops all along them. The shops are built of mud, or mixed mud and chaff. They have every kind of roof: reeds, old branches, yellow maize plants piled up into a thatch or heaped on reed or pole rafters. Some roofs are mounds of pale, gritty earth, and from this soil weeds and grass are growing. The booths sell fruit, vegetables, meat, manufactured goods; and the men, many of them Afghan, sit in the doorways watching the world go by, or perhaps lie on beds made of string and poles and placed outside the booths. Sometimes friends join them, and then these groups of men sit and gossip and stare at the cars and the traffic — the murderous traffic of Peshawar. But soon the sides of the road swarm with Mujahideen, and now many of them are armed, because Peshawar is being left behind. Hundreds of them, then thousands, then it seems that all this mass of people are Mujahideen. Among the men moves an occasional woman. You have to force yourself to notice them: their garb, like their gait, is designed for invisibility. A woman in a burka, interestingly, has a freer, more casual walk than one who is veiled. A burka covers from head to foot; it fits close around the head, with a little grille for the eyes, and then flows out around her as she walks. The woman inside is in a different world: she is observing, not seen — really invisible. (It goes without saying that burkas are used for all kinds of dangerous or shady transactions. The authorities on the frontiers between Pakistan and Afghanistan look at hands and feet: Is this

a Mujahid or a journalist trying to get into Afghanistan?) A woman in a
veil — that is, a cloth thrown across her mouth, leaving only her eyes
visible — acquires a scurrying, furtive look. It is painful to see a woman
you have been talking with, a human being, a person, transformed in
this way. . . .

Soon we were in a little village of the mud houses the refugees make   12
for themselves, and now began one of the muddles that seem unavoidable
in that part of the world. We had been invited to visit the commander
and also his family. Again, we had been told that it was permitted to film
his women. But he was not there. His aides did not know what had
happened to him; he had not been home for three days. He had gone
off into the fighting in the valley, they thought. His mother and wife
were worried about him. (He turned up next day, apologetic but not
explanatory about the incident.) The aides knew nothing about filming
the family.

Again, we three women were taken into the women's quarters at the
back. These women were much better off than most: they had space. A
big mud wall enclosed a large yard, where three horses were feeding on
maize stalks like those we had seen carted along the roads for fodder.
There were chickens. In a niche in the mud wall was a little garden
about two yards square, with jasmine and roses: dry, dusty, but it was a
garden. Two young women, the wives of the commander and his brother,
also a commander, were both pregnant, and were nursing babies, and
each had a larger child as well. The older children were playing with a
bird in a small string cage. It was like a partridge. It was their pet: I think
it had a hard time of it. Both young women were beauties of a certain
Afghan type: they had heart-shaped faces with wide cheekbones, and full,
sensuous mouths but with short upper lips showing white teeth. Their
large green eyes, frank and direct and candid, were a world away from
the dark, secretive eyes of their Pakistani neighbors. They walked and
held themselves like mountain women.

There was an old woman in command of everything — sixty years
old, the commander's mother. She was formidable. What we had been
told of the surprises of purdah at once came to life: we had not even sat
down before she flung up her skirt to show her naked stomach. It was
swollen. She had a growth. It was not painful, she said, but not operable.
She had visited a clinic run by the doctors in exile from Kabul, but they
had very few medicines. We asked these young women if two of us might
film and photograph them, but their husbands were not present to give
permission. The old woman and the children — yes, that was different.

The two families lived in two smallish rooms with a veranda joining them. The walls were of cement, unpainted. Matting covered the floors. In one corner was a great pile of bedding, reaching almost to the ceiling, and the usual mattresses around the walls were covered with bright cloth. The women wore pretty, bright dresses, earrings, necklaces, bangles. This was cheap jewelry, of beads, plastic. When the war began, the women of Afghanistan stripped themselves of their good jewelry, anything of value, and gave it to the fighters to buy guns and arms. Pack animals loaded with this jewelry were driven over the mountains to the camps in Pakistan. Women arriving as refugees in the camps were unlikely to have much left; what they did have was sold for food. The bazaars of Peshawar were full of their necklaces, bracelets, earrings. I bought a necklace: twenty-one complicated copper pendants sewn onto a brocade braid. It has the intensely private, personal look and feel of an article much used. It is made to be worn close around the throat. It lies on a table in my room and seems to pull my eyes toward it. "Don't forget me," it says.

It was the old woman who did the talking: animated, vigorous, con- 16 fident. When her sons went into battle, they left the children in her care, not their wives'. Their story began, of course, "And then the Russians bombed us and destroyed our food and we came across the mountains." Their life here, she said, was poor and dull. At home, they had everything — everyone was happy in Afghanistan before the Catastrophe. Now they never left this camp. Where could they go? And they had no clothes. The children had only what they were wearing now — little cotton dresses and shirts and pants. The winter was coming. "Besides," said the old woman, "we all feel safe here, surrounded by our Mujahideen. In Peshawar, people get killed by KHAD, by the Russians."

We asked about the bands of women fighters we had heard about in Europe. Had they heard of them? Did they exist?

"Oh, yes," said the old woman at once. "There is one near Herat." She herself came from Herat. "This woman commander is called Maryam. She was the only child of her father, who said, 'I have only one child, no son, and she must go to Jihad.' He tied his ammunition belt around her, and his men accepted her. She is famous. She is as brave as a man. She says, 'When I find a man as brave as I am, I will marry him.' But she is thirty-five years old, and, of course, she cannot marry until we win the war. She is very clever, this woman commander. For instance, once, when she knew that the Russians were coming, she made the village people drive cows and chickens across a bridge. The Russian soldiers are badly fed, and she knew they would stop to chase the cows and chickens. When they got out of the tanks, her soldiers killed them all. Another time, the Russians came and she said to them, 'Come in, you are our guests. Sit down.' They sat down, and she and her soldiers poured gasoline around the place and set fire to it, and the soldiers burned to death. And there is another woman commander in Panjshir. I have heard of her."

The old woman said that two thousand of her tribe were killed in Herat; twenty-six were killed by napalm as they stood in prayer. "Herat is wearing white," she said. When Afghans say someone is wearing white, it means he has his shroud on — is ready to die. She said, "Why does not the world complain about the destruction of Herat? It was so beautiful, and now it is rubble. Why do you let the Russians behave like savages? And Paghman, too — it was so beautiful." Paghman, outside Kabul, was once full of gardens, orchards, and irrigation systems. It has been devastated by bombing.

The women kept offering us tea, which we refused, for their offering   20
meant that they had no tea; if they had had any, it would simply have been brought in. Sitting there with them, all so friendly and sociable and gossipy, inside walls that shut out the world, and with the big, brave armed men out there in front, I found myself thinking, "Ah well, why not leave it all to the men?" (It was exactly as I once felt after five days in the Middlesex Hospital in London, cosseted and protected. Coming out, I could not believe I'd ever be able to deal with the traffic, the streets, the struggle of daily life. This state of mind lasted a day or two.) I am sure that it would be easy to fall victim to purdah and soon begin to think that no other way of life was possible.

Later, we began to ask all the Mujahideen we met about Maryam, but they only smiled politely. They told us that the women help the Mujahideen all the time in the war. In the towns, they conceal the Mujahideen, find them hiding places from the Russians, carry ammunition and messages — the war could not go on without the women. But a woman commander! They wouldn't hear of it. But, of course, she would be "invisible" — like a woman in a burka.

There is a tradition of women warriors in Afghanistan. For instance, there was one called Malalai. She is a heroine, with schools named after her. Girls are called Malalai. At a famous battle, at Maiwand, in 1880, the English General G. R. S. Burrows was winning. The Afghans had been marching all night and were tired. The Afghans say that Malalai, a peasant girl, called the soldiers cowards and walked out in front of them carrying the flag toward the British lines. She was killed, but her death energized the Afghans, and they won the battle.

The day after we failed to find the commander whose family we visited, he appeared, and took us back to the same area to see some newly established camps. Again, we drove until we had left behind the green, fertile fields and the irrigation systems and the fat, contented animals, and were in a desert place, full of red blowing dust, stones, dry gullies, rocky ridges. The good ground available for refugee camps had been used up. Poor land or desert or mountain areas were all the refugees could find now.

One of the political parties had supplied tents, some of them ragged. 24 They were scattered about in the dust, over the ridges, a few among some sparse desert shrubs. These people had come out of Afghanistan, over the mountains, six weeks earlier. It had been very hot, and twenty babies and small children had died. Some of the tents had low walls of hard mud around them, but most had only a little soil roughly piled up. The tents were floored with bare earth. There was nothing in them except a few cooking pots. Not much food: there was a little flour in bags hanging from the corners of the tents. Flour and salt. "Salt is cheap," said the commander, grim. A lorry came once a day with water — enough to drink, but not enough to wash with. There were latrine pits here and there between the tents. They were about a yard long, two feet deep. They had no covers; there was nothing to use as covers. The sun rapidly dried the deposits, which thereafter blew about with the dust.

Even in this awful place, the women were kept separate from the men. They and the young girls were crowded in the opening of their tents, watching the men and the boys, who were everywhere, and the very small girls. A girl of about ten loses her freedom and has to join the women; before that, she is as free as she will ever be in her life. When we Western women went toward the women's tents, we were surrounded by a mass of women and children begging for medicines — any medicines. This is partly because the poorer and more ignorant they are the greater is their uncritical respect for Western medicine — they have never heard of the scandals that make us careful about the drugs we take. Partly, they are indeed badly in need of medicines. "And so the Russians bombed our villages and destroyed the crops standing in our fields, and we came over the mountains . . . " And during the weeks of journeying the women of all ages and the children of all ages, with little food or water, fell ill, got diarrhea, broke limbs, suffered from nervous disorders, could not sleep. There were untreated wounds from the bombing. And there were no medicines — none. They begged and begged, and all we had was a few aspirins, which they bore off as if they were some kind of miracle.

Some of them were anxious to tell their stories, believing that if the world knew, help would be forthcoming. As always, every story began, "The Russians bombed our village, and we came over the mountains to this place." A woman said that when the Russians found people in a village they slit the women's stomachs, and killed the children, "for fun." One said that the Russians found a girl baking bread on the edge of a village when they attacked, and they threw her into her own oven and burned her to death. And laughed. Did we know that the Russians piled live people in heaps, poured petrol over them, and set them alight? Did we know that the Russians put people alive into pits, heaped earth over them, and then drove tanks back and forth over them until there wasn't any more movement? The atrocity stories went on and on. "Do you want to hear more?" the commander demanded, fiercely. We said no, thinking of people in the West who had already supped so full of horrors not their own and, alas, might start suffering from "compassion fatigue."

EXPLORATIONS

1. According to Lessing, what is the common theme of every conversation with the Mujahideen? What is the common beginning of every narrative by Afghan refugee women?

2. What Western preconceptions and prejudices about the Afghans does Lessing mention? What observations of hers bring out the uniqueness of the Afghan people and of the individuals she meets?

3. Why does Lessing fear Westerners' "suffering from 'compassion fatigue'"? What steps does she take to guard against this problem in her account?

CONNECTIONS

1. What observations in Lessing's essay suggest that she agrees with Czeslaw Milosz's statement in "American Ignorance of War": "Man tends to regard the order he lives in as *natural*"? How does each author use descriptive details to jar her or his readers out of complacency into sympathy with people in a war zone? (Give at least two examples from each essay.)

2. Lessing says of the Mujahideen: "They have that brand of sardonic humor special to people up against it: black and wry and shocking — like Jewish humor." What evidence for or against this concept of Jewish humor do you find in Amos Oz's "If There Is Justice" (p. 180)? How do you think being "up against it" influences what people perceive as funny?

3. In "Life Behind the Veil" (p. 267), Cherry and Charles Lindholm describe purdah — the seclusion of women — in the Swat region of Pakistan. After reading their essay and Lessing's, what advantages do you think purdah has for a society during wartime? What are its disadvantages?

ELABORATIONS

1. Should the United States support the Mujahideen more heavily? Should we send humanitarian aid? military aid? soldiers? Why or why not? Write an essay arguing for your position in this controversy.

2. What part(s) do Afghan men play in the resistance? What part(s) do women play? How does each sex help and hinder the other? Write an essay comparing and contrasting the sexes' roles in the Afghan Jihad.

ROGER ROSENBLATT

Children of Cambodia

Journalist and essayist Roger Rosenblatt was born in 1940 in New York, where he now lives with his family. His book *Children of War* (1983), in which "Children of Cambodia" appears, took him to Thailand, Hong Kong, Israel, Lebanon, Greece, and Northern Ireland. In addition to winning the 1984 Robert F. Kennedy Book Award, *Children of War* was nominated for the 1983 National Book Critics Circle Award. Rosenblatt studied at New York University and Harvard University; he taught English and American literature at Harvard from 1963 to 1973 and was a Fulbright scholar in 1965–66. For two years he served as director of education at the National Endowment for the Humanities in Washington, D.C. He then became a columnist and literary editor for the *New Republic,* switched to the *Washington Post,* and finally moved to *Time* magazine, where he is a senior writer and essayist.

Cambodia first came to the attention of many Americans during the Vietnam War, when U.S. troops — supporting democratic South Vietnam — crossed its border to pursue Communist Vietcong guerrillas. As Rosenblatt notes, enmities in the region go back many centuries: the Khmer dominated the peninsula that now comprises Thailand, Laos, Cambodia, and Vietnam from the ninth to thirteenth centuries, losing its east and west coasts finally to invading Siamese and Vietnamese. France took control of most of the region in the mid-1800s. Prince Norodom Sihanouk ruled Cambodia from 1941 through its independence from France in 1953 until pro–United States Lon Nol seized power in 1970. In the early 1970s American troops left Vietnam; North Vietnam brought the South under Communist rule in 1975. That same year, in Cambodia, the Communist Khmer Rouge ousted the Lon Nol government. Then commenced the brutal regime of Pol Pot, who forced people out of the cities and towns to clear jungle and forest, and slaughtered not only his opponents but intellectuals and anyone else not aligned with his ideology. Over a million Cambodians were executed or died of hardship. Four years later, just as the United States recognized Pol Pot's government, Vietnam invaded Cambodia and forced Pol Pot and his troops into the jungles, setting up an austere Communist regime.

(For more background on Cambodia and Vietnam, see p. 383.)

The road to Khao I Dang is a looping highway extending from Bangkok east southeast 150 miles to the Thai-Cambodian border. . . .

Socua assumes the task of telling me about the region. Socua is herself Khmer. She prefers the term *Khmer* to *Cambodian*, as do her countrymen, yet they also prefer *Cambodia* to *Kampuchea*, since that is the name Pol Pot gave the country after his takeover in April 1975. Wherever possible, they seek to draw a distinction between the peaceful, dignified people once known as the Khmer and the murderers who called themselves the Khmer Rouge. Socua is in her midtwenties, self-confident, attractive, her black hair cut short like a flapper's. A refugee herself, she lived and studied in San Francisco, and only recently came to Thailand to work with other refugees. Because of the war between the Khmer Rouge and the invading Vietnamese, travel to her homeland is impossible. She tells me that most of the people in Khao I Dang would also prefer to return home rather than be dispersed abroad.

For the present hope of returning is out of the question. The Vietnamese and Khmer Rouge are stalking each other in the jungles, leaving the innocent majority of Khmer terrorized, helpless, and starving. The Thais, suffused with traditional hatred of the Vietnamese and with traditional contempt for the Khmer, sell weapons to the Khmer Rouge. These are largely U.S. weapons. I discover that my country is in the idiotic and shameful position of recognizing the Khmer Rouge in the UN, arming them in the jungles, and accepting their victims as refugees. As a sidelight to the Cambodian war, the Thai government does nothing to restrain the Thai pirates from raping and slaughtering the Vietnamese boat people, including children, whose junks stray into Thai waters. Later in Hong Kong I read of a thirteen-year-old Vietnamese girl raped over and again by Thai pirates who passed her around. In seven days aboard the West German rescue ship she did not smile once. The nurses wept when they first saw her.

On a map one can see how close these now famous nations are — 4 Thailand, Laos, Vietnam, Cambodia — pressed together as tightly as four midwestern American states. The Thais first won independence from the Khmer in 1238. It has taken awhile to hone these enmities. . . .

Many of the houses rest on stilts here. Socua tells me that in Cambodia the height of one's house signifies how rich and important he is. The height of a house is often increased by piling roof upon roof. "If one wishes to determine how powerful you are, he will not ask directly, which would be rude. He will ask instead how many roofs your house has." At least that was so when Cambodia still had gradations of self-esteem. That is gone now, Socua says. War has changed her people. A country known for centuries for docility, gentleness, and pride — "known mainly for smiling" — is ravaged now, the people shaken, their former values ruined and cast away. "Still, you will see vestiges of the old dignity in Khao I Dang. Whenever parents want to discipline their children, all they do is remind them: 'You are Khmer. Behave like Khmer.'" From a very early age, Socua says, the children are taught to honor, in this order, the land, the nation, their dead ancestors, their parents, their village, including their friends. "They continue to do so, even in a place like Khao I Dang." . . .

In the middle of the morning on October 13, we arrive in Khao I Dang, swarmed immediately by small girls calling "Buy, please, buy," and selling wooden birds on wooden perches. Socua guides us through the children. She points to a huddle of Khmer adults waiting by the gate to be moved in trucks to other camps. Their faces are lifeless. At its largest Khao I Dang held over 120,000 refugees. That population is reduced to 40,000 now, a number that sounds more manageable, given the small-town size of the camp, about seventy square acres. Behind the neat rows of straw-roofed huts rises the mountain Khao I Dang, or "spotted bitch mountain" or simply "spotted mountain"; evidently it translates both ways. Socua leads Matthew and me along Phnom Penh Road, a mud path named to recall the homeland of the Khmer. Their camp looks like an ancient village to me. Women in *sampots* skitter by with naked babies riding on their hips. Monks in yellow gowns sit cross-legged on long bamboo tables, their shaved heads lowered in contemplation. We arrive on a holiday, the last days of the Buddhist Lent. Everyone smiles at us openly, the children tagging along. Some are in tatters. I find them astonishingly beautiful.

"They think you'll take them home with you," says Socua. "Take care to say nothing that would indicate you might."

Neil Boothby greets us at the Children's Center, a long, dirt-floor hut   8
the size of a mess hall in an army camp. We wired Neil from Bangkok to say why we were coming. He has already engaged an interpreter for us. Socua is thus free to work elsewhere in the camp. She will arrange a dance performance by the children later in the day. Our interpreter, Khav Yuom, called Yuom, is a man so small and fresh-faced he could pass for a child himself. In fact, I take him for a teenager until I look at him more earnestly. Yuom is in his midtwenties. Partly because he looks like a boy, he not only managed to escape from the Khmer Rouge himself but to smuggle his wife and mother out of the country as well. He goes to get Ty Kim Seng, a ten-year-old who also escaped Pol Pot's soldiers and who arrived at Khao I Dang about a year ago. Ty Kim Seng is one of several children Neil has lined up for me to meet. . . .

"He always talked fairly freely, even when he first came to the camp and looked like this." Neil slides a sheet of paper toward me across the kitchen table where we sit. It is a crayon drawing of a bright orange skeletal figure with a grim mouth in an open frown. Round teardrops fall from the skeleton's eyes. Ty Kim Seng drew this picture shortly after he arrived at Khao I Dang. It refers to the time when the boy was eight and was forced to join one of the mobile work teams instituted by Pol Pot for the Khmer children's "education and well-being." When Ty Kim Seng first walked down into Khao I Dang, he was nearly dead from malnutrition.

No longer, Ty Kim Seng enters the hut alongside Yuom and greets me with a *wai*, a small bow of homage in which one's hands are pressed together as if in prayer and raised to one's face, the fingertips stopping at about eye level. I return the gesture, asking Yuom with my eyes if I have done the *wai* correctly. I soon realize he would never risk discourtesy by telling me if I erred. Yuom and Ty Kim Seng take the bench on the opposite side of the kitchen table, and we begin to talk above the squeals of the children outside the hut. The boy is visible to the middle of his chest. He wears a white sport shirt. His face is bright brown, his head held in balance by a pair of ears a bit too large for the rest. The effect is scholarly, not comical. . . . I ask a few introductory questions to which at first he gives only brief answers.

"Are your parents living?"

"No. They are dead."   12

"What work did they do in Cambodia?"

"My father was a doctor. My mother did housework."

"Would you also like to be a doctor someday?"

"No. I would like to be an airplane pilot." He tells me that once in   16
1974 he flew in an airplane from his village to Phnom Penh.

"Was it exciting?"

"It was wonderful." He smiles at last.

In fact, I had not needed to ask him if his parents were living. Neil gave me Ty Kim Seng's background earlier while we waited for the boy. Ty Kim Seng's father was shot to death by a Pol Pot firing squad, for no reason other than that he was a doctor. The policies of the Khmer Rouge included the execution of all Cambodian intellectuals. The definition of a Cambodian intellectual was quite flexible. It included dancers, artists, the readers of books. Under Pol Pot it was a capital offense to wear eyeglasses, which signified one might be able to read. At the age of five Ty Kim Seng watched his father being taken away in a helicopter. A few days later the body of his father was returned to his village, also by

helicopter. For a long while in Khao I Dang, Ty Kim Seng only drew
pictures of helicopters.

His mother died of starvation a few years later. By then, Ty Kim Seng   20
belonged to the mobile work team and he no longer lived at home. His
mother remained in their village, in which nearly everyone was starving.
Much of the country was starving. Ty Kim Seng received word that his
mother was very weak, and he managed to be taken to her. The night
before she died he came to her bedside and saw how swollen she was,
how weak her voice, with what difficulty she was breathing. The woman
held her son's hand and told him that very soon now he was going to be
an orphan, that he would have to be strong and look out for himself.

Then her eyes focused more clearly for a moment, and she said to
her son: "Always remember your father's and mother's blood. It is calling
out in revenge for you." She then told him to leave her room and to try
to sleep.

At the time, Ty Kim Seng was keeping a diary, on which he would
rely as a source of solace. He described this diary to Neil, but he had
lost it by the time he came to Khao I Dang. In it he would begin his
entries, "Dear Friend, I turn to you in my hour of sorrow and trouble."
On the night his mother spoke to him he could not sleep, and he wrote
in his diary how helpless and frightened he felt. In the morning his
mother was dead. He knelt at her bed and he prayed. Then he walked
to the house of a neighbor and asked that man to bury his mother beside
his father in the village cemetery. Ty Kim Seng brought a shirt with him
as payment for this service.

The neighbor and his wife carried Ty Kim Seng's mother in their arms
to the burial ground, the boy walking several paces behind them. Ty
Kim Seng was himself quite weak and thin. The neighbors buried his
mother, burned incense, and departed. Then the boy knelt by the grave
and burned three incense sticks of his own. Finally, he took a handful
of dirt from each of his parents' graves, poured it together in his hands,
and beseeched his dead parents to look after him. Afterward, he returned
to the mobile team.

"Do you feel your parents' spirit inside you now?"   24

"Yes, it talks to me. It tells me that I must gain knowledge and get a
job." He says that knowledge makes people good.

"Does your spirit tell you to take revenge?"

"Yes," solemnly.

"So, will you go back to Cambodia one day and fight the Khmer   28
Rouge?"

"No. That is not what I mean by revenge. To me revenge means that I must make the most of my life."

I place before him one of the other pictures he drew when he arrived at Khao I Dang, one that Neil showed me before, along with the skeleton drawing. "What is happening here, Ty Kim Seng?"

The drawing is of three boys, stick figures, standing to the side of several gravestones at night. The background consists of a large mountain with a leering yellow moon resting on its peak. Perched on a tree is an oversized owl, whose song, says Ty Kim Seng, is mournful.

"One day I left my mobile team to go find food for myself, to look for yams. I was very hungry. I met two boys, and together we came upon a mass grave of thirty bodies. They were piled up and rotting. The Khmer Rouge soldiers found me. I lied and told them I had gone for firewood. But they punished me. They bound my hands to a bamboo stick behind my back. I was tied up without food for several days."

He is asked what it is that makes a man strong. He tells me, "a spirit." Is there a spirit within him? "Yes. I talk to my spirit. I tell my spirit that I must study diligently and work in order to find a home in America. Or perhaps in France." Yuom explains that France is much on Ty Kim Seng's mind these days, because he has recently learned that his older brother lives there. The boy hopes to join his brother in France eventually, though for the present that is unlikely. The refugee allotments for all countries are quite low now.

"Is the spirit that makes you strong that of your mother and father?"

"Yes. My spirit told me how to find my way to the border when I escaped from the mobile team." Neil told me that before making his way to Thailand, the boy walked more than sixty miles to Phnom Penh, hoping for news of his brother. I see him doing so as he talks, traveling mainly at night to avoid detection, the small face alert in the dark. I ask him if he believes his spirit will always guide him toward the right destinations. He says yes, definitely. "One day it will lead me home."

Presenting his drawing of the orange skeleton, I ask if he would explain it too. "I drew this after the death of my mother," he says softly. "I ate leaves then. That is why there is a tree in the picture."

"If you drew yourself today, would the picture be different?"

"Yes, very different." He looks happier. "Here I have food. And there would be a smile on my face."

"Would you do a self-portrait for me now?" Unhesitating, he moves to a long worktable under a window at the far end of the hut. An elder provides him with paper and crayons, and he works in silence. The noise of the other children has abated momentarily, the only sound being an occasional squawk of a late-rising rooster. Soon the boy returns and presents me with his drawing, which is not a self-portrait at all, but a bright blue airplane with green doors, green engines, and a red nose and tail.

"But where are *you*, Ty Kim Seng?"   40

"I am the pilot!" He points himself out enthusiastically. "We are flying to France!"

Yuom brings a second child to the table. I am beginning to feel like a village official, a census taker. At the window beside me, a square hole in the wall, little faces pop up and down, vivid with curiosity. Nop Narith performs the *wai*. He is Ty Kim Seng's size and age, has shaggy black hair and great buck teeth that gleam in a smile. He holds his left arm below the table. Nop Narith had polio when he was younger, and the arm is withered. Both his parents are dead.

"When the soldiers came to my house, they took our whole family away. Me they took to a mobile team. I never saw my parents again. But I have a photograph of my father. My father was worried that I could not take care of myself. Yet I feel guarded by his spirit. I dreamed that I saw him, and he promised that his spirit would protect me. In the dream he told me to gain knowledge and to take revenge on his killers."

I ask him what is the happiest time he has known. The Lon Nol   44 regime, he says, because that is when his family prospered. Lon Nol deposed Norodom Sihanouk and was himself overthrown by the Khmer Rouge. "We had air conditioning then." I ask what to him is the most important thing in the world. He answers, "Diamonds and gold."

"Which would you rather have, a peaceful time or diamonds and gold?"

"Peace is worth more than gold," he says.

"Your father's spirit told you to gain knowledge. Does knowledge lead to peace?" He says that it does. "Your father's spirit also told you to seek revenge against Pol Pot's soldiers. Is it your plan to do that?" Again he says yes.

"What do you mean by revenge?"   48

The boy responds at once: "Revenge is to make a bad man better than before."

Two more children come to talk with me, and they, like Ty Kim Seng and Nop Narith, define revenge either as self-improvement or as working to instill virtue in others. I wish to ask Neil about this. When I considered the subject of revenge in Athens, I only noted its absence in the children

I had met up to that point. I was defining vengeance conventionally. It did not occur to me that the idea could ever be applied in such a way as to make it an instrument of beneficence or generosity. Was this something cultural, I wondered. Something derived from Khmer history or from Buddhist doctrine? The Theravada version of Buddhism practiced by the Khmer centers on the Four Noble Truths, which define wisdom as abjuring worldly desires. Perhaps so worldly a desire as revenge would be thought to impede salvation. . . .

A twelve-year old girl, Meng Mom, approaches the table next. She is puffy-cheeked and very shy. She toys with her purple sleeve throughout our conversation and only smiles and looks straight at me when I mention that her gold circular earrings are becoming. No other subject I introduce elicits a response. She will not speak of her father, who is long missing, or of life under Pol Pot. She will not make small talk. Yuom tries his utmost to encourage her. Still, nothing. Then once again I bring up the problematical question: "Meng Mom, why do men make wars?"

Suddenly she blurts out, "There are lot of bad men in the world."   52

"How does someone manage to remain good if so many men are bad?"

"Good must fight the bad."

"Can good and bad exist in the same person?"

"No. Not together. They are in separate places. The good must beat   56 the bad." All this is said quite rapidly. Then she is silent again.

I begin to suspect that the intensity with which the children contemplate the idea of good and evil residing in the same person has some connection with their unorthodox views of revenge as charity. That morning one of the other children I spoke with, Gnem Thy Rak, a boy of sixteen, told of watching a Khmer Rouge soldier cut a man's throat in the jungle. When I asked what it is that makes someone do so dreadful a thing, he like the other children responded that some people are born with a good spirit inside them, some with a bad one, and that these two warring spirits cannot coexist in the same person. He added further that there are many more bad spirits than good ones in Cambodia these days. To the question, then, of how the good may ever prevail, he replied, "The good spirit must revenge the bad spirit," meaning, I gathered, that while good and evil are discrete qualities, it is still possible for virtue to triumph by exerting its influence on the corrupted spirit.

The idea is admirable but illogical. If the world is divided between the predetermined good and the predetermined wicked, then how would either be susceptible to change by the other? Would it not have been simpler for these children to allow that good and evil do exist in some proportions in everyone and that the problem of mastery is a continuous struggle? In order to answer that with a sure "yes," one would have to appreciate the depth and extent of the evil these children have witnessed and experienced. And clearly, some of the things perpetrated by the Pol Pot regime were so far beyond the imagination that the idea of a good spirit coexisting with that degree of evil must have seemed intolerable. Was it possible, then, that the children made their neat division of the spirits because they felt that no people who behaved like the Khmer Rouge could conceivably have any goodness in them?

Still, that would not account for the deep anxiety in their eyes and voices as they confronted this issue. What might explain it, however, was their knowledge that those who were carrying on the acts of murder and torture were neither strangers nor foreign invaders but were their own people, their neighbors, perhaps their relatives. This odd fact pertained in Northern Ireland and in the Middle East as well, but the depth and extent of destruction in those places was nothing like Cambodia. The term genocide has been used carelessly and indiscriminately since 1945, but what Pol Pot did was genocide, tens of thousands killed in a sweep. Some now call it "autogenocide." The killers and the victims were one people: the same skin, the same hands. How does one explain such a thing to the satisfaction of one's conscience except to contend that some people must be born with one spirit, and some with another? To believe otherwise would be to suggest that Ty Kim Seng's father had in himself the capacity to be his own executioner, that Ty Kim Seng and Nep Phem and Meng Mom had that same capacity. It was a terrible thing to concede.

Could their idea of revenge thus be a way of dealing with the fear of   60 evil in themselves? If they could see how dangerous a good and gentle people can become, was it not possible that the only form of revenge to which they might be susceptible would be the reassertion of greater goodness and mercy? Revenge, conventionally defined, cannot be taken against oneself. If hate destroys the hater, it does so doubly when the enemy is within. "Revenge is to make a bad man better than before," said Nop Narith. What the children meant by revenge might be that revenge is a self-healing act, a purification into compassion and wisdom, as Buddhism itself prescribes. Revenge is to be taken against fate, against a whole world of incomprehensible evil. Living well, in a moral sense, is the best revenge. Logical or not, such a thought was at least a way of avoiding the essential nightmare that each of us is his own beast in the jungle.

EXPLORATIONS

1. How do Rosenblatt's young Cambodian interviewees define "revenge"? What explanation does Rosenblatt suggest for their unusual views?

2. What happened to Ty Kim Seng and Nop Narith after Pol Pot's soldiers took over their villages? What happened to their parents? How did Ty Kim Seng get to Khao I Dang?

3. What aspects of Cambodian culture make this an unlikely country for war and genocide? What factors in the region's history make the war there not so surprising?

CONNECTIONS

1. Rosenblatt narrates his visit to Khao I Dang in the present tense, whereas Doris Lessing narrates her visit to Peshawar in the past tense. How do these strategies create different effects? What techniques do both Rosenblatt and Lessing use to make their narratives vivid?

2. Rosenblatt writes: "I discover that my country is in the idiotic and shameful position of recognizing the Khmer Rouge in the UN, arming them in the jungles, and accepting their victims as refugees." What explanation do you think Czeslaw Milosz would suggest for this tragic dilemma? What recommendations might he make to the individuals responsible for American policy in Southeast Asia?

3. The *Observations* by William Broyles, Jr., and Barbara Ehrenreich contrast sharply with the views about violence expressed by the children Rosenblatt interviews. What do you think are the reasons for the difference? What conclusions do you draw about people's (or men's) innate love of war?

ELABORATIONS

1. Examine George Gilder's *Observation* suggesting that the United States in a sense won the war in Vietnam. How do you think Rosenblatt would reply to Gilder? Which writer's viewpoint is closer to your own, and why? Write an essay summarizing the conflict between them and arguing on behalf of the position you agree with.

2. Rosenblatt and Doris Lessing both describe the changes war wreaks on people's lives. What dreams, regrets, scars, daily struggles, and fears for the future do the Afghan refugees in Peshawar, Pakistan, share with the Cambodians in Khao I Dang, Thailand? Write an essay defining what it means to be a war refugee.

SHELLEY SAYWELL

Women Warriors of El Salvador

Shelley Saywell was born in Ottawa, Canada, and now lives with her husband in Toronto. She is a television researcher and producer whose credits include *The Ten Thousand Day War,* an acclaimed documentary series about the war in Vietnam. Saywell is currently senior producer and writer for the Canadian Broadcasting Company series *Going Great.* "Women Warriors of El Salvador" comes from her book *Women in War* (1985); to research it she traveled to Britain, France, the United States, Italy, and the Soviet Union.

Saywell interviewed the women she calls Ileana and Maria in Toronto, where they had been sent to recuperate from imprisonment, torture, and their husbands' deaths. Saywell writes: "Both women are twenty-five years old, both are mothers, and both have spent the past decade fighting for the revolutionary forces in El Salvador." She describes Ileana as "the more political" of the two: "She is a small woman with large dark eyes and a soft voice. She wears no makeup, and nondescript clothes." Maria, who speaks no English, "wears makeup and colorful clothes. She looks small and fragile. . . . Still a devout Catholic, Maria believes that revolution in El Salvador has little to do with Marxism. 'There are Marxists and socialists fighting,' she concedes, 'but there are also many of us who believe in democracy. We have united because revolution is the only way to end the tyranny.'"

The Republic of El Salvador is a nation the size of Massachusetts, south of Guatemala and Honduras in Central America. Like the rest of the region, it was controlled for centuries by Spain, from which it became independent in 1821. Saywell writes: "The war in El Salvador is a passionate subject, going back a hundred years to the 1880s, when the government decreed laws that recognized only private property, thereby effectively destroying the traditional communal landownership of the peasants. . . . Today the rich largely control the government and an economy that is described by experts as the most inegalitarian in that part of the world." San Salvador is the nation's capital.

Ten years ago Ileana was a fifteen-year-old high school student in San Salvador, a deeply religious Catholic, reared in a middle-class home, who liked rock-and-roll, boys, and nice clothes. Today she is a committed revolutionary, living underground, rotating between the city and the countryside where she carries out organizational work and participates in armed actions against the government.

"I believe now that armed confrontation is the only way for El Salvador, even if it is the most painful way, because all the political expressions of the people have been suppressed, all the peaceful means of protest have been attacked, and even our archbishop was killed for his views. What other way is there to change things? The only way left is to pick up our guns and fight for a better life."

After eighteen months of safety and rest in Canada, her choice to return was in many ways more difficult than her decision to become a revolutionary in the first place, because now she knows all too well what being there means. "It frightens me," she said before leaving, "because here I've grown used to being safe, and I've lost many of the instinctive defense habits I once had in El Salvador, the things that I used to do automatically to keep safe. Here you can walk down the street day or night, sit in a restaurant, talk about politics, and your life is not endangered. I feel that I need more preparation, that I'm no longer ready to face the confrontation. I have to find the strength to leave my daughter, knowing I might not return, and then both her parents will be dead."

She looks at me with wide eyes but speaks with the hardened resolve   4
of a veteran revolutionary who has robbed banks, kidnapped men, and killed. She has done these things because "I believe that only revolution can bring about the changes we need in our country."

The guerrilla war in El Salvador has veteran Vietnam correspondents shivering with déjà vu in the tropical jungle. American involvement continues to escalate in the region, and there is equal evidence of aid and military advisers from the Socialist bloc. Families are divided; sons and daughters fight each other. The television images are hardly distinguishable from the scenes the world watched not so long ago from Southeast Asia. But comparisons with Vietnam serve only to remind us that protracted civil wars become part of wider geopolitical cold war — and that millions of people die.

Ileana's father was a politician and businessman throughout his active life. His beliefs were to greatly influence the fate of his family and the choices made by his children. "He was involved in the struggle in his time," she says. "As a politician he saw too clearly the poverty and desperation of most of the people of El Salvador. He spoke up about it and was imprisoned and 'disappeared' several times. Finally he was exiled from the country. El Salvadorans have been opposing the regime for decades. In 1932 the peasants rebelled against their low wages and loss of employment. Thirty thousand were massacred by the military and landowners. Because of my father's activities in the 1950s, we went to live in Guatemala for a while. Ever since I was a child we have lived in fear of what was going to happen to us. After we returned from Guatemala my father decided not to get involved in politics anymore. He could not take imprisonment or torture at his age. When we kids became active he told us to be careful. He is scared for us, but he supports us."

Ileana's mother was never really involved: "She really didn't understand anything, even after all those years with my father. Now they are separated, but even when she was with him she didn't understand. Still, she is very good-hearted and always helps us when we need her."

There had always been revolutionary currents, predominantly stem-   8
ming from the middle class. The seeds of the present state of civil war were sown in 1970 when university students and professors began to protest against the excesses and corruption of the government, including nepotism, electoral frauds, payoffs by the rich for legislation of benefit to them, and suppression by threats, torture, and murder of opposition politicians and clergy.

In a country where the vast majority of the population is Catholic, priests and nuns working among the lower class also became opponents of the regime. They began to organize Christian-based rural communities that were in effect communes where peasants could collectively manage such needs as medical services and education. It was through church groups that Ileana and Maria became involved in their war.

Ileana remembers: "I was religious then, at fifteen. I belonged to a Church group and did social work in the community. It was at that time that many of the priests began to preach that our rulers were not good. The Church became more and more involved in the problems of the people — not spiritually, but in day-to-day life — and then they began to talk about it."

It was 1975 when Maria, also fifteen, joined a Church group in the town of Aguilares. "My father was from the lower middle class," she says. "He works as the overseer of a manor, and so from childhood I lived on manors and saw how the peasants lived, the kind of work they were subjected to and the problems they had just to feed their large families. I started studying in the nearby town of Aguilares, and that is when I first came into contact with Father Rutilio Grande."

Grande, a Salvadoran Jesuit, had arrived in Aguilares in 1972. In the   12
rich, sugar-growing regions outside the town the peasants were unable to

get more than three or four months' labor each year, backbreaking work that helped provide the average annual income per family of seven hundred dollars. The rampant malnutrition of their children affected him deeply. He and three other priests began organizing rural communities and preached that "they must not live in conditions of such tremendous inequality that the very Fatherhood of God is denied." During the next four years Father Rutilio led peasants in several strikes and sit-ins at the haciendas in the vicinity.

Maria remembers the effect Grande had on the people: "He told us that in the Bible it says that people must not be exploited, people must not be oppressed. A hacienda in the area was an example of the way people lived. The peasants who worked there during harvest season were starving to death, and the rich widow who owned the estate would not allow most of it to be cultivated because she wanted it to be a memorial to her dead husband. The peasants had no running water, no electricity in their one-room huts. They had no education for their children, no medical care. Father Rutilio and three co-workers visited the widow and suggested an agreement for sharecropping in which the peasants would pay her for the use of her land. She refused, and so we organized a takeover of the hacienda. About two hundred peasants simply squatted on her land. We put up armed sentinels at different points, and we were prepared to confront the authorities." Maria was armed. Asked about weapons training, she said she had already been taught to shoot by her father, for recreation and hunting on the hacienda. Her parents believed her still a student who dutifully came home on weekends. But she had quit school and devoted all her time to the cause.

It was May 1975. The peasants remained on the estate for three months. They had begun to cultivate the land when the area was surrounded and attacked by the Security Forces in the middle of the night. "One of our sentinels had fallen asleep on guard," says Maria. "The troops were already inside the estate when our second sentry gave us the warning. We had prepared for this and had our escape routes planned. Each of us who was armed was responsible for leading out a small group of peasants — about fourteen or fifteen people. Others were assigned to cover our retreat. About fifteen minutes after we heard the warning, helicopters came and began dropping barrels of flaming gasoline on us. Our plastic, plywood shacks caught fire immediately. A lot of people were badly burned. We walked . . . ran, through the night. We had to cross a river. One of the women was in labor. She gave birth during the night." Maria led her group to a prearranged location where they met up with the others the next day. The peasants were told to disperse and remain silent about their involvement in the takeover.

Asked if they weren't expecting that kind of reaction to the illegal takeover of the hacienda, Maria said, "We were of course expecting the authorities to come and make us leave. What we didn't expect was that the army would attack us in the middle of the night with helicopters and flaming gasoline. I was very scared after that backlash, but my older brother, who was also involved, said to me, 'Sure you can stay home and Daddy will pay for your studies. You'll have something to eat. But what about the other people?'"

Father Rutilio Grande continued his work among the peasants. He 16 organized literacy classes in which Maria and other young students helped teach the children. But the local landowners had by now had enough of the priests in Aguilares who, they said, "were instigating class warfare," and the members of the Christian movement realized that there would be further violence.

"We were given training, told what to do if we were captured and questioned, how to respond, to make up a story quickly. They taught us how to deal with many problems. Throughout the rest of 1975 we led demonstrations in Aguilares. We went to the high schools and got more students involved."

In the capital, San Salvador, dissent was brewing in schools and universities. In July 1975 the army attacked a student demonstration protesting the government expenditure of three million dollars to host a Miss Universe Pageant. The army blocked off the streets to those trying to escape and opened fire on the crowds. Twelve students were killed, eighty wounded, and twenty-four "disappeared." Ileana: "It was a peaceful demonstration, and they attacked us with tanks! People were screaming, in complete panic. It was terrifying. We joined together with other protest groups and decided on a joint action. Several days later we took over one of the cathedrals of San Salvador. We did it to denounce the army and what it had done at the demonstration. We asked the government to state who was responsible for the killing, and that the chief of police and the army be forced to resign.

"The one thing we did succeed in was getting attention, letting people know the truth. Because all the newspapers are controlled by the rich people, when things like that happened they would write a lot of lies. For example, if the army killed one hundred people, they would write that three people died in a crossfire between guerrillas and the army.

"This joint action was important because it brought several groups 20 together — peasants, students, teachers, labor unions, and people from the ghettos. We discussed a revolution which would change the whole basis of society. We had learned that it was impossible to achieve reforms in the existing government. They would never change. By 1975 we were thinking of armed revolution. Several political groups formed armed sections and began taking armed actions against the government. They began in the cities, and then more and more grew in the countryside. I left the Church group. It was good, but I didn't think it was doing enough. That is when I joined the Revolutionary Popular Front."

By the end of that year there were many groups of opposition to the government, several with their own guerrilla armies. Eventually the left wing and liberals united and formed the Democratic Revolutionary Front (FDR) whose military arm was the Farabundo Marti Front for National Liberation (FMLN), named after the most famous communist leader of the 1932 peasant rebellion. . . .

In 1976, at sixteen years of age, Maria married one of the *compañeros* ("comrades-in-arms") with whom she had participated in several actions. She says she married so young because of the situation in her family home. "I had not been able to discuss anything with my parents. I couldn't tell them what I was doing, thinking, or feeling. I was completely absorbed in the revolution and often endangered, and yet I went home on weekends and pretended to be a meek, obedient little school girl. Getting married was my freedom from this double life." She adds, "My husband was a few years older than me, and it was an intense relationship: we believed in the same things and took the same risks."

Shortly thereafter Maria had her first baby, a daughter. Asked if becoming a mother had led her to consider leaving the movement, to avoid the risks, she said no. "Having a child reinforced my commitment. As a mother I felt even more strongly about helping to create a new society for our children to grow up in." But only fifteen days after the baby was born, she and her husband were arrested in Aguilares. "We were caught spraying slogans on a wall. I was not mistreated, just interrogated. They asked my why I was doing this, who my family was. I told them my uncle was a colonel in the Security Forces and hoped that would carry some weight. After two weeks they released us.

"After we were released from jail we stayed in Aguilares for two more   24
months. Then Father Rutilio told us we should relocate and begin living underground. The police had our number, they were watching us, so we moved to another district and went 'underground.'"

Ileana was also married that year, to a man she had met in the cathedral takeover in August 1975. He had subsequently joined the guerrillas. "For the first four months we lived separately. Then the organization authorized us to live together, but we were told to be careful because it would be dangerous for us to be identified together. That is because he was a known guerrilla, while I was still working in the open. I was only home one or two days a week. The rest of the time I was in the countryside. It was a difficult period. I felt as though I didn't have any home. I was always traveling from one place to another, sleeping here and there, and worrying about my husband while we were apart."

In a political climate where ten thousand people became *desaparecidos*, or "disappeared," each year, working underground in the city created enormous stress. Maria says: "It was very tense. We constantly had to change our names and identities. We were always on the move. Sometimes I would forget what name I had used with different people. I would run into someone and not know how to respond, desperately trying to remember what I had told them about myself. But the nature of our work gave me energy. I found it so rewarding. I got used to the pressure."

Maria's work was still with Christian groups. "We had contacts in different parishes with different priests and we would join them in their discussion groups. We worked in their parishes in the shantytowns or slums. We discussed ways of helping the poor. We related the Bible to the reality in which we were living. We helped the poor with their sick children, and even with their household chores." In 1977, she and her husband left this work and joined the People's Army. The move was a personal reaction to the assassination of Father Rutilio Grande on 12 March 1977. He was gunned down as he drove to Sunday mass.

That year the military government of Colonel Arturo Molina had 28 launched an all-out campaign to terrorize and kill parish priests and nuns. Anonymous pamphlets dropped into the street blamed the war on "Marxist priests." The slogan ran, "Be a patriot! Kill a priest!" When Rutilio Grande was killed, the newly appointed Archbishop Romero, a man noted for his moderation, openly condemned the Molina government. Molina had come to power in 1972 in a particularly scandalous election. Though his opponent, Napoleón Duarte, was ahead at the polls by two to one, Molina's well-placed supporters in the previous administration stopped all election broadcasts and finally pronounced the colonel president. The Christian Democrats were outraged by the flagrant fraud. Molina's answer was to have Duarte arrested, imprisoned, and tortured, although he was released when international pressure was brought to bear.

A month before his death Grande had told a crowd, "Nowadays it is dangerous and practically illegal to be an authentic Christian in Latin America. I greatly fear that very soon the Bible and the Gospel will not be allowed within the confines of our country. Only the bindings will arrive, nothing else, because all the pages are subversive — they are against sin." Despite a government-declared state of siege, over a hundred thousand people risked their lives to attend Grande's funeral at a San Salvador cathedral. Eight bishops, Archbishop Romero, and four hundred priests held mass for the slain father.

For Maria, who had known and loved the priest, it was a deep personal loss. It seemed that the last vestiges of humanity had been swept away, and in their place the war became uglier and uglier. That year when President Molina retired, his minister of defense, General Carlos Humberto Romero, was "elected" president in his place. The priest-killing campaign continued. Priests were found decapitated, disfigured by battery acid, and otherwise mutilated. In Aguilares the army launched an attack in which several more Jesuits were murdered, and code-named it Operation Rutilio.

"Things really heated up," recalls Ileana. "Women in large numbers began to join the revolutionary movement. I think they found this final obscenity impossible to condone or ignore. . . . We had some problems with chauvinism in the beginning. The men didn't want us to join, or they wanted us to stay in subservient roles. But soon they realized the importance of having as many people fighting as possible, and they changed a bit. I think it actually helped make male-female relationships more equal." . . .

Maria and her husband were asked to open a supermarket in San   32
Salvador that would serve as a cover for shipping supplies to the guerrillas. "We lived over the store — my husband, our two daughters, and two of my husband's sisters. Our house became a meeting place and the kids used to help camouflage it. When we were having a meeting one of us would go out and play with the kids on the street in front of the houses, making sure the coast was clear. We all carried guns for personal protection. We knew if we were searched by the authorities we would be killed. I used to carry a huge bag with all this kids' stuff in it — talcum powder, diapers, baby bottles. I hid my gun and pamphlets underneath. Sometimes I would even put my gun in my baby's diapers. The soldiers never thought of checking in the baby's diapers.

"The supermarket was a good front. We had a delivery van and I used to deliver goods to the groups in the countryside. I took them everything

— shoes, beans, and Kotex. Kotex was used for dressing wounds because if we took real bandages it would be too obvious. . . ."

In July 1979 the Sandinista revolution in neighboring Nicaragua succeeded in overthrowing dictator Anastasio Somoza. "When we saw them succeed," says Ileana, "it gave us hope. I really didn't believe they could succeed so quickly. We thought if they can do it, we can too. But on the other hand, the United States learned a lot from the Nicaraguan revolution. Now they are applying that knowledge to El Salvador, giving enormous aid to the government for the military. They began sending in military advisers."

In Washington the Carter administration was sore on the point of human rights abuses, perpetrated by the Romero regime in San Salvador, which were making it increasingly difficult to get military aid bills through Congress. Washington needed a more moderate government in El Salvador. On 15 October 1979 a military-civilian junta overthrew the ruling regime in a brief coup d'état. The junta was comprised of younger, more moderate officers, and a number of representatives of opposition parties were appointed to the cabinet. The new government immediately began land reforms designed to restore land to the peasants. The reforms were ill-fated from the start. Army troops sent to redistribute parcels of land took over haciendas, helped themselves to the goods, then systematically murdered peasants who came to claim their new plots. Payoffs and threats protected the estates of the richest families.

One by one the more moderate civilian politicians were forced out of 36
office by the military leaders who controlled the army. One such politician, Hector Dada Hirezi, wrote in his letter of resignation: "The facts are indisputable proof of the conclusion. We have been unable to stop the repression, and those who commit acts of repression in defiance of the junta's authority remain unpunished; the promised dialogue with the popular organizations has not come about; the possibilities of generating reforms supported by the people have retreated beyond our grasp."

Six months after the new junta took power, the archbishop of San Salvador, Archbishop Oscar Amulfo Romero y Galdames, was assassinated as he gave mass. *Time* and *Newsweek* magazines recounted the carnage that followed when thousands of people attended his funeral and army troops opened fire into the crowds. Three weeks after the archbishop's assassination the United States government committed another $5.7 million in military aid to the ruling junta. By this time it was estimated that in the country of five million people, two thousand people a week were dying in the war.

Ileana was caught in 1980. She says, "I can't tell you everything, but I was at the house of one of our *compañeros* for a meeting. The army found out about us and came and surrounded the house. We heard the trucks and jeeps pull up, and out stormed dozens of soldiers with machine guns. We considered holding them off and trying to escape, but when we realized we were surrounded we surrendered. They arrested everyone in the house.

"I was taken to the National Guard's secret jail, where they interrogate political prisoners, and kept there for one week. I was raped repeatedly and tortured with electric shocks. I was three months pregnant, but thank God it didn't show. I knew if they found out it would be worse. They would have tried to hurt the baby, to abort it or something. They would have asked me who the father was. They continually threatened to kill me and my family. Sometimes I had to answer them, but I would just tell them things that they already knew, like where I had studied. Other times I would make up stories. I always thought about what I was saying and tried not to endanger the others.

"They didn't treat me better because I was a woman. To them there   40 was no difference. I think for women it was worse. They thought we were worthless, so they wanted to defile us. I was constantly pawed, threatened with rape or raped. They were pigs." She pauses, then adds, "I know this sounds hard to believe. I was very lucky because many, many people never get out of those clandestine jails. I tried to keep myself together by telling myself how many others were in the same situation I was in. It made me stronger. When I was being tortured I kept thinking of my friends who had gone through this, as an example to keep me brave. I kept thinking that they had held out in even worse situations. . . .

"My husband didn't know I had been arrested until I was sentenced and sent to the penal institution. Of course he couldn't come to see me. But it was a regular prison run by the Ministry of Justice, so I had visitors every Sunday. My family came and brought me some things — milk, because I was pregnant. I was kept there for four months."

On 5 March 1980 Napoleón Duarte, the Christian Democrat who had run against Colonel Arturo Molina in 1972, been arrested and later exiled, agreed to head the eroding junta. Those who considered Duarte a moderate could not understand why he chose to become a part of the corrupt and brutal government, but those who knew him well have said that his tremendous ego eventually dictated his quest for leadership, even at the helm of a mutinous group of military leaders.

One of Duarte's first public statements was that "the Security Forces had been trained for fifty years to do things 'the other way.'" He said it would take "time to change things." He refused to negotiate with the FMLN despite the fact that Mexico, several European governments, and many Salvadoran clergy recommended that he do so. Instead, he declared the country in a state of siege.

By 1980 the revolutionary forces had greatly expanded and were said   44
to have gained widespread public support. They claimed in that year that 40 percent of their leadership were women, and women were increasingly adopting military roles in the war. A women's military school was opened, offering a twenty-day training course to all women between sixteen and twenty-two years of age. At least two all-women battalions were formed, and Maria fought with one of them for a few months in the guerrilla-controlled zones of the countryside. . . .

The women taught Maria many new maneuvers. "For example, how to cross a river using ropes. We would throw the ropes like lassos, and swing ourselves across the river holding the rope with one arm and our grenades and weapons with the other. We covered each other as we made our way. We left these ropes on the trees and periodically went to check to make sure they were not rotting and the knots were still secure. Work was the same as in the mixed guerrilla groups," she says. "But when the enemy was killed or ambushed by the women's battalions they found it more demoralizing. They consider women worthless.

"We used this to our advantage. Whenever we successfully killed a number of army troops we always put out communiqués saying that we were responsible. We wanted to rub it in.

"I found that the all-women battalion was even more disciplined than the mixed units. For example, if we were given an order not to smoke all day because we were staked out somewhere, we wouldn't. If it had been men, someone would have found a way to sneak a cigarette. Women were more punctual about meeting times and places, too."

Maria says that despite their youth most of the women combatants   48
had children, who were left in care of their families or friends. "Women still did most things during their pregnancies," she says. "It was just for a short time after the baby was born that they couldn't do all the things they normally did." She shows an easy acceptance of motherhood, at any age or in any circumstances, that "is prevalent in El Salvador. It just doesn't seem onerous to us to have babies. We don't wait for the right time and place." Despite the availability of birth control, both Maria and Ileana said that most women wanted to become pregnant because it was

psychologically uplifting to give birth when so much death was going on around them.

Ileana had been released from jail and had given birth to a daughter. Six months later her husband was killed. "They came at five in the morning to murder him," she says. "That is when the death squads operate. Dawn is the most terrifying time for all of us. We would lie awake and half expect to hear the loud knocks and yells at the door. I hid myself and the baby while he went to hold them off. They took him away and shot him. Members of the organization came for me and took me to a safe place. I stayed in El Salvador for seven more months before they got me out to Canada."

The FMLN planned to instigate a general offensive in January 1981 for which Maria and her husband had been training in the countryside's "liberated zones." They were told to return to the city in December 1980 to help coordinate the uprising there. On the first of December four American Catholic nuns were assassinated by members of the government forces. American President Jimmy Carter condemned the murders and ordered all military and economic aid to the junta suspended. Five weeks later, on 3 January 1981, two American economic aid consultants with the American Institute for Free Labor Development (AIRFLD) were shot to death in a hotel coffee shop, presumably by government enforcers of the agrarian "reform" program: the Americans had been privy to information that exposed corruption within the program. Washington leaders were outraged at the excesses, which were causing an uproar at home and making it increasingly difficult to get public support for American aid to the regime.

On 10 January Maria and her husband waited at home for their final orders. The next day guerrillas overran a classical music radio station and broadcast an appeal to the people of the country to rise up in a general insurrection.

A number of guerrilla units operating in the capital launched hit-and-run attacks against police and military targets. Maria was assigned to a unit attacking the air force base. "The base is located a little way from the center of the city. We were to go in and plant the explosives, liquidate the guards, and get as many of their munitions as we could. I was in charge of distributing arms to different groups after we got hold of them.

"The offensive began at seven o'clock in the evening, when there would be a minimum of patrol cars, and the majority of people would be at home. That way there would be fewer civilian casualties. We managed to attack the air base and get the weapons. But we were identified. They saw our car and the license plate number. We returned home and hid the armaments in the back room."

The general insurrection had failed. The army had mobilized within the capital and imposed martial law and a dusk-to-dawn curfew. The FMLN had poorly coordinated their own forces and had counted, unrealistically it seemed, on the majority of the people in the city to rise up. In the countryside guerrilla gains were substantial, but in the cities the uprising was a failure.

The following morning the army surrounded Maria's home. "We heard their tanks and trucks and patrol cars surrounding the house. The trucks were full of soldiers. There were six adults and six children there, and we were all captured.

"I was taken to a cell where I was raped and beaten. For a few days 56 they kept me inside a gas drum, and when they took me out for interrogation I would be tied hands and feet on metal bars, suspended horizontally with bags of sand on my stomach and then beaten. They used psychological torture as well. They would bring in my children, point pistols at their heads, and ask me to talk. . . . I would make up things to trick them for a while.

"I was being kept at the National Police headquarters. In the beginning they said that they had documents to back up all their accusations. They told me they had spoken to my parents and that my parents had told them to kill me, had said bitter things about me, that I was a terrorist and should be killed.

"I was given electrical shocks, attached to all parts of my body. I was raped many times. I had tried to prepare psychologically for this. I had answers ready for them, a lot of garbage that they already knew or that was fabricated."

After two and a half months at the National Guard headquarters she was removed to Ilopango Prison for women political prisoners. Her children were allowed into the custody of relatives, her husband imprisoned elsewhere. The cell at Ilopango was her world for the next two years, during which time she participated in three hunger strikes that badly affected her health. The electric shocks had caused partial paralysis in her legs, which she is only now recovering from.

"Our capture was broadcast on the Liberation Radio, a station run by 60 the FMLN. The archbishop, the Red Cross, and Amnesty International began to lobby for our release. Because of the six children who had been taken at the same time there was a lot of across-the-board-pressure on the government not to let us 'disappear' — not to kill us. That is the only reason I am still alive. In April 1983 I was released from prison. My husband was already dead — he was killed at some point during those two years. I left my children with my relatives and came to Canada. I was sent here by the FMLN to recuperate, basically. This is a recovery period."

Since Maria has been in Canada, the civil war has escalated in El Salvador. The Reagan administration continues to pour large amounts of military aid into the country despite continued pressure and documentation, by human rights organizations, of the junta's atrocities. The killings continue, indiscriminately; laborers, priests and nuns, students, suspected leftists, and even foreign journalists are targets. The majority of the killing is attributed to the right-wing death squads operating for Napoleón Duarte's government. He has ruled continuously since 1980 and was "elected" to office in June 1984 when he ran against an ultra-rightist candidate without any challenge from FMLN candidates. As one foreign journalist wrote: "The government's stand — and Duarte's — is that the guerrillas must lay down their guns and join an electoral process set up by the government. For the guerrilla movement, the problem with this stance is that it may mean both literal and figurative suicide. Literal because leftists could not campaign in El Salvador without getting murdered. . . . The left could never afford to lose an election, and the U.S. government would never allow it to win."

The FMLN has moved noticeably further to the left and undoubtedly receives financial support from the Socialist bloc. One American journalist who traveled deep into guerrilla zones recently was asked by local villagers if he was the guerrillas' Russian adviser. It is apparent that despite the many political beliefs that united to form the FMLN, it has now turned for help to those who are sympathetic — typically the Socialist countries. Once again a civil war fought only because of brutal internal oppression has become a battleground for the superpowers. Still, women like Ileana and Maria remain convinced that the only way to effect change in their country is to fight.

"It is such a strange state of consciousness to leave that reality and come to this one," says Maria. "I don't think I have really adapted at all. There are always reminders. I am never without the presence of El Salvador. If I am eating a good meal, I think about those who don't have enough to eat there, people so poor that they eat roots and weeds. I think of my children every minute. It has not been a tranquil time here, either. . . ."

"It is an area of strategic importance to the United States," Ileana told 64 me before she returned, "so they continue to support the government and ignore the human rights abuses. I think the war will continue for a long time. Mothers are fighting, kids are fighting, priests and nuns are fighting or helping us to fight. We won't give up. We have tried to negotiate, but it never works. It is not to their advantage to come to an agreement with us. They have all the power and all the wealth, so why should they? They just go on suppressing the movement and increasing their military strength."

In late 1984 Napoleón Duarte arranged the first meeting to discuss future negotiations between his government and leaders of the FMLN. The meeting was positive, if only in bringing the two sides together, and all agreed to meet again.

Meanwhile war and rumors of war escalate throughout the region. The Sandinista government of Nicaragua fears an attack from the United States, whose government has accused them of disrupting the balance of power in Central America and arming the revolutionaries in El Salvador.

Maria: "We are willing to die to change the basis of our society, to feed and educate our children, to end the murders, the terror, and the oppression. You might not understand that, here. But there, it is another reality."

EXPLORATIONS

1. How did Maria and Ileana first become involved in the war? What was the focus of their early efforts on behalf of their fellow Salvadorans?

2. What incident pushed each woman out of peaceful social activism into acceptance of armed confrontation? What subsequent actions by the government persuaded Ileana, and Maria, that revolution is the only way to achieve reforms?

3. What reasons does Maria give for marrying at age sixteen? What other factors appear to have influenced her and Ileana to marry within a year of becoming involved in the war? What positive and negative effects have their marriages had on their work in the movement?

CONNECTIONS

1. Like Roger Rosenblatt, Saywell has based her account of a foreign war on interviews. How are the two writers' purposes similar? How is their use of interview material different? How would the impact of "Women Warriors of El Salvador" change if Saywell chose a format like Rosenblatt's?

2. Doris Lessing writes of her visit with Afghan refugee women: "Sitting there with them, all so friendly and sociable and gossipy, inside walls that shut out the world, and with the big, brave men out there in front, I found myself thinking, 'Ah well, why not leave it all to the men?'" What reasons do Maria and Ileana give for not leaving it all to the men? Judging from Germaine Greer's description of Cuba some thirty years after the revolution (p. 441), what do Salvadoran women stand to gain over the long term from fighting as equal partners with men? What do they, and their culture, stand to lose?

3. What similarities do you notice between the Salvadoran governments described by Saywell and the Philippine government described by James Fenton (p. 422)? What changes do you think would have to take place in El Salvador (and in American foreign policy, if relevant) for Duarte's government to be deposed without violence, as Marcos's was?

ELABORATIONS

1. In both the Philippines' nonviolent revolution and El Salvador's ongoing violent revolution, the Roman Catholic church has been active and influential. Write an essay comparing and contrasting the church's role in these two upheavals.

2. "Both Maria and Ileana said that most women wanted to become pregnant," reports Saywell, "because it was psychologically uplifting to give birth when so much death was going on around them." How are Salvadoran attitudes toward childbearing and child care in a war zone, as described by these women, different from those in the early kibbutzim described by Bruno Bettelheim (p. 14)? Write an essay describing and explaining the contrast.

ALBALUCÍA ÁNGEL

The Guerrillero

Born in Colombia in 1939, Albalucía Ángel is a novelist and folksinger as well as a short story writer. Her first book, *Los girasoles en invierno* (*Sunflowers in Winter*), won the "Esso" Prize in Bogotá in 1966. The translator of "The Guerrillero," Alberto Manguel, describes her work as more like that of Lewis Carroll than that of her famous fellow Colombian Gabriel García Márquez. This "looking-glass" quality is evident not only in Ángel's 1972 novel *Dos veces Alicia* (*Twice Alice*) but in the following dialogue between a woman and herself.
(For background on Colombia, see p. 493.)

Now you'll see, Felicidad Mosquera, when they all arrive with their machetes, threatening, asking you where in hell has he hidden himself, then you'll confess. They'll ask. They'll force you to betray him because if you won't talk they'll take the old folks, like they did two days ago with your friend Cleta, remember, or they'll put your hands into the fire, like Calixta Peñalosa, or they'll slice open your belly, after all — all of them — have used your body. That's how it is, Felicidad. That's how it is. You should have gone with him, then you wouldn't have suffered. You wouldn't be dragging yourself around, crying and moaning, looking for anything that might do as a weapon, pushing the few bits of furniture against the door. That night, when Sebastian Martinez's dogs began to howl as if they'd smelled the devil, and you saw him there, suddenly, standing ever so still, his trousers in shreds and his white shirt all bloody, then you should have spoken, said anything, any excuse to make him whisper good-night and creep back where he'd come from, but no, too bad it didn't happen that way. Bad luck, Felicidad. You made him come in without a word, you pulled up a chair for him, he let himself fall heavy as lead, and then you saw the other wound on his skull; *I'm tired*, was all he mumbled; and then collapsed like a horse on the floor. Whatever got into your head, Felicidad Mosquera? What evil star dazzled you then, what evil wind blew through your heart to stir up the fire, to blind you? Because you were blind, blind. The shivers you felt when you looked upon his face and realized he was so handsome. That you liked his black mustache. The nervous urgency with which you went to

boil water and prepare the herb plasters, somehow wasn't yours. Because
you've always been coolheaded. A watchful heart. Careful. You never
let yourself be trapped into these things. Whatever happened to you, tell
me. Whatever came over you when instead of saying good-bye, once he
felt better, and began to go out at night to take a walk, to get firewood,
offering to pump water, instead of saying yes, well thank you, see you
sometime, you said no, it was no trouble, why didn't he stay a few more
days. What happened, damn you. I can't understand. Felicidad Mosquera, I don't recognize you any longer. I never thought you'd change
this fast, go from black to white, as you did, from one day to the other.
Because the trembling you felt when he looked at you with his dark eyes,
or the stammering, like a little girl, when he asked for the salt and barely
touched you with his fingers as you put it in his hand, everything in you
turned upside down, the current changed, your cables crossed, so how
in God's name didn't you notice it. Putting salt into another person's
hand is stupid, brings bad luck. Bad tidings. And what about that day
when instead of letting him go off on his own to get some air, you
flushed, all red in the face, when he offered to walk together for a while,
and crossing the bridge he held your waist, because it shakes so much
was his excuse, but you felt how the heat boiling on his skin began to
seep into you, burning, hurting, a cry inside you. A deep, deep moan.
They're coming, Felicidad Mosquera. They'll come shouting that they
know. Kicking everything in the house, as they did with Prospero Mon-
toya's wife, when they left her stuck inside the well, her belly sliced open
and the baby inside. They won't let you make the slightest move. When
they arrive like that they're all ready to kill you. To leave no trace. They'll
say they know so that you go for it. But only God and you are witnesses.
The only witnesses of the meeting in the fields, on the riverbank, between
the scented sheets; who else will swear if only you felt the delight, the
sex entering your body, searching your smoothness, changing you into
streams, twilight, sea; who else will know the movement of your thighs,
burning, your hands searching; touching the groin forcing sweetly your
way into life. Who else heard his groans. His loving search. His long,
drawn-out orgasm as you sank into a silence of moist membranes, a
quick throb of blood, a hurried quiver of muscles, which then relaxed
rippling through the entire body, an inside scream bursting upwards, like
a torrent. And who's to judge you, Felicidad Mosquera, if only God and
you can swear that this is true. No one will dare. They can search your
very innards, cut you in two with their machetes, drill into your senses,
pierce your heart, they will find nothing. Not a whisper. Don't look like

that. Throw your fear overboard. Don't curse any more: He's far away and all that counts is that he lives and carries on fighting. You won't say a word. Not even if they set fire to your shack, ram themselves into you, or bottles, or do what they did to others to drive you crazy; take courage, Felicidad Mosquera, don't cry or moan any more. Open the door yourself. Stand upright in the doorway. Hold their eyes.

EXPLORATIONS

1. Who is the man Felicidad Mosquera recalls so vividly? Why is he dangerous to her? How is she dangerous to him?

2. What does Felicidad believe is about to happen? What are her worst fears? What are her highest hopes? How does she rate her chances of surviving?

3. Why is it so important to Felicidad that no one but herself knows what happened between her and her lover? Given the danger she is facing, why do you think she lets herself dwell on the pleasure of sex?

CONNECTIONS

1. What comments about torture by Ileana in Shelley Saywell's "Women Warriors of El Salvador" suggest why Felicidad Mosquera thinks about her friends at this terrifying moment? What function do Felicidad's friends fulfill for the story's author?

2. Like her fellow Colombian Gabriel García Márquez, Ángel writes about a doomed affair at a moment of political upheaval. What other resemblances do you notice between "The Guerrillero" and García Márquez's "Death Constant Beyond Love" (p. 493)?

3. At what point, and from what clues, could you tell that Felicidad Mosquera is talking to herself? How would the story's effect change if Angel had written it as an internal dialogue, like Nathalie Sarraute's "My First Sorrow" (p. 109), instead of as a monologue? — that is, if she had two voices going back and forth instead of a single voice?

ELABORATIONS

1. Write a press release for a hypothetical government-controlled newspaper about the events narrated in "The Guerrillero." Then, switching viewpoints, write a report for a hypothetical underground newsletter.

2. Recall a moment in your past when you felt that your fate hung in the balance. What were your hopes? regrets? fears? Write a second-person monologue like "The Guerrillero" in which you combine a narrative of the situation with indications of your emotional response to it.

MILOVAN DJILAS

Ideas Against Torture

Milovan Djilas was born in the small Eastern European kingdom of Montenegro (now part of Yugoslavia) in 1911. At eighteen he went to the University of Belgrade in Yugoslavia's capital, where he won recognition for his poems, short stories, and revolutionary activities. Joining the then illegal Communist Party in 1932, he was arrested, imprisoned, and released; he became a partisan leader, a general, and finally one of the four chiefs of the Communist Yugoslav government until the Central Committee expelled him in 1954. Over the twenty years following, Djilas was continually in and out of prison for writings critical of Marshal Tito's bureaucracy. After a brief trip to this country and Great Britain in 1968, Djilas and his wife were refused passports and so have remained in Belgrade. "Ideas Against Torture" comes from his most recent book, *Of Prisons and Ideas* (1986), translated from the Serbo-Croatian by Michael Boro Petrovich.

The Socialist Federal Republic of Yugoslavia was created after World War II when the partisan fighter Josip Broz, known as Marshal Tito, executed his main competitor and established himself at the head of a Communist government. Yugoslavia, which lies north of Greece, south of Austria and Hungary, and across the water from Italy, comprises several former provinces of the Austro-Hungarian Empire plus the state of Montenegro. Unified as Yugoslavia after the empire's collapse following World War I, it was invaded by Germany in 1941. Both the Soviet Union and Great Britain supported Marshal Tito, and Tito maintained ties with Western as well as Eastern Europe when he became president. He died in 1980; the Party leadership and presidency now rotate among the heads of Yugoslavia's member republics and provinces.

A fighting man possessed of faith in an idea need not fear, and has no reason to fear, prison, torture, or even death. He will survive. He will live on in the lives of his comrades, in the life of the idea. Nevertheless, he will be all the more confident and able to bear torture all the more easily if he is familiar with certain "weak points" innate to the act itself and those who practice it.

First, no torture has ever been devised that a victim dedicated to an idea and ready to die for it cannot withstand. Torturers are seldom possessed of a particularly inventive imagination in devising their terrors. Most frequently they find it easiest to follow long-trodden paths and make use of those tried and true methods handed down from the past. They rely on ready-made instruments: whips, truncheons, sandbags, needles, castor oil, electric currents, and the like. It is common, of course, especially where torture is not standard procedure, for the police to use whatever instruments may be at hand — pencils (for jabbing between fingers), drawers (for crushing hands), chairs (for jamming bodies against walls), and, most frequently, to be sure, the most direct, handiest instrument of all, their fists.

Second, the victim will often be more terrified by his imagination of the event than by the event itself. This being so, he should exert every effort not to think about torture or any of its particular methods. Such efforts, alas, are all too frequently less powerful than the imagination, which, since it secretly nurtures the will to live, cannot be completely suppressed. If the victim is lucky enough to be put in a cell with other prisoners, he will have a chance to talk, to swap stories, to while away the time in idle games and so keep his wilder flights of fancy under control. But if he is alone in a cell, he must fill his time as best he can — by cleaning the cell, by taking care of his personal hygiene, and the like. For it is time that is the intractable sworn enemy of the prisoner. And though time in a single cell — even without books, without pen and paper, without anything of one's own — passes faster than it does in a common jail pen, it is more deadly because of its killing monotony.

In the period before torture, as well as between bouts, it is the very 4 uneventfulness of time that fires the imagination and intensifies torment into seemingly unbearable pain. Consequently, one must learn to stifle the imagination from the start, to trick it and to master it. As soon as one's feelings give signs of taking over, one must force oneself to think of something else and to think of it constantly, persistently, all the time. Occupy your mind so that it doesn't occupy you. It will finally submit. It is not separate from the will, however limitless and unrestricted in its choice of subject it may seem to be. And even in the most difficult, most adverse circumstances, even if both hands and feet are shackled and one is exposed all night to the cries of tortured victims and the curses of guards, one must make one's mind concentrate on insignificant concrete things — spots on the ceiling, say — with a steady stare, until one's surroundings and all their details utterly vanish.

Third, all individual acts of torture have their limits, just as our bodies have limits of endurance. When the infliction of pain reaches the outer limits, the body and spirit protect themselves by lapsing into unconsciousness. In those moments of unconsciousness even torments become sweet, turning into the most subtle, spiritual joys imaginable. This is the beginning of the victory over torturers and tortures alike.

Fourth, one should never be afraid of dying while being tortured. In any case, there would be no point to it. Most torturers employed by the police are careful and experienced. The sadists are much rarer than rebels against authority and potential political criminals believe. Brutality, violence, and self-assertion are part and parcel of a policeman's profession, qualities which in time become habit, an adjunct of the personality. Such qualities do not necessarily take over the personality to such a degree that it gives in to murderous passions and mindless caprice. This restraint is particularly true of the political police, for they are controlled by political leaders as well as by their own politically disciplined organization. As a rule, political police do not kill or even torture if they are not ordered to do so and if such practices do not conform to the policy of the dictator and the oligarchy. The police — the political police in particular — are generally intelligent, experienced, and moderate, even in the practice of torture. It is virtually by sheer chance that a prisoner dies while undergoing torture, unless specific orders have been given to deal with him without regard for his life. And no one anywhere can ever be made safe from accidental death.

EXPLORATIONS

1. What does Djilas cite as the greatest dangers to a torture victim? What does he cite as a potential victim's greatest fears? What does he mean in paragraph 2 by "withstand" torture?

2. Djilas writes mostly in the third person, referring to "the victim" and "one." How would his essay's impact change if he had written it in the first person, about his own experience, or in the second person, giving advice? What does he gain (and lose) by using a matter-of-fact rather than a dramatic tone?

3. What is the meaning of Djilas's title, "Ideas Against Torture"?

CONNECTIONS

1. In what ways does Felicidad Mosquera in Albalucía Ángel's "The Guerrillero" follow Djilas's advice? In what ways does she violate it? What do you think Djilas would say about her attitude change from the beginning to the end of the story?

2. Having read Shelley Saywell's "Women Warriors of El Salvador" and Albalucía Ángel's "The Guerrillero," what points would you add to Djilas's list to make it as applicable to women torture victims as to men?

3. Djilas suggests that torture is easier to bear if one is prepared for it. In "American Ignorance of War," Czeslaw Milosz suggests that Americans view war as unreal because of their lack of experience with it. What aspects of Mark Baker's *Observation* suggest that Americans who found the Vietnam War unbearable might have stood the strain better if they had been better prepared? What kinds of preparation might have helped?

ELABORATIONS

1. Aside from failing to crush their victims, what dangers do torturers face? Judging from the other selections you have read, what seem to be the usual reasons why someone becomes a torturer? Can one human being deliberately inflict pain on others over an extended period and stay human? Write an essay that is similar in form to Djilas's, consisting of points that a potential torturer should keep in mind.

2. Djilas talks of the pain and fear that torture entails; yet he states: "No torture has ever been devised that a victim dedicated to an idea and ready to die for it cannot withstand." Maria and Ileana in Shelley Saywell's "Women Warriors of El Salvador" were tortured both physically and emotionally; yet they withstood it. Is there an idea you are dedicated enough to die for? If you were kidnaped by terrorists, or captured in a war, or imprisoned for your beliefs, how would you stand up to torture? to brainwashing? Choose one of these scenarios, and write an essay indicating how and why you would (or would not) resist successfully.

FRANK O'CONNOR

Guests of the Nation

Frank O'Connor was born Michael John O'Donovan in Cork, Ireland, in 1903. The only son of a hardworking (and hard-drinking) laborer, he took his mother's maiden name when he became a writer. O'Connor was largely self-educated; he produced his first "collection" of poems, biographies, and essays at age twelve. In his teens he joined the Irish Republican Army (IRA) and fought in the civil war from 1919 until 1921, when a treaty ended seven centuries of the island's occupation by neighboring England. However, the IRA went on fighting to bring Ulster (Northern Ireland, still under British rule) into the Irish Free State. O'Connor was arrested and imprisoned. On his release in 1923 he became a librarian and joined the nationalistic literary revival sweeping Ireland. He became a friend and colleague of such prominent Irish writers as George Russell (known as Æ), William Butler Yeats, John Millington Synge, Sean O'Casey, and Sean O'Faoláin. As a director with Yeats of the Abbey Theatre Company in Dublin, O'Connor was at the hub of contemporary Irish literature. He left the theater after four years in protest against censorship; in the 1940s the Irish government banned a number of his books. With side trips to teach at Harvard, Northwestern, and Stanford universities, O'Connor continued to write and to fight censorship until his death of a heart attack in Dublin in 1966. "Guests of the Nation" is one of his first and best known stories; it was adapted into a play that premiered on Broadway in 1958. The conflict it depicts is still going on, in the form of a bitter battle between Ulster's Protestants and Catholics over remaining under British (Protestant) rule versus joining the rest of (Catholic) Ireland.

At dusk the big Englishman Belcher would shift his long legs out of the ashes and ask, "Well, chums, what about it?" and Noble or me would say, "As you please, chum" (for we had picked up some of their curious expressions), and the little Englishman 'Awkins would light the lamp and produce the cards. Sometimes Jeremiah Donovan would come up of an evening and supervise the play, and grow excited over 'Awkins's cards (which he always played badly), and shout at him as if he was one of our own, "Ach, you divil you, why didn't you play the tray?" But, ordinarily,

Jeremiah was a sober and contented poor devil like the big Englishman Belcher, and was looked up to at all only because he was a fair hand at documents, though slow enough at these, I vow. He wore a small cloth hat and big gaiters over his long pants, and seldom did I perceive his hands outside the pockets of that pants. He reddened when you talked to him, tilting from toe to heel and back and looking down all the while at his big farmer's feet. His uncommon broad accent was a great source of jest to me, I being from the town as you may recognize.

I couldn't at the time see the point of me and Noble being with Belcher and 'Awkins at all, for it was and is my fixed belief you could have planted that pair in any untended spot from this to Claregalway and they'd have stayed put and flourished like a native weed. I never seen in my short experience two men that took to the country as they did.

They were handed on to us by the Second Battalion to keep when the search for them became too hot, and Noble and myself, being young, took charge with a natural feeling of responsibility. But little 'Awkins made us look right fools when he displayed he knew the countryside as well as we did and something more. "You're the bloke they calls Bonaparte?" he said to me. "Well, Bonaparte, Mary Brigid Ho'Connell was arskin abaout you and said 'ow you'd a pair of socks belonging to 'er young brother." For it seemed, as they explained it, that the Second used to have little evenings of their own, and some of the girls of the neighborhood would turn in, and seeing they were such decent fellows, our lads couldn't well ignore the two Englishmen, but invited them in and were hail-fellow-well-met with them. 'Awkins told me he learned to dance "The Walls of Limerick" and "The Siege of Ennis" and "The Waves of Tory" in a night or two, though naturally he could not return the compliment, because our lads at that time did not dance foreign dances on principle.

So whatever privileges and favors Belcher and 'Awkins had with the 4 Second they duly took with us, and after the first evening we gave up all pretense of keeping a close eye on their behavior. Not that they could have got far, for they had a notable accent and wore khaki tunics and overcoats with civilian pants and boots. But it's my belief they never had an idea of escaping and were quite contented with their lot.

Now, it was a treat to see how Belcher got off with the old woman of the house we were staying in. She was a great warrant to scold, and crotchety even with us, but before ever she had a chance of giving our guests, as I may call them, a lick of her tongue, Belcher had made her his friend for life. She was breaking sticks at the time, and Belcher, who hadn't been in the house for more than ten minutes, jumped up out of his seat and went across to her.

"Allow me, madam," he says, smiling his queer little smile; "please allow me," and takes the hatchet from her hand. She was struck too parlatic[1] to speak, and ever after Belcher would be at her heels carrying a bucket, or basket, or load of turf, as the case might be. As Noble wittily remarked, he got into looking before she leapt, and hot water or any little thing she wanted Belcher would have it ready for her. For such a huge man (and though I am five foot ten myself I had to look up to him) he had an uncommon shortness — or should I say lack — of speech. It took us some time to get used to him walking in and out like a ghost, without a syllable out of him. Especially because 'Awkins talked enough for a platoon, it was strange to hear big Belcher with his toes in the ashes come out with a solitary "Excuse me, chum," or "That's right, chum." His one and only abiding passion was cards, and I will say for him he was a good card player. He could have fleeced me and Noble many a time; only if we lost to him, 'Awkins lost to us, and 'Awkins played with the money Belcher gave him.

'Awkins lost to us because he talked too much, and I think now we lost to Belcher for the same reason. 'Awkins and Noble would spit at one another about religion into the early hours of the morning; the little Englishman as you could see worrying the soul out of young Noble (whose brother was a priest) with a string of questions that would puzzle a cardinal. And to make it worse, even in treating of these holy subjects, 'Awkins had a deplorable tongue; I never in all my career struck across a man who could mix such a variety of cursing and bad language into the simplest topic. Oh, a terrible man was little 'Awkins, and a fright to argue! He never did a stroke of work, and when he had no one else to talk to he fixed his claws into the old woman.

I am glad to say that in her he met his match, for one day when he tried to get her to complain profanely of the drought she gave him a great comedown by blaming the drought upon Jupiter Pluvius (a deity neither 'Awkins nor I had ever even heard of, though Noble said among the pagans he was held to have something to do with rain). And another day the same 'Awkins was swearing at the capitalists for starting the German war, when the old dame laid down her iron, puckered up her little crab's

8

---

[1]Paralytic. — ED.

mouth, and said, "Mr. 'Awkins, you can say what you please about the war, thinking to deceive me because I'm an ignorant old woman, but I know well what started the war. It was that Italian count that stole the heathen divinity out of the temple in Japan, for believe me, Mr. 'Awkins, nothing but sorrow and want follows them that disturbs the hidden powers!" Oh, a queer old dame, as you remark!

So one evening we had our tea together, and 'Awkins lit the lamp and we all sat in to cards. Jeremiah Donovan came in too, and sat down and watched us for a while. Though he was a shy man and didn't speak much, it was easy to see he had no great love for the two Englishmen, and I was surprised it hadn't struck me so clearly before. Well, like that in the story, a terrible dispute blew up late in the evening between 'Awkins and Noble, about capitalists and priests and love for your own country.

"The capitalists," says 'Awkins, with an angry gulp, "the capitalists pays the priests to tell you all abaout the next world, so's you won't notice what they do in this!"

"Nonsense, man," says Noble, losing his temper, "before ever a capitalist was thought of people believed in the next world."

'Awkins stood up as if he was preaching a sermon. "Oh, they did, did   12 they?" he says with a sneer. "They believed all the things you believe, that's what you mean? And you believe that God created Hadam and Hadam created Shem and Shem created Jehoshophat? You believe all the silly hold fairytale abaout Heve and Heden and the happle? Well, listen to me, chum. If you're entitled to 'old to a silly belief like that, I'm entitled to 'old to my own silly belief — which is, that the fust thing your God created was a bleedin' capitalist with mirality and Rolls-Royce complete. Am I right, chum?" he says then to Belcher.

"You're right, chum," says Belcher, with his queer smile, and gets up from the table to stretch his long legs into the fire and stroke his mustache. So, seeing that Jeremiah Donovan was going, and there was no knowing when the conversation about religion would be over, I took my hat and went out with him. We strolled down towards the village together, and then he suddenly stopped, and blushing and mumbling, and shifting, as his way was, from toe to heel, he said I ought to be behind keeping guard on the prisoners. And I, having it put to me so suddenly, asked him what the hell he wanted a guard on the prisoners at all for, and said that so far as Noble and me were concerned we had talked it over and would rather be out with a column. "What use is that pair to us?" I asked him.

He looked at me for a spell and said, "I thought you knew we were keeping them as hostages." "Hostages — ?" says I, not quite understanding. "The enemy," he says in his heavy way, "have prisoners belong' to us, and now they talk of shooting them. If they shoot our prisoners we'll shoot theirs, and serve them right." "Shoot them?" said I, the possibility just beginning to dawn on me. "Shoot them exactly," said he. "Now," said I, "wasn't it very unforeseen of you not to tell me and Noble that?" "How so?" he asks. "Seeing that we were acting as guards upon them, of course." "And hadn't you reason enough to guess that much?" "We had not, Jeremiah Donovan, we had not. How were we to know when the men were on our hands so long?" "And what difference does it make? The enemy have our prisoners as long or longer, haven't they?" "It makes a great difference," said I. "How so?" said he sharply; but I couldn't tell him the difference it made, for I was struck too silly to speak. "And when may we expect to be released from this anyway?" said I. "You may expect it tonight," says he. "Or tomorrow or the next day at latest. So if it's hanging round here that worries you, you'll be free soon enough."

I cannot explain it even now, how sad I felt, but I went back to the cottage, a miserable man. When I arrived the discussion was still on, 'Awkins holding forth to all and sundry that there was no next world at all and Noble answering in his best canonical style that there was. But I saw 'Awkins was after having the best of it. "Do you know what, chum?" he was saying, with his saucy smile. "I think you're jest as big a bleedin' hunbeliever as I am. You say you believe in the next world and you know jest as much abaout the next world as I do, which is sweet damn-all. What's 'Eaven? You dunno. Where's 'Eaven? You dunno. Who's in 'Eaven? You dunno. You know sweet damn-all! I arsk you again, do they wear wings?"

"Very well then," says Noble, "they do; is that enough for you? They do wear wings." "Where do they get them then? Who makes them? 'Ave they a fact'ry for wings? 'Ave they a sort of store where you 'ands in your chit and tikes your bleedin' wings? Answer me that."   16

"Oh, you're an impossible man to argue with," says Noble. "Now listen to me — " And off the pair of them went again.

It was long after midnight when we locked up the Englishmen and went to bed ourselves. As I blew out the candle I told Noble what Jeremiah Donovan had told me. Noble took it very quietly. After we had been in bed about an hour he asked me did I think we ought to tell the Englishmen. I having thought of the same thing myself (among many others) said no, because it was more than likely the English wouldn't shoot our men, and anyhow it wasn't to be supposed the Brigade who were always up and down with the Second Battalion and knew the Englishmen well would be likely to want them bumped off. "I think so," says Noble. "It would be sort of cruelty to put the wind up them now." "It was very unforeseen of Jeremiah Donovan anyhow," says I, and by Noble's silence I realized he took my meaning.

So I lay there half the night, and thought and thought, and picturing myself and young Noble trying to prevent the Brigade from shooting 'Awkins and Belcher sent a cold sweat out through me. Because there were men on the Brigade you daren't let nor hinder without a gun in your hand, and at any rate, in those days disunion between brothers seemed to me an awful crime. I knew better after.

It was next morning we found it so hard to face Belcher and 'Awkins   20 with a smile. We went about the house all day scarcely saying a word. Belcher didn't mind us much; he was stretched into the ashes as usual with his usual look of waiting in quietness for something unforeseen to happen, but little 'Awkins gave us a bad time with his audacious gibing and questioning. He was disgusted at Noble's not answering him back. "Why can't you tike your beating like a man, chum?" he says. "You with your Hadam and Heve! I'm a Communist — or an Anarchist. An Anarchist, that's what I am." And for hours after he went round the house, mumbling when the fit took him "Hadam and Heve! Hadam and Heve!"

I don't know clearly how we got over that day, but get over it we did, and a great relief it was when the tea things were cleared away and Belcher said in his peaceable manner, "Well, chums, what about it?" So we all sat round the table and 'Awkins produced the cards, and at that moment I heard Jeremiah Donovan's footsteps up the path, and a dark presentiment crossed my mind. I rose quietly from the table and laid my hand on him before he reached the door. "What do you want?" I asked him. "I want those two soldier friends of yours," he says reddening. "Is that the way it is, Jeremiah Donovan?" I ask. "That's the way. There were four of our lads went west this morning, one of them a boy of sixteen." "That's bad, Jeremiah," says I.

At that moment Noble came out, and we walked down the path together talking in whispers. Feeney, the local intelligence officer, was standing by the gate. "What are you going to do about it?" I asked Jeremiah Donovan. "I want you and Noble to bring them out: you can tell them they're being shifted again; that'll be the quietest way." "Leave me out of that," says Noble suddenly. Jeremiah Donovan looked at him hard for a minute or two. "All right so," he said peaceably. "You and Feeney collect a few tools from the shed and dig a hole by the far end of the bog. Bonaparte and I'll be after you in about twenty minutes. But whatever else you do, don't let anyone see you with the tools. No one must know but the four of ourselves."

We saw Feeney and Noble go round to the houseen where the tools were kept, and sidled in. Everything if I can so express myself was tottering before my eyes, and I left Jeremiah Donovan to do the explaining as best he could, while I took a seat and said nothing. He told them they were to go back to the Second. 'Awkins let a mouthful of curses out of him at that, and it was plain that Belcher, though he said nothing, was duly perturbed. The old woman was for having them stay in spite of us, and she did not shut her mouth until Jeremiah Donovan lost his temper and said some nasty things to her. Within the house by this time it was pitch dark, but no one thought of lighting the lamp, and in the darkness the two Englishmen fetched their khaki topcoats and said good-bye to the woman of the house. "Just as a man mikes a 'ome of a bleedin' place," mumbles 'Awkins, shaking her by the hand, "some bastard at Headquarters thinks you're too cushy and shunts you off." Belcher shakes her hand very hearty. "A thousand thanks, madam," he says, "a thousand thanks for everything . . ." as though he'd made it all up.

We go round to the back of the house and down towards the fatal bog.   24 Then Jeremiah Donovan comes out with what is in his mind. "There were four of our lads shot by your fellows this morning so now you're to be bumped off." "Cut that stuff out," says 'Awkins, flaring up. "It's bad enough to be mucked about such as we are without you plying at soldiers." "It's true," says Jeremiah Donovan, "I'm sorry, 'Awkins, but 'tis true," and comes out with the usual rigmarole about doing our duty and obeying our superiors. "Cut it out," says 'Awkins irritably. "Cut it out!"

Then, when Donovan sees he is not being believed he turns to me, "Ask Bonaparte here," he says. "I don't need to arsk Bonaparte. Me and Bonaparte are chums." "Isn't it true, Bonaparte?" says Jeremiah Donovan solemnly to me. "It is," I say sadly, "it is." 'Awkins stops. "Now, for Christ's sike. . . ." "I mean it, chum," I say. "You daon't saound as if you mean it. You knaow well you don't mean it." "Well, if he don't I do," says Jeremiah Donovan. "Why the 'ell sh'd you want to shoot me, Jeremiah Donovan?" "Why the hell should your people take out four prisoners and shoot them in cold blood upon a barrack square?" I perceive Jeremiah Donovan is trying to encourage himself with hot words.

Anyway, he took little 'Awkins by the arm and dragged him on, but it was impossible to make him understand that we were in earnest. From which you will perceive how difficult it was for me, as I kept feeling my Smith and Wesson and thinking what I would do if they happened to put up a fight or ran for it, and wishing in my heart they would. I knew if only they ran I would never fire on them. "Was Noble in this?" 'Awkins wanted to know, and we said yes. He laughed. But why should Noble want to shoot him? Why should we want to shoot him? What had he done to us? Weren't we chums (the word lingers painfully in my memory)? Weren't we? Didn't we understand him and didn't he understand us? Did either of us imagine for an instant that he'd shoot us for all the so-and-so brigadiers in the so-and-so British Army? By this time I began to perceive in the dusk the desolate edges of the bog that was to be their last earthly bed, and, so great a sadness overtook my mind, I could not answer him. We walked along the edge of it in the darkness, and every now and then 'Awkins would call a halt and begin again, just as if he was wound up, about us being chums, and I was in despair that nothing but the cold and open grave made ready for his presence would convince him that we meant it all. But all the same, if you can understand, I didn't want him to be bumped off.

At last we saw the unsteady glint of a lantern in the distance and made towards it. Noble was carrying it, and Feeney stood somewhere in the darkness behind, and somehow the picture of the two of them so silent in the boglands was like the pain of death in my heart. Belcher, on recognizing Noble, said "'Allo, chum" in his usual peaceable way, but 'Awkins flew at the poor boy immediately, and the dispute began all over again, only that Noble hadn't a word to say for himself, and stood there with the swaying lantern between his gaitered legs.

It was Jeremiah Donovan who did the answering. 'Awkins asked for the twentieth time (for it seemed to haunt his mind) if anybody thought he'd shoot Noble. "You would," says Jeremiah Donovan shortly. "I wouldn't, damn you!" "You would if you knew you'd be shot for not doing it." "I wouldn't, not if I was to be shot twenty times over; he's my chum. And Belcher wouldn't — isn't that right, Belcher?" "That's right, chum," says Belcher peaceably. "Damned if I would. Anyway, who says Noble'd be shot if I wasn't bumped off? What d'you think I'd do if I was in Noble's place and we were out in the middle of a blasted bog?" "What would you do?" "I'd go with him wherever he was going. I'd share my last bob with him and stick by 'im through thick and thin."

"We've had enough of this," says Jeremiah Donovan, cocking his revolver. "Is there any message you want to send before I fire?" "No, there isn't, but . . ." "Do you want to say your prayers?" 'Awkins came out with a cold-blooded remark that shocked even me and turned to Noble again. "Listen to me, Noble," he said. "You and me are chums. You won't come over to my side, so I'll come over to your side. Is that fair? Just you give me a rifle and I'll go with you wherever you want."

Nobody answered him.

"Do you understand?" he said. "I'm through with it all. I'm a deserter or anything else you like, but from this on I'm one of you. Does that prove to you that I mean what I say?" Noble raised his head, but as Donovan began to speak he lowered it again without answering. "For the last time have you any messages to send?" says Donovan in a cold and excited voice.

"Ah, shut up, you, Donovan; you don't understand me, but these 32 fellows do. They're my chums; they stand by me and I stand by them. We're not the capitalist tools you seem to think us."

I alone of the crowd saw Donovan raise his Webley to the back of 'Awkins neck, and as he did so I shut my eyes and tried to say a prayer. 'Awkins had begun to say something else when Donovan let fly, and, as I opened my eyes at the bang, I saw him stagger at the knees and lie out flat at Noble's feet, slowly, and as quiet as a child, with the lantern light falling sadly upon his lean legs and bright farmer's boots. We all stood very still for a while watching him settle out in the last agony.

Then Belcher quietly takes out a handkerchief, and begins to tie it about his own eyes (for in our excitement we had forgotten to offer the same to 'Awkins), and, seeing it is not big enough, turns and asks for a loan of mine. I give it to him and as he knots the two together he points with his foot at 'Awkins. "'E's not quite dead," he says, "better give 'im another." Sure enough 'Awkins's left knee as we see it under the lantern is rising again. I bend down and put my gun to his ear; then, recollecting myself and the company of Belcher, I stand up again with a few hasty words. Belcher understands what is in my mind. "Give 'im 'is first," he says. "I don't mind. Poor bastard, we dunno what's 'appening to 'im now." As by this time I am beyond all feeling I kneel down again and skillfully give 'Awkins the last shot so as to put him forever out of pain.

Belcher who is fumbling a bit awkwardly with the handkerchiefs comes out with a laugh when he hears the shot. It is the first time I have heard him laugh, and it sends a shiver down my spine, coming as it does so inappropriately upon the tragic death of his old friend. "Poor blighter," he says quietly, "and last night he was so curious abaout it all. It's very queer, chums, I always think. Naow, 'e knows as much abaout it as they'll ever let 'im know, and last night 'e was all in the dark."

Donovan helps him to tie the handkerchiefs about his eyes. "Thanks, 36 chum," he says. Donovan asks him if there are any messages he would like to send. "Naow, chum," he says, "none for me. If any of you likes to write to 'Awkins's mother you'll find a letter from 'er in 'is pockct. But my missus left me eight years ago. Went away with another fellow and took the kid with her. I likes the feelin' of a 'ome (as you may 'ave noticed) but I couldn't start again after that."

We stand around like fools now that he can no longer see us. Donovan looks at Noble and Noble shakes his head. Then Donovan raises his Webley again and just at that moment Belcher laughs his queer nervous laugh again. He must think we are talking of him; anyway, Donovan lowers his gun. "'Scuse me, chums," says Belcher, "I feel I'm talking the 'ell of a lot . . . and so silly . . . abaout me being so 'andy abaout a 'ouse. But this thing come on me so sudden. You'll forgive me, I'm sure." "You don't want to say a prayer?" asks Jeremiah Donovan. "No, chum," he replies, "I don't think that'd 'elp. I'm ready if you want to get it over." "You understand," says Jeremiah Donovan, "it's not so much our doing. It's our duty, so to speak." Belcher's head is raised like a real blind man's, so that you can only see his nose and chin in the lamplight. "I never could make out what duty was myself," he said, "but I think you're all good lads, if that's what you mean. I'm not complaining." Noble, with a look of desperation, signals to Donovan, and in a flash Donovan raises his gun and fires. The big man goes over like a sack of meal, and this time there is no need of a second shot.

I don't remember much about the burying, but that it was worse than all the rest, because we had to carry the warm corpses a few yards before we sunk them in the windy bog. It was all mad lonely, with only a bit of lantern between ourselves and the pitch blackness, and birds hooting and screeching all round disturbed by the guns. Noble had to search 'Awkins first to get the letter from his mother. Then having smoothed all signs of the grave away, Noble and I collected our tools, said good-bye to the others, and went back along the desolate edge of the treacherous bog without a word. We put the tools in the houseen and went into the house. The kitchen was pitch black and cold, just as we left it, and the old woman was sitting over the hearth telling her beads. We walked past her into the room, and Noble struck a match to light the lamp. Just then she rose quietly and came to the doorway, being not at all so bold or crabbed as usual.

"What did ye do with them?" she says in a sort of whisper, and Noble took such a mortal start the match quenched in his trembling hand. "What's that?" he asks without turning round. "I heard ye," she said. "What did you hear?" asks Noble, but sure he wouldn't deceive a child the way he said it. "I heard ye. Do you think I wasn't listening to ye putting the things back in the houseen?" Noble struck another match and this time the lamp lit for him. "Was that what ye did with them?" she said, and Noble said nothing — after all what could he say?

So then, by God, she fell on her two knees by the door, and began   40 telling her beads, and after a minute or two Noble went on his knees by the fireplace, so I pushed my way out past her, and stood at the door, watching the stars and listening to the damned shrieking of the birds. It is so strange what you feel at such moments, and not to be written afterwards. Noble says he felt he seen everything ten times as big, perceiving nothing around him but the little patch of black bog with the two Englishmen stiffening into it; but with me it was the other way, as though the patch of bog where the two Englishmen were was a thousand miles away from me, and even Noble mumbling just behind me and the old woman and the birds and the bloody stars were all far away, and I was somehow very small and very lonely. And anything that ever happened [to] me after I never felt the same about again.

EXPLORATIONS

1. What conflicting political loyalty divides Belcher and 'Awkins from the other characters in "Guests of the Nation"? At what point and in what way does this division cease to be a real one? What conflicting religious loyalty theoretically divides these characters? How does author O'Connor make this division, too, a false one?

2. In the middle of "Guests of the Nation" the narrator learns that the Englishmen are hostages who may soon be shot, in spite of his and Noble's long acquaintance with them. "And what difference does it make?" asks Jeremiah Donovan. What is the answer to this question, which the narrator is "struck too silly" to give him?

3. The story's first section ends with the old woman of the house telling 'Awkins that "nothing but sorrow and want follows them that disturbs the hidden powers!" What theme(s) in the story does this statement reflect?

CONNECTIONS

1. O'Connor, like Milovan Djilas in "Ideas Against Torture," writes about dying for an idea. How are these two authors' views on this subject different? Cite evidence in each selection indicating the author's views.

2. How is the dilemma faced by O'Connor's characters similar to that of the Cambodians interviewed by Roger Rosenblatt in "Children of Cambodia"? What explanation does Rosenblatt offer for the children's feelings about violence that might also apply to Bonaparte's attitude toward killing his prisoners?

3. What ideas about war and nationalism are expressed in both "Guests of the Nation" and Shelley Saywell's "Women Warriors of El Salvador"? What do both accounts suggest about the motivation of those who kill their fellow citizens?

4. How is the ending of O'Connor's story similar to that of William H. Sullivan's *Observation*? What thematic similarities can you discern in these two pieces?

ELABORATIONS

1. Write an essay about the functions in "Guests of the Nation" of the ongoing religious argument between 'Awkins and Noble: its importance to the plot, to character development, and to the story's theme.

2. Have you ever obeyed an order, or yielded to pressure, to do something you believed was wrong? How did you feel about it at the time? afterward? Write an essay about the incident, with attention to the issues of loyalty raised by O'Connor.

RYSZARD KAPUŚCIŃSKI

Carlotta

Ryszard Kapuściński (pronounced *Rish*-ard Kap-ush-*chin*-ski) was
born in 1932 in Pinsk, which was then part of Poland and is now part
of the Soviet Union. His family fled in 1940, with the Russians advancing
from one direction and the Germans from the other. Both his home and
his school were burnt-out ruins: "There were fifty boys in the class, and
between us we had one book which the teacher would read and pass
round." He became an activist, joining a Communist youth organization,
and entered the University of Warsaw in 1950. After receiving his master's
degree, Kapuściński worked for a Warsaw youth journal, from which he
was fired for writing an exposé on a showcase factory; however, his article
provoked an investigation and ultimately won him the Golden Cross of
Merit. He became a foreign correspondent, then joined the Polish Press
Agency, traveling to India, Pakistan, and Afghanistan, Japan and China,
Latin America, and Africa. "I have personally witnessed twenty-seven
revolutions," he says. Kapuściński turned many of his observations into
books, including his widely praised *The Emperor* (1978), a collage of
interviews with Haile Selassie's courtiers following the Ethiopian emper-
or's downfall in 1974. From 1974 to 1981 he served as deputy editor in
chief of the weekly magazine *Kultura* ("culture"), leaving to resume free-
lance writing. "Carlotta" comes from *Jeszcze dzien zycia* (1976; *Another
Day of Life,* 1987), translated from the Polish by William R. Brand and
Katarzyna Mroczkowska-Brand.

The war in Angola during which Kapuściński met Carlotta is now in
a new phase. Angola, south of Zaire and north of South Africa on Africa's
eastern coast, was occupied by Bantu tribes when the Portuguese arrived
in 1583. After heavy Portuguese immigration in the early twentieth century, a guerrilla war began in 1961. In 1974 Portugal offered independence, but violence continued between the Zaire-based National Front
for the Liberation of Angola (FNLA), the Soviet-backed Popular Movement for the Liberation of Angola (MPLA), and the National Union for
Total Independence of Angola (UNITA), supported by the United States
and South Africa. Cuban and Soviet aid helped the MPLA win control
and establish a Marxist government. UNITA continues to try to overthrow
that government, and to seek U.S. help in doing so.

Benguela: a sleepy, almost depopulated city slumbering in the shade of acacias, palms, and kipersols. The villa neighborhoods are empty, the houses locked up and drowned in flowers. Indescribable residential luxury, a dizzying excess of floor space, and, in the streets before the gates, orphaned cars — Chevrolets and Alfa Romeos and Jaguars, probably in running order although nobody tries to drive them. And nearby, a hundred meters away, the desert — white and glimmering like a salt spill, without a blade of grass, without a single tree, beyond redemption.

I spent some time walking the border of the two quarters, and then I went downtown. I found the lane in which the general staff for the central front was quartered in a spacious two-story villa. In front of the gate sat a guard with a face monstrously swollen by periostitis, groaning and squeezing his head, obviously terrified that his skull would burst. There was no way to communicate with such an unfortunate; nothing existed for him at that point. I opened the gate. In the garden boxes of ammunition, mortar barrels, and piles of canteens lay on the flower beds in the shade of flaming bougainvilleas. Further on, soldiers were sleeping side by side on the veranda and in the hall. I went upstairs and opened a door. There was nothing but a desk inside, and at the desk sat a large, powerfully built white man: [MPLA] Comandante Monti, the commander of the front.

He was typing a request to Luanda for people and weapons. The only armored personnel carrier he had at the front had been knocked out the day before by a mercenary. If the enemy attacked now with their own armored personnel carrier, he would have to give ground and retreat.

Monti read the letter that I had brought him from Luanda, ordered   4
me to sit down — on the windowsill, because there were no chairs — and went on typing. A quarter of an hour later there were footsteps on the stairs and four people came in, a television crew from Lisbon. They had come here for two days and afterwards they would return to Portugal in their plane. The leader of the crew was Luis Alberto, a dynamic and restless mulatto, sharp and gusty. We immediately became friends. Monti and Alberto knew each other from way back since they both came from Angola and perhaps even from right here in Benguela. So we didn't have to waste any time making introductions and getting to know one another.

Alberto and I wanted to drive to the front, but the rest of the crew — Carvalho, Fernandez, and Barbosa — were against it. They said they had wives and children, they had begun building houses outside Lisbon (near Cascais, a truly beautiful spot), and they weren't going to die in this mad, senseless war in which nobody knew anything, the opponents couldn't tell each other apart until the last second, and you could be blown away without any fighting simply because of the crazy screwups, the lack of information, the laziness and callousness of blacks for whom human life had no value.

In other words, they expressed a desire to live.

A discussion began, which is what Latins love most of all. Alberto tried to sell them on the argument that they would shoot a lot of tape and make a lot of the money they all needed so badly. But it was Monti who finally assuaged them by saying that at that time of day — it was almost noon — there was no fighting on the front. And he gave the most straightforward explanation in the world: "It's too hot."

Outside the window the air was rippling like tin in a forge; every   8
movement demanded effort. We started getting ready to hit the road. Monti went downstairs, woke up one of the soldiers, and sent him into town where, somewhere, there were drivers and cars. A Citroën DS and a Ford Mustang turned up. Monti wanted to make it nice for us, so he designated as our escort a soldier named Carlotta.

Carlotta came with an automatic on her shoulder. Even though she was wearing a commando uniform that was too big for her, you could tell she was attractive. We all started paying court to her immediately. In fact, it was Carlotta's presence that persuaded the crew to forget about their houses outside Lisbon and travel to the front. Only twenty years old, Carlotta was already a legend. Two months earlier, during the uprising in Huambo, she had led a small MPLA detachment that was surrounded by a thousand-strong UNITA force. She managed to break the encirclement and lead her people out. Girls generally make excellent soldiers — better than boys, who sometimes behave hysterically and irresponsibly at the front. Our girl was a mulatto with an elusive charm and, as it seemed to us then, great beauty. (Later, when I developed the pictures of her, the only pictures of Carlotta that remained, I saw that she wasn't so beautiful. Yet nobody said as much out loud, so as not to destroy our myth, our image of Carlotta from that October afternoon in Benguela. I simply looked up Alberto, Carvalho, Fernandez, and Barbosa and showed them the pictures of Carlotta taken on the way to the front. They looked at them in silence and I think we all chose silence so we wouldn't have to comment on the subject of good looks. Did it mean anything in the end? Carlotta was gone by then. She had received an order to report to the front staff, so she put on her uniform, combed out her Afro, slung the automatic over her shoulder, and left. When Co-mandante Monti, four Portuguese, and a Pole saw her in front of staff headquarters, she seemed beautiful. Why? Because that was the kind of mood we were in, because we needed it, because we wanted it that way. We always create the beauty of women, and that day we created Carlotta's beauty. I can't explain it any other way.)

The cars moved out and drove along the road to Balombo, 160 kilometers to the east. To tell the truth, we all should have died on the winding road, full of switchbacks that the drivers took like madmen; it was a miracle that we got there alive. Carlotta sat beside the driver in our car and, since she was used to that kind of driving, she kidded us a little. The force of the wind threw her head back, and Barbosa said he would hold on to Carlotta's head so the wind wouldn't tear it off. Carlotta laughed, and we envied Barbosa. At one of the stops, Fernandez proposed that Carlotta move to the back with us and sit on our knees, but she refused. We rejoiced out loud at his defeat. After all, Fernandez had clearly wanted Carlotta to sit on his own lap, which would have ruined everything since she didn't belong to anyone and we were creating her together, our Carlotta.

She had been born in Roçadas, not far from the border of Namibia. She had received her military training a year ago in the Kabinda forest. She wants to become a nurse after the war. That's all we know about this girl who is now riding in the car holding an automatic on her knees, and who, since we have run out of jokes and calmed down for a moment, has become serious and thoughtful. We know that Carlotta won't be Alberto's or Fernandez's, but we don't yet know that she will never again be anybody's.

We have to stop again because a bridge is damaged and the drivers have to figure out how to get across. We have a few minutes, so I take a picture of her. I ask her to smile. She stands leaning against the bridge railing. Around us lie fields, meadows perhaps — I don't remember.

After a while we drove on. We passed a burned-out village, an empty town, abandoned pineapple and tobacco plantations. Then a profusion of tamarisk shrubs that evolved into a forest. It got worse, because we were driving to the front on a road that had been fought over, and there were corpses of soldiers scattered on the asphalt. They aren't in the habit of burying the fallen here, and the approach to every combat zone can be recognized by the inhuman odor of decaying bodies. Some additional fermentation must take place in the putrid humidity of the tropics, because the smell is intense, terrible — so stunning that, no matter how many times I went to the front, I always felt dizzy and ready to vomit. We had jerrycans full of extra gasoline in the lead car, so we stopped and poured some on the corpses, and covered them with a few dry branches and roadside bushes; then the driver fired his automatic into the asphalt at such an angle that sparks flew and a fire started. We marked our route to Balombo with these fires.

Balombo is a little town in the forest that keeps changing hands. Neither side can settle in for good because of the forest, which allows the enemy to sneak to within point-blank range under cover and suddenly attack the town. This morning Balombo was taken by an MPLA detachment of a hundred people. There is still shooting in the surrounding woods because the enemy has retreated, but not very far. In Balombo, which is devastated, not a single civilian remains — only these hundred soldiers. There is water, and the girls from the detachment approach us freshly bathed, with their wet hair wound around curling papers. Carlotta admonishes them: they shouldn't behave as if preparing to go out for the evening; they ought to be ready to fight at all times. They complain that they had to attack in the first wave because the boys were not eager to advance. The boys strike their foreheads with their hands and say the girls are lying. They are all sixteen to eighteen years old, the age of our high school students or of the fighters in the Warsaw uprising. Part of the unit is joyriding up and down the main street on a captured tractor. Each group makes one circuit and hands the wheel over to the next one. Others have given up contending for the tractor and are riding around on captured bicycles. It is chilly in Balombo because it lies in the hills; there is a light breeze and the forest is rustling.

As the crew films, I walk along with them, snapping pictures. Carlotta, who is conscientious and doesn't let herself be carried away in the euphoria of victory sweeping the detachment, knows that a counterattack could begin at any time, or that snipers lurking under cover could be taking aim at our heads. So she accompanies us all the time with her automatic at the ready. She is attentive and taciturn. We can hear the tops of her boots rubbing together as she walks. Carvalho, the cameraman, films Carlotta walking against the background of burned-out houses, and later against a background of strikingly exuberant adenias. All of this will be shown in Portugal, in a country that Carlotta will never see. In another country, Poland, her pictures will also appear. We are still walking through Balombo and talking. Barbosa asks her when she'll get married. Oh, she can't say — there's a war on. The sun sinks behind the trees; twilight is approaching and we must leave. We return to the cars, which are waiting on the main street. We're all satisfied because we have been to the front, we have film and pictures, we are alive. We get in as we did when we drove here: Carlotta in front, we in the back. The driver starts the motor and puts the car in gear. And then — we all remember that it was exactly at that moment — Carlotta gets out of the car and says she is staying. "Carlotta," Alberto says, "come with us. We'll take you out to supper, and tomorrow we'll take you to Lisbon." Carlotta laughs, waves good-bye, and signals the driver to start.

We're sad. 16

We drive away from Balombo on a road that grows darker and darker, and we drive into the night. We arrive late in Benguela and locate the one restaurant still open; we want something to eat. Alberto, who knows everyone here, gets us a table in the open air. It's splendid — the air is cool and there's an ocean of stars in the sky. We sit down hungry and exhausted and talk. The food doesn't come for a long time. Alberto calls, but it's noisy and nobody hears us. Then lights appear at the corner and a car comes round and brakes sharply in front of the restaurant. A tired, unwashed soldier with a dirt-smeared face jumps out of the car. He says that immediately after our departure there was an attack on Balombo and they have given up the town; in the same sentence, he says that Carlotta died in the attack.

We stood up from the table and walked into the deserted street. Each of us walked separately, alone; there was nothing to talk about. Hunched over, Alberto went first, with Carvalho behind him and Fernandez on the other side of the street, with Barbosa following and me at the end. It was better for us to reach the hotel that way and disappear from each other's sight. We had driven out of Balombo at a crazy speed and none of us had heard the shooting begin behind us. And so we hadn't been fleeing. But if we had heard the shots, would we have ordered the driver to turn back so we could be with Carlotta? Would we have risked our lives to protect her, as she had risked hers to protect us in Balombo? Maybe she had died covering us as we drove away, because the boys were chasing around on the tractor and the girls were doing their hair when the enemy appeared out of nowhere.

We are all culpable in Carlotta's death, since we agreed to let her stay behind; we could have ordered her to return. But who could have foreseen it? The most guilty are Alberto and I: we are the ones who wanted to go to the front, so Monti gave us an escort — that girl. But can we change anything now, call it off, run the day backwards?

Carlotta is gone. 20

Who would have thought that we were seeing her in the last hour of her life? And that it was all in our hands? Why didn't Alberto stop the driver, get out, and tell her: Come with us because otherwise we'll stay and you'll be responsible! Why didn't any of us do that? And is the guilt any easier to bear because it is spread among the five of us?

Of course it was a tragic accident. That's how, lying, we will tell the story. We can also say there was an element of predestination, of fate, to it. There was no reason for her to stay there, and furthermore it had been agreed from the start that she would return with us. In the last second she was prompted by some indefinable instinct to get out of the car, and a moment later she was dead. Let's believe it was fate. In such situations we act in a way we can't explain afterwards. And we say, Your Honor, I don't know how it happened, how it came to that, because in fact it began from nothing.

But Carlotta knew this war better than we did; she knew that dusk, the customary time for attack, was approaching, and that it would be better if she stayed there and organized cover for our departure. That must have been the reason for her decision. We thought of this later, when it was too late. But now we can't ask her about anything.

We knock on the hotel door, which is already locked. The owner, a   24 massive old black man, opens up and wants to hug us because we've made it back in one piece; he wants to ask us all about it. Then he looks at us carefully, falls silent, and walks away. Each of us takes his key, goes upstairs, and locks himself in his room.

EXPLORATIONS

1. What is Carlotta's official position? Why does she go to the front with a journalist and a television crew? Why does she stay at the front instead of returning with them?

2. Kapuściński says that "we created Carlotta's beauty" and "we were creating her together, our Carlotta." In what sense(s) is this a professional creation? — that is, what functions besides escort does Carlotta serve for Kapuściński and the Portuguese TV crew? How does her death affect her usefulness to them?

3. What does Kapuściński say about who is fighting in Angola, and why? How would the essay's focus change if he included more data about the war? What does he emphasize instead?

CONNECTIONS

1. What elements of plot and theme does "Carlotta" share with Frank O'Connor's "Guests of the Nation"? What role(s) does the narrator play in each story? How would the impact of each story change if the author had written as a third-person recorder of events instead of a first-person participant?

2. What ideas about women's involvement in war and their response to it appear in both "Carlotta" and Shelley Saywell's "Women Warriors of El Salvador"? How would the effect of Kapuściński's narrative be different if its central character were male instead of female?

3. "Carlotta," like Mark Baker's *Observation*, derives a good deal of its impact from the narrator's use of descriptive details. What function do such details serve in each piece? Which details did you find most striking and memorable?

ELABORATIONS

1. Imagine that you are Carlotta, a soldier assigned to escort five foreign journalists to the front. Write a first-person narrative about the same events Kapuściński describes, from Carlotta's point of view.

2. Kapuściński shows us a woman participating in a war as a soldier; so does Shelley Saywell. Mark Baker's *Observation* shows us a woman participating in a war as a nurse. American presidents who send soldiers into foreign wars often refer to them as "our boys" or "these brave young men." Do you think the United States would have accepted a president's sending "our girls" into battle in Southeast Asia? into any current war zone? Why or why not? How is (or isn't) the commitment of fighting different from the commitment of nursing? Write an essay exploring the question of women's roles in war.

CHINUA ACHEBE

Civil Peace

Chinua Achebe was born in Ogidi, Eastern Nigeria, in 1930. His first novel, *Things Fall Apart* (1959), has sold over two and a half million copies; he has since published three more novels, a volume of short stories (*Girls at War and Other Stories,* 1972), and a volume of poetry (*Beware, Soul-Brother,* 1972). Formerly director of external broadcasting for the Nigerian Broadcasting Corporation, Achebe has taught at the University of Nigeria, Nsukka; at the Universities of Massachusetts and Connecticut in the United States; and at the University of Guelph in Ontario, Canada. He holds honorary doctorates from the Universities of Stirling, Southampton, Kent, and Guelph. Achebe is coeditor of *Okike: An African Journal of New Writing,* founded in 1971. "Civil Peace" originally appeared in *Okike* 2.

Nigeria, a center for the Portuguese and British slave trade from the fifteenth century on, came under British control after 1861. A century later Nigeria regained its independence as a republic within the British Commonwealth; most of its governments since then have been military. In 1967 the Eastern Region seceded, proclaiming itself the Republic of Biafra. Civil war followed, with casualties of over a million — including many "Biafrans" (mostly Ibos) who starved despite international relief efforts. In 1970 the secessionists capitulated. "Civil Peace" takes place during that postwar period.

(For more background on Nigeria, see p. 66.)

Jonathan Iwegbu counted himself extraordinarily lucky. "Happy survival!" meant so much more to him than just a current fashion of greeting old friends in the first hazy days of peace. It went deep to his heart. He had come out of the war with five inestimable blessings — his head, his wife Maria's head, and the heads of three out of their four children. As a bonus he also had his old bicycle — a miracle too but naturally not to be compared to the safety of five human heads.

The bicycle had a little history of its own. One day at the height of the war it was commandeered "for urgent military action." Hard as its loss would have been to him he would still have let it go without a thought had he not had some doubts about the genuineness of the officer. It wasn't his disreputable rags, nor the toes peeping out of one blue and one brown canvas shoe, nor yet the two stars of his rank done obviously in a hurry in biro [ballpoint] that troubled Jonathan; many good and heroic soldiers looked the same or worse. It was rather a certain lack of grip and firmness in his manner. So Jonathan, suspecting he might be amenable to influence, rummaged in his raffia bag and produced the two pounds with which he had been going to buy firewood which his wife, Maria, retailed to camp officials for extra stockfish and cornmeal, and got his bicycle back. That night he buried it in the little clearing in the bush where the dead of the camp, including his own youngest son, were buried. When he dug it up again a year later after the surrender all it needed was a little palm-oil greasing. "Nothing puzzles God," he said in wonder.

He put it to immediate use as a taxi and accumulated a small pile of Biafran money ferrying camp officials and their families across the four-mile stretch to the nearest tarred road. His standard charge per trip was six pounds and those who had the money were only glad to be rid of some of it in this way. At the end of a fortnight he had made a small fortune of one hundred and fifteen pounds.

Then he made the journey to Enugu and found another miracle 4 waiting for him. It was unbelievable. He rubbed his eyes and looked again and it was still standing there before him. But, needless to say, even that monumental blessing must be accounted also totally inferior to the five heads in the family. This newest miracle was his little house in Ogui Overside. Indeed nothing puzzles God! Only two houses away a huge concrete edifice some wealthy contractor had put up just before the war was a mountain of rubble. And here was Jonathan's little zinc house of no regrets built with mud blocks quite intact! Of course the doors and windows were missing and five sheets off the roof. But what was that? And anyhow he had returned to Enugu early enough to pick up bits of old zinc and wood and soggy sheets of cardboard lying around the neighborhood before thousands more came out of their forest holes looking for the same things. He got a destitute carpenter with one old hammer, a blunt plane, and a few bent and rusty nails in his tool bag to turn this assortment of wood, paper, and metal into door and window shutters for five Nigerian shillings or fifty Biafran pounds. He paid the pounds, and moved in with his overjoyed family carrying five heads on their shoulders.

His children picked mangoes near the military cemetery and sold them to soldiers' wives for a few pennies — real pennies this time — and his wife started making breakfast akara balls for neighbors in a hurry to start life again. With his family earnings he took his bicycle to the villages around and bought fresh palm wine which he mixed generously in his rooms with the water which had recently started running again in the public tap down the road, and opened up a bar for soldiers and other lucky people with good money.

At first he went daily, then every other day, and finally once a week, to the offices of the Coal Corporation where he used to be a miner, to find out what was what. The only thing he did find out in the end was that that little house of his was even a greater blessing than he had thought. Some of his fellow ex-miners who had nowhere to return at the end of the day's waiting just slept outside the doors of the offices and cooked what meal they could scrounge together in Bournvita tins. As the weeks lengthened and still nobody could say what was what Jonathan discontinued his weekly visits altogether and faced his palm-wine bar.

But nothing puzzles God. Came the day of the windfall when after five days of endless scuffles in queues and counterqueues in the sun outside the Treasury he had twenty pounds counted into his palms as ex-gratia award for the rebel money he had turned in. It was like Christmas for him and for many others like him when the payments began. They called it (since few could manage its proper official name) *egg-rasher*.

As soon as the pound notes were placed in his palm Jonathan simply   8
closed it tight over them and buried fist and money inside his trouser pocket. He had to be extra careful because he had seen a man a couple of days earlier collapse into near-madness in an instant before that oceanic crowd because no sooner had he got his twenty pounds than some heartless ruffian picked it off him. Though it was not right that a man in such an extremity of agony should be blamed yet many in the queues that day were able to remark quietly at the victim's carelessness, especially after he pulled out the innards of his pocket and revealed a hole in it big enough to pass a thief's head. But of course he had insisted that the money had been in the other pocket, pulling it out too to show its comparative wholeness. So one had to be careful.

Jonathan soon transferred the money to his left hand and pocket so as to leave his right free for shaking hands should the need arise, though by fixing his gaze at such an elevation as to miss all approaching human faces he made sure that the need did not arise, until he got home.

He was normally a heavy sleeper but that night he heard all the neighborhood noises die down one after another. Even the night watchman who knocked the hour on some metal somewhere in the distance had fallen silent after knocking one o'clock. That must have been the last thought in Jonathan's mind before he was finally carried away himself. He couldn't have been gone for long, though, when he was violently awakened again.

"Who is knocking?" whispered his wife lying beside him on the floor.

"I don't know," he whispered back breathlessly. 12

The second time the knocking came it was so loud and imperious that the rickety old door could have fallen down.

"Who is knocking?" he asked them, his voice parched and trembling.

"Na tief-man and him people," came the cool reply. "Make you hopen de door." This was followed by the heaviest knocking of all.

Maria was the first to raise the alarm, then he followed and all their 16 children.

"*Police-o! Thieves-o! Neighbors-o! Police-o! We are lost! We are dead! Neighbors, are you asleep? Wake up! Police-o!*"

"You done finish?" asked the voice outside. "Make we help you small. Oya, everybody!"

"*Police-o! Tief-man-so! Neighbors-o! we done loss-o! Police-o! . . .*"

There were at least five other voices besides the leader's. 20

Jonathan and his family were now completely paralyzed by terror. Maria and the children sobbed inaudibly like lost souls. Jonathan groaned continuously.

The silence that followed the thieves' alarm vibrated horribly. Jonathan all but begged their leader to speak again and be done with it.

"My frien," said he at long last, "we don try our best for call dem but I tink say dem all done sleep-o . . . So wetin we go do now? Sometaim you wan call soja? Or you wan make we call dem for you? Soja better pass police. No be so?"

"Na so!" replied his men. Jonathan thought he heard even more voices 24 now than before and groaned heavily. His legs were sagging under him and his throat felt like sandpaper.

"My frien, why you no de talk again. I de ask you say you wan make we call soja?"

"No."

"Awrighto. Now make we talk business. We no be bad tief. We no like for make trouble. Trouble done finish. War done finish and all the katakata wey de for inside. No Civil War again. This time na Civil Peace. No be so?"

"Na so!" answered the horrible chorus. 28

"What do you want from me? I am a poor man. Everything I had went with this war. Why do you come to me? You know people who have money. We . . ."

"Awright! We know say you no get plenty money. But we sef no get even anini. So derefore make you open dis window and give us one hundred pound and we go commot. Orderwise we de come for inside now to show you guitar-boy like dis . . ."

A volley of automatic fire rang through the sky. Maria and the children began to weep aloud again.

"Ah, missisi de cry again. No need for dat. We done talk say we na   32
good tief. We just take our small money and go nwayorly. No molest. Abi we de molest?"

"At all!" sang the chorus.

"My friends," began Jonathan hoarsely. "I hear what you say and I thank you. If I had one hundred pounds . . ."

"Lookia my frien, no be play we come play for your house. If we make mistake and step for inside you no go like am-o. So derefore . . ."

"To God who made me; if you come inside and find one hundred   36
pounds, take and shoot me and shoot my wife and children. I swear to God. The only money I have in this life is this twenty-pounds *egg-rasher* they gave me today . . ."

"OK. Time de go. Make you open dis window and bring the twenty pound. We go manage am like dat."

There were now loud murmurs of dissent among the chorus: "Na lie de man de lie; e get plenty money . . . Make we go inside and search properly well . . . Wetin be twenty pound? . . ."

"Shurrup!" rang the leader's voice like a lone shot in the sky and silenced the murmuring at once. "Are you dere? Bring the money quick!"

"I am coming," said Jonathan fumbling in the darkness with the key   40
of the small wooden box he kept by his side on the mat.

At the first sign of light as neighbors and others assembled to commiserate with him he was already strapping his five-gallon demijohn to his bicycle carrier and his wife, sweating in the open fire, was turning over akara balls in a wide clay bowl of boiling oil. In the corner his eldest son was rinsing out dregs of yesterday's palm wine from old beer bottles.

"I count it as nothing," he told his sympathizers, his eyes on the rope he was trying. "What is *egg-rasher*? Did I depend on it last week? Or is it greater than other things that went with the war? I say, let *egg-rasher* perish in the flames! Let it go where everything else has gone. Nothing puzzles God."

EXPLORATIONS

1. Why does Jonathan Iwegbu count himself extraordinarily lucky? What does his definition of luck say about the condition of other Biafrans? Who seems to have come out on top in this war, and who has come out on the bottom?

2. What has been the war's effect on currency? What kind of money is most plentiful in Biafra? What kind is most valuable?

3. Where does the name *egg-rasher* come from? How does Jonathan Iwegbu's *egg-rasher* embody the theme of "Civil Peace"? Why is this an appropriate title for the story, and for the situation in Biafra when the story takes place?

CONNECTIONS

1. What central value expressed by Achebe in "Civil Peace" is also expressed by Ryszard Kapuściński in "Carlotta" and by Frank O'Connor in "Guests of the Nation"? In each selection, what characters bear the guilt for the story's climactic tragedy? Why do (or don't) we as readers regard each set of guilty characters as villains?

2. "Which world is 'natural'?" asks Czeslaw Milosz. "That which existed before, or the world of war?" Look closely at Milosz's examples of how war changes human perceptions, and at Achebe's examples. What changes noted in "American Ignorance of War" are illustrated in "Civil Peace"?

3. Wole Soyinka's "Nigerian Childhood" (p. 66) is a vivid example of the blend of Western and African traditions described by Ezekiel Mphahlele in "Tradition and the African Writer" (p. 344). How does Achebe — also writing about Nigeria — portray that dual heritage? What items in "Civil Peace" represent native African tradition? What items represent British colonial tradition?

ELABORATIONS

1. What does Jonathan Iwegbu mean by "Nothing puzzles God"? Write an essay explaining this expression's significance in "Civil Peace" by examining the specific contexts in which Iwegbu uses it, as well as the story as a whole.

2. The saying "Necessity is the mother of invention" is amply borne out during a war. Using "Civil Peace," Shelley Saywell's "Women Warriors of El Salvador," and other selections from Part Six as sources, write an essay illustrating human ingenuity under wartime and postwar stress.

GÜNTER GRASS

Resistance

Günter Grass is respected for his poetry and plays, but best known for his novels. Born in the Polish city of Danzig in 1927, Grass saw the Nazis take over his hometown; he joined the Hitler Youth, fought with the German army, and became a prisoner of war while still in his teens. Much of his writing is concerned with German politics. He established his literary reputation with the Danzig Trilogy, three novels beginning with *The Tin Drum* (1959) that examine various reactions among Germans to the rise of Nazism, the horrors of World War II, and their lasting backlash of guilt. Grass's fiction typically mixes realism and absurdity; in his own childhood Nazi indoctrination followed a grounding in traditional folklore from his mother. His later work — including "Resistance" — tends to focus on contemporary German culture and society.

Grass comments in this essay: "It has again become possible that for the third and last time, war can be started from Germany." The first time was World War I, launched in 1914 by Kaiser ("emperor") Wilhelm II. France, Britain, and their allies (including the United States after 1917) defeated Germany in 1919, at a cost of over 10 million lives. Within a dozen years Adolf Hitler had become head of the National Socialist German Workers' (Nazi) Party. Worldwide financial depression struck in 1929; the Depression encouraged extremism, and by 1933 Hitler had gained enough clout to be named chancellor by Germany's President Hindenburg. Upon Hindenburg's death the next year, Hitler became *Führer* ("leader"), with dictatorial powers. He immediately began persecuting Jews and by the late 1930s was annexing territory. When his troops attacked Poland in 1939, Britain and France declared war. Nazi death camps murdered 6 million Jews; altogether, the war killed over 45 million. Germany surrendered in 1945 and was divided by the victorious allies into the Federal Republic of Germany (West Germany), controlled by the United States, France, and Britain, and the German Democratic Republic (East Germany), controlled by the Soviet Union.

The Federal Republic's Bundeswehr, referred to by Grass, comes from *bund* (federal) and *wehr* (defense). Pershing missiles, supplied by the United States to Germany, are part of the North Atlantic Treaty Organization's (NATO) European defense; they caused bitter controversy when the German government accepted them. As this book goes to press, it appears likely that Grass will get his wish: Germany's Pershing missiles are targeted for removal as part of a U.S.-Soviet arms control agreement.

"Resistance" was translated from the German by Michael Hofmann.

They are here: against the wishes of the majority of the people, by the wishes of a parliamentary majority. They are referred to as weapons, but they are instruments of genocide. They are here ostensibly for our security, but they increase the risk of a nuclear holocaust in Europe. Though they are stationed here, decisions regarding their deployment and possible use are taken far away, where we have no say. They are supposed to strengthen our defenses, but they have been designed for an aggressive first strike. Their presence here is explained by the need to "close the gap," but the deployment of corresponding systems in the other Germany and in Czechoslovakia is also called "closing the gap"; so that on both sides the "gap" will go on being "closed" — far beyond the threshold of madness already. They are called medium-range missiles. Representative of all the other accumulated power of destruction, they give a picture of the condition of mankind as it spends billions on preparing an end for itself; the deadly logic of self-destruction spares no expense.

I am not sure if this terminal development can still be arrested. After last November's debate in the *Bundestag*, the Lower House of the German Parliament, which was concerned less with the criminal dangers of the new missile systems than with "loyalty to NATO" and keeping our word to the United States, my doubts hardened into fear: the people governing us are fools. Overtaxed by the gritty day-to-day of politics, they take refuge in a majority decision that hands the responsibility for life and death to our major allies, and commits us to silence and acquiescence. The stance of this parliamentary majority is one that I can only condemn as pathetic or insane.

They clearly don't know what they're doing. Accustomed only to following matters of detail, they have become criminals acting out of conviction. And when they cry, "There is a price to pay for freedom!" then one begins to worry seriously about both freedom and its price.

But who can protect us from those who will protect freedom to death?   4
How can a process be arrested, when its terminal tendency appears virtually preordained? Isn't it already apparent how the peace movement is slowing down, flagging, impotent? Do we still have the exact words to express our horror? Are we not faced daily with the cynicism (and the submissive kowtowing to government statements) of the press and television which credit the government's security forces for the failure of the peace movement and the nonappearance of the promised "hot autumn" of protest? And medium-range missiles? Nuclear warheads? They're all old news — fish-and-chip paper, in the journalists' slang. But is it true?

Are we learning to live with them, as we've learned to live with the poison gas stockpiled in the Pfälzer Wald, and with over five thousand tactical nuclear weapons that have been on West German soil for years? And — I ask myself — am I not sated too by all these protests, by the almost identical appeals, the recurring lists of the names of protesting public figures — my own name always among them?

For that reason, because exhaustion and weariness were to be anticipated, our motto must now be "Learning to Resist." There are people — the Poles, for instance — who don't need to learn, because their history is a history of resistance. But the Germans have time and again failed to resist. German history is a history of the failure to resist. But can it be learned? Can it be drummed into people through lessons? Do we in Germany — since we are so helplessly smitten with pedagogy — have to make resistance a special subject?

It cannot simply be prescribed. But whoever sees nonviolent resistance as the only way of opposing the prevailing insanity (which even includes genocide in its calculations of nuclear fatalities), will decide on that course for himself, and carry it out himself. Like me too. That is why I must talk about myself and my own experience, my hopes and disappointments, and insights which I can no longer evade.

In the summer of 1944, aged sixteen, I became a soldier. I arrived at the barracks in shorts, with a cardboard suitcase. When my training was completed — seventeen by now — I was sent to the Eastern Front. After several days of seemingly pointless to-ing and fro-ing, and after we had finally withdrawn, the whole company came under fire from a battery of Soviet rockets (known as "Stalin's organ pipes"). The company — consisting only of jeeps, small tanks, and light artillery — had retreated to a forest of young trees. The Soviet barrage lasted for about three minutes. When it was over, half the company had been killed or maimed. Most of the dead and injured were seventeen, like myself.

Ever since, I've known what fear is. Ever since, I've known that it's only by chance that I am alive. Ever since, any war has appeared conceivable to me. And after the war, my generation found it easy to say the imploring words, "No more war!" 8

But this "No more war!" — this attitude of include-me-out — wasn't enough. The decision to rearm was taken, first in the Federal Republic, then in the German Democratic Republic, despite the voices of opposition, despite the lessons of history. The division of the country was deepened as the West German Army over here, the Federal Defense, and the "The People's Army" over there, were incorporated into the military alliances of the two great power blocs. This reality is part of the postwar history of both German states. In each case, it was justified by the constitutional imperative of national self-defense. (Article 26, paragraph 1 of the *Grundgesetz* forbids a war of aggression and any preparation towards such a war.) Many citizens who had spoken out against rearmament accepted the Federal Defense and the membership of NATO, because they believed the assurances that the weapon systems, the army maneuvers and the war strategies would be exclusively for the purpose of defense. I too was satisfied with such explanations, and put my hopes in disarmament and a reduction of tension.

Only now, too late, and to my horror, do I realize that I should have been alerted — and reminded of Orwell's "Newspeak" — by the strategical "concepts" of the military: like that of so-called "forward defense." But it was only when it became transparently clear that the United States and NATO claimed the right to an atomic "first strike" that I understood the deception, and reverted to my original "No": "no more war!"

The Pershing II nuclear missile is a first strike weapon. Accepted by the West German government (as a member of NATO), the new missile transforms the theoretical basis of the Federal Defense. It no longer serves to protect us, as a defense; it has been harnessed to a strategy of aggression. We are therefore talking about a breach of the Constitution. Since the deployment of Pershing IIs began, the Federal Defense is no longer engaged in defensive duties; transgressing Article 26 of the *Grundgesetz*, it is outside the law. We are obliged by the Constitution to resist this perversion.

Not indiscriminately, though. Without violence. It is not blanket 12 opposition but specific and targeted resistance that is needed. This must be directed against a Federal Defense which has been cheated of its defensive mission: because it has been put in the service of NATO's first strike strategy, because the soldiers of the Bundeswehr are being improperly used, because they are already being discounted as casualties in the Pentagon's war-offensive plans.

In the same way thousands of doctors refuse to prepare emergency services in readiness for a nuclear war, so in future I shall practice what is termed "demoralizing the armed forces." I will call on my sons and their friends to refuse to do their military service. In my writing and my speeches, I will introduce and reiterate, unambivalently, the same unwillingness to support an unconstitutional force. In answer to questions from foreign journalists, I will henceforth deny West Germany's commitment to peace, because, through the NATO twin-track decision, through the deployment of first strike weapons, it has again become possible that for the third and last time, war can be started from Germany.

This is the resistance I intend to learn. I will resist, and encourage others to resist, until West Germany is free from nuclear weapons — both tactical and strategic — and free from agents of chemical and bacteriological warfare. Only in this way is it possible for me, and for us, to help the Federal Defense to return to its constitutional duty, exclusively to defend West Germany. It is not new weapons and additional nuclear warheads that we need, but radical democrats, who will stand by West Germany's Constitution, and, still more, who will protect this Constitution from the idiocy of our rulers.

Twice now, writers from the two Germanies have met, first in East Berlin, then in West Berlin. The meetings were heated, because the mania for armaments has gripped both East and West, occupying minds and militarizing thought. But all of us realized that SS 20s and Pershing II missiles are equally horrifying. In the end our talks failed because each side expected the other to take the first step out of the vicious circle. Nevertheless, the Academy of Arts in Berlin sent out invitations for a third meeting, this time in Heilbronn, one of the sites of this accursed development. The writers from the German Democratic Republic did not show up; some didn't want to, others were not allowed to. For the present, then, we will have to learn how to resist without them.

EXPLORATIONS

1. What is Grass's position on Germany's acceptance, as a NATO member, of American Pershing II nuclear missiles on its soil? What was his position on Germany's acceptance of NATO weapons before the Pershing II? Why has he changed his mind?

2. What do the terms *genocide* and *holocaust* mean with regard to World War II? What do they mean in the present context? What impact does Grass achieve by using those terms in his opening paragraph?

3. A Latin expression that has persisted into our century is *Quis custodiet ipsos custodes?* — "Who will keep the keepers themselves?" or "Who's guarding the guards?" In what form does Grass present this question? What answer does he suggest?

CONNECTIONS

1. Both Grass and Chinua Achebe write about the loss of control, ceding one's fate to distant officials who seem perilously careless of it. How does Grass's response to his political impotence differ from Jonathan Iwegbu's? What do you think are the reasons for the difference?

2. Compare and contrast Grass's attitude toward violence with that of Frank O'Connor narrator in "Guests of the Nation." How are they different, and why? How are they alike, and why?

3. Grass writes: "Ever since, I've known what fear is. Ever since, I've known that it's only by chance that I am alive. Ever since, any war has appeared conceivable to me." What is the cause for each of these effects? What train of thought links this sequence of statements? What thesis does Grass's essay share with Czeslaw Milosz's "American Ignorance of War"?

ELABORATIONS

1. Grass's essay presents a fairly wide range of defense strategies West Germany might choose against nuclear war. What strategy falls at each end of the spectrum? What other options lie in between? Write an essay identifying and evaluating at least three positions West Germany could take. What are the advantages and disadvantages of each one? Which choice do you think is most advisable, and why?

2. In "Resistance," Grass speaks of the "exhaustion and weariness" brought on by too many almost-identical protests against nuclear weapons. In "The Afghan Resistance," Doris Lessing speaks of Westerners' "compassion fatigue" from hearing too many foreign horror stories. Write your own essay explaining why people's commitment to acting on their beliefs often weakens over time. Should activists like Grass and Lessing accept this erosion of support as inevitable or try to arrest it? What steps — if any — can and should be taken?

PART SEVEN

WE ARE ALL
FOREIGNERS

◇◆◇◆◇

Paul Harrison, *The Westernization of the World*

V. S. Naipaul, *Entering the New World* (IVORY COAST)

Edward T. Hall, *Proxemics in the Arab World* (ARAB WORLD)

Kate Millett, *Arriving in Tehran* (IRAN)

Guan Keguang, *A Chinese Reporter on Cape Cod*
(CHINA/UNITED STATES)

Orville Schell, *Shanghai* (CHINA)

Andrea Lee, *The Beriozka* (SOVIET UNION)

David K. Shipler, *Western Things* (SOVIET UNION)

Stanisław Lem, *Being Inc.* (POLAND/UNITED STATES)

"OH, EAST IS EAST, AND WEST IS WEST, AND NEVER THE TWAIN SHALL meet," wrote Rudyard Kipling in 1889. *East* for Kipling and his fellow Britons meant colonies such as India, Malaya, and Hong Kong. *West* was home — Europe, England, the hub of civilization.

Now, most European colonies are independent nations. Indeed, one former colony — the United States — has come to epitomize the West. As travel shrinks the globe, Westerners increasingly realize that, far from holding a monopoly on civilization, we can learn much from other cultures.

Yet when we encounter foreign customs and ideas, our first response may not be appreciation but alienation. In "Woman as Other" (p. 241), Simone de Beauvoir notes: "The native traveling abroad is shocked to find himself in turn regarded as a 'stranger' by the natives of neighboring countries." What causes this us-them reaction? Is it useful or dangerous?

In the twentieth-century global village, where our fate is inseparable from our neighbors', we do well to recognize that our culture has no innate moral superiority to theirs. To most of the world's people, we — not they — are the foreigners.

Part Seven looks at foreignness by comparing the comments of Americans and Europeans abroad with foreigners' views of the West. We begin with challenging observations by British writer Paul Harrison in "The Westernization of the World." V. S. Naipaul, a native of Trinidad, watches the balance tilt between the Ivory Coast's African heritage and French colonial legacy in "Entering the New World." Edward T. Hall, in "Proxemics in the Arab World," explains why Arabs and Americans consider each other pushy. American feminist Kate Millett's "Arriving in Tehran" tells of her reactions to Iran, where young Islamic soldiers brandish machine guns beside a Sheraton Hotel pool. "A Chinese Reporter on Cape Cod" describes Guan Keguang's surprise at the value placed by U.S. employers on being "aggressive, talented, and hungry." American journalist Orville Schell, in "Shanghai," is equally bemused by two young Chinese motorcyclists' obsession with Western clothes, cars, and cigarettes. As a student in the Soviet Union, Andrea Lee has mixed feelings about using her American passport as a ticket to scarce luxuries in "The Beriozka." David K. Shipler interprets the Soviets' fascination with "Western Things" as nonpolitical: The Russians don't envy our democracy, only our Levis and stereos. A final veiled comment from behind the Iron Curtain is offered by Polish writer Stanisław Lem in "Being Inc.," a review of an imaginary American science fiction novel in which all-powerful corporations arrange every citizen's life from birth to death as he or she wishes. ❖

PAUL HARRISON

The Westernization
of the World

Paul Harrison is a free-lance writer and journalist based in London. He has traveled widely in Asia, Africa, and Latin America, visiting twenty-eight developing countries. He has contributed frequently to the *Guardian, New Society,* and *New Scientist,* and to publications of major United Nations agencies, such as the World Health Organization, the Food and Agriculture Organization, UNICEF, and the International Labor Organization. He is a contributor to *Encyclopaedia Britannica.* Harrison attended Manchester Grammar School and took master's degrees at Cambridge University and the London School of Economics. His interest in the Third World began in 1968 when he was lecturing in French at the University of Ife, Nigeria. He is married with two children.

"The Westernization of the World" comes from Harrison's 1981 book *Inside the Third World,* as do these biographical notes. Harrison based his book on research and travel between 1975 and 1980, visiting Sri Lanka, Upper Volta and the Ivory Coast, Colombia and Peru, Brazil, Indonesia and Singapore, India, Bangladesh, and Kenya. "In some ways it was a mad enterprise to attempt to cover so much ground," he admits. However, "The underdevelopment of countries and of human beings cannot be compartmentalized if it is to be fully grasped. It is a total situation, in which every element plays a part."

Like many commentators, Harrison refers to underdeveloped countries and their citizens collectively as the Third World. The term has more than one definition: nations in Africa, Asia, and Latin America that are not heavily industrialized and have a low standard of living; nations that are not aligned with either the Communist or the non-Communist bloc. Shiva Naipaul (see p. 337) writes: "Whatever the confusions, we do, I believe, have a picture of the exemplary Third World denizen: he lives a hand-to-mouth existence, he is indifferent to the power struggles of the mighty ones, and he is dark-skinned." Naipaul adds, "To blandly subsume, say, Ethiopia, India, and Brazil under the one banner of Third Worldhood is as absurd and as denigrating as the old assertion that all Chinese look alike." Still, keeping in mind the dangers noted by Simone de Beauvoir of dividing humanity into "us" and "them" (see p. 241), we can use the concept of the Third World to examine, as Harrison does, certain tendencies shared by nations that are otherwise dissimilar.

The bourgeoisie has, through its exploitation of the world market, given a cosmopolitan character to production and consumption in every country.

— Karl Marx

In Singapore, Peking opera still lives, in the back streets. On Boat Quay, where great barges moor to unload rice from Thailand, raw rubber from Malaysia, or timber from Sumatra, I watched a troupe of traveling actors throw up a canvas-and-wood booth stage, paint on their white faces and lozenge eyes, and don their resplendent vermilion, ultramarine, and gold robes. Then, to raptured audiences of bent old women and little children with perfect circle faces, they enacted tales of feudal princes and magic birds and wars and tragic love affairs, sweeping their sleeves and singing in strange metallic voices.

The performance had been paid for by a local cultural society as part of a religious festival. A purple cloth temple had been erected on the quayside, painted papier-mâché sculptures were burning down like giant joss sticks, and middle-aged men were sharing out gifts to be distributed among members' families: red buckets, roast ducks, candies, and moon cakes. The son of the organizer, a fashionable young man in Italian shirt and gold-rimmed glasses, was looking on with amused benevolence. I asked him why only old people and children were watching the show.

"Young people don't like these operas," he said. "They are too old-fashioned. We would prefer to see a high-quality Western variety show, something like that."

He spoke for a whole generation. Go to almost any village in the   4
Third World and you will find youths who scorn traditional dress and sport denims and T-shirts. Go into any bank and the tellers will be dressed as would their European counterparts; at night the manager will climb into his car and go home to watch TV in a home that would not stick out on a European or North American estate. Every capital city in the world is getting to look like every other; it is Marshall McLuhan's global village, but the style is exclusively Western. And not just in consumer fashions: the mimicry extends to architecture, industrial technology, approaches to health care, education, and housing.

To the ethnocentric Westerner or the Westernized local, that may seem the most natural thing in the world. That is modern life, they might think. That is the way it will all be one day. That is what development and economic growth are all about.

Yet the dispassionate observer can only be puzzled by this growing world uniformity. Surely one should expect more diversity, more indigenous styles and models of development? Why is almost everyone following virtually the same European road? The Third World's obsession with the Western way of life has perverted development and is rapidly destroying good and bad in traditional cultures, flinging the baby out with the bathwater. It is the most totally pervasive example of what historians call cultural diffusion in the history of mankind.

Its origins, of course, lie in the colonial experience. European rule was something quite different from the general run of conquests. Previous invaders more often than not settled down in their new territories, interbred, and assimilated a good deal of local culture. Not so the Europeans. Some, like the Iberians or the Dutch, were not averse to cohabitation with native women: unlike the British, they seemed free of purely racial prejudice. But all the Europeans suffered from the same cultural arrogance. Perhaps it is the peculiar self-righteousness of Pauline Christianity that accounts for this trait. Whatever the cause, never a doubt entered their minds that native cultures could be in any way, materially, morally, or spiritually, superior to their own, and that the supposedly benighted inhabitants of the darker continents needed enlightening.

And so there grew up, alongside political and economic imperialism,   8
that more insidious form of control — cultural imperialism. It conquered not just the bodies, but the souls of its victims, turning them into willing accomplices.

Cultural imperialism began its conquest of the Third World with the indoctrination of an elite of local collaborators. The missionary schools sought to produce converts to Christianity who would go out and proselytize among their own people, helping to eradicate traditional culture. Later the government schools aimed to turn out a class of junior bureaucrats and lower military officers who would help to exploit and repress their own people. The British were subtle about this, since they wanted the natives, even the Anglicized among them, to keep their distance. The French, and the Portuguese in Africa, explicitly aimed at the "assimilation" of gifted natives, by which was meant their metamorphosis into model Frenchmen and Lusitanians, distinguishable only by the tint of their skin.

The second channel of transmission was more indirect and voluntary. It worked by what sociologists call reference-group behavior, found when someone copies the habits and life-style of a social group he wishes to belong to, or to be classed with, and abandons those of his own group. This happened in the West when the new rich of early commerce and industry aped the nobility they secretly aspired to join. Not surprisingly the social climbers in the colonies started to mimic their conquerors. The returned slaves who carried the first wave of Westernization in West Africa wore black woolen suits and starched collars in the heat of the dry season. The new officer corps of India were molded into what the Indian writer Nirad Chaudhuri has called "imitation, polo-playing English sub-alterns," complete with waxed mustaches and peacock chests. The elite of Indians, adding their own caste-consciousness to the class-consciousness of their rulers, became more British than the British (and still are).

There was another psychological motive for adopting Western ways, deriving from the arrogance and haughtiness of the colonialists. As the Martiniquan political philosopher, Frantz Fanon, remarked, colonial rule was an experience in racial humiliation. Practically every leader of a newly independent state could recall some experience such as being turned out of a club or manhandled on the street by whites, often of low status. The local elite were made to feel ashamed of their color and of their culture. "I begin to suffer from not being a white man," Fanon wrote, "to the degree that the white man imposes discrimination on me, makes me a colonized native, robs me of all worth, all individuality. . . . Then I will quite simply try to make myself white: that is, I will compel the white man to acknowledge that I am human." To this complex Fanon attributes the colonized natives' constant preoccupation with attracting the attention of the white man, becoming powerful like the white man, proving at all costs that blacks too can be civilized. Given the racism and culturism of the whites, this could only be done by succeeding in their terms, and by adopting their ways.

This desire to prove equality surely helps to explain why Ghana's   12
Nkrumah built the huge stadium and triumphal arch of Black Star Square in Accra. Why the tiny native village of Ivory Coast president Houphouët-Boigny has been graced with a four-lane motorway starting and ending nowhere, a five-star hotel and ultramodern conference center. Why Sukarno transformed Indonesia's capital, Jakarta, into an exercise in gigantism, scarred with six-lane highways and neofascist monuments in the most hideous taste. The aim was not only to show the old imperialists, but to impress other Third World leaders in the only way everyone would recognize: the Western way.

The influence of Western life-styles spread even to those few nations who escaped the colonial yoke. By the end of the nineteenth century, the elites of the entire non-Western world were taking Europe as their reference group. The progress of the virus can be followed visibly in a room of Topkapi, the Ottoman palace in Istanbul, where a sequence of showcases display the costumes worn by each successive sultan. They begin with kaftans and turbans. Slowly elements of Western military uniform creep in, until the last sultans are decked out in brocade, epaulettes, and cocked hats.

The root of the problem with nations that were never colonized, like Turkey, China, and Japan, was probably their consciousness of Western military superiority. The beating of these three powerful nations at the hands of the West was a humiliating, traumatic experience. For China and Japan, the encounter with the advanced military technology of the industrialized nations was as terrifying as an invasion of extraterrestrials. Europe's earlier discovery of the rest of the world had delivered a mild culture shock to her ethnocentric attitudes. The Orient's contact with Europe shook nations to the foundations, calling into question the roots of their civilizations and all the assumptions and institutions on which their lives were based.

In all three nations groups of Young Turks grew up, believing that their countries could successfully take on the West only if they adopted Western culture, institutions, and even clothing, for all these ingredients were somehow involved in the production of Western technology. As early as the 1840s, Chinese intellectuals were beginning to modify the ancient view that China was in all respects the greatest civilization in the world. The administrator Wei Yüan urged his countrymen to "learn the superior technology of the barbarians in order to control them." But the required changes could not be confined to the technical realm. Effectiveness in technology is the outcome of an entire social system. "Since we were knocked out by cannon balls," wrote M. Chiang, "naturally we became interested in them, thinking that by learning to make them we could strike back. From studying cannon balls we came to mechanical inventions which in turn lead to political reforms, which lead us again to the political philosophies of the West." The republican revolution of 1911 attempted to modernize China, but her subjection to the West continued until another Young Turk, Mao Tse-tung, applied that alternative brand of Westernization: communism, though in a unique adaptation.

The Japanese were forced to open their border to Western goods in 1853, after a couple of centuries of total isolation. They had to rethink fast in order to survive. From 1867, the Meiji rulers Westernized Japan with astonishing speed, adopting Western science, technology, and even manners: short haircuts became the rule, ballroom dancing caught on, 16 and *moningku* with *haikara* (morning coats and high collars) were worn. The transformation was so successful that by the 1970s the Japanese were trouncing the West at its own game. But they had won their economic independence at the cost of losing their cultural autonomy.

Turkey, defeated in the First World War, her immense empire in fragments, set about transforming herself under that compulsive and ruthless Westernizer, Kemal Atatürk. The Arabic script was abolished and replaced with the Roman alphabet. Kemal's strange exploits as a hatter will probably stand as the symbol of Westernization carried to absurd lengths. His biographer, Lord Kinross, relates that while traveling in the West as a young man, the future president had smarted under Western insults and condescension about the Turkish national hat, the fez. Later, he made the wearing of the fez a criminal offense. "The people of the Turkish republic," he said in a speech launching the new policy, "must prove that they are civilized and advanced persons in their outward respect also. . . . A civilized, international dress is worthy and appropriate for our nation and we will wear it. Boots or shoes on our feet, trousers on our legs, shirt and tie, jacket and waistcoat — and, of course, to complete these, a cover with a brim on our heads. I want to make this clear. This head covering is called a hat."

EXPLORATIONS

1. What general cause, and what three specific channels, does Harrison cite as responsible for the Third World's Westernization? What differences between Western newcomers and Third World natives seem to have most strongly affected relations between them?

2. "By the end of the nineteenth century," writes Harrison, "the elites of the entire non-Western world were taking Europe as their reference group." How does he explain the initial westward tilt of countries that were never colonized? What explanation does he give, or hint at, for their present continuing interest in Western ways?

3. Early in his essay Harrison asks the central question: "Why is almost everyone following virtually the same European road?" What are the characteristics of this "European road"? What are the origins of the specific examples the author cites?

4. What types of evidence does Harrison present for his assumptions about Western homogeneity? Do you think his evidence justifies his conclusions? Why or why not?

CONNECTIONS

1. In paragraphs 11–12 Harrison proposes an explanation for the sort of excess that David Lamb describes in "The New African Chiefs" (p. 414). What similar ideas appear in both essays? In what respects (if any) do these two authors disagree? After reading both selections, what recommendations would you make to a U.S. ambassador newly assigned to one of the countries mentioned by Lamb and Harrison?

2. Look back at Shiva Naipaul's "The Palmers" (p. 337). Which of Harrison's statements apply to Mr. and Mrs. Palmer? What evidence in Naipaul's essay suggests that black as well as white Kenyans are imitating Western customs and values? How do the two groups' purposes differ?

3. What Western influences on the Third World appear in Jill Gay's "Patriotic Prostitutes" (p. 383)? Which of the explanations cited by Harrison (if any) suggests why and how Southeast Asian governments came to support prostitution? What additional explanation(s) does Gay offer for Westernization in this part of the Third World?

4. In paragraph 9 Harrison mentions Christian missionary schools as one means by which "cultural imperialism began its conquest of the Third World." What does Ezekiel Mphahlele have to say about European Christianity's influence on Africa in "Tradition and the African Writer" (p. 344)? What evidence for or against Harrison's statements appears in Wole Soyinka's "Nigerian Childhood" (p. 66)?

ELABORATIONS

1. In "Woman as Other" (p. 241), Simone de Beauvoir analyzes men's view of women in terms that could also apply to the West's view of the Third World. Write an essay using de Beauvoir's ideas about the Self and the Other to interpret and expand on Harrison's observations. Illustrate your statements with examples drawn from your reading elsewhere in this book.

2. Harrison focuses on Westernization in non-Western countries. What explanation (if any) does he offer for the spread of a single cultural trend all over Europe and North America? On the basis of Harrison's theories, plus evidence from other selections you have read, write an essay identifying causes and effects behind the West's homogeneity.

V. S. NAIPAUL

Entering the New World

V. S. Naipaul, like his brother Shiva (see p. 337), was born in Trinidad of Indian descent but has lived most of his life in England. Feeling stifled on his small native island, which lies off the coast of Venezuela and constitutes half the Republic of Trinidad and Tobago, Naipaul vowed to escape. In 1950, at the age of eighteen, he left for Oxford University on a government scholarship. At twenty-one he became a broadcaster for the Caribbean Service of the British Broadcasting Company (BBC). He wrote three novels, two of which were in print by the time he was twenty-six. At twenty-nine he published what is widely considered his masterpiece, *A House for Mr. Biswas.* Since then Naipaul has lived in India, Africa, South America, and the Middle East as well as England. He has written twenty books, the majority nonfiction, and won both critical praise and a number of literary awards, including England's prestigious Booker Prize. Naipaul currently lives with his wife, Patricia Hale, whom he met at Oxford, and writes alone in a Wiltshire cottage. "Entering the New World" comes from "The Crocodiles of Yamoussoukro," a narrative about his travels in the Ivory Coast, published as part of his 1984 book *Finding the Center.*

The Ivory Coast (République de la Côte d'Ivoire) lies almost directly across the Atlantic Ocean from Trinidad, between Liberia and Ghana on Africa's Gulf of Guinea. A former French colony, it gained independence in 1960. Economic (particularly agricultural) diversification, foreign investment, and close ties to France have helped make the Ivory Coast the most prosperous of tropical African nations. Naipaul's meeting with Ebony takes place in the capital city — then Abidjan, now Yamoussoukro.

"Volta" is Upper Volta, which also became independent of France in 1960; its name was changed to Burkina Faso in 1984. Landlocked in the southwest African savannah north of the Ivory Coast, Burkina Faso has a largely agricultural economy but only 10 percent arable land; several hundred thousand of its farm workers migrate every year to the Ivory Coast and Ghana. Benin — another French colony until 1960 — lies east of the Ivory Coast beyond Ghana and Togo.

In the morning I was telephoned from the hotel lobby by a man called Ebony. He said he had heard from Busby that a writer was in Abidjan, and he had come to meet this writer. He, Ebony, was himself a poet.

I went down to see him. He was a cheerful young man of regal appearance, with the face of a Benin bronze, and he was regally attired, with a brightly patterned skullcap and a rich African tunic. He said the skullcap and tunic were from Volta. His family employed laborers from Volta and he had always, even as a child, liked their clothes.

He had been a journalist, he said, but he had given it up, because in the Ivory Coast journalism was like smoking: it could damage your health. He liked the joke; he made it twice. But he was vague about the journalism he had done. He said he was now a government servant, in the department of the environment. He had written a paper on things that might be done environmentally in the Ivory Coast. But after twelve months he had heard nothing about his paper. So now he just went to the office and from time to time he wrote poetry.

He said, "I have a theory about African administrations. But it is 4 difficult and will take too long to tell you."

He had come to see me — and the hotel was a good way out of the town — because he was sociable; because he wanted to practice his English; and because, as a poet and intellectual, he wanted to try out his ideas.

I offered coffee. He offered me a cola nut, the African token of friendship. I nibbled at my grubby, purple-skinned nut: bitter. He chewed his zestfully, giving little dry spits of chewed husk to his left and right, and then at the end of his chew taking out the remainder of the husk with his fingers and placing it on the ashtray.

He asked why I had come to the Ivory Coast. I said because it was successful and French.

He said, "Charlemagne wasn't my ancestor."   8

I felt it had been said before, and not only by Ebony. He ran on to another idea. "The French run countries like pigsties. They believe that the sole purpose of men is to eat, to go to the toilet, and to sleep." So the French colonialists created bourgeois people. Bourgeois? "The bourgeois want peace, order. The bourgeois can fit into any political system, once they have peace. On the other hand, the British colonialists created entrepreneurs." Entrepreneurs? "Entrepreneurs want to change things." Entrepreneurs were revolutionaries.

Antithesis, balance: the beauty rather than the validity of a thought: I thought I could detect his French training. I began to examine his ideas of the bourgeois and the entrepreneur, but he didn't encourage me. He said, playfully, it was only an idea.

Starting on another cola nut — he had a handful in his tunic pocket — he said, "Africans live at peace with nature. Europeans want to conquer or dominate nature."

That was familiar to me. I had heard similar words from young Muslim   12
fundamentalists in Malaysia: ecological, Western romance bouncing back like a corroborating radio signal from remote, inactive worlds. But that again was an idea Ebony didn't want to stay with.

Ebony said, "I saw white men for the first time when I was fourteen or fifteen, when I went to school. That was the first time I discovered the idea of racial superiority. African children are trained not to look elders in the eye. It is disrespectful. At school the French teachers took this to be a sign of African hypocrisy."

What was the point of this story?

Ebony said, "So I thought my French teachers inferior."

I felt this racial story, with its triumphant twist, had previously had a   16
sympathetic foreign listener. And it turned out that there was a Scandinavian woman journalist who had made a great hit with Ebony. She was now in Spain and Ebony earnestly asked me — two or three times — to look her up and pass on his regards.

Ebony said, "When my father sent me to the school, do you know what he said? He said, 'Remember. I am not sending you to the school to be a white man or a Frenchman. I am sending you to enter the new world, that's all.'"

I felt that in his own eyes Ebony had done that. . . . Ebony said he had no money, no car. The salary he got from the government was less than the rent he paid. He had come to the hotel on his bicycle. But I thought he was relaxed, a whole man. He knew where he was, how he had got there, and he liked the novelty of what he saw. There was no true anxiety behind his scattered ideas. At any rate he was less anxious than a romantic or concerned outsider might have wished him to be. Ideas about Africa, words, poetry, meeting foreigners — all this was part of his relishing of life, part of his French-inspired role as intellectual, part of the new world he had happily entered.

He went away on his bicycle, and I took a taxi later to a beach restaurant at the other end of the city, beyond the industrial and port area. The lunch there, and the French style of the place, were usually worth the fare and the journey in the midday heat through the traffic and the crowds. But today it wasn't so.

It was more than a matter of an off day. The waiters, impeccable the 20 day before, were casual, vacant. There were long delays, mistakes, some of the portions were absurdly small; the bill, when it came, was wrong. Someone was missing, perhaps the French or European manager. And with him more than good service had gone: the whole restaurant idea had vanished. An elaborate organization had collapsed. The waiters — Ivorian: these jobs were lucrative — seemed to have forgotten, from one day to the next, why they were doing what they did. And their faces seemed to have altered as well. They were not waiters now, in spite of their flowered tunics. Their faces and manners radiated various degrees of tribal authority. I saw them as men of weight in the village: witch doctors, herbalists, men who perhaps put on masks and did the sacred dances. The true life was there, in the mysteries of the village. The restaurant, with its false, arbitrary ritual, was the charade: I half began to see it so.

Ebony had been told by his father: "I am not sending you to the school to become a white man. I am sending you to enter the new world."

The new world existed in the minds of other men. Remove those men, and their ideas — which after all had no finality — would disappear. Skills could be taught. What was fragile — to men whose complete, real life lay in another realm of the spirit — was faith in the new world.

EXPLORATIONS

1. "The new world existed in the minds of other men," writes Naipaul. "Remove those men, and their ideas — which after all had no finality — would disappear." What incidents during the author's lunch at a "French" restaurant trigger this conclusion? What assumption does Naipaul make about the restaurant to explain the incidents? On what evidence does he base that assumption?

2. What opinion does Ebony express of the European colonial influence in Africa? What statements reveal his opinion? What are the apparent sources of his views?

3. What statements by Naipaul encourage us as readers to focus on the style rather than the content of Ebony's remarks? What impression of Ebony does Naipaul give us in the first half of his essay? How do you think he means our impression to change in the second half?

CONNECTIONS

1. What statements by Paul Harrison in "The Westernization of the World" are echoed by Naipaul and Ebony? How does Naipaul's assessment of Western influence on the Third World differ from Harrison's?

2. Like Ezekiel Mphahlele in "Tradition and the African Writer" (p. 344), Naipaul investigates the impact of a dual heritage on an African writer. What evidence in "Entering the New World" suggests that Ebony has faced the same conflict between native and European influences as Mphahlele? How does Naipaul suggest that Ebony has (or has not) resolved his dilemma?

3. "Entering the New World," Mphahlele's "Tradition and the African Writer" (p. 344), Wole Soyinka's "Nigerian Childhood" (p. 66), and Nadine Gordimer's "Africa Emergent" (p. 465) all depict Africans living in former European colonies. According to these writers, what qualities make up a traditional African consciousness or character? What qualities were brought into Africa by European colonizers?

4. Look back at Shiva Naipaul's "The Palmers" (p. 337). What statements by and about Mr. and Mrs. Palmer indicate that they, like V. S. Naipaul, perceive the European "new world" in Africa as fragile and impermanent? What other evidence in "The Palmers" supports or conflicts with this idea?

ELABORATIONS

1. Reread Ebony's comments in paragraph 9 on French versus British colonies. On the basis of the selections you have read in this book, do you agree with Ebony that "the British colonialists created entrepreneurs"? Choosing examples from Australia, India, Kenya, Malaysia, Nigeria, South Africa, and any other countries you think are relevant, write an essay either supporting or refuting Ebony's statements about British colonies.

2. Have you ever eaten in a restaurant, or patronized a store, where you unexpectedly became aware of the "real" life of someone waiting on you? Have you ever held a job, attended a class, or participated in a social function where an unplanned event shattered the group's customary identity? Write an essay using your experience to illustrate Naipaul's comments about the fragility of worlds that exist mainly in someone's mind.

EDWARD T. HALL

Proxemics in the Arab World

Edward T. Hall was born in Webster Groves, Missouri, in 1914. His affinity for travel began early: His education took him from Pomona College to Columbia University, and he has taught at institutions from the University of Denver to Harvard Business School as well as worked for the U.S. State Department. Hall's special interest is proxemics, the study of people's responses to spatial relationships. He has done anthropological fieldwork in Micronesia, the southwestern United States, and Europe. "Proxemics in the Arab World" comes from his book *The Hidden Dimension* (1966).

The term *Arab* generally refers to any of the Semitic peoples living in Arabia, the peninsula between Africa and the Asian continent, or in northern Africa (see p. 256). The Arab League, formed in 1945, overlaps these geographic boundaries: Egypt, Iraq, Jordan, Lebanon, Saudi Arabia, and Syria were founding members, and Algeria, Kuwait, Libya, Morocco, Sudan, Tunisia, and Yemen have joined since. (Yemen, currently divided into the northern Yemen Arab Republic and the southern People's Democratic Republic of Yemen, signed a league-sponsored unification agreement in 1979.) Although all the Arab countries are predominantly Islamic, not all Islamic countries are Arab; noteworthy exceptions include Turkey (see p. 279), Pakistan (see p. 267), Afghanistan (see p. 519), and Iran (see pp. 76 and 621).

In spite of over two thousand years of contact, Westerners and Arabs still do not understand each other. Proxemic research reveals some insights into this difficulty. Americans in the Middle East are immediately struck by two conflicting sensations. In public they are compressed and overwhelmed by smells, crowding, and high noise levels; in Arab homes Americans are apt to rattle around, feeling exposed and often somewhat inadequate because of too much space! (The Arab houses and apartments of the middle and upper classes which Americans stationed abroad commonly occupy are much larger than the dwellings such Americans usually inhabit.) Both the high sensory stimulation which is experienced in public places and the basic insecurity which comes from being in a dwelling that is too large provide Americans with an introduction to the sensory world of the Arab.

Pushing and shoving in public places is characteristic of Middle Eastern culture. Yet it is not entirely what Americans think it is (being pushy and rude) but stems from a different set of assumptions concerning not only the relations between people but how one experiences the body as well. Paradoxically, Arabs consider northern Europeans and Americans pushy, too. This was very puzzling to me when I started investigating these two views. How could Americans who stand aside and avoid touching be considered pushy? I used to ask Arabs to explain this paradox. None of my subjects was able to tell me specifically what particulars of American behavior were responsible, yet they all agreed that the impression was widespread among Arabs. After repeated unsuccessful attempts to gain insight into the cognitive world of the Arab on this particular point, I filed it away as a question that only time would answer. When the answer came, it was because of a seemingly inconsequential annoyance.

While waiting for a friend in a Washington, D.C., hotel lobby and wanting to be both visible and alone, I had seated myself in a solitary chair outside the normal stream of traffic. In such a setting most Americans follow a rule, which is all the more binding because we seldom think about it, that can be stated as follows: as soon as a person stops or is seated in a public place, there balloons around him a small sphere of privacy which is considered inviolate. The size of the sphere varies with the degree of crowding, the age, sex, and the importance of the person, as well as the general surroundings. Anyone who enters this zone and stays there is intruding. In fact, a stranger who intrudes, even for a specific purpose, acknowledges the fact that he has intruded by beginning his request with "Pardon me, but can you tell me . . . ?"

To continue, as I waited in the deserted lobby, a stranger walked up   4
to where I was sitting and stood close enough so that not only could I easily touch him but I could even hear him breathing. In addition, the dark mass of his body filled the peripheral field of vision on my left side. If the lobby had been crowded with people, I would have understood his behavior, but in an empty lobby his presence made me exceedingly uncomfortable. Feeling annoyed by this intrusion, I moved my body in such a way as to communicate annoyance. Strangely enough, instead of moving away, my actions seemed only to encourage him, because he moved even closer. In spite of the temptation to escape the annoyance, I put aside thoughts of abandoning my post, thinking, "To hell with it. Why should I move? I was here first and I'm not going to let this fellow drive me out even if he is a boor." Fortunately, a group of people soon

arrived whom my tormentor immediately joined. Their mannerisms explained his behavior, for I knew from both speech and gestures that they were Arabs. I had not been able to make this crucial identification by looking at my subject when he was alone because he wasn't talking and he was wearing American clothes.

In describing the scene later to an Arab colleague, two contrasting patterns emerged. My concept and my feelings about my own circle of privacy in a "public" place immediately struck my Arab friend as strange and puzzling. He said, "After all, it's a public place, isn't it?" Pursuing this line of inquiry, I found that in Arab thought I had no rights whatsoever by virtue of occupying a given spot; neither my place nor my body was inviolate! For the Arab, there is no such thing as an intrusion in public. Public means public. With this insight, a great range of Arab behavior that had been puzzling, annoying, and sometimes even frightening began to make sense. I learned, for example, that if A is standing on a street corner and B wants his spot, B is within his rights if he does what he can to make A uncomfortable enough to move. In Beirut only the hardy sit in the last row in a movie theater, because there are usually standees who want seats and who push and shove and make such a nuisance that most people give up and leave. Seen in this light, the Arab who "intruded" on my space in the hotel lobby had apparently selected it for the very reason I had: it was a good place to watch two doors and the elevator. My show of annoyance, instead of driving him away, had only encouraged him. He thought he was about to get me to move.

Another silent source of friction between Americans and Arabs is in an area that Americans treat very informally — the manners and rights of the road. In general, in the United States we tend to defer to the vehicle that is bigger, more powerful, faster, and heavily laden. While a pedestrian walking along a road may feel annoyed he will not think it unusual to step aside for a fast-moving automobile. He knows that because he is moving he does not have the right to the space around him that he has when he is standing still (as I was in the hotel lobby). It appears that the reverse is true with the Arabs who apparently *take on rights to space as they move*. For someone else to move into a space an Arab is also moving into is a violation of his rights. It is infuriating to an Arab to have someone else cut in front of him on the highway. It is the American's cavalier treatment of moving space that makes the Arab call him aggressive and pushy.

The experience described above and many others suggested to me that Arabs might actually have a wholly contrasting set of assumptions

concerning the body and the rights associated with it. Certainly
the Arab tendency to shove and push each other in public and to feel
and pinch women in public conveyances would not be tolerated by
Westerners. It appeared to me that they must not have any concept
of a private zone outside the body. This proved to be precisely the
case.

In the Western world, the person is synonymous with an individual   8
inside a skin. And in northern Europe generally, the skin and even the
clothes may be inviolate. You need permission to touch either if you are
a stranger. This rule applies in some parts of France where the mere
touching of another person during an argument used to be legally defined
as assault. For the Arab the location of the person in relation to the body
is quite different. The person exists somewhere down inside the body.
The ego is not completely hidden, however, because it can be reached
very easily with an insult. It is protected from touch but not from words.
The dissociation of the body and the ego may explain why the public
amputation of a thief's hand is tolerated as standard punishment in Saudi
Arabia. It also sheds light on why an Arab employer living in a modern
apartment can provide his servant with a room that is a boxlike cubicle
approximately 5 by 10 by 4 feet in size that is not only hung from the
ceiling to conserve floor space but has an opening so that the servant can
be spied on.

As one might suspect, deep orientations toward the self such as the
one just described are also reflected in the language. This was brought
to my attention one afternoon when an Arab colleague who is the author
of an Arab-English dictionary arrived in my office and threw himself into
a chair in a state of obvious exhaustion. When I asked him what had
been going on, he said: "I have spent the entire afternoon trying to find
the Arab equivalent of the English word 'rape.' There is no such word
in Arabic. All my sources, both written and spoken, can come up with
no more than an approximation, such as 'He took her against her will.'
There is nothing in Arabic approaching your meaning as it is expressed
in that one word."

Differing concepts of the placement of the ego in relation to the body
are not easily grasped. Once an idea like this is accepted, however, it is
possible to understand many other facets of Arab life that would otherwise
be difficult to explain. One of these is the high population density of
Arab cities like Cairo, Beirut, and Damascus. . . . While it is probable
that Arabs are suffering from population pressures, it is also just as possible
that continued pressure from the desert has resulted in a cultural adap-

tation to high density which takes the form described above. Tucking the ego down inside the body shell not only would permit higher population densities but would explain why it is that Arab communications are stepped up as much as they are when compared to northern European communication patterns. Not only is the sheer noise level much higher, but the piercing look of the eyes, the touch of the hands, and the mutual bathing in the warm moist breath during conversation represent stepped-up sensory inputs to a level which many Europeans find unbearably intense.

The Arab dream is for lots of space in the home, which unfortunately many Arabs cannot afford. Yet when he has space, it is very different from what one finds in most American homes. Arab spaces inside their upper-middle-class homes are tremendous by our standards. They avoid partitions because Arabs *do not like to be alone.* The form of the home is such as to hold the family together inside a single protective shell, because Arabs are deeply involved with each other. Their personalities are intermingled and take nourishment from each other like the roots and soil. If one is not with people and actively involved in some way, one is deprived of life. An old Arab saying reflects this value: "Paradise without people should not be entered because it is Hell." Therefore, Arabs in the United States often feel socially and sensorially deprived and long to be back where there is human warmth and contact.

Since there is no physical privacy as we know it in the Arab family, 12 not even a word for privacy, one could expect that the Arabs might use some other means to be alone. Their way to be alone is to stop talking. Like the English, an Arab who shuts himself off in this way is not indicating that anything is wrong or that he is withdrawing, only that he wants to be alone with his own thoughts or does not want to be intruded upon. One subject said that her father would come and go for days at a time without saying a word, and no one in the family thought anything of it. Yet for this very reason, an Arab exchange student visiting a Kansas farm failed to pick up the cue that his American hosts were mad at him when they gave him the "silent treatment." He only discovered something was wrong when they took him to town and tried forcibly to put him on a bus to Washington, D.C., the headquarters of the exchange program responsible for his presence in the United States.

Like everyone else in the world, Arabs are unable to formulate specific rules for their informal behavior patterns. In fact, they often deny that there are any rules, and they are made anxious by suggestions that such is the case. Therefore, in order to determine how the Arab sets distances, I investigated the use of each sense separately. Gradually, definite and distinctive behavioral patterns began to emerge.

Olfaction occupies a prominent place in the Arab life. Not only is it one of the distance-setting mechanisms, but it is a vital part of a complex system of behavior. Arabs consistently breathe on people when they talk. However, this habit is more than a matter of different manners. To the Arab good smells are pleasing and a way of being involved with each other. To smell one's friend is not only nice but desirable, for to deny him your breath is to act ashamed. Americans, on the other hand, trained as they are not to breathe in people's faces, automatically communicate shame in trying to be polite. Who would expect that when our highest diplomats are putting on their best manners they are also communicating shame? Yet this is what occurs constantly, because diplomacy is not only "eyeball to eyeball" but breath to breath.

By stressing olfaction, Arabs do not try to eliminate all the body's odors, only to enhance them and use them in building human relationships. Nor are they self-conscious about telling others when they don't like the way they smell. A man leaving his house in the morning may be told by his uncle, "Habib, your stomach is sour and your breath doesn't smell too good. Better not talk too close to people today." Smell is even considered in the choice of a mate. When couples are being matched for marriage, the man's go-between will sometimes ask to smell the girl, who may be turned down if she doesn't "smell nice." Arabs recognize that smell and disposition may be linked.

In a word, the olfactory boundary performs two roles in Arab life. It [16] enfolds those who want to relate and separates those who don't. The Arab finds it essential to stay inside the olfactory zone as a means of keeping tab on changes in emotion. What is more, he may feel crowded as soon as he smells something unpleasant. While not much is known about "olfactory crowding," this may prove to be as significant as any other variable in the crowding complex because it is tied directly to the body chemistry and hence to the state of health and emotions. . . . It is not surprising, therefore, that the olfactory boundary constitutes for the Arabs an informal distance-setting mechanism in contrast to the visual mechanisms of the Westerner.

One of my earliest discoveries in the field of intercultural communication was that the position of the bodies of people in conversation varies with the culture. Even so, it used to puzzle me that a special Arab friend seemed unable to walk and talk at the same time. After years in the United States, he could not bring himself to stroll along, facing forward while talking. Our progress would be arrested while he edged ahead, cutting slightly in front of me and turning sideways so we could see each other. Once in this position, he would stop. His behavior was explained when I learned that for the Arabs, to view the other person peripherally is regarded as impolite, and to sit or stand back-to-back is considered very rude. You must be involved when interacting with Arabs who are friends.

One mistaken American notion is that Arabs conduct all conversations at close distances. This is not the case at all. On social occasions, they may sit on opposite sides of the room and talk across the room to each other. They are, however, apt to take offense when Americans use what are to them ambiguous distances, such as the four- to seven-foot social-consultative distance. They frequently complain that Americans are cold or aloof or "don't care." This was what an elderly Arab diplomat in an American hospital thought when the American nurses used "professional" distance. He had the feeling that he was being ignored, that they might not take good care of him. Another Arab subject remarked, referring to American behavior, "What's the matter? Do I smell bad? Or are they afraid of me?"

Arabs who interact with Americans report experiencing a certain flatness traceable in part to a very different use of the eyes in private and in public as well as between friends and strangers. Even though it is rude for a guest to walk around the Arab home eying things, Arabs look at each other in ways which seem hostile or challenging to the American. One Arab informant said that he was in constant hot water with Americans because of the way he looked at them without the slightest intention of offending. In fact, he had on several occasions barely avoided fights with American men who apparently thought their masculinity was being challenged because of the way he was looking at them. . . . Arabs look each other in the eye when talking with an intensity that makes most Americans highly uncomfortable.

As the reader must gather by now, Arabs are involved with each other   20 on many different levels simultaneously. Privacy in a public place is foreign to them. Business transactions in the bazaar, for example, are not just between buyer and seller, but are participated in by everyone. Anyone who is standing around may join in. If a grownup sees a boy breaking a window, he must stop him even if he doesn't know him. Involvement and participation are expressed in other ways as well. If two men are fighting, the crowd must intervene. On the political level, *to fail to intervene* when trouble is brewing is to take sides, which is what our State Department always seems to be doing. Given the fact that few people in the world today are even remotely aware of the cultural mold that forms their thoughts it is normal for Arabs to view *our* behavior as though it stemmed from *their* own hidden set of assumptions.

In the course of my interviews with Arabs the term *tomb* kept cropping up in conjunction with enclosed space. In a word, Arabs don't mind being crowded by people but hate to be hemmed in by walls. They show a much greater overt sensitivity to architectural crowding than we do. Enclosed space must meet at least three requirements that I know of if it is to satisfy the Arabs: there must be plenty of unobstructed space in which to move around (possibly as much as a thousand square feet); very high ceilings — so high in fact that they do not normally impinge on the visual field; and, in addition, there must be an unobstructed view. It was spaces such as these in which the Americans referred to earlier felt so uncomfortable. One sees the Arab's need for a view expressed in many ways, even negatively, for to cut off a neighbor's view is one of the most effective ways of spiting him. In Beirut one can see what is known locally as the "spite house." It is nothing more than a thick, four-story wall, built at the end of a long fight between neighbors, on a narrow strip of land for the express purpose of denying a view of the Mediterranean to any house built on the land behind. According to one of my informants, there is also a house on a small plot of land between Beirut and Damascus which is completely surrounded by a neighbor's wall built high enough to cut off the view from all windows!

Proxemic patterns tell us other things about Arab culture. For example, the whole concept of the boundary as an abstraction is almost impossible to pin down. In one sense, there are no boundaries. "Edges" of towns, yes, but permanent boundaries out in the country (hidden lines), no. In the course of my work with Arab subjects I had a difficult time translating our concept of a boundary into terms which could be equated with theirs. In order to clarify the distinctions between the two very different defini-tions, I thought it might be helpful to pinpoint acts which constituted trespass. To date, I have been unable to discover anything even remotely resembling our own legal concept of trespass.

Arab behavior in regard to their own real estate is apparently an extension of, and therefore consistent with, their approach to the body.

My subjects simply failed to respond whenever trespass was mentioned. They didn't seem to understand what I meant by this term. This may be explained by the fact that they organize relationships with each other according to closed social systems rather than spatially. For thousands of years Moslems, Marinites, Druses, and Jews have lived in their own villages, each with strong kin affiliations. Their hierarchy of loyalties is: first to one's self, then to kinsman, townsman, or tribesman, coreligionist and/or countryman. Anyone not in these categories is a stranger. Strangers and enemies are very closely linked, if not synonymous, in Arab thought. Trespass in this context is a matter of who you are, rather than a piece of land or a space with a boundary that can be denied to anyone and everyone, friend and foe alike.

In summary, proxemic patterns differ. By examining them it is possible   24
to reveal hidden cultural frames that determine the structure of a given people's perceptual world. Perceiving the world differently leads to differential definitions of what constitutes crowded living, different interpersonal relations, and a different approach to both local and international politics. There are in addition wide discrepancies in the degree to which culture structures involvement, which means that planners should begin to think in terms of different kinds of cities, cities which are consistent with the proxemic patterns of the peoples who live in them.

EXPLORATIONS

1. According to Hall, why do Arabs seem pushy to Americans? Why do Americans seem pushy to Arabs? What contrasting concept of the person underlies this mutual misunderstanding?

2. What kinds of data does Hall use as the basis for his conclusions about Arab versus Western concepts of personal space? How would the credibility of his findings change (if at all) if Hall depended on statistical data instead of the types of information he draws on here?

3. Who is Hall's apparent intended audience? What clues in his essay enable you to tell? To publish "Proxemics in the Arab World" in an Arab magazine, what changes in presentation would Hall need to make?

4. At what points does Hall treat northern Europeans and Americans together as more or less identical Westerners? At what points does he speak separately of one group or the other? At what points, if any, does he draw conclusions about one group from data relating to the other?

CONNECTIONS

1. In V. S. Naipaul's "Entering the New World," Ebony mentions the contrasting significance of eye contact to African children and their French teachers. What does looking someone in the eye mean to each group? According to Hall, what role does eye contact play among Arabs?
2. Hall cites ignorance as the central factor in misunderstandings between members of dissimilar cultures. Where and how does Paul Harrison blame ignorance for cross-cultural conflict in "The Westernization of the World"? What observations by V. S. Naipaul in "Entering the New World" show that he has familiarized himself with customs in the country he is visiting?
3. Look back at John David Morley's "Acquiring a Japanese Family" (p. 36). How are Japanese concepts of personal space involving the home and family similar to Arab concepts? What explanation does Hall suggest for the Arab attitude? What explanation can you suggest for the Japanese attitude?

ELABORATIONS

1. Hall's essay is filled with examples of misunderstandings between Arabs and Westerners based on contrasting ideas about personal space. At the political level such misunderstandings can be dangerous to international relations. Based on all the selections you have read about Arab countries, write an essay recommending guidelines for men and women representing the U.S. government in the Middle East.
2. Hall touches on Western concepts of public and private space mainly as a standard of comparison for his investigation of contrasting Arab concepts. Write an essay in which you classify and examine various attitudes toward personal space in the United States. Use examples from your own experience, and from Hall's essay if you wish, as illustrations.

KATE MILLETT

Arriving in Tehran

The feminist writer Kate Millett is best known for her 1970 book *Sexual Politics*. Millett was born in St. Paul, Minnesota, in 1934 and educated at the University of Minnesota and Oxford University. She currently divides her time between her New York City loft and her farm in upstate New York. Long active in political and artistic causes, including CAIFI (the Committee for Artistic and Intellectual Freedom in Iran), Millett accepted the request of Iranian feminists to speak at their International Women's Day celebration after the shah's downfall. "Arriving in Tehran" comes from her book about that visit, *Going to Iran* (1982), a collaboration with photographer Sophie Keir.

The shahs' dynasty began in 1925 with military leader Reza Khan; he abdicated in 1941 in favor of his son. Shah Mohammad Reza Pahlavi expanded his control of Iran in 1953 after Premier Mohammed Mossadegh, whose nationalization of the oil industry had prompted a British blockade, was overthrown. The shah — a U.S. ally — instituted economic and social reform, but he also arrested thousands and executed hundreds of political opponents. Conservative Muslim protests erupted into violence in 1978. After several unsuccessful changes of government, the shah fled to Egypt in early 1979; he died there the next year. Meanwhile, the exiled religious leader Ayatollah Ruhollah Khomeini returned to Iran, becoming head of the government in late 1979. Political turmoil, arrests, and executions have continued, while mounting religious fanaticism has isolated Iran from most of the rest of the world.

(For more background on Iran, see p. 76.)

The first sight of them was terrible. Like black birds, like death, like fate, like everything alien. Foreign, dangerous, unfriendly. There were hundreds of them, specters crowding the barrier, waiting their own. A sea of chadori, the long terrible veil, the full length of it, like a dress descending to the floor, ancient, powerful, annihilating us. And the men beside them too, oddly enough, nondescript in their badly cut Western suits, a costume that had none of the power of an Arab robe. And in giving themselves this bit of "Westernism," this suit that looks, like the suits on men in Japan, never really right since it is an adopted clothing, a deference to the wealth and political force of another section of persons,

621

the men announce their alliance with the "new," the world of business and technology, currency and bureaucratic forms and industrialism. Relegating women to the old, the traditional, the tribal garment. In Japan it is ceremonial and decorative, here merely punitive and abject. The men control them, insignificant as they appear, hardly visible before the splendor and drama of the chador.

Yet if the women were alone they would be wonderful; awesome, even frightening — for there is a mana[1] of antiquity in the sight of their chador, the length, the ferocity of that fall of black cloth, the masses of them like the chorus in Greek tragedy. You would never be close to it; these women seem utterly closed to women. Here in this public place defended by their robes, the fabric held tightly under the chin, much of the face hidden by the fold of cloth as it peaks over the forehead or is folded hard against forehead obscuring it altogether. And the hair hidden, the friendliness of hair, from woman to woman, its personality, its sexual innocence, the signal of animal humanity.

Yet the chador is theater, some theater of women so old I no longer know it. Before this garment was forced upon us for our shame, it must have been our pride; before it was compelled upon us, we must have worn it out of self-love, vanity, grace, thoroughly conscious how glamorous it could be in evening, how seductive. A glance thrown from it, the way it frames the face, reveals the bones, accentuates, turns every face into mystery, eyes, eyebrows speaking. Effective. As all frames are. As all costume heightens. And it is surely costume, the thrill of theater in it. But the threat too.

Look at them and they do not look back, even the friendly curiosity   4
with which women regard each other. Still wearing the cloth of their majesty, they have become prisoners in it. The bitterness, the driven rage behind these figures, behind these yards of black cloth. They are closed utterly. The small, hardly visible men in their suits have absolute control here.

I wonder if the women on the airplane on the way here have ducked back into their headscarves or have dared to enter this crowd without them. I understand now their fear. This is real, and I had only thought they were squeamish, sissy. The crowd before us is adamant, like an ancient obdurate wall of conformity. And behind them you already see

---

[1]An elemental natural force embodied in a person. — ED.

the guns. Big ones. Machine guns carried in the arms of militia, some in uniform, some not, but equally ferocious, insanely proud of the object they hold, its authority; new, superbly new, the importance it gives them, the masculinity in a country now in a paroxysm of masculinity. Here is the crowning emblem. Always just about to go off. From the way they hold it you doubt their knowledge of the weapon, are sure it is recently acquired. Their fingers are on the trigger, actually on the trigger, they even carry it and walk along with their fingers on the trigger, naive belief in the magic of the safety catch. Out hunting I once nearly shot a friend by that sort of credulity. The way guns are carried here, displayed, the arrogance of it, the swagger, has even in the half-hour going through customs made me angry and frightened ten times over. How oppressive the size of these weapons, not your policeman's little pistol covered by a holster, but huge, bigger than carbines, faster, more delightful to their possessor, more intimidating to all others.

There are guns everywhere, and when you look around, you discover that they are often pointed at you. In a moment our friends will appear, we'll be out of this, our eyes darting along the faces at the barricade. That moment of truth when you reach the barricade after customs and your friend calls out your name and you smile and people watch you and you are both self-consciously embarrassed and delighted. And saved, crossing over into their arms, you become a private person, no longer stared at, but claimed. For everyone stares at us, we are foreigners, foreign women, the men staring in thousands of ways, the women staring inscrutably from the chador but when we look at them they look away; shut, disapproving.

We are even becoming something of a public spectacle; the fact that we are not being met is becoming public knowledge, the fact of our being unclaimed. When it is so obvious we expect it, our look of anticipation, our assurance that Kateh will be here, that Khalil will have called her. An article of faith to us. And of course she won't be wearing a chador, she'll look like us, she'll be easy to recognize. The people are pressing behind us, we cannot stand here forever searching the crowd behind the barrier, examined and rejected by each of them as we scan one after another for a fellow spirit. Perhaps Kateh sent someone else, Caifi are always doing things like that, one person's busy, another one is dispatched to an airport to pick up an arrival. Who looks the right type? Sort of hip, radical, young, studentlike, the appropriate clothing. There are only two young women without chador in the whole crowd. We are examining it from the back now, having so spectacularly failed the applause moment of being greeted before the throng. In fact we are trying to disappear in it, so intense are the stares.

I stand by the bags, feeling absurd in my English bobby's cape, in 8 shape a chador without a hood, my head an object of reproach, my very existence somehow an affront. The happy traveler. With a submachine gun trained on her from the guard at the front door. He is actually pointing this thing at me, I say to myself, Sophie gone off to page our friends; here is your adventure in Iran you were so crazy to have against all your friends' better judgment, your mother's warning, trying to grin at the guard, trying to be so obviously harmless he will dismiss me and get on to something better.

Travelers are trying to leave through his door, he is giving them the runaround, insisting they use another door, strutting his petty power, being a nuisance, exciting himself to wrath with that weapon in his hands. His superior comes over, dashing type in a jumpsuit, smaller but more glamorous gun, probably Air Force paratrooper, the crack troops here, they armed the insurgents on the great day of the Revolution — 21 Bahman (February).

See it all historically; a newly armed populace of course will be fascinated, even childishly fascinated with its weapons, the power they represent, having been shoved around for years by creeps with guns, they will all too easily strut and be insolent having their own — but not in the same entire abuse of power. These are the militia, not the shah's Savak.[2] You would never have been permitted to enter this airport at all in the old days; and you are an oddity, so calm down. Sit down, in fact, if you want to stop drawing attention. There are other unfortunates whose friends have failed to arrive, it's probably just traffic. I console myself with tobacco and smile at the woman on the next bench. She smiles back. We have arrived in the late evening, the exchange is closed, we have no Iranian money, only one phone number and address in Tehran. If this is not just a little mix-up, it could be a dead end. Rather humbling. Very frightening.

Sophie says it's a little more serious than that, she had begged a coin to use the phone; Kateh's mother had no idea we were coming, Kateh isn't home. Though she speaks little English, Kateh's mother has conveyed her sense that we are dangerous, she recognizes her daughter knows

---

[2]Secret police. — ED.

us but it is unwise to speak on the phone, and it would be more graceful perhaps to betake ourselves to a hotel and straighten everything out in the morning. Well, all right, a hotel, I seem to have forgotten that there are hotels, though without money it may be hard to get to one. Sophie dispatches me to the travelers' aid, where a good-looking man with a gun hears my sad tale and changes a twenty-dollar bill. He is going to "The States" in two weeks, he can use the money. Going to Virginia, he says. I tell him Virginia is lovely just now, the blossoms should be out. He says they won't be out here for quite a while, it's been a very cold winter. We are getting along famously, it is almost normal.

Even the guns and the checkpoints on the way to the hotel he has   12 sent us to seem plausible. The hotel itself is overly so — a Sheraton. All one's fantasies of real Persian hotels, beautiful and subtle as Japanese inns — all that out the window. That we have a roof over our heads, running water, a bed after two days of airplane. That is enough. Though it sets the teeth on edge to look at the Arya Sheraton. Awful monumental concrete pile, American anonymous modern transported here, in fact the whole neighborhood is such, and in the days after, as we drove through the city we discovered more dismal "new" buildings than I have ever seen anywhere else in the world. The shah was in a rage of producing this stuff, to make an entire city of totalitarian modern, a monument to himself, to the conquerors who sponsored him, a tribute to Western imperialism, destroying all indigenous buildings, leaving only these skeletons of half-built towers we see through the windows of our room.

The Sheraton is sandbagged in front. More sandbags in the lobby. Young men with machine guns lolling about to "defend" it from some anonymous attackers. The hotel is nearly deserted. Merely a dozen guests lost in its towers. The hotel staff seem unhappy. Under guard. This is no way to run a place of hostelry, they seem to say. One is even quite open with Sophie over his dissatisfaction. . . .

A man comes to bring us towels and we mistake him for a subversive force, howling, "Holy, holy, holy," outside our door. We say we don't want any. Further awkwardness in checking out, the room immaculate, still without towels. At the elevator we meet the towel man having another go at it. A go at us too, elaborate attempts to shake our hands, then to kiss us; we tire of international goodwill and close the elevator door, expecting the worst from the management. Our sudden departure. Explain it as best we can.

Dinner is in the basement, Sheraton's Italian-grotto motif, arranged somewhere else for somewhere else or nowhere at all. The swimming pool just outside the windows is equally "international" in flavor, equally flavorless. Its invitation to the sun, to drinks by poolside, to languor and relaxation, are now only symptoms of decadence. It is also decadent to ask the waiter for a drink. "Alcohol is no longer served," he rebukes me. "But it's on the menu." Until a few days ago you could have a drink here, now it's against the law. Doesn't that seem a pity? I ask him, acknowledging the power of the state over our lives, but curious to know if there is any sense of how arbitrary it all is. Doesn't he think many of the people having dinner here would like to have a beer or a glass of wine with their food, even a little whiskey beforehand? Does he drink himself, does he know how it relaxes you when you're tired, nervous, frustrated? What will it do to a whole population to be without this little pleasure, to have it made against the law? I wheedle, but he's not buying any. The very fact that I dare to discuss Muslim law is impiety. The people at the next table stare and then smile; they are in agreement with us probably as he reports our scandalous remarks.

We suffer through dinner: everything one would hate about a Western   16 multinational corporation is here: the mediocre tasteless food (neither Western nor Eastern nor food), the showy swimming pool to intimidate the poor, the hot, the dusty, the millions who would never be permitted in the door, even the phony decor. And nothing redeemable is left either; the food seems deliberately disimproved and carelessly served, the pleasure of the pool is lost forever since you are sure they will never fill it again. Two corny Western-style bars and you can't have even one drink. As if everything that might be fun is now governmentally interdict. What an odd way to liberate a place. Instead of confiscating the imperialist fat-cat stuff and democratizing the enjoyment of it — instead, what few pleasures it offered have all been forbidden. To everyone.

The just resentment against foreign things, foreign money, foreign arrogance has run its course to a kind of xenophobia. The young mili-tiamen surround us up at the desk and demand to know where we are going. Are we American? Sophie is quick to claim her Canadian dispen-sation. I answer that I am American, as if it were a crime for which I am expected to take responsibility. Why are we going out at night? Our friends are coming to get us. We are bourgeois foreigners according to them. We ask if they are socialists, leftists. We get little satisfaction here. They are the Islamic revolution, they are from the Komiteh. An earlier bunch — they have just changed guard — had felt like leftist students; these now feel like Khomeini types, the good boys at the mosque who Khalil says are replacing the leftists — but to a woman both give off the same threat, the same obdurate male stance. I ask them about the women.

Becoming suspicious thereby. Why ask about that? I want to know what the women will gain by the revolution. "We got rid of the shah." "Of course, and the women helped to do it, but what will it be like for women now?" "Our women are happy. They do what we want." Another laughs. How easy and infuriating this humor over women, how universal. "That's happiness?" "Why you ask about this?" a third demands, gun in hand. "Because I'm a feminist." A dangerous thing to say, but I risk it, having talked to them long enough now to have established contact, they are unlikely even to arrest me.

We are waiting for our friends, hours of waiting; we still don't know it, but it is only the beginning of our days of waiting. Sophie is talking to the desk clerk, a very different conversation from mine with the militia. Pouring out to her all his detestation of the new regime, his frustration and that of his colleagues — no one comes to the hotel anymore, no one wants to be bossed by the soldiers, denied a drink. The Intercontinental is getting all their business, it is still almost a hotel rather than a branch of the police and the state, it still sells alcohol, it is full of reporters. Sophie makes a mental note to stay at the Intercontinental if she is ever in need of a hotel. She's a reporter; he must tell her what it's like here. And listens to the man's woes. He develops a great interest in her. Becoming inquisitive, becoming forward, offering his services, would we like him to act as our interpreter during our visit here? Sophie decides he's a spy. I decide our friends are never coming long before one of them, Bahram, calls to say there are thirty-two checkpoints to get through between us, and they think it too dangerous. It has taken them this long just to locate a car.

"Are they always this inefficient, these friends of yours in Caifi?" Sophie is miffed. We have been two hours in the lobby exposed to hotel clerks and soldiery. The humiliation of reregistering lies ahead of us; having checked out, we must now check in again. "I can't understand what's the matter, they're always wonderful to work with." Trying to imagine what it means to get through thirty-two checkpoints; coming here, they didn't stop our cab, but would they stop Caifi, search, question? Thirty-two times. Of course they couldn't come. We are being inconsiderate, we are failing to notice that this is a country under armed guard only a few weeks after an insurrection; if we are not in the midst of a revolution, we are at least in the midst of a counterrevolution, which, because so much is still in flux, might still come out all right.

We have only to wait and see, we have only to be patient, going to 20 bed at the Sheraton, talking into our tape recorder, the day a confusing mass behind us. We are rather alone in Tehran.

EXPLORATIONS

1. How would you summarize Millett's emotional response at the airport to the Iranian women in chadori? to the Iranian men in suits? What relationship does she assume exists between these men and women? Do you think the evidence in her essay justifies her assumption? Why or why not?

2. A central feature of "Arriving in Tehran" is the guns carried by militia. What do Millett's references to guns reveal about the social and political atmosphere of Iran as she experiences it? What specific value-laden words indicate how she feels about those guns and the people carrying them?

3. Within her first six paragraphs Millett utilizes the full range of persons available to writers in English. At what points does she use the first-person singular *I*, and with what effect? Where does she use the first-person plural *we*? Whom does she appear to mean by *we*? At what points does she use the second-person *you*? What audience is she addressing as *you* in each instance?

4. "Arriving in Tehran" depicts two types of alienation: that of an American entering a foreign country, and that of a feminist confronted by a male-dominated culture. How might Millett's reactions be different if she were already familiar with Iran? if she felt neutral about the power balance between the sexes?

CONNECTIONS

1. Millett's response to Iran centers on her sense of being barred, as a foreign woman, from communicating with either women or men. What obstacles impeded Edward T. Hall's communication with Arabs? What role do women play in "Proxemics in the Arab World"? After reading Millett's essay, what factors do you think Hall may have overlooked in his assessment of neighboring cultures?

2. Compare the restaurant scene in Millett's paragraph 15 with V. S. Naipaul's restaurant scene in "Entering the New World." What similar observations and conclusions appear in both? What role does Naipaul play in his scene, and how does his role affect the scene's impact? What role does Millett play in her scene, and how does her role affect the scene's impact?

3. What evidence of Third World Westernization, as described by Paul Harrison in "The Westernization of the World," appears in "Arriving in Tehran"? Which Western artifacts and customs are left over from the shah's regime, and which ones are part of Khomeini's Iran? What causes identified by Harrison seem to have shaped the shah's attitude toward Western ways? How does the Khomeini regime's attitude evidently differ from the shah's?

4. Look back at Doris Lessing's comments on women's clothing in "The Afghan Resistance" (p. 519). Which of Lessing's observations and reactions are similar to Millett's? Which ones are different? What can you tell about each writer's biases from the contrast in their descriptions of the burka or chador?

ELABORATIONS

1. Given Paul Harrison's theories about the Westernization of the world, and given the West's present defense buildup, what do you think Harrison would predict regarding the effects of the arms race on Iran? How is the impact likely to be different under Khomeini from what it would have been under the shah? Write an essay using Harrison's and Millett's observations, other relevant selections from this book, and your own knowledge as the basis for a speculative look into the future.

2. The selections in this book by Millett, Doris Lessing (p. 519), Naila Minai (p. 256), Cherry and Charles Lindholm (p. 267), Yashar Kemal (p. 279), and Gholam-Hossein Sa'edi (p. 76) all contain observations on sex roles. Synthesize the information in these essays and stories, and write an essay comparing and contrasting Middle Eastern men's and women's perceptions of each other with those in the United States.

GUAN KEGUANG

A Chinese Reporter on Cape Cod

Born in China in 1938, Guan Keguang graduated from Shanghai International Studies University in 1960 and was assigned to teach there. He became an associate professor in the English department, first teaching literature and linguistics (his field of research), then shifting to journalism in 1983. Guan took a leave from his position as deputy director of the university's journalism program to visit the United States in 1986. Having previously visited this country with an exchange program, he returned at the invitation of the *Pittsburgh Post Gazette,* which arranged for him to tour various American newspapers. Guan's travels took him to Hyannis, Massachusetts, where he decided to stay and write a weekly column for the *Cape Cod Times* during the winter of 1986–87. In June 1987 he accepted a job with the *Asian Wall Street Journal* in New York.

Guan's presence in the United States reflects China's opening up to Western contact since Mao Zedong's death. For comments on the change, see the introductory notes to the following selection, Orville Schell's "Shanghai" (p. 635). For additional background on China, see pp. 220 and 450.

Next to the newsroom in the *Cape Cod Times* main office building there is a "lunchroom." My colleagues and I sometimes go there to buy something to eat or drink from the vending machines.

The experience has been quite a novelty for me. I put in some coins, push a button, and out comes what I want.

The machines offer a variety of food and drinks. Many of them are new to me and the labels don't tell me much about what's inside. The operation is simple and automatic. But so many decisions!

Such a process epitomizes what I have experienced while struggling hard to adapt my traditional ways of thinking and doing things to an American environment, which demands constantly considering alternatives and making decisions.   4

This has been no easy job for me.

For almost half a century I have lived in a culture where choices and decisions are made by authorities and circumstances rather than by individuals and personal preferences.

It's OK for young children to have things arranged for them by their parents, because they are inexperienced in life and not wise enough to make important decisions. But when they reach their late teens they don't like to be treated that way — even in China. They yearn for independence and freedom, as the recent demonstrations have shown. They are frustrated when things don't go their way and they find themselves helpless and unable to do anything about their fate.

When the time comes to enter the work force, however, reality sets   8
in. They are assigned a job, and that's it. Moreover, the job assignment determines where you must live.

If you have completed twelve years' schooling, but you fail in the college entrance examination and are not admitted, the government will assign you a job — perhaps as a factory worker, a store clerk, or a bus driver. Very likely that will be you lifelong job, because you can't freely pick and choose or change your job. Once you are in a job you will have to stick to it, unless the authorities want to transfer you to another job. You could negotiate with the authorities, but the government always has the final say.

Students do have an opportunity to state their preference among university and courses of study — and if you pass your exams with flying colors, with scores much higher than others, you will be admitted into a department of a university of your own choice. But once you get into a university you stay in your major for four or five years without a break. You do not change your major. You take the courses given to you, pass all the exams, behave well and toe the party line, earn your bachelor's degree and graduate.

Then, you just wait until a job is assigned to you. During the waiting period, students with "connections" seek to influence the decision. A few succeed. In any event, until the decision is made, you will not know where you will go and what your lifelong career will be.

Your job assignment notice is more than a certificate with which you   12
report for duty. It is also a certificate for your residence registration and your daily necessity rations. If you don't like the job assigned to you and refuse to take it, you are jobless. Because you don't have an official permission to live in any place other than where the job is, you won't get your ration coupons.

Your choice, therefore, is very simple: to eat or not to eat.

Every graduate is guaranteed a job. Each job affords the same starting salary. Engineer, schoolteacher, office clerk, truck driver, scientist — the difference in salary is negligible. That is the socialist way.

No matter if you like it or not, you stay with your job.

No matter if you are liked or not, you stay with your job.   16

If you are not very ambitious, life can be very easy for you. Its pace won't be so maddeningly fast as it is here in America. You don't have to worry about choosing alternatives or making decisions. You don't have to worry about getting laid off.

Since you don't have much to choose from and everything is planned and arranged for you, you will be better off if you take things easy. As an old Chinese saying goes: "Those who are content are forever happy."

People like that — who have been content to let their decisions be made for them — would find it hard to get used to the American life-style, to keep their eyes open to opportunities, to be searching constantly for a better job, a better place to live. Such a way of life would be too risky, too precarious, too challenging.

Our old tradition taught us to be humble, modest, unassuming, mod-   20 erate, and passive. Even when a Chinese host treats a guest to a dinner consisting of twelve courses and costing half of his monthly salary, he still apologizes repeatedly to the guest between the courses for the "in-adequate" meal he has prepared for his honorable guest. Meanwhile, the guest politely and humbly refuses to accept the food his host keeps piling up on his dish, because he feels he shouldn't assume that he deserves so much good food and he should leave more good stuff for the host family, even though he is very hungry at the moment and he likes the food immensely.

The other day while I was going through the classified ads in the magazine *Editor & Publisher*, I came across ads placed by publications in search of "aggressive, talented, hungry" reporters.

What could I do if I wanted such a position?

If I were hungry, I would try every face-saving means not to admit it.

It I were talented, I would (or should) be modest enough not to   24 advertise it.

Even if I were desperately in need of the position, I still wouldn't know how to be aggressive.

I wonder if I should take a crash course, teaching me how to be aggressive, talented, and hungry.

EXPLORATIONS

1. Why does Guan regard American vending machines as extraordinary? What larger aspect of American culture do they represent in his essay? Why are most Americans less imtimidated by the choices presented by vending machines than Guan is?

2. Guan writes, "For almost half a century I have lived in a culture where choices and decisions are made by authorities and circumstances rather than by individuals and personal preferences." China became officially Communist in 1949. Which of the social phenomena described by Guan came under state control at that point? Which ones were controlled even before the revolution, and by what "authorities and circumstances"?

3. What aspects of Chinese life — as Guan describes it — would you have a hard time adjusting to, and why?

CONNECTIONS

1. How does Guan's response to the United States resemble Kate Millett's response to Iran in "Arriving in Tehran"? What are each writer's obvious biases? What aspects of American life do you think Guan has exaggerated, or overreacted to, because of his biases? What aspects of Iranian life do you suspect Millett has exaggerated or overreacted to because of her biases?

2. In "Entering the New World," V. S. Naipaul writes of Ebony: "He knew where he was, how he had got there, and he liked the novelty of what he saw. . . . He was less anxious than a romantic or concerned outsider might have wished him to be." What statements in "A Chinese Reporter on Cape Cod" paint a similar picture of Guan? Why might a "romantic or concerned outsider" wish him to be more anxious than he seems?

3. Look back at "Chairman Mao's Good Little Boy" by Liang Heng and Judith Shapiro (p. 450). Liang's father, like Guan, was a reporter. What comments in Liang and Shapiro's narrative suggest that the senior Liang's views about his job, and working in general, were much the same as Guan's?

ELABORATIONS

1. "Chairman Mao's Good Little Boy" (p. 450) was written after Liang Heng
   had emigrated to the United States; "A Chinese Reporter on Cape Cod" was
   written while Guan was on leave from his job in Shanghai. How does Guan's
   essay exemplify the relationship he describes between the Chinese individual
   and the state? How does Liang and Shapiro's essay exemplify a Chinese
   native's having adapted "traditional ways of thinking and doing things to an
   American environment"? Write an essay using both the content and the
   approach of these two selections to compare and contrast Guan's and Liang's
   attitudes toward China.

2. Guan writes of traditional Chinese: "People like that — who have been content
   to let their decisions be made for them — would find it hard to get used to
   the American life-style, to keep their eyes open to opportunities, to be searching constantly for a better job, a better place to live. Such a way of life would
   be too risky, too precarious, too challenging." Are all (or most) Americans as
   avid for change as Guan assumes? Write an essay classifying the reasons and
   the ways some Americans "let their decisions be made for them" to avoid a
   life-style that seems "too risky, too precarious, too challenging."

ORVILLE SCHELL

Shanghai

Orville Schell, born in New York City in 1940, received his bachelor's degree from Harvard University in 1962 and then spent several years in the Far East studying Chinese. Along with his graduate work at National Taiwan University, Schell served as Asian correspondent for the *Atlantic*, *Look*, *Harper's*, the *New Republic*, the *Boston Globe*, and the *San Francisco Chronicle*. In 1964–65 he worked for the Ford Foundation's Indonesia field office in Djakarta. Returning to the United States, Schell received a master's degree from the University of California at Berkeley in 1967. Since then he has written for *The New Yorker*, *Rolling Stone*, *Life*, *Look*, the *Atlantic*, and many other publications. He has also written and edited several books on China, commenting: "I write about China because it is an alternative. Although not a plug-in substitute for our problems, it shows that there are indeed utterly different ways to do things." The following essay, "Shanghai," comes from his 1980 book *"Watch Out for the Foreign Guests!"*

Perhaps the best introduction to "Shanghai" is Schell's own summary of recent changes in China: "When I first went to China, in 1975, Mao Zedong and the so-called Gang of Four, led by Mao's wife, Jiang Qing, were still firmly in power. The shadow of the Chinese Communist Party fell across all aspects of life, freezing the Chinese people in a combination of fear and socialist rectitude. Politics was 'in command.' To put one's own interests above those of the Party and the task of 'building socialism' was a dangerous form of heresy. And to be branded a heretic in a land where there were few places to hide and fewer ways to escape was a grim prospect indeed. . . . After Mao's death, in 1976, . . . the country cautiously began a cultural transformation. Like a piece of paper in a fire, whose edges slowly burn before the flames finally move inward to incinerate the center, old-style Chinese Communism was beginning to be consumed by change. Western influences were penetrating China's protective isolationism. . . . Politics slowly receded in importance as China's leadership implemented a new political 'line' stressing a pragmatic approach to rebuilding the country's economy rather than class struggle."

(For more background on China, see pp. 220 and 450.)

The strings of Christmas-tree-like lights strung up and down the main thoroughfares of Shanghai have just blinked out. It is 10 P.M. The first evening of a three-day holiday celebrating the thirtieth anniversary of the founding of the People's Republic of China is drawing to a close.

The huge crowds of people who only an hour ago filled the streets of Shanghai to overflowing have now disappeared. People's Square, a vast parade ground in the center of the city reclaimed from an old English horse-racing track after liberation, is now almost empty.

This year, unlike so many past years when politics were "in command," there will be no fanfare or parades here at People's Square to celebrate China's Communist anniversary. The only suggestion of those tumultuous days of Maoist adoration is the massive portrait of the departed chairman that hangs behind the reviewing stand next to a likeness of his replacement, Hua Guofeng. In back of this oversized icon, the dark bleachers of the old race track still rise, evoking an ambience of times past.

A motorcycle and sidecar bearing two white-uniformed agents from   4
the Public Security Bureau cruises down the parade grounds.

There is an autumnal coolness in the night air. I walk alone, savoring the solitude and openness of the square, having spent the day amidst endless crowds of people walking along the Bund, once the center of foreign commerce in China.

I sit down to rest under one of the ornate lampposts which dot the square, when off in the distance I hear a buzzing that sounds like several amplified mosquitoes.

I get up, curious to see what nocturnal phenomenon is making this noise, and spot three figures on mopeds hurtling down the far side of the square, running a slalom course among the lampposts. When the riders reach the far end of the parade grounds, they loop back and begin to weave in and out of the row of lampposts in which I am standing.

I watch them as they navigate their way toward me at full throttle,   8
hunkered down over the handlebars of their mopeds like apprentice Hell's Angels.

The first youth to reach my particular lamppost wears wraparound sunglasses, despite the darkness. It is not until he has almost passed me that he takes a quick glance in my direction, smiles, and waves. Then, before he reaches the next lamppost, his rear brake light blinks on. He stops and circles back. As he pulls up in front of me, he looks around to see if the coast is clear, then comes to a stop.

"Hey, foreign friend!" he says, hailing me with a broad, friendly smile.

"Would you like to have a ride?" He gestures toward the purring moped.

"Sure."

He dismounts. I get on. After a moment of instruction, I twist the 12
throttle back on this toy-sized Chinese chopper and aim myself toward
Chairman Mao's portrait across the square.

The two-stroke engine rattles and pops as I gain speed. The cool night
air sweeps back my hair. I have a sensation of immense freedom on the
90 cc machine in the middle of the expansive square — of being able to
turn in any direction at any time without obstruction — a feeling that is
enjoyable precisely because it seems so incongruous here in China.

I pass one lone couple walking and holding hands. They do a cartoon
double take as I rifle by: a foreign devil, hell-bent-for-leather in the
middle of Shanghai.

"Not bad, not bad," my congenial host says as I glide back toward the
lamppost where he has been waiting. I dismount. He receives his bike
back with obvious affection.

The name of my newfound friend is Shen Yongzhang. He is a tall, 16
good-looking youth in his early twenties. He sports a neatly trimmed
Clark Gable mustache, a tight-fitting cashmere shirt, which is unbuttoned
halfway down his chest, and skintight, baby-blue bell-bottom trousers.

"Are you a student?" he asks.

"No. I'm a writer."

"Where are you from?" He kills the engine of his moped.

"The United States."   20

"Oh. Wonderful! Where do you think my trousers come from?"

He smiles proudly as I lean down to examine his bell-bottoms.

"Look. Look here," he adds before I can respond. He fumbles at one
of his back patch pockets until he locates a small label sewn into the
seam. It appears to say LEVIS.

"Do you see that? Now tell me. Where do you think these pants come 24
from?"

"Well, it looks like they must come from the U.S.," I reply obligingly.

"No! No! Wrong!" He surprises me with the vehemence of his denial.
Then shifting his weight from one hip to the other over his bike, he says
triumphantly, "I made them myself, including the label. I made a pattern
of some pants that an overseas Chinese friend had, cut out the cloth,
and sewed them up myself."

He gets off his bike. Kicks down the stand. Does a complete turnaround
with elbows slightly raised as if he were fashion modeling a new line of
sports clothes.

"Not bad, huh?" He is grinning from ear to ear.   28

Examining Shen Yongzhang's pants more carefully, I can see that although convincing from a distance, they are indeed homemade. Not only is the machine stitching wavy, but in one place the inseam is coming unsewn. Nor is the LEVIS label an original but a replication done with a ballpoint pen on white cotton tape.

Unlike most Chinese youths who wear their hair in practical crew cuts, Shen wears his hair smartly trimmed, pomaded, and swept back in a fashionable wave so that tonsorially, he looks as if he might have come out a commercial filmed in Hong Kong or Singapore.

Of course, Shen does not know the West firsthand. His imitations are constructed on the basis of limited information. He is like a man enclosed in an isolated room trying to sketch the full dimensions of the outside world according to what he can see through the keyhole. Given such incomplete knowledge, the authenticity of his disguise is, in fact, no small triumph. Through sheer dedication and enthusiasm, he has some-how managed to create this enclave of Western affectation in the middle of China.

He remounts his moped and rests his elbows on its diminutive han-   32
dlebars in a way which is at once cavalier and winsome: although he is a handsome young man who has mastered coolness, he nonetheless seems to be a gentle and pleasant person at heart.

What is disorienting about Shen is that despite his look of cultivated aloofness, he exhibits none of the negativism or sullen sarcasm that one usually associates with his pose and style of dress in the West. His friendly exuberance and openness are completely at odds with the image his clothes create.

"How much would a motorbike like mine cost in America?" he asks, taking a scrap of rag out from under the seat and buffing the shiny black gas tank.

"It's quite difficult to make a comparison."

"Well, how many years' wages would it cost?" he persists.   36

"Probably less than a month's wages for an average worker."

Shen pauses to digest the import of what I have said. Finally, he says almost reverentially, "I saved five years for this one. It's made in Jinan, Shandong Province. This one cost me six hundred and eighty yuan [about $450 in 1980]. I saved since I graduated from middle school. Now I work for the city at a power plant on the night shift. But since this is holiday, I have a few nights off."

Three more motorcycles and sidecars filled with Public Security police officers ride into the square and head toward us. Shen stops talking and without turning his head follows their progress out of the corner of his eye.

"It's OK," he says, lowering his voice. But not until after they have   40 traversed the square and turned out on Tibet Road does he continue.

"It's OK. We're just making friends, aren't we? Our two countries are friends now, right? So why shouldn't we talk?" he asks rhetorically, as if he himself needed assurance that our conversation was not still considered a nefarious activity.

"Do the agents from the Public Security Bureau mind if you're out here on your bikes racing around at night?" I ask.

"Oh, it's all right," replies Shen diffidently. "But we wouldn't have dared do it during the Gang of Four. It was considered really bourgeois. They would have hounded us and criticized us for not being home studying politics."

"What about now?"   44

"Well," he begins, just as one of his confreres peels up and stops beside us with a skid. "We can do what we want now. Getting rid of the Gang of Four was like a second liberation for us."

Shen turns to his friend, Li Baomin, and introduces him to me. He is also wearing dark glasses, bell-bottom pants, and a tailored cotton shirt.

Again, several Public Security Bureau motorcycles turn into People's Square.

"They're just cruising," says Li. "Here, let's walk over toward the   48 reviewing stand. If you're not walking they think you're up to no good."

Both youths get off their mopeds and begin to push them by the handlebars. We start walking across the square as the motorcycles bear down on us.

"If they should stop, just speak Chinese and they'll think you're a student," says Shen. "They don't bother foreign students. Don't tell them you are a writer." Then, taking a comb out of his pocket, he gives his pomaded hair a few artful licks and pats it as if to make sure he is properly groomed should a confrontation arise.

"Just look in the other direction," says Li through the side of his mouth. "That way they won't be able to see that you're a foreigner."

I turn my head. The motorcycles glide by.   52

"Do you have much opportunity to talk with foreigners?"

"Not really," answers Shen dispiritedly. "We'd like to. There are a lot of young people now who just go up to foreigners on the Bund. They want to practice English. Everyone wants to speak English. But, unfortunately, we don't know how." He looks with resignation at Li. "When we were in middle school there were no classes in English, so we never learned."

The admission that he cannot speak any English seems to depress Shen. Indeed, it is ironic that these two youths, whose appearance suggests such accomplishment in the pursuit of foreign styles, cannot speak the language of the world they seek to imitate. Nor does it seem likely that, as power plant workers, Shen and his friend will ever learn. It is the fatal flaw in their efforts to transform themselves. Like actors, they are eternally fated to play characters they can never become.

Suddenly the floodlights which have been bathing the visages of Chair-   56
man Mao and Hua in bright light blink off. It is after midnight. Besides the other two mopeds which continue their frenzied buzzing around People's Square, there is virtually no one else out.

Shen offers Li and me cigarettes. I refuse politely.

"Hey! What about American cigarettes?" he asks, regaining some of his early joviality. "What about Loto Pai [Camels] and Luji Pai [Lucky Strike]?"

"And what about American cars?" asks Li. "Do you have a Fu-te [Ford] or a Da-zhe [Dodge]?"

Both youths ask their questions not to elicit answers but to display   60
proudly their knowledge of such forbidden foreign goods.

"Did you know that the government now allows Chinese people to buy foreign cars and import them?" asks Shen. "All that you need is the foreign currency. I heard of one person who got it from a relative in Hong Kong. But so far I don't think there are more than a few people who have them."

"Does everyone own a car in America?" queries Li.

"Yes. In fact, some people have two."

Again our conversation is interrupted as several more Public Security   64
Bureau motorcycles pull into the square. They pause and watch the other mopeds speeding around at the far end.

"They're patrolling again," advises Li. He looks over at the notebook in which I am writing.

"It would be better to put that away. If they come by and see someone talking to us and writing things down, they'll probably think you're a spy. There are still a lot of spies running around."

"But Li and I both feel very friendly to foreigners," Shen hastens to add, lest I take umbrage at even the merest suggestion that I am a spy.

"I'm not sure why they always talk so much about spies. I mean, who are these spies? You're not Russian. You're an American." He laughs.

"Sometimes," adds Li, "I think that all those cadres are a little too much. They can't even tell the difference between a foreigner and a spy, but if they catch you talking with a foreigner, they start rumors about you."

"Does everyone in the United States have cassette tape recorders?" asks Shen, shifting the conversation back to concrete affairs.

"Most anyone who wishes to have one can afford it, but since radio stations play popular music all day long, most people don't bother with them."

"Do you like disco music?" Before I can answer, Shen adds, "We're very fond of it. Sometimes we can get cassettes with disco music from overseas Chinese who visit Shanghai."

"Do you like to dance then?"

"Of course," responds Shen brightly. "But the government won't allow it in public any more. They closed down the only dance hall in Shanghai last spring. Now there is no place to go except our own homes, which are so cramped."

"I suppose you go dancing every night in the United States," Li says somewhat enviously.

"One can. But most people don't," I explain, trying to be truthful without utterly deflating the expectations of these two Western enthusiasts about the El Dorado from which I come.

"Do your friends like to drink a lot?" asks Shen as we finally reach the reviewing stand at the side of the square.

"Some do. How about young people here in Shanghai? Do they like to drink a lot?"

"No. Oh, no," says Shen and Li almost in unison. "Young people don't drink much in China. But we love to smoke cigarettes." With satisfaction, Shen exhales a large cloud of smoke into the night air. He again offers me a Double Happiness cigarette which, since I do not smoke, I refuse.

"Hey! Don't be so polite!" he protests. "If we're going to be friends, you can't be so polite," and again offers the cigarettes, whch I decline as tactfully as I can.

The last lights on the ornate lampposts, which have been serving as the slalom course, blink off. It is after one in the morning.

Seeing no further signs of Public Security Bureau motorcycles, I take out my notebook to exchange addresses with Li and Shen. As I write, both of them admire my American-made felt-tip pen. I ask if they would like to have it.

"No. No. We don't want it," they quickly protest, making me suddenly feel like a GI trying to dispense gum and nylons to the ravaged natives.

Neither youth, however, has the slightest compunction about giving his address.

"If you have time, come and see us. Anytime," says Shen, a cigarette 84 rakishly drooping from his mouth as he kick-starts his moped.

"OK. We'll be going." Li smiles and gives a quick wave. Then both youths open their throttles with a decisive twist and buzz down the center of People's Square, past the darkened portraits of the two chairmen.

EXPLORATIONS

1. What is the significance of the three-day Chinese holiday to Schell? to Shen Yongzhang? What is the significance of People's Square to Schell? to Shen?

2. What statements by Shen Yongzhang and Li Baomin show a sense of freedom under China's post-Mao government? What statements indicate that this freedom is limited?

3. Schell describes his nighttime adventure in the present tense. How would its impact change if he used the past tense? How would the essay's structure and effect change if Schell wrote it as a third-person report on current Chinese customs instead of as a first-person narrative?

CONNECTIONS

1. After reading Guan Keguang's "A Chinese Reporter on Cape Cod," what features of Shen Yongzhang's life would you guess were decided for him by the Party? What features has he evidently decided on for himself? Judging from "Shanghai" and from comments by Guan (who comes from Shanghai) about Chinese teenagers' yearning for independence, why do you think Shen's moped is worth five years' savings to him?

2. In what respects does "Shanghai" bear out Paul Harrison's theories about the Westernization of the world? Which elements in Shen Yongzhang's and Li Baomin's mimicry of American culture evidently reflect a national trend? Which elements are individual, and what seems to be their purpose?

3. In "Arriving in Tehran," what vision of post-shah Iran does Kate Millett give as a reason for wanting to visit that country? In what ways does reality fail to match her vision? What vision do Shen and Li have of the West that makes them copy American styles? In what ways does their vision conflict with reality? Why do they, or don't they, hope to visit the United States? What do you think would disappoint them most if they did come here?

ELABORATIONS

1. Based on "Shanghai," Guan Keguang's "A Chinese Reporter on Cape Cod," Liang Heng and Judith Shapiro's "Chairman Mao's Good Little Boy" (p. 450), Beverley Hooper's "Falling in Love with Love" (p. 220), and Ruth Sidel's "The Liu Family" (p. 21), write an essay describing what a day in your life would be like — your home, family, and friends, your activities, ambitions, and frustrations — if you lived in China. You may (but need not) use the form of a diary entry, a letter to a pen pal, or an article for an English-language magazine.

2. Guan Keguang writes that teenagers in China "yearn for independence and freedom. . . . They are frustrated when things don't go their way and they find themselves helpless and unable to do anything about their fate." Is this an accurate description of Shen Yongzhang and Li Baomin? Write an essay comparing those two Chinese teenagers' dreams, plans, and prospects with those of the characters in Satoshi Kamata's "Six Months at Toyota" (p. 360), Mario Vargas Llosa's "Sunday, Sunday" (p. 145), or Gholam-Hossein Sa'edi's "The Game Is Over" (p. 76).

ANDREA LEE

The Beriozka

Andrea Lee was born in Philadelphia in 1953; she received her bachelor's and master's degrees in English from Harvard University. In 1978–79, as graduate students, she and her husband spent a year in the Soviet Union. There she began writing *Russian Journal* (1979), from which comes "The Beriozka." Lee's sketchy knowledge of Russian quickly became fluent. "The fact that we both spoke Russian and were allowed to live among Russian students — for eight months in Moscow State University and two months at Leningrad State — made it easy for us to make a number of Russian friends from outside the restricted circles normally accessible to foreigners," she remarks in her foreword. In 1980 Lee received the Front Page Award for Distinguished Journalism given by the Newswomen's Club of New York. She has published several short stories concerning the dilemma of growing up well-to-do and black. Lee and her husband now live in Rome.

(For background on the Soviet Union, see the headnote to the following selection and pp. 48, 139, and 213.)

The diplomatic food store on Vasilevsky Island is located on an exceedingly drab industrial street where there are several factories, and a steady stream of poorly dressed men and women going by with huge bundles of food and necessities in bulging plastic suitcases or net bags. Many of these people slow down to stare as they pass the diplomatic store, which has the veiled, suggestive appearance of all Soviet *beriozki*. On this muddy street, filled with pits and rubble and lined with shabby buildings, the unmarked store window, with its snowy pleated draperies over a tasteful arrangement of pebbles that looks almost Japanese, is a mysterious and angelic presence, a visitation of luxury to a world that lives without it. Outside the store are often parked a few shiny foreign automobiles with diplomatic or business-community license plates — or equally shiny Soviet cars, usually the discreet black Volga. These are minutely examined by the heavily laden passersby. Occasionally a workman with a gnarled frostbitten face will eye the cars and spit scornfully, muttering, "Foreigners!"

Inside, the shop consists of two rooms, and to enter them from the street is like passing into another dimension; the carefully decorated interior, in fact, has a suggestion of the feeling of intimacy and luxury found in an expensive Western boutique. The larger room holds every expensive brand of European and American beer, wine, liquor, cigarette, and candy, all artistically set out on mirrored shelves that reflect the soft lighting and the red carpet on the floor. There is a section devoted to Soviet beverages — Armenian and Georgian wines and brandies, flavored vodkas, the rare "balsam" liqueur from the Baltic region — many of which are unobtainable on the open market. In front of the shelves are a couple of comfortable armchairs, and near these is an attractive laminated wooden desk where normally sit two pretty English-speaking Soviet girls in stylish Western outfits. These girls greet customers, sizing them up with the expertise of snobbish salespeople around the world; sometimes, depending on the apparent rank of the customer, they actually fill and push the little shopping carts. (We students are definitely not important enough to have our carts pushed. Living among Russians and arriving on foot as we do, we form the lowest of the castes allowed in the store, slightly below, say, the African diplomats, who receive only the most perfunctory smiles from the young women.)

The second, smaller room is filled with canned goods — usually German, Russian, or Bulgarian — and an array of marvelous fresh meats, dairy products, and produce, all of which are Russian, and most of which are superior to anything one can buy on the open market or at the *rynok*. The beef is all prime, the hamburger particularly, so lean that fat must be added to it. There is liver, which Russians love, and which is almost impossible to buy for rubles, since it is reserved for restaurants serving foreigners and stores like this one. In the produce section are big bags of hothouse cucumbers and tomatoes, the same vegetables that have been selling for ten to fifteen rubles a kilo in the peasant markets this winter. In general, the prices at the diplomatic store are very low. The payment procedure is this: the foreigner pays his own currency for a booklet of ruble coupons redeemable for goods only in these special stores. Right now, a diplomatic ruble costs about a dollar forty. Even with the disadvantageous exchange rate, the store is full of bargains: a bottle of Cointreau costs about three rubles; a sack of precious tomatoes, about two rubles; a bottle of Starorusskaya (considered one of the best Russian vodkas), a ruble fifty.

Last week when I was at the store, a middle-aged foreign woman from   4 the Brahmin caste that receives obsequious service from the salesgirls was doing some shopping. She had a finely made-up, rather imperious face, and was swathed in handsome sheared beaver, the kind of coat Russians rarely see, because the best Russian furs are exported. One of the sales-girls, a curly-headed blonde in a denim jumper, was pushing her cart and urging her to buy some lettuce. "It's just in today, madame," she said in her birdlike English. "Greenhouse lettuce! Our first this winter!"

"I don't know," said the woman, also in English but with an ambiguous European accent. "So far I've not been very impressed with your Soviet vegetables. But send some to me tomorrow." She raised a thin hand to her lips, and I saw her fingers glittering with diamonds. At the desk, the other salesgirl, a redhead, gently packed the woman's few purchases into a plastic bag, totted up the bill in graceful flourishes on a piece of paper, and reverently received the coupons. As the woman went out, the blond salesgirl sighed, and then said to her companion in rapid Russian, "That coat — oh, my goodness! And the boots, did you see the boots? All the women are wearing that style now. What a life!"

I had been pushing my own cart around. When I came up to the desk, they treated me with absentminded civility, and I felt very annoyed. I was annoyed partly because I, too, longed for a fur coat and diamonds, but mostly because I knew that these young women shared with me a knowledge of the contrast between the two worlds of the Soviet Union: the hidden world where luxury and snobbery reign for privileged Russians — and especially for foreigners — and the harsh life of the working class on the outside, where even the plastic shopping bags from the *beriozki* are coveted luxuries. The workers on the street can't see inside the diplomatic store, and the foreigners, climbing into their cars and driving back to their segregated luxury apartments, can't possibly know what life is like for the average Russian. But I, trudging through the streets, speaking Russian and visiting Russian friends, know what both sides are like, and so do these young women, far better than I. So how, I wondered, could they sit there, so prettily painted and manicured, ready to shepherd rich women around this mirrored, carpeted room, without any trace of ugly cynicism crossing their faces? I told myself it was the universal Soviet pragmatism I've seen so clearly in Valerii and my other friends: the philosophy is to find your niche, make your adjustments, and then live without considering it. Like Intourist guides, and other Russians whose jobs involve close contact with foreigners, the salesgirls probably have KGB affiliations and probably, also, the privilege of shopping in the special "closed" stores for upper-level Russians. They are young, pretty girls, and the diplomatic-store job is clearly quite a pleasant one.

Just as I was leaving the store last week, something happened that occasionally occurs in these special stores. Normally, the doorman, a short, fat man with bulging eyes and a grotesquely upturned nose, is on guard to keep ordinary Russians from entering, but at that moment he was pausing to smoke a foreign cigarette and to lean over the desk to say something confidential to the two girls; the door, moreover, was open to allow some of the fresh balmy afternoon into the store. An old woman dressed in a worn black wool coat, a gray wool scarf, and a pair of rubber-shod *valenki* — unmistakably a woman from that stream of populace passing in the grimy street outside — appeared suddenly in the doorway. "*Ostorozhno!* [Watch out!]" hissed one of the salesgirls, and the guard leaped over to the door and began to back the old woman out, speaking in a firm, officious voice as if to a child. "Now, grandmother, this isn't for you. This is a special store, for foreigners . . ." The *babushka* pretended to be deaf and slow-witted, but it was clear that she knew what she was doing, and had been drawn there out of curiosity. As the guard backed her out, her head swiveled around and she took in the whole glittering two rooms. It was amazing to watch her wrinkled red face, on which there struggled a remarkable mixture of astonishment and avidity, as if she'd just discovered, and longed to plunder, an entirely new world.

EXPLORATIONS

1. What are the advantages and disadvantages to Lee of being a foreigner in the Soviet Union? Which of these advantages and disadvantages are not shared by the "middle-aged foreign woman from the Brahmin caste" whom she observes in the beriozka?

2. How do the beriozka employees treat different types of foreign customers differently? What seem to be the reasons for the distinction? How do other Russians evidently feel about the beriozka customers, and why?

3. Lee speaks of "the contrast between the two worlds of the Soviet Union" — luxury for the powerful and "the harsh life of the working class." How are the criteria for membership in the upper stratum different in the Soviet Union and the United States? Why do you think Lee, an upper-middle-class black American, is "annoyed" by the Soviets' acceptance of such a gap between wealth and poverty?

CONNECTIONS

1. What response to foreigners is shared by the Russian young women at the beriozka and the Chinese young men in Orville Schell's "Shanghai"? How are their responses different? On the basis of Schell's experience in China, and other reading you have done on the Soviet Union, where and how do you think Lee might be able to start a serious conversation with the young women from the beriozka? What factors might make such a conversation impossible under any circumstances?

2. In "The Beriozka," as in most of the preceding selections, clothing plays a central role in people's assessment of foreigners. What message does the European shopper's clothing convey to the Russian girls? to Lee? What do we learn about the young Chinese in "Shanghai" from Orville Schell's remarks about their clothing? What is revealed about the Iranians in "Arriving in Tehran," and about Kate Millett's sense of herself, by their clothing? In "Entering the New World," what does V. S. Naipaul suggest about Ebony with his comments on the poet's clothing? Quote key phrases by each author.

3. What official Soviet attitude toward foreigners, and toward Westerners in particular, is reflected by the beriozka? How do you think Paul Harrison would explain this attitude, based on his theories in "The Westernization of the World"? Into which of his categories does the Soviet Union fall?

ELABORATIONS

1. In "Woman as Other" (p. 241 and repeated in Part Seven's introduction on p. 598) Simone de Beauvoir writes: "The native traveling abroad is shocked to find himself in turn regarded as a 'stranger' by the natives of neighboring countries." Judging from "The Beriozka" and Paul Harrison's "The Westernization of the World," what qualities help travelers insulate themselves from this shock? Under what circumstances would you expect the insulation to be ineffective? Among visitors and immigrants to our country, who is treated most and least like the Other, and why? Drawing on these and other selections you have read, write an essay identifying the qualities that seem to increase and decrease culture shock for strangers in a strange land.

2. How different is the Soviet beriozka — its employees, its customers, its displays of goods, its reasons for existing — from an exclusive shop in the United States? Using "The Beriozka" as a model, a standard of comparison, or both, write an essay describing a visit you have made to a store that caters to wealthy customers or some other special group, such as military personnel.

DAVID K. SHIPLER

Western Things

Born in 1942 in Orange, New Jersey, David K. Shipler has worked for the *New York Times* since 1966. He received his bachelor's degree from Dartmouth College in 1964; two years later he married and became a news clerk at the *Times*. He rose to reporter in 1968, and in 1973 he became a foreign correspondent in Saigon. His next posting was Moscow, where he served first as foreign correspondent and then as bureau chief from 1977 to 1979. From there he went to Jerusalem as *Times* bureau chief. In 1982 Shipler was a corecipient of the George Polk Award for foreign reporting for his coverage of the war in Lebanon. He spent the year 1984–85 as a visiting scholar at the Brookings Institution in Washington, D.C. Shipler was named chief diplomatic correspondent for the *Times* in 1987. His books include *Russia: Broken Idols, Solemn Dreams* (1983), from which "Western Things" is taken, and *Arab and Jew: Wounded Spirits in a Promised Land* (1987). He and his family live in Chevy Chase, Maryland, near Washington.

Like China (see p. 635), the Soviet Union has been opening up in recent years to Westerners and their ideas. With new political leadership has come a receptivity to capitalist tenets and tactics that would have shocked the revolutionary souls of Lenin and Mao. Soviet General Secretary Mikhail Gorbachev, who became Communist Party leader in 1985, has introduced a policy of *glasnost,* or openness, which in some ways echoes the détente that relaxed international tensions in the early 1970s. So far, *glasnost* has brought new arms-control proposals, the release of several political dissidents, broader media coverage, less censorship and more international exchange in the arts, and greater freedom of movement for foreign visitors. (Perhaps as a counterbalance, Gorbachev also seems to be a strong supporter of the KGB, the Soviet secret police.) Among Gorbachev's top priorities is domestic economic reform: improving food and housing, and raising the quality of Soviet industries' products and operations (see Hedrick Smith's "*Skoro Budet* — It'll Be Here Soon," p. 374). These and other proposed changes are hard to implement in the heavily centralized Soviet system, a problem which may encourage some of the quasi-capitalist experimentation that has worked so well for China.

Russia for centuries has looked out upon the Western world through a blended sense of infatuation and inferiority, drawn by the material wealth and cultural novelty, repelled by the disharmony of pluralism, terrified by the fluidity of ideas that rage outside the gates. This has been no easy gaze of detachment but a raw obsession driven by the Russians' conflicting emotions about themselves. Gripped by an aching inadequacy, cloistered by an ancient chauvinism, Russia remains intrigued by Western life and largely immune to it.

In the decade of the 1970s the openings provided by détente exposed Soviet society to more Western, especially American, influence than at any other period since the Bolshevik Revolution. American banks and businesses set up offices in Moscow to promote trade. Tourists, students, scientists, scholars, performers, and journalists poured in from Western Europe, Canada, and the United States. And a more restricted and selective flow of Russians went westward, bringing back an array of impressions unvarnished by the politics of their textbooks and newspapers. But the qualities in America that the Russians came to admire were not those that many Americans had hoped to export. A powerful lust developed for the material goods and popular styles of American society, a craving for the exotic artifacts of the consumer culture. In Moscow and other major cities a lucrative black market flourished in jeans, rock records, chewing gum, and American cigarettes. Faddish teenagers slapped English words into Russian slang and sported dungaree jackets with American flags sewn on the sleeves. The Voice of America, which the authorities stopped jamming from September 1973 to September 1980, became a daily source of news for millions of Russians, including many high officials.

But the idea of democracy never gained much favor, even in the quiet of personal attitudes. Few Russians comprehended the principles of a free press, free elections, open debate, and individual liberties; few could grasp the curious American notion that government was to be distrusted and contained and kept out of private lives. And those who understood often found the ideas distasteful, productive only of disorder. Black-marketeering was much more popular than political dissent, though just as dangerous: Many more Soviet citizens were willing to risk imprisonment for buying and selling jeans than for advocating free speech.

The lessons of this came to me slowly. It is easy to be dazzled by the   4
semi-illicit jazz concert, held in a trade union hall at the farthest outskirts of Moscow, the tickets passed out hand to hand by members and friends of the local bands and combos that are assembling for a long night of Dixieland and saxophone blues and tuneless improvisation. The kids are

mostly college students with connections, dressed in demin and suede, jammed into the seats, where they listen intensely but impassively, letting whatever emotions the music rouses stir quietly beneath an implacable surface. A long-haired young man onstage, alone with his saxophone, begins to undress slowly as he warbles and screeches and toots and squawks. He has a bushy, Gabby Hayes mustache, and he is supposed to be funny, free, unrestrained, wonderfully impulsive. He takes off his dungaree jacket, revealing a raspberry red undershirt. He writhes, makes faces, yells into the microphone, gets down on his knees, and plays unmusically. The kids around me are intrigued, but many are contemptuous; they think it is stupid and undisciplined, and the applause he gets at the end is scattered, perfunctory. They have good taste; they like the accomplished groups. Above the stage hangs a red and white banner: LET US FULFILL OUR PERSONAL TASKS IN THE 3RD YEAR OF THE FIVE-YEAR PLAN.

It is easy to be enthralled by the excitement of a crowd of Muscovites pushing, clamoring for places at a performance of the London Symphony. It is easy to imagine that in the craving of travel to the West, in the passion to read Western literature (even trash), in the stalwart lining up at dawn to get into a State Department exhibition on American life, Russians are expressing their rebelliousness, their discontent, their yearning for the freewheeling cultural and political values of the Western world. Only gradually did I see that the phenomenon did not often run that deep. "It is the only opportunity for them to look through a window," Irina Brailovsky explained to me. "It is as if you lived in a little room with the same people, the same point of view, and no visitors. All of a sudden there's a window, so you rush to it to look out, even if you don't like what's on the other side." The attraction to the tangible, the shimmering superficiality, leaves impulse and attitude at the depths unchanged.

This is a hard discovery for Americans, one we often resist, for its implications corrode our creed that freedom is man's natural state, that all other conditions are abnormal, that the innate reflex of human beings is to strive against their bonds. After a time in Russia we become embarrassed by the nakedness of our naïveté. And on some level, perhaps, we hate the Russians for giving the lie to our innermost assumptions about mankind.

The disjointed reactions to the outside world, the dissonance of infatuation and contempt, expressed themselves in several rather symbolic episodes. Irina McClellan, the Moscow schoolteacher who married an American, found herself vilified as *Amerikanka*, ("American woman"), by neighbors in her communal apartment, people who were anti-Semitic

Russian nationalists, she said, but who shamelessly acquired every possible electronic or wearable item from the West and Japan. They talked
about these goods constantly and seemed to see no inconsistency between
their material and social views. Irina laughed about this in that wry
fashion that has become the trademark of the dissident who has learned
how closely these bitter situations come to comedy.

One December, as the New Year approached, Russians in contact   8
with Westerners began their annual rite of agitation and lobbying for the
item of prestige and currency known as the business calendar, which was
to be used in schemes of favoritism and bribery so complex that only a
bazaar merchant could unravel them. Soviet employees of the American
Embassy and news organizations put in their bids for Pan Am calendars.
The annual shipment of Swissair calendars was stolen from Sheremetyevo
Airport, as usual. And a carton of Chase Manhattan Bank calendars was
delivered to the bank's offices in the Metropole Hotel near Red Square,
setting off a remarkable chain of events. The bank's secretary in the outer
office buzzed the bank's representative, David Buckman, on the inter-
com. She told him the calendars had arrived. Five minutes later she
appeared in Buckman's office to explain, quietly, that the gentleman who
listens to the telephones had heard the conversation about the calendars
and wondered if he might have a few. "I figured I'd smoke him out,"
Buckman told me later. So he had his secretary tell the KGB man that
he, Buckman, would present him with some calendars if he came personally to get them. Minutes later the man was there, shaking hands and
smiling, receiving his calendars, taking Buckman down the hall to show
him his room equipped with telephone paraphernalia and a reel-to-reel
tape recorder. Thereafter, when Buckman came to work each morning,
the KGB man would lean out of his room and wave greetings.

In the winter of the United States bicentennial year, plastic bags with
the bicentennial seal were being given out at a mobbed American exhibition to all Muscovites who had the fortitude to line up long enough in
the freezing cold to make it into the pavilion. The plastic bag became
an instant sign of status, proof that the citizen who carried it had caught
a glimpse through that window into the outside world. At the height of
this frenzy, on a boulevard some distance from the exhibition, a traffic
policeman spotted a black Chevrolet Impala with the distinctive license
plate that designated a diplomat of the American variety — black nu-
merals on white, beginning with the telltale code D-04. The Chevrolet
was being driven by a Soviet chauffeur, and the policeman waved him
over. The chauffeur got out, walked back to converse with the cop, then

returned, explaining to his American Embassy passenger that he was being accused of crossing a solid line presumably painted somewhere beneath the snow.

"Did you get a ticket?" the passenger asked.

"I don't know yet," the driver replied. "He said if I got back here with a plastic bag before he goes off duty at two P.M., he'd tear the ticket up."

One cannot expect all uniformed or plainclothes guardians of Soviet insularity to maintain indifference as tantalizing fragments of American life flit past them. So relatives visiting prisoners sometimes slip the guards packages of American chewing gum in exchange for a longer time with their loved ones. Packs of Marlboros and Winstons become currency for favors from the most officious bureaucrats. A hapless tourist, ahead of me in a customs line, found his *Playboy* magazine intercepted at the airport as pornography; the customs inspectors (several were needed for such a serious purpose) leafed through the journal with considerable slowness, studying each page to be sure that the momentous step of confiscation, which they were about to take, was thoroughly justified. An American diplomat once had the temerity to offer a copy of *Playboy* to a KGB "militiaman" on guard outside his apartment house. The officer accepted it with alacrity. Later, as the American returned home, another officer, who had just come on duty, asked if he had another *Playboy* to spare. No, the diplomat apologized. "Well," said the guard, "do you have a gin and tonic?" The American got him one.

In certain suave circles of the middle elite, American styles became overt fads. A friend of mine whose parents were both medical professors told me that at her sister's fifteenth birthday party, all the boys and girls, who clustered separately, wore American jeans — every one of them. At a prestigious Moscow architectural institute's annual dance the students one year built a huge model of a pair of dungarees to tower over the dance floor — the centerpiece of their decorations and a totem in the idolatry of the age. An American woman shocked her Russian maid by removing and throwing away a leather Lee patch that was coming loose from a pair of jeans. The patch was the whole idea, the maid said, and snapped it up to sew on a pair of her son's.

EXPLORATIONS

1. According to Shipler, what aspects of Western culture are most admired or coveted in the Soviet Union, and why? What conflicts does his essay suggest between the Communist ideal of equality and the personal goals of individual Russians?

2. What Western assumptions and attitudes are not shared by most Russians? What evidence in Shipler's essay suggests that chauvinism (excessive or blind patriotism) is a factor in these differences of opinion? What other factors play a role?

3. In paragraph 4 Shipler describes a "semi-illicit jazz concert" in Moscow. What point is this paragraph evidently meant to convey? What words and phrases appear to reflect Shipler's views about the music and musicians more than the audience's?

CONNECTIONS

1. What ideas about the Soviet Union appear in both "Western Things" and Andrea Lee's "The Beriozka"? How do Shipler's reasons for being in the Soviet Union differ from Lee's? How do these two writers' viewpoints, focuses, and conclusions differ?

2. How do you think Shipler would interpret the Chinese view of the West that emerges in Orville Schell's "Shanghai"? On what points would Schell and Shipler be likely to agree? to disagree?

3. According to Edward T. Hall in "Proxemics in the Arab World," both Arabs and Westerners consider each other "pushy." After reading "Western Things," what labels do you think both Russians and Westerners might apply to each other, and why?

ELABORATIONS

1. What central conclusion about Western influence on non-Western countries is reached by Shipler? by Paul Harrison in "The Westernization of the World"? by V. S. Naipaul in "Entering the New World"? On the basis of these three selections, and any others you wish to draw on, write an essay (a) indicating how citizens of foreign countries perceive the United States, and (b) suggesting ways for our government, private citizens, or both to make future dealings abroad as positive and productive as possible.

2. In describing Russians' passion for imported calendars, plastic bags, and brand-name jeans, Shipler is not introducing us to a new or strictly foreign phenomenon. What imported goods in the United States have taken on a status value that exceeds their innate worth? What makes these objects so highly prized? Write an essay classifying one or more categories of "non-Western things" that people in this country covet.

STANISŁAW LEM

Being Inc.

Stanisław Lem is a man of many contradictions. Known for his futur-istic stories and novels involving intergalactic travel, he dislikes traveling and has spent most of his life in the ancient Polish city of Krakow. Lem was born in 1921 in Lvov, eighteen years before Poland was overrun and divided by Germany and the Soviet Union — events that triggered World War II. Lem originally studied medicine but switched to a literary career in the 1940s, channeling his scientific flair into cybernetics and space exploration, which he blends with philosophy and parody. His novels, stories, and screenplays have been translated into almost thirty languages (Lem reads English but does not speak it). "Being Inc.," translated from the Polish by Michael Kandel, comes from Lem's 1979 collection *A Perfect Vacuum*. It is an example of one story form at which he excels: the mock book review, in this case of a novel by the mythical American Alastair Waynewright. Although its setting is the United States, Lem has never traveled to this country (in spite of numerous invitations) and has no wish to do so. However, in 1983 he and his wife and son moved to Vienna, partly so that his son could attend an American high school there. The move followed Lem's refusal to become a member of the government-sponsored writers' union after the suppression of Solidarity (although he has never openly supported the movement). He has not decided yet whether to stay in the West or return to Poland.

(For more background on Poland, see p. 488.)

When one takes on a servant, his wages cover — besides the work — the respect a servant owes a master. When one hires a lawyer, beyond professional advice one is purchasing a sense of security. He who buys love and not merely strives to win it, also expects caresses and affection. The price of an airplane ticket has for some time included the smiles and seemingly genial courtesy of attractive stewardesses. People are in-clined to pay for the "private touch," that feeling of being *intime*, taken care of, liked, which constitutes an important ingredient in the packaging of services rendered in every walk of life.

But life itself does not, after all, consist of personal contacts with servants, lawyers, employees of hotels, agencies, airlines, stores. On the contrary: the contacts and relationships we most desire lie outside the sphere of services bought and sold. One can pay to have computer assistance in selecting a mate, but one cannot pay to have the behavior one chooses in a wife or husband after the wedding. One can buy a yacht, a palace, an island, if one has the money, but money cannot provide longed-for events — on the order of: displaying one's heroism or intelligence, rescuing a divine creature in mortal danger, winning at the races, or receiving a high decoration. Nor can one purchase goodwill, spontaneous attraction, the devotion of others. Innumerable stories bear witness to the fact that the desire for precisely such freely given emotions gnaws at mighty rulers and men of wealth; in fairy tales he who is able to buy or use force to obtain anything, having the means for this, abandons his exceptional position so that in disguise — like Hārūn ar-Rashīd, who went as a beggar — he may find human genuineness, since privilege shuts it out like an impenetrable wall.

So, then, the one area that has not yet been turned into a commodity is the unarranged substance of everyday life, intimate as well as official, private as well as public, with the result that each and every one of us is exposed continually to those small reversals, ridiculings, disappointments, animosities, to the snubs that can never be paid back, to the unforeseen; in short, exposed — within the scope of our personal lot — to a state of affairs that is intolerable, in the highest degree deserving a change; and this change for the better will be initiated by the great new industry of life services. A society in which one can buy — with an advertising campaign — the post of president, or a herd of albino elephants painted with little flowers, or a bevy of beauties, or youth through hormones, such a society ought to be able to put to rights the human condition. The qualm that immediately surfaces — that such purchased forms of life, being unauthentic, will quickly betray their falseness when placed alongside the surrounding authenticity of events — that qualm is dictated by a naïveté totally lacking in imagination. When all children are conceived in the test tube, when then no sexual act has as its consequence, once natural, procreation, there disappears the difference between the normal and the aberrant in sex, seeing as no physical intimacy serves any purpose but that of pleasure. And where every life finds itself under the solicitous eye of powerful service enterprises, there disappears the difference between authentic events and those secretly arranged. The distinction between natural and synthetic in adventures, successes, failures, ceases to exist when one can no longer tell what is taking place by pure accident, and what by accident paid for in advance.

This, more or less, is the idea of A. Waynewright's novel, *Being Inc.*   4

The mode of operation of that corporate entity is to act at a distance: its base cannot be known to anyone; clients communicate with Being Inc. exclusively by correspondence, in an emergency by telephone. Their orders go into a gigantic computer; the execution of these is dependent on the size of the client's account, that is, on the amount of the remittance. Treachery, friendship, love, revenge, one's own good fortune and another's adversity may be obtained also on the installment plan, through a convenient credit system. The destinies of children are shaped by the parents, but on the day he comes of age each person receives in the mail a price list, a catalog of services, and in addition the firm's instruction booklet. The booklet is a clearly but substantively written treatise, philosophical and sociotechnological — not the usual advertising material. Its lucid, elevated language states what in an unelevated way may be summarized as follows.

All people pursue happiness, but not all in the same way. For some, happiness means preeminence over others, self-reliance, situations of permanent challenge, risk, and the great gamble. For others it is submission, faith in authority, the absence of all threat, peace and quiet, even indolence. Some love to display aggression; some are more comfortable when they can be on the receiving end of it. Many find satisfaction in a state of anxiety and distress, which can be observed in their inventing for themselves, when they have no real worries, imaginary ones. Research shows that ordinarily there are as many active individuals as passive in society. The misfortune of society in the past — asserts the booklet — lay in the fact that society was not able to effect harmony between the natural inclinations of its citizens and their path in life. How often did blind chance decide who would win and who lose, to whom would fall the role of Petronius,[1] and to whom the role of Prometheus.[2] One must seriously doubt the story that Prometheus did not expect the vulture. It is far more likely, according to modern psychology, that it was entirely for the purpose of being pecked in the liver that he stole the fire of heaven. He was a masochist; masochism, like eye coloring, is an inborn trait and nothing to be ashamed of; one should matter-of-factly indulge it and utilize it for the good of society. Formerly — explains the text in scholarly tones — blind fate decided for whom pleasures would be in store, and for whom privation; men lived wretched lives, because

---

[1]Roman satirist of the first century. — ED.

[2]Greek mythological hero who stole fire from the gods and gave it to humans, for which he was chained to a rock where his liver was torn out by a vulture. — ED.

he who, fond of beating, is beaten, is every bit as miserable as he who, desirous of a good thrashing, must himself — forced by circumstances — thrash others.

The principles of operation of Being Inc. did not emerge in a vacuum: matrimonial computers have for some time now been using similar rules in matchmaking. Being Inc. guarantees each client the full arrangement of his life, from the attaining of his majority until his death, in keeping with the wishes expressed by him on the form enclosed. The Company, in its work, avails itself of the most up-to-date cybernetic, socioengineering, and informational methods. Being Inc. does not immediately carry out the wishes of its clients, for people often do not themselves know their own nature, do not understand what is good for them and what is bad. The Company subjects each new client to a remote-monitor psychotechnological examination; a battery of ultrahigh-speed computers determines the personality profile and all the proclivities of the client. Only after such a diagnosis will the Company accept his order.

One need not be ashamed of the content of the order; it remains forever a Company secret. Nor need one fear that the order might, in its realization, cause harm to anyone. It is the Company's job to see that this does not happen; let it trouble its electronic head over that. Mr. Smith here would like to be a stern judge handing out sentences of death, and so the defendants who come before him will be people deserving nothing less than capital punishment. Mr. Jones wishes he could flog his children, deny them every pleasure, and in addition persist in the conviction that he is a just and upright father? Then he shall have cruel and wicked children, the castigation of whom will require half his lifetime. The Company grants all requests; sometimes, however, one must wait on line, as when the desire is to kill a person by one's own hand, since there are a surprising number of such fanciers. In different states the condemned are dispatched differently; in some they are hanged, in others poisoned with hydrogen cyanide, in still others electricity is used. He who has a predilection for hanging finds himself in a state where the legal instrument of execution is the gallows, and before he knows it he has become the temporary hangman. A plan to enable clients to murder with impunity in an open field, on the grass, in the privacy of the home, has not as yet been sanctioned by the law, but the Company is patiently working for the institution of this innovation as well. The Company's skill in arranging events, demonstrated in millions of synthetic careers, will surmount the numerous difficulties that presently bar the way to these murders on order. The condemned man, say, notices that the door of his cell on death row is open; he flees; the Company agents, on the lookout, so influence the path of his flight that he stumbles on the client in circumstances the most suitable for both. He might, for example, attempt to hide in the home of the client while the latter happens to be engaged in loading a hunting rifle. But the catalog of possibilities which the Company has compiled is inexhaustible.

Being Inc. is an organization the like of which is unknown in history. This is essential. The matrimonial computer united a mere *two* persons and did not concern itself with what would happen to them after the tying of the knot. Being Inc., on the other hand, must orchestrate enormous groupings of events involving thousands of people. The Company cautions the reader that its actual methods of operation are *not* mentioned in the brochure. The examples given are purely fictitious! The strategy of the arranging must be kept in absolute secrecy; the client must never be allowed to find out what is happening to him naturally and what by the aid of the Company computers that watch unseen over his destiny.

Being Inc. possesses an army of employees; these make their appearance as ordinary citizens — as chauffeurs, butchers, physicians, engineers, maids, infants, dogs, and canaries. The employees must be anonymous. An employee who at any time betrays his incognito, i.e., who discloses that he is a bona fide member of the team of Being Inc., not only loses his post but is pursued by the Company to his grave. Knowing his habits and tastes, the Company will arrange for him such a life that he will curse the hour in which he perpetrated the foul deed. There is no appealing a punishment for the betrayal of a Company secret — not that the Company intends this statement as a threat. No, the Company includes its *real* ways of dealing with bad employees among its trade secrets.

The reality shown in the novel is different from the picture painted in the promotional pamphlet of Being Inc. The advertisements are silent about the most important thing. Antitrust legislation in the U.S.A. forbids monopolies; consequently Being Inc. is not the only life arranger. There are its great competitors, Hedonica and the Truelife Corporation. And it is precisely this circumstance that leads to events unprecedented in history. For when persons who are clients of different companies come into contact with one another, the implementation of the orders of each may encounter unforeseen difficulties. Those difficulties take the form of what is called "covert parasitizing," which leads to cloak-and-dagger escalation.

Suppose that Mr. Smith wishes to shine before Mrs. Brown, the wife

of a friend, to whom he feels an attraction, and he selects item No. 396b
on the list: saving a life in a train wreck. From the wreck both are to
escape without injury, but Mrs. Brown thanks only to the heroism of
Mr. Smith. Now, the Company must arrange a railway accident with
great precision and in addition set up an entire situation in order that
the named parties, as the result of a series of apparent coincidences, ride
in the same compartment; monitors located in the walls, the floor, and
the backs of the seats in the coach, feeding data to the computer that —
concealed in the lavatory — is programming the action, will see to it
that the accident takes place exactly according to plan. It must take place
in such a way that Smith *cannot not* save the life of Mrs. Brown. So
that he will not know what he is doing, the side of the overturned coach
will be ripped open in the very place where Mrs. Brown is sitting, the
compartment will fill with suffocating smoke, and Smith, in order to get
out, will first have to push the woman through the opening, thereby
saving her from death by asphyxiation. The whole operation presents no
great difficulty. Several dozen years ago it took an army of computers,
and another of specialists, to land a lunar shuttle meters from its goal;
nowadays a single computer, following the action with the aid of a concert
of monitors, can solve the problem set it with no trouble.

If, however, Hedonica or Truelife has accepted an order from the   12
husband of Mrs. Brown, which asks that Smith reveal himself to be a
scoundrel and a coward, complications ensue. Through industrial espi-
onage Truelife learns of the railway operation planned by Being; the most
economical thing is to hook into someone else's arrangemental plan, and
it is precisely in this that "covert parasitizing" consists. Truelife introduces
into the moment of the wreck a small deviation factor that will be
sufficient to have Smith, when he shoves Mrs. Brown out of the hole,
give her a black eye, tear her dress, and break both her legs into the
bargain.

Should Being Inc., thanks to its counterintelligence, learn of this
parasitizing plan, it will take corrective measures, and thus will begin the
process of operational escalation. In the overturning coach inevitably it
comes to a duel between two computers — the one belonging to Being,
in the lavatory, and the one belonging to Truelife, hidden perhaps under
the floor of the coach. Behind the potential deliverer of the woman and
behind her, the potential victim, stand two Molochs of electronics and
organization. During the accident there is unleashed — in fractions of a
second — a monstrous battle of computers; it is difficult to conceive what
colossal forces will be intervening on one side in order that Smith push

heroically and rescuingly, and, on the other, that he push ungallantly and tramplingly. More and more reinforcements are brought in, till what was to have been a small exhibition of manliness in the presence of a woman turns into a cataclysm. Company records note the occurrence, over a period of nine years, of two such disasters, called GASPs (Galloping Arrangementive Spirals). After the last GASP, which cost the parties involved nineteen million dollars for the electrical energy, steam, and waterpower expended in the course of thirty-seven seconds, an agreement was reached on the strength of which an upper limit to arrangementing was set. It may not comsume more than 10^{12} joules per client-minute; excluded also from the actualization of services are all forms of atomic energy.

Against this background runs the action proper of the novel. The new president of Being Inc., young Ed Hammer III, is personally to look into the case of the order submitted by Mrs. Jessamine Chest the eccentric heiress-millionairess, since her demands, of an outré nature, not to be found in any catalog, go beyond the reach of all the rungs in the Company's administrative ladder. Jessamine Chest desires life in its full authenticity, purged of all arranging interference; for the fulfillment of this wish she is prepared to pay any price. Ed Hammer, against the advice of his advisers, accepts the assignment; the task, which he puts before his staff — how to arrange the total absence of arranging — proves more difficult than any so far tackled. Research reveals that nothing like an elemental spontaneity in life has existed for a long time. Eliminating the preparations for any particular arrange-plan brings to light the remnants of other, earlier ones; events unscenarioed are not to be found even in the bosom of Being Inc. For, as it turns out, the three rival enterprises have thoroughly and reciprocally arranged one another; that is, they have filled with their own trusted men key positions in the administration and on the board of directors of each competitor. Aware of the danger created by such a discovery, Hammer turns to the chairmen of both the other enterprises, whereupon there is a secret meeting in which specialists having access to the main computers serve as advisers. This confrontation makes it possible, finally, to ascertain the true state of affairs.

In the year 2041, throughout the length and breadth of the U.S.A., not a man can eat a chicken, fall in love, heave a sigh, have a whiskey, refuse a beer, nod, wink, spit — without higher electronic planning, which for years in advance has created a preestablished disharmony. Without realizing it, in the course of their competition the three billion-dollar corporations have formed a One in Three Persons, an All-Powerful

Disposer of Destiny. The programs of the computers make up a Book of Fate; arranged are political parties, arranged is the weather, and even the coming into the world of Ed Hammer III was the result of specific orders, orders that in turn resulted from other orders. No one any longer can be born or die spontaneously; no one any longer can on his own, by himself, from beginning to end, live anything, because his every thought, his every fear, his every pain, is a short sequence of algebraic calculations run through the computer. Empty now are the concepts of sin, retribution, moral responsibility, good and evil, because the full arrangementation of life excludes nonnegotiable values. In the computerized paradise created thanks to the hundred-percent utilization of all the human qualities and their incorporation into an infallible system, only one thing was missing — the awareness of the inhabitants that this was precisely how things stood. And therefore the meeting of the three corporate heads has been planned also by the main computer, which — providing them with this information — presents itself now as the Tree of Knowledge lit up with electricity. What will happen next? Should this perfectly arranged existence be abandoned in a new, second flight from Eden, in order to "start once more from the beginning"? Or should man accept it, renouncing once and for all the burden of responsibility? The book offers no answer. It is, therefore, a metaphysical burlesque, whose fantastic elements nevertheless have some connection with the real world. When we disregard the humoristic humbug and the elephantiasis of the author's imagination, there remains the problem of the manipulation of minds, and particularly of that kind of manipulation which does not lessen the full subjective sense of spontaneity and freedom. The thing will certainly not come about in the form shown in *Being Inc.*, but who can say whether fate will spare our descendants other forms of this phenomenon — forms perhaps less amusing in description but not, it may be, any less oppressive.

EXPLORATIONS

1. What is the one request that the corporation Being Inc. cannot fulfill? Why is this request impossible to grant?
2. What is the central point of Lem's first two paragraphs in "Being Inc."? What dilemma is posed in his last paragraph? How is the point made in the opening paragraphs essential to the concluding dilemma?

3. What message(s) do you draw from "Being Inc."? What advantages does Lem gain by presenting his ideas in the form of a mock book review rather than an essay or story?

4. What aspects of American culture, as it exists in the real world today, does Lem seem to view as dangerous? How would the impact of his parody change if Lem had made the book's author and setting European or Japanese instead of American?

CONNECTIONS

1. Some of Lem's readers and acquaintances have suggested that he has stayed on good terms with Poland's government by disguising his criticism of it — for instance, by writing about American generals when he means Polish or Soviet generals. Recall the selections you have read about life in the Soviet bloc, particularly Guzel Amalrik's "A Visit with Andrei at the Labor Camp" (p. 479) and Janine Wedel's "Polish Line Committees" (p. 488). What aspects of "Being Inc." could be interpreted as veiled criticisms of Soviet Communism? (Cite the not-so-veiled criticisms by other writers that Lem's book review echoes.)

2. What fears about powerful institutions are shared by Lem in "Being Inc." and Julio Cortázar in "Regarding the Eradication of Crocodiles from Auvergne" (p. 436)? How do you think Lem rates the relative threat of corporations versus governments, and why? What evidence in Cortázar's story indicates whether he would agree with Lem's position?

3. Czeslaw Milosz, like Lem, saw his Polish homeland invaded by Germany, devastated in World War II, and subsequently annexed by the Soviet Union. What ideas about political power appear in both Milosz's "American Ignorance of War" (p. 513) and "Being Inc."? What ideas about Americans appear in both essays?

4. Lem writes: "In fairy tales he who is able to buy or use force to obtain anything, having the means for this, abandons his exceptional position so that in disguise . . . he may find human genuineness, since privilege shuts it out like an impenetrable wall." Look back at Gabriel García Márquez's "Death Constant Beyond Love" (p. 493). How does privilege shut out human genuineness for Senator Onésimo Sánchez? What is his response? How does Lem's concept of the burdens of power differ from García Márquez's?

ELABORATIONS

1. "The thing will certainly not come about in the form shown in *Being Inc.*" concludes Lem in his persona of reviewer. What assumptions made by mythical author Alastair Waynewright strike you as implausible? possible? likely? What ideas presented in *Being Inc.* are most and least intriguing? Write a review of Waynewright's book that serves the conventional purpose of critiquing its flaws and its appeal for potential readers, rather than recapitulating its content, as Lem has done.

2. "Being Inc." is a good example of the maxim that every work of fiction starts with the author's asking "What if . . .?" Think of a "What if . . .?" question you have wondered about. Using Lem's parody as a model, write a mock review of a book (fiction or nonfiction) that supposedly explores your question. Start by outlining the imaginary book before you begin to review it. You may also want to look at some real book reviews for reference.

3. In "Shanghai" Shen Yongzhang and Li Baomin tell Orville Schell that drinking is rare among young people in China but smoking is common. In "Arriving in Tehran" Kate Millett describes the contrast between Iranian men in suits and women in chadori. In "The Beriozka" Andrea Lee finds the finest Soviet products reserved for foreigners, while in "Western Things" David K. Shipler tells of Soviet officials vying for imported status symbols. Choose a country you have read about in Part Seven and elsewhere in this book, and write an essay classifying its Western tendencies: Which facets of its culture are imported? Are they old or recent? intact or blended with native traditions? Which trends are nationwide and which represent local or individual choice? How significant is age? sex? race? social class? politics? religion? What function or purpose is accomplished by imitations of the West? (You may also use Paul Harrison's "The Westernization of the World" as a resource.)

Acknowledgments *(Continued from page iv)*

Jack Agueros, "Halfway to Dick and Jane," from the book *The Immigrant Experience* by Thomas Wheeler. Copyright © 1971 by Dial Press, Inc. Reprinted by permission of Doubleday, a division of Bantam, Doubleday, Dell Publishing Group, Inc.

Guzel Amalrik, "A Visit with Andrei at the Labor Camp." Reprinted by permission of Avon Books from *Kontinent 4: Contemporary Russian Writers*, edited by George Bailey. Copyright © 1982 by Kontinent Verlag GmbH. English translation copyright © 1982 by Avon Books. Published by arrangement with Kontinent Verlag GmbH.

Albalucía Ángel, "The Guerrillero." Reprinted from *Other Fires: Short Fiction by Latin American Women*. English translation copyright © 1986 by Alberto Manguel. Used by permission of Clarkson N. Potter, Inc.

Mark Baker, from *Nam: The Vietnam War in the Words of the Men and Women Who Fought There*. Copyright © 1981 by Mark Baker. By permission of William Morrow & Company, Inc.

Russell Baker, from "September 6, Labor Day." Copyright © 1969 by The New York Times Company. Reprinted by permission.

Bruno Bettelheim, "Why Kibbutzim?" Reprinted by permission of Macmillan Publishing Company from *The Children of the Dream: Communal Child-Rearing and American Education*. Copyright © 1969 by Macmillan Publishing Company.

Susan Brownmiller, from *Femininity*. Copyright © 1983 by Susan Brownmiller. Reprinted by permission of Linden Press, a division of Simon & Schuster, Inc.

William Broyles, Jr., from "Why Men Love War." Reprinted by permission of International Creative Management, Inc.

Richard Cohen, from "Suddenly I'm the Adult?" *Psychology Today*, May 1987.

Julio Cortázar, "Regarding the Eradication of Crocodiles from Auvergne," excerpted from *Around the Day in Eighty Worlds*. Copyright © 1986 by Julio Cortázar. Translated by Thomas Christensen. Published by North Point Press and reprinted by permission.

Bill Cosby, from *Fatherhood*. Reprinted by permission of Doubleday & Company, Inc.

Vincent Crapanzano, "Growing Up White in South Africa," from *Waiting: The Whites of South Africa*. Copyright © 1983 by Vincent Crapanzano. Reprinted by permission of Random House, Inc.

Simone de Beauvoir, "Woman as Other," from *The Second Sex*, translated by H. M. Parshley. Copyright 1952 by Alfred A. Knopf, Inc. Reprinted by permission of the publisher.

Sri Delima, "Black-and-White Amah," from *As I Was Passing*, Volume II. Published by Berita Publishing SDN.BHD, Kuala Lumpur.

Annie Dillard, from *Encounters with Chinese Writers*. Copyright © 1984 by Annie Dillard. Reprinted by permission of Wesleyan University Press.

Isak Dinesen, excerpts from "Daguerreotypes." © 1979 by The Rungstedlund Foundation. Reprinted by permission of the publisher, The University of Chicago Press.

Milovan Djilas, "Ideas Against Torture," from *Of Prisons and Ideas*. Copyright © 1984 by Milovan Djilas; English translation copyright © 1986 by Harcourt Brace Jovanovich, Inc. Reprinted by permission of the publisher.

Gayle Early, "The Hazards of Being Male," excerpted with permission from the *Chico News & Review* (July 11, 1985).

Barbara Ehrenreich, from "Iranscam: The Real Meaning of Oliver North," *Ms.* Magazine, May 1987. Reprinted by permission of the author.

James Fenton, excerpts from "The Philippine Election," as published in *Granta 18*. Copyright © 1986 by James Fenton. Reprinted by permission of Literistic, Ltd.

Thelma Forshaw, "The Demo," from *An Affair of Clowns*. Reprinted by permission of the author.

Betty Friedan, from *The Second Stage*. Copyright © 1981 by Betty Friedan. Reprinted by permission of Summit Books, a division of Simon & Schuster, Inc.

Kapuściński; English translation copyright © 1987 by Harcourt Brace Jovanovich, Inc. Reprinted by permission of the author.

Yashar Kemal, "A Dirty Story," from *Anatolian Tales*. Reprinted by permission of the publisher, Collins Harvill.

Carol Kleiman, from "My Home Isn't Broken — It Works." *Ms.* Magazine, November 1984. Reprinted by permission of the author.

David Lamb, "The New African Chiefs," from *The Africans*. Copyright © 1983 by David Lamb. Reprinted by permission of Random House, Inc.

William Least Heat Moon, from *Blue Highways: A Journey into America*. Copyright © 1982 by William Least Heat Moon. Reprinted by permission of Little, Brown and Company, Inc., in association with the Atlantic Monthly Press.

Andrea Lee, "The Beriozka," from *Russian Journal*. Copyright © 1981 by Andrea Lee. Reprinted by permission of Random House, Inc.

Stanisław Lem, "Being Inc.," from *A Perfect Vacuum*. Copyright © 1971 by Stanisław Lem; English translation copyright © 1979, 1978 by Stanisław Lem. Reprinted by permission of Harcourt Brace Jovanovich, Inc.

Doris Lessing, from *The Wind Blows Away Our Words*. Copyright © 1987 by Doris Lessing. Reprinted by permission of Random House, Inc.

Liang Heng and Judith Shapiro, "Chairman Mao's Good Little Boy," from *Son of the Revolution*. Copyright © 1983 by Liang Heng and Judith Shapiro. Reprinted by permission of Alfred A. Knopf, Inc.

Elliot Liebow, from *Tally's Corner: A Study of Negro Streetcorner Men*. Copyright © 1967 by Little, Brown and Company, Inc. Reprinted by permission of Little, Brown and Company, Inc.

Cherry Lindholm and Charles Lindholm, "Life Behind the Veil," as published in *Science Digest*, Summer 1980. Reprinted by permission of the authors.

Sophronia Liu, "So Tsi-fai." Originally appeared in *Hurricane Alice*, Vol. 2, No. 4 (Fall 1986). Copyright © 1986 by Sophronia Liu. Reprinted by permission of the author.

Andrew H. Malcolm, "Snowbird," from *The Canadians*. Copyright © 1985 by Andrew Malcolm. Reprinted by permission of Times Books, a division of Random House, Inc.

Ved Mehta, "Pom's Engagement," from *The Ledge Between the Streams*. Reprinted by permission of W. W. Norton & Company, Inc. Copyright © 1982, 1983, 1984 by Ved Mehta.

Kate Millett, "Arriving in Tehran," from *Going to Iran*. Reprinted by permission of Georges Borchardt, Inc. Copyright © 1982 by Kate Millett.

Czeslaw Milosz, "American Ignorance of War," from *The Captive Mind*. Copyright 1951, 1953 by Czeslaw Milosz. Reprinted by permission of Alfred A. Knopf, Inc.

Naila Minai, "Women in Early Islam," from *Women in Islam*. Seaview Books, 1981.

Mishima Yukio, "The Boy Who Wrote Poetry," from *Shi O Kaku Shōnen*. Copyright 1954 Yoko Mishima. All rights reserved. Translated by Ian Levy. Used with permission.

Alberto Moravia, "The Chase," from *Command, and I Will Obey You*. English translation copyright © 1969 by Martin Secker & Warburg Ltd. Reprinted by permission of Farrar, Straus and Giroux, Inc.

John David Morley, "Acquiring a Japanese Family," reprinted from *Pictures from the Water Trade: Adventures of a Westerner in Japan*. Copyright © 1985 by John David Morley, reprinted by permission of the Atlantic Monthly Press.

Ezekiel Mphahlele, "Tradition and the African Writer," retitled from "African Literature: What Tradition?" from *Voices in the Whirlwind and Other Essays*. Copyright © 1967, 1969 by Ezekiel Mphahlele. Reprinted by permission of Hill and Wang, a division of Farrar, Straus and Giroux, Inc.

Vladimir Nabokov, excerpt from *Speak, Memory*. Copyright 1966 by Vladimir Nabokov. Reprinted by permission of the Estate of Vladimir Nabokov.

Shiva Naipaul, "The Palmers," from *North of South: An African Journey.* Copyright © 1979 by Shiva Naipaul. Reprinted by permission of Simon & Schuster, Inc.

V. S. Naipaul, "Entering the New World," from *Finding the Center: Two Narratives.* Copyright © 1984 by V. S. Naipaul. Reprinted by permission of Alfred A. Knopf, Inc.

R. K. Narayan, "Trail of the Green Blazer," from *Malgudi Days.* Copyright © 1981, 1982 by R. K. Narayan. All rights reserved. Reprinted by permission of Viking Penguin Inc.

Robert Nisbet, from "Besieged by the State." Copyright © 1984 by *Harper's Magazine.* All rights reserved. Reprinted from the June issue by special permission.

Michael Novak, from "The Family out of Favor." Copyright © 1976 by *Harper's Magazine.* All rights reserved. Reprinted from the April issue by special permission.

Frank O'Connor, "Guests of the Nation," from *Collected Stories.* Copyright © 1981 by Harriet O'Donovan Sheehy, Executrix of the Estate of Frank O'Connor. Reprinted by permission of Alfred A. Knopf, Inc.

David Owen, "Work Marriage," excerpted from the Reports & Comment section of the *Atlantic,* February 1987. Reprinted by permission of the author.

Amos Oz, "If There Is Justice," from *Elsewhere, Perhaps.* Copyright © 1966 by Sifriat Poalim; English translation copyright © 1973 by Harcourt Brace Jovanovich, Inc. Reprinted by permission of Harcourt Brace Jovanovich, Inc.

Octavio Paz, "My Life With the Wave," from *Arenas movedizas.*

David W. Plath, "Tomoko on Her Television Career," from *Long Engagements: Maturity in Modern Japan.* Excerpted with the permission of the publishers, Stanford University Press. © 1980 by the Board of Trustees of the Leland Stanford Junior University.

Mario Puzo, "Italians in Hell's Kitchen," from the book *The Immigrant Experience* by Thomas Wheeler. Copyright © 1971 by Dial Press, Inc. Reprinted by permission of Doubleday, a division of Bantam, Doubleday, Dell Publishing Group Inc.

Santha Rama Rau, "Boris's Romance," from *My Russian Journey.* Copyright © 1959 by Vasanthi Rama Rau Bowers. Reprinted by permission of Harper & Row, Publishers, Inc.

Richard Rodriguez, from *Hunger of Memory.* Copyright © 1982 by Richard Rodriguez. Reprinted by permission of David R. Godine, Publisher.

Anne Roiphe, excerpts from "Confessions of a Female Chauvinist Sow," published by *New York Magazine.* Copyright © 1972 by Anne Roiphe. Reprinted by permission of Brandt & Brandt Literary Agents, Inc.

Roger Rosenblatt, "Children of Cambodia." Originally appeard in slightly different form with the title "The Road to Khao I Dang" in *The Yale Review* (April 1983); later in the book *Children of War.* Copyright © 1983 by Roger Rosenblatt. Reprinted by permission of Doubleday, a division of Bantam, Doubleday, Dell Publishing Group, Inc.

Gholam-Hossein Sa'edi, "The Game Is Over," from *Dandil: Stories from Iranian Life.* Copyright © 1981 by Gholam-Hossein Sa'edi. Reprinted by permission of Random House, Inc.

Nathalie Sarraute, "My First Sorrow," from *Childhood,* translated by Barbara Wright. Reprinted by permission of the author and George Braziller, Inc., New York. Originally published by Editions Gallimard, Paris.

Shelley Saywell, "Women Warriors of El Salvador," from *Women in War.* Copyright © Shelley Saywell, 1985. Reprinted by permission of Penguin Books Canada Limited.

Orville Schell, "Shanghai," from *Watch Out for the Foreign Guests.* Copyright © 1980 by Orville Schell. Reprinted by permission of Pantheon Books, a division of Random House, Inc.

Gail Sheehy, from *Passages: Predictable Crises of Adult Life.* Copyright © 1974, 1976 by Gail Sheehy. Reprinted by permission of the publisher, E. P. Dutton, a division of NAL Penguin Inc.

David K. Shipler, "Western Things," from *Russia: Broken Idols, Solemn Dreams.* Copyright ©

1983 by David K. Shipler. Reprinted by permission of Times Books, a Division of Random House, Inc.

Marjorie Shostak, "Nisa's Marriage," excerpted by permission of the author and publishers from *Nisa: The Life and Words of a !Kung Woman*. Cambridge, Massachusetts: Harvard University Press. Copyright © 1981 by Marjorie Shostak.

Ruth Sidel, "The Liu Family," from *Families of Fengsheng: Urban Life in China*. Copyright © 1974 by Ruth Sidel. All rights reserved. Reprinted by permission of Viking Penguin Inc.

Olga Silverstein, from "The Good Mother: An Interview with Olga Silverstein." *Vogue*, June 1987. Courtesy *Vogue*. Copyright © 1987 by The Condé Nast Publications Inc.

Adam Smith, from "The Myth, Fable, and Reality of the Working Woman." Copyright © 1984 by Adam Smith. Reprinted with permission from *Esquire*.

Hedrick Smith, "*Skoro Budet* — It'll Be Here Soon," from *The Russians, Revised Edition*. Copyright © 1983 by Hedrick Smith. Reprinted by permission of Times Books, a division of Random House, Inc.

Wole Soyinka, "Nigerian Childhood," from *Ake: The Years of Childhood*. Copyright © 1982 by Wole Soyinka. Reprinted by permission of Random House, Inc.

Gloria Steinem, "If Men Could Menstruate," from *Outrageous Acts and Everyday Rebellions*. Copyright © 1983 by Gloria Steinem. Reprinted by permission of Henry Holt and Company, Inc.

William H. Sullivan, reprinted from *Obbligato, 1939–1979, Notes on a Foreign Service Career*. by permission of W. W. Norton & Company, Inc. Copyright © 1984 by William H. Sullivan.

Studs Terkel, from *Working: People Talk About What They Do All Day and How They Feel About What They Do*. Copyright © 1972, 1974 by Studs Terkel. Reprinted by permission of Pantheon Books, a division of Random House, Inc.

Frank Trippett, from "The Trivial State of the States." Copyright 1978 Time Inc. All rights reserved. Reprinted by permission from *Time*.

Mario Vargas Llosa, "Sunday, Sunday," originally entitled "Dia Domingo," by Mario Vargas Llosa. Copyright © 1959 by Mario Vargas Llosa. Reprinted by permission of the author and Carmen Balcells Agency.

Alice Walker, from "Telling the Black Woman's Story." *The New York Times Magazine*, January 8, 1984.

Claudia Wallis, from "The Child-Care Dilemma." Copyright 1987 Time Inc. All rights reserved. Reprinted by permission from *Time*.

Bruce Weber, from "Alone Together: The Unromantic Generation." Copyright © 1987 by The New York Times Company. Reprinted by permission.

Janine Wedel, "Polish Line Committees," from *The Private Poland*. Copyright © 1986 by Janine Wedel. Reprinted with permission of Facts on File, Inc., New York.

Vicki Williams, from "The View from $204 a Week," as published in *Newsweek*, January 18, 1982.

Tom Wolfe, excerpt from "The Me Decade and the Third Great Awakening," from *Mauve Gloves & Madmen, Clutter & Vine*. Copyright © 1976 by Tom Wolfe. Reprinted by permission of Farrar, Straus and Giroux, Inc.

Zhang Xinxin and Sang Ye, "The Hunter," from *Chinese Profiles*, Beijing: Panda Books.

GEOGRAPHICAL INDEX

AFRICA

Angola: Carlotta (Ryszard Kapuściński), 576
Botswana: Nisa's Marriage (Marjorie Shostak), 172
Ivory Coast: Entering the New World (V. S. Naipaul), 606
Kenya: The Palmers (Shiva Naipaul), 337
Nigeria: Civil Peace (Chinua Achebe), 584; Nigerian Childhood (Wole Soyinka), 66
South Africa: Africa Emergent (Nadine Gordimer), 465; Growing Up White in South Africa (Vincent Crapanzano), 58; Tradition and the African Writer (Ezekiel Mphahlele), 344
Zaire: The New African Chiefs (David Lamb), 414

ASIA

Afghanistan: The Afghan Resistance (Doris Lessing), 519
Cambodia: Children of Cambodia (Roger Rosenblatt), 530
China: Chairman Mao's Good Little Boy (Liang Heng and Judith Shapiro), 450; A Chinese Reporter on Cape Cod (Guan Keguang), 630; Falling in Love with Love (Beverley Hooper), 220; The Hunter (Zhang Xinxin and Sang Ye), 321; The Liu Family (Ruth Sidel), 21; Shanghai (Orville Schell), 635
Hong Kong: So Tsi-fai (Sophronia Liu), 127
India: Our Side of the Fence and Theirs (Gyanranjan), 28; Pom's Engagement (Ved Mehta), 162; Trail of the Green Blazer (R. K. Narayan), 331
Iran: Arriving in Tehran (Kate Millett), 921; The Game Is Over (Gholam-Hossein Sa'edi), 76
Israel: If There Is Justice (Amos Oz), 180; Why Kibbutzim? (Bruno Bettelheim), 14
Japan: Acquiring a Japanese Family (John David Morley), 36; The Boy Who Wrote Poetry (Mishima Yukio), 115; Six Months at Toyota (Satoshi Kamata), 360; Tomoko on Her Television Career (David Plath), 351
Malaysia: Black-and-White Amah (Sri Delima), 9
Pakistan: Life Behind the Veil (Cherry Lindholm and Charles Lindholm), 267
Philippines: The Philippine Election (James Fenton), 422; Patriotic Prostitutes (Jill Gay), 383
South Korea: Patriotic Prostitutes (Jill Gay), 383

Soviet Union: The Beriozka (Andrea Lee), 644; Boris's Romance (Santha Rama Rau), 213; Liza and Family (Carola Hansson and Karin Lidén), 48; *Skoro Budet* — It'll Be Here Soon (Hedrick Smith), 374; A Visit with Andrei at the Labor Camp (Guzel Amalrik), 479; Western Things (David K. Shipler), 649
Thailand: Patriotic Prostitutes (Jill Gay), 383
Turkey: A Dirty Story (Yashar Kemal), 279

AUSTRALIA

The Demo (Thelma Forshaw), 391

EUROPE

Denmark: From "Daguerreotypes" (Isak Dinesen), 204
France: My First Sorrow (Nathalie Sarraute), 109; Regarding the Eradication of Crocodiles from Auvergne (Julio Cortázar), 436; Woman as Other (Simone de Beauvoir), 241
Ireland: Guests of the Nation (Frank O'Connor), 564
Italy: The Chase (Alberto Moravia), 249
Poland: American Ignorance of War (Czeslaw Milosz), 513; Being Inc. (Stanisław Lem), 656; Polish Line Committees (Janine Wedel), 488
West Germany: Resistance (Günter Grass), 591
Yugoslavia: Ideas Against Torture (Milovan Djilas), 560

NORTH AMERICA

Canada: Snowbird (Andrew H. Malcolm), 313
Cuba: In Cuba (Germaine Greer), 441
El Salvador: Women Warriors of El Salvador (Shelley Saywell), 540
Mexico: My Life with the Wave (Octavio Paz), 234

SOUTH AMERICA

Argentina: The Stolen Party (Liliana Heker), 132
Colombia: Death Constant Beyond Love (Gabriel García Márquez), 493; The Guer-rillero (Albalucía Ángel), 556
Peru: Sunday, Sunday (Mario Vargas Llosa), 145

OTHER

Czarist Russia: From *Speak, Memory* (Vladimir Nabokov), 139
The Arab World: Proxemics in the Arab World (Edward T. Hall), 611
The Islamic World: Women in Early Islam (Naila Minai), 256

INDEX OF
AUTHORS AND TITLES

Achebe, Chinua, *Civil Peace*, 584
Acquiring a Japanese Family
(Morley), 36
Afghan Resistance, The (Lessing), 519
Africa Emergent (Gordimer), 465
Agueros, Jack, 104
Amalrik, Guzel, A *Visit with Andrei at
the Labor Camp*, 479
American Ignorance of War
(Milosz), 513
Ángel, Albalucía, *The Guerrillero*, 556
Arriving in Tehran (Millett), 621

Baker, Mark, 506
Baker, Russell, 308
Being Inc. (Lem), 656
Beriozka, The (Lee), 644
Bettelheim, Bruno, *Why
Kibbutzim?*, 14
Black-and-White Amah (Delima), 9
Boris's Romance (Rama Rau), 213
Boy Who Wrote Poetry, The
(Mishima), 115
Brownmiller, Susan, 197
Broyles, William, Jr., 508
Byrne, David, 505

Carlotta (Kapuściński), 576
Chairman Mao's Good Little Boy
(Liang and Shapiro), 450
Chase, The (Moravia), 249
Children of Cambodia (Rosenblatt), 530
Chinese Reporter on Cape Cod, A
(Guan), 630

Civil Peace (Achebe), 584
Cohen, Richard, 106
Cortázar, Julio, *Regarding the
Eradication of Crocodiles from
Auvergne*, 436
Cosby, Bill, 3
Crapanzano, Vincent, *Growing Up
White in South Africa*, 58

"Daguerreotypes" (Dinesen), 204
Death Constant Beyond Love (García
Márquez), 493
de Beauvoir, Simone, *Woman as
Other*, 241
Delima, Sri, *Black-and-White Amah*, 9
Demo, The (Forshaw), 391
Dillard, Annie, 413
Dinesen, Isak, *"Daguerreotypes,"* 204
Dirty Story, A (Kemal), 279
Djilas, Milovan, *Ideas Against
Torture*, 560

Early, Gayle, 198
Ehrenreich, Barbara, 510
Entering the New World (V. S.
Naipaul), 606

Falling in Love with Love
(Hooper), 220
Fenton, James, *The Philippine
Election*, 422
Forshaw, Thelma, *The Demo*, 391
Friedan, Betty, 309

Galbraith, John Kenneth, 409
Game Is Over, The (Sa'edi), 76
García Márquez, Gabriel, *Death
    Constant Beyond Love,* 493
Gay, Jill, *Patriotic Prostitutes,* 383
Gilder, George, 509
Goodman, Ellen, 7
Gordimer, Nadine, *Africa
    Emergent,* 465
Grass, Günter, *Resistance,* 591
Greer, Germaine, *In Cuba,* 441
Gross, Amy, 200
Growing Up White in South Africa
    (Crapanzano), 58
Guan Keguang, *A Chinese Reporter on
    Cape Cod,* 630
Guerrillero, The (Ángel), 556
Guests of the Nation (O'Connor), 564
Gyanranjan, *Our Side of the Fence and
    Theirs,* 28

Hall, Edward T., *Proxemics in the Arab
    World,* 611
Hansson, Carola, and Karin Lidén,
    Liza and Family, 48
Harrison, Paul, *The Westernization of
    the World,* 599
Heker, Liliana, *The Stolen Party,* 132
Hooper, Beverley, *Falling in Love with
    Love,* 220
Howard, Jane, 5
Hunter, The (Zhang and Sang), 321

Ideas Against Torture (Djilas), 560
If There Is Justice (Oz), 180
In Cuba (Greer), 441

Justin, Dena, 195

Kamata, Satoshi, *Six Months at
    Toyota,* 360
Kane, Joe, 195
Kapuściński, Ryszard, *Carlotta,* 576
Kemal, Yashar, *A Dirty Story,* 279
Kleiman, Carol, 4

Lamb, David, *The New African
    Chiefs,* 414
Least Heat Moon, William, 407

Lee, Andrea, *The Beriozka,* 644
Lem, Stanisław, *Being Inc.,* 656
Lessing, Doris, *The Afghan
    Resistance,* 519
Liang Heng and Judith Shapiro,
    *Chairman Mao's Good Little
    Boy,* 450
Lidén, Karin, and Carola Hansson,
    Liza and Family, 48
Liebow, Elliot, 306
Life Behind the Veil (Lindholm and
    Lindholm), 267
Lindholm, Cherry and Charles, *Life
    Behind the Veil,* 267
Liu, Sophronia, *So Tsi-fai,* 127
Liu Family, The (Sidel), 21
Liza and Family (Hansson and
    Lidén), 48

Malcolm, Andrew H., *Snowbird,* 313
Mehta, Ved, *Pom's Engagement,* 162
Millett, Kate, *Arriving in Tehran,* 621
Milosz, Czeslaw, *American Ignorance of
    War,* 513
Minai, Naila, *Women in Early
    Islam,* 256
Mishima Yukio, *The Boy Who Wrote
    Poetry,* 115
Moravia, Alberto, *The Chase,* 249
Morley, John David, *Acquiring a
    Japanese Family,* 36
Mphahlele, Ezekiel, *Tradition and the
    African Writer,* 344
My First Sorrow (Sarraute), 109
My Life with the Wave (Paz), 234

Nabokov, Vladimir, Speak,
    Memory, 139
Naipaul, Shiva, *The Palmers,* 337
Naipaul, V. S., *Entering the New
    World,* 606
Narayan, R. K., *Trail of the Green
    Blazer,* 331
New African Chiefs, The (Lamb), 414
Nigerian Childhood (Soyinka), 66
Nisa's Marriage (Shostak), 172
Nisbet, Robert, 410
Novak, Michael, 3

O'Connor, Frank, *Guests of the
Nation*, 564
Our Side of the Fence and Theirs
(Gyanranjan), 28
Owen, David, 199
Oz, Amos, *If There Is Justice*, 180

Palmers, The (S. Naipaul), 337
Patriotic Prostitutes (Gay), 383
Paz, Octavio, *My Life with the
Wave*, 234
Philippine Election, The (Fenton), 422
Piercy, Marge, 308
Plath, David, *Tomoko on Her Television
Career*, 351
Polish Line Committees (Wedel), 488
Pom's Engagement (Mehta), 162
Proxemics in the Arab World (Hall), 611
Puzo, Mario, 305

Rama Rau, Santha, *Boris's
Romance*, 213
*Regarding the Eradication of Crocodiles
from Auvergne* (Cortázar), 436
Resistance (Grass), 591
Rodriguez, Richard, 305
Roiphe, Anne, 201
Rosenblatt, Roger, *Children of
Cambodia*, 530

Sa'edi, Gholam-Hossein, *The Game Is
Over*, 76
Sang Ye and Zhang Xinxin, *The
Hunter*, 321
Sarraute, Nathalie, *My First
Sorrow*, 109
Saywell, Shelley, *Women Warriors of El
Salvador*, 540
Schell, Orville, *Shanghai*, 635
Shanghai (Schell), 635
Shapiro, Judith, and Liang Heng,
*Chairman Mao's Good Little
Boy*, 450
Sheehy, Gail, 105
Shipler, David K., *Western Things*, 649
Shostak, Marjorie, *Nisa's Marriage*, 172
Sidel, Ruth, *The Liu Family*, 21
Silverstein, Olga, 105

Six Months at Toyota (Kamata), 360
Skoro Budet — *It'll Be Here Soon* (H.
Smith), 374
Smith, Adam, 195
Smith, Hedrick, Skoro Budet — *It'll Be
Here Soon*, 374
Snowbird (Malcolm), 313
So Tsi-fai (Liu), 127
Soyinka, Wole, *Nigerian Childhood*,
66
Speak, Memory (Nabokov), 139
Steinem, Gloria, 196
Stolen Party, The (Heker), 132
Sullivan, William H., 505
Sunday, Sunday (Vargas Llosa), 145

Tomoko on Her Television Career
(Plath), 351
Tradition and the African Writer
(Mphahlele), 344
Trail of the Green Blazer
(Narayan), 331
Trippett, Frank, 405
Terkel, Studs, 310

Vargas Llosa, Mario, *Sunday,
Sunday*, 145
*Visit with Andrei at the Labor Camp,
A* (Amalrik), 479

Walker, Alice, 305
Wallis, Claudia, 6
Weber, Bruce, 307
Wedel, Janine, *Polish Line
Committees*, 488
Westernization of the World, The
(Harrison), 599
Western Things (Shipler), 649
Why Kibbutzim? (Bettelheim), 14
Williams, Vicki, 406
Wolfe, Tom, 106
Woman as Other (de Beauvoir), 241
Women in Early Islam (Minai), 256
Women Warriors of El Salvador
(Saywell), 540

Zhang Xinxin and Sang Ye, *The
Hunter*, 321

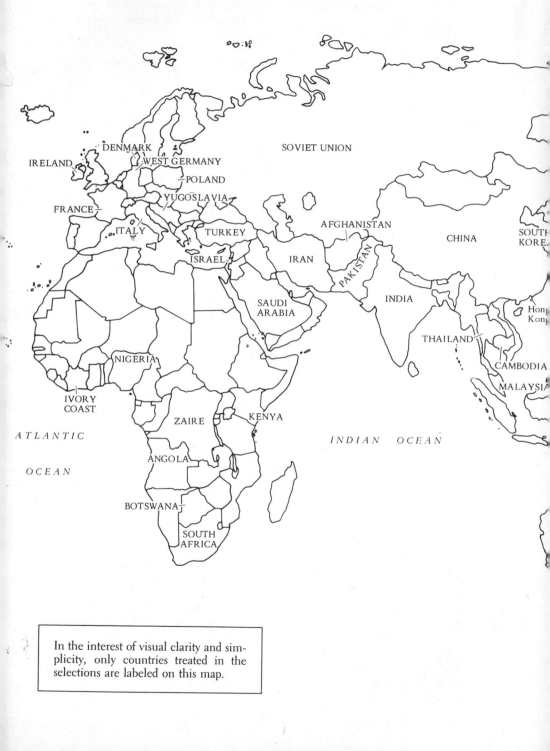

ARCTIC

IRELAND
DENMARK
WEST GERMANY
POLAND
FRANCE
YUGOSLAVIA
ITALY
TURKEY
ISRAEL
IRAN
AFGHANISTAN
PAKISTAN
SAUDI ARABIA
INDIA
SOVIET UNION
CHINA
SOUTH KOREA
Hong Kong
THAILAND
CAMBODIA
MALAYSIA
NIGERIA
IVORY COAST
ZAIRE
KENYA
ANGOLA
BOTSWANA
SOUTH AFRICA

ATLANTIC

OCEAN

INDIAN OCEAN

In the interest of visual clarity and simplicity, only countries treated in the selections are labeled on this map.